Financial Institutions and Markets

A Reader

Edited by

Robert W. Kolb

School of Business Administration
University of Miami

 Kolb Publishing Company   Miami, Florida

A list of sources appears on pp. 409–410 at the end of this text.

Printed in the United States of America.

Library of Congress Catalog Card Number   90–091891

ISBN: 1–878975–02–1

K Kolb Publishing Company
7175 S.W. 47th Street, Suite 210   Miami, Florida 33155
KOLB (305) 663-0550   FAX (305) 663-6579

Preface

The current financial scene is witnessing radical change in virtually every dimension. The United States faces a financial scandal of unprecedented magnitude in the thrift industry. Europe prepares to commit to economic union among countries that have traditionally been foes. Around the world, new financial instruments and techniques revolutionize the management of financial institutions and other businesses. Against this background, technological developments draw geographically diverse markets into a single network, as financial markets become truly global. *Financial Institutions and Markets: A Reader* surveys these exciting developments. This text collects some of the most timely and accessible articles on the changing financial scene in a single convenient volume.

Dramatic world developments in finance have stimulated intense discussion and have increased the pace of financial analysis. Part of this heightened activity has resulted in numerous articles on the changing financial scene. For the collector of readings on financial institutions and markets, current trends create an embarrassment of riches. The problem facing the editor is to select wisely among hundreds of excellent discussions. Selecting relatively few articles from the vast number available requires some principle of selection. To be included in this volume, an article was screened with three principal criteria in mind.

Timeliness   Today's financial scene is one of immediacy. Old articles about financial institutions and markets are as exciting and important as yesterday's stale beer. If an article is not current, it is not here. Every article in this book was published in 1989 or later.

Accessibility   To be accessible, an article cannot be too technical, too mathematical, or too stuffed with jargon. This reader attempts to convey the immediacy and excitement that today's finance offers. Putting the reader to sleep does not accomplish this task. Accordingly, each article was carefully screened to ensure its accessibility.

Content   An article can be still warm from the press and can be as accessible as a comic strip. However, to deserve inclusion in a readings book, the article must also possess meaningful content. I believe that every article in this book is rich in content and can stimulate the reader's interest in financial institutions and markets. Of the three criteria listed, meaningful content is the most important.

This text contains thirty–six articles that meet these criteria admirably. They are grouped here into the five sections shown below, along with a listing of the most important topics covered by each section.

Section I   The Financial System and Central Banking

Money and Monetary Policy ▾ Inflation ▾ The Payments System ▾ The U.S. as a Debtor Nation

Section II   Financial Markets

Junk Bonds ▾ Stocks and Corporate Financing ▾ Financial Market Volatility ▾ Mezzanine Finance ▾ Derivative Instruments and Their Applications

Section III   The Thrift Crisis and Deposit Insurance Reform

Origins of the Crisis ▾ FIRREA (Financial Institutions Reform, Recovery, and Enforcement Act of 1989) ▾ Potential Cures

Section IV   Management and Policy Issues for Financial Institutions

Interstate Banking ▾ Foreign Competition ▾ Principal–Agent Conflicts ▾ Small Bank Issues ▾ ATMs ▾ International Lending ▾ Corporate Lending

Section V   International Financial Markets and Instruments

Globalization of Financial Services ▾ Europe in 1992 ▾ Exchange Rates

Each section begins with a brief essay that covers the major issues addressed in the section. The section introduction also includes a brief summary of each article.

I wish to thank several individuals who were instrumental in bringing this book to life. Joe Rodriguez designed the cover and Andrea Coens edited the manuscript. Sol Roskin and Robin Hood at Hallmark Press printed the book and gave valuable assistance in taking the book through the production cycle. The greatest thanks goes to the authors of the articles included here and to the publications where these articles originally appeared. It is customary to praise others for making a book possible. For this book, such praise has special meaning. The creativity and diligent efforts of the authors represented in this text really did make this book possible.

Robert W. Kolb
University of Miami

Contents

Section I
The Financial System and Central Banking

The eight readings of Section I consider the big picture of financial institutions and markets. These articles develop an overview of the macroeconomy and the role of the Federal Reserve System. For the most part, these readings consider systemic issues, such as the nature of money and the importance of inflation. They also focus on the payments system, which affects the entire financial sector. Readings in this section also consider the role of the United States in the world economy. Overall, the articles in this section provide a comprehensive view of financial institutions and markets and the broadest level—the nation's economy and the role of our national economy in the world marketplace.

In "Monetary Aggregates: A User's Guide," John R. Walter distinguishes different monetary aggregates—measures of the money supply. While these measures have evolved, each attempts to measure the supply of money in a meaningful way. Measuring the money supply accurately is important to everyone trying to understand macroeconomic developments. While linkages between money and real economic activity continue to be debated, most economists agree that the money supply can potentially affect many phases of economic life. For example, unwise changes in the money supply could cause unemployment or stimulate inflation. Similarly, a wise monetary policy could help the nation achieve high employment, stable prices, and moderate interest rates. Thus, money affects every element of the economy and policy makers require the meaningful monetary aggregates that Walter describes.

The velocity of money is the ratio of nominal national income to the money supply. If the supply of money can affect real economic activity, such as income, then velocity provides a conceptual link between the money supply and income. In "Money and Velocity in the 1980s," John B. Carlson and John N. McElravey survey the changing relationship between national income and the money supply. Prior to the 1980s, velocity was quite stable. However, in the 1980s, this relationship became unsettled. As Carlson and McElravey show, this change in velocity led the Federal Reserve to alter the way it measures the money supply for purposes of monetary policy.

Inflation is a persistent increase in the general level of prices. The important point in this definition is the focus on the general level of prices, not the price change of a single commodity such as beef or gasoline. Over time, prices generally seem to drift higher, giving an inflationary tendency. Michelle R. Garfinkel asks, "What Is an 'Acceptable' Rate of Inflation?—A Review of the Issues." Like almost every issue in economics, inflation involves costs and benefits. Surging prices hurt some economic agents and benefit others. As Garfinkel points out, zero inflation might be the most desirable target, but the costs to the economy necessary to achieve zero inflation may be undesirably high.

One cost associated with inflation is the tendency of the stock market to perform poorly. In an inflationary period, one might expect stock prices to rise along with the general level of prices. After all, stock ownership represents title to the underlying real assets of corporations. However, a considerable body of evidence shows that stock prices do not rise as quickly as the general price level in inflationary times. In "The Stock Market and Inflation: A Synthesis of the Theory and Evidence," David P. Ely and Kenneth J. Robinson consider the reasons for the failure of stock prices to keep up with general price level surges.

The payments system is the nationwide system for paying checks and transferring funds electronically. During the business day, banks are allowed to overdraw their reserve account with the Federal Reserve without paying interest. This means that the Federal Reserve extends credit to banks for part of each business day. If a bank fails while overdrawn, the Federal Reserve is left holding the bag. This is payments system risk. In "Payments System Risk: What Is It and What Will Happen If We Try To Reduce It?," R. Alton Gilbert analyzes payments system risk and reports on the Federal Reserve's new examination of its risky position.

One fine day in 1985 the United States became a net debtor nation. That is, since that day in 1985 the United States has owed foreigners more than foreigners owe the United States. This change from being a large net creditor to a large net debtor is the focus of "The U.S. as a Debtor Country: Causes, Prospects, and Policy Implications," by Stephen A. Meyer. Meyer addresses two concerns. First, some fear that this debt may reduce living standards for future Americans. Second, some observers fear large foreign debt causes high inflation rates, such as those experienced by some other debtor nations.

Throughout the 1980s, the United States has acquired more goods and services from foreigners than we have sold abroad. This phenomenon generates a trade deficit. If we, as a nation, consume more than we produce, we must finance that additional consumption by borrowing or by selling assets. During the 1980s, the United States did both. We have already seen that Meyer addresses the debt issue. In his paper, "Is America Being Sold Out?," Mack Ott addresses the sale of U.S. assets to foreign interests. Both Meyer and Ott realize that national borrowing can be good. For example, acquiring capital from abroad would be wise if we have productive uses for the capital. In other words, if investment projects in the United States generate a risk–adjusted rate of return that exceeds the cost of the funds, then borrowing the funds is a wise business decision. This is exactly the issue that stimulates the greatest debate in discussions of our debtor status and sales of assets to foreigners.

The discount rate is the rate of interest that banks pay to borrow from a Federal Reseve Bank. At one time, the Federal Reserve Board changed the discount rate to affect the supply of money. In recent years, the Fed has attempted to affect the money supply by buying or selling securities. E. J. Stevens, in his paper "Setting the Discount Rate," considers the current role of the discount rate and suggests that the discount rate might be managed more effectively to provide an additional tool for influencing the money supply.

Article 1

MONETARY AGGREGATES: A USER'S GUIDE

John R. Walter

The monetary aggregates are measures of the nation's money stock. The most narrowly defined monetary aggregate, M1, is the sum of the dollar amounts of currency and nonbank travelers checks in circulation, plus checkable deposits. M2 includes M1 plus overnight repurchase agreements, overnight Eurodollar deposits, general purpose and broker/dealer money market fund balances, money market deposit accounts, and savings and small time deposits. M3 is the sum of M2 and large time deposits, term repurchase agreements, term Eurodollar deposits, and balances in money market funds employed solely by institutional investors. Analysts study the relationships among these monetary measures and other macroeconomic variables, such as national income, employment, interest rates, and the price level. These relationships are then used to forecast changes in economic activity, interest rates, and inflation. The Board of Governors of the Federal Reserve System defines the aggregates and calculates and reports their values.

This article explains the origin and evolution of the monetary aggregates and discusses how they are prepared and released, how they are used, and when and why they are revised. Information on the monetary base is also included.

How the Monetary Aggregates Evolved

Over the years economists have proposed many different groupings of financial assets into something called "money." No single definition of money has been universally acceptable. Two approaches have been used to define money. The first is to identify what financial assets are commonly used for certain purposes. Analysts using this approach generally include as money financial assets serving (1) as a medium of exchange, i.e., assets widely acceptable in payment for goods, services, and debts, and (2) as a store of value. A second approach to defining money is to find the groupings of financial assets the movements of which are most closely correlated with the movements of certain macroeconomic variables such as national income, employment, and prices. Both approaches have contributed to the development of the monetary aggregates constructed by the Federal Reserve. A brief chronology of the evolution of these measures is given below.

In 1944 the Board of Governors of the Federal Reserve System began reporting monthly data on two types of exchange media, (1) currency outside of banks, and (2) demand deposits at banks, i.e., non-interest-bearing deposits transferable by check or convertible into cash "on demand." It also reported the sum of these two. The Board's expressed intent in reporting the data was "to increase the information available to the public on current changes . . . in the nation's money supply." In time the sum of currency outside banks and demand deposits came to be called M1, the narrowest of the Fed's monetary aggregates.

Until 1971 M1 was the only monetary aggregate for which estimates were published by the Board of Governors. In that year, however, the Board began reporting data for two additional aggregates, M2 and M3. Interest in these latter variables reflected the growing importance of the monetary aggregates in formulating monetary policy. It also reflected the view among some economists that the appropriate definition of money should include assets capable of providing a temporary store of value. Accordingly, M2 was defined to include M1 plus savings deposits at commercial banks and time deposits at commercial banks except large negotiable certificates of deposit. Similarly M3 was defined as the sum of M2 and deposits at mutual savings banks and savings and loan associations.

In 1975, the Board began publishing data for even broader collections of financial assets, namely M4 and M5. M4 included M2 plus large negotiable certificates of deposit. M5 was the sum of M3 and large negotiable certificates of deposit.

The decade of the 1970s witnessed the development of many financial instruments. Some of the new assets were close substitutes for demand deposits, namely negotiable order of withdrawal (NOW) accounts which are interest-bearing checkable accounts, savings accounts featuring automatic transfer to checking accounts (ATS accounts), credit union share draft accounts, and money market mutual funds with checking privileges. These new accounts began to be used as exchange media but were not counted in M1 until 1980.

The introduction of these new assets also coincided with what some economists interpreted as changes in the relationships between the monetary aggregates and economic variables such as income, employment, and prices. These apparent changes provided some of the Fed's motivation for modifying its definitions of the aggregates in 1980.[1] At that time the Fed replaced its M1 definition of money with M1A and M1B. M1A was equivalent to the old M1, including only currency and demand deposits; M1B included all of M1A plus NOW and ATS balances at banks and thrifts, credit union share draft balances, and demand deposits at mutual savings banks.[2] At the same time old M2 through M5 were replaced with new measures of M2 and M3. New M2 included all of M1B and a number of other assets that are easily convertible to transaction account deposits or that can be used in transactions to a limited degree. These were overnight repurchase agreements (RPs) issued by commercial banks and certain overnight Euro-dollars held by nonbank U.S. residents, money market mutual fund shares, and savings and small-denomination time deposits at all depository institutions.[3] New M3 added to M2 large-denomination time deposits at all depository institutions and term RPs at commercial banks and savings and loan associations.

In January 1982 the Board of Governors stopped reporting M1A and redesignated M1B as M1. Since then the definitions have been modified only slightly. Table I shows the current magnitudes of M1, M2, and M3.

Monetary Base

The monetary base is composed of currency held by the public and in vaults of depository institutions, plus reserves of depository institutions. In 1968 the Federal Reserve Bank of St. Louis began publishing figures on the monetary base. In 1979 the Board of Governors of the Federal Reserve System also began publishing data on a somewhat different version of the monetary base.

The base can be viewed as the foundation upon which the superstructure of deposits is erected. An increase in the reserves component of the base allows the system of depository institutions to expand deposits. Initially, an increase in reserves—resulting from open market operations or loans by the Fed—

leads to an increase in "excess" reserves, that is, reserves beyond the amount needed to meet reserve requirements at depository institutions. These institutions use the excess reserves to make loans and investments which soon become deposits. When these deposits are spent and redeposited, they create additional excess reserves and lead to the extension of more loans. Through a multiplicative process the money supply is increased by a multiple of the Fed's original addition to the monetary base. The extent to which the money stock increases upon an increase in the monetary base depends on the percentages of required and excess reserves held by depository institutions and on the public's holdings of cash relative to deposits.[4]

As noted above, the Board of Governors' and the St. Louis Federal Reserve Bank's estimates of the monetary base differ, and do so in three respects. First, the Board and St. Louis adjust the base differently to cleanse it of changes that are simply the result of changes in reserve requirements.[5] Second, the Board and St. Louis account for vault cash differently. Third, they seasonally adjust their estimates differently.[6]

Preparation and Release of Monetary Data

The Board of Governors constructs its estimates of the monetary aggregates from information supplied by depository institutions, the U.S. Treasury, money market mutual funds, New York State investment companies, nonbank issuers of travelers checks, and foreign central banks. Some of these institutions report every week, others report less frequently. Some report in an abbreviated form not available to larger institutions. To produce weekly and monthly estimates of the aggregates, the Board estimates missing data where detail or frequency of reporting

---

[1] See Board of Governors (June 1976) and Board of Governors (January 1979), p. 24.

[2] M1A excluded demand deposits held by foreign commercial banks and foreign official institutions while old M1 did not.

[3] For a thorough discussion of RPs see Stephen A. Lumpkin's article "Repurchase and Reverse Repurchase Agreements" in Cook and Rowe (1986), pp. 65-80.

[4] Humphrey (1987) describes the theory of deposit expansion and its history. Most introductory level college money and banking texts provide a basic discussion of how monetary actions of the Fed affect the base and the money stock. Burger (1971) goes into great detail.

[5] For example, when the reserve requirement against business time deposits with maturities of 2-1/2 to 3-1/2 years was dropped in April 1983, the amount of reserves banks were required to hold declined by $80 million. In order to prevent a corresponding increase in excess reserves the Fed concurrently withdrew this $80 million through open market operations, leading to an identical decline in the monetary base. The Board of Governors and the Federal Reserve Bank of St. Louis then eliminated this $80 million decline in their adjusted monetary base data.

[6] Burger (1979) discusses the causes of the differences between the Board of Governors' and St. Louis' monetary base estimates.

Table I

COMPONENTS OF THE MONETARY AGGREGATES AND MONETARY BASE AND THEIR LEVELS
August 1988
Billions of dollars

M1	**782.5**
Currency	207.2
Travelers checks	7.2
Demand deposits	290.0
Other checkable deposits	278.1
M2	**3032.0**
M1	782.5
Overnight RPs	64.9
Overnight Eurodollars	15.8
MMF balances (general purpose and broker/dealer)	231.2
MMDAs	517.1
Savings deposits	433.8
Small time deposits	985.2
M3	**3847.3**
M2	3032.0
Large time deposits	514.7
Term RPs	121.0
Term Eurodollars	102.4
MMF balances (institution only)	84.0
Monetary Base	**271.2**
Currency	207.2
Reserves	61.1

Sources: Data for M1, M2, M3 and their components are from Board of Governors of the Federal Reserve System H.6 release, "Money Stock, Liquid Assets, and Debt Measures," dated October 6, 1988. Data for Monetary Base are from Board of Governors of the Federal Reserve System H.3 release, "Aggregate Reserves of Depository Institutions and the Monetary Base," dated October 6, 1988. The Currency figure shown below Monetary Base is from H.6 while the Reserves figure is from H.3.

Explanation: M2 and M3 both differ from the sums of their components because these aggregates are seasonally adjusted by adjusting the non-M1 components of M2 and the non-M2 components of M3 as blocks. Several of these components are not reported in seasonally adjusted form while those that are have been adjusted individually. Monetary Base differs from its components because the currency component the Board uses in its Monetary Base computation includes some adjustments excluded from the H.6 currency figure. The Board does not publish the currency portion of Monetary Base separately.

Other checkable deposits are negotiable order of withdrawal (NOW) accounts, automatic transfer service (ATS) accounts, credit union share draft accounts, and demand deposits at thrift institutions.

RPs, repurchase agreements, are loan arrangements in which the borrower sells the lender securities with an agreement to repurchase them at a future date.

Eurodollars are dollar-denominated deposits issued to U.S. residents by foreign branches of U.S. banks worldwide.

MMF, money market mutual funds, are funds investing in money market instruments, offered by investment companies.

MMDA, money market deposit accounts, are savings deposits on which only a limited number of checks can be drawn each month.

Savings deposits are liabilities of depository institutions that do not specify a date of withdrawal or a time period after which deposited funds may be withdrawn, although depository institutions must reserve the right to require at least seven days written notice before withdrawal of savings deposits.

Time deposits are liabilities of depository institutions payable on a specified date, or after a specified period of time or notice period, which in all cases may not be less than seven days following the date of deposit.

Term, as in Term RPs and Term Eurodollars, means maturities of greater than one day.

The *Reserves* component of Monetary Base is total reserves of depository institutions with Federal Reserve Banks plus vault cash used to satisfy reserve requirements and is adjusted for reserve requirement changes.

For a detailed description of each of the components of M1, M2, and M3 see any recent H.6 release or footnotes to the table entitled "Money Stock, Liquid Assets, and Debt Measures," in the statistical section of a recent *Federal Reserve Bulletin.* For a detailed description of the Reserves component of Monetary Base see the footnotes to the H.3 release, or footnotes to the table entitled "Reserves and Borrowings, Depository Institutions" in the statistical section of a recent *Federal Reserve Bulletin.* The Federal Reserve Bank of Richmond's *Instruments of the Money Market* includes a chapter for each of the major money market instruments, including Eurodollars, RPs, and MMF, listed above.

The Federal Reserve, in its H.6 release and in the tables of its *Federal Reserve Bulletin,* publishes estimates of liquid assets and total debt of nonfinancial sectors with the monetary aggregates even though these are not considered monetary aggregates. The liquid assets measure is called L and is made up of M3 plus U.S. savings bonds, short-term Treasury securities, commercial paper, and bankers acceptances. The aggregate labeled "Debt" includes the debt of the U.S. government, state and local governments, and private nonfinancial sectors. L first appeared in the *Federal Reserve Bulletin* in 1980, with Debt following in 1984. Items in L and Debt fall outside of the category of assets that most economists would call money.

---

are lacking. Table II lists, by component, sources of data used by the Board to calculate the monetary aggregates.

The Board of Governors reports figures for M1, M2, and M3 each week (usually on Thursday afternoon at 4:30 eastern time). Reported values are weekly averages of daily figures for the week ending ten days earlier. The Board publishes both seasonally adjusted and not seasonally adjusted data. Revisions of the seasonally adjusted aggregates can be large due to changing seasonal patterns over time.[7]

---

[7] For a discussion of the difficulties of seasonal adjustment see Hein and Ott (1983).

The Board of Governors releases its most recent estimates of the monetary base every two weeks. These figures are two-week averages of daily figures for the two weeks ending eight days earlier. The Board publishes a seasonally adjusted monetary base figure adjusted for changes in reserve requirements, a not seasonally adjusted base figure adjusted for changes in reserve requirements, and a not seasonally adjusted figure not adjusted for reserve requirement changes. The St. Louis Federal Reserve Bank also releases a new estimate of the average monetary base every two weeks. It provides only a base figure adjusted for reserve requirement changes and for seasonal change.

Table II

SOURCES OF DATA USED BY THE BOARD OF GOVERNORS IN THE ESTIMATION OF THE MONETARY AGGREGATES AND THE MONETARY BASE

Component	Description of Component	Source of Data on Component and Frequency
M1		
Currency	Currency and coin in the hands of the nonbank public.	Consolidated Statement of Condition of All Federal Reserve Banks (H.4.1)—weekly; vault cash data from Report of Transaction Accounts, Other Deposits and Vault Cash (FR 2900)—weekly, and Quarterly Report of Selected Deposits, Vault Cash, and Reservable Liabilities (FR 2910Q).
Nonbank travelers checks	Travelers checks issued by institutions other than banks. Included in M1 because they can be used directly for purchases.	Report of Travelers Checks Outstanding (FR 2054)—monthly.
Demand deposits and Other checkable deposits	Checkable deposits including regular non-interest-bearing checking accounts, NOW balances, ATS balances, and credit union share draft balances.	FR 2900; FR 2910Q; Reports of Condition and Income (Call Reports)—quarterly; internal Federal Reserve float data; Weekly Report of Assets and Liabilities for Large Banks (FR 2416).
M2		
M1		
Overnight repurchase agreements	Overnight and continuing contract repurchase agreements (RPs) issued by commercial banks. Included in M2 because they are generally considered short-term investments used in managing demand deposit balances.	Report of Selected Borrowings (FR 2415)—weekly; Annual Report of Repurchase Agreements (FR 2090A); Weekly Report of Assets of Money Market Mutual Funds (FR 2051A); Weekly Report of Assets for Selected Money Market Mutual Funds (FR 2051C).
Overnight Eurodollars	Overnight Eurodollars issued to U.S. residents by foreign branches of U.S. banks worldwide. Short-term investments like RPs.	Report of Selected Deposits in Foreign Branches Held by U.S. Residents (FR 2050)—weekly; FR 2051A; FR2051C.
Money market mutual fund (MMF) balances (general purpose and broker/dealer)	Often checkable, but included in M2 rather than M1 because turnover rates are more like savings instruments than transactions instruments.	Investment Company Institute (ICI) gathers FR 2051A and FR 2051C for Fed covering all MMFs.
Money market deposit accounts (MMDAs)	Limited check writing features and turnover rates like savings rather than transactions accounts cause Fed to include this asset in M2 rather than M1.	FR 2900; FR 2910Q; Call Reports.
Savings deposits	Passbook and telephone transfer accounts.	FR 2900; FR 2910Q; Call Reports; FR 2416.
Small time deposits	Time deposits at depository institutions with denominations less than $100,000. Includes RPs with denominations less than $100,000.	FR 2900; FR 2910Q; Call Reports; Monthly Survey of Selected Deposits and Other Accounts (FR 2042); Report of Repurchase Agreements on U.S. Government and Federal Agency Securities (FR 2090Q)—quarterly; FR 2090A.
M3		
M2		
Large time deposits	Time deposits at depository institutions with denominations of $100,000 or more. Held largely by institutions.	FR 2900; FR 2910Q; Call Reports; FR 2416; FR 2051A; FR 2051C.
Term RPs	Denominations $100,000 or greater with more than one day maturity. Held largely by institutions rather than individuals.	FR 2415; FR 2090A; Call Reports; FR 2051A; FR 2051C.
Term Eurodollars	More than one day maturity, held largely by institutions rather than individuals.	Weekly Report of Foreign Branch Liabilities to, and Custody Holdings for, U.S. Residents (FR 2077); information from Bank of Canada and Bank of England; FR 2051A; FR 2051C.
MMF balances (institution only)	Balances held by institutions rather than individuals.	FR 2051A; FR 2051C.
Monetary Base		
Currency	Currency and coin in the hands of the nonbank public plus currency and coin in bank vaults not used to satisfy reserve requirements.	H.4.1; FR 2900; FR 2910Q; Call Reports.
Reserves	Reserves of depository institutions held with Federal Reserve Banks plus vault cash used to satisfy reserve requirements.	FR 2900; H.4.1.

The Board of Governors publishes historical series of the monetary aggregates and many of the components making up the aggregates. These series are periodically updated to reflect revisions or redefinitions of the aggregates. Both the Board and the St. Louis Fed produce historical series for the base. Table III lists the monetary aggregates and their component series as well as the monetary base and its component series available from the Board and St. Louis.

How The Monetary Aggregates Data Are Used

The Fed's legislative mandate is to set a monetary policy consistent with high employment, stable prices, and moderate long-term interest rates. In semiannual testimony to Congress, the Chairman of the Board of Governors of the Federal Reserve System reports the targets set by the Federal Open Market Committee (the Fed's monetary policy-making body)[8] for growth of the monetary aggregates. The Chairman also relates these targeted growth rates to forecasted rates of unemployment, output growth, and inflation. Because of concern with the instability of the behavior of M1, the Federal Open Market Committee has not specified an M1 target range since 1986, although it has continued to set target ranges for M2 and M3.

The Federal Reserve cannot directly control the quantity of money. It can, however, control

---

[8] The President of the Federal Reserve Bank of New York is a permanent voting member of the Federal Open Market Committee while the other eleven Federal Reserve Bank presidents share four voting memberships on a rotating basis. All seven members of the Board of Governors are also permanent voting members.

Table III

AVAILABILITY OF TIME-SERIES ON MONETARY AGGREGATES AND COMPONENTS MAKING UP MONETARY AGGREGATES

Series	Weekly Averages Available Beginning: sa	nsa	Monthly Averages Available Beginning: sa	nsa
Aggregates				
M1	1/75	1/75	1/59	1/47*
M2	1/81	1/81	1/59	1/59
M3	1/81	1/81	1/59	1/59
Monetary Base—Board				
Adjusted	1/59**	1/59**	1/59	1/59
Unadjusted		1/59**		1/59
Monetary Base—St. Louis				
Adjusted	1/72**	1/72**	1/50	1/29
Unadjusted		1/72**		1/19
Components of Ms				
Currency	1/75	1/75	1/59	1/47*
Demand deposits	1/75	1/75	1/59	1/47*
Other checkable deposits	1/75	1/75	1/63	1/63
Overnight RPs		1/75		11/69
Overnight Eurodollars		12/79		2/77
MMMF (general purpose and broker/dealer)		2/80		11/73
MMMF (institution only)		2/80		4/74
Nonbank travelers checks	1/75	1/75	1/59	1/59
Savings deposits	1/81	1/81	1/59	1/59
Small time deposits	1/81	1/81	1/59	1/59
Large time deposits	1/81	1/81	1/59	1/59
MMDA		12/82		12/82
Term RPs		1/75		10/69
Term Eurodollars		12/79		1/59
Components of Base				
Reserves—Board				
Adjusted	1/59**	1/59**	1/59	1/59
Unadjusted		1/59**		1/59
Reserves—St. Louis				
Adjusted			1/50	1/47
Currency—St. Louis		1/72**		1/50

Sources: Board of Governors of the Federal Reserve System, H.6, "Historical Money Stock Data," March 1988; Board of Governors of the Federal Reserve System, H.3, "Reserves of Depository Institutions, Historical Data," June 1988; Banking and Monetary Statistics, 1941-1970, Board of Governors of the Federal Reserve System, 1976; The Federal Reserve Bank of St. Louis.

* Data from 1/47 until 12/70 can be found in Banking and Monetary Statistics, 1941-1970, Board of Governors of the Federal Reserve System, 1976, while data for 1/59 to current are available from Board of Governors of the Federal Reserve System, H.6, "Historical Money Stock Data," March 1988. Definitions used in these two sources differ.

** Weekly data are available until 2/84, after which only biweekly data are available.

sa = Seasonally adjusted

nsa = Not seasonally adjusted

variables that influence short-term interest rates, namely the quantity of reserves held by depository institutions and the monetary base, and thereby influence the growth rate of the aggregates. Greater provision of reserves through Federal Reserve open market purchases of securities tends to push down the federal funds rate and other short-term interest rates. Lower interest rates, in turn, help determine the quantities of the monetary aggregates demanded by the private sector. Downward pressure on federal funds and other rates makes holding money balances, which pay no or low rates of interest, less costly. The lower cost of holding money increases the quantity of money demanded. Assuming money supply equals money demand, the result is an increase in the level of monetary aggregates. Changes in the aggregates normally are followed by temporary changes in aggregate output and employment and by permanent changes in prices.[9] Chart 1 illustrates the relationship between M2 and the price level. As is conventional in such comparisons, M2 is shown per unit of real output, i.e., is divided by real GNP, to adjust for growth in the economy.[10]

The monetary aggregates have been watched closely by those attempting to predict Fed policy moves.[11] In periods when the Fed sought tight control of the growth rate of the aggregates, unusually fast or slow money growth has generated expectations of subsequent policy actions by the Fed to arrest or reverse these movements. In such periods, the financial markets react to the announcement of the weekly M1 figure. The announcement of a higher than expected M1 figure, for example, leads market participants to increase their estimate of the probability that the Fed will put upward pressure on the funds rate, and other short-term rates rise in reaction to these changed expectations.[12]

Many economists study the aggregates to improve their understanding of the links between monetary growth and changes in other macroeconomic variables. Prior to the 1980s empirical studies generally found stable relationships between M1 growth and inflation and GNP growth. These findings were important to the Fed's decision to place more emphasis on the monetary aggregates in monetary policymaking during the 70s and early 80s. With the financial deregulation and disinflation of the early 1980s

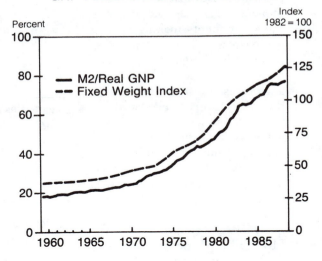

M2/REAL-GNP AND GNP FIXED WEIGHT PRICE INDEX

however, studies began to find that the once stable relationships between M1 growth and inflation and GNP growth were breaking down. These findings led the Federal Reserve in 1982 to de-emphasize M1 in its monetary policymaking process.[13] Recent studies, however, suggest that changes due to disinflation and deregulation have had a smaller effect on M2 than on M1 growth, and that the relationship between M2 growth and inflation has remained fairly stable.[14] In his February 1989 testimony before Congress the Chairman of the Board of Governors stated that "over the long haul there is a close relationship between money [M2] and prices." The Fed, consistent with the view that further reductions in the growth rate of M2 are necessary to achieve long-run price stability, reduced its target range for M2 in both 1988 and 1989.[15]

Revisions to the Monetary Aggregates

Major revisions to the published data on the monetary aggregates occur for four reasons. First, the data are revised as reporting or processing errors are discovered. Second, the aggregates are revised annually to incorporate "benchmark" changes. Third, the seasonally adjusted data are revised annually to incorporate new seasonal adjustment factors. Finally, the historical series are revised whenever there is a redefinition of the aggregates.

---

[9] See Board of Governors (July 1988), pp. 419-20, and Broaddus (1988), pp. 45-49.

[10] Friedman (1969), p.177.

[11] Loeys (1984).

[12] Walter (1988), pp. 222-25.

---

[13] Friedman (1988) and Bernanke and Blinder (1988).

[14] Hetzel and Mehra (1988), Mehra (1988), and Reichenstein and Elliott (1987).

[15] Greenspan (April 1989) and Board of Governors (March 1989).

With thousands of institutions reporting to the Federal Reserve System on a weekly basis, it is impossible for the Fed to find and correct all errors before the first release of monetary aggregate data. As errors are discovered the Board revises the data. Most revisions occur within the first month following initial release of a figure, although some can take place months later.

As noted above, to produce estimates of the monetary aggregates the Board of Governors must estimate the deposits held in financial institutions not reporting on a weekly basis. Most of these institutions do report data on a quarterly or annual basis, however. When these quarterly or annual figures become available, they provide points of reference, or "benchmarks," which the Board uses to make more accurate estimates for intervening dates. The Board makes these benchmark revisions to the aggregates each February.

The monetary aggregates are seasonally adjusted to remove those movements that tend to recur at the same time each year, such as the temporary increases in transactions balances before Christmas and before the due date for tax payments. To determine the proper seasonal adjustment factors to apply to a given month's or week's aggregates the Board normally uses data on the aggregates for three years before and three years after the month or week in question. No later data are available for the most recently released aggregates so the Board forecasts fifteen months of the data and appends it to the actual aggregate data. As time passes, the estimates of the seasonal factors can be made more accurately as forecasted data are replaced by actual data and as data errors are corrected and new benchmarks become available. Each February, the Board re-estimates the seasonal factors for the data series used in the monetary aggregates and revises the seasonally adjusted data accordingly.[16]

As discussed earlier, the Federal Reserve changes the definitions of its aggregates from time-to-time following financial market innovations and regulatory changes that affect the way money is held. Some definitional changes are minor and produce only small revisions in the aggregates; others, such as those occurring during the early 1980s, lead to major revisions. When the Fed changes the definitions of the monetary aggregates, it revises the historical data to be consistent over the whole period of the series. (For a list of the beginning dates of various series see Table III.) Previously published data, however,

may not bear the same definitions. Thus when comparing data at different dates, users should take care to determine that the data definitions are consistent.

Sources of Data

Monetary aggregate data are available from many sources. On each Friday *The Wall Street Journal* publishes a table giving the money stock data released on Thursday afternoon. Historical data can be found in the *Federal Reserve Bulletin*, in the Board of Governor's H.6 release, in the Board's annual historical supplement to the H.6, "Historical Money Stock Data," in the Federal Reserve's *Banking and Monetary Statistics, 1914-1941*, *Banking and Monetary Statistics, 1941-1970*, and *Annual Statistical Digest* for years since 1970.

Historical data on the monetary base are available directly from the St. Louis Federal Reserve Bank and from the Board of Governors, or in the Board's H.3 release as well as the Board's historical supplement to the H.3, "Reserves of Depository Institutions, Historical Data." Normally, on Friday, *The Wall Street Journal* publishes a table including the most recent figures on the monetary base from the H.3 release.

Suggestions for Further Reading

Most college level money and banking texts discuss the monetary aggregates and the monetary base and their relationship to economic variables. James N. Duprey's "How the Fed Defines and Measures Money" in the Spring-Summer 1982 issue of the *Quarterly Review* of the Federal Reserve Bank of Minneapolis, examines the aggregates and discusses their construction. "Data Sources Used In Constructing the U.S. Monetary Aggregates," a 1984 monograph by Cynthia Glassman of the Board of Governors of the Federal Reserve System, details the sources used in the estimation of the monetary aggregates. The debate among economists over the best definition of money is discussed in Alfred Broaddus's "Aggregating the Monetary Aggregates: Concepts and Issues" in the *Economic Review* of the Federal Reserve Bank of Richmond, November/December 1975.

The footnotes found in the Board of Governor's weekly H.6 release provide detailed definitions of the aggregates. The H.6 release also describes components included in each of the aggregates and reports their estimated levels over time.

The February 1980 *Federal Reserve Bulletin* article "The Redefined Monetary Aggregates" by Thomas Simpson, describes the events and intellectual forces that led the Fed to redefine its aggregates in 1980

---

[16] Lawler (1977), Hein and Ott (1983), pp. 16-20, and Cook (1984), pp. 22-25.

and specifies how the redefinition was accomplished. This article includes time series charts showing the growth of the pre-1980 aggregates and the post-1980 aggregates.

A Monetary History of the United States, 1867-1960, by Milton Friedman and Anna Schwartz provides a seminal discussion of how changes in growth of the money stock have affected the American economy. The authors discuss and make use of the Fed's monetary aggregates throughout much of the book. *Monetary Statistics of the United States*, also by Friedman and Schwartz, provides estimates of the quantity of money for the period 1867-1968 and discusses sources and methods of construction of historical money stock estimates. This volume also devotes more than 100 pages to alternative approaches to the definition of money.

The *Federal Reserve Bulletin* and the Board of Governors' *Annual Report* generally document and explain definitional changes in the monetary aggregates. *Banking and Monetary Statistics, 1941-1970*, published by the Board of Governors, includes a detailed discussion of the Fed's money stock measures.

"The Monetary Base—Explanation and Analytical Use," by Leonall C. Anderson and Jerry L. Jordan, in the August 1968 Federal Reserve Bank of St. Louis *Review*, explains the construction of the St. Louis version of the monetary base and points out why that concept is of importance to monetary economists. The Board of Governors' H.3 release gives a complete definition of the Board's monetary base in its footnotes. Carl M. Gamb's "Federal Reserve Intermediate Targets: Money or the Monetary Base?" in the January 1980 Federal Reserve Bank of Kansas City *Economic Review*, discusses the pros and cons of use of the monetary base in monetary control and provides a good review of the Board's and St. Louis' construction of the base.

References

Anderson, Leonall C., and Jerry L. Jordan. "The Monetary Base—Explanation and Analytical Use." Federal Reserve Bank of St. Louis *Review* 50 (August 1968): 7-11.

Bernanke, Ben S., and Alan S. Blinder. "Credit, Money, and Aggregate Demand." *American Economic Review* 78 (May 1988): 435-39.

Board of Governors of the Federal Reserve System. "A Proposal for Redefining the Monetary Aggregates." *Federal Reserve Bulletin* 65 (January 1979): 13-42.

——————. *Banking and Monetary Statistics, 1914-1941*. Washington, 1976.

——————. *Banking and Monetary Statistics, 1941-1970*. Washington, 1976.

——————. "Implementing Monetary Policy." *Federal Reserve Bulletin* 74 (July 1988): 419-29.

——————. "Improving the Monetary Aggregates." Report of the Advisory Committee on Monetary Statistics. June 1976.

——————. "Monetary Aggregates and Money Market Conditions in Open Market Policy." *Federal Reserve Bulletin* 57 (February 1971): 79-95.

——————. "Monetary Policy Report to the Congress." *Federal Reserve Bulletin* 74 (August 1988): 517-33.

——————. "Monetary Policy Report to the Congress." *Federal Reserve Bulletin* 75 (March 1989), forthcoming.

——————. "Money Stock Revisions." (Annual historical supplement to the Board of Governors of the Federal Reserve System release H.6, "Money Stock, Liquid Assets, and Debt Measures"). March 1988.

——————. "New Monetary and Banking Statistics." *Federal Reserve Bulletin* 30 (February 1944): 134.

——————. "Notes to Table 1.21." *Federal Reserve Bulletin* 72 (November 1986): A14.

——————. "Reserves of Depository Institutions." (Annual historical supplement to the Board of Governors of the Federal Reserve System release H.3, "Aggregate Reserves of Depository Institutions and the Monetary Base"). June 1988.

——————. *69th Annual Report*, 1982. Washington: Board of Governors, 1983.

——————. *The Federal Reserve System: Purposes & Functions*. 7th ed. Washington: Board of Governors, 1984.

Broaddus, Alfred. "Aggregating the Monetary Aggregates: Concepts and Issues." Federal Reserve Bank of Richmond *Economic Review* 61 (November/December 1975): 3-12.

——————. *A Primer on the Fed*. Richmond: Federal Reserve Bank of Richmond, 1988.

Broaddus, Alfred, and Marvin Goodfriend. "Base Drift and the Longer Run Growth of M1: Experience from a Decade of Monetary Targeting." Federal Reserve Bank of Richmond *Economic Review* 70 (November/December 1984): 3-14.

Burger, Albert E. "Alternative Measures of the Monetary Base." Federal Reserve Bank of St. Louis *Review* 61 (June 1979): 3-8.

——————. *The Money Supply Process*. Belmont, California: Wadsworth Publishing Co., Inc., 1971.

Cook, Timothy Q. "The 1983 M1 Seasonal Factor Revisions: An Illustration of Problems That May Arise in Using Seasonally Adjusted Data for Policy Purposes." Federal Reserve Bank of Richmond *Economic Review* 70 (March/April 1984): 22-33.

Cook, Timothy Q., and Timothy D. Rowe, eds. *Instruments of the Money Market*, 6th ed. Richmond: Federal Reserve Bank of Richmond, 1986.

Duprey, James N. "How the Fed Defines and Measures Money." Federal Reserve Bank of Minneapolis *Quarterly Review* (Spring-Summer 1982), pp. 10-19.

Federal Reserve Bank of St. Louis. "Monetary Trends." Various dates.

——————. "U.S. Financial Data." Various dates.

Friedman, Benjamin M. "Monetary Policy Without Quantity Variables." *American Economic Review* 78 (May 1988): 440-45.

Friedman, Milton. *The Optimum Quantity of Money and Other Essays*. Chicago: Aldine Publishing Company, 1969.

Friedman, Milton, and Anna Jacobson Schwartz. *A Monetary History of the United States, 1867-1960*. Princeton, N.J.: Princeton University Press, 1963.

——————. *Monetary Statistics of the United States, Estimates, Sources, Methods*. New York: National Bureau of Economic Research, 1970.

Gambs, Carl M. "Federal Reserve Intermediate Targets: Money or the Monetary Base?" Federal Reserve Bank of Kansas City *Economic Review* 65 (January 1980): 3-15.

Glassman, Cynthia A. "Data Sources Used in Constructing the U.S. Monetary Aggregates." Paper presented at 21st Meeting of Technicians of Central Banks of the American Continent. Washington: Board of Governors of the Federal Reserve System, Division of Research and Statistics, Financial Reports Section, 1984.

Greenspan, Alan. "Statement before the Committee on Banking, Finance and Urban Affairs, U.S. House of Representatives, February 21, 1989." *Federal Reserve Bulletin* 75 (April 1989), forthcoming.

Hein, Scott E., and Mack Ott. "Seasonally Adjusting Money: Procedures, Problems, Proposals." Federal Reserve Bank of St. Louis *Review* 65 (November 1983): 16-24.

Hetzel, Robert L., and Yash P. Mehra. "The Behavior of Money Demand in the 1980s." Federal Reserve Bank of Richmond, June 1988. Photocopy.

Humphrey, Thomas M. "The Theory of Multiple Expansion of Deposits: What It Is and Whence It Came." Federal Reserve Bank of Richmond *Economic Review* 73 (March/April 1987): 3-11.

Lawler, Thomas A. "Seasonal Adjustment of the Money Stock: Problems and Policy Implications." Federal Reserve Bank of Richmond *Economic Review* 63 (November/December 1977): 19-27.

Lindsey, David E., and Henry C. Wallich. "Monetary Policy." In *The New Palgrave, A Dictionary of Economics*, edited by John Eatwell, Murray Milgate, and Peter Newman, vol. 3. London: The MacMillan Press Limited, 1987, pp. 508-15.

Loeys, Jan G. "Market Views of Monetary Policy and Reactions to M1 Announcements." Federal Reserve Bank of Philadelphia *Business Review* (March/April 1984), pp. 9-17.

Mehra, Yash P. "The Forecast Performance of Alternative Models of Inflation." Federal Reserve Bank of Richmond *Economic Review* 74 (September/October 1988): 10-18.

McCarthy, F. Ward, Jr. "Basics of Fed Watching." In *The Handbook of Treasury Securities*, edited by Frank J. Fabozzi. Chicago: Probus, 1987.

Reichenstein, William, and J. Walter Elliott. "A Comparison of Models of Long-Term Inflationary Expectations." *Journal of Monetary Economics* 19 (May 1987): 405-25.

Simpson, Thomas D. "The Redefined Monetary Aggregates." *Federal Reserve Bulletin* (February 1980): 97-114.

Stone, Courtenay C., and Jeffrey B. C. Olson. "Are the Preliminary Week-to-Week Fluctuations in M1 Biased?" Federal Reserve Bank of St. Louis *Review* 63 (December 1978): 13-20.

Taylor, Herb. "What Has Happened to M1?" Federal Reserve Bank of Philadelphia *Business Review* (September/October 1986), pp. 3-14.

Walter, John R. "How to Interpret the Weekly Federal Reserve Data." In *The Financial Analyst's Handbook*, 2nd. ed., edited by Sumner N. Levine. Homewood, Illinois: Dow Jones-Irwin, 1988.

Article 2

Money and Velocity in the 1980s

by John B. Carlson and
John N. McElravey

Prior to 1980, a sharp slowdown in the money supply was expected to be associated with a downturn in economic activity. Indeed this concern was still expressed by some analysts in 1987 and 1988 as the growth rates of money supply measures M1 and M2 slowed precipitously.[1] Nevertheless, the economy has remained strong, despite the problems caused by the 1988 drought.

Recent evidence suggests that money growth is becoming more variable, reflecting increasing sensitivity of some bank deposits to changes in interest rates. In turn, this interest-rate sensitivity has affected the behavior of the velocity of money—the ratio of nominal income to money—and hence has affected the link between money and economic activity.

This *Economic Commentary* discusses how the newly emerging patterns in the velocities of M1 and M2 ultimately reflect the effects of financial deregulation and disinflation. Given the degree of the interest-rate sensitivity of money, and the uncertainty about how interest rates may need to vary in response to shocks to the economy, it has become difficult for policymakers to prespecify an appropriate growth rate for the nation's money supply over

the short run. This problem is also discussed.

■ Velocity Trends

The relationship of money to nominal income was once thought to be one of the most stable relationships in economics. This was evident in the behavior of M1 velocity. From 1959 to 1980, M1 velocity grew smoothly along a 3-percent trend (see chart 1). While M1 velocity was systematically related to interest rates, the impact of interest-rate changes appeared relatively small.

In effect, a substantial slowdown in M1 growth during this period was usually associated with a slowdown in aggregate spending and, therefore, in economic activity. This tendency for changes in M1 growth to mirror changes in economic activity made it a useful guidepost for monetary policy. Indeed, the Federal Reserve increasingly relied on M1 as a gauge for monetary policy during the 1970s.

The apparent stability of the M1 velocity trend, however, was not inherent. During the current decade, M1 velocity has varied substantially with changes in interest rates (see chart 2). Moreover, while M1 velocity has declined since 1982, it is not evident that it is following any identifiable trend path. The case of M2 velocity is somewhat

The behavior of money has changed greatly in the 1980s. This article identifies the newly emerging patterns in money and its relationship to economic activity. These new patterns, largely a consequence of both deregulation and disinflation, reveal an increased sensitivity of money to interest rates. The implications for the role of money in the monetary policy process are also discussed.

different. It had a systematic relationship to interest rates in the short run before 1980, but was, and continues to be, relatively stable over long periods.[2]

■ Opportunity Cost and the Aggregates

The substantial interest sensitivity of the monetary aggregates (M1, M2) and their velocities is being confirmed in studies of money demand.[3] In these studies, money demand is viewed as a function of its opportunity cost—the foregone interest income of holding lower-yielding money balances. As this cost of holding money rises, the demand for money falls (and velocity increases). The opportunity cost of a given deposit typically is measured by the difference between the market interest rate on a relatively risk-free, short-term asset (such as the 3-month Treasury bill) and the rate paid on that deposit (its *own-rate*).

Prior to financial deregulation, beginning in the late 1970s, virtually all checkable deposits were noninterest bearing. Thus, the opportunity cost of M1 balances—comprised of currency and checkable deposits—was essentially equal to the Treasury-bill rate. Interest rates drifted upward over most of the postwar period. Rate levels at the trough of each recession were higher than at the previous trough (see chart 2). Money balances continually became more expensive to hold as interest rates and inflation rose. Economizing on money balances motivated individuals and businesses to find innovative ways to arrange portfolios and to execute transactions while keeping a minimum of checkable deposits.

Some innovations during the 1970s circumvented regulations on financial institutions. Interest-rate ceilings, for instance, kept banks from paying higher rates as market rates increased. New deposit-like instruments, such as money market mutual funds, were created to meet the demand of investors for higher yields on their funds, while maintaining their liquidity.

Also, cash management practices of businesses evolved as the rising opportunity cost made bank deposits less attractive relative to market instruments. Banks began to offer arrangements through which their corporate customers could conveniently purchase securities owned by the bank on an overnight basis and thereby earn market yields on funds otherwise held in noninterest-bearing deposits. The net effect of the evolution of these innovations and practices was that less and less money was held for the same amount of transactions and, by definition, velocity increased.

■ **Disinflation and Financial Deregulation**

Disinflation and financial deregulation greatly affected the opportunity cost of money and its velocity. Disinflation resulted in sharply falling interest rates, reversing the upward trend that dated back to the 1950s. Deregulation allowed banks to compete more effectively for funds by offering interest-bearing checking accounts and market rates of interest on saving and time deposits. The opportunity cost of most bank deposits fell markedly after 1982 when market rates fell and when banks priced deposits more competitively.

The combined impact perhaps was greatest on individual checking accounts. For these deposits, the opportunity cost fell from a high of 18 percent in 1980 to almost zero in 1986. Because banks can now price these deposits competitively, it would seem doubtful that their opportunity cost would ever soar as high as it did in the early 1980s. Moreover, the long-run, 3-percent growth trend in M1 velocity now appears to have been an artifact of secularly rising inflation and interest rates in a regulated environment. On the other hand, the long-run trendless nature of M2 velocity seems unaffected by the events of the 1980s.

What is curious is that, in the short run, most bank deposits appear more interest sensitive now than before deregulation. In principle, banks can, if they wish, alter most of their own deposit rates promptly in response to changes in market rates and thereby keep the opportunity cost of various deposits constant. With this kind of behavior, interest-rate changes should have less effect on aggregates of these deposits. This would seem especially likely for M2 because there are no interest ceilings on 83 percent of its deposits.

In fact, however, banks do not adjust all their deposit rates one-for-one with movements in market rates. Experience after deregulation indicates that repricing of some types of deposits is quite sluggish. Banks tend to raise rates on some deposits more slowly than on

others in response to rising market rates. For example, the own-rate on other checkable deposits (OCDs) rises more slowly because it increases a bank's cost of funds more than an increase in the own-rate on time deposits. This is because a change in the rates paid on OCDs affects all existing balances, whereas a change in the rates paid on time deposits affects only newly acquired deposits.[4]

The net impact of these tactics is that bank deposits have become more interest sensitive. Some have speculated that this may reflect the increased sophistication of most deposit holders and the improved information and communications technologies that have made funds transfers more convenient. Even if opportunity costs were less affected by changes in interest rates now than before deregulation, deposit holders are much more conscious and aware of alternative assets. Thus, they are more likely to respond to changes in opportunity cost.

■ **Recent Patterns**

The opportunity cost of OCDs fell substantially with the decline in the Treasury-bill rate from 1984 until early 1987. The decline in opportunity cost spurred rapid growth in these accounts. As rates started rising in 1987, however, OCD growth dropped off sharply. Market rates declined after the stock-market crash, and OCDs surged during the first half of 1988. OCD growth moderated as short-term rates climbed in the second half of 1988. The own-rate on OCDs has not kept pace with the increase in market rates, so that the opportunity cost has again widened. The interest sensitivity of OCDs accounts for a large part of the post-1980 variability of M1 velocity.

Own-rates on savings deposits and money market deposit accounts (MMDAs) in M2 also have been slow to adjust to changes in market rates, making their opportunity costs variable. The opportunity costs of OCDs, MMDAs, and savings deposits all have risen sharply during 1988. It seems likely that deposit holders would shift

CHART 1

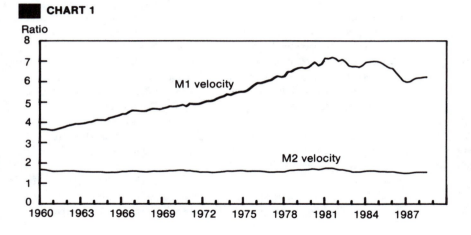

CHART 1

Ratio

M1 velocity

M2 velocity

SOURCE: Board of Governors of the Federal Reserve System.

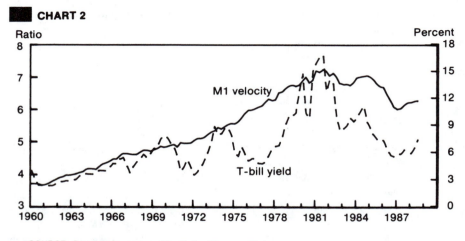

CHART 2

Ratio   Percent

M1 velocity

T-bill yield

SOURCE: Board of Governors of the Federal Reserve System.

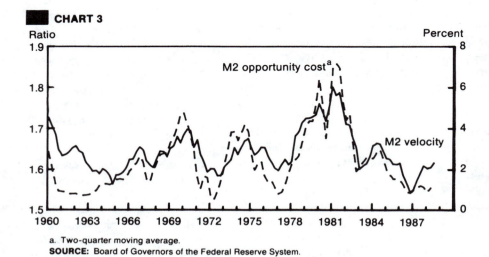

CHART 3

Ratio   Percent

M2 opportunity cost[a]

M2 velocity

a. Two-quarter moving average.
SOURCE: Board of Governors of the Federal Reserve System.

out of these assets into more competitively priced instruments. These accounts, which comprise a large segment of M2, are responsible for much of the recent slowdown in M2 growth in the second half of 1988.

Rates paid on small time-deposits, also a large part of M2, have been more responsive to market rates, and their opportunity cost has varied less than that of the nontime deposits. As a consequence, small time-deposits have grown more rapidly than the others, though not enough to offset weakness in the other M2 components in the second half of 1988.

Reviewing the experience of the past three years provides a good example of how the portfolio effects of M2 opportunity cost work (see chart 3). Interest rates, opportunity cost, and inflation were approaching their lows in 1986. M2 grew at a rapid rate and, at the end of the year, its level was above the upper bound of the annual target range established for it by the Federal Reserve.

Although growth in the economy remained strong in 1987, M2 still fell substantially below the bottom of its annual target range because interest rates and opportunity cost rose, and inflation accelerated. Falling market interest rates after the stock-market crash spurred M2 growth to about 8 percent through June 1988. A series of policy tightening moves by the Federal Reserve during the spring and summer raised market rates, which led to M2 growth below the midpoint of its 1988 range by late in the year.

■ **Policy Implications**
As the traditional relationship between M1 and nominal income broke down, M1 became less useful in the monetary policy process. The Federal Reserve's Federal Open Market Committeee (FOMC) dropped M1 from its reported objectives in 1987; M2 has received the most attention since then. In February, the FOMC chooses and reports its targets for M2 and other financial objectives for 1989. The Com-

mittee chose a tentative target range of 3 to 7 percent for M2 last July.

While M2 seems to be durably related to nominal income over periods of 18 months or longer, its substantial sensitivity to interest-rate changes makes its usefulness as a short-run target questionable. M2's target ranges were widened in 1988, from 3 to 4 percentage points, to allow for the uncertainty about how interest rates may need to vary in response to unanticipated economic conditions. As the past several years have shown, the large short-run variability of M2 may be consistent with a steadily growing economy.

As Federal Reserve Chairman Alan Greenspan noted in his testimony before Congress in February 1988, one should not conclude that the Federal Reserve is giving up on monetary targeting.[5] The FOMC will continue to interpret incoming information on the monetary aggregates in conjunction with other data on the performance of the economy to determine the best course for monetary policy. If the net result of policy actions is to substantially change the level of interest rates, however, the FOMC might be willing to tolerate M2 growth outside its specified ranges.

Finally, the difficulty posed by interest sensitivity of M2 is strictly a problem over the short run. The relationship between M2, prices, and income remains intact over the long run. Consequently, targets for M2 may prove to be especially useful in achieving the longer-term policy objective of price stability.

■ **Footnotes**

1. See the *Federal Reserve Bulletin*, any recent issue, for definitions of these measures. Generally, M1 includes balances used in making transactions, while M2 includes M1 plus household savings assets.

2. In fact, even with the increased volatility in the 1980s, the velocity of M2 appears to be stationary around a constant mean level, although it may be more interest sensitive.

3. See Moore, George R., Richard D. Porter, and David H. Small, "Modeling the Disaggregated Demands for M2 and M1 in the 1980's: The U.S. Experience," a paper presented at the Federal Reserve Board Conference on Monetary Aggregates and Financial Sector Behavior in Interdependent Economies, May 1988.

4. For a thorough analysis of deposit-rate behavior see Moore et al.

5. Congressional testimony of Alan Greenspan, Chairman, Board of Governors of the Federal Reserve System; February 23, 1988; Monetary Policy Objectives for 1988.

John B. Carlson is an economist at the Federal Reserve Bank of Cleveland. John N. McElravey is a research analyst at the Bank.

Article 3

Michelle R. Garfinkel

Michelle R. Garfinkel is an economist at the Federal Reserve Bank of St. Louis. Thomas A. Pollmann provided research assistance.

What Is an "Acceptable" Rate of Inflation?—A Review of the Issues

"Our strategy continues to be centered on moving toward, and ultimately reaching, stable prices, that is, price levels sufficiently stable so that expectations of change do not become major factors in key economic decisions."

Alan Greenspan, *Testimony to House Committee on Banking, Finance, and Urban Affairs*, January 24, 1989

RECENT fears of increased future inflationary pressures, heightened by high rates of capacity utilization, have generated a large body of commentary concerning what level of inflation would be desirable or at least acceptable.[1] While there appears to be a general consensus that a rise in the rate of inflation is not desirable, whether or not many would agree with Mr. Greenspan's statement above is not clear. Indeed, his statement makes a stronger suggestion that even the current rate of inflation is not acceptable.[2]

This article points out three central issues for determining what constitutes an "acceptable" rate of inflation. The first issue concerns the costs of inflation. The second issue is whether, despite these costs, inflation's benefits are suffi-

ciently large to justify some positive rate of inflation. The final issue concerns the costs of reducing inflation. Even if there were convincing reasons for ultimately eliminating inflation, some analysts would argue that a positive inflation could be acceptable in the short-run; the optimal time path along which a long-run goal of zero inflation is achieved depends on the temporary costs of adjustment to reach that goal eventually.

WHAT ARE THE COSTS OF INFLATION?

Examining the effects of inflation sheds light on why price stabilization is a primary objective of monetary policy. This section focuses on

---

[1]See, for example, Clark (1989) and Stein (1989).

[2]Mr. Greenspan expressed this view more clearly in his testimony to Congress in February 1989: ". . . let me stress that the current rate of inflation, let alone an increase, is not acceptable, and our policies are designed to

reduce inflation in coming years." [Greenspan (1989), p. 274.] Elsewhere, he has been quoted as suggesting that the ultimate objective of the Fed is to eradicate inflation [Murray (1989)].

Table 1

Some Effects of Inflation

Anticipated Inflation	**Unanticipated Inflation**
1. Inflation tax on money balances: transfers resources from money holders to government and reduces money demand.	1. Reduction in real value of gross return from holding nominal debt: transfers resources from net monetary creditors to net monetary debtors.
2. Inflation-induced increase in marginal income taxes: transfers resources from taxpayers to the government and reduces labor supply.	2. Reduction in real wages if wages are fixed in nominal terms: transfers resources from labor to employers.
3. Taxation of nominal interest income: transfers resources from savers to the government and reduced savings.	**Inflation Uncertainty**
4. Interaction with tax incentives: reduces cost of borrowing and increases debt finance.	1. Increase in reluctance to enter into nominal wage contracts and increase in cost of nominal wage contract negotiations: increases indexation of nominal contracts and reduces real economic growth.
5. Costs of price adjustments: produces excessive relative price variability and a misallocation of resources.	2. Increase in risk premia of longer maturity nominal bonds: causes a movement from longer to shorter term maturities and increases the real cost of capital.
	3. Increase in incentive to hedge against unanticipated inflation: transaction costs incurred in attempts to hedge against risk associated with inflation uncertainty and distortions in asset accumulation.
	4. Confusion about source of price movements: causes excessive relative price variability and a misallocation of resources.

some of the relevant effects given existing institutional arrangements in the United States.[3] These effects, as summarized in table 1, are organized by their source: the effects arising from anticipated (or expected) inflation and those arising from unanticipated inflation (or the difference between actual inflation and expected inflation) and the associated uncertainty about future inflation.

The Effects of Anticipated Inflation

Much of modern macroeconomic research has been devoted to examining how expectations affect economic decisions. In contrast to the idea that only "surprises" or unanticipated events can have real effects, economic theory suggests that even fully anticipated inflation can distort economic decisions. These "distortions" are said to be the costs of anticipated inflation. A useful way to focus solely on the effects of anticipated inflation is to assume that the future sequence of changes in the general price level is known in advance.[4]

Anticipated inflation influences the allocation of resources in the economy primarily through two types of tax effects. First, inflation effectively imposes a tax on money balances equal to the

---

[3]For a more exhaustive list and detailed analysis of the effects of inflation, see Fischer and Modigliani (1978). Also, Kessel and Alchian (1962) provide a useful discussion of inflation's consequences. For a survey of the earlier literature concerning the theory of inflation, see Laidler and Parkin (1975).

[4]This assumption is made purely for expositional ease. When uncertainty is introduced in the discussion, the effects of anticipated inflation mentioned in this section are simply added to those effects arising from the unanticipated component of inflation and those effects arising from uncertainty. It should be noted that the assumption of certainty does not preclude a variable inflation rate.

reduction of purchasing power of money holdings. For example, an individual holding $100 throughout 1988, when the inflation rate was around 4 percent, lost about $4 in purchasing power.[5]

Since inflation imposes a tax on money balances, it reduces individuals' demand for money.[6] Because individuals will attempt to economize on money holdings during periods of inflation by making extra trips to the bank or automatic teller machine, inflation is said to generate "shoe-leather costs." But the costs of the inflation tax are not merely the physical resources and time expended to avoid the inflation tax, as that term suggests. The total cost or the "gross burden" of the inflation tax more importantly includes the increase in the price paid to maintain real money balances and the value of lost services otherwise provided by money. Inflation, however, generates revenue to the government that indirectly accrues to individuals. The "excess burden" is the difference between the total costs and the government's revenues. Under some plausible assumptions, a

rough estimate of this excess burden from a "small" inflation tax of 5 percent is about $13.4 billion or about 0.3 percent of gross national product (GNP) per year.[7]

The excess burden of the inflation tax on money balances is only part of the total welfare cost associated with inflation. The second type of tax effect arises as anticipated inflation interacts with the structure of the existing income tax system, exacerbating the distortions contained therein. Since the progressive income tax system is not completely indexed against increases in the price level, inflation will subject individuals' incomes to higher average and marginal tax rates. Even if wages fully adjust to inflation so that the real (before-tax) wage rate is approximately constant, an individual's real, after-tax income will decline.[8]

Although one would expect that, through the so-called "bracket-creep" effect, anticipated inflation would influence and distort individual's labor supply decisions, empirical evidence on the effects of marginal taxes suggests that anticipated inflation has little effect on aggregate

---

[5]Inflation as measured by the consumer price index for all urban consumers was 4.4 percent during 1988, while other measures indicate that inflation was between 3.0 percent and 4.5 percent. The current dollar loss of purchasing power of $100 is calculated by the following equation:

$$P_{t+1} \left(\frac{100}{P_t} - \frac{100}{P_{t+1}} \right)$$, where P_t is the general

price level in time t. Since the rate of inflation, π_t, equals

$\frac{P_{t+1} - P_t}{P_t}$, the loss in purchasing power in current dollar

terms equals $100\,\pi_t$. As noted below, the tax on money balances generates revenue to the government.

[6]Another way to see why inflation reduces the demand for money is by noting that inflation increases the opportunity cost of holding those balances. The opportunity cost is the revenue forgone by holding money rather than securities yielding a nominal interest rate, R. (The assumption that money does not yield interest is not important here. As argued by Tatom (1979), among others, even checkable deposits that pay interest are subject to the inflation tax.) Suppose, for example, that there is no expected future inflation. Then the nominal rate paid on a security is its real yield, r. An individual holding $100 in cash balances for transaction services forgoes the real interest payment, $100r, that would have been obtained if he instead bought a $100 bond. In this case, the opportunity cost of holding money balances is r per dollar. Now suppose that inflation, π, in the next period is expected to be positive. The nominal yield on the bond R, will increase roughly by the amount of expected inflation to compensate lenders for the expected loss in purchasing power of the initial loan; the nominal yield will equal the real rate plus an expected inflation premium. (Strictly speaking, $R = (1 + r)(1 + \pi)-1$. Simply adding the real rate of interest and the rate of inflation will be a reasonable approximation provided that the product of the real rate of interest and the rate of inflation,

$r\pi$, is of a small order of magnitude.) The higher nominal rate forgone by holding money implies that the opportunity cost of holding money has increased.

[7]This estimate is intended to give only a rough order of magnitude of the excess burden of inflation. The estimate assumes that the current stock of money (M1) is about $780 billion and that the interest elasticity of the demand for money is -.15. This latter assumption means that when the opportunity cost of holding money increases 1 percent, the quantity of money demanded falls .15 percent. Thus, assuming the real rate of interest is 3 percent, the demand for money would increase by 25 percent to $975 billion if inflation were zero. It should be noted that the estimate of the welfare cost ignores the fact that total "tax" borne by the individual money holder does not go entirely to the government. Since the banking system receives part of the revenue from the inflation tax through money creation, the estimate above understates the excess burden. See Tatom (1976, 1979) and Fischer (1981b) for more detailed discussions of estimating the excess burden of the inflation tax on money balances.

[8]In a preliminary study, Baye and Black (1988) table II, p. 480, estimate that the "bracket-creep-induced inflation tax rate," defined as the difference between the rate of change in gross income necessary to keep utility constant and the associated rate of change in consumption expenditures, ranges from 0.2 percent to 2.4 percent between 1972 and 1981. Furthermore, they find that changes in the tax code during this period, intended to mitigate the bracket-creep effect, were largely offset by simultaneous increases in Social Security taxes (pp. 481-82).

labor supply.[9] Furthermore, to the extent that the current income tax system has become partially indexed by recent tax reform, the effects of inflation in terms of the bracket creep effect have been partially mitigated.[10]

Nonetheless, recent tax reform has not fully insulated individuals from the tax effects of anticipated inflation. Anticipated inflation produces an overstatement of interest income subject to taxation. The nominal interest rate required by lenders includes two components. The first component, r, is a payment to the lender for not consuming today and, hence, constitutes income. The second component, π, is a premium to compensate the lender for the anticipated lost purchasing power of the principal due to inflation. Because the latter component serves to preserve the value of the principal, it is not income in an economic sense. Yet, like income, it is taxed.

To see how an increase in anticipated inflation increases an individual's tax liability for a given before-tax real return, consider the following example. Suppose, first, that no inflation is expected and the marginal income tax rate is 25 percent. A one-year loan that yields a 3 percent (real) return to an individual before taxes generates an after-tax real return of 2.25 percent. If, instead, the anticipated rate of inflation were 2 percent, with the real interest rate on the one-year loan remaining at 3 percent, and the nominal yield rising to 5 percent (the real rate of interest plus the rate of inflation that would be required when abstracting from tax considerations), then the after-tax real rate of return to the lender would fall to 1.75 percent. A rise in the anticipated inflation rate to 5 percent would erode the expected (and actual) return dramatically to 1 percent.

Lenders will demand a nominal return higher than the original real interest rate plus the rate

of inflation to be compensated for the increased future tax liability arising from an increase in anticipated inflation. In the example above, for the lender to supply the same dollar amount of loans as when expected inflation was zero, the same after-tax real return of 2.25 percent would be required; this, in turn, would require a rise in the nominal return from 3 percent to 9.67 percent when expected inflation rises to 5 percent. Hence, the nominal rate of interest must rise by more than the rate of inflation to induce the lender to forgo the same amount of current consumption. If, however, nominal interest rates did not rise enough to keep the after-tax real rate the same when inflation rises, savings would be reduced. It has been estimated that the distortionary effect of a 10 percent rate of inflation on savings over a 20-year period produces a total welfare loss (total cost net of additional revenues to the government in present value terms) of about 7 percent of current savings or, assuming that savings is 10 percent of GNP, about 0.7 percent of current GNP.[11]

Tax incentives combined with anticipated inflation distort financial decisions. Because nominal interest payments on debt are tax-deductible and dividends are effectively taxed twice, anticipated inflation will induce corporations to finance an expansion of their operations by creating debt rather than issuing additional stock. If nominal interest rates do not adjust to anticipated inflation enough to maintain a fixed, after-tax real rate of return, then an increase in anticipated inflation can induce individuals to finance a greater proportion of their consumption and asset purchases with debt.[12] This bias for debt finance, which increases with anticipated inflation, could be costly if, by increasing future debt obligation as a fraction of expected future cash flows, it increases the chances of future default.

---

[9]See, for example, Hausman (1981), who finds that the tax-induced effects on wages do not significantly reduce aggregate labor supply. Inflation's effect on the marginal tax rate could similarly have an insignificant effect on labor supply.

[10]Tatom (1985) discusses the impact of the partial indexation of the income tax system on real tax liabilities. As discussed by Tatom, the currently used method of indexation does not fully mitigate the bracket creep effect because the indexation of tax brackets is calculated using past increases in the general price level. Furthermore, some deductions, credits and adjustments that can be made for tax purposes have maximum dollar limits or nominal ceilings that are not indexed. Even assuming a constant real income before taxes, an expected rise in the

price level implies that a larger portion of real income will be subject to taxes. Without increasing the marginal tax rate, anticipated inflation increases the average tax liability.

[11]Fischer (1981b), p. 23. As he notes, however, the estimate is rough and could be as large as 2 percent to 3 percent of GNP under slightly different, although still plausible, assumptions.

[12]Even if nominal rates fully adjusted to increases in anticipated inflation so as to not affect the after-tax real return, an increase in anticipated inflation decreases the cost of debt finance to firms provided that the corporate marginal tax rate exceeds the individual marginal tax rate.

The impact of anticipated inflation on economic behavior is not restricted solely to inflation-induced tax effects. Specifically, by changing prices, some firms incur lump-sum or "menu" costs. Even if these costs are small, real-world price adjustments occur at discrete times rather than continuously. Assuming that price changes are not sychronized, anticipated inflation (and deflation) can generate relative price changes in the short run. Since these inflation-induced relative price changes do not reflect real, fundamental changes in the economy, they can create a misallocation of resources, resulting in a welfare loss in addition to the explicit costs of changing prices.[13]

The Effects of Unanticipated Inflation and Uncertainty

Unanticipated inflation also can result in a misallocation of resources. Its impact on individuals' behavior, however, is less obvious. In particular, although unanticipated inflation primarily redistributes wealth among people, it is the uncertainty associated with these possible future redistributions that distorts economic behavior. Before discussing these distortionary effects, this section focuses on the distributional effects of unanticipated inflation.

To examine the distributional effects, while initially abstracting from the effects of uncertainty *per se*, suppose there is a one-time shock to the level of inflation. The shock is temporary in the sense that, after one period, the rate of inflation will return to the previously expected time path.[14] This unanticipated inflation influences the distribution of wealth through contracts that fix future nominal cash flows, especially debt contracts.

When debt contracts are fixed in nominal terms, the main effect of unanticipated inflation is to redistribute real wealth to net monetary debtors at the expense of net monetary creditors.[15] Not suspecting the possibility of a divergence between actual and expected inflation, a lender would demand a rate of return that compensates him only for not consuming today and for the lost purchasing power of the initial borrowings due to anticipated inflation. When actual inflation exceeds anticipated inflation, the lender unexpectedly suffers a loss on his loan; the purchasing power of the return on the loan falls below that expected at the time the loan was made.

For example, suppose an individual, who expects zero inflation over the next period, requires a 5 percent nominal (and real) return next period in exchange for lending $100 today. Regardless of next period's inflation, the lender will receive $105 in the next period. If there is a 5 percent (unanticipated) inflation, then the purchasing power of the $105 payment to the lender is identical to that of the $100 lent. In this case, the real net return is zero.

Just as unanticipated inflation erodes the real purchasing power of the return from the loan, it reduces the real liability of the debtor. Along the same lines, if nominal wages specified in labor contracts are fixed for an interval of time, unanticipated inflation reduces an individual's real wage while increasing an employer's income net of the wage bill in real terms.

Although the redistribution of wealth due to unanticipated inflation is important to the individual before and after the fact, it is not easy to say anything meaningful about the welfare implications of the realized or *ex post* redistrib-

---

[13]Mankiw (1985) demonstrates that, in the presence of even small price adjustment costs, optimizing behavior by price-setting firms can produce sticky prices that are inefficient from a social welfare perspective in a deflationary period. He shows, however, that sticky prices in an inflationary period could be more efficient than fully flexible prices. Since price-setting firms produce at lower-than-socially-optimal levels, sticky prices in an inflationary period reduce the wedge between actual and socially optimal output levels.

[14]If the level of inflation were permanently increased above its previously expected and actual level, but the possibility of a future shock were arbitrarily close to zero, the discussion to follow is virtually unchanged. It should be noted, however, that the discussion implicitly assumes that, when contracts are signed, individuals do not perceive the possibility of shock in the future. Hence, the discussion is about a counterfactual and can be misleading. Specifically, if individuals suspected that such a shock might occur

(with a positive probability), they would adjust their behavior, so that the terms of the contract reflect the possibility of a future shock. The implicit assumption is made for expositional purposes, and the possible adjustments in behavior are discussed in turn.

[15]A net monetary creditor's (debtor's) holdings of fixed nominally denominated assets are greater (less) than his holdings of nominally denominated liabilities. See, for example, Kessel and Alchian (1962). Alchian and Kessel (1959) present evidence that the market value of equity of firms classified as net monetary creditors tends to fall during inflationary periods. The converse holds for net monetary debtors.

utions.[16] The losses due to unanticipated inflation are matched by others' gains, so that there is no net change in wealth associated with the redistribution. In an expected or *ex ante* sense, however, the possible (and arbitrary) redistributions have aggregate welfare implications, because they distort behavior, especially that of individuals who dislike risk.

Uncertainty associated with inflation manifests itself quantitatively and qualitatively in both nominal and real contracts. In the presence of fixed nominal wage contracts, uncertainty associated with future inflation can depress the supply and demand for labor. As greater inflation uncertainty increases the difficulties and costs of forecasting future inflation, wage negotiations become more complex and costly. Consequently, without nominal wage indexation when future inflation becomes more uncertain, individuals and firms are less willing to lock themselves into fixed nominal contracts.

But the effects of inflation uncertainty will be partially alleviated as labor markets adjust. Greater uncertainty about future increases in the general price level gives risk-averse individuals and firms an incentive to increase the degree of indexation in wage contracts and to reduce the duration of the contract. The increased degree of indexation and the shortening of the length of the nominal contracts increases the responsiveness of nominal wages to unanticipated inflation.[17] Nevertheless, a recent empirical study, which accounts for the greater wage indexation induced by greater inflation uncertainty, indicates that an increase in inflation uncertainty similar to that which occurred

roughly between the 1960s and the 1970s would reduce growth in real GNP in the long term by approximately 2 percent.[18]

Inflation uncertainty also affects the demand and supply of nominally denominated debt of different maturities. Risk-averse lenders might be less willing to purchase a long-term nominal bond over short-term nominal bonds. As forecasting future inflation becomes more difficult with longer time horizons, the opportunity cost of holding a longer-term nominal bond is more uncertain. In addition, a given permanent unexpected movement in the rate of inflation will have a greater impact on the market value of the longer-term bond and, consequently, a greater impact on the realized rate of return from selling that bond. To compensate lenders for taking on additional risk, the required nominal yield on a bond with a longer maturity will embody a greater risk premium.

The uncertainty associated with future inflation creates an element of uncertainty about real, future rates of return on all investments whose returns are not fixed in real terms. The more uncertain are the future rates of inflation, holding all else constant, the greater the risk premia for all bonds of any given maturity.[19] As the required nominal yields on instruments of all maturities increase with greater inflation uncertainty, the cost of capital financed by nominal debt increases. Not all investments, however, are fixed in nominal terms. The risk-averse individual can hedge, at least partially, against unanticipated inflation by investing in projects or holding financial instruments whose actual and expected real returns are relatively

---

[16]Such a value judgment would depend on the specified social welfare function—in particular, the relative weights assigned to each individual's utility. Nonetheless, the decline in wealth experienced by some in a period of positive unanticipated inflation does not necessarily provide sufficient justification, in terms of a Pareto efficient criterion, for a ''forced'' transfer of resources to restore the initial distribution of wealth.

[17]When the economy is subject to real as well as to nominal disturbances, however, complete wage indexation is not desirable. See Gray (1976) for example. Also, see Holland (1984b) for a more detailed discussion of the effects of inflation uncertainty on labor markets.

[18]Holland (1988), p. 478-80. This is a cumulative effect over a number of years (e.g. 2 to 6 years). In general, however, there is mixed evidence about the effects of inflation uncertainty on output growth. For example, Jansen (1989) finds that the conditional variance of inflation as a measure of inflation uncertainty has no significant impact on real output growth.

[19]Taylor (1981), among others, finds a positive relation between the average rate of inflation and the variability of inflation across nations and through time. This stylized fact, however, does not imply any causal link between the two. Moreover, greater variability does not imply greater uncertainty. Nevertheless, preliminary evidence indicates that inflation variability is positively related to uncertainty, as measured by the variance of the forecast errors from survey data or from an econometric model for predicting future inflation, or as measured by the dispersion of inflationary expectations within a survey. But Jansen (1989) recently found no statistical relation between inflation and the conditional variance of inflation. See Taylor (1981) and Holland (1984a), who review the existing evidence on the relations between average inflation, the variability of inflation and uncertainty.

independent of future rates of inflation, such as human capital, homes and corporate stocks.[20]

Even a complete hedge against unanticipated inflation would not eliminate the welfare costs of uncertainty, however. Substantial transaction costs can be incurred by those who attempt to eliminate the risk associated with future inflation from their portfolios. In any case, as individuals and firms attempt to hedge against unanticipated movements in the general price level, inflation uncertainty can distort asset accumulation and the aggregate allocation of resources.[21]

Another distorting feature of the uncertainty associated with price movements arises when information about the source of price movements is not available without costs. If information were costless to obtain, the appropriate response to a given increase in prices is clear. For example, an unanticipated temporary increase in observed prices correctly attributed to monetary policy (a nominal factor), rather than to an increase in demand for some goods relative to others (a real factor), would not alter the decisions of producers in the absence of nominal rigidities. If it is costly, however, to distinguish between general price movements produced by nominal factors from those created by real factors, price movements will be "noisy." Confusion about the source of a given price movement and the appropriate response will produce excessive relative price variability, resulting in a misallocation of resources.[22]

WHY NOT A ZERO RATE OF INFLATION?

While any positive inflation has a large number of distortionary effects, a zero inflation rate might not necessarily be desirable—even in the long run. First, the various measures of inflation (for example, the consumer price index and the GNP implicit price deflator) do not control perfectly for quality improvement of products over time. To the extent that the lower and higher quality versions of goods are treated as comparable, the difference in their prices will be measured as inflation; the resulting measure will tend to overstate the actual inflation rate. Given this positive bias in inflation measures, it has been suggested that a 2 percent inflation rate measured by the usual price indexes would be associated with roughly stable prices.[23] Moreover, some would contend that inflation also has some important benefits like providing a cheaper source of government revenue or creating higher output and employment, so that the long-run desirable rate of inflation is not zero, but positive.

Optimal Taxation

Some have argued that inflation is required for optimal taxation.[24] The inflation tax provides

---

[20]While homes appear to be good hedges against expected and unexpected inflation, the evidence for human capital is inconclusive, at least for the long run. Moreover, a puzzling negative relation between stock returns and expected as well as unexpected inflation has been widely documented, but not resolved. See, for example, Fama and Schwert (1977).

[21]See Jaffee and Kleiman (1977) for a more detailed discussion of the effects of inflation uncertainty on the allocation of resources.

[22]To be sure, relative price variability need not be a cost. To the extent that relative price movements signal real disturbances to the economy, those movements contain important information facilitating an efficient allocation of resources. Fischer (1981a) provides a summary of competing approaches to explaining the relation between the average inflation rate and relative price variability. Taylor (1981) and Fischer (1981b) do not find evidence indicating a causal relation between inflation and variability of relative prices. Rather, Taylor (1981) and Fischer (1981a) find evidence consistent with the notion that the positive relations between average inflation, the variability of inflation and relative price variability in the 1970s have been driven by supply shocks (for example, energy and food shocks). Taylor (1981) also finds that accommodative monetary policies aiming to stabilize output and employment in light of real disturbances to the economy contributed in a large part to the increased variability of inflation in the 1970s. Furthermore, Fischer (1981a) concludes that policy shocks that could have created confusion about the source of price movements do not appear to be associated with lower aggregate economic activity.

[23]Friedman (1969), p. 47. According to Friedman (1969), however, a negative inflation rate (about 2 percent deflation) correctly measured would be optimal. In this case, a zero inflation rate, as measured by the various price indices would be a desirable target. (See Alchian and Klein (1973) for a critical assessment of the appropriateness of the price indexes for policy.)

[24]See, for example, Phelps (1973). The government's revenue from the production of money is the nominal rate of interest times the stock of the monetary base (total reserves plus currency). Using the fact that the ratio of the monetary base to the money stock (M1) is about 40 percent and assuming that the real interest rate is about 3 percent, the revenue with a 5 percent inflation tax on a stock of M1 of $780 billion is about $25 billion per year in current dollar terms. The inflation tax alone generates $15.6 billion per year. It is important to note that unanticipated inflation implicitly generates additional revenue to the government (a net monetary debtor) through its effect on the real value of public debt. By reducing the purchasing power of interest payments on outstanding debt, unanticipated inflation lowers the real liability of the government and the amount of revenue to be raised through income taxes.

the government an alternative source of revenue to other explicit and distorting taxes—for example, income taxes.[25] The theory of optimal taxation suggests that, to finance a given level of public expenditures, the government should trade off the costs of distortions arising from inflation against those arising from other taxes.[26] From this perspective, the optimal inflation tax rate equates the marginal cost per dollar of revenue from the inflation tax and from other distorting taxes.

Recent empirical evidence on the marginal costs of the inflation tax and other taxes, however, casts doubt on the relevance of the optimal taxation theory to justify a positive rate of inflation. These studies suggest that the marginal cost per dollar revenue of the inflation tax at any positive rate of inflation exceeds that for alternative taxes set at plausible rates.[27] In other words, inflation does not necessarily provide a cheaper source of government revenue. Furthermore, the interaction between inflation and the distortions produced by the tax system suggests that the marginal cost of income taxes could be positively related to the rate of inflation; thus, lowering the inflation tax not only would reduce the welfare losses associated with the inflation tax, but make income taxation a cheaper source of government revenue.[28]

The Inflation and Unemployment Trade-off

The older argument used to justify positive inflation hinges on the so-called Phillips curve trade-off between inflation and unemployment. Figure 1, which depicts the apparent trade-off that emerged in the 1960s, could be interpreted as suggesting that, by tolerating a higher level of inflation, society could benefit from lower levels of unemployment.

One possible story behind such an interpretation is that an expansionary monetary policy that increases the general price level can increase output if nominal wages are relatively fixed. With fixed nominal wages, a rise in inflation can induce firms to increase output. This incentive arises because the firm's marginal profit—that is, the change in real revenues net of the change in the real wage bill realized by expanding output—increases with unanticipated inflation. If nominal wages were not fixed, they would adjust quickly to the increase in prices to maintain a given real wage rate; output and unemployment would be essentially independent of inflation. But, according to the trade-off view, the existence of nominal wage contracts means that, by generating inflation, the government can decrease the rate of unemployment and thereby enhance social welfare.

The possibility of exploiting the trade-off between inflation and unemployment with monetary policy, however, depends on the way in which inflationary expectations are formed and incorporated into nominal wages. If inflation is correctly anticipated and incorporated into wage contracts, then real output will be independent of inflation in the long run. Even if the government were to generate inflation un-

---

[25]If there were non-distorting taxes, then the excess burden of the inflation tax discussed above would render inflation an "inefficient" tax. But, in the absence of non-distorting taxes as a source of revenue to the government, the optimal rate of inflation could be positive. Browning (1987), table 1, p. 16, estimates that in 1984 the total welfare cost associated with the distortionary effects of the labor tax ranged from $55.9 billion to $212.6 billion under various assumptions. As a percentage of tax revenues from labor, the welfare loss ranged from 7.5 percent to 28.5 percent, well below the inflation-induced welfare loss as a percentage of revenues from the inflation tax (about 86 percent).

[26]In recent studies, Mankiw (1987) and Poterba and Rotemberg (1988) test the implications of the hypothesis that the government optimally trades off the distortions from explicit income taxes and inflation. While Mankiw finds preliminary evidence supporting the hypothesis for the United States, Poterba and Rotemberg, who look at different nations, do not find conclusive evidence. That the hypothesis is not fully supported by the data might be a result of the maintained assumption that the distortionary effects of the explicit tax system are independent of the distortionary effects of the inflation tax. Given the discussion above, this assumption seems inappropriate.

[27]For example, Tatom (1976), p. 20, shows that marginal cost per dollar revenue of the inflation tax, assuming that the elasticity of demand for money is − .15, is 44 percent. This estimate is not conditional on the inflation rate, but it is highly sensitive to the assumed elasticity of demand for money. For example, an elasticity of − .25 would imply a marginal cost of 83.33 percent. Browning (1987), table 2, p. 21, shows that the marginal welfare cost from taxes on labor earnings ranges from 9.9 percent to 33.2 percent under the assumption that labor supply is not highly responsive to the marginal income tax rate (see footnote 9).

[28]It should be noted, however, that since the marginal cost of taxes on labor earnings is positively related to the marginal tax rate, the theory of optimal taxation in light of the evidence on marginal welfare costs does not necessarily imply a zero rate of inflation. Nevertheless, if the marginal cost of the inflation tax were positively related to inflation, the optimal rate of inflation would more likely be zero.

Figure 1
The Inflation-Unemployment Trade-off

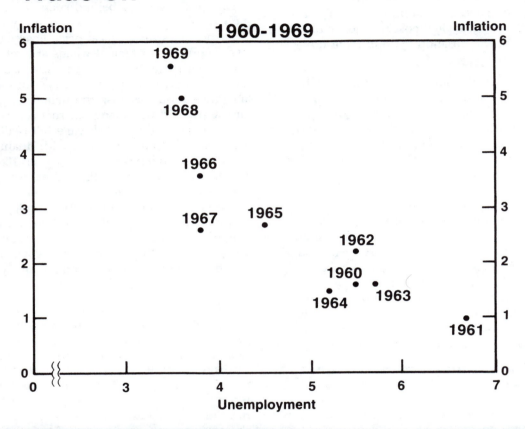

expectedly, the increase in output and decrease in unemployment would only be transitory. Subsequent wage changes would restore the original level of the real wage. As a consequence, the original profit rate would be restored, with output and unemployment returning to their original equilibrium or "natural" levels; the trade-off between unemployment and inflation would not exist in the long run.[29]

Indeed, figure 2, which plots the combinations of unemployment and inflation in the 1970s and the 1980s, does not support the existence of a long-run trade-off. While a short-run trade-off might exist, whether or not it is operative for the purpose of enhancing social welfare is un-

clear. Attempts to "fool" individuals systematically, by continuously creating surprise inflation so as to exploit the short-run trade-off, would not improve the welfare of all individuals because, although some individuals experience unexpected wealth gains, others suffer wealth losses. In addition, attempts to repeatedly fool individuals would increase the costs associated with inflation due to increased inflation uncertainty.

Moreover, as individuals and firms adjust to the higher inflation uncertainty, the trade-off becomes less favorable, because greater inflation uncertainty increases incentives for indexation. With greater wage indexation, a given

[29]See Fischer (1977), for example. The notion that real output and employment are independent of the inflation rate in the long run (a vertical Phillips curve) is known as the "Natural Rate Hypothesis."

Figure 2
The Inflation-Unemployment "Trade-off"

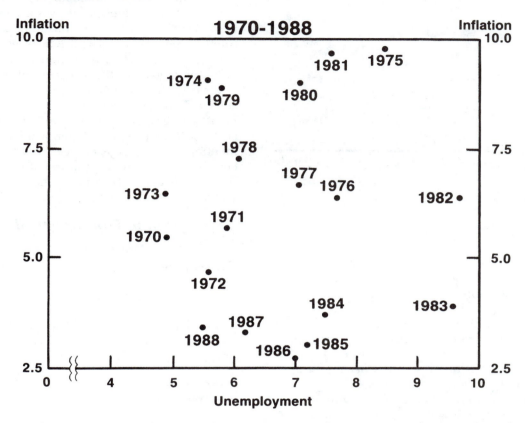

amount of surprise inflation will have a smaller transitory effect on output and employment as nominal wages become more responsive to actual inflation. Accordingly, the trade-off becomes steeper. If attempts to exploit the trade-off also increases average inflation, the trade-off shifts outward, so that a given rate of inflation will be associated with a higher rate of unemployment.

WHAT ARE THE COSTS OF REDUCING INFLATION?

The suggested benefits of inflation seem hardly compelling to justify any positive, sustained inflation. The long-run desirability of achieving stable prices, however, does not necessarily mean that the current rate of inflation is unac-

ceptable. Specifically, the latter discussion suggests that policies to reduce inflation and ultimately achieve the long-run desirable inflation rate can be costly. That is, any short-run trade-off between inflation and unemployment implies that anti-inflationary policies will produce temporary increases in unemployment.

Are The Costs Too High?

Table 2 shows the inflation rate, as measured by the GNP implicit price deflator, and the civilian unemployment rate; it indicates that the large reduction in inflation from 1979 to 1988 was accompanied by significantly large rates of unemployment. These observed high rates of unemployment, however, can overstate the costs of the anti-inflationary policy. Regardless of the current inflation rate or its prospective

Table 2
Unemployment and Inflation, 1979-88

Year	Civilian unemployment	Inflation[1]
1979	5.8%	8.9%
1980	7.1	9.0
1981	7.6	9.7
1982	9.7	6.4
1983	9.6	3.9
1984	7.5	3.7
1985	7.2	3.0
1986	7.0	2.7
1987	6.2	3.3
1988	5.5	3.4

SOURCE: *Economic Report of the President* (1989) and *Economic Indicators* (January 1989).

[1]Percentage change from the previous year in the GNP price deflator.

path, temporary unemployment is an efficient response to fundamental changes in the economy, as individuals search for new jobs. Consequently, the "natural" rate of unemployment (the rate of unemployment consistent with a steady inflation) can be positive. It has been estimated that, assuming the natural rate of unemployment is 6·percent, the decline in inflation from 9 percent in 1980 to 3.2 percent in the middle of 1987 was associated with about 2.4 percentage points of "excess" unemployment per percentage-point reduction in inflation.[30]

Similarly constructed estimates have been used to suggest that reducing inflation is unacceptable on efficiency grounds:

> The damage that high unemployment does to economic efficiency is enormous and inadequately appreciated. By contrast, the harm that inflation

inflicts on the economy is often exaggerated; and those costs which are not mythical can be minimized or even eliminated by indexing. Hardheaded devotion to the principle of efficiency thus argues for worrying less about inflation and running a high-pressure economy in which jobs are plentiful.[31]

By definition, excess unemployment is inefficient, because it implies that resources, otherwise available to increase consumption opportunities, have been wasted. But excess unemployment is only a transitional cost as the economy adjusts to the long-run desirable inflation rate. When the inflation goal is finally achieved and sustained, the excess unemployment will disappear. In contrast, the welfare costs associated with inflation are incurred indefinitely—that is, each year in which the economy's institutional features (for example, the explicit tax system) make the distortionary effects of inflation discussed above relevant.[32]

The Optimal Time Path of Reducing Inflation

Among the important questions that policymakers must face is the timing of anti-inflationary policy actions to reach the long-run desirable inflation rate. Given the initial inflation rate, the speed with which the desirable inflation rate is reached partly determines the cost of that policy.

One recent study shows that there are large differences in the costs of policies that vary with respect to their timing[33]. On the basis of various models, this study calculates the costs of several policies to bring inflation from 7.5 percent to zero. The costs of the policies are estimated in terms of output losses using a relationship known as Okun's law that translates each percentage point of excess unemployment into a 3.2 percent reduction in real output. For example, employing a Phillips curve model, this study

[30]Friedman (1988), p. 66. Each percentage point of unemployment above the natural rate (or that in a "fully employed" economy, with a steady inflation rate) constitutes a percentage point of "excess" unemployment. Of course, because the natural rate of unemployment is not observed and is subject to change during the evolution of the economy subject to permanent and transitory real shocks, one could argue that Friedman's estimate understates (or overstates, for that matter) the welfare loss associated with the reduction of inflation in the 1980s.

[31] Blinder (1987), p. 65.

[32]Of course, not all anti-inflationary policies can be justified. Rather, without a careful evaluation of the costs and benefits of reducing inflation, a monetary policy that pro-

duces an inflation above (or below) the optimal rate does not easily follow from an efficiency criterion. As pointed out by Meyer and Rasche (1980, p. 14), among others, however, if the benefits from eliminating inflation (or identically, the costs of sustaining inflation) increase at the same rate of real potential output, then any anti-inflationary policy would be justified, irrespective of the policy's costs, provided that the costs are finite and that the initial gain from such a policy is positive.

[33]Meyer and Rasche (1980).

found that a gradual policy to eliminate inflation over a 23-year period could generate a discounted cumulative output loss of $1 trillion (in 1972 terms), whereas a policy that reached the inflation goal in 11 years could result in a discounted cumulative output loss of $1.5 trillion.[34]

The relation between the time path and the costs of the policy depends on the dynamic relation between unemployment and inflation. In addition to the degree to which the economy is indexed, this dynamic relation depends on the credibility of the anti-inflationary policy and expectations about future inflation. If, as assumed in the Phillips curve model, expectations depend on past inflation, a given inflation-reducing policy will be more costly; with nominal rigidities in the economy and a sluggish adjustment of expectations, the short-term trade-off between inflation and unemployment can be large. To achieve a specific reduction in inflation over a given time span can require higher levels of unemployment and greater output losses. If inflationary expectations are forward-looking and the policy is credible, however, the link between inflation and unemployment is weaker; in this case, unemployment is less responsive to movements in inflation. Accordingly, credible anti-inflationary policies will be less costly in terms of output losses than incredible ones.[35]

The time path of the anti-inflationary policy is also important because it determines the speed with which the gains from such a policy are realized fully. For example, a gradual policy that eliminates inflation over 50 years might not generate significant output losses, but the present discounted value of the benefits from that policy could be infinitesimally small.

CONCLUSION

Analyses of the acceptability of any particular positive inflation should start by asking what is the optimal rate of inflation. In reviewing the various effects and costs of inflation, this article questions the validity of the notion that any positive inflation could be desirable as a long-run phenomenon. The surprisingly large number of distortionary effects resulting from inflation weakens the possible justifications for sustained positive inflation.

The long-run desirability of zero inflation need not imply, however, that a positive rate of inflation is never acceptable for any period. The transitional costs of reducing inflation over a short period could be considerably large relative to the benefits of quickly eradicating inflation. But the costs of fighting the current inflation do not preclude the desirability of an anti-inflationary policy, either. Indeed, the steady reduction in monetary aggregate growth since 1987 (measured by M1, M2 or the adjusted monetary base) suggests that the trade-off has been faced, at least implicitly. In any case, the acceptability of an inflation in excess of the long-run desirable rate depends on the appropriately measured net benefits of alternative paths to achieve the ultimate inflation goal.

REFERENCES

Alchian, Armen A., and Reuben A. Kessel. "Redistribution of Wealth Through Inflation," *Science* (September 4, 1959), pp. 535-39.

Alchian, Armen A., and Benjamin Klein. "On a Correct Measure of Inflation," *Journal of Money, Credit and Banking* (Part 1, February 1973), pp. 173-81.

Baye, Michael R., and Dan A. Black. "The Microeconomic Foundations of Measuring Bracket Creep and Other Tax Changes," *Economic Inquiry* (July 1988), pp. 471-84.

Blinder, Alan S. *Hard Heads, Soft Hearts: Tough-Minded Economics for a Just Society* (Addison-Wesley, 1987).

Browning, Edgar K. "On the Marginal Welfare Cost of Taxation," *American Economic Review* (March 1987), pp. 11-23.

Clark, Lindley H. Jr. "Why Don't We Aim for Zero Inflation?" *Wall Street Journal*, February 9, 1989.

Cukierman, Alex. "Central Bank Behavior and Credibility: Some Recent Theoretical Developments," this *Review* (May 1986), pp. 5-17.

Fama, Eugene F., and G. William Schwert. "Asset Returns and Inflation," *Journal of Financial Economics* (November 1977), pp. 115-46.

Fischer, Stanley. "Relative Shocks, Relative Price Variability, and Inflation," *Brookings Papers on Economic Activity* (1981a), pp. 381-431.

---

[34]Ibid., pp.7-8.

[35]Taylor (1983) shows that even if overlapping wage contracts temporarily fix nominal wages, a policy that gradually reduces inflation can be relatively costless provided that expectations about future inflation are rationally formed and everyone believes that the policy will actually be implemented. See Cukierman (1986) and references cited therein for analyses of the institutional and economic factors that tend to detract from the credibility of anti-inflationary policies. These analyses suggest that, without a perfect resolution of the credibility problem, the economy is likely to be characterized by an "inflationary bias." Fischer and Summers (1989) show how by decreasing the marginal costs of inflation, the government, recognizing the importance of its reputation, can reduce that bias. Without reputational considerations, however, reducing the costs of inflation can increase the inflationary bias.

_____ . "Towards an Understanding of the Costs of Inflation: II," in Karl Brunner and Allan H. Meltzer, eds., *The Costs and Consequences of Inflation*, Carnegie-Rochester Conference Series on Public Policy (North-Holland, Autumn 1981b), pp. 5-42.

_____ . "Long-Term Contracts, Rational Expectations, and the Optimal Money Supply Rule," *Journal of Political Economy* (February 1977), pp. 191-206.

Fischer, Stanley, and Franco Modigliani. "Towards an Understanding of the Real Effects and Costs of Inflation," *Weltwirtschaftliches Archiv* (Band 114, 1978), pp. 810-33.

Fischer, Stanley, and Lawrence H. Summers. "Should Governments Learn to Live With Inflation?" *American Economic Review* (May 1989), pp. 382-87.

Friedman, Benjamin M. "Lessons on Monetary Policy from the 1980s," *Journal of Economic Perspectives* (Summer 1988), pp. 51-72.

Friedman, Milton. "The Optimum Quantity of Money," *The Optimum Quantity of Money and Other Essays* (Aldine, 1969), pp. 1-50.

Gray, Jo Anna. "Wage Indexation: A Macroeconomic Approach," *Journal of Monetary Economics* (April 1976), pp. 221-35.

Greenspan, Alan. "1989 Monetary Policy Objectives," Testimony to the Congress (February 21, 1989) in *Federal Reserve Bulletin* (April 1989), pp. 272-77.

Hausman, Jerry A. "Labor Supply," in Henry J. Aaron and Joseph A. Pechman, eds., *How Taxes Affect Economic Behavior* (Brookings Institution, 1981), pp. 27-72.

Holland, A. Steven. "Indexation and the Effect of Inflation Uncertainty on Real GNP," *Journal of Business* (October 1988), pp. 473-84.

_____ . "Does Higher Inflation Lead to More Uncertain Inflation?" this *Review* (February 1984a), pp. 15-26.

_____ . "The Impact of Inflation Uncertainty on the Labor Market," this *Review* (August/September 1984b) pp. 21-28.

Jaffee, Dwight M., and Ephraim Kleiman. "The Welfare Implications of Uneven Inflation," in Erik Lundberg, ed., *Inflation Theory and Anti-Inflation Policy* (Macmillan, 1977), pp. 285-307.

Jansen, Dennis W. "Does Inflation Uncertainty Affect Output Growth? Further Evidence," this Review (July/August 1989), pp. 43-54.

Kessel, Reuben A., and Armen A. Alchian. "Effects of Inflation," *Journal of Political Economy* (December 1962), pp. 521-37.

Laidler, David E., and Michael Parkin. "Inflation: A Survey," *Economic Journal* (December 1975), pp. 741-809.

Mankiw, N. Gregory. "The Optimal Collection of Seigniorage: Theory and Evidence," *Journal of Monetary Economics* (September 1987), pp. 327-41.

_____ . "Small Menu Costs and Large Business Cycles: A Macroeconomic Model of Monopoly," *Quarterly Journal of Economics* (May 1985), pp. 529-37.

Meyer, Laurence H., and Robert H. Rasche. "On the Costs and Benefits of Anti-Inflation Policies," this *Review* (February 1980), pp. 3-14.

Murray, Alan. "Fed's Goal is to Cut Inflation to Zero, Greenspan Says," *Wall Street Journal*, March 28, 1989.

Phelps, Edmund S. "Inflation in the Theory of Public Finance," *Swedish Journal of Economics* (March 1973), pp. 67-82.

Poterba, James M., and Julio J. Rotemberg. "Inflation and Taxation with Optimizing Governments," National Bureau of Economic Research Working Papers Series, 2567 (April 1988).

Stein, Herbert. "Inflation is Here, Still," *Wall Street Journal*, March 6, 1989.

Tatom, John A. "Federal Income Tax Reform in 1985: Indexation," this *Review* (February 1985), pp. 5-12.

_____ . "The Marginal Welfare Cost of the Revenue From Money Creation and the 'Optimal' Rate of Inflation," *The Manchester School* (December 1979), pp.359-68.

_____ . "The Welfare Cost of Inflation," this *Review* (November 1976), pp. 9-22.

Taylor, John B. "Union Wage Settlements During a Disinflation," *American Economic Review* (December 1983), pp. 981-93.

_____ . "On the Relation Between the Variability of Inflation and the Average Inflation Rate," in Karl Brunner and Allan H. Meltzer, eds., *The Costs and Consequences of Inflation*, Carnegie-Rochester Conference Series on Public Policy (North-Holland, Autumn 1981), pp. 57-86.

Article 4

David P. Ely
Assistant Professor
San Diego State University

Kenneth J. Robinson
Economist
Federal Reserve Bank of Dallas

The Stock Market and Inflation:
A Synthesis of the Theory and Evidence

One of the more puzzling anomalies found in financial markets is the poor performance of the stock market during periods of inflation. The failure of equities to maintain their value during inflationary time periods is considered anomalous as stocks, representing claims to *real* assets, should provide a good hedge against inflation. Moreover, if the so-called "Fisher" effect holds, stocks should be positively related to measures of expected inflation as well.

As shown in Chart 1, during the rapid inflation years of the 1970s, movements in U.S. stock prices failed to keep pace with movements in the general level of prices. This pattern has also been found in a number of other countries. Table 1 contains correlation coefficients between real stock returns and inflation for the Group of Seven countries using monthly data over the period 1950–1986. As that table shows, a significant negative relationship holds during at least one extended subperiod for all except one of the countries listed. And a significant negative relationship is found in four of the seven countries for the overall period of 1950–1986. Against this backdrop, it is not surprising that "inflation fears" were cited as a possible contributing factor to the stock market crash of October 1987.[1]

A number of studies have documented the inverse relationship between real common stock returns and various measures of both actual and expected inflation.[2] The literature is generally divided, however, over the reasons why equities might fail to maintain their value during periods of inflation. This paper surveys the two main arguments that have been advanced as possible explanations for this observed anomaly in the U.S. stock market. First, the so-called "tax-effect" hy-

pothesis is examined. This hypothesis focuses on the treatment of depreciation and the valuation of inventories in periods of inflation. Particularly, share prices fail to keep pace with inflation because inflation increases corporate tax liabilities and thus reduces after-tax earnings. Here, inflation can be said, in an econometric sense, to "cause"—or more precisely to temporally precede—movements in stock prices.

The "proxy-effect" hypothesis is the alternative explanation for why real stock returns are negatively correlated with inflation. In its current form, this hypothesis involves two assumptions—one that cyclical variations in output and earnings growth are positively correlated, and the other that monetary policy is countercyclical. The central tenet here is that lower stock returns signal lower expected future output and earnings growth, which, in turn, initiates a countercyclical policy response by the central bank. Individuals anticipate the expansion in the money supply and thus anticipate future inflation, which leads to an increase in *current* inflation. So, when stock re-

The authors would like to thank Mike Cox, Joe Haslag and Scott Hein for helpful comments without implicating them in our conclusions.

[1] The Report of the Presidential Task Force on Market Mechanisms *(1988, p. I-13)* states that *"It is meaningless whether or not these inflation fears were justified, for it is clear that for as long as financial authorities were responding to the inflation threat—whether real or imagined..."* the equity market might suffer.

[2] See Bodie *(1976)*, Nelson *(1976)*, and Fama and Schwert *(1977)*.

Chart 1
Annual CPI and S&P 500
Common Stock Price Index

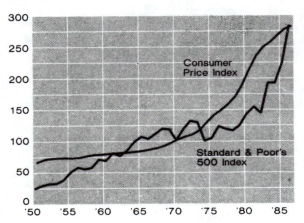

Sources of Primary Data: Standard & Poor's Corporation.
U.S. Bureau of Labor Statistics.

Table 1
Real Stock Returns and Inflation:
Various Periods

Country	1950-1959	1960-1969	1970-1979	1980-1986	1950-1986
United States	−0.05	−0.28*	−0.24*	−0.34*	−0.25*
Japan	−0.08	−0.21*	−0.33*	−0.26*	−0.20*
West Germany	−0.05	−0.19*	−0.02	−0.12	−0.09
France	−0.24*	−0.12	−0.005	−0.15	—0.13*
United Kingdom	−0.02	−0.16	−0.06	−0.08	−0.04
Italy	−0.26*	−0.16	−0.29*	−0.09	−0.20*
Canada	−0.06	−0.12	−0.04	−0.26*	−0.03

* Significant at the 1-percent level.

turns fall, inflation increases. Although inflation in this case, is negatively correlated with stock returns, more precisely, stock returns temporally precede inflation. Thus, in an econometric sense, they are said to "cause" inflation.[3]

In the following analysis, a simple model of stock-price determination is offered. (*See the accompanying box for a description.*) This model can be used to highlight the role that inflation has played in determining both stock prices and stock returns in the U.S. economy. In the context of this model, the tax-effect hypothesis is first examined, with emphasis on particular features of the U.S. Tax Code that may have given rise to inflation's adverse effect on equity markets. This is followed by an exposition of the proxy-effect hypothesis, which shows how monetary policy may have historically contributed to the anomalous relationship between stock returns and inflation.

Tax-effect hypothesis: the firm's perspective

Adherents of the tax-effect hypothesis argue that the adverse effect of inflation on share prices stems primarily from two sources—inflation's effect on after-tax earnings of firms and inflation's effect on individuals' portfolio allocation. This section considers the first of these two sources.

From the standpoint of firms, inflation has a detrimental effect due primarily to two features of the U.S. Tax Code. The first of these features is the treatment of depreciation. Traditionally, the value of the depreciation deduction allowed for firms has been based on the original or "historic cost" of an asset, and *not* on its full replacement value. In a period of rising prices, then, the value of the depreciation allowance becomes inadequate and real corporate tax liabilities increase. In this way, inflation leads to a reduction in real after-tax earnings of firms and a consequent reduction in real dividends and stock prices.

Also contributing to the adverse effect of inflation on the firm is the treatment of inventory valuation under U.S. tax laws. When inventories are valued under FIFO (or first-in-first-out) accounting, inflation leads to an understatement of the costs of replacing these inventories. As is the case under the use of historic-cost accounting for depreciation charges, inflation raises the effective corporate tax burden, thus depressing net earn-

ings. Each of the above two factors—depreciation allowances and inventory valuation—acts to make inflation a penalty to firm profitability; consequently, inflation penalizes a firm's dividends and share prices.

There is, however, one potential *benefit* to firm profitability from rising prices. Namely, at higher rates of inflation, nominal interest rates are higher. And, since firms are allowed to deduct the full nominal interest payments on debt, accounting profits are in this regard reduced by inflation.

The net corporate tax burden caused by inflation thus depends on a comparison of the *penalty* arising from historic-cost accounting methods to the *benefit* arising from the deductibility of nominal interest payments on debt. Using simulation analysis, Hasbrouck (1983) finds that, under tax laws in effect through 1980, the loss due to historic-cost accounting outweighs the leverage gain at low inflation rates. Hasbrouck estimates that the corporate tax-maximizing inflation rate is in the range of 7–9 percent. Beyond these rates, inflation actually reduces the corporate tax burden since gains resulting from the use of debt financing outweigh the effects of historic-cost accounting.[4] It is worth noting that from 1973 to 1980, when real stock prices tended to fall, the rate of inflation averaged 9.2 percent per year. Interpreted in light of Hasbrouck's esti-

---

[3] *Modigliani and Cohn (1979) offer a third explanation. Investors commit two "major errors" in evaluating stocks during periods of inflation. First, investors are said to be unable to distinguish between real and nominal rates of return in the valuation of equities. Second, market participants fail to realize the gain that flows from a depreciation in the value of corporate debt outstanding in a time of inflation. In essence, Modigliani and Cohn argue that investors suffer from a form of "money illusion." This framework is ignored in the current analysis as it is outside the generally accepted paradigm of market efficiency and thus has not generated much interest.*

[4] *Maher and Nantell (1983) argue that there is no offset possible from debt usage as the premium that must be paid to bondholders in the face of inflation exceeds the tax advantages of debt financing. The crucial assumption for this result to hold is that the bondholder's marginal tax rate must exceed the corporate tax rate.*

A Model of Share Price Determination

This box outlines a simple model of stock-price determination helpful for illustrating the relationship between stock prices and inflation. In order to focus attention on the issues considered in this article—specifically, on the tax-effect hypothesis and on the proxy-effect hypothesis—certain simplifying assumptions are made.

In general, the price of a firm's stock today can be expressed as the present discounted value of expected future dividends (Brealey and Myers 1984, Chap. 4). That is,

$$(1) \qquad V_t = \sum_{i=1}^{\infty} \frac{DIV_{t+i}^e}{(1+R)^i}$$

where V_t equals the dollar price of the firm's stock today, DIV_{t+i}^e equals the firm's nominal expected future dividend (dividend in period $t+i$), and R represents the nominal rate (presumed constant over time) at which market participants discount these expected future cash flows (or the rate of return required by investors).

Consider first the numerator of this expression. There are essentially two ways that expected dividends can grow over time. One of these is through growth in expected *real* earnings, and the other is through inflation. That is, $DIV_{t+i}^e = div_{t+i}^e * P_{t+i}^e$ where div_{t+i}^e represents real earnings of the firm in period $t+i$ and P_{t+i}^e is the expected price level in period $t+i$. Since the purpose of this paper is to investigate the relationship between *inflation* and the stock market, both actual and expected real earnings will be provisionally treated as constant over time. This allows div_{t+i}^e to be expressed simply as div in all periods.

For simplicity, it is also assumed that inflation, π, is constant over time and fully anticipated. Under these assumptions, P_{t+i}^e

can be rewritten simply as $P_t(1+\pi)^i$. This allows expected nominal dividends to be separated into its two components, real dividends and the general level of prices, so $DIV_{t+i}^e = div*P_t(1+\pi)^i$.

Turning now to the denominator of this expression, the nominal rate of discount can be separated into its two components—inflation and the (constant) real rate of discount (r)—by making use of the Fisher relationship. That is, $1+R$ equals $(1+r)(1+\pi)$.

With these simplifications, the value of the firm's stock can then be expressed as:

$$(2) \qquad V_t = \sum_{i=1}^{\infty} \frac{div * P_t (1+\Pi)^i}{(1+r)^i (1+\Pi)^i},$$

which, upon simplification, reduces to:

$$(3) \qquad V_t = \frac{div \cdot P_t}{r}$$

As equation 3 makes clear, stock prices will not increase proportionately with an increase in the general price level if inflation is associated with either (1) a reduction in real dividends of the firm, or (2) an increase in individuals' discount rate. Equation 3 is thus helpful in explaining both the tax-effect hypothesis and the proxy-effect hypothesis. The tax-effect hypothesis, for example, is represented in equation 3 as the case where either (1) div is reduced, or (2) r is increased due to an increase in P_t. The proxy-effect hypothesis, on the other hand, is represented as the case where an anticipated reduction in GNP growth causes a reduction in div and V_t, which is associated with an increase in P_t. In the text we will discuss more fully the underlying bases for each of these hypotheses.

mates, stock prices fell during a period in which inflation had risen to roughly its corporate tax-maximizing rate, indicating the possibility of an adverse tax-effect at work.

Tax-effect hypothesis: individuals' perspective

The foregoing discussion pertains to the adverse effect that inflation can have on stock prices due solely to its direct effect on firms' profitability. Inflation was shown to potentially lower firms' real dividends which, as seen from Equation 3, prevents stock prices from keeping pace with the general level of prices. Chart 2 illustrates this hypothesized link between inflation and stock prices.

There are, however, other methods by which taxes and inflation can interact to lower firms' stock prices. One of these methods, as outlined by Martin Feldstein (1980 a & b), pertains to the manner in which tax rules and inflation interact to raise individuals' effective rate of discount. Feldstein's argument relies principally on the assumption that individuals invest in a wide range of alternative assets (stocks, bonds, land, gold, owner-occupied housing, tax-free instruments, etc.). Furthermore, although inflation generally reduces firm profitability and thus reduces the rate of return on stocks, it tends to raise the relative return offered on a variety of other assets. (In fact, as Feldstein points out, individuals may actually experience an increase in their net real yield on some assets during inflation).

Therefore, since they: (1) must pay income tax on both dividends and capital gains; (2) must pay taxes on nominal interest income from corporate bonds; and (3) may invest in a much wider range of alternative investments, individuals will substitute out of corporate stocks and bonds in times of rising prices. The effect of this substitution is to increase the real cost to firms of raising capital or, viewed alternatively, to increase the real rate at which individuals discount their before-tax dividends received from firms (r). As seen in equation (3), this effect of inflation on individuals' rate of discount reinforces that outlined previously on firms' dividends, so that real stock prices would be further depressed in periods of inflation.[5] Chart 2 illustrates this added

effect of inflation on stock prices.

Tax-effect hypothesis: empirical evidence

While the theoretical justification for the tax-effect hypothesis is generally acknowledged, formal empirical evidence is more problematic. As shown previously, when firms' computation of taxes is based on historic-cost accounting methods for both depreciation and cost of goods sold, tax-deductible firm costs differ from the current costs of factors of production. It follows that real *aggregate* corporate tax liabilities, then, should vary directly with the rate of inflation. Following this line of reasoning, Gonedes (1981) attempts to assess the impact of both expected and unexpected inflation on various measures of the aggregate real corporate tax burden over the period 1929–1974. Contrary to expectations, Gonedes presents evidence that appears to be inconsistent with the tax-effect hypothesis.[6] Specifically, aggregate corporate tax liabilities over the period from 1929–1974 are found to be unrelated to various measures of inflation—-rather than positively affected by inflation—and thus not in support of the tax-effect hypothesis.

Gonedes attributes the lack of empirical verification of a tax effect at work to an implicit "indexing" that has occurred over the period 1929–1974. Indexing the tax code with respect to both depreciation and inventory charges would eliminate the effect of inflation on share prices. Gonedes argues that de facto indexation has been

---

[5] Friend and Hasbrouck (1982) criticize the ad hoc nature of Feldstein's approach to share-price determination. Using a model based on expected utility maximization, along with different values of the tax and risk parameters, Friend and Hasbrouck arrive at the same qualitative conclusions as Feldstein. That is, inflation places downward pressure on share prices due to tax effects, but the magnitude of the effect is discovered to be much smaller than what follows from Feldstein's model. Feldstein (1982) acknowledges the usefulness of deriving the price investors are willing to pay per share on the basis of expected utility maximization, but rejects as "implausible" some of the parameter values assumed by Friend and Hasbrouck.

[6] Gordon (1983) also finds little evidence in support of a tax effect at work.

Chart 2

Tax-Effect Hypothesis

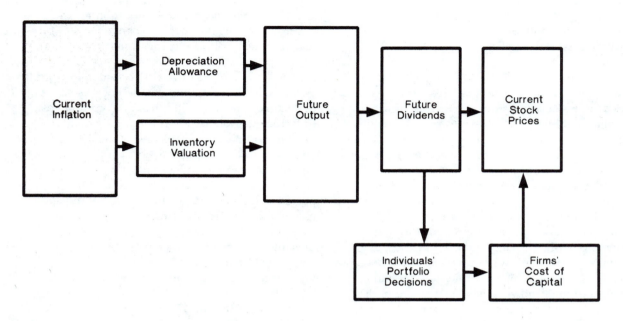

Proxy-Effect Hypothesis

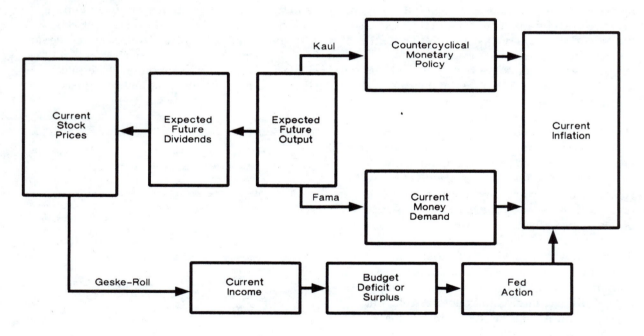

achieved through such factors as: (1) The implementation of accelerated depreciation schedules; (2) Various subsidies, such as the Investment Tax Credit; and (3) Decreasing the service lives on depreciable assets, all of which occurred simultaneously over the period 1929-1974.

Recall that, during times of inflation, the *net* corporate tax burden depends on both a penalty arising from historic-cost accounting methods and a benefit arising from the deductibility of nominal interest payments on corporate debt. If inflation is unanticipated, an additional benefit is available from the unforeseen decline in the real value of a firms' outstanding debt. Over the time period November 1977 through December 1982, Pearce and Roley (1988) examine the impact of unanticipated inflation on firms' share prices by considering these potential penalties and benefits. Historic-cost accounting of inventories is found to adversely affect stock prices. But, depreciation expenses are not a significant factor in explaining movements in share prices. Finally, the magnitude of a firms' outstanding debt is found to have a positive affect on share prices, indicating that inflation, in part, reduced the real value of firms' liabilities.

Tax-effects hypothesis: recapitulation of theory and evidence

The failure of changes in share prices to keep pace with movements in the overall level of prices could be attributed to certain features of the tax system. Particularly, the use of historic-cost accounting drives a wedge between tax-deductible costs and current costs of the factors of production. As a result, taxable profits increase at a faster pace than inflation, which puts downward pressure on equity prices. Empirical evidence of a tax effect at work is mixed and does not generally come out in support of the tax-effects hypothesis. Also, evidence that relies on simulation analysis is usually quite sensitive to the assumptions regarding the *effective* corporate tax burden.[7] Further, if it *is* the tax structure which is the driving force behind the seemingly anomalous relationship between inflation and stock prices in the U.S., then it is puzzling to observe (*see Table 1*) basically the same phenomenon across countries despite variation in tax laws.

An alternative framework: the proxy-effect hypothesis

In view of the criticisms of the tax-effect hypothesis, an alternative framework has developed to explain why inflation and stock values are inversely related. This explanation—known as the proxy-effect hypothesis—argues that expected future output growth and current inflation are inversely correlated. Inflation is said to be merely "proxying" for expected output or earnings growth in statistical tests of the relationship between stock returns and inflation. According to the proxy-effect hypothesis, any significant inverse relationship between these two variables is spurious, because it is induced by a *direct* relationship between stock returns and expected output growth together with an *inverse* relationship between expected future output growth and inflation. In contrast to the tax-effect hypothesis, the proxy-effect hypothesis claims that inflation has not been a causal factor in the performance of real stock prices but, rather, the relationship between inflation and stock prices is spurious.

Understanding the proxy-effect hypothesis requires exposition of the purported links in two contemporaneous chains of causality. Each chain begins with an increase or decrease in the rate of growth of expected future output. In one case this chain runs to expected future dividends and thus to current stock returns and in the other case, to expected future inflation and thus to current inflation. The link between expected future output growth and current stock returns is straightforward and requires little explanation. The purported link between expected future output growth and current inflation is not commonly acknowledged and requires further elaboration. In what follows, three explanations are reviewed to show how movements in expected future output may be related to current inflation.

[7] See the discussion in Friend and Hasbrouck (1982) and Feldstein (1982) for an example of the importance of assumed parameter values.

The proxy-effect hypothesis: linkage through money demand

The proxy-effect hypothesis was first introduced by Eugene Fama (1981). Fama's explanation for the inverse relationship between expected economic activity and current inflation follows from two key assumptions—(1) that individuals are "rational" in the sense of making use of all available current information relevant to their money and financial decisions, and (2) that individuals' current demand for money is related to future real economic activity and current interest rates.[8] Then, assuming that the money supply, real economic activity, and interest rates are exogenous, this demand for money, in effect, becomes a vehicle for the transmission of expected future inflation to current inflation.

In order to explain this more fully, consider the case where individuals' expectations of future output growth are revised downward. The lowering in expected future output growth leads to a lowering in expected future dividends and has the direct and immediate effect of reducing current stock returns. But also, the decline in expected future output growth leads to a decrease in money demand currently and thus an excess supply of money. Following Fama's assumption that interest rates and the money supply are exogenous, the excess supply of money is accompanied by an increase in the price level to restore monetary equilibrium. Essentially, the forward-looking nature of individuals' money demand generates an inverse relationship between current inflation and expected future growth in GNP. This enables a decrease in future output growth to cause *both* a decline in current stock returns and an increase in current inflation.

In terms of the model developed earlier, and summarized in equation 3, a reduction in expected future output and earnings growth lowers *div* with the direct effect of lowering V_t.[9] But also, the reduction in anticipated future output growth raises P_t. Chart 2 outlines this purported linkage of the proxy-effect hypothesis (identified as the Fama scenario). Any observed relation between stock returns and current or expected inflation then, according to this theory, is purely spurious, with no causal chain from inflation to stock returns.[10]

The proxy-effect hypothesis: linkage through debt monetization

Geske and Roll (1983), who relax the assumption of an exogenous money supply, have suggested an extension of Fama's argument. These authors posit, in fact, that a "reverse causality" actually drives the inverse relationship between stock returns and inflation. In contrast to earlier work which hypothesized a causative influence of inflation on stock returns (and in contrast to Fama's model in which inflation and stock returns are spuriously related), it is stock returns which "cause" inflation.[11]

Geske and Roll weave a sequence of events by which this reverse causality comes about. In order to illustrate the Geske-Roll hypothesis, consider the case where expectations regarding future GNP growth are lowered. Stock prices decrease in response to projections of slower growth which leads to a decline in both personal and corporate income. Government tax revenues then decline which leads to a deficit in government revenue. That is, Geske and Roll suggest that a decline in expected future economic activity should be fol-

---

[8] It should be pointed out that it is not common in economic models to assume that the demand for money currently is related to future economic activity, and, on this basis, Fama has been criticized. It is worth noting, however, that Fama's results could also be obtained in a more standard framework where, instead of Fama's assumption (2), current money demand is assumed to be related to current income and current interest rates, but with individuals being forward looking in decisions regarding interest rates. In this case, a decline in expected future output growth would lead to a perceived future excess supply of money and thus to a perceived increase in future inflation and interest rates (equivalently a decrease in future bond prices). Expecting such an increase in future interest rates, individuals may bid up interest rates today (bond prices fall) as they sell bonds in order to avoid a future capital loss. Again, the demand for money currently would fall leading to an excess supply of money and inflation.

[9] This application of the proxy-effect hypothesis assumes that the expected growth rate of future output was initially zero, so that a decline in the growth rate amounts to an anticipated contraction in GNP.

lowed both by a decline in government revenue *and* by an increase in the federal budget deficit. The next step in the Geske-Roll model involves the central bank. When deficits begin to grow, government debt outstanding increases. The central bank chooses to monetize a portion of this debt, thus leading to inflation. Since this debt monetization is anticipated by rational individuals, a decline in the stock market will cause an increase in expected future inflation. Therefore, stock returns are inversely correlated with expected future inflation.

Geske and Roll point out that changes in expected inflation tend to be highly correlated with unexpected inflation. This explains the negative association between stock returns and unexpected inflation which Fama (1981) found puzzling. Finally, through individuals' forward-looking behavior, the increase in expected future inflation is transmitted to current inflation as well. It is through this extended chain of causality, then, that lower current stock returns cause an increase in current inflation. In terms of the model developed earlier, *div* first falls (due to an anticipated cyclical contraction in output). The reduction in *div* drives V_t down, which ultimately leads to an increase in P_t. Chart 2 shows this hypothesized chain of events (identified as the Geske-Roll scenario).

The proxy-effect hypothesis: linkage through countercyclical monetary policy

The Fama model excludes any response by the monetary authority while Geske and Roll stress a policy response of debt monetization. An extension of these arguments is developed by Kaul (1987) who agrees that the relationship between stock returns and inflation is spurious. Following Fama, Kaul stresses the importance of the money demand linkage in his analysis but is also willing to incorporate a response of the monetary authorities. Unlike Geske and Roll, however, this response does not hinge exclusively on the practice of debt monetization. Rather, Kaul presumes that the central bank follows a *countercyclical* money supply process.

The full sequence of events as viewed by Kaul occurs as follows. First, expected future output declines which is signaled by a fall in stock prices. The Fed then responds with a countercyclical policy which results in an increase in the money supply. This causes both an increase in current inflation and an upward revision in inflation expectations. As a result, there is an observed inverse relationship between stock returns and both actual and expected inflation.

Kaul's version of the proxy effect hypothesis thus incorporates two commonly accepted effects of a perceived reduction in future GNP growth. For one, the anticipated slowing lowers current stock returns. For another, the anticipated slowing causes a current monetary expansion, and thus inflation. These two alone are sufficient to generate the inverse relationship often found between stock returns and inflation. The inverse relationship between expected future GNP growth and current inflation now is the result of the equilibrium process in the monetary sector. In terms of the model developed earlier, *div* first declines (due to an anticipated decline in GNP) which lowers V_t. But also, the decline in *div* stimulates a countercyclical response on the part of the monetary authorities which raises P_t. Chart 2 shows this hypothesized connection between stock prices and inflation (identified as the Kaul scenario).

[10] Benderly and Zwick (1985) agree with Fama that the relationship between stock returns and inflation is spurious. Unlike Fama though, Benderly and Zwick argue that the relationship runs from inflation to expected output growth. These authors base their conclusion on a real balance model of output in which changes in aggregate demand are related to lagged changes in real money balances.

[11] One should take note of the subtle distinction in Geske and Roll's use of the term "cause" here. Really, there is not reverse causality in the sense previously described for the tax-effect hypothesis because the sequence of events does not begin with stock prices. It begins with movements in expected future output. Actually, then, the relationship between current inflation and stock returns is here, too, spurious because both inflation and stock returns are ultimately driven by a decline in expectations of future GNP growth. Movements in stock prices, however, do precede movements in inflation and in this sense can be said to cause inflation.

Proxy-effect hypothesis: the empirical evidence

Empirical evidence on the proxy-effect hypothesis is extensive and generally may be delineated into the categories outlined above in reviewing the theoretical linkages between stock returns and inflation. In what follows, we will review the empirical evidence on the proxy-effect hypothesis beginning with the evidence on the linkage through money demand, as theorized by Fama.

Recall that the key to the spurious relationship between inflation and stock returns in Fama's hypothesis is that movements in expected future economic activity cause movements in both expected and current inflation. Empirical evidence relating real stock returns to both expected and unexpected inflation reveal a significant negative relationship. However, in multiple tests which also include real expected output growth, expected inflation looses its significance in explaining stock returns. This evidence suggests a spurious relationship between expected future inflation and current stock returns. Note also that *unexpected* inflation remains significant in nearly all of Fama's tests (all but those using annual data), and the expected inflation term looses significance in explaining real stock returns only when the growth rate of the monetary base is added to the set of explanatory variables. Fama points out that his measure of expected inflation is highly correlated with monetary base growth. Therefore, it is possible that one proxy for expected inflation has simply replaced another and the puzzling relationship between stock returns and inflation remains.

Turning now to empirical evidence on other views of the proxy-effect hypothesis, recall that Geske and Roll view current stock prices as driving current inflation through a practice of debt monetization by the central bank. Geske and Roll offer as empirical evidence a series of "transfer-functions" which purport to establish the linkage between stock prices and inflation in their model. For the most crucial element of this linkage, however—the practice of debt monetization—Geske and Roll do not offer compelling evidence. Empirical verification of the existence of debt monetization by the Federal Reserve is mixed, at best.[12] Geske and Roll point out that "...the detectable effect of Federal Reserve System Treasury debt holdings on the Fed's issuance of base money is very small in estimated magnitude; however, it *is* significant." The failure to discover a very substantial degree of debt monetization is blamed on "the incredible short-term churning of the Fed's asset portfolio."[13]

Kaul (1987) presents empirical evidence for the United States, as well as for Canada, the United Kingdom and Germany, consistent with the central tenets of the proxy-effect hypothesis. Regression results indicate a positive relationship between stock returns and expected real activity. Inflation and expected real activity are found to be negatively related, Kaul argues, due to both a countercyclical monetary policy response and to the practice of debt monetization.

Just as Geske and Roll's results hinge on the practice of debt monetization, Kaul's conclusions rely on a consistent countercyclical policy response which is anticipated by individuals. In estimates of both base-growth and monetary-aggregate growth equations, Kaul includes the unemployment rate to capture this policy response. In the four countries analyzed, however, the unemployment rate is generally insignificant in explaining money growth.

Evidence of central bank behavior from reaction functions casts doubt about the consistency of Federal Reserve policymaking, making it difficult to derive a generally accepted model of central-bank behavior.[14] Moreover, throughout most of the 1970's, the Fed engaged in federal funds rate targeting, which tends to result in a *procyclical* policy. Also, the current procedure of targeting on borrowed reserves, in effect since the fall of 1982, represents a return to funds rate targeting.[15] Clearly, a procyclical policy results in either a *positive* relationship between stock re-

---

[12] See Allen and McCrickard (1988) and Joines (1988). For additional support of the inconclusive evidence of debt monetization, see the references in McMillin (1986).

[13] Geske and Roll (1983, p. 22)

[14] For a summary of the reaction function literature, see Barth Sickles and Wiest (1982).

[15] See Gilbert (1985) and Thornton (1988).

turns and inflation or, at best, no relationship. Yet there has been an inverse relationship between stock returns and inflation in the United States during the 1970's and 1980's, as Table 1 shows, despite evidence of a procyclical policy stance by the central bank. These findings cast further doubt on the validity of Kaul's hypothesis.

Summary and conclusions

Equities, representing claims to real assets, should prove to be good hedges against inflation. Moreover, if future inflation can be at all foreseen, stock-market returns should be positively related to expected inflation as well. During much of the post-war time period, however, a well-documented tendency exists for equities to perform poorly during periods of inflation. Two main schools of thought have arisen to explain this anomaly.

The first of these appeals to particular features of the tax code in the United States as the primary factor behind the failure of equities to maintain their value during inflation. Historic-cost accounting for both depreciation and inventories results in an overstatement of corporate profits during periods of inflation. As a result, real corporate tax liabilities increase, which decreases net earnings. A simple model of share price determination then predicts downward pressures on real equity values during periods of inflation. While theoretically valid, empirical evidence for a tax effect at work is inconclusive.

The second school of thought appeals to the monetary sector as a vehicle through which the inverse stock return-inflation relationship occurs. A combination of money demand effects, along with both the practice of debt monetization and countercyclical monetary policy responses by the central bank is said to give rise to an inverse relationship between stock returns and inflation. Again, empirical evidence for this model is problematic.

References

Allen, Stuart D., and Donald L. McCrickard, (1988), "Deficits and Money Growth in the United States: A Comment," *Journal of Monetary Economics* 21 (January): 143–153.

Barth, James, Robin Sickles, and Philip Wiest, (1982), "Assessing the Impact of Varying Economic Conditions on Federal Reserve Behavior," *Journal of Macroeconomics* 4 (Winter): 47–70.

Benderly, Jason, and Burton Zwick, (1985), "Inflation, Real Balances, Output, and Real Stock Returns," *American Economic Review* 75 (December): 1115–1123.

Bodie, Zvi (1976), "Common Stocks as a Hedge Against Inflation," *Journal of Finance* 31 (May): 459–470.

Brealey, Richard, and Stewart Myers (1984), *Principles of Corporate Finance* (New York: McGraw-Hill).

Fama, Eugene F. (1981), "Stock Returns, Real Activity, Inflation and Money," *American Economic Review* 71 (September): 545–565.

———— and G. William Schwert, (1977), "Asset Returns and Inflation," *Journal of Financial Economics* 5 (November): 115–146.

Feldstein, Martin (1980a), "Inflation, Tax Rules and the Stock Market," *Journal of Monetary Economics* 6 (July): 309–331.

———— (1980b), "Inflation and the Stock Market," *American Economic Review* 70 (December): 839-847.

———— (1982), "Inflation and the Stock Market: Reply," *American Economic Review* 72 (March): 243–246.

Friend, Irwin, and Joel Hasbrouck (1982), "Inflation and the Stock Market: Comment," *American Economic Review* 72 (March): 237–242.

Geske, Robert, and Richard Roll (1983), "The Fiscal and Monetary Linkage between Stock Returns and Inflation, "*Journal of Finance* 38 (March): 1–33.

Gilbert R. Alton, (1985), "Operating Procedures for Conducting Monetary Policy," Federal Reserve Bank of St. Louis *Review*, (February): 13–21.

Gonedes, Nicholas J. (1981), "Evidence on the 'Tax Effects' of Inflation under Historical Cost Accounting Methods, "*Journal of Business* 54 (April): 227–270.

Gordon, Myron G. (1983), "The Impact of Real Factors and Inflation on the Performance of the U.S. Stock Market from 1960-1980," *Journal of Finance* 38 (May): 553–563.

Hasbrouck, Joel (1983) "The Impact of Inflation Upon Corporate Taxation," *National Tax Journal* 36 (March): 65–81.

Joines, Douglas H. (1988), "Deficits and Money Growth in the United States: Reply, *Journal of Monetary Economics* 21 (January): 155–160.

Kaul, Gatam (1987), "Stock Returns and Inflation: The Role of the Monetary Sector," *Journal of Financial Economics* 18 (June): 253–276.

Maher, Michael, and Timothy J. Nantell (1983), "The Tax Effects of Inflation: Depreciation, Debt and Miller's Equilibrium Tax Rates," *Journal of Accounting Research* 21 (Spring): 329–340.

McMillin, W. Douglas (1986), "Federal Deficits, Macrostabilization Goals, and Federal Reserve Behavior," *Economic Inquiry* 24 (April): 257–269.

Modigliani, Franco, and Richard A. Cohn (1979), "Inflation, Rational Valuation and the Market," *Financial Analysts Journal* (March/April): 24–36.

Nelson, Charles R. (1976), "Inflation and Rates of Return on Common Stocks, *Journal of Finance* 31, no. 2, (May): 471–483.

Pearce, Douglas K., and V. Vance Roley (1988), "Firm Characteristics, Unanticipated Inflation, and Stock Returns," *Journal of Finance* 43 (September): 965–981

Report of The Presidential Task Force on Market Mechanisms (1988) (Washington, D.C.: Government Printing Office, January).

Thornton, Daniel L. (1988), "The Borrowed-Reserves Operating Procedure: Theory and Evidence," Federal Reserve Bank of St. Louis *Review*, (January/February): 30–54.

Article 5

R. Alton Gilbert

R. Alton Gilbert is an assistant vice president at the Federal
Reserve Bank of St. Louis. Dawn M. Peterson provided research
assistance.

Payments System Risk: What Is It and What Will Happen If We Try To Reduce It?

BOTH commercial banks and the Federal Reserve assume a certain amount of risk in participating in the payments system. This paper provides an introduction to payments system risk and the public policy issues involved in limiting the risk. Using simple balance sheet entries to illustrate, the paper will examine how policies intended to reduce payments system risk would affect banks and bank customers.

PAYMENTS SYSTEM RISK: WHAT IS IT?

Many banks overdraw their reserve accounts at the Federal Reserve during part of each business day as they process payments within the payments system. The Federal Reserve is concerned about the extent of this intraday credit for several reasons. First of all, since it does not charge interest on the intraday credit it extends, it is providing this overdraft facility at no cost to banks and, thus, may be overused by banks. Second, and more important, it is possible, though unlikely, that a bank could fail while its reserve account is overdrawn. In this event, the Federal Reserve would become a general creditor of the failed bank. Finally, the Fed is concerned with the risk that banks assume through their participation in private wire transfer systems. Current Federal Reserve policy is de-

signed to limit the risk assumed by Reserve Banks as well as commercial banks who participate in private systems for their electronic payments. (See appendix 1 for a description of that policy.)

Federal Reserve Daylight Overdraft Risk and the Operation of Fedwire

While various types of transactions affect the reserve balances of banks, daylight overdrafts generally reflect large transactions through Fedwire, the wire transfer system operated by the Federal Reserve System. Institutions with reserve or clearing accounts at a Reserve Bank may transfer their reserve balances to other institutions that have similar accounts. These transfers, which averaged $605 billion per business day in 1987, are processed electronically through Fedwire.

Federal Reserve Banks transfer reserves to receiving banks even if the reserve balance of the sending bank is insufficient to cover the transfers. Transfers over Fedwire are "final" when the receiving banks are notified of the transfers. Thus, if a sending bank should fail while its reserve account was overdrawn, the Federal Reserve would have no claim on banks that received reserves from the failed bank over Fedwire.

U.S. Treasury and agency securities also are transferred among banks over Fedwire. Ownership records of these securities are maintained in each Federal Reserve Bank's computer system. Banks can transfer securities held in their names to other institutions through these computers, a system called "book-entry." A transfer of securities in book-entry form can be arranged either in conjunction with a transfer of reserves of equal value or as a separate transaction. Such securities transactions contribute to daylight overdrafts, since typically the reserve accounts of banks are debited when their book-entry securities accounts are credited. Transfers of book-entry securities over Fedwire averaged $312 billion per day in 1987.

The Federal Reserve measures its exposure to payments system risk by simply summing the maximum daylight overdraft each day across all banks. In 1987, the Fed's exposure to daylight overdrafts averaged $112 billion, approximately 53 percent of which can be attributed to transactions involving book-entry government securities.[1] Some specific features of this risk measure should be noted. First, unlike conventional risk measures, the Federal Reserve's measure does not incorporate the probability that a bank will fail while in an overdraft position or the probability of Fed losses in such situations.[2] Since the Federal Reserve has never incurred a loss on daylight overdrafts, the probability of losses in the future are quite low.

Second, it exceeds the actual sum of reserve account overdrafts at any point during the day; the maximum overdrafts of individual banks typically occur at different times during the day. Third, it represents the loss that the Federal Reserve would incur on a given day if all banks with overdrawn reserve accounts failed when their overdrafts were at maximum levels and the Federal Reserve recovered nothing.

Systemic Risk and the Operation of CHIPS

The Clearing House Interbank Payments System (CHIPS) is an electronic payment system operated by the New York Clearing House. It currently is the only private electronic payment system in operation in the United States. CHIPS has about 140 members, which include U.S.-chartered banks and foreign banks. Members of CHIPS send and receive payment messages during the day; no funds are actually transferred to cover these payment messages, however, until the end of the day. Net obligations are settled at day's end through Fedwire transfers in the reserve accounts of CHIPS participants. Banks in net debit positions on CHIPS at the end of the day (value of payment messages sent exceeds the value of payment messages received) transfer funds from their accounts at Reserve Banks to a reserve account maintained by the clearing house at the Federal Reserve Bank of New York, while banks in net credit positions receive reserve transfers from that account. The value of payment messages processed by CHIPS averaged $555 billion per day in 1987.

Systemic risk refers to the risk that the failure of one bank will cause one or more other banks to fail. One way that this could happen is through participation in CHIPS. If a bank fails while in a net debit position on CHIPS, other CHIPS participants could suffer losses as well, depending on the procedures in force for dealing with such a default. Payments over Fedwire, in contrast, involve no systemic risk. The Federal Reserve would absorb any losses resulting from failures by banks with overdrawn reserve accounts.

The Federal Reserve measures the payments system risk assumed by CHIPS participants as the sum of their *maximum* net debit positions during the day on CHIPS. This measure averaged $43.7 billion in 1987.

To relate this measure to systemic risk is difficult, however; under current CHIPS rules, payment messages do not reflect intraday extensions of credit among banks but provisional payments which may be unwound at the end of the day. If a bank could not cover its net debit position on CHIPS at the end of the day, all payment messages to and from that bank would be canceled; new net debit and credit positions would then be calculated for the remaining CHIPS participants, and payments would be made to cover these revised positions. Unwinding CHIPS payments because of a defaulting bank, however, could expose the remaining CHIPS participants to losses if their de-

---

[1]Daylight overdrafts attributed to transactions in book-entry securities are calculated as follows. A bank is in a net credit position on book-entry securities transfers if the value of securities transferred to the bank's book-entry securities account exceeds the value of securities transferred out of that account to other banks. The book-entry overdraft of a bank for each day equals its largest net credit position on securities transfers that occurs while the reserve account of the bank is overdrawn.

[2]In conventional definitions, risk is specified in terms of the probability distribution of returns on an investment. Under one definition, risk may be measured as the variance of the distribution of returns. See Rothschild and Stiglitz (1970).

positors had withdrawn balances credited to their accounts during the day based on payment messages from the defaulting bank. These banks in turn may be unable to recover the funds withdrawn by their depositors during the day.[3]

Federal Reserve Policy on Payments System Risk

In recent years, the Federal Reserve Board has taken actions to limit its own risk and the systemic risk involved in CHIPS. The Federal Reserve induced CHIPS to require each bank in its system to establish bilateral net debit limits with each other CHIPS participant, beginning in 1984. Under another program that went into effect in March 1986, the Federal Reserve requires banks to set limits on their daylight overdrafts across Fedwire and CHIPS. (See appendix 1 for details of these policies.) The Fed is currently studying proposals to establish an explicit or implicit price for daylight overdrafts of reserve accounts.

HOW PAYMENTS AFFECT RISK

This section uses simple balance sheets of hypothetical banks to illustrate how transactions through the payments system affect the exposure of the Federal Reserve and commercial banks to potential losses. The illustrations involve federal funds transactions and transactions among CHIPS participants. Appendix 2 illustrates how the payment practices of banks that serve government securities dealers and those that issue and redeem commercial paper affect their reserve overdrafts.

Federal Funds Transactions

Banks that borrow federal funds overnight are concerned primarily about their reserve balances as of the end of the day, rather than during the day, for two reasons. First, the Federal Reserve is more tolerant of daylight overdrafts of reserve accounts than of negative reserve balances at the close of business. Second, the intraday reserve balances do not count toward meeting reserve requirements; only those balances held at the end of the business day do.

Banks that borrow overnight federal funds typically receive reserves from the lending banks over Fedwire late in the day; they return the requisite reserve balances the following morning. Such

transfers can cause the borrowing banks to overdraw their reserve balances during the day.

The balance sheet entries in table 1 illustrate how federal funds transactions affect the risk borne by the Federal Reserve. Each bank begins the day with deposits of $100 and reserves of $10. With a 10 percent reserve ratio, excess reserves are zero. During the previous business day, Bank A borrowed $25 from Bank B through the federal funds market. Before the end of business on the previous day, Bank B transferred $25 over Fedwire from its reserve account to the account of Bank A. This transaction created a liability for Bank A (federal funds purchased) and shifted $25 of the assets of Bank B from reserve balances to federal funds sold.

The first transaction by Bank A in the current day is a transfer of $25 from its reserve account to the reserve account of Bank B, returning the funds it had borrowed overnight; this eliminates the liability of federal funds purchased by Bank A. Since the balance in the reserve account of Bank A was only $10 at the start of the day, the transfer of $25 makes its reserve account overdrawn by $15. This presents no problem for Bank A, however, since it plans to borrow $25 through the federal funds market later in the day to eliminate its reserve overdraft and meet its reserve requirement of $10.

If Bank A borrows the $25 in the federal funds market, the lending bank(s) will transfer the reserves to the account of Bank A in the afternoon. Given the time gap between the transfer of funds to lending banks in the morning and the transfer of reserves to Bank A in the afternoon, the Federal Reserve effectively lends $15 to Bank A during part of the business day by permitting the reserve overdraft.

The Fed is a general creditor of Bank A while its reserve account is overdrawn. To illustrate the risk it assumes in permitting daylight overdrafts, suppose that participants in the federal funds market find out that the value of Bank A's assets have declined by $15 just after Bank A transfers $25 to Bank B. After this information becomes known, Bank A will be unable to borrow reserves in the federal funds market at prevailing market rates. The agency that chartered Bank A must decide whether it is solvent. If Bank A is declared solvent and has assets to pledge as collateral, it could

---

[3]The legal status of claims by the banks against their depositors in such situations is currently unclear. See Mengle (1989).

Table 1

Risk Created by the Transfer of Reserve Balances in Overnight Federal Funds Transactions

Balance sheets at start of day:

Bank A				Bank B			
Reserves	$ 10	Deposits	$100	Reserves	$ 10	Deposits	$100
Other assets	125	Federal funds purchased	25	Federal funds sold	25	Net worth	10
		Net worth	10	Other assets	75		

Bank A sends $25 of its reserve balances to Bank B over Fedwire:

Bank A				Bank B			
Reserves	− $ 15	Deposits	$100	Reserves	$ 35	Deposits	$100
Other assets	125	Federal funds purchased	0	Federal funds sold	0	Net worth	10
		Net worth	10	Other assets	75		

Value of other assets at Bank A reduced by $15:

Bank A				Bank B			
Reserves	− $ 15	Deposits	$100	Reserves	$ 35	Deposits	$100
Other assets	110	Federal funds purchased	0	Federal funds sold	0	Net worth	10
		Net worth	− 5	Other assets	75		

receive a loan from the Federal Reserve to cover its reserve overdraft. If the supervisory agency declares Bank A insolvent, it will be closed. If Bank A is closed and liquidated, the depositors get first claim on the $110 of "other assets." In this case, the Federal Reserve will receive $10 against the $15 overdraft of the reserve account and, thus, will lose $5.

If the Federal Reserve had known that Bank A was in poor financial condition, it would have required the bank to pledge collateral against its overdrafts.[4] By requiring collateral, the Fed shifts the risk to other parties. Suppose, in this case, that Bank A had pledged $15 of its riskless assets to the Federal Reserve to cover its overdrafts. When the bank fails, the Fed would hold the $15 in collateral

to cover any losses. The loss of $5 would be borne by uninsured depositors or the Federal Deposit Insurance Corporation (FDIC). Thus, requiring collateral against reserve overdrafts does not necessarily protect the public sector; it may simply shift the loss from the Federal Reserve to the FDIC.

Transactions Among CHIPS Participants

In the case illustrated in table 1, the Federal Reserve assumes the risk. Banks also assume risk by participating in CHIPS. The interbank risk exposures created through the processing of payment messages through CHIPS are illustrated in table 2.

In the first transaction of the day, a depositor of Bank A sends $25 to a depositor of Bank B in the

---

[4]Task Force (1988), pp. 65–69.

Table 2

Risk Created by the Transfer of Funds over CHIPS

Balance sheets at start of day:

Bank A				Bank B			
Reserves	$ 10	Deposits	$100	Reserves	$ 10	Deposits	$100
Other assets	100	Net worth	10	Other assets	100	Net worth	10

Depositor at Bank A transfers $25 to depositor of Bank B, transaction over CHIPS:

Bank A				Bank B			
Reserves	$ 10	Deposits	$ 75	Reserves	$ 10	Deposits	$125
Other assets	100	Reserves payable	25	Reserves receivable	25	Net worth	10
		Net worth	10	Other assets	100		

Depositor at Bank B transfers $25 to depositor of Bank C, over CHIPS:

Bank B				Bank C			
Reserves	$ 10	Deposits	$100	Reserves	$ 10	Deposits	$125
Reserves receivable	25	Reserves payable	25	Reserves receivable	25	Net worth	10
Other assets	100	Net worth	10	Other assets	100		

form of a wire transfer over CHIPS. Bank A debits the deposit account of that customer for $25. Because banks do not report their balance sheets on an intraday basis, there is no official term for the offsetting liability entry in this transaction. In this case, we will call it "reserves payable." For Bank B, deposit liabilities and an asset item called "reserves receivable" each increase by $25.

In the next transaction, a depositor of Bank B directs it to send $25 to a customer of Bank C. After the second transaction, Bank B is even with CHIPS. If there were no more transactions over CHIPS that day involving Bank B, the settlement for CHIPS transactions would have a zero impact on the reserve account of Bank B. Bank A, in contrast, would have its reserve account debited for $25, while Bank C would have its account credited by $25. Bank A would have to increase its reserve balance before the time for settlement of CHIPS payments to facilitate settlement.

Suppose that, before the end of the day, adverse publicity prevents Bank A from borrowing $25 in the federal funds market. This situation could create a liquidity problem for Bank B. If Bank A cannot obtain sufficient reserves to cover its net debit position on CHIPS, current rules call for unwinding all transactions involving Bank A and settling the transactions among the remaining CHIPS participants. This settlement would involve a transfer of $25 in reserves from Bank B to Bank C. Such a net settlement cannot take place, however, because Bank B has only $10 in its reserve account. Thus, unless the Federal Reserve lends $25 to Bank A or Bank B, all CHIPS transactions for the day would be canceled.

Simulation exercises indicate that the unwinding of transactions with one large CHIPS participant that cannot meet its payment obligations would make a high percentage of other participants unable to meet their commitments on

CHIPS without additional reserves.[5] In these exercises, some banks that become illiquid have no direct transactions with the defaulting bank. Thus, as illustrated in table 2, a default by Bank A keeps Bank C from receiving its payments over CHIPS, because the default by Bank A makes Bank B illiquid.

As the central bank, the Federal Reserve is responsible for preventing such a liquidity crisis. In our example, the Fed could lend reserves either to Bank A or Bank B. If it considers Bank A to be solvent, it could lend the $25 and take collateral. The $25 added to the reserve account of Bank A facilitates the net settlement on CHIPS. If Bank A turns out to be insolvent, the collateral protects the Federal Reserve from loss, transferring it instead to the general creditors and the FDIC.

Alternatively, the Federal Reserve could prevent a liquidity crisis by lending $25 to Bank B, allowing Bank B to meet its required reserves and CHIPS obligation to Bank C. Even if the Fed prevents a liquidity crisis by lending $25 to Bank B, the default of Bank A could make Bank B insolvent. This is an example of systemic risk involved in the operation of the payments system. Suppose that the transfer of $25 from Bank B to Bank C is initiated by the depositor of Bank B who received $25 from Bank A. Bank B makes this transfer before discovering the default by Bank A. At this time, it is not clear whether the courts would permit Bank B to regain these funds from its depositor.[6] If Bank B's loss exceeds $10, it is bankrupt.

Suppose, instead, that this depositor of Bank B holds the extra $25 in its demand deposit account at Bank B until the end of the day. The transfer of reserves from Bank B to Bank C was initiated by a different depositor of Bank B. When Bank A's default is discovered, Bank B could cancel the $25 in reserves receivable and reverse the $25 credit to its demand deposit liabilities. In this case, the unwinding of the CHIPS transaction has no adverse effect on the net worth of Bank B.

THE EFFECTS OF POSSIBLE CHANGES IN POLICY

Changes in policy on payments system risk are being discussed within the Federal Reserve System and the private sector. This section illustrates the effects of two possible policy changes: explicit fees on reserve account overdrafts and interest-earning reserve balances required to cover part or all of daylight overdrafts.[7]

Federal Reserve policymakers have indicated that such changes would be adopted only after CHIPS has developed arrangements for ensuring the execution of payments on that system that they consider acceptable.[8] This section also illustrates the implications of such an arrangement for banks.

Explicit Pricing of Daylight Overdrafts of Reserve Accounts

One way to reduce Federal Reserve risk would be to charge a fee on daylight overdrafts. If the fee were high enough, banks would reduce the size of their overdrafts by changing their practices for making payments.

Responses of Banks to Pricing Daylight Overdrafts — Perhaps the easiest and least expensive change for most of the relatively large banks would involve routing more of their wire transfers of funds through CHIPS rather than Fedwire. There are other ways for banks to reduce their reserve account overdrafts. They could purchase more of their federal funds as term federal funds or under rollover arrangements that involve paying a daily rate but eliminating the daily transfer of reserve balances. Pricing total daylight overdrafts of reserve balances (including book-entry overdrafts) would impose costs on the clearing banks, which they would pass on to the government securities dealers they serve. The dealers could reduce book-entry daylight overdrafts by building smaller inventories of securities during the day or holding larger inventories overnight. Banks that act as agents in issuing commercial paper could charge

---

[5]Humphrey (1986).

[6]Mengle (1989).

[7]For discussions of these possible changes from Federal Reserve sources, see Belton, et al. (1987), Corrigan (1987), Johnson (1988), Task Force (1988) and Mengle, et al. (1987). For discussions of these issues by those in the private sector, see Flannery (1987), Faulhaber, et al. (1989) and Large Dollar Payments System Advisory Group (1988). Governor Wayne D. Angell of the Federal Reserve Board has proposed another approach to revising policy on payments system risk. Under the Angell proposal, the Federal Reserve would prohibit daylight overdrafts. Transfers of reserves that would make the reserve balance of a bank negative would be funded as discount window loans. To provide banks incentives to hold enough reserves to prevent overdrafts, the Federal Reserve would pay interest on excess reserves, but at a rate below the discount rate. See VanHoose (1988).

[8]Johnson (1988), p. 15.

issuers for the fees on overdrafts or delay payments to issuers until they receive payments from purchasers.

Effects in Financial Markets — Pricing daylight overdrafts could have a variety of indirect effects in the financial markets. Banks that lend in the overnight federal funds market could find that their reserves are being returned later the following day. The time value of intraday reserves might lead to the development of an intraday federal funds market, with lenders making reserve balances available to borrowers for only part of the business day. Some analysts think this could lead to greater variability in an overnight federal funds rate and other interest rates.[9]

Banks could limit the size of their daylight overdrafts by delaying wire transfers of funds for depositors that do not demand immediate delivery of funds; or, they might charge an extra fee to depositors that demand immediate delivery.

Clearing banks would charge government securities dealers for the cost of the fee on daylight overdrafts. Government securities dealers, in turn, would increase the transaction costs of buying and selling government securities. Interest rates on government securities would rise somewhat relative to yields on alternative investments, increasing the Treasury's cost of servicing the national debt.

How banks react to daylight overdraft fees could affect market yields on other financial instruments. For instance, the fee on overdrafts would increase the costs to banks acting as agents for firms that issue commercial paper. The responses by the agent banks could increase the costs to firms of raising funds by issuing commercial paper.[10]

Supplemental Balance Requirement

The Federal Reserve could impose an implicit price on daylight overdrafts by requiring the banks that overdraw their reserve accounts to hold supplemental reserve balances. These requirements would be set to cover part or all of their daylight overdrafts. The suggested interest rate to be paid on the supplemental balances would be slightly below the federal funds rate, thus creating an opportunity cost of holding supplemental reserves. This cost would have the same implications for bank behavior and financial markets as an equal explicit fee on daylight overdrafts.

The implications of a supplemental reserve requirement can be examined by adjusting the balance sheet entries in table 1. In this case, Bank A would be required to increase its average end-of-day reserve balance by $15. A reserve balance of $25 at the start of the day would eliminate the risk of Federal Reserve loss because Bank A's reserve balance would not fall below zero after the $25 transfer.

The method by which Bank A raises the $15 supplemental balance affects the distribution of potential losses among participants in the banking industry. Suppose, for example, Bank A sold some assets to obtain the $15 in additional reserves. This response would raise the risk-adjusted capital ratio of Bank A, unless it shifted the remaining $110 of other assets into categories with higher risk weights. A rise in Bank A's risk-adjusted capital ratio would reduce the FDIC's potential losses.[11]

Suppose, instead, that Bank A raises the $15 in supplemental reserves by increasing federally insured deposits from $100 to $115. This response would increase the potential losses faced by the FDIC.[12]

Bank A also could raise the additional $15 in the term federal funds market. The claims of those selling term federal funds to Bank A would be subordinate to the claims of Bank A's depositors. Thus, the supplemental balance requirement would shift risk to those banks supplying the term

---

[9]Task Force (1988), pp. 103–14.

[10]To illustrate the potential effects on the cost of issuing commercial paper, suppose the Federal Reserve charges 100 basis points at an annual rate on the maximum daylight overdraft of each bank. See Mengle, et al. (1987) for the basis for such a rate. If an agent bank continues the timing of payments described in appendix 2 in issuing and redeeming commercial paper, the overdrafts fee would cost $54.79 per $1 million of commercial paper issued and redeemed. If the banks pass this cost on to the issuers, the annual cost of raising funds by issuing commercial paper every 30 days would rise by 7 basis points.

[11]A risk-based capital ratio is calculated as a measure of capital divided by weighted assets, with weights assigned as approximations to relative risk. Reserves have a weight of zero. See "Proposals for International Convergence" (1988).

[12]Assume that these additional federally insured deposits have a zero reserve requirement. To illustrate the implications for FDIC risk, suppose that after Bank A transfers $25 to Bank B, there is a public announcement of events that reduce the value of the assets of Bank A by $15. Bank A fails and the FDIC becomes the receiver. As receiver, the FDIC obtains assets worth $110 and assumes liabilities of $115, for a net loss of $5. In this case, therefore, the supplemental balance requirement shifts risk from the Federal Reserve to the FDIC.

federal funds, increasing the systemic risk in the banking system.

Of course, supplemental balance requirements also would give banks an incentive to reduce the size of the intraday movements in their reserve balances, since the interest rate paid on the balances would be below the marginal return on other assets and below the interest rate on federal funds. The supplemental balance requirement would be reduced to the extent that a bank kept its reserve balance positive throughout the business day. Suppose, for instance, that Bank A changes its intraday pattern of payments so that, with the supplemental requirement of $15, its reserve balance never falls below $5. The Federal Reserve might reduce its supplemental balance requirement to $10, thus reducing the opportunity cost of Bank A.

Provisions for Settlement Finality of Payments over CHIPS

Settlement finality would involve procedures for ensuring the execution of payments (avoid unwinding payments involving a defaulting bank) and the allocation of losses in the event of a default by a CHIPS participant.[13] If losses are spread widely among CHIPS participants, the failure of a CHIPS participant to meet its payment obligation would probably not cause other banks to fail.

The implications of settlement finality arrangements for payments system risk are illustrated using the balance sheet entries in table 2. In this illustration, CHIPS is presumed to have formed a bankers' bank, which is a cooperative venture that performs banking services for CHIPS members. This institution processes payment messages for its members as debit and credit entries to their demand deposit accounts at the bankers' bank.[14] The illustration is based on some general principles of settlement finality arrangements that have been considered for several years.[15]

The hypothetical arrangement requires members of CHIPS as a group to pledge enough collateral with their bankers' bank to cover the largest net debit position of any one participant. This is based on the idea that a default by one large participant would disrupt the operation of CHIPS. Since there has never been a default by a CHIPS participant, however, a default by one large participant is an unlikely event. Collateral requirements for CHIPS participants in excess of the largest net debit of an individual CHIPS participant could be interpreted as an excessive degree of precaution.

In table 2, the largest net debit position is $25. To cover this position (and to allow some margin for error), CHIPS requires each of the three banks to pledge $10 of their interest-earning assets with CHIPS in the form of Treasury securities.

Suppose that after CHIPS processes the transactions described in table 2, an announcement indicates a $15 loss in the value of Bank A's assets. Under the settlement finality arrangement, CHIPS would use the collateral posted by its participants to raise $25, either by selling part of the collateral

---

[13]Discussions of the finality of payments on private wire transfer systems mention three aspects of finality. Sender finality makes each message over the payments system final when sent. Payment messages cannot be canceled later in the day. The rules for payment messages on CHIPS include sender finality.

Settlement finality refers to procedures that would ensure the settlement of payments if a participant defaults on its net debit at the end of the day. CHIPS does not have settlement finality procedures in place at this time. Under current procedures, CHIPS would cancel all payments by the bank that defaults, as well as all payments to that bank, and calculate new net debit or credit positions for the remaining participants. This section illustrates the implications of adopting a form of settlement finality.

Under receiver finality, credits to the deposit accounts of the customers of CHIPS participants would be final when the receiving banks receive payments messages over CHIPS. If a sending bank defaults, the receiving bank would have no recourse to its depositors. CHIPS rules do not include receiver finality. For additional discussion of these aspects of the finality of payments, see Humphrey (1986) and Belton, et al. (1987).

[14]CHIPS has considered developing a bankers' bank to ensure that payment obligations over CHIPS would be treated as net rather than gross obligations in the case of a default by a CHIPS participant. See Kantrow (1988). To illustrate the signifi-

cance of the distinction between gross and net obligations, suppose a bank fails while it is in a net credit position on CHIPS payments. If CHIPS obligations are treated legally as net obligations, CHIPS participants would make a payment to the receiver of the failed bank for the amount of the net debit position. The receiver of the failed bank might sue CHIPS participants based on gross obligations. Under a successful suit by the receiver, those that had sent payment messages to the failed bank would have to pay the gross amount of those payments, and those who received payment messages from the failed bank would become its general creditors for the amount of the gross transfers from the failed bank. This treatment of CHIPS participants would increase the recovery rate of the failed bank's other general creditors. There have been no such cases to indicate whether the courts would uphold payments to the receiver based on gross payments.

Suppose, in contrast, that CHIPS payments are processed through demand deposit accounts at the bankers' bank for CHIPS. Under that arrangement, the only claim of the receiver of the failed bank would be for the positive balance of the failed bank in its demand deposit account at the bankers' bank.

[15]Mengle (1989).

or using the securities as collateral for a loan at the Federal Reserve discount window. CHIPS would then transfer the $25 to the reserve account of Bank B, facilitating the payment from Bank B to Bank C. In turn, the bankers' bank of CHIPS would hold the $10 in collateral posted by Bank A and have a $15 claim against Bank A as a general creditor. Losses on the $15 claim against Bank A would thus be spread between Bank B and Bank C. Neither bank would be forced into bankruptcy by a complete loss on the $15 claim.

From the Federal Reserve's perspective, this settlement finality arrangement is better than the procedure that currently would be used to deal with a default by a CHIPS participant — unwinding payments involving the bank. If this settlement finality arrangement were in place, the unwinding of payments, which would disrupt the flow of payments in the economy, could be avoided. If a discount window loan was necessary to avoid a liquidity crisis in the banking system, the collateral would be available through the CHIPS organization. The Federal Reserve would not have to decide which banks should receive discount window loans.

By making the risk to CHIPS participants more explicit, the arrangement would give CHIPS participants stronger incentives to exclude banks in relatively poor financial condition from their system. Banks that are excluded would route their wire transfers through Fedwire, thus reducing systemic risk. Finally, the spreading of potential losses would limit the chances of the failure of one bank causing others to fail. It is not possible to determine whether the risk of bank failure is lower under current CHIPS procedures or under this proposed procedure for settlement finality. Such a comparison depends on the extent to which depositors of CHIPS participants draw down the intraday credits to their demand deposit accounts and the success that banks would have in collecting from those depositors in case of a default by a CHIPS participant.

CONCLUSIONS

All banks assume some risk by participating in the payments system. The payment practices that generate this risk were developed in an environment in which there was no interest charge on intraday credit and, until recently, no constraints on the magnitude of intraday credit. There have been no losses to the Federal Reserve or to members of private wire transfer systems resulting from the daylight credit exposures. The Federal Reserve, however, has adopted a policy on payments system risk which includes limits on the daylight overdrafts of individual banks.

The Fed has been considering possible changes in its policy to reduce its own risk and provide incentives for banks to change the payment practices that tend to create the intraday risk exposures. One proposed approach involves a fee on daylight overdrafts of reserve accounts. A second approach, which involves an implicit price on daylight overdrafts, requires additional reserve balances at the banks which regularly overdraw their reserve accounts during the day. The Federal Reserve would pay interest on these supplemental reserve balances at a rate just below the federal funds rate. Under either approach, CHIPS would be required to work out an arrangement that is satisfactory to the Federal Reserve to ensure the finality of its payments.

The objective of changing the policy on payments system risk is to reduce the risk of the Federal Reserve without creating a large increase in systemic risk — the risk that the failure of one bank will cause the failure of other banks, thus disrupting the operation of the payments system. The type of settlement finality arrangement desired by the Federal Reserve would ensure the execution of payments over CHIPS in the event of a default by a CHIPS participant and spread any losses so widely among other CHIPS participants that one bank failure is unlikely to lead to the failure of other CHIPS participants.

REFERENCES

Association of Reserve City Bankers. *Report of the Working Group of the Association of Reserve City Bankers on Book-Entry Daylight Overdrafts* (June 1986).

Belton, Terrence M., et al. "Daylight Overdrafts and Payments System Risk," *Federal Reserve Bulletin* (November 1987), pp. 839–52.

Corrigan, E. Gerald. *Financial Market Structure: A Longer View* (Federal Reserve Bank of New York, January 1987).

Faulhaber, Gerald R., Almarin Phillips, and Anthony M. Santomero. "Payment Risk, Network Risk and the Role of the Fed," in David B. Humphrey, ed., *U.S. Payment System: Efficiency, Risk and the Role of the Federal Reserve System* (Kluwer, 1989).

Flannery, Mark J. "Payments System Risk and Public Policy," Mimeo, University of North Carolina at Chapel Hill, November 30, 1987.

Humphrey, David B. "Payments Finality and Risk of Settlement Failure," in Anthony Saunders and Lawrence J. White, ed., *Technology and the Regulation of Financial Markets* (Lexington Books, 1986).

Johnson, Manuel H. "Challenges to the Federal Reserve in the Payments Mechanism," *Issues in Bank Regulation* (Summer 1988), pp. 13–16.

Kantrow, Yvette D. "Big NY Banks May Spin Off Chips Network," *American Banker* (June 27, 1988), pp. 1, 23.

Large-Dollar Payments System Advisory Group. *A Strategic Plan for Managing Risk in the Payments System*, Report to the Payments System Policy Committee of the Federal Reserve System, Board of Governors of the Federal Reserve System, August 1988.

Mengle, David L. "Legal and Regulatory Reform in Electronic Payments: An Evaluation of Finality of Payment Rules," in David B. Humphrey, ed., *U.S. Payment System: Efficiency, Risk and the Role of the Federal Reserve System* (Kluwer, 1989).

Mengle, David L., David B. Humphrey, and Bruce J. Summers. "Intraday Credit: Risk, Value and Pricing," Federal Reserve Bank of Richmond *Economic Review* (January/February 1987), pp. 3–14.

"Proposals for International Convergence of Capital Measurement and Capital Standards." *Issues in Bank Regulation* (Winter 1988), pp. 3–12.

Rothschild, Michael, and Joseph E. Stiglitz. "Increasing Risk: I. A Definition," *Journal of Economic Theory* (September 1970), pp. 225–43.

Task Force on Controlling Payments System Risk. *Controlling Risk in the Payments System*, Report to the Payments System Policy Committee of the Federal Reserve System, Board of Governors of the Federal Reserve System, August 1988.

VanHoose, David. "The Angell Proposal: An Overview," staff paper, Board of Governors of the Federal Reserve System (June 1988).

Appendix 1
Current Federal Reserve Policy on Payments System Risk

Currently, the Federal Reserve uses specific limits on daylight overdrafts of reserve accounts and net debit positions on private wire transfer systems to reduce payments system risk. The limits on net debit positions apply to any private wire transfer system that settles the net positions of its participants through transfers of balances in reserve or clearing accounts at Reserve Banks. Since CHIPS is the only such system in operation, the following description refers only to it, but would apply to any such system developed in the future.[1]

Bilateral Net Credit Limits on CHIPS

The Federal Reserve requires each participant on CHIPS to set a limit on its net credit position on message transfers with each of the other participants in the system. Funds transfer messages that violate these bilateral net credit limits are rejected by the computer system that processes payment messages. CHIPS participants have had bilateral credit limits since October 1984.

Sender Net Debit Caps on CHIPS

The Federal Reserve requires CHIPS to establish limits on the net debit positions of each partici-

pant with all other participants on the system. CHIPS sets this limit for each participant at 5 percent of the sum of all bilateral credit limits for that participant extended by all other CHIPS participants.[2] CHIPS established these sender net debit caps in October 1985.

Cross-System Caps

Each bank that occasionally has daylight reserve overdrafts is required to adopt a cap on its cross-system daylight overdraft. Cross-system refers to the daylight overdraft position on Fedwire and CHIPS. The relevant overdraft position for this cap is the sum of a bank's funds-related overdraft of its reserve account and its net debit position on CHIPS at each moment during the day. Each bank sets its cap by placing itself in one of the possible categories indicated in table A1; banks are directed to consider their creditworthiness, credit policies and operational control and procedures. Each possible rating has corresponding caps for both the one day and two-week average maximum daylight overdraft, each as a percentage of primary adjusted capital. These percentages have been

---

[1]For an analysis of the effects of these credit limits on daylight overdrafts and the operation of the payments system, see Belton, et al. (1987).

[2]There are additional details involved in determining these limits. See Belton, et al. (1987).

Table A1

Caps on Daylight Overdrafts Across Payments Systems (multiples of adjusted primary capital)

Self-assessment category	Cap applied to	Period caps in effect		
		March 27, 1986 to January 13, 1988	January 14, 1988 to May 18, 1988	May 19, 1988 to present
High	Two-week average	2.000	1.700	1.500
	Single day	3.000	2.550	2.250
Above average	Two-week average	1.500	1.275	1.125
	Single day	2.500	2.125	1.875
Average	Two-week average	1.000	0.850	0.750
	Single day	1.500	1.275	1.125
Limited	Two-week average	0.500	0.425	0.375
	Single day	0.500	0.425	0.375

NOTE: Adjusted primary capital for U.S.-chartered banks is the sum of primary capital less all intangible assets and deferred net losses on loans and other assets sold.
SOURCE: Federal Reserve Bulletin (November 1987), p. 843.

reduced over time to make them more effective in constraining overdrafts.

Book-Entry Securities Transfers

In calculating the relevant measure of overdrafts for the cross-system caps, the Federal Reserve nets out the value of book-entry securities credited to the account of the bank. This step exempts daylight overdrafts generated through securities transactions from the limits imposed by the caps. The Federal Reserve has allowed this distinction to avoid disrupting the market for U.S. government securities.

Appendix 2
Additional Illustrations of Payments and Risk

Transfers for Depositors Over Fedwire

Wire transfers of funds for depositors may cause banks to overdraw their reserve accounts, as table A2 illustrates. A depositor instructs Bank A to pay $25 to a depositor of Bank B in the form of a wire transfer. Since the initial reserve balance is only $10, the $25 transfer makes the reserve account of Bank A overdrawn by $15. As in table 1 in the text, an announcement of a $15 decline in the value of the assets of Bank A would force the Federal Reserve to absorb a $5 loss.

Table A2

Risk Created by Transferring Depositor's Funds over Fedwire

Balance sheets at start of day:

Bank A				Bank B			
Reserves	$ 10	Deposits	$100	Reserves	$ 10	Deposits	$100
Other assets	100	Net worth	10	Other assets	100	Net worth	10

Bank A sends $25 of depositor's money to Bank B over Fedwire:

Bank A				Bank B			
Reserves	− $ 15	Deposits	$ 75	Reserves	$ 35	Deposits	$125
Other assets	100	Net worth	10	Other assets	100	Net worth	10

Value of other assets at Bank A reduced by $15:

Bank A				Bank B			
Reserves	− $ 15	Deposits	$ 75	Reserves	$ 35	Deposits	$125
Other assets	85	Net worth	− 5	Other assets	100	Net worth	10

Securities Transfers

A few banks incur large daylight overdrafts because of the transactions they conduct for customers that deal in U.S. government securities. These transactions warrant special examination. A few large banks (called clearing banks) specialize in serving government securities dealers; these banks generate a large share of the total daylight overdrafts of bank reserve accounts. In the second quarter of 1988, for example, four clearing banks accounted for about 70 percent of the daylight overdrafts attributable to transactions in book-entry securities.

Business Practices of Dealers and Clearing Banks — Government securities dealers who buy and sell securities for their customers have no direct access to the book-entry system for transferring ownership of government securities. Instead, they maintain book-entry securities accounts and demand deposit accounts with commercial banks that serve as their clearing banks for securities transfers.

Daylight overdrafts of the clearing banks' reserve accounts reflect the practices of the government securities dealers in managing their inventories of governments securities. Dealers hold large inventories of securities during the day to meet the anticipated demands of their customers. To minimize the cost of holding the inventories, the dealers sell most of their securities by the end of the day through repurchase agreements. The investors who enter into these agreements "own" the securities overnight and "resell" them to dealers early the next day. Thus, the dealers build their inventories of government securities in the morning of each business day by receiving securities returned by the overnight repo investors and buying additional securities offered for sale.[1]

The following features of the business practices of government securities dealers explain why they generally wait until early afternoon to begin run-

[1]For a more complete discussion of the practices of clearing banks and dealers, see Association of Reserve City Bankers (1986).

ning down their inventory of securities. Salesmen for a dealer make commitments to deliver specific securities to its customers by the end of the day. The dealer is then vulnerable to losses if it cannot fulfill these commitments. The customers receive interest on the promised securities for that day, even if the dealer does not make delivery. The customers, however, make payments to the dealers only when the securities are delivered. The dealer would fail to make delivery if it could not locate the desired securities in its inventory or in the market, or if it sent the wrong securities to a customer and had them returned. Each dealer attempts to minimize the probability of such "fails" by waiting until early afternoon to direct its clearing bank to send its securities to the book-entry accounts of the banks that serve the customers that have bought them.

Another reason the dealers hold their securities until early afternoon involves potential profits from special orders. On some days, certain issues of government securities are in relatively high demand. The dealers can make larger profits if they have securities available to meet these special orders. In contrast to the specific requirements for special orders, dealers may substitute a wide variety of securities as acceptable collateral for repos.

Effects on Intraday Reserve Balances — These dealer practices affect the intraday patterns of their demand deposit balances and the reserve balances of the clearing banks that serve them. When a repo investor returns the securities to the dealer, there is an increase in the securities account of the dealer at its clearing bank and an equal reduction in its demand deposit account. On the books of the Federal Reserve, there is an increase in the securities in the book-entry account of the clearing bank and a reduction in the reserve account of the clearing bank. The same transactions occur when the dealer buys securities to hold in its inventory that day. The dealer builds its inventory of securities by overdrawing its demand deposit account during the day. The dealers do not control the timing of these inflows of securities to their accounts and the outflows from their demand deposit accounts, since the party that holds the securities initiates the transfer of securities and reserves through the Fedwire system.

The process of overdrawing reserve and deposit accounts is reversed later in the day as the dealers sell their inventories of securities. The reserve accounts of the clearing banks rise as the book-entry securities are transferred to the accounts of other banks and reserve balances are simultaneously transferred to the accounts of the clearing banks. The timing of transactions in book-entry securities for the dealers causes the reserve accounts of the clearing banks to be overdrawn by billions of dollars during part of the day.

Implications for Risk — The clearing banks extend credit to government securities dealers during the day by allowing them to overdraw their demand deposit accounts. The banks limit their risk by obtaining a lien against the securities held for the account of the dealers. Thus, a clearing bank could claim the securities credited to the account of a dealer to cover any losses on its deposit overdraft.[2]

The Federal Reserve has considered various methods of establishing liens against the securities in the book-entry accounts of banks but has not initiated such collateral arrangements. Thus, the Fed is vulnerable to losses on the full amount of a bank's reserve overdraft, whether the overdraft was generated through funds transfers or transactions in book-entry securities.[3]

The risk implications of book-entry overdrafts can be illustrated by examining the balance sheet entries in table A2. Bank A is a clearing bank for a governments securities dealer. The dealer receives $25 in book-entry securities and has its demand deposit account debited by $25, leaving it overdrawn at that time. Suppose the dealer goes bankrupt after this transaction is completed. Bank A claims the $25 in securities that were credited to the securities account of the dealer to cover any possible losses on the deposit overdraft. The bank is spared any losses, and the Federal Reserve suffers no losses.

This book-entry daylight overdraft, however, does leave the Federal Reserve vulnerable to a loss on the reserve overdraft. Suppose that after the dealer receives the $25 in book-entry securities, there is an announcement that implies a $15 loss in the value of the other assets of Bank A, as in the other illustrations. Under current arrangements, the Fed has no claim on the $25 in book-entry securities that had been transferred to Bank A, to offset its $5 loss. Thus, collateral agreements between clearing banks and the dealers make Federal Reserve losses due to defaults by government securities dealers unlikely, but the daylight reserve

---

²Task Force (1988), p. 69.

³Task Force (1988), p. 70–72.

Table A3

The Effects of Issuing Commerical Paper on the Balance Sheet of an Agent Bank

Balance sheets at start of day:

Bank A				Bank B			
Reserves	$ 10	Deposits	$100	Reserves	$ 10	Deposits	$100
Other assets	100	Net worth	10	Other assets	100	Net worth	10

Bank A transfers $25 to Bank B, credited to the account of the firm that issues commercial paper:

Bank A				Bank B			
Reserves	− $ 15	Deposits	$100	Reserves	$ 35	Deposits	$125
Reserves receivable	25			Other assets	100	Net worth	10
Other assets	100	Net worth	10				

Bank A receives $25 from purchaser of commercial paper:

Bank A				Bank B			
Reserves	$ 10	Deposits	$100	Reserves	$ 10	Deposits	$100
Reserves receivable	0			Other assets	100	Net worth	10
Other assets	100	Net worth	10				

overdrafts of the clearing banks expose the Fed to potential losses in the event of large, unanticipated declines in the value of the assets of the clearing banks themselves.

A lien by the Federal Reserve against the book-entry securities in the accounts of the clearing banks might have little practical significance in limiting Fed risk. Suppose the public learns during the day that a clearing bank may be bankrupt. Would the Federal Reserve suddenly seize the book-entry securities in the account of the clearing bank? Doing so would disrupt the business of the government securities dealers served by the clearing bank and, given the high concentration of business among clearing banks, would disrupt trading in the whole government securities market. The Fed and the other federal supervisory authorities have been reluctant to close large commercial banks because of their effects on other depository institutions and the financial markets in general. A lien on the book-entry securities of banks might make the supervisory authorities more reluctant to close a large bank that also serves as a clearing bank for government securities dealers.

Issuing and Redeeming Commercial Paper

The timing of payments by banks involved in issuing and redeeming commercial paper creates reserve overdrafts.[4] Several banks act as agents for firms that issue commercial paper. The agent banks collect funds from those purchasing the commercial paper and transfer them to the accounts of those firms issuing the paper. When the paper matures, the agent banks collect from the

---

[4]For a discussion of how daylight overdrafts reflect transactions in commercial paper and other financial instruments, see Large-Dollar Payments System Advisory Group (1988).

paper issuers and make payments to the holders of the paper.

When a firm issues commercial paper, the agent bank generally pays the firm before it receives payment from those buying the paper. During the period between the payment to the issuer and the receipts from the purchasers, the reserve account of the agent bank falls by the amount of the funds raised by issuing the commercial paper. The reserve balance of the agent bank also falls by the face amount of the issue when the paper matures; the agent bank generally makes payment to those holding the paper before receiving payment from the issuer.

The effects of these transactions on the balance sheet of the agent bank are illustrated in table A3. A firm raises $25 by issuing commercial paper. Bank A is the agent bank, and both the issuer and purchaser of the paper have their demand deposit accounts at Bank B. Early in the day on which the commercial paper is issued, Bank A transfers $25 to Bank B, to be credited to the demand deposit account of the issuer. After that transaction, the reserve account of Bank A is overdrawn by $15. In this example, the offsetting transaction is a $25 increase in an account called "reserves receivable." Later that day, the purchaser of the paper arranges for Bank B to send $25 to Bank A over Fedwire, eliminating the reserve overdraft by the end of the day. As in the other balance sheets, the Federal Reserve is a general creditor of Bank A while its reserve account is overdrawn.

Article 6

The U.S. as a Debtor Country: Causes, Prospects, and Policy Implications

*Stephen A. Meyer**

One and a quarter trillion dollars—that is roughly the value of claims on the United States accumulated by foreigners from 1982 through 1988. Their purchases of U.S. assets far exceeded U.S. residents' purchases of foreign assets, turning the United States into a net foreign debtor in 1985. By the end of 1988, foreign ownership of assets in the U.S. exceeded our ownership of foreign assets by about $530 billion.

---

*Stephen A. Meyer is Vice President and Associate Director of Research at the Federal Reserve Bank of Philadelphia.

Our growing status as a net debtor has raised various concerns. A major one is that future generations of Americans may face lowered living standards because they will be forced to service the foreign debt we have accumulated. A second concern is that our large foreign debt might bring the U.S. very high inflation rates in the future, like those experienced recently by some of the world's debtor nations.

To assess the validity of these concerns, we first need to understand the economic factors that generated large net capital inflows into the United States. That understanding will enable us to analyze the implications for future living standards and inflation. We also will be able to evaluate the prospects for reversing our position as a net debtor and weigh the role economic policies can play in that process. (See *Glossary*, pp. 30-31, for definitions of terms that appear above and elsewhere in this article.)

LARGE CURRENT ACCOUNT DEFICITS MADE THE U.S. A NET DEBTOR

A direct link exists between the current account balance and international capital flows. Understanding that link is critical to understanding how the U.S. became a net debtor.

What Does It Mean to Be a Net-Debtor Country?

There is widespread confusion about what the Commerce Department's figures mean when they show that the U.S. is a net foreign debtor. Technically, those figures show that foreigners' ownership of claims on the U.S. (including land, buildings, firms, stocks, bonds, and other financial instruments) exceeds U.S. residents' ownership of claims on foreign countries. The important point here is that *all* foreign assets and liabilities are included in this calculation, not just debt instruments.

About 30 percent of U.S. foreign "debt" is accounted for by foreign ownership of stock issued by U.S. corporations and by foreign direct investments in the United States (such as foreign-owned land, office buildings, and manufacturing and distribution facilities in the United States). For example, automobile factories built in the U.S. by Japanese auto companies show up in the official figures as foreign claims on the United States. Corporate stocks and direct investments account for nearly the same percentage of U.S. claims on foreigners.

That some of our foreign assets and "debts" are actually real investments matters for three reasons. First, direct investments produce goods and services in the U.S. and thereby generate the stream of dividends or profits that are paid to foreigners. In the process, direct investments generate output and employment in the U.S., benefiting residents as well as nonresidents. Second, while direct investments generate a stream of profits or dividends that flow to their owners, direct investments do not normally require a contractually fixed stream of payments to foreigners (such as are required by interest payments on a bond). Instead, foreign direct investments in the U.S. pay high returns when profits are strong in the U.S. and lower returns when profits are weak. In effect, we pay more to foreigners when we can best afford to. Third, direct investments are valued at their "book value" (historical acquisition cost) in the official figures, unlike financial instruments, which usually are valued at their current market value. Using book value results in a large understatement of the true value of foreign direct investments owned by U.S. residents, but a much smaller understatement of the true value of foreign-owned direct investments in the United States. Thus, valuing foreign direct investments at their book value results in a large overstatement of the true size of the U.S. net-debtor position. These three points argue that the true burden that will arise from the need to service our foreign "debts" is likely to be smaller than estimates based on official Commerce Department figures seem to suggest.

Making these and other technical adjustments to the official figures suggests that the U.S. net-foreign-liability position was at least $350 billion *smaller* at the end of 1987 than the official figures show.* Despite the ambiguities in the official figures, however, it is clear that the balance between U.S. claims on foreigners and U.S. liabilities to foreigners has changed dramatically during the 1980s. From a large net-foreign-asset position in 1982, the U.S. almost certainly shifted to a net-foreign-liability position at the end of 1988.

---

*For a discussion of these issues and other measurement problems in the official statistics, and also for corrected estimates of U.S. foreign assets and liabilities, see Michael Ulan and William G. Dewald, "Deflating U.S. Twin Deficits and the Net International Investment Position," Planning and Economic Analysis Staff Working Paper 12 (Bureau of Economic and Business Affairs, U.S. Department of State, 1989).

When the U.S. imports more than it exports and runs a current account deficit, as it has each year since 1982, our receipts from abroad fall short of our payments to foreigners. To finance the excess of foreign payments over receipts, the U.S. must borrow from foreigners or sell assets to them. In each case, financial capital flows into the United States. At the same time, either our liabilities to foreigners rise or our holdings of foreign assets decline, so our *net* foreign asset position declines.[1]

Current Account Deficits and Matching Capital Inflows Reflected Macroeconomic Imbalances. Fundamentally, the large capital inflows into the U.S. during the 1980s resulted from a shortfall of national saving relative to the demand for funds to finance real invest-

[1] A standard source for information on the U.S. trade and current account balances, and on the foreign assets and liabilities of the U.S., is the *Survey of Current Business*, published monthly by the Bureau of Economic Analysis, U.S. Department of Commerce. The March, June, September, and December issues contain detailed information on the U.S. current account balance and its components. The June issue also includes details on foreign assets and liabilities of the United States.

ment in buildings, equipment, structures, and inventories. The excess of investment spending over national saving was financed by an inflow of capital from abroad.

National saving (the sum of personal saving, business saving, and government saving) declined as a share of GNP during the 1980s. National saving declined from 16.2 percent of GNP in 1980 and 17 percent in 1981 to a little more than 12 percent in 1987 before rising somewhat in 1988. Business saving did not decline relative to GNP; it was just about the same share of GNP in 1987 and 1988 as in 1980 and was higher between 1981 and 1986. But personal saving fell from about 5 percent of GNP at the beginning of the 1980s to less than 2.5 percent in 1987. And government *dis*saving in the form of budget deficits (for all levels of government combined) grew from a little more than 1 percent of GNP to an average of almost 3.5 percent in 1982 through 1986, then declined in 1987 and 1988. Thus, about half of the decline in national saving relative to GNP was caused by falling personal saving rates and about half by rising government budget deficits.

TABLE 1
Personal and Government Saving Fell Relative to GNP While Investment Rose

	Investment Spending (% of GNP)	National Saving (% of GNP)	National Saving (% of GNP)		
			Business	Personal	Government
1980	16.0	16.2	12.5	5.0	-1.3
1981	16.9	17.0	12.8	5.2	-1.0
1982	14.1	14.1	12.7	4.9	-3.5
1983	14.8	13.6	13.6	3.8	-3.8
1984	17.6	13.5	13.5	4.4	-2.8
1985	16.0	13.3	13.4	3.1	-3.3
1986	15.6	12.4	12.9	3.0	-3.4
1987	15.5	12.2	12.4	2.3	-2.4
1988	15.4	13.2	12.2	3.0	-2.0

While the national saving rate fell, investment spending rebounded from its 1982 low as the economy recovered from recession. Investment spending grew especially strongly in 1983 and 1984, rising to 17.6 percent of GNP, then fell back to about 15.8 percent of GNP from 1985 through 1988. The resulting imbalance between investment spending and national saving has exceeded $100 billion each year since 1984, generating the need for a capital inflow from abroad.[2]

The large current account deficits and matching deterioration in the U.S. net-foreign-debt position also reflected a decline in the international competitiveness of U.S. firms from 1980 to 1985, most of which was caused by the more than 50 percent increase in the value of the dollar during that period. That rise in the dollar's value, which has since been reversed, meant that firms in the U.S. could buy various goods abroad and import them into the U.S. at a lower cost than they would incur by producing the goods here. The resulting increase in U.S. imports, and the accompanying decline in exports, accounts for most of the growth in our current account deficit.

The imbalance between national saving and investment was an important cause of the dollar's appreciation. The shortfall of national saving relative to investment spending helped drive up real (inflation-adjusted) interest rates in the United States. The rise in real interest rates, in turn, contributed to the rise in the dollar's value that reduced U.S. international competitiveness. The interplay between these

factors produced the large current account deficits and matching capital inflows of the 1980s. Those capital inflows cumulated to produce our net-foreign-liability position of $530 billion—almost 11 percent of GNP—at the end of 1988.[3]

WILL OUR NET-DEBTOR STATUS REDUCE OUR FUTURE STANDARD OF LIVING?

Our growing net-debtor status has raised worries that we will have to transfer to foreigners so much of our future income—in the form of interest and dividend payments to foreign owners of claims on the U.S.—that we will end up with a falling standard of living. Whether the U.S. faces reduced living standards depends upon how the capital inflows of the 1980s were used—in particular, whether they financed investment or consumption. And the answer also depends upon our future savings behavior.

If Capital Inflows Financed Additional Investment, Our Future Standard of Living Is Likely to Rise. Additional spending on new investment in plant and equipment generates higher output and incomes by making workers more productive and by creating new jobs. Only part of the increased output and income accrues to foreign investors in the form of interest and dividend payments. The remainder of the higher incomes flows to workers in the U.S. in the form of wages and salaries and to governments in the U.S. in the form of tax revenues.

Foreign capital inflows can finance additional investment either directly or indirectly. They can finance additional investment directly if they are used to build new factories,

---

[2]Data on U.S. national income and product, including saving and investment spending, are available monthly in the *Survey of Current Business*. Those data show that personal saving has been declining as a share of GNP since the mid-1970s, when it peaked at 6.5 percent. For more detail on the behavior of private and government saving in the U.S., see Behzad Diba, "Private-Sector Decisions and the U.S. Trade Deficit," this *Business Review* (September/October 1988).

[3]A shortfall of national saving relative to desired investment spending in one country can generate foreign capital inflows into that country only if other countries' saving exceeds their investment spending. That has been true for Germany, Japan, and other countries during the 1980s.

office buildings, and other structures, or if they are used to purchase new equipment. Foreign capital inflows can finance new investment indirectly if they are used to buy financial instruments (such as stocks and bonds) from Americans, who will then be able to use the funds to finance investment.

But if Capital Inflows Financed Consumption, Our Future Living Standards May Be Reduced. If the inflow of foreign capital financed only current consumption spending, including consumption by the government, then we incur future payments to service the accumulated foreign debt but gain no offsetting increase in future incomes. In this case, our future standard of living will be lower *than it otherwise would have been*, but it still may be higher than today's. Continuing technological progress and real investment financed by domestic savings will raise our future standard of living, unless interest and dividend payments to foreigners rise more than our GNP. Thus there *is* a possibility that foreign capital inflows could produce a burden on future generations in the form of a lowered standard of living, if those capital inflows are used to finance consumption spending rather than new investment.

More Than Half of the Capital Inflow Was Used to Finance Increased Net Investment. By comparing the net capital inflows during the 1980s with the increase in the amount of *net* investment spending undertaken in the United States, we can determine how much of the capital inflows were used, directly or indirectly, to finance additions to the capital stock. During 1980 and 1981, when there was virtually no net capital flow, net investment spending by U.S. businesses averaged about $150 billion per year. From 1984 to 1988 there were sizable net foreign capital inflows averaging a little more than $126 billion per year. Net investment increased to an average of about $221 billion per year over this period, better than $70 billion per year higher than in 1980-

81.[4] On average, then, about 55 percent of the net foreign capital inflow from 1984 to 1988 was used, directly or indirectly, to finance additional net investment.

There is another way to look at this issue: although national saving declined from 16.6 percent of GNP in 1980-81 to about 13.2 percent in 1984-88, net investment was unchanged as a share of GNP; net investment averaged 5.2 percent of GNP during the earlier period and also during the latter years. The implication is that foreign capital inflows allowed the U.S. capital stock to grow at the same rate from 1984 through 1988 as during 1980 and 1981, despite the drop in national saving relative to GNP. In

---

[4]We omit data for 1982 and 1983 from this comparison because investment spending was depressed during those years as a result of the 1981-82 recession. It would be misleading to attribute either the drop in investment spending from 1981 to 1982, or the increase from 1983 to 1984, to changing foreign capital inflows. If we were to include data for 1982 and 1983, it would appear that nearly 80 percent of the foreign capital inflow financed additional net investment.

TABLE 2
More Than Half of Net Capital Inflows Were Used to Finance Added Investment

	Net Capital Inflow Per Year ($ billion)	Net Investment Spending Per Year ($ billion)
1980-81	-4.4	150.5
1984-88	126.3	220.9
		Increase = 70.4

the absence of foreign capital inflows, a drop in national saving relative to GNP would have to be accompanied by a drop in investment relative to GNP. The inflow of capital from abroad allowed continuing growth in the capital stock, which is likely to mean rising living standards in the future. Nevertheless, more of the returns to that new capital will accrue to foreigners, so our standard of living will grow less rapidly than if net investment had been financed by domestic saving rather than foreign saving.

A simple back-of-the-envelope calculation will give a feeling for the potential size of this effect. The ratio of net foreign debt to GNP for the U.S. was almost 11 percent at the end of 1988. Whether that ratio rises or falls in the future, and by how much, will be critical in determining the size of the burden. If that ratio rises, indicating that our net foreign debt is growing faster than our GNP, then a rising share of our total incomes will accrue to foreigners.

Projections by various economic forecasting services of the likely future paths of GNP and the current account deficit suggest that the ratio of our net foreign debt to GNP might gradually rise to 15 percent of GNP, or perhaps to as much as 20 percent, before it begins to decline sometime late in the 1990s.[5] As a result, we would need to transfer a rising share of each year's GNP to foreigners to make the interest and dividend payments that go with our net-debtor status. The projections indicate that net interest and dividend payments to foreigners might peak at as much as 1 percent of GNP. That is the potential burden of our position as a net foreign debtor.

We can gain some perspective on the size of this potential burden by noting that net interest

---

[5]These figures, and other numbers cited below, are based upon long-term economic projections published during the winter of 1988-89 by DRI/McGraw-Hill and The WEFA Group.

and dividend payments to foreigners are projected to rise from about $4 billion in 1988 to as much as $90 billion in 10 years' time. But over the same 10 years our GNP is projected to roughly double, rising by nearly $5 *trillion*. Some of that growth in measured GNP reflects price increases rather than production of more goods and services, and some of that growth is needed to maintain our existing standard of living as the U.S. population grows. But even after adjusting for inflation and population growth, the projections suggest that per capita real GNP less net interest and dividend payments to foreigners is likely to grow about 16 percent by 1998.

That is not to say that our growing net-foreign-debtor position will have no effect upon Americans' future living standards, however. According to these projections, growing net interest and dividend payments to foreigners will leave our per capita real income roughly 1 percent lower at the turn of the century than it would be in the absence of those payments. Such an effect is small, but noticeable.

While the projections upon which these calculations are based are necessarily subject to great uncertainty, they do give a feeling for the size of the future burden of our net-debtor position. Americans are not likely to face a lower standard of living than we enjoy today. Still, our standard of living will grow a little less quickly as a result of our growing net-debtor position.

WILL OUR FOREIGN DEBT CAUSE HIGH INFLATION?

While it is unlikely that our growing net foreign debt will mean a lower standard of living than we have today, the concern remains that our net-debtor status might generate strong inflationary pressures like those in some other debtor countries. This concern raises two related questions. First, does the U.S. face the temptation to generate higher inflation because doing so could reduce the real value of its foreign debts? And second, if foreigners were to become unwilling to continue accumulating claims on the U.S., as has happened with some other debtor countries, would the result be a debt crisis that generates high inflation in the United States?

Can We Inflate Away Our Foreign Debt? One important difference between the U.S. and other debtor countries is that much of our foreign debt is denominated in our own domestic currency while theirs is not. That fact raises the possibility that the U.S. could inflate away the real value of its foreign debt by generating higher domestic inflation so that each dollar owed to foreigners would buy fewer U.S. goods.

In assessing this possibility, it is important to note that it is only fixed-rate, long-term nominal debt whose real value can be reduced by higher inflation. That is, the real value of fixed-income securities with fixed value at maturity, such as long-term bonds, can be reduced by higher inflation. But the real value of shares of stock in U.S. firms and of real assets such as buildings, factories, or land cannot reliably be reduced by inflation; their dollar values tend to rise along with prices of goods and services. And the real value of short-term or floating-rate debt cannot be reduced by higher inflation, because interest rates on such debt would rise along with the inflation rate, thereby compensating the holder of such debt for the higher inflation. Indeed, higher inflation would actually increase the burden of servicing short-term or floating-rate claims held by foreigners, because it would quickly raise the required interest payments on such debt.

Fixed-rate, long-term debt, whose value can be reduced by higher inflation, accounts for at most 20 percent of foreign claims on the United States.[6] The bulk of U.S. liabilities to foreigners

---

[6]Twenty percent is almost certainly an overestimate. Very little data on the maturity structure of foreign claims on the U.S. are available. The 20 percent figure is an estimate

consists of short-term debt, equity, and investments in real property. Thus, the U.S. cannot effectively inflate away the real value of its foreign debt, even though most of that debt is denominated in U.S. dollars.

That the U.S. cannot inflate away its foreign debt may not be enough to prevent inflationary pressures. Some of the world's debtor countries have suffered very high inflation, even though their foreign debts are largely floating-rate debt denominated in currencies other than their own so that their domestic inflation does not reduce the real value of their foreign debt. Those episodes of very high inflation seem to follow or accompany debt crises, in which foreign lenders become unwilling to continue accumulating claims on a particular country.

Would the U.S. Face Very High Inflation if It Could No Longer Borrow From Foreigners? Although very high inflation seems to be connected with debt crises, episodes of very high inflation actually have little to do with the presence of foreign debt, or with debt crises, per se. Rather, very high inflation reflects a lack of well-developed internal capital markets, governments' inability to collect taxes effectively, and governments' responses to debt crises.

Many of the world's debtor countries had large government budget deficits that they financed mostly by borrowing from foreigners,

---

derived by treating all U.S. government notes and bonds plus all U.S. corporate and other bonds held by foreign official and foreign private investors as long-term, fixed-rate claims, and dividing that sum by total foreign claims on the United States. (Data on foreign holdings of U.S. government debt are available in the *Treasury Bulletin*; data on foreign ownership of U.S. corporate bonds are given in the June issue of the *Survey of Current Business*.) This method for estimating how much of foreign claims on the U.S. is fixed-rate, long-term debt almost certainly produces an overestimate because much of the stock of U.S. government notes outstanding at any point in time actually has a fairly short time remaining to maturity. The rest of foreign claims on the United States, other than those cited above, are either short-term or are real assets.

especially from international banks and multilateral organizations. After issuing so much foreign debt that lenders became unwilling to provide additional funds, or became unwilling to provide as large a flow of new lending as in earlier years, many of those countries found that their domestic capital markets could not absorb enough new debt to finance ongoing government budget deficits as large as those previously financed by borrowing from foreigners. Policymakers in those countries then faced a choice between reducing government spending, raising taxes to finance that spending, or simply printing new money to finance the excess of government spending over revenues. Those governments that printed money to finance continuing budget deficits generated high inflation.[7] On the other hand, those

debtor countries that responded to the reduced availability of foreign funds by reducing their budget deficits, thereby avoiding rapid growth of their money supplies, did not experience rapid inflation.

Thus, it is not foreign debt per se, or even the inability to issue new foreign debt, that causes high inflation in debtor countries. Rather, it is continuing rapid expansion of the money supply, usually to finance large government budget deficits, that causes high inflation.

Should we expect our government budget deficits to generate high inflation in the United States? In applying the lesson from those debtor countries that have experienced very high inflation, there are three points to bear in mind. First, the U.S. has well-developed domestic

[7]For a more thorough discussion of these problems, with details of particular countries' experiences, see Thomas J. Sargent, "The Ends of Four Big Inflations," in Robert Hall

(ed.), *Inflation*, NBER and University of Chicago Press (1982), and also Rudiger Dornbusch and Stanley Fischer, "Stopping Hyperinflations Past and Present," NBER Working Paper #1810 (1986).

Comparing the U.S. to High-Inflation Debtor Countries

While foreign claims on the U.S. are large, they are much smaller relative to the size of our economy than is true for those debtor countries that have suffered very high inflation. More importantly, the growth rate of the money supply in the United States is much, much lower than in high-inflation debtor countries.

In most of the debtor countries that have experienced very high inflation, large and continuing government budget deficits caused a large shortfall of domestic saving relative to investment spending. That shortfall was financed primarily by borrowing abroad. Accordingly, those countries accumulated very large foreign debts relative to their GNP and foreigners eventually became unwilling to continue lending at the same pace.

The size of the foreign debt was not itself the cause of high inflation, however. Nor was foreigners' reluctance to continue lending the cause of high inflation. Rather it was governments' response to the reduced availability of foreign funds that was critical. When foreigners became unwilling to continue lending to the same extent, some governments responded by creating large amounts of new money to finance continuing large budget deficits. Those governments that did so generated high inflation. Comparing the U.S. to Argentina, Bolivia, Brazil, Peru, and South Korea makes the point clear. In contrast to the United States, the first four of these debtor countries have experienced very high inflation because their governments generated very rapid growth of their money supplies.

South Korea, too, has a large foreign debt relative to the size of its economy; its government, however, did not allow very rapid money growth. Thus South Korea, like the United States, did not experience high inflation. The difference in monetary policy, not in the level of foreign debt, is what separates debtor countries that experienced high inflation from those that did not.

financial markets. The U.S. government has had no difficulty financing its deficits by issuing debt in these markets, although some of that debt has been purchased by foreigners. And no such difficulty is likely to arise as long as investors perceive that the U.S. budget deficit will shrink further relative to GNP.

Second, the shortfall of national saving relative to investment has been much smaller over the past 15 years for the U.S. than for the major debtor countries that have experienced very high inflation. As a result, the foreign debt of the U.S. is much smaller relative to our GNP than is the case for those countries. And the money supply has grown much less rapidly in the United States than in those countries.

Third, the U.S. Treasury cannot finance its deficit by printing new money. The power to issue new money in the U.S. is vested in the Federal Reserve System, which is prohibited by law from issuing new money to purchase newly issued debt directly from the U.S. Treasury.[8] Thus we should not expect budget deficits to generate very high growth rates of the money supply or very high inflation in the United States. Still, the inflationary experience of many debtor countries makes clear the importance of conducting monetary policy so as to avoid very rapid growth of the money supply, even when government deficits put pressure on financial markets.

---

[8]There is a minor exception (contained in 31 United States Code, section 5301; act of September 13, 1982) that allows the Federal Reserve to buy up to $3 billion of securities directly from the U.S. Treasury when the President of the United States declares an economic emergency. This amount is tiny relative to the roughly $230 billion of government securities that the Federal Reserve System held during the summer of 1989 — securities that were acquired in the open market during the normal course of monetary policy operations.

Large Foreign Debts Need Not Mean High Inflation

	Argentina	Bolivia	Brazil	Peru	S. Korea	U.S.
Total external debt (public and private) as % of GNP (1986)	59	103	43	62	47	22
Avg. saving shortfall (I - S) as % of GNP						
(1973-80)	0.6	6.8	4.6	4.3	6.0	0.0
(1980-86)	4.7	8.7	3.3	4.4	3.0	1.5
Average money growth (broad money: M2) (% per year, 1980-86)	302	643	176	101	18	9
Average inflation (% per year, 1980-86)	326	684	157	100	5	4

Sources: *World Development Report 1988* (World Bank, Washington, D.C., 1988);
Survey of Current Business, June 1988 (U.S. Department of Commerce, Washington, D.C.)

Continued Increases in Net Foreign Debt Might Lead to Slightly Higher Inflation. Although the buildup of foreign claims on the U.S. is unlikely to generate high inflation, future debt increases might contribute to modestly higher inflation for several years. Theoretical models of exchange-rate behavior suggest that if U.S. current account deficits do not shrink and our net-foreign-debtor position continues to grow rapidly as a result, then the dollar would tend to depreciate gradually over time. Such gradual but continuing depreciation would be expected to make inflation as measured by the Consumer Price Index a little higher than it would be otherwise. The reason is that the dollar's depreciation would contribute to rising prices for imports and for import substitutes produced domestically.

WHAT ARE THE PROSPECTS FOR REVERSING OUR NET-DEBTOR STATUS?

We have seen that the costs of our net-debtor status, whether it affects our future living standards or inflation, are likely to be small. Still, a long-run economic perspective suggests that it may be desirable for the U.S. to eventually reverse its net-debtor position and return to being a net foreign creditor.

When large numbers of those in the "baby boom" generation begin to retire, roughly 25 to 30 years from now, they will need a large stock of assets—domestic or foreign—upon which to draw in order to finance their consumption during retirement. Americans can accumulate such a stock of assets by saving more to finance more domestic investment, or by saving more and using the funds to lend to foreigners or buy assets from foreigners. Those foreign assets can later be sold back, in exchange for the goods that members of the baby-boom generation will want to consume during their retirement. Such behavior by individuals would imply that the U.S. would need to accumulate a positive net-foreign-asset position—a position that would eventually be drawn down to finance imports of consumer goods after the baby-boom generation retires.

Reducing Our Net-Debtor Position Will Require National Saving to Exceed Investment Spending. We saw earlier that the foreign capital inflows that produced our net-debtor status reflected a shortfall of national saving relative to investment. To reduce our net-foreign-debt position, we must generate capital outflows either to repay foreign debt or to acquire foreign assets. To generate capital outflows, national saving must exceed investment in the United States. Are there forces at work in the U.S. economy that will raise national saving relative to investment spending?

Recall that national saving is composed of personal saving, business saving, and government saving in the form of budget surpluses. Both personal saving and government saving seem likely to rise in the future.

The U.S. Personal Saving Rate Should Rise Over the Next 20 Years. Historical evidence clearly indicates that the bulk of personal saving in the U.S. is done by people 45 to 64 years old. During the past 20 years, the share of the U.S. population in that age group has fallen to a low of about 18.5 percent, and personal saving as a share of GNP has fallen too. The U.S. Census Bureau projects that as the baby-boom generation grows older, the share of those aged 45 to 64 is likely to grow to about 23 percent of the population by the year 2000 and then rise still further. Thus, the U.S. personal saving rate is likely to rise over time, contributing to a rise in national saving relative to GNP. How much personal saving will rise is not known, however.

Government Saving Is Likely to Increase Too. Large government budget deficits, especially at the federal level, as well as a declining personal saving rate, contributed to the decline in national saving relative to GNP during the 1980s. While large federal budget deficits were to be expected when the U.S. economy was in recession from 1980 to 1982 (because reces-

TABLE 3

Demographic Trends Suggest Personal Saving Will Rise

	Share of U.S. Population Ages 45 to 64 (%)	Personal Saving as Share of GNP (%)
1970	21.5	5.7
1975	20.3	6.0
1980	19.1	5.0
1985	18.8	3.1
1987	18.6	2.3
1988	18.7	3.0
1990	18.7	—
1995	20.2	—
2000	23.0	—

sions produce lower incomes and profits and thus lower federal revenues), large budget deficits now that the economy is at or close to full employment suggest a need for corrective policies. Those corrective policies are embodied in the Gramm-Rudman-Hollings deficit reduction legislation, which commits the U.S. government to eliminate its budget deficit by 1993. Even if that target is not met fully, the government budget deficit seems quite likely to shrink relative to GNP over the next few years, as it has since 1986.[9]

Continuing to reduce the budget deficit, or even running a budget surplus, would raise national saving relative to investment spending and thereby help transform current account deficits and net capital inflows into current account surpluses and net capital outflows. Such capital outflows will be required if

---

[9]Part of the reduction in the federal budget deficit reflects the growing surplus of the Social Security trust fund. That surplus is projected to continue growing at least through the end of the century, contributing to higher government saving.

we are to reduce our net foreign liabilities and eventually return to being a net foreign creditor.

One way to reduce the shortfall of national saving relative to investment spending would be to reduce investment. Few people would argue that the U.S. should cut investment spending, because doing so would reduce our future standard of living. In addition, the U.S. already uses a smaller share of its GNP for investment purposes than do other major industrial countries. If we do not wish to reduce investment spending relative to GNP, our focus in eliminating the shortfall of national saving relative to investment must be on generating higher savings. Whether national saving will eventually rise enough to exceed investment spending, and thereby generate capital outflows from the U.S., remains an open question. Private saving is expected to rise relative to GNP in coming years, as is government saving. To close the shortfall of saving relative to investment without reducing investment as a share of GNP, national saving's share of GNP must rise by about 2.2 percentage points from its level in 1988 (or 2.8 points from its average level for the years from 1983 through 1988). Such an increase is possible, but not certain.

THE ROLE OF MONETARY POLICY

While it is clear that fiscal policy can help reduce or reverse our net-foreign-liability position by continuing to reduce the budget deficit, nothing in the preceding discussion seems to suggest much of a role for monetary policy. In fact, monetary policy can play an important role by promoting sustainable economic growth and low inflation. Too-rapid growth in the demand for goods and services in the U.S., and the attendant rise in inflationary pressures, would tend to increase our trade and current account deficits and thus contribute to higher foreign debt. But a recession, while it would reduce imports, would tend to increase the burden of our existing foreign debt because interest and dividend payments to foreigners would become a greater share of our diminished GNP.

Another way of stating the role of monetary policy—and of fiscal policy as well—is that policymakers can promote an eventual reduction in our net foreign debt by adopting policies to ensure that the domestic components of demand for U.S. goods and services (especially consumer spending and government purchases) grow less rapidly than the economy's capacity to produce goods and services. By doing so, policymakers would allow U.S. firms to meet growing export orders without generating stronger inflationary pressures. If government deficits continue to shrink as a share of GNP, and if personal saving rates increase appreciably as demographic trends suggest, then the domestic components of demand will grow more slowly; so, in the future it may not be necessary to use monetary policy to restrain growth in demand so as to reduce our net foreign debt.

GLOSSARY

Current account balance - a broad measure of the difference between the international receipts and payments that result from transactions with foreigners. It includes the difference between our exports and imports (the trade balance), and it also includes "factor payments" such as interest and dividends, and outright gifts such as charitable donations and foreign aid. The U.S. current account balance is the difference between our receipts from foreigners and our payments to foreigners that result from all transactions *except* purchases or sales of assets (whether stocks and bonds and other financial assets, or real assets such as land and buildings and factories).

Capital inflow into the U.S. - financial capital flows into the United States when residents of the U.S. borrow abroad or when they sell existing assets to foreigners.

Capital outflow from the U.S. - financial capital flows out of the United States when residents of the U.S. lend to foreigners or when they buy existing assets from foreigners.

Net capital inflow into the U.S. - the capital inflow from abroad minus the capital outflow.

Foreign claims on the U.S. - the total value of foreign-owned assets in the U.S., including the value of loans to U.S. residents.

U.S. claims on foreigners - the total value of assets outside of the U.S. that are owned by U.S. residents, including loans to foreigners.

U.S. net-foreign-asset position - U.S. claims on foreigners minus foreign claims on the United States. A country with a positive net-foreign-asset position is a "net foreign creditor."

U.S. net-foreign-liability position - foreign claims on the U.S. minus U.S. claims on foreigners. A country with a positive net-foreign-liability position (and thus a negative net-foreign-asset position) is a "net foreign debtor." The United States is now a net foreign debtor.

SUMMARY

A look at the causes and implications of the U.S. becoming a net-debtor country yields four conclusions. First, our standard of living is unlikely to decline, although it may grow less rapidly because of the need to service our liabilities to foreigners. Second, our net-debtor status is unlikely to cause very high inflation rates like those experienced by some of the world's debtor countries. Third, we can reduce, and eventually reverse, our net-debtor position if we save a greater proportion of our incomes in the future—especially if the baby-boom generation saves more as it enters middle age. And fourth, the government can help if it continues to reverse the budget deficit as a share of GNP, and if it chooses monetary and fiscal policies that promote sustainable, noninflationary economic growth.

Personal saving - that part of households' current after-tax income that is not spent to buy goods and services. This is the part of current income that is deposited in financial institutions, used to buy additional financial assets, or otherwise lent out. When we aggregate personal saving for the economy as a whole, we net out new consumer borrowing from the flow of new saving done by households.

Business saving - that part of businesses' revenues that is not paid out to workers, lenders, suppliers, or owners. Alternatively, the funds that are retained as cash on hand, deposited in financial institutions, or lent out. Business saving is comprised largely of retained earnings and depreciation or amortization allowances.

Government saving - the consolidated government budget surplus for all levels of government. When governments run a budget surplus they use the excess of revenue over outlays either to retire debt they had issued previously, or they buy financial assets. When governments run budget deficits, they dissave and issue new debt or money.

National saving - the sum of personal, business, and government saving. Conceptually, national saving represents the quantity of funds that can be used to finance domestic investment or that can be lent to foreigners.

Real investment - the purchase and installation of new machinery and equipment, the construction or expansion of buildings and structures, and the accumulation of additional inventory.

Net investment - gross (total) investment spending by businesses less an estimate of economic depreciation. Economic depreciation is the amount of the capital stock that wears out or becomes useless. Thus net investment is a measure of the amount by which investment spending increases the stock of capital in the economy.

Article 7

Mack Ott

Mack Ott is a senior economist at the Federal Reserve Bank of St. Louis. Erik A. Hess provided research assistance.

Is America Being Sold Out?

THE LAST time the U.S. current account balance was in surplus was in 1981. During the seven years 1982-88, U.S. deficits averaged over $100 billion. Capital inflows from foreign investors have reduced the U.S. foreign investment position steadily from a net U.S. claim of $141.1 billion at the end of 1981 to net foreign claims on the United States of $368.2 billion at the end of 1987.

Much of the commentary on this reversal has presumed the loss of U.S. economic sovereignty, declining opportunities for American labor, and a reduction in the U.S. standard of living. In rebutting these concerns, analysts have generally concentrated on selected aspects of the phenomenon. For example, recent articles have focused on the relative pace of foreign direct investment, in particular, Japanese direct investment, while others have singled out the benefits of capital inflows for both American investors and labor[1]

This article takes a broader perspective to review the full range of concerns about foreign investment, both from a logical and an empirical vantage. The public concerns about the flow of foreign investment and its anxiety about the implications of the U.S. net international debtor status are each addressed. We begin with an overview of recent public opinion polls about foreign investment in the United States, and then consider the data on foreign investment. The potential for a foreign takeover of the U.S. economy and the pattern of foreign investment in the United States relative to U.S. investment abroad are examined.

FOREIGN INVESTMENT IN THE UNITED STATES IN THE 1980s

In assessing the implications of foreign investment in the United States during the 1980s, it is useful to examine three dimensions of the foreign capital inflows. First is the *perception* of foreign investment as reported by the media and recorded in public opinion polls. Since perceptions are often as important as facts, it is appropriate to begin with them. If there were no perceived threat, it is unlikely that any policy actions would be considered; certainly, the threat of foreign ownership of U.S. assets would not be an issue in the public forum. Second is the *pattern* of foreign investment. The concern seems to be chiefly that foreigners will obtain control of certain U.S. industries vital to

---

[1]Anderson (1988) focuses on direct investment misperceptions, Little (1988) discusses the relatively small magnitude of both direct and portfolio investment, Makin (1988b) discusses the Japanese investment patterns in the United States, Rosengreen (1988) discusses direct investment by foreigners and compared with U.S foreign direct investment and Weidenbaum (1988) argues that capital inflows are beneficial. Francis (1988) recounts an interview with Milton Friedman in which he argues that the U.S. foreign asset position is understated to the extent that he doubts the U.S. is a net debtor. Ulan and Dewald (1989) estimate adjustments to obtain a corrected U.S. net international investment balance. From a different vantage, Hweko and Chediek (1988) describe the ruinous consequences following Argentine dictator Juan Peron's drive for ''economic independence'' through import substitution and restrictions on foreign investment.

---

national security, industries traditionally dominated by U.S. firms, or high-technology industries. Third is the reported *magnitude* of foreign investment. If the magnitude of such investment is negligible, there cannot be much threat to U.S. overall interests. If the magnitude is substantial, the inflow of foreign capital must be evaluated on its merits.

The Perception of Foreign Investment in the United States

Opinion polls unambiguously reveal that the American public is concerned about increased foreign ownership of U.S. firms and real estate.[2] A poll by the Roper Organization in March 1988 found that 84 percent of the respondents thought that foreign companies buying more companies and real estate in America is not "a good idea for the U.S." In the same poll, by a 49 percent to 45 percent plurality, respondents disapproved of new jobs for Americans in foreign-owned plants, and at least 72 percent thought that foreign companies' investments should be restricted.[3] In May 1988, a CBS News/New York Times survey found that 51 percent of a national sample agreed that the "increase in foreign investment poses a threat to American economic independence."[4] Similar findings were reported by other polling firms.[5]

Moreover, the uneasiness is not limited to Americans outside of the opinion-making elite. Last year, Sen. James Exon of Nebraska supported legislation "to give the Pentagon the right to veto" foreign takeovers of defense contractors; this provision was ultimately incorporated in the 1988 trade act. The political attractiveness of the issue is very strong:

Actions from Japanese land purchases in Hawaii to a British corporate takeover attempt in Pittsburgh fuel grass-roots worries. 'The farther away you get from Washington,' the greater the reaction 'that America

should belong to Americans,' says one antitakeover group official.[6]

The political furor and public uneasiness continue in early 1989. A controversial bill calling for greater disclosure by foreign investors was scheduled for a quick vote in the House of Representatives but was withdrawn by the Speaker of the House after an "explosion of protest in the Bush administration."[7] In a survey for the Washington Post-ABC News Poll in mid-February 1989, "Forty-five percent said Japanese citizens should not be allowed to buy property in the United States, and eight of 10 said there should be a limit on how many U.S. companies the Japanese should be allowed to buy."[8]

The Pattern of Foreign Investment in the United States in the 1980s

There has been pronounced opposition to direct investment in the United States by foreigners, especially the Japanese. Direct investment is defined as a 10 percent or greater ownership share in a firm. Foreign direct investment in American firms has been the focus of the greatest unease. Such investment can take place either through stock purchases or the creation of new enterprises in the United States by foreigners, with or without U.S. partners. The seriousness of this concern is exemplified by excerpts from an editorial by Malcolm Forbes:

BEFORE JAPAN BUYS TOO MUCH OF THE U.S.A.
We must instantly legislate a presidentially appointed Board of Knowledgeables whose approval would be required before *any* foreign purchase of any significance would be allowed of *any* consequential U.S. company—regardless of size. . . .It's one thing for the Japanese and Germans and others to buy U.S. government bonds to finance our huge trade imbalances with them. But it's a

---

[2]For a comprehensive accounting of this view, see Tolchin and Tolchin (1988). Other briefer accounts, supporting in varying degrees the Tolchins' concerns, are in Baer (1988), Burgess (1989), Fierman (1988), Jenkins (1988), Norton (1988), O'Reilly (1988), Skrzycki (1988), and "Mr. Greenspan on the Gas Tax" (1988). Even those who make their skepticism obvious—such as Friedman (1988), Kinsley (1988), Makin (1988a,b), "Buying into a Good Thing" (1988)—imply that the notion has received such frequent airing as to become conventional wisdom.

[3]Baer (1988), p.24.

[4]"Opinion Roundup" (1988).

[5]Hamilton, Frederick & Schneiders reported that "78 percent of Americans favor laws limiting foreign investment in

real estate and business" [Jenkins, p. 45] and Smick Medley & Associates found that "nearly 80 percent of Americans outside of the opinion-making elite would like to limit foreign buying, and 40 percent want to halt it altogether. 'Joe America is nervous and suspicious,' says the firm's president, David Smick. 'He is worried about losing control over his destiny.'" [Fierman, p.54]

[6]Jaroslovsky (1988).

[7]Birnbaum (1989).

[8]Morin (1989).

Figure 1
U.S. vs. Foreign Direct Investment

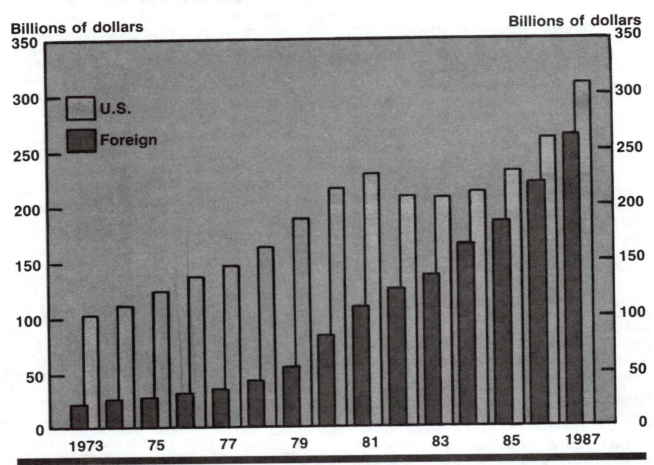

whole and totally impermissible other thing for them to use their vast billions of dollars to buy great chunks of America's big businesses, or take over the high-tech, medical or other strategic, vital U.S. concerns.[9]

Figure 1 shows that since the advent of floating exchange rates in the early 1970s, foreign direct investment in the United States has grown faster than U.S. direct investment abroad—an annual growth rate of 18.7 percent vs. 7.6 percent. Consequently, the relative size of foreign direct investment has risen—from about 22 percent of U.S. foreign direct invest-

ment in 1975 to about 85 percent in 1987. Of the $41.5 billion of direct U.S. investment by foreigners in 1987, nearly half, $19.1 billion, was in U.S. manufacturing.

The Magnitude of Foreign Investment in the United States in the 1980s

Table 1 shows the estimated composition of foreign investment in the United States and of U.S. investment abroad at the end of 1975 and 1980-87.[10] These data reveal that, since 1975,

[9]Forbes,(1988).Similar views are recounted in Makin (1988b) and expressed throughout Tolchin and Tolchin (1988).

[10]Note that the U.S. government gold stock reported in table 1 is vastly understated relative to its market value. In the table, the official U.S. government gold entry is computed

using an accounting price of $42.22 per troy ounce. If its value were computed using a value closer to its market value in the 1980s, say $400 per ounce, the entry in table 1 for U.S. official gold would be about $100 billion rather than $11 billion.

Table 1

The Composition of Foreign Investment in the United States and U.S. Investment Abroad (billions of dollars)

	1975	1980	1981	1982	1983	1984	1985	1986	1987
Foreign investment in the United States	$220.9	$500.8	$578.7	$688.0	$784.4	$829.6	$1060.9	$1340.7	$1536.0
Official	86.9	176.1	180.4	189.1	194.5	199.3	202.6	241.7	283.1
U.S. Government securities	63.6	118.2	125.1	132.6	137.0	143.0	143.4	177.3	219.0
Private, nonbank	77.6	173.3	202.3	243.4	284.7	350.0	474.4	620.7	684.7
Direct investment	27.7	83.0	108.7	124.7	137.1	164.6	184.6	220.4	261.9
Private and non-U.S.- Treasury securities	45.7	74.1	75.1	93.0	113.8	127.3	206.2	308.8	344.4
U.S. Treasury securities	4.2	16.1	18.5	25.8	33.8	58.2	83.6	91.5	78.4
U.S. bank liabilities	42.5	121.1	165.4	228.0	278.3	312.2	354.5	451.6	539.4
Other	13.9	30.4	30.6	27.5	26.9	31.0	29.4	26.6	28.8
U.S. investment abroad	$295.1	$607.1	$719.8	$824.9	$873.9	$896.1	$950.3	$1071.4	$1167.8
Official	16.2	26.8	30.1	34.0	33.7	34.9	43.2	48.5	45.8
Gold	11.6	11.2	11.2	11.1	11.1	11.1	11.1	11.1	11.1
Private, nonbank	159.0	278.0	291.7	283.2	291.0	300.6	343.1	392.8	455.6
Direct investment	124.0	215.4	228.4	207.8	207.2	211.5	230.2	259.6	308.9
Securities	34.9	62.6	63.4	75.5	83.8	89.1	112.8	133.2	146.7
U.S. bank claims	59.8	203.9	293.5	404.6	434.5	445.6	447.4	507.3	547.9
Other	18.3	34.7	35.8	28.6	35.1	30.0	29.0	33.3	30.1
Net foreign assets in the United States	−$74.2	−$106.3	−$141.1	−$136.9	−$89.4	−$3.5	$110.7	$269.2	$368.2

SOURCE: Scholl (1988), table 2.

foreign assets in the United States have increased much faster than U.S. assets abroad. This pattern of faster foreign asset growth is even more pronounced if the comparison is made from 1981, the last year of an American trade surplus, to 1987. From a net claim on foreigners of $141.1 billion, the United States has become the world's largest debtor, with estimated net liabilities to foreigners of $368.2 billion. During this interval, foreign assets increased by 165 percent compared with 62 percent for U.S. assets abroad.

The disparity in accumulation is even greater for assets held by private investors, that is, total foreign investment less U.S. securities held by foreign governments and central banks. Over the seven years 1981-87, private foreign investment in the United States more than tripled, from $398 billion to $1253 billion. The bulk of these capital inflows have gone into foreign holdings of U.S. securities— corporate stocks and bonds and government notes and bonds— and liabilities of U.S. banks—deposits by foreigners. Together, these two asset categories account for about three-fourths of the increase in private foreign investment in the United States, $643 billion of the $855 billion total.

The size of the foreign claims raises another issue, the cost of servicing the net foreign indebtedness. Peter Drucker (1988) has called this "the looming transfer crisis":

> ...ours is the only major industrial country that has a significant *foreign* indebtedness, not only governmental but private as well, and that therefore has a significant foreign exchange requirement. By 1991 we will need close to $1 billion to cover our foreign exchange remittances, about $500 million for the federal debt....And there is no way to earn that in our foreign transactions. No way. Even if we balance our trade, we won't have that much surplus.

Starkly put, Drucker believes that the accumulation of U.S. assets by foreigners will force the United States to repudiate its debts, either directly, indirectly by inflation or by reducing the nominal value of the dollar: "As long as we can knock down the dollar without domestic inflation, I think that is the best thing to hope for." Such a policy would be injurious not only to foreign investors but to U.S. interests as well. To see why, consider why foreigners invest in the United States and how U.S. labor and investors each benefit from such investment.

WHY DO FOREIGNERS INVEST IN THE UNITED STATES?

There are three reasons for foreign investment in the United States or for U.S. investment abroad: greater profit, lower risk and the trade deficit. The first, greater profit, is the fundamental reason, as it is for any other investment choice. The investor chooses one asset over another because it has a higher risk-adjusted rate of return. Both critics of foreign investment such as the Tolchins (1988) and defenders of unimpeded capital flows such as Makin (1988a,b) and Poole (1988) are agreed: Foreign investment is motivated primarily by profit.[11] Speaking of the capital flows from Japan and Europe to the United States, Poole observes that:

> Two rate of return conditions are relevant. First, Japanese saving invested in the United States is in the interest of the U.S. if the rate of return we pay to the Japanese is less than the return we earn on the invested capital, and there is no evidence that this condition is not met. Second, Japanese investment in the United States is in the interest of Japan if the rate of return Japan receives in the United States is greater than the rate of return available in Japan. Given the declines in Japan's growth rate and investment share, and evidence that the rate of return in the Japanese equity and fixed income markets is extremely low, it is highly likely that both of these rate-of-return conditions were met from 1981 to 1985, and perhaps later. For Europe, it seems clear that the declining investment share is a supply-side problem; incentives to produce are too low because of high marginal tax rates and labor market rigidities. Europe also provides substantial subsidies to weak and inefficient enterprises. U.S. policies have, if anything, raised European growth in the 1980s by providing a large market for European exports. Thus, the two rate-of-return conditions discussed for Japan also apply to Europe.[12]

One important implication of Poole's discussion is that Drucker's concern about being able to finance the U.S. foreign obligations becomes moot.

---

[11]"Political leaders should remember that foreign investors are very anxious to invest in the United States, and that they invest primarily for market share and profits, and everything else is secondary." [Tolchin and Tolchin (1988),

p.271] See also Poole (1988), p.44.

[12]Poole (1988), pp.45-6.

The second motivation for foreign investment is to reduce the risks of wealth loss due to unforeseen exchange rate changes.[13] This proposition is simply an extension of the risk reduction principle of portfolio diversification to international alternatives. Portfolio diversification—spreading wealth across several assets rather than a single security—reduces losses due to unforeseen events.

Similarly, exchange rate risk can be hedged by holding several assets denominated in different currencies rather than all in a single currency. The investor's wealth is insured against rising or falling by the full amount of any unforeseen exchange rate change. A corollary of this is that multinational firms can reduce the unforeseen variability of their production costs and market sales by producing and selling in several countries rather than in a single one.

The third reason for foreign investment is that it accompanies trade deficits. Foreign investment induced by higher yields or portfolio diversification occurs whether or not international trade is in balance; however, trade deficits imply that net foreign investment *must* occur in the amount by which trade is in deficit.[14] Yet it would be incorrect to infer from this accounting identity that trade deficits cause foreign capital inflows. In other words, foreign investment is not undertaken simply to finance the trade deficit; indeed, it may well be that the capital inflows cause trade deficits:

> The international accounts too, are more likely be driven from the capital side than the merchandise side. In this era of instant capital transactions, a year's worth of world trade amounts to only a

week's worth of capital flows. The U.S. trade deficit arose when U.S. banks stopped exporting capital to developing nations, and when, because of the Reagan tax cuts, the U.S. economy was the only growth opportunity in the world. These developments resulted in a tremendous net capital inflow; the deficit in merchandise trade was necessary to balance the equation.[15]

Thus, capital flows appear to be generated by investors' self-interested profit-seeking. There is broad agreement that, whatever other effects international capital flows may have on domestic economies, foreign investment makes investors and sellers of assets wealthier than they would be if their investment and sales were restricted to domestic assets and buyers. Nonetheless, this leaves open the issue of how labor is affected by international capital flows.

BENEFITS TO DOMESTIC LABOR OF FOREIGN INVESTMENT

Labor and the owners of capital share the value added in production created by transforming raw materials into output. Capital is just a generic term for the tools, buildings, land, patents, copyrights, trademarks and goodwill that labor uses to convert one set of goods—raw materials—into another—finished output. The value of each factor of production in a market economy is its opportunity cost, that is, what the raw materials, labor or capital could produce in their most profitable alternative application.

In most cases, labor and capital are complementary, so that an increase in the quantity of one raises the productivity, hence, the value

---

[13]Anticipated changes in exchange rates are reflected in the differences between the rates of return on assets in different currencies. For example, if it is widely anticipated that the British pound sterling will decline by 5 percent in exchange value vs. the dollar in the coming year, then the interest rate on British securities will be 5 percent higher than the interest rate on U.S. securities of similar risk. This relation between interest and exchange rates is known as interest rate parity; for a discussion, see Koedijk and Ott (1987), pp. 5-7.

[14]Actually, the recorded capital inflows—the capital account balance—have been persistently smaller than the broadest measure of the trade deficits—the current account balance—throughout the 1980s. This error—the statistical discrepancy—has averaged over $20 billion annually, which is between one-seventh and one-fifth of the current account deficit. For a review of the relation between the international trade and capital accounts and the statistical discrepancy, see Ott (1988), pp 3-13.

[15]Bartley (1988). See also Tatom (1987, 1989). Poole (1988), p. 42, points out that "the issue of causation is complex and should be discussed with care." Heller (1989), p. 2, notes that foreigners are financing attractive investments for which U.S. total saving is insufficient:

...the [domestic government] deficit is still substantial in relation to domestic savings and uses up funds that are needed for private sector investment. Thus far the US economy has enjoyed the confidence of foreign investors, preventing serious 'crowding-out' of the private sector in financial markets.

Wayne Angell, Heller's colleague on the Board of Governors of the Federal Reserve System, also has observed that the capital inflows are beneficial:

"I'm not irritated or upset about capital inflows into the United States. Capital inflows do tend to increase our productivity." "Capital Inflows Called Helpful" (1988)

of the services, of the other. For example, providing an auto mechanic or a carpenter with more tools increases the amount or quality of work they can accomplish; this increase in productivity leads to a rise in their wages, or, at the same wages, to an increase in the number of them employed.

Consequently, to the extent that foreign investment is an increment of capital that would otherwise not be available for labor to use, the foreign capital must unambiguously be beneficial to labor.[16] Equally true, the availability of foreign capital lowers the cost of capital to owners; this makes additions to plant and equipment cheaper, makes possible some investment projects that otherwise would not occur and raises the value of firms.[17] Thus, even if the foreign capital does not directly affect the ownership of the firm, it benefits labor and asset owners by lowering interest rates, the cost of capital.

This discussion can be summarized in five postulates about the expected gains and losses from the addition of foreign capital:

(i)   Labor gains as the incremental capital raises the productivity of labor, increasing the amount of labor that can be employed or the wages of those who are employed;

(ii)   Owners of firms—the shareholders— benefit by the lower interest rates implied by higher asset prices;

(iii)   Consumers gain as a result of the lower prices of goods implied by the increased labor productivity;

(iv)   The profitability of financial intermediaries may decline since the value of their services in bringing borrowers and lenders together is inversely related to the supply of capital. Moreover, the entry of foreign financial intermediaries makes the industry more competitive, which also tends to reduce the rate return;

(v)   Savers may lose interest income as a result of lowered interest rates due to the greater capital availability. This loss is offset, to some extent, as they receive capital gains on their existing fixed-rate portfolio holdings for the same reason as in (ii).

Since foreign investment raises the amount of capital available, labor productivity rises as does the absolute income of labor. Labor is better off with more capital than with less, and the nationality of the investor is a matter of indifference to labor.[18]

THE MYTHICAL THREAT OF WITHDRAWAL OF FOREIGN CAPITAL

In early 1989, the U.S. economy continues its longest peacetime expansion on record, so the dangers of foreign investment are posed as the potential calamity of an abrupt foreign withdrawal. This scenario was described by a

[16]Recent media discussions of worker views on foreign ownership of their firms have revealed a general absence of hostility by workers and their unions, emphasizing instead the benefits of the employment made possible by the capital inflow. Holusha (1989) quotes two automobile workers at the Nummi joint venture of Toyota and General Motors as follows:

"I can't honestly say I like it better [than when it was a G.M. plant], but I'm working and that's better."
and
"We got a second chance here, and we are trying to take advantage of it. Many people don't get a second chance."

The Tolchins'(1988) single out Volkswagen of America as being "a notable exception to the anti-union flavor of many foreign owned companies." (p. 178) Ironically, the other foreign automakers castigated by the Tolchins continue operations and employment of labor in the United States, while Volkswagen ceased U.S. production in 1988.

[17]The elimination of restrictions on foreign ownership can raise the wealth of domestic asset owners, as recently illustrated in a policy change by Nestle, a Swiss corporation; see Dullforce (1988a). In late November 1988, Nestle announced that, henceforth, it would sell registered shares to any buyer, whether or not that buyer was a Swiss resident. As a result of the eradication of the distinction between its two types of common stock, registered (formerly restricted to residents) and bearer (available to

nonresidents), common shares of both types now sell for about the same price. Before the change, bearer shares had sold for about twice the price of registered shares. See Financial Times Market Staff (1988). Removing the restriction on foreign buyers' ability to buy the resident shares realized a 40 percent wealth gain for Swiss resident shareholders. Nestle reportedly makes up about 11 percent of the capitalized value of the Swiss stock market shares, and its decision may influence other Swiss corporations' equity policies. This change opens up the possibility of foreign ownership of Swiss corporations; apparently, Swiss Nestle stockholders are willing to bear this cost. The Governor of the Swiss National Bank also has argued that the market for financial assets in Switzerland must not discriminate on the nationality of the buyer if the country is to remain an important center for capital transactions; see Dullforce (1988c). Similar arguments are offered in a discussion of the European Community's eradication of capital restrictions by Greenhouse (1988).

[18]In the 1988 Presidential campaign, the Democratic candidate, Michael Dukakis, told a group of workers at a St. Louis automotive parts plant, "Maybe the Republican ticket wants our children to work for foreign owners....but that's not the kind of a future Lloyd Bentsen and I and Dick Gephardt and you want for America." The workers addressed by the candidate had been employed by an Italian corporation for 11 years. "Dukakis-Bentsen-Gephardt" (1988).

Figure 2
U.S. Dollar Exchange Rates vs. Japan, U.K. and West Germany

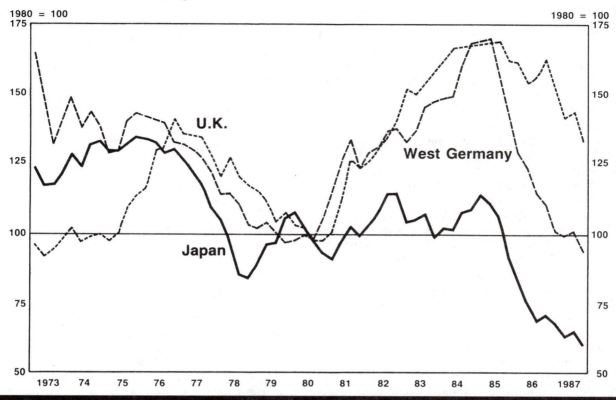

This scenario entails the confluence of four events: a decline in the dollar's exchange value; a cyclical decline in U.S. interest rates; a withdrawal and subsequent re-entry of foreign investment; and a banking crisis induced by the

foreign withdrawal. Thus, to evaluate the dangers posed by foreign ownership of U.S. assets, one must investigate not just the likelihood of each of these events but their joint likelihood, including whether they are mutually consistent.

Decline of the Dollar

From its peak in February 1985, the exchange value of the dollar averaged against the principal industrial currencies has fallen more than 40 percent.[20] As shown in figure 2, it has fallen by about one-third against the pound, by almost one-half vs. the yen and by over two-fifths in terms of the Deutsche mark. Yet, there has been no sign of a widespread flight from

prominent New York investment banker as follows:

> The dollar will eventually fall, he notes, and when it does and interest rates decline in a period of recession, foreign investors would withdraw their portfolio investments, triggering a banking crisis. These foreign investors then could use their inflated portfolios to make direct investments of American industry at "bargain basement prices. . . .We will have financed our deficit by putting up permanent assets."[19]

---

[19]Attributed to Felix Rohatyn, p.28, in Tolchin and Tolchin (1988); this scenario is repeated nearly verbatim on pp. 197-98 and again on p. 201. See also Baer (1988), Fierman (1988), Jenkins (1988), Makin (1988a,b) and Norton (1988).

[20]The trade-weighted exchange rate of the dollar against the other Group of Ten countries plus Switzerland hit a peak of 158.43 (1973 = 100.00) in February 1985; it was below 90.0 in late 1987 and has a value of 91.88 in January 1989, a 42 percent decline from its early 1985 peak.

dollar assets. Even the record stock-market crash of October 1987, when the dollar's exchange value was at its nadir, did not suffice to trigger a massive withdrawal of foreign capital.[21]

Cyclical Decline of U.S. Interest Rates

Generally, differences in interest rates in one currency vs. another are just sufficient to offset the anticipated depreciation of the higher-interest currency vs. the lower-interest currency as reflected in their forward exchange rate.[22] While interest rates do decline in recessions, the benefit to an investor from selling U.S. assets and shifting to another currency at such times is limited by the likely state of other economies. The world's major economies are so economically integrated that periods of recession in the U.S. economy are generally also periods of recession in the other economies in which attractive substitute investments would be available. Consequently, to the extent that both interest rates and asset prices were to fall in the U.S. economy, the same pattern is likely to have occurred in the rest of the industrial economies as well, so a shift from U.S. to foreign assets would accrue no profit. If other economies' asset prices and interest rates had not fallen with those in the United States, then the depreciation of the dollar's exchange rate would obviate the benefit of such a withdrawal.

Withdrawal and Subsequent Re-entry of Foreign Investment

Investors withdrawing their funds from U.S. assets must do it in two steps—first selling the asset and then using the cash (dollar) proceeds to buy another asset, either another U.S. asset or a foreign currency. An investor selling an asset from a portfolio is, by that action, buying something else—a stock, a bond, a piece of real estate, a quantity of money denominated in some currency.[23] When the dollar proceeds are exchanged for foreign currency, some other investors will acquire the original asset and the U.S. dollars. In the spirit of the scenario, if only domestic U.S. investors are buying the U.S. assets from the prior foreign owners, both a U.S. capital outflow and a sharply declining dollar exchange rate will occur. The capital outflow can only occur if the United States has a trade surplus.[24] In reality, massive withdrawals of foreign capital cannot occur in the short run. Prices and exchange rates adjust first; international payments flows adjust with a substantial lag. Nonetheless, if this unlikely abrupt swing from trade deficit to surplus were to occur because of the foreigners' panic sales, the assets would end up in U.S. investors' hands at considerably lower prices. If foreigners repurchased them shortly thereafter, the result would be increased prices and an appreciation of the exchange value of the dollar with the resulting profit accruing to domestic owners.

---

[21]In part, this is simply an illustration of the interconnectedness of the world's economies. All major stock market around the globe crashed together:

All major world markets declined substantially in that month [October 1987], which is itself an exceptional fact that contrasts with the usual modest correlations of returns across countries....The United States had the fifth *smallest* decline, i.e., the fifth best performance, in local currency units. However, because the dollar declined against most currencies, the U.S. performance restated in a common currency was only 11th out of 23....[A]n attempt was made to ascertain how much of October's crash could be ascribed to the normal response of each country's stock market to a worldwide marketmovement. A world market index was constructed and found to be statistically related to monthly returns in every country during the period from the beginning of 1981 up until the month before the crash. The magnitude of market response differs materially across countries. The response coefficient, or "beta" was *by far* the most statistically significant explanatory variable in the October crash. It swamped the influences of the institutional market characteristics. Roll (1989), pp.65-6

[22]This relation between interest rate differences and anticipated exchange rate changes (primarily due to inflation rate differences) is called covered interest parity (CIP). The evidence supporting the absence of profitable speculative opportunities due to CIP is overwhelming. While there is also evidence of risk premia in interest differentials, such evidence also suggests that these premia are a return for the cost of risk-bearing, not a pure profit. See Koedijk and Ott (1987).

[23]The scenario at this point makes a distinction between foreign investors' portfolio and direct investment: "...withdraw their portfolio investments...then could use their inflated portfolios to make direct investments at bargain basement prices..." This presumes a distinction between bond and stock prices which is inconsistent. According to the scenario, the dollar and all other U.S. asset prices fall, so it would be irrelevant where foreign investors' portfolios were initially invested. Moreover, since direct investment is simply a 10 percent or greater holding in a corporation, the distinction between "portfolio" and "direct investment" holdings of common shares is one of degree, not of kind.

[24]It is unlikely, but conceivable that a swap of U.S. assets for foreign assets could take place without any impact on the balance of payments; however, this would require that the assets exchange in exactly balanced total values, the value of U.S. assets sold equaling the value of foreign assets sold. In contrast, the scenario being reviewed postulates a declining dollar, suggesting that the U.S. assets are no longer as desirable as they were at their prior prices. Consequently, with falling U.S. asset prices and foreigners engaging in net sales, a capital outflow is implied. This can only occur if the trade balance is registering a surplus.

Banking Crisis[25]

Here the scenario presumes that foreigners, having sold their portfolios, then convert their dollar deposits to nondollar currencies. To do so, they must buy these currencies from others who, in turn, end up holding dollar deposits. This would put downward pressure on the dollar's exchange rate and would be associated with a capital outflow from the United States. Such substantial withdrawals—even if replaced dollar for dollar in aggregate—would increase the uncertainty entailed in asset-liability management decisions at *individual* depository institutions.

In particular, this uncertainty would complicate the matching of the duration of assets and deposit liabilities. The likely response of depository institutions to these portfolio shifts would be an increase in their demand for reserves, reflected in a rise of the federal funds rate. Yet, the stress of an abrupt rise in deposit turnover—whether or not it is associated with a net outflow of funds from depository institutions—does not necessarily imply a banking crisis. Such an implication would require that the Federal Reserve take no action to accommodate an abrupt shift in the public's portfolio preferences. The Fed can and has accommodated such increases in the public's demand for liquidity and the rise in depository institutions' demand for reserves.[26]

Overview of the Foreign Withdrawal Myth

In summary, the scenario is extremely likely to occur. It is internally inconsistent and depends on inept U.S. monetary policy actions and irrational investment behavior by both domestic and foreign investor. Since interest rates are linked through integrated international capital markets, the presumed low U.S. interest rates and a depreciating dollar are inconsistent. Investors, U.S. resident and foreign, are unlikely to believe that the U.S. monetary authorities would be passive in the event of a U.S. banking crisis. They could profit by buying U.S. assets at prices temporarily depressed by any general foreign withdrawal and subsequently selling them back to other chagrined but wiser foreign investors. In short, rational expectations and the profit motive induce competitive behavior which nullifies the threat of widespread foreign capital withdrawal, the same profit motive that induced the foreign investment in the first place.[27]

HAS FOREIGN DIRECT INVESTMENT CHALLENGED CONTROL OF DOMESTIC U.S. INDUSTRIES?

Misperceptions about the distribution of foreign ownership pervade discussions about foreign investment in the United States. First, as can be seen in table 1, most foreign investment is concentrated in portfolio and bank deposits. In 1987, foreigners held only about 17 percent of their U.S. assets in direct investment; if official assets are excluded, the share of direct investment rises to about 21 percent. In contrast, U.S. direct investment abroad is about 26 percent of the total or 27 percent of private investment. As the table shows, U.S. direct investment abroad exceeds foreign direct investment in the United States. Moreover, the excess of U.S. direct investment widened in 1987 to $47 billion from $39.2 billion at the end of 1986.

The acceleration of U.S. foreign direct investment beginning with 1985 is obvious in figure 1. U.S. foreign direct investment fell from 1981 to 1982 and was stagnant until 1985; during this

---

[25]A "banking crisis" can be defined as a widespread loss of confidence in the solvency of depository institutions resulting in runs on banks or abrupt rises in interest rates to deter withdrawals. From the public's point of view, such shifts in portfolio preferences away from deposits can be characterized as an increase in liquidity preference. Such a crisis could very well be precipitated by sharp declines in stock and bond prices if deposit holders feared that banks' direct losses on portfolio investments or indirect losses through loans secured by securities endangered their deposits.

[26]For example, by a combination of increased open market purchases of U.S. securities and the indication of greater accommodation through the discount window, the Fed obviated a potential liquidity crisis in the U.S. financial system following the October 1987 stock market crash.

[27]Another interpretation of this scenario is that it is simple lobbying for restrictions on foreign buyers and foreign intermediaries. The scenario is intended to engender doubt about the benefits of unhindered foreign capital inflows. The policy implication contingent on finding the scenario credible would be to restrict U.S. investment by foreigners and foreign investment intermediaries. These restrictions would lower the supply of capital and raise interest rates and other costs of financing domestic investment and corporate restructuring. As a result, the services of domestic financial intermediaries would rise in value. In short, the argument is of a piece with all regulatory arguments for restrictions on entry or output—that the increased safety, purity or quality of the licensed practitioners justifies the reduced supply and higher cost. See Stigler (1971).

period, foreign direct investment in the United States accelerated. Since 1985, however, U.S. investment abroad has outpaced foreign direct investment in the United States. While there is a lively debate about why this resurgence of U.S. direct investment has occurred, most analysts argue that it reflects the tax reforms of 1986:

> Nonresidential [U.S.] fixed investment rose substantially in 1983-84, but reached a peak in 1985 and then fell somewhat. The tax reform discussion, which began in earnest with the Treasury I tax proposal in November 1984, killed the investment boom. Further evidence for this view is that U.S. direct investment abroad rose substantially at the same time.[28]

The second misperception about foreign direct investment in the United States is the apparent belief that the Japanese are the principal foreign direct investors.[29] This notion is incorrect. As figure 3a indicates, Japanese direct investment in the United States ranks a distant third behind that of the British and the Dutch. In fact, the European Community holds about three-fifths of the foreign direct investment in the United States—$157.7 billion of the $261.9 billion in 1987—nearly five times the Japanese stake. Of the total investment, direct, portfolio and bank deposits, Burgess (1988) notes that "at the end of 1987, Europeans had holdings of $785 billion, compared to Japan's $194 billion ...[of] assets of all kinds—wholly owned companies, stocks, bonds, bank deposits, real estate."

The third misperception is that foreign direct investment is concentrated in the manufacturing sector. As shown in figure 3a and 3b, the share of U.S. direct investment by foreigners in manufacturing is just over one-third, 35 percent, slightly less than the 41 percent share of U.S. direct investment abroad in manufacturing. In terms of country shares, the Japanese have less than one-sixth of their U.S. direct investment in manufacturing. The top four areas of direct investment show substantial similarity. In descending order, manufacturing, trade, petroleum and finance are the largest foreign direct investment areas in the United States, while manufacturing, petroleum, finance and wholesale are the largest U.S. direct investment areas abroad.

Considered at the level of individual firms, the Japanese record is even less obtrusive. Rosengren (1988) reports that Japan's acquisition of 94 U.S. companies during 1978-87 ranked fifth compared with the 640 taken over by the British, 435 by the Canadians, 150 by the Germans and 113 by the French. Considering the year 1987, the Japanese tied for fifth place with the Germans at 15 acquisitions, well behind the pace of the British (78), the Canadians (28), the French (19), and the Australians (17). Rosengren argues that these company purchases tend to be reciprocal in two respects. First, the U.S. list of companies purchased has nearly the same country rank order as the foreign purchases in the United States, and the particular industries also were similar for the U.S. and foreign direct. Second, both U.S. and foreign firms tend to make acquisitions of firms in their own industries as a means of extending their markets.

The upshot of Rosengren's study is that foreign acquisitions of U.S. firms have exhibited much the same patterns as U.S. acquisitions of foreign firms with a twist reflecting the increasing international integration of business: "[M]any of the foreign acquisitions are partnerships between foreign investors and U.S. banks and investment companies."[30]

IS THERE ANY CREDIBLE DANGER FROM FOREIGN CAPITAL?

Any credible threat from foreign investment must ultimately depend on the share of foreign

---

[28]Poole (1988), p. 46. See also Tatom (1987, 1989).

[29]For example, see O'Reilly (1988). This view also is implicit in the excerpt of the editorial by Malcolm Forbes (1988) on pages 48-49. Its inaccuracy is addressed in Makin (1988b) and Rosengren (1988).

[30]Rosengren (1988), p. 50, illustrates this with a clear example of the financial integration of takeovers:

> Classifying an acquisition as "foreign" can be misleading since the bulk of the purchase may be financed by a domestic company. Depending on how the deal is structured, those who provide the financing may have a substantial stake in the outcome of the acquisition. For example, when Beazer, a British company announced its $1.85 billion hostile bid for Koppers, much of the financing was provided by a U.S. company, Shearson/American Express. Shearson/American Express not only provided $500 million in debt financing, it also agreed to purchase 46 percent of equity.

Figure 3a
Distribution of Foreign Direct Investment in the United States, ($261.9 Billion), 1987

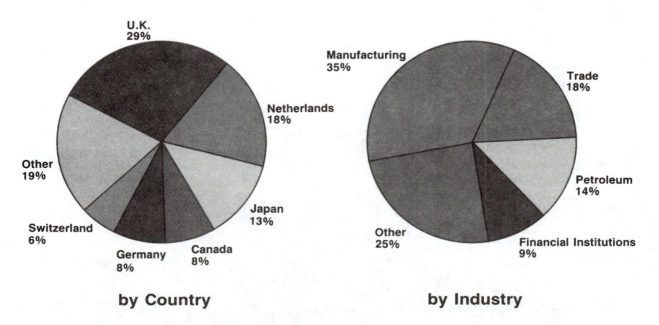

by Country

by Industry

Figure 3b
Distribution of U.S. Direct Investment Abroad, ($308.8 Billion), 1987

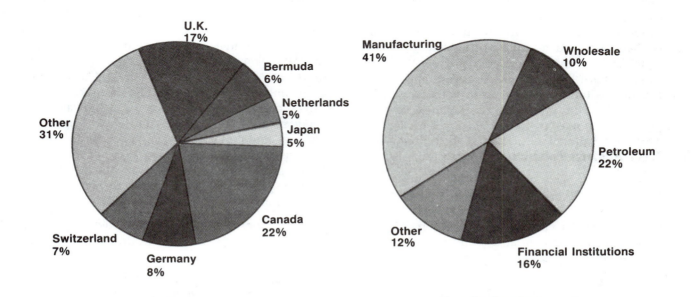

by Country

by Industry

Figure 4
U.S. Net Reproducible Fixed Capital Stock at Market Prices

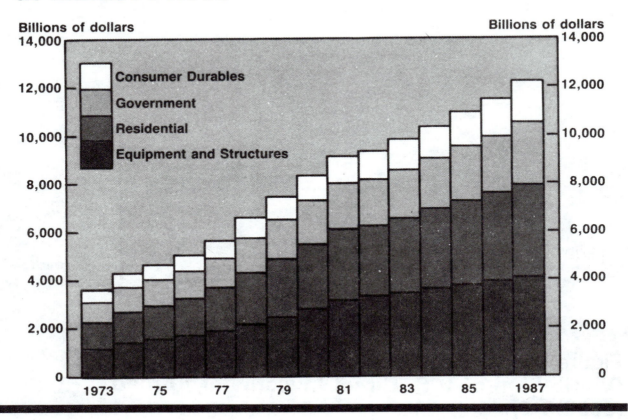

Billions of dollars

Billions of dollars

Legend:
- Consumer Durables
- Government
- Residential
- Equipment and Structures

ownership of the stock of U.S. assets. That is, a small proportional share of U.S. capital held by foreigners is sufficient to preclude the possibility that foreign investment in the United States is deleterious. In this section, we show that the foreign share of U.S. capital, current and prospective, is too small to support the critics' concern.

The Miniscule Share of Foreign Ownership of U.S. Capital

The market value and the composition of the U.S. reproducible fixed net capital stock from 1973 to 1987 is shown in figure 4. From 1973, when its market value was $3.6 trillion, it has grown to $12.2 trillion at the end of 1987. During the period of large U.S. current account

deficits beginning in 1982, its annual increase has averaged more than $0.5 trillion—that is, more than five times the average capital inflow—an annual growth rate of about 5.5 percent. Its composition in 1987 was $4.1 trillion of producers' plant and equipment, $2.4 trillion of government capital, $4.0 trillion of residential capital and $1.7 trillion of consumer durable goods such as automobiles, household furnishings and equipment.[31] For purposes of this analysis, we will consider the share of the net U.S. reproducible tangible capital stock (less consumer durables) that the net foreign investment could command as collateral.

The composition of U.S. assets held abroad and foreign assets held in the United States are shown in table 1. Considered as a potential

---

[31]Government capital, valued at its current estimated replacement cost, consists of government buildings, plant and equipment used in government production and roads,

bridges, waterway improvements, etc. State and local governments hold about two-thirds of the public capital stock and the federal government one third.

Figure 5
Ratio of Net Foreign Assets to Net Reproducible Capital Stock Excluding Consumer Durables

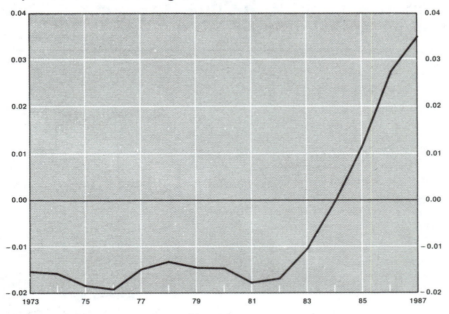

claim collateralized by the U.S. capital stock, the estimated foreign holding of U.S. claims at year-end 1987, $1.54 trillion, was about 12.5 percent of the U.S. reproducible capital stock and 14.6 percent of the nonconsumer capital stock. Considered as a claim on the producer capital stock, $4.1 trillion, it amounted to a 37.4 percent claim. Subtracting estimated U.S. assets abroad at year-end 1987, $1.17 trillion, from the foreign claims yields net foreign assets in the United States, $0.37 trillion, so that the percentage foreign claim on the net U.S. reproducible nonconsumer capital stock at the end of 1987 was 3.5 percent.

In summary, the net current share of U.S. assets owned by foreigners is implausibly low to substantiate any potential cornering of U.S. asset markets. Even so, this leaves open the question of whether the trend of increasing foreign ownership poses any such likelihood.

Sustained Capital Inflows Are Insufficient to Threaten U.S. Economic Sovereignty

The U.S. Commerce Department estimates that the U.S. international investment position became a net foreign claim in 1985 for the first time since 1914, -$110.7 billion (see table 1). Figure 5 shows this net foreign investment claim as a share of the net U.S reproducible nonconsumer capital stock. Reflecting the U.S. trade deficits during the 1980s, the foreign claim has grown at an average of over $80 billion per year since 1981. Since becoming a net claim, the foreign percentage claim has risen to 3.5 percent of this U.S. wealth measure.

Even if the capital inflows persisted indefinitely at their 1988 level of about $120 billion, this need not result in an eventual foreign control of the U.S. economy in the sense of majority foreign ownership of U.S. nonconsumer assets. This is because the U.S. capital stock also is growing. If either the inflation of replacement prices of physical capital or real capital accumulation is fast enough, the share of foreign capital could rise for a period of years and then decline. The maximum the foreign share would attain and the time at which it would top out vary with the assumed rates of capital stock growth and the rate of capital price appreciation.

Figure 6
Foreign Share of Net U.S. Reproducible Capital Stock Excluding Consumer Durables Collaterized by Net Foreign Investment with Constant Capital Inflows and Declining Capital Inflows

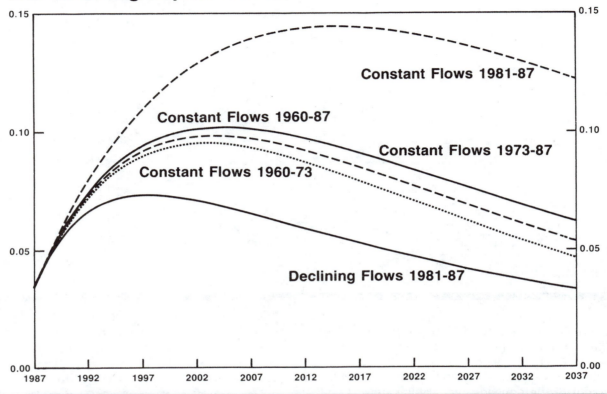

The U.S. capital stock grows each year by the amount by which gross investment in new buildings, roads, housing and industrial plant and equipment exceeds the scrappage and depreciation of the existing stock. The market value of this stock also rises with inflation. As was shown in chart 4, the estimated market value of the U.S. nonconsumer capital stock grew from $7.9 trillion at the end of 1981 to $10.5 trillion at the end of 1987. Over this period, the implicit annual rate of inflation of capital stock replacement cost has averaged

about 2.3 percent, and the annual growth of the real net stock (at 1982 prices) has averaged about 2.2 percent. The sum of these two effects in the 1980s has implied a nominal capital stock growth rate of 4.5 percent. Combining these recent trends, we can determine the long-term consequences of a continued capital inflow.[32]

As shown in figure 6, under these assumptions, which are most favorable to the threat scenario, the foreign share actually would rise to a maximum of 14.4 percent in the year 2015

---

[32]The period 1981-87 and the constant $120 billion inflow are used in this discussion as they maximize the growth of and the peak share attained by foreign capital. More plausible rates are considered below. Nonetheless, the fact that even indefinitely sustained capital inflows of over $100 billion would be insufficient to support any traumatic restructuring of the U.S. economy is consistent with Mussa's conjecture about surprisingly large equilibrium

U.S. current account deficits: As a result of the higher growth rate of the U.S. population, its relatively younger age distribution, the size of the U.S. economy and its attractive investment opportunities, "...we should have an equilibrium current account deficit of roughly one percent of our GNP." See Mussa (1985, p.146). In terms of the 1988 level of GNP of $5 trillion, this would imply an equilibrium capital inflow of $50 billion.

and then decline.[33] Since the assumed sustained capital inflow is probably larger than most analysts would assume, this is a worst-case scenario. For example, under growth and inflation rates averaged over the the full floating-rate era, 1973-87, the constant $120 billion capital inflow would generate a peak share of 10.2 percent in 2004. Finally, if the capital inflow declines over the near future as it has since 1987, then the foreign share would peak in 1997 at about 7.3 percent.

Consequently, the growth of the foreign share of U.S. capital, while large by 20th century experience, does not approach the share necessary to corner the market. Even when expressed as a claim on a subset of U.S. wealth—excluding consumer durable goods, land, and human capital—and presuming an investment pattern which foreign investment has not exhibited, the share of foreign investment does not present a credible takeover threat to the American economy.

IS THE UNITED STATES REALLY A NET DEBTOR?

Much of the concern about the economic security of the United States was triggered by the Department of Commerce estimate that the U.S. net international investment position became negative in 1985 (see table 1). The proximate cause of the declining U.S. net investment position is the U.S. current account deficits since 1981. There is no question that the U.S. international investment balance has declined as a result of the relatively faster foreign investment in the United States than U.S. investment abroad. In other words, there is no question that the net capital flows have been into the United States. Conversely, there is a very real question whether the U.S. position has yet become negative. The primary basis for this skepticism is that direct investment is recorded at its historic cost, which understates the current market value by amounts that grow over the years.

Recently, Ulan and Dewald (1989) have estimated the net U.S. investment position [NIIP] adjusting for the understatement of U.S. direct foreign investment:

> When direct investment is revalued to market, we estimate that the U.S. NIIP as about $400 to $600 billion more than the official NIIP indicates through the end of 1987, though, by all but the earnings measure, the NIIP is below its peak values of 1980 or 1981.[34]

In terms of the official Commerce Department data reported in table 1, this would imply that the U.S. position at the end of 1987 was a net U.S. claim on foreigners of between $31 and $231 billion. If the midpoint of this range is used as the appropriate point estimate, then given the estimated $120 billion capital inflow in 1988, the United States still held a net claim on foreigners as of the end of 1988.

CONCLUSION

The joint implication from analysis of the three aspects of foreign investment in the United States—the effects on labor and investors, the threat of withdrawal, and the relative size of the foreign claim—is that the capaital inflows are beneficient. The capital inflows benefit labor and management, entrepreneurs and investors alike. Workers benefit from the greater abundance of tools; the increased capital raises labor's produc-

---

[33]The year t^* foreign share, $s(t^*)$, of the U.S. nominal non-consumer capital stock is the ratio of the sum of the initial foreign net holding, $368.2 billion, of the nominal capital stock plus the integral of the annual capital inflow, $120 billion, reduced by the rate of inflation of capital stock replacement cost, to the growing real capital stock whose 1987 value is $10,514.3 billion:

$$s(t^*) = \frac{(\$368.2 + \$120 \int_0^{t^*} e^{-ut}dt\,)}{\$10,514.3\ e^{gt^*}}$$

where $s(t^*)$ = share of net U.S. nonconsumer capital collateralized against net foreign investment at end of year t^*;

u = implicit rate of inflation of net capital stock's replacement cost;

g = growth rate of real net capital stock due to investment, foreign and domestic.

[34]Ulan and Dewald use three different methods to estimate the capital gains in the U.S. foreign direct investment and the foreign direct investment in the United States: stock price indexes, corporate earnings, investment goods price deflators. Their estimates based on the capitalization provide the largest estimate of the U.S. undervaluation and provide the clearest rebuttal of the transfer problem outlined by Drucker (1988). Their adjustments omit the U.S. gold stock, which would add about $90 billion to the U.S. position as reported by the Commerce Department (see note 3 above); however, they also do not allow for a potential write-down of U.S.bank holdings of LDC debt which they report would reduce the U.S. investment position by about $50 billion.

tivity and increases its employment or wages. Management benefits from the greater capital availability and lower interest rates; the capital inflows facilitate long-range planning, and the rise in labor productivity enhances management productivity as well. Entrepreneurs benefit from the lower interest rates due to a greater abundance of capital; this increases the range of profitable projects and new firm startups. And investors benefit since a more capital-abundant economy is a richer economy, regardless of who owns the capital.

The United States has imported capital throughout the 1980s, but far from signaling an economy in decline, such investment by foreigners is a measure of the economy's vigor. William Baumol aptly sums up this positive aspect of foreign capital inflows: "...relatively declining nations send their funds abroad because their decline makes it profitable to invest elsewhere."[35] Clearly, foreign investment in the United States does not signify the selling out of America.

REFERENCES

Anderson, Gerald H. "Three Common Misperceptions about Foreign Direct Investment," *Economic Commentary*, Cleveland Federal Reserve Bank, July 15, 1988.

Baer, Donald. "Anxiety in America's Heartland," *U.S. News and World Report* (April 25, 1988), p 24.

Bartley, Robert L. "Whither Voodoo Economics?" *Wall Street Journal*, August 18, 1988.

Birnbaum, Jeffrey H. "Wright Angers Some With Call for Vote On More Disclosure by Foreign Investors," *Wall Street Journal*, February 17, 1989.

Burgess, John. "British Investments in the U.S. Out-pace Japan's, Study Finds," *Washington Post*, January 27, 1989.

"Buying into a Good Thing." *National Review* (October 14, 1988), p.17.

"Capital Inflow Called Helpful." *New York Times*, May 25, 1988.

Drucker, Peter. "The Looming Transfer Crisis," *Institutional Investor*, June 6, 1988, p. 29.

"Dukakis-Bensten-Gephardt," *Wall Street Journal*, October 11, 1988.

Dullforce, William. "Swiss Life Wins Battle for LaSuisse," *Financial Times*, August 8, 1988a.

_____ . "Nestle to End Foreign Shares Discrimination," *Financial Times*, November 18, 1988b.

_____ . "Nestle Breaks Market Mold," *Financial Times*, November 22, 1988c.

Fierman, Jaclyn. "The Selling of America (Cont'd)," *Fortune* (May 23, 1988), pp. 54-64.

Financial Times Market Staff. "Nestle Bearers Plummet after Hours on Shock News," *Financial Times*, November 18, 1988.

Forbes, Malcolm S. "Before Japan Buys Too Much of the USA," *Forbes* (January 25, 1989), p. 17.

Francis, David R. "US Not a Debtor Nation, But the Idea Doesn't Worry Economist," *Christian Science Monitor*, July 2, 1988.

Friedman, Milton. "Why the Twin Deficits Are a Blessing," *Wall Street Journal*, December 14, 1988.

Greenhouse, Steven. "Europeans Adopt Plan to End Curbs on Capital FLows," *New York Times*, June 17, 1988.

Heller, H. Robert. "Mr. Heller Examines the US Economy and Monetary Policy," Speech at the University of St. Gallen, February 2, 1989, *BIS Review*, no. 35 1989, pp.1-7.

Hewko, John, and Jorge Chediek. "The Economic and Political Awakening of Argentina's Peronists," *Wall Street Journal*, March 11, 1988.

Holusha, John. "No Utopia, but to Workers It's a Job," *New York Times*, January 29, 1989.

Jaroslovosky, Rich. "Foreign Takeovers Emerge as an Increasingly Hot Political Issue," *Wall Street Journal*, April 1, 1988.

Jenkins, Holman, Jr. "Anxiety Rises as Foreigners Buy American," *Insight* (March 28, 1988), pp. 44-45.

Kinsley, Michael. "Deficits : Lunchtime Is Over," *Time* (October 3, 1988), pp 27-28.

Koedijk, Kees, and Mack Ott. "Risk Aversion, Efficient Markets and the Forward Exchange Rate," this *Review* (December 1987), pp. 5-13.

Little, Jane Sneddon. "Foreign Investment in the United States: A Cause for Concern?" *New England Economic Review* (July/August 1988), pp 51-58.

Makin, John H. "Is Foreign Investment Taking Over America?" *Washington Post*, February 28, 1988a.

_____ . "Japan's Investment in America: Is It a Threat?" *Challenge* (November/December 1988b), pp. 8-16.

"Mr.Greenspan on the Gas Tax." *Washington Post*, March 7, 1988.

Morin, Richard. "Americans Rate Japan No. 1 Economic Power," *Washington Post*, February 21, 1989.

Mussa, Michael. "Commentary on 'Is the Strong Dollar Sustainable?' " in *The U.S. Dollar —Recent developments, Outlook, and Policy Options* (Federal Reserve Bank of Kansas City, October 1985).

Niehans, Jurg. *International Monetary Economics*, (John Hopkins University Press, 1984).

Norton, Robert E. "Fleeing from the Almighty Dollar," *U.S. News and World Report* (June 13, 1988), pp 47-48.

"Opinion Roundup." *Public Opinion*, (November/December 1988), p.29.

O'Reilly, Brian. "Will Japan Gain Too Much Power?" *Fortune* (September 12, 1988), pp. 150-153.

Ott,Mack. "Have U.S. Exports Been Larger than Reported," this *Review* (September/October 1988), pp. 3-23.

[35]"Buying into a Good Thing," (1988). Another economist, Jurg Niehans, expresses the idea in the context of net investment this way: "Countries are debtors if their investment opportunities are greater than their wealth and are creditors if their wealth exceeds their investment opportunities." Niehans (1984), p. 107

Poole, William. "U.S. International Capital Flows in the 1980s," in *Shadow Open Market Committee,* March 1988, pp. 42-47.

Roll, Richard W. "The International Crash of 1987," in Robert Kamphuis, Roger Kormendi and J.W. Henry Watson, eds., *Black Monday and the Future of Financial Markets* (Mid America Institute, October 1988), pp. 37-70.

Rosengren, Eric S. "Is the United States for Sale? Foreign Acquisitions of U.S. Companies," *New England Economic Review* (November/December 1988), pp. 47-56.

Scholl, Russell B. "The International Investment Position of the United States in 1987," *Survey of Current Business* (June 1988), pp. 76-84.

Skrzycki, Cindy. "America on the Auction Block," *U.S. News and World Report* (March 30, 1987), pp. 56-58.

Stigler, George. "Theory of Regulation," *Bell Journal of Economics and Management Science* (Spring 1971), pp 3-21.

Tatom, John A. "Will a Weaker Dollar Mean a Stronger Economy?" *Journal of International Money and Finance,* 1987, pp 433-47.

_____ . "U.S. Investment in the 1980s: the Real Story," this *Review,* (March/April 1989), pp. 3-15.

Tolchin, Martin, and Susan Tolchin. *Buying into America— How Foreign Money Is Changing the Face of Our Nation,* (Times Books, 1988).

Ulan, Michael, and William G. Dewald. "The U.S. Net International Investment Position: The Numbers Are Misstated and Misunderstood," U.S. State Department mimeo, February 199.

Weidenbaum, Murray. "Foreign Investment Could Be an Asset, Not a Liability," *Christian Science Monitor,* August 24, 1988.

Article 8

Setting the Discount Rate

by E.J. Stevens

An uncommonly wide spread existed in the first half of this year between the federal funds rate, the rate that banks pay to borrow from one another, and the discount rate, the rate that banks pay to borrow from a Federal Reserve Bank.

The federal funds rate rose more than 300 basis points (three percentage points) over the 12 months ending in March 1989. The discount rate, on the other hand, was raised by a total of only 100 basis points over that same period: 50 basis points in August 1988 and another 50 basis points in February of this year. As a result, the spread between the federal funds rate and the discount rate sometimes exceeded 275 basis points, although it has declined recently.

A rate spread wider than even 200 basis points is unusual (see table 1). In the past, such extreme values typically emerged only in periods when the discount rate had reached a kind of plateau (see figure 1). Prior to 1983, these discount-rate plateaus all occurred near business-cycle peaks. Since 1983, plateaus and their associated wide rate spreads emerged during the periods of restrictive monetary policy that have interrupted the long-run disinflationary downward trend of nominal interest rates in the U.S. economy.

This year's wide rate spread thus was only the latest in a series of such episodes. These have alternated with contrasting periods of relatively close comovement of the funds rate and the discount rate. It is tempting to look for a uniform explanation of this historical pattern: perhaps policymakers typically underestimate peak interest rates and then get "locked in" to a discount-rate level for fear that even a small increase will be misinterpreted as a major tightening of policy; perhaps a higher rate would disadvantage small banks; perhaps restrictive policy requires a wide spread.

The trouble with such explanations is that none of them seems sufficiently universal to account for all of the episodes of unusually wide spreads in the past 25 years. However, such speculation does raise a more fundamental question: for monetary policy purposes, does it make any difference what the level of the discount rate is?

When the Federal Reserve Banks opened for business 75 years ago, raising and lowering the discount rate was conceived of as the principal monetary policy tool for tightening and loosening the supply of reserves. But, in the 1920s, open market operations took over this policy function, now managed by the Federal Open Market Committee (FOMC). [1]

Open market purchases and sales of U.S. government securities add and drain reserves directly, effectively

An independently determined discount rate seems irrelevant as long as open market operations implement monetary policy. This suggests moving the discount rate frequently in alignment with market rates. Instead, however, the Federal Reserve could use the discount rate as an independent tool to enrich the policy process. In so doing, the central bank could improve the reliability of short-term policy information available to the public and prevent market activity based on faulty assumptions about policy intentions.

determining the level of the federal funds rate. The level of the discount rate relative to the funds rate simply influences the proportion of total reserves that are created through discount-window borrowing. Open market operations could always compensate for fluctuations in borrowing, thereby maintaining effective long-run control of total bank reserves and the monetary base.

Monetary policy can be thought of as a decision to provide a particular amount of reserves to the banking system; policy actions are reflected in the federal funds rate and other money market interest rates as demand interacts with supply. An independently determined discount rate seems irrelevant: in the long run, if the monetary base and market interest rates get where they have to go, policy has been implemented.

Hence the question: is there a rationale for using the discount rate as an independent monetary policy tool, rather than simply moving the discount rate to keep it aligned with the key FOMC-determined federal funds rate at which banks borrow from one another? This *Economic Commentary* explains one rationale: accepting all other current monetary policy arrangements as given, changes in the discount rate could be used to convey useful information about monetary policy to the public.

■ **Current Mechanics and Subsidiary Issues**
The mechanics of setting the discount rate are not complicated. The Board of Directors of each of the 12 Federal Reserve Banks is required to recommend a rate setting for its Bank to the Board of Governors of the Federal Reserve System no less frequently than every two weeks. [2] If the Board of Governors approves the recommendation, typically it will notify any of the other 12 Banks that have not made the same recommendation so that their Boards of Directors have an opportunity

to act simultaneously. If the Board of Governors thinks that a change is called for when none of the 12 Banks has recommended a change, it may make informal efforts to elicit a recommendation.

The discount rate has been lower than the federal funds rate during most of the past 25 years without ever generating much borrowing. [3] Reluctance of banks to borrow from the discount window, despite a favorable rate spread, has two primary explanations. One is that Reserve Banks limit the circumstances under which a bank may use the borrowing privilege, reinforced by careful scrutiny of the frequency and amount that any bank actually borrows. The other is that banks fear damage to their market reputations if it were to become known that they were placing substantial reliance on this nonmarket source of funds.

A frequent suggestion over the years has been that, as a matter of policy, the discount rate should always lie *above* the federal funds rate and other money market rates, so that borrowing would entail a penalty. A related idea is to eliminate most administrative oversight, counting on the penalty aspect to keep borrowing to a minimum level consistent with those infrequent occasions when a bank is unable to access market sources of funds. [4]

Another suggestion that would eliminate administrative overhead is to set the discount rate itself automatically, whether above or below market rates, by some formula linking it to market rates. Counterarguments emphasize the potential organizational costs of such a change. In particular, the directors of Reserve Banks, who receive only nominal remuneration for their service to the nation, are thought to be attracted to their positions chiefly by their role in maintaining prudent national monetary policy. [5] A related thought is that involving the Reserve Banks in the rate-setting process also lends weight to the positions of their presidents within the FOMC.

All of these arguments raise important issues, but none gets to our fundamental question. Regardless of who sets the discount rate and whether it should be above or below market rates, and assuming that it is not to be fixed at a permanent level for all time, is there a rationale for using the rate as a policy tool independent of open market operations? If there is not, then the best basis for setting the rate would seem to be to keep it aligned with market rates that reflect monetary policy. But if there is such a rationale, then on what basis should rate-setting decisions be made?

■ **The Discount Rate as a Source of Policy Information**
Changes in the discount rate can improve the reliability of policy information available to markets. This "announcement effect" will improve the Federal Reserve's chances of getting the funds rate where it has to go, of getting the monetary base where it has to be, and of getting the whole spectrum of interest rates, monetary aggregates, credit flows, income, and output where they have to go in order to implement policy and achieve its implicit or explicit inflation-rate objective.

The reason the discount rate can enrich the policy process is that markets operate in an uncertain environment. Policy actions depend on what policymakers foresee, and market actions depend on what market participants foresee and think that the Fed foresees. The better informed markets are about Fed intentions, the more effortlessly markets will reach equilibrium.

Sources of information about policy intentions are readily enumerated. Twice a year, the FOMC's Humphrey-Hawkins report to Congress includes information about the economic outlooks of FOMC members, FOMC targets for growth of monetary aggregates, and discussion of broader

TABLE 1   FEDERAL FUNDS RATE MINUS DISCOUNT RATE—
FREQUENCY DISTRIBUTION OF THE RATE SPREAD[a]

Size of Spread (basis points)	Frequency (no. of mos.)	Percent of cases	Cumulative percent
>300	13	4%	4%
>250, <300	22	8%	11%
>200, <250	11	4%	15%
>150, <200	21	7%	22%
>100, <150	27	9%	31%
>50, <100	66	22%	54%
>0, <50	70	24%	78%
<0	64	22%	100%
	294	100%	

a. Monthly average rates, January 1965 to June 1989.
SOURCE: Board of Governors of the Federal Reserve System.

monetary policy objectives. While fresh when delivered, this information is 26 weeks old before it is updated by another Humphrey-Hawkins report.

The policy record of each FOMC meeting is released after the next succeeding meeting. It provides only historical information about policy intentions because it is about six weeks old when delivered, and 12 weeks old when updated. Further qualitative information might be sought in the occasional speeches and other statements of FOMC members, but these necessarily represent individual views, not statements of FOMC policy.

Weekly and monthly data for the targeted monetary aggregates become available with only a two-week delay. For considerable periods in the past, these data provided important information about prospective open market

policy actions. This was because deviations of incoming data (and of market projections of future data) from target paths implied by the policy record would suggest the impending need for tighter or easier policy.

This is no longer the case. Deposit-rate deregulation and reversal of the postwar upward trend of interest rates in the 1980s introduced substantial uncertainty into relationships between the monetary aggregates and national output and prices. Deviations of monetary aggregates from target paths within the annual ranges no longer play a central role in determining FOMC actions, at least on a dependable short-run basis. The annual target ranges themselves are quite broad, so that an equally broad spectrum of monetary aggregate levels may be consistent with the targets.

The level of the federal funds rate and the nature of open market operations can be observed on a daily basis. Careful scrutiny of these items, either directly or through the judgment of professional Fedwatchers, provides a contemporaneous signal of current policy. This signal is not clear, however, because interpretation of the items is always uncertain and never unanimous. Moreover, the signal reflects only today's policy setting; it says little about future policy actions.

In this situation, an occasional increase or decrease in the discount rate could certify that policymakers viewed recent levels or changes in the federal funds rate not as incidental or temporary, but as the necessary consequence of ongoing monetary policy. One reason for changing the rate would be a perception in the Federal Reserve that markets were misinterpreting policy intentions. The other would be a recognition in the Federal Reserve that its own outlook had changed, from less to more certainty about the joint implications of its objective and its economic outlook for the direction or extent of future changes in the funds rate. Within these guidelines, the discount rate might be changed with varying frequency, and result in variable spreads from the funds rate.

The information content of a discount-rate change need not be restricted to the direction and size of the change: discount-rate changes typically are announced in a press release that includes a brief explanation of the action. For example, "In the light of inflationary pressures in the economy, the Federal Reserve Board announced…an increase in the discount rate…(2/24/89)." Such brief statements can provide the public with some sense of direction about policy, whereas open market operations are conducted without any accompanying explanation for adding or draining reserves.

FIGURE 1 THE FEDERAL FUNDS RATE AND THE DISCOUNT RATE

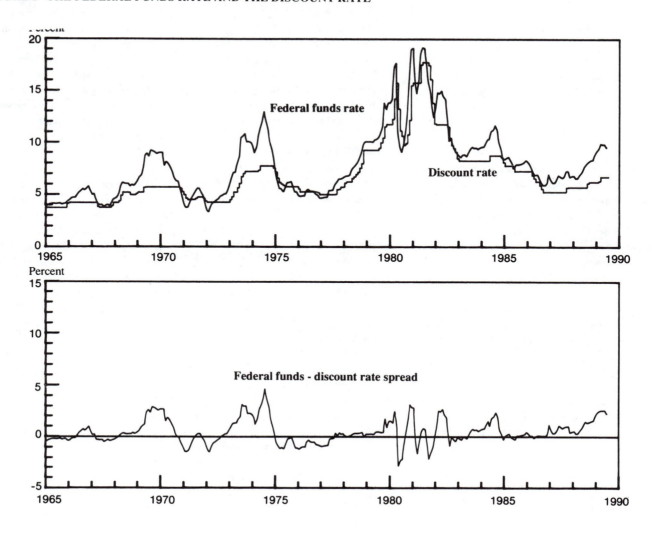

NOTE: The level of the discount rate between March 17, 1980, and November 17, 1981, includes a surcharge in addition to the basic rate. This surcharge varied between 0 and 4 percent, levied on borrowing by banks with deposits in excess of $500 million. It was intended to discourage frequent use of the discount window and to encourage large banks to adjust their loans and investments quickly in response to market conditions.

SOURCE: Board of Governors of the Federal Reserve System.

In any case, the discount-rate-setting mechanism provides a means of conveying useful policy information. The directors of a District Bank could recommend a change in the rate to inform the Board of Governors of the direction they believe monetary policy should take to achieve FOMC objectives. An actual change in the discount rate, approved by the Board of Governors, could be used to assure fuller incorporation of an easier

or tighter future monetary policy than might otherwise be reflected in current financial-market prices. Resetting the rate may thereby impose immediate losses, but prevent future days or weeks of market activity based on incorrect or less-certain policy assumptions.

■ **Past Changes in the Rate**
With hindsight, many past changes in the discount rate have the appearance

of routine attempts to keep it aligned with the federal funds rate (see figure 1). Nonetheless, alignment has been far from perfect. Contrary to popular belief, the discount rate is not necessarily the bellwether of the federal funds rate and of closely associated market rates. In fact, it was adjusted in only a quarter of the months plotted in the figure. Markets may have received useful policy information from the Federal

Reserve in those months in which the discount rate was changed, but not in the others.[6]

The usefulness of information conveyed by a change in the discount rate need not be uniform over time. In particular, the operating procedure employed by the FOMC to guide open market operations might influence the effect of discount-rate changes. When the funds rate is the direct target of daily open market operations, there should be little market uncertainty about the "equilibrium" funds rate. This is because the Federal Reserve can enter the market to add or drain reserves on a daily basis whenever the funds rate varies from the FOMC's desired equilibrium.

Uncertainty should be greater when open market operations seek to provide only a predetermined amount of non-borrowed reserves. In this case, the market must discover an equilibrium funds rate consistent with the FOMC open market policy setting because the FOMC explicitly will tolerate some variance in the funds rate. Changes in the discount rate may provide information that helps the market find the right funds rate in this latter case, while no such information is needed in the former case, when the funds rate is the direct policy target.

In either case, changes in the discount rate may provide information about the short-run future, affecting rates on securities with maturities longer than overnight federal funds. Failure to detect information effects uniformly in past discount-rate changes would not disprove the information rationale for managing the discount rate. An adverse finding says only that the rate was not managed this way during some time periods in the past or, if it was, that the result was too small to be detected.

■ Conclusion

Delayed release of the FOMC policy record is an important basis for the potential usefulness of the discount rate as an independent tool of monetary policy. Reasons for, contingencies attached to, and any dissents from the FOMC policy record guiding open market operations until the next meeting could provide much of the flavor of policy outlook that now might be attributed to changes in the discount rate. But delayed release makes the policy record useful largely as an historical document.

Immediate release of the policy record could make changes in the discount rate less informative, except to the extent that fundamental changes in policy thinking between meetings might warrant an immediate signal to markets. Frequent changes to maintain alignment with the funds rate would seem to be the appropriate way to manage the discount rate if immediate release of the policy record provided more information about the basis for policy actions than currently is the case.

Inertia in the discount rate is the source of its power, but this poses a danger. By allowing a wide or narrow spread between market rates and an unchanged discount rate to build up over a longer and longer interval, a change in the rate, when it comes, might suggest a major innovation in policy thinking. Apprehension of market overreaction could then make a rate-change decision increasingly difficult for the Board of Governors, even though the language of a rate-change announcement can be used to shape its interpretation. On the other hand, changing the rate frequently and in minor amounts to avoid this danger would trivialize the tool into a routine device for rate alignment.

Setting the discount rate inescapably involves this choice between inertia and alignment. Directors' recommendations to change the discount rate could be a tool for conveying useful information from the public to policymakers. Actual discretionary changes in the discount rate could be a tool for conveying useful information to the public about the near-term intentions of monetary policy.

Under this scenario for managing the rate, an unusually wide spread of the funds rate above a relatively stable discount rate would have an explanation. It would suggest a persistent tendency for policymakers to be, or to want to be seen to be, both more surprised than the market at the need for tighter policy, as well as dubious that so restrictive a policy would continue to be needed.

■ Footnotes

1. The Banking Act of 1935 created the current form of the FOMC to control open market operations. The Committee consists of the seven members of the Board of Governors of the Federal Reserve System, the president of the Federal Reserve Bank of New York, and, on an annual rotating basis, four of the presidents of the other 11 Federal Reserve Banks. (The Cleveland Bank president serves every other year, alternating with the president of the Chicago Bank.) The FOMC now meets eight times each year, with additional meetings as necessary (typically by telephone conference).

2. This rate recommendation is for the level of the basic discount rate borrowers pay for adjustment credit and seasonal credit.

3. Adjustment borrowing has averaged 1.9% of total reserves over the past 25 years, with a standard deviation of 1.6%.

4. An extension of this idea is that the discount window for adjustment credit could be closed completely. Banks in exigent circumstances that prevent access to market sources of liquidity would run overnight overdrafts, making up the reserve deficiency on succeeding days. Presumably they would also have to pay the penalty for such overdrafts, currently the larger of $50, or the larger of 10% or a rate 2 percentage points above the federal funds rate, *in addition to* making up the deficiency.

5. Directors' rate recommendations sometimes are thought to reflect regional rather than national conditions, but this seems unlikely as a general rule. Directors know that there is no basis for maintaining regional differences in interest rates in the modern world of integrated global money and capital markets. Also, the expertise of many directors is not about the regional economy, but about national and global conditions in the industries in which they are employed.

6. Substantial effort has gone into the search for evidence that past discount-rate changes conveyed new information and therefore had an impact on securities prices, with at least partial success. Citations and a useful summary of the evolution of these efforts can be found in Timothy Cook and Thomas Hahn, "The Information Content of Discount Rate Announcements and Their Effect on Market Interest Rates," *Journal of Money, Credit, and Banking*, vol. 20, no. 2 (May 1988), pp. 167-180.

E. J. Stevens is an assistant vice president and economist at the Federal Reserve Bank of Cleveland. The author thanks John Carlson, William Gavin, Owen Humpage, and Mark Sniderman for useful discussion. Susan Black provided able research assistance.

The views stated herein are those of the author and not necessarily those of the Federal Reserve Bank of Cleveland or of the Board of Governors of the Federal Reserve System.

Section II
Financial Markets

Two powerful movements swept financial markets in the United States during the 1980s. First, there was debt, more debt, and lots of risky debt. The market for risky debt expanded wildly and contracted with suddenness as Drexel Burnham Lambert collapsed and Donald Trump scrambled to avoid bankruptcy. Second, there was a tidal wave of financial innovation, including the maturation of the interest rate futures market, the establishment and flourishing of stock index futures, and the development of sophisticated special instruments. This section highlights these two major trends in financial markets.

In "The High–Yield Debt Market: 1980–1990," Richard H. Jefferis, Jr. traces the debt market through the 1980s and into the 1990s with the collapse of Drexel. (Drexel Burnham Lambert, led by Michael Milken, was largely responsible for the success of the high–yield/high–risk debt market. Now Drexel is bankrupt and disbanded and Milken has pled guilty to a variety of securities market felonies.) As Jefferis notes, high–yield debt may be in partial eclipse today, but the market succeeded due to basic and persisting economic forces. Therefore, Jefferis believes that risky debt will find a continuing role in a more cautious market.

Some observers of the debt market believe that corporations rely too much on debt. Ben Bernanke examines this issue in his article "Is There Too Much Corporate Debt?" Bernanke uses an allegory of Goofus and Gallant, who start similar businesses, but use different levels of debt. Bernanke show how the higher level of debt financing can lead to the socially optimal allocation of resources. However, as Bernanke notes, the high leverage that keeps Gallant working while Goofus plays may also lead to financial distress for the economy as a whole.

The term "junk bond" is a pejorative term for "high–yield debt." In his paper, "The Case for Junk Bonds," Eric S. Rosengren accepts the pejorative (and quite common) name for the bonds and defends them. In essence, Rosengren argues that the junk bond market emerged as a partial replacement for commercial bank lending and is due to legitimate economic forces that are likely to continue. Therefore, Rosengren concludes, attempts to regulate the junk bond market will probably be unproductive and may impede the growth of small firms.

With Anthony Saunders' article "Why Are So Many New Stock Issues Underpriced?," we turn from the debt market to the stock market. By "new stock" Saunders refers to stock that is newly issued, as opposed to existing shares. Considerable evidence suggests that newly issued stock is underpriced because the stock price increase after issuance exceeds the appropriate risk–adjusted return. Saunders reviews the evidence supporting this view and asks a deeper question: What does this underpricing suggest about the regulation of investment banking firms and commercial banks? (Currently, the Glass–Steagall Act limits commercial bank participation in issuing new stock.) Saunders concludes that repeal of Glass–Steagall could result in fairer pricing for newly issued stock.

In a department store or hotel, the mezzanine is a middle range of floors. In a popular financial analogy, capital structure is like a hotel. Equity occupies the lower floors and senior debt resides in the penthouse. Financial innovation can fill the middle floors with a new approach to corporate financing. John R. Willis and David A. Clark tour these floors in their article, "An Introduction to Mezzanine Finance and Private Equity." They define mezzanine financing to include various forms of subordinated debt and preferred stock. Almost always, mezzanine financing is private and includes some equity participation. Willis and Clark illustrate mezzanine financing with an actual application.

On October 19, 1987 the stock market lost about twenty–five percent of its value. In the 1980s, other days of great drama also helped call the investor's attention to financial market risk, or volatility. Sean Becketti and Gordon H. Sellon address the changing risk of financial markets in their paper, "Has Financial Market Volatility Increased?" They consider stocks, interest rates, and exchange rates. They find that stock market volatility did not increase during the 1980s. While this might seem surprising given some of the dramatic events, this result of Becketti and Sellon corroborates a number of other studies. For interest rates and exchange rates, however, they reach a different conclusion. The volatility of both interest and exchange rates did increase during the 1980s.

A market is efficient with respect to some information set if prices in that market fully reflect the information. Economists study whether particular markets reflect different kinds of information. An efficient market is desirable because prices that reflect information lead to better allocation of scarce resources and can increase the general level of well–being in an economy. Stephen F. Leroy reviews some recent challenges to market efficiency in "Capital Market Efficiency: An Update." While economists have long tended to accept market efficiency for major U.S. capital markets, Leroy joins the growing chorus of economists that find fault with the model of efficiency.

One of the great financial innovations of recent years has been the emergence of interest-rate and stock index futures. These markets have flourished because they offer exciting speculative opportunities and provide powerful techniques for reducing financial risk. In two studies, Charles S. Morris shows how to use futures to control interest rate risk and stock market risk. As Morris notes in his paper, "Managing Interest Rate Risk with Interest Rate Futures," these are powerful instruments. Successful control of interest rate risk requires knowledge and care. Similarly, as Morris explains in "Managing Stock Market Risk with Stock Index Futures," stock index futures offer new techniques for handling stock market risk. However, for the unwary, they also present new risks.

Financial innovation has created entirely new classes of risk–control products. Prominent among these are "Interest–Rate Caps, Collars, and Floors," which is also the title of an article by Peter A. Abken. Caps, collars, and floors are three techniques for managing interest rate risk. Each pertains to an agreement in which the interest rate fluctuates or floats with market conditions, and each limits the extent and direction of the change in the interest rate. A cap limits the maximum interest rate that a borrower must pay, while a floor guarantees a minimum rate of interest to a lender. A collar embodies both a cap and a floor, limiting the increase and decrease in interest rates during the agreement period. Abken carefully defines caps, collars, and floors and illustrates their use.

Article 9

The High-Yield Debt Market: 1980-1990

by Richard H. Jefferis, Jr.

The February collapse of Drexel Burnham Lambert, which followed five months of turmoil in the junk bond market, signaled the end of a six-year period of sustained growth of that market. Prices of lower-grade bonds declined sharply from September 1989 through February 1990. In the secondary market, some investors found it difficult to locate buyers for their securities. In the primary market, new issues during January 1990 were only one-third of their value a year earlier. New issues during all of 1989 decreased by 11 percent from the 1988 total of $27 billion, while mutual fund investment in high-yield bonds fell from $34 billion to $28 billion.[1] These events, triggered by financial distress in a number of leveraged buyouts that included the slide of the Campeau Corporation into bankruptcy, have engendered predictions of the demise of the modern high-yield market.[2]

This *Economic Commentary* reviews the growth of that market from virtual nonexistence in 1980 to nearly $200 billion by the end of the decade, and assesses the impact of recent events on its viability. Three trends in debt formation that contributed to the rapid expansion of the high-yield market are discussed. The first is the overall growth of the economy, which contributed to the rapid expansion of both equity and debt during the 1980s. The second is the substitution of credit-market debt for bank loans in the balance sheets of middle-market customers who had not

previously enjoyed access to the bond market. The third is the wave of leveraged restructuring induced by the Tax Reform Act of 1986.

Volume patterns in the bond market, especially the high-yield market, suggest that the third phenomenon may have played itself out. The tax code, however, still provides both investors and corporations with a strong incentive to elect debt rather than equity as a vehicle for financing new investment. Moreover, the dynamic middle-market customers who fueled the growth of this market prior to 1986 continue to represent profitable lending opportunities. The high-yield market will shrink if investors, shaken by recent events, withdraw their capital, but the economic forces that created the market persist, and it is quite unlikely that high-yield bonds will disappear altogether.

■ Economic Growth and Debt Formation

Between 1980 and 1989, nominal gross national product expanded at an annual rate of 7 percent. Businesses spent $3.6 trillion on new plant and equipment during this period, while outstanding credit-market debt on the balance sheets of domestic nonfinancial corporations increased by $1.2 trillion. Other factors influenced the formation of credit-market debt during the 1980s, but the contribution of economic growth to this phenomenon should not be overlooked.

Did the collapse of Drexel Burnham Lambert in February signal the end of the high-yield debt market? Considering that the economic forces responsible for creating the market remain in place, it is unlikely that junk bonds will disappear any time soon.

FIGURE 1 INVESTMENT AND DEBT FORMATION IN THE 1980s

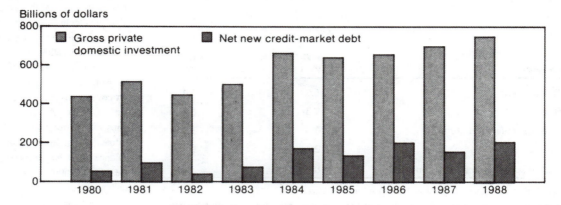

Billions of dollars

■ Gross private domestic investment ■ Net new credit-market debt

SOURCES: U.S. Department of Commerce, Bureau of Economic Analysis; and Board of Governors of the Federal Reserve System.

FIGURE 2 STANDARD & POOR'S 500 INDEX, 1965-1989

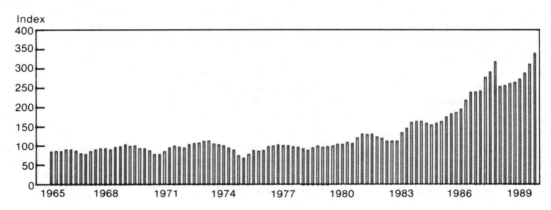

Index

SOURCE: Standard & Poor's Corporation.

Figure 1 shows gross private domestic investment and net new credit-market debt over the course of the decade.[3] As always, new debt formation closely tracks the behavior of investment.[4] (The year of the Tax Reform Act is an obvious exception.) Figure 2 portrays the behavior of equity prices, an indicator of expected future investment opportunities. Equity markets supplied firms with a strong positive signal about the value of investment opportunities throughout the 1980s, contributing to the willingness of businesses to borrow.

■ **Credit-Market Debt and Bank Loans**

It is convenient for the sake of discussion to partition the decade into three time periods, although the division is

somewhat arbitrary. The first period is 1980–1982, which precedes the growth of the high-yield market and serves as a useful reference point. During the second period, between 1983 and 1985, high-yield bonds became a significant component of new corporate lending, capturing an increasing share of a growing debt market from commercial banks. The Tax Reform Act of 1986 marks the beginning of the third period, when the composition of the high-yield market shifted from middle-market firms seeking to finance new investment toward tax-driven restructuring.

Bank loans and corporate bonds make up the bulk of debt on the corporate balance sheet throughout the decade, as they have during the entire postwar period. Balance-sheet data indicate that the combined market share of these

two sources of funding remained steady during the 1980s, never varying outside a range of 70 to 75 percent. There was, however, a clear trend toward the use of credit-market debt throughout the decade. Figure 3 shows the steady decline of a composite of bank loans, finance company debt, and mortgage debt relative to security market debt that began in the 1970s.[5]

The share of these items in outstanding debt understates trends in new lending activity. Figure 4 portrays the year-to-year change in outstanding bank loans, corporate bonds, and speculative-grade bonds during the 1980s.[6] Between 1980 and 1982, bank lending accounted for 57 percent of net new corporate credit, while bonds accounted for only 36 percent of that amount. The share of bank lending in net new credit fell by

TABLE 1   CHARACTERISTICS OF HIGH-YIELD ISSUERS
Annual Growth Rates, 1980-1986 (Percent)

Category	High-Yield Firms	Other Firms
Employment	6.7	1.4
Sales	9.3·	6.2
Sales (manufacturing firms)	5.6	3.8
Capital spending	12.4	9.9
Capital spending (manufacturing firms)	10.6	3.8

SOURCE: G. Yago (1988—see footnote 7). All figures are percentages.

half, to 26 percent, between 1983 and 1985, while the share of bonds remained steady at 35 percent. Between 1986 and 1988, bank lending accounted for only 15 percent of new credit, while the share of bonds nearly doubled to 61 percent.

The overall growth in debt, and the substitution of bonds for bank loans, fueled the growth of the high-yield market. New issues of speculative-grade bonds rose from $1.5 billion in 1982 to $15 billion during 1984. During this period, Drexel Burnham Lambert underwrote virtually 100 percent of the new issues. The strategy that proved so successful at Drexel was the marketing of debt, issued by middle-market firms that had previously depended on banks for credit, directly to sophisticated investors. Insurance companies and pension funds provided most of the capital absorbed by the high-yield market between 1982 and 1984. By 1986, the public had become involved more directly through mutual funds.

The leveraged buyouts and leveraged restructurings of recent years have focused attention on a type of high-yield issuer that differs significantly from the representative borrower of 1983–1986. In a broad survey of U.S. industrial firms covering the period 1980–1986, Yago profiles the issuers of high-yield bonds and contrasts these firms with other U.S. industrial companies.[7] Table 1 presents some of the findings from this study. Firms in the sample that used high-yield finance are dynamic enterprises, with growth in

sales, employment, and investment that exceeds that of other industrials. Only 3 percent of the firms in the sample that issued high-yield debt used the proceeds for merger or acquisition activity.

The forces that resulted in the substitution of credit-market debt for bank loans on corporate balance sheets during this period are poorly understood. Plausible explanations include a regulatory burden for banks, conservatism in lending induced by the onus of Third-World debt, and advances in information technology that made it possible for investors to monitor the performance of smaller firms directly, making it unnecessary to rely on banks for those services. The evidence necessary to discriminate among these explanations has not yet been accumulated.

It is, however, possible to dismiss on the basis of currently available evidence at least one other explanation of the substitution of bonds for bank debt. Thrift institutions received significant new investment powers under legislation passed in the early 1980s, which enabled them to invest in high-yield bonds.[8] Some thrifts became active investors in the high-yield market. However, thrift industry investment in high-yield issues, which peaked at a total of $13 billion in 1986, accounted for only 8 percent of outstanding high-yield issues during that year. Thrift holdings of high-yield debt were never a significant portion of either total thrift industry assets or outstanding high-yield debt.

■ **The Tax Reform Act of 1986**
The biggest year of the decade in the high-yield debt market was not 1988, when leveraged buyout activity reached its zenith, but rather 1986, when the U.S. Congress enacted what may well be the most significant revisions of the tax code in this century. Two features of the Tax Reform Act provide corporations with a strong incentive to substitute debt for equity on the corporate balance sheet. At the corporate level, the curtailment of non-debt tax shields such as the investment tax credit and depreciation allowances eliminated important alternatives to debt for protecting corporate earnings from taxation.[9] At the personal level, the abolishment of preferential treatment for capital gains enhanced the after-tax value of debt relative to equity.[10] The combination of these factors provided a strong impetus for increased leverage between 1986 and 1989.

Financial economists have long believed that the financial structure of corporations is sensitive to the tax environment. When corporate taxes are calculated, interest payments to investors who hold debt are deductible, while dividend payments to investors who hold equity are not. This feature of the tax code provides firms with a powerful incentive to finance investment through the issue of debt. That incentive is mitigated by firms' preference for the flexibility associated with equity (or equivalently, an aversion to the financial distress that may result from excess leverage), and by the availability of tax deductions other than interest payments on debt. Changes in the tax code that reduce the availability of non-debt tax shields tilt the balance between debt and equity in favor of increased debt.

Hard empirical evidence concerning the relationship between the tax code and corporate financial structure has heretofore proved elusive, probably because of measurement problems inherent in financial accounting, and the imprecise timing of tax code revisions. But the Tax Reform Act resulted in such a drastic, instantaneous change in

FIGURE 3   DEBT STRUCTURE OF U.S. NONFINANCIAL CORPORATIONS

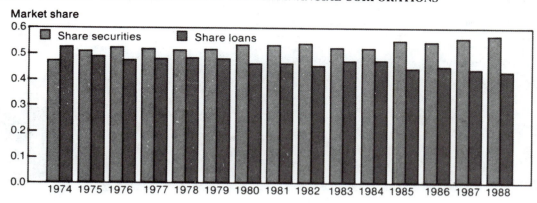

Market share

SOURCE: Balance Sheets for the U.S. Economy, Board of Governors of the Federal Reserve System.

FIGURE 4   NET CHANGE IN BONDS AND BANK LOANS ON THE CORPORATE BALANCE SHEET

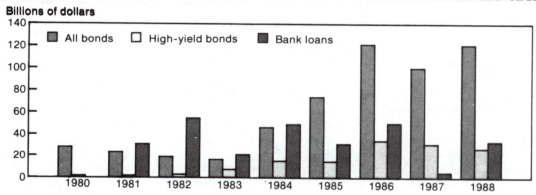

Billions of dollars

SOURCES: Board of Governors of the Federal Reserve System; and E. Altman (1989—see footnote 14).

the tax environment that it has been possible to detect a response in corporate financial policy. A recent study using a diverse set of U.S. industrial companies documents a $140 increase in outstanding debt in response to each $100 decrease in non-debt tax shields associated with the Tax Reform Act.[11] Moreover, the observed response of individual firms depends on the dividend policy of the firm prior to the change, suggesting that changes in the personal tax code also affected the financial structure of corporations.

It is also possible to observe a response to the Tax Reform Act in aggregate data. The deviation in the relationship between investment activity and debt formation that is apparent in figure 1 has already been noted. Commercial and industrial lending, and new issues of both investment-grade bonds and

speculative-grade bonds, all increased sharply in 1986. Equity repurchases surged the following year: net issues of equity were negative in 1987. The accumulation of debt following tax reform increased the ratio of debt to equity in all nonfinancial corporations from 0.67 to 0.75 between 1985 and 1988.

■ **Leverage, Debt Quality, and Defaults**

The accumulation of debt in the 1980s represents a significant increase in the fixed obligations of corporations. However, during a period when the value of debt on the corporate balance sheet grew by 150 percent, the market value of equity increased by 175 percent, so that the debt-to-equity ratio of nonfinancial corporations actually declined slightly over the past 10 years. As figure 5 shows, debt-to-equity ratios are

currently less than they were during much of the 1970s, a time when stock prices were depressed.[12] Although leverage in U.S. industrial corporations is greater than it was during the 1950s and 1960s, the shift toward more debt in capital structures occurred during the 1970s, not the 1980s.

Nor has there been any widespread decline in debt quality, despite frequent reports to the contrary in the popular press. Moody's Investor Services reports that issues rated Aaa (the firm's highest rating) constituted the most rapidly expanding category of bonds between 1977 and 1989. Issues rated B (the lowest rating for which figures are reported) did take second place in the growth sweepstakes, but by 1989, Aaa issues represented 33 percent of all outstanding issues rated by Moody's, while B-rated issues constituted only 8 per-

FIGURE 5 LEVERAGE IN NONFINANCIAL CORPORATIONS

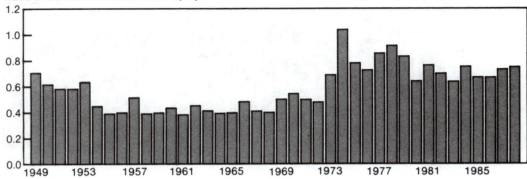

Ratio of debt to market value of equity

SOURCE: Balance Sheets for the U.S. Economy, Board of Governors of the Federal Reserve System.

cent of the total.[13] (Recall that the high-yield category was minuscule compared to the investment-grade category at the beginning of the decade.)

This is not to say that high-yield debt is of the same quality as investment-grade debt. Recent defaults among firms that experienced leveraged buyouts during the 1980s have called our attention to a simple fact: high-yield bonds bear high yields because they are riskier than investment-grade bonds. A number of studies report 10-year cumulative default rates on B-rated issues of 30 percent. In contrast, investment-grade issues enjoy cumulative default rates on the order of 1 or 2 percent.[14] The greater default rates associated with high-yield bonds should not surprise investors: Hickman reported a similar discrepancy in default rates for the 1900–1943 period in his 1958 study. (The default rates reported by Hickman are higher than the modern experience for both investment-grade issues and speculative-grade issues. At least part of the difference is attributable to the fact that the Great Depression is included in his sample.)

A feature of default experience that is far more significant than the average default rate is the sensitivity of defaults to overall business conditions. Defaults among high-quality issues are not especially sensitive to economic growth. In contrast, defaults among lower-grade issues are affected significantly by the

level of business activity. The implication of this sensitivity is that the onset of a recession is likely to be associated with financial distress among a number of high-yield issuers. The $6 billion in total 1989 defaults, which occurred during a year when economic growth slowed but did not stop, are a reminder of this fact.

The possibility of widespread financial distress among corporate borrowers merits careful consideration from policymakers. Recent analyses of the severe economic depressions that marked the nineteenth century and the first part of the twentieth century suggest that the collapse of credit markets played an important role in these episodes.[15] But the mechanism that induced the collapse of credit appears to have been a significant deflation, or downward revision in expected inflation, which decreased corporate revenues while the value of debt obligations remained fixed, leaving borrowers unable to pay their bills or obtain new credit. The behavior of the money supply and the price level in the United States during the postwar period indicates that this scenario is unlikely, although not impossible.

Moreover, the nonchalant reception that the bankruptcy of Drexel Burnham Lambert received in credit markets suggests that isolated incidents are not apt to trigger a panic.[16]

■ **Conclusion**

The spectacular growth of corporate debt during the 1980s was accompanied by the equally spectacular growth of the high-yield bond market. Attributing these phenomena to fads or to greed ignores the fact that neither explanation represents a new force on Wall Street or in the world at large. Financial innovation and the significant restructuring of the U.S. tax code are explanations that hold up much better to careful scrutiny. Recent events are likely to result in increased caution among investors, but the high-yield bond market was created by forces that persist today, and it is unlikely to follow into oblivion the firm credited with its inception.

■ **Footnotes**

1. Price and volume statistics were supplied by IDD Information Services.

2. There was an active market in the U.S. for below-investment-grade bonds between 1900 and 1945. See W. Braddock Hickman, *Corporate Bond Quality and Investor Experience*. Princeton: The Princeton University Press and the National Bureau of Economic Research, 1958.

3. Business investment in plant and equipment is taken from table C-54 of the Economic Report of the President, February 1990. Credit-market debt figures are from Balance Sheets for the U.S. Economy, Board of Governors of the Federal Reserve System, October 1989.

4. The difference between investment and credit-market debt is accounted for by retained earnings.

5. The first composite consists of debt created through intermediaries, while the second focuses on securities issued directly by the firm. The appropriate category for some items (mortgage debt and tax-exempt bonds) is not always clear, but the trend is not sensitive to variations in the definition of the two categories.

6. The data for changes in bank loans and outstanding bonds are from Balance Sheets for the U.S. Economy, op. cit. The overall bond category is comprehensive, encompassing private placements, speculative-grade debt, and convertible debt. The speculative-grade debt figures are for public, nonconvertible debt only, as reported in E. Altman, "The Nature of the Market for High-Yield Bonds: Nature of the Market and Effect on Federally Insured Institutions," Washington, D.C.: U.S. Government Printing Office, May 1988. If private placements were included in the speculative-grade debt series, it would be significantly greater.

7. See Glen Yago, Testimony submitted to the U.S. General Accounting Office hearings on high-yield bonds, U.S. General Accounting Office, 1988.

8. The Garn-St Germain Act of 1982 provided thrift institutions with the authority to participate in a wide variety of new investment activities, including investment in high-yield bonds.

9. The elimination of the investment tax credit alone was designed to raise an additional $118 billion in revenue at the corporate level between 1987 and 1991. See Joint Committee on Taxation, "Summary of Conference Agreement on HR 3838, The Tax Reform Act of 1986," August 29, 1986.

10. Prior to 1986, 60 percent of long-term capital gains were exempt from taxation. Individuals currently enjoy a greatly reduced incentive for realizing profits in the form of capital gains rather than interest or dividends.

11. See D. Givoly, C. Hayn, A. Ofer, and O. Sarig, "Taxes and Capital Structure: Evidence from Firms' Response to the Tax Reform Act of 1986," Working Paper, Northwestern University, December 1989. By observing individual firms before and after the Tax Reform Act, these authors are able to circumvent some of the measurement problems that plagued previous studies and document a number of responses to the tax-law revision.

12. The impact of rising equity prices on this relationship is reflected in the value of the Standard & Poor's 500 index, which increased by 210 percent between 1979 and 1989. Equity repurchases explain why the market value of outstanding equity grew less rapidly than equity prices. Figures for debt and equity values are from Balance Sheets for the U.S. Economy, Board of Governors of the Federal Reserve System.

13. "Historical Default Rates of Corporate Bond Issuers: 1970 Through 1988," Moody's Investor Services, July 1989.

14. See E. Altman, "Measuring Corporate Bond Mortality and Performance," *Journal of Finance*, vol. 44 (September 1989), pp. 909-22; P. Asquith, D. Mullins, and E. Wolff, "Original Issue High Yield Bonds: Aging Analyses of Defaults, Exchanges and Calls," *Journal of Finance*, vol. 44 (September 1989), pp. 923-52; and Moody's, op. cit. All of these studies report similar figures.

15. See B. Bernanke, "Nonmonetary Effects of the Financial Crisis in the Propagation of the Great Depression," *American Economic Review*, vol. 63 (1983), pp. 257-76; and Charles Calomiris and R. Glenn Hubbard, "Price Flexibility, Credit Availability, and Economic Fluctuations: Evidence from the United States, 1894-1909," *Quarterly Journal of Economics*, vol. 104 (August 1989), pp. 429-52.

16. Historically, widespread banking panics not accompanied by a severe downward revision in price expectations are quite rare. Runs against individual banks associated with fears of financial weakness (that were often warranted) were much more frequent. See Charles Calomiris and Charles Kahn, "Demandable Debt as the Optimal Banking Contract," Working Paper, Northwestern University, July 1989.

Richard H. Jefferis, Jr. is a visiting scholar at the Federal Reserve Bank of Cleveland.

The views stated herein are those of the author and not necessarily those of the Federal Reserve Bank of Cleveland or of the Board of Governors of the Federal Reserve System.

Article 10

Is There Too Much Corporate Debt?

Ben Bernanke*

Borrowing by U.S. corporations has increased dramatically in recent years. The outstanding debt of nonfinancial corporations rose 70 percent between 1983 and 1988, more than two-thirds faster than growth of nominal GNP. Highly leveraged transactions, such as the $25 billion takeover of RJR Nabisco, routinely make the front pages.

Heavy borrowing such as this has raised the

issue of whether corporate debt has become excessive. Congress has been considering whether changes should be made in the tax law to try to reduce the rate of corporate debt accumulation. The Federal Reserve has been studying the implications of debt growth for monetary policy and banking system oversight.

In evaluating the debt situation there are many issues to consider, but two questions lie at the heart of the debate. First is the "micro" issue: do high levels of debt increase the efficiency of firms, as some proponents of high leverage have claimed? Then there is the

*Ben Bernanke is a Professor of Economics at Princeton University. He wrote this article while he was a Visiting Scholar in the Research Department of the Federal Reserve Bank of Philadelphia.

"macro" issue: does increased corporate debt reduce the stability of the country's financial and economic system?

THE MICRO ISSUE:
DOES DEBT PROMOTE EFFICIENCY?

The traditional explanation for why corporations use debt as a source of finance is debt's tax advantage: interest payments made by a firm are tax-deductible, while dividend payments are not. Offsetting this advantage are the costs of bankruptcy and reorganization that may be incurred should the firm not be able to meet the stipulated interest payments. According to the traditional view, the optimal ratio of debt to equity is the one that just balances these two costs.

More recently, however, financial economists have gone beyond this traditional view to focus on the possibly beneficial effects of debt issuance on managerial performance.[1] This point can be illustrated by a simple example.

A Tale of Two Twins. Suppose that there are two potential entrepreneurs, who (like the two characters in a well-known children's magazine) are named Goofus and Gallant.[2] Goofus and Gallant plan to start ice cream stands on opposite sides of town. The necessary equipment for a stand costs $1,000, and since the entrepreneurs each have only $100, they must obtain some outside finance.

Goofus finances his ice cream stand through stock issuance: that is, he finds some friends to put up $900, in exchange for which he promises them 90 percent of the profits. Gallant issues debt instead; he gets a friend to lend him $900, for which Gallant promises to pay $100 in annual interest. Both boys thus have enough capital to get their businesses going.

[1]The classic article that introduced this approach is Jensen and Meckling (1976).

[2]The characters Goofus and Gallant are copyrighted by *Highlights for Children*, and their names are used with permission.

Things go along well enough at first for both entrepreneurs. But the summer days are hot, and scooping ice cream is hard work. Goofus says to himself, "I've made $100 profit at my stand already this week. If I were to keep working through the weekend, I could make another $100. But I have to share 90 percent with my partners—so that extra $100 really means only $10 for me! I'm not really willing to work the weekend for less than a $25 personal profit, so I think I'll quit and go fishing."

On the other side of town, Gallant is also having a crisis of conscience; he is developing scooper's elbow from serving so much ice cream. He loves to fish as much as Goofus does. Should he quit working? He says to himself, "The $100 I have earned so far is enough to cover the interest payment on my loan. From now on, any profits the ice cream stand earns are mine to keep. If I worked through the weekend, I could earn another $100; that's more than the $25 I would be willing to pay to knock off and go fishing." So Gallant goes back to work.

The two entrepreneurs have faced the same quandary, but have made different decisions. It is important to understand that, in both cases, it is economically efficient to keep the ice cream stand in operation through the weekend, in that the $100 in extra profit that could be earned is greater than the $25 value the proprietor of each stand places on his leisure. Yet, of the two, only Gallant does the "right" thing and keeps working.

Incentives to Do The Right Thing. In the children's magazine, Gallant's decisions to do the right thing stem from his superior moral character. In this example, morality has nothing to do with it; both boys make their decisions based on their calculations of personal gain. The difference between Goofus and Gallant is the way in which they have financed their ventures. By financing with equity, Goofus has created a situation in which his personal rewards are relatively insensitive to the profits of the company; a $100 increase in profits increases his personal return by only $10. This reduces Goofus's incentive to work hard and make decisions that are in the interest of the company. In contrast, once the interest payment is made, Gallant's personal returns fluctuate dollar for dollar with the profits of the company; he thus has a strong incentive to take actions that maximize the company's profits.

Indeed, in this particular example, Gallant would do the right thing (keep working) as long as he was financed at least 60 percent by debt. With 60 percent ($600) in debt, there would be 40 percent ($400) in total equity. Gallant's $100 in original capital would give him 25 percent of that equity, giving him a 25 percent share of the firm's profits. With a 25 percent share, Gallant would be just indifferent between working through the weekend (which nets him an extra .25 x $100 = $25) or going fishing (which is worth $25 to him). With anything above 60 percent debt finance, he would keep working.

Changing the Mode of Financing. We can add another chapter to the story of Goofus and Gallant. At the end of the summer, both boys notice that the debt-financed ice cream stand is more profitable than the equity-financed stand, and that this extra profitability is due entirely to the way in which the stands are financed. This implies that pure profits can be earned by a capital restructuring—a change in the mode of finance—of Goofus's operation. This restructuring can be accomplished if someone takes out a loan and uses the borrowed money to buy back the shares from Goofus's shareholders; this changes the stand's financing from equity to debt. The share buyback is particularly attractive at the current market price for Goofus's company's shares, which—because Goofus is always going fishing—is low. But the buyback would be profitable even if the acquirers had to pay the current stockholders some premium for their shares; the acquirers would simply be sharing with the current shareholders some of the profits expected to be produced by the restructuring.

The capital restructuring of Goofus's stand would work equally well if performed by Goofus, by Gallant, or by someone else.[3] In any case, the swapping of debt for equity is called a *leveraged buyout*, or LBO. If done by Goofus, the current manager of the operation, it could also be called a *management buyout*; if done by Gallant, it would be called a *takeover* (a hostile takeover, if Goofus resisted and tried to hold on to the company). The key point is that, in either case, the leverage of the company (its ratio of debt to equity) would increase, and this would lead to more efficient and profitable operations.

The Recent Explosion of Debt. The parable of Goofus and Gallant illustrates the idea that the financial structure of firms influences the incentives of "insiders" (managers, directors, and large shareholders with some operational interest in the business) and that, in particular, high levels of debt may increase the willingness of insiders to work hard and make profit-maximizing decisions. This incentive-based approach makes a valuable contribution to our understanding of a firm's capital structure. But while this theory might explain why firms like to use debt in general, does it explain why the use of debt has increased so much in recent years?

Michael Jensen, a founder and leading proponent of the incentive-based approach to capital structure, argues that it can.[4] Jensen focuses on a recent worsening of what he calls the "free cash flow" problem. Free cash flow is defined as the portion of a corporation's cash flow that

---

[3]This assumes, first, that Gallant has time to operate both stands and, second, that Gallant has enough profits from operating his own stand to buy out Goofus's share.

[4]For a summary of Jensen's views, see Jensen (1988). Jensen's article is part of a *Journal of Economic Perspectives* special symposium on takeovers, which provides an excellent and balanced introduction to this subject.

it is unable to invest profitably within the firm. Companies in industries that are profitable but no longer have much potential for expansion—the U.S. oil industry, for example—have a lot of free cash flow.

Why is free cash flow a problem? Jensen argues that managers are often tempted to use free cash flow to expand the size of the company, even if the expansion is not profitable. This is because managers feel that their power and job satisfaction are enhanced by a growing company; so given that most managers' compensation is at best weakly tied to the firm's profitability, Jensen argues that managers will find it personally worthwhile to expand even into money-losing operations. In principle, the board of directors and shareholders should be able to block these unprofitable investments; however, in practice, the fact that the management typically has far more information about potential investments than do outside directors and shareholders makes it difficult to second-guess the managers' recommendations.

How More Leverage Can Help. The problem of free cash flow is precisely analogous to the problem in the Goofus and Gallant example. Just as Goofus was willing to sacrifice company profits in order to pursue his personal goals (going fishing), so the company manager with lots of free cash flow may attempt to use that cash to increase his power and perquisites, at the expense of the shareholders. Jensen argues that the solution to the free-cash-flow problem is the same as the solution to the Goofus-Gallant problem: more leverage. For example, suppose that management uses the free cash flow of the company, plus the proceeds of new debt issues, to repurchase stock from the outside shareholders—that is, to do a management buyout. This helps solve the free-cash-flow problem in several ways. First, as in the Goofus and Gallant example, the personal returns of the managers are now much more closely tied to the profits of the firm, which gives them incentives to be more effi-

cient. Second, the re-leveraging process removes the existing free cash from the firm, so that any future investment projects will have to be financed externally; thus, future projects will have to meet the market test of being acceptable to outside bankers or bond purchasers. Finally, the high interest payments implied by re-leveraging impose a permanent discipline on the managers; in order to meet these payments, they will have to ruthlessly cut money-losing operations, avoid questionable investments, and take other efficiency-promoting actions.

According to Jensen, a substantial increase in free-cash-flow problems—resulting from deregulation, the maturing of some large industries, and other factors—is a major source of the recent debt expansion. Jensen also points to a number of institutional factors that have promoted increased leverage. These include relaxed restrictions on mergers, which have lowered the barriers to corporate takeovers created by the antitrust laws, and increased financial sophistication, such as the greatly expanded operations of takeover specialists like Drexel Burnham Lambert Inc. and the development of the market for "junk bonds."[5] Jensen's diagnosis is not controversial: it's quite plausible that these factors, plus changing norms about what constitutes an "acceptable" level of debt, explain at least part of the trend toward increased corporate debt.[6] However, the im-

---

[5]Junk bonds, more properly called below-investment-grade or high-yield bonds, have been used in a number of large corporate restructurings. For a discussion of the junk-bond market and the uses of junk bonds in takeovers, see Loeys (1986).

[6]One important piece of evidence in favor of this explanation is that net equity issues have been substantially negative since 1983. This suggests that much of the proceeds of the new debt issues is being used to repurchase outstanding shares. This is what we would expect if corporations are attempting to re-leverage their existing assets, rather than using debt to expand their asset holdings.

plied conclusion—that the debt buildup is beneficial overall to the economy—is considerably more controversial.

Criticisms of the Incentive-based Rationale for Increased Debt. Jensen and other advocates of the incentive-based approach to capital structure have made a cogent theoretical case for the beneficial effects of debt finance, and many architects of large-scale restructurings have given improved incentives and the promise of greater efficiency as a large part of the rationale for increased leverage. The idea that leverage is beneficial has certainly been embraced by the stock market: even unsubstantiated rumors of a potential LBO have been sufficient to send the stock price of the targeted company soaring, often by 40 percent or more. At a minimum, this indicates that stock market participants *believe* that higher leverage increases profitability. Proponents of restructuring interpret this as evidence that debt is good for the economy.

There are, however, criticisms of this conclusion. First, the fact that the stock market's expectations of company profitability rise when there is a buyout is not proof that profits *will* rise in actuality. It is still too soon to judge whether the increased leverage of the 1980s will lead to a sustained increase in profitability. One might think of looking to historical data for an answer to this question. But buyouts in the 1960s and 1970s were somewhat different in character from more recent restructurings, and, in any case, the profitability evidence on the earlier episodes is mixed.

Even if the higher profits expected by the stock market do materialize, there is contention over where they are likely to come from. The incentive-based theory of capital structure says they will come from improved efficiency. But some opponents have argued that the higher profits will primarily reflect transfers to the shareholders from other claimants on the corporation—its employees, customers, suppliers, bondholders, and the government. For example, Andrei Shleifer and Lawrence Summers, in a soon-to-be-published study, present evidence that the premium received by shareholders of Trans World Airlines, when it was taken over, was paid for twice over by the wage concessions wrested from three TWA unions. Customers may be hurt if takeovers are associated with increased monopolization of markets.[7] Bondholders have been big losers in some buyouts, as higher leverage has increased bankruptcy risk and thus reduced the value of outstanding bonds. The government may have lost tax revenue, as companies, by increasing leverage, have increased their interest deductions (although there are offsetting effects here, such as the taxes paid by bought-out shareholders on their capital gains). The perception that much of the profits associated with re-leveraging and buyouts comes from "squeezing" existing beneficiaries of the corporation explains much of the recent political agitation to limit these activities.[8]

Another possible explanation for the effect of LBOs on stock prices is that the announcement of a buyout provides information about, but does not directly affect, the firm's future prospects. Suppose that the management of a publicly owned pharmaceutical firm has secret information about a revolutionary new drug discovered in its laboratories. This highly profitable new opportunity, being secret, is not

---

[7]McAndrews and Nakamura (1989) present a model in which increased leverage by existing firms can help deter potential competitors from entering the market.

[8]Not much systematic empirical work on the "squeezing" hypothesis has been done to date. In a careful study of 76 companies' management buyouts, Kaplan (1988) found that most of the value gained from the buyout was due to increased operating income and tax benefits, and that the transfers from bondholders were small. However, the study considered only the first two years' experience of each firm after its buyout, and lack of data prevented measurement of the buyout's effects on employees, suppliers, and customers.

reflected in the firm's stock price. The management of this company has a strong incentive to do a buyout, because it knows the stock is currently underpriced relative to the firm's future profits. But if the managers attempt a buyout, this will reveal to the public that the management thinks the stock is underpriced—which will cause the stock price to be bid up. This means that the managers will have to share some of the profits from their inside information with the shareholders. Profits may indeed rise after the buyout—reflecting the introduction of the new drug—but this increase in profits would not be in any way caused by the increase in leverage associated with the buyout. Similar arguments apply if the buyout is initiated by a competitor or someone else who might have better information about the firm than do stock market investors.

The debt buildup can also be criticized from the perspective of incentive-based theories themselves. Two points are worth noting: first, the principal problem that higher leverage is supposed to address is the relatively weak connection between firms' profits and managers' personal returns, which reduces managers' incentives to take profit-maximizing actions. But if this is truly the problem, it could be addressed more directly—without subjecting the company to serious bankruptcy risk—simply by changing managerial compensation schemes to include more profit-based incentives. Robert Vishny and Andrei Shleifer (1988) argue that the approach of tying managers' pay to profits is limited by legal precedents that allow shareholders to sue if managerial compensation is "excessive"; however, if managerial incentives are really the problem, it does seem that more could be done in this direction.

The Downside of Debt Financing. A second point, made by the original Jensen-Meckling (1976) article and many since then, is that increased debt is not the optimal solution to all incentive problems. For example, it has been shown, as a theoretical proposition, that managers of debt-financed firms have an incentive to choose riskier projects over safe ones; this is because firms with fixed-debt obligations enjoy all of the upside potential of high-risk projects but share the downside losses with the debt holders, who are not fully repaid if bad investment outcomes cause the firm to fail.

That high leverage does not always promote efficiency can be seen when highly leveraged firms suffer losses and find themselves in financial distress. When financial problems hit, the need to meet interest payments may force management to take a very short-run perspective, leading them to cut back production and employment, cancel even potentially profitable expansion projects, and sell assets at fire-sale prices. Because the risk of bankruptcy is so great, firms in financial distress cannot make long-term agreements; they lose customers and suppliers who are afraid they cannot count on an ongoing relationship, and they must pay wage premiums to hire workers.

These efficiency losses, plus the direct costs of bankruptcy (such as legal fees), are the potential downside of high leverage. In terms of the ice cream stand, if Gallant does not earn enough to make his interest payment, he may be tempted to skimp on the ice cream or even serve the cracked cones, sacrificing future sales to increase short-run income and avoid bankruptcy. Or he may simply choose to stop working, letting the stand go into default. Maybe a highly leveraged Gallant isn't so gallant after all!

THE MACRO ISSUE: SPILLOVERS AND MULTIPLIERS

Most discussion of corporate debt has focused on the microeconomic efficiency issues. However, the macroeconomic implications of debt are also important. There are several possible (although speculative) scenarios under which high corporate debt could contribute to macroeconomic dislocations.

One scenario is a "liquidity crisis." In

1970, the bankruptcy of the Penn Central railroad, and Penn Central's resulting default on its short-term borrowings, caused a temporary, sharp decrease in new lending in the commercial-paper market. Prompt action by the Federal Reserve stabilized the situation. However, the potential for a similar episode, possibly on a larger scale, exists.

This potential arises from the fact that many firms count on being able to "roll over" their short-term debt (that is, re-borrow) as it comes due. If, for some reason, lenders became worried about bankruptcy risk and refused to roll over maturing debt, then these firms (even though they might be fundamentally solvent) would find themselves illiquid—that is, short of cash to make promised payments.

In most cases, firms would respond to this by taking loans on lines of credit previously negotiated with banks; however, that would spread the illiquidity problem to the banking system, as banks suddenly were subjected to large demands for credit. To ease such a liquidity crisis, the Federal Reserve would have to provide more funds to the financial system, either through the discount window, as it did during the Penn Central episode, or through open-market operations.

Perhaps a more disturbing scenario is a "solvency crisis." Suppose that, for reasons unrelated to financial structure, the economy were to enter a serious recession, leading to falling earnings and (perhaps) rising interest costs. Given high leverage inherited from the past, some firms might find it difficult to service their debt. Firms in financial distress are likely to retrench, cutting back employment, production, and investment. This would reduce total demand, worsening the recession and leading to financial problems in other firms. Thus, the initial recessionary shock could be magnified by high leverage; in the language of traditional Keynesian macroeconomic analysis, the "multiplier" relating the size of the initial disturbance to the size of the resulting recession will have increased.

Distressed Firms Can Have Far-reaching Effects. The difference between the microeconomic and macroeconomic perspective is that in the macroeconomic approach, we are concerned not only with the effects of financial distress on the distressed firm itself, but with the effects of the distressed firm's actions on other firms. If there are "spillovers" from one firm to another (for example, if the shutdown of a large employer in a town affects the town's economy more generally), then financial distress will increase the multiplier. Higher leverage thus has the potential to increase the vulnerability of the economy to destabilizing shocks. Importantly, the possible effects of spillovers and multipliers will not be taken into account by individual firms when they choose their preferred level of debt.

Are these scenarios likely? Nobody knows for sure, but there are several ways to argue that they are not very likely.

First, it should be pointed out that, despite the rapid increase in debt, corporate debt-to-equity ratios (measured in market-value terms) have not changed much during the 1980s. Indeed, Ben Bernanke and John Campbell (1988), using a sample of 1,400 large U.S. nonfinancial corporations, showed that debt-to-equity ratios in the 1980s remain well below their peaks, which occurred during the 1973-74 recession. The relative stability of the debt-to-equity ratio reflects the bull market in stocks of the 1980s, which allowed stock values to keep up with the high rate of debt issuance. From this perspective, debt burdens have not really increased.

However, even though debt-to-equity ratios have not increased, another measure of debt burden—the ratio of interest payments to total cash flow—has grown significantly. Bernanke and Campbell found this measure of interest burden to be about 50 percent higher in the mid-1980s than in the 1970s; several studies report that this ratio is currently close to its 1981-82 recession high, despite the long expansion that has occurred since the end of 1982.

How do we reconcile the fact that the interest-payments-to-earnings ratios (and debt-to-earnings ratios) have grown while debt-to-equity ratios have not? Mechanically, the answer is that both debt and stock values have grown much faster than earnings. The high ratio of stock prices to current earnings—sometimes called the P/E ratio—implies optimism on the part of investors about future earnings.[9] The stock market can be interpreted as saying that, even though current interest burdens are high, earnings are likely to rise enough in the future for firms to meet their debt obligations.

If we take the stock market's prediction at face value, then, a liquidity crisis or solvency crisis cannot be called a likely event; a reasonable expectation is that the corporate debt will be serviced. This doesn't mean that macroeconomic problems due to debt are not possible, however; it only means that they should be thought of as a sort of worst-case scenario. Nevertheless, good policymaking requires attention to worst-case as well as average outcomes. Indeed, it is during crisis situations in which good policies are most important.

The Likelihood of Macroeconomic Debt Problems. To get an idea of what might happen in a worst-case situation, Bernanke and Campbell (1988) simulated the effects of a recession in their sample of large firms. They asked what would have happened if the changes in cash flow, stock prices, and interest rates that actually occurred in the recessions of 1973-74 and 1981-82 had occurred again in 1986, affecting the very same firms in their sample.

Those two recessions were found to have different effects in the simulations. In the 1973-74 scenario, the stock market declines sharply; the simulation shows that in this type of recession more than 10 percent of the large firms would become technically insolvent, in the sense that the market value of their assets would fall below the market value of their debt.[10] In the 1981-82 scenario the stock market is fairly stable, but cash flow falls and interest rates rise; in this case Bernanke and Campbell found that about 10 percent of their firms would be unable to meet interest obligations without further borrowing. In the terminology introduced above, a 1973-74-type recession would create the potential for a solvency crisis, while a 1981-82-type recession might lead to a liquidity crisis.

Overall, then, the high share prices of U.S. corporations—not to mention the willingness of lenders to accept the high leverage of borrowing corporations—suggest that knowledgeable investors consider a macroeconomic debt crisis unlikely. However, unlikely is not the same as impossible; the Bernanke-Campbell simulations suggest that macroeconomic debt problems could be triggered by recessionary shocks of a magnitude that has been experienced twice in the last decade and a half.[11] This risk could possibly be ameliorated in the short run by aggressively expansionary monetary and fiscal policies, but only at the cost of higher inflation and potentially greater instability in the long run.

[9]If the stock market is "efficient," then the price of a share should represent the present discounted value of current earnings and future expected earnings. If the P/E ratio is high, then either interest rates are low (which they currently are not), or future earnings are expected to be high relative to current earnings.

[10]If the value of assets is less than the value of debt, then the debt cannot be repaid; the firm must either eventually go bankrupt or be reorganized.

[11]Another quantitative objection to the possibility of a macroeconomic debt crisis is that much of the recent debt buildup has occurred in cyclically insensitive sectors, such as food processing and services (see Roach, 1988). While this is true, it is also true that debt burdens have increased in cyclically sensitive sectors, like durable goods, as well. The simulations reported in the text implicitly take into account any shifting sectoral composition of debt.

Has Debt Become Less Risky? An alternative way to question the possibility of a macroeconomic debt crisis is to argue that, because of changes in the financial environment, a given level of debt poses less risk in 1989 than it would have in, say, 1974. Here is a concrete example: a recent development is the use of what is called "strip financing," in which investors in a firm commit to holding a fixed combination of the firm's debt and equity instruments. The idea is to minimize conflict between debt holders and shareholders (who, under strip financing, are one and the same), thus reducing the potential cost of financial distress and reorganization. Another development, stressed by Jensen, is that financial firms involved in arranging buyouts are in some cases retaining some stake in the management of the LBO firm; thus, the financial firm will have an incentive to assist the reorganization process should the LBO fall into financial trouble.

It is certainly true that the safety of any given level of debt depends on the financial environment. Japanese corporations, for example, have borne much higher levels of debt than their U.S. counterparts without experiencing problems. This works because most Japanese corporate debt is in the form of bank loans, and the large banks take an active role in the management of the firms to which they lend. Should a firm experience difficulties, the bank assists in obtaining new finance or in reorganization; at the same time, the bank is well placed to oversee whatever management or strategy changes the firm must make. These sorts of practices, which contrast with traditional "arm's length" lending in the United States, make high debt burdens safer.

Whether the U.S. financial environment has in fact moved substantially in the Japanese direction is an open question. Oversight of corporate management by the financial firm that arranged the LBO is a step toward the Japanese model; however, it is not clear at this point how widespread this practice is. Working in the other direction is the fact that increasing corporate reliance on below-investment-grade (junk) bonds has come at the expense of corporate use of bank loans. Since junk bonds tend to be held by mutual funds, insurance companies, and other institutions not directly involved in the management of the firms to which they lend, the use of junk bonds (in place of bank loans) may strengthen the traditional "arm's length" tendency of U.S. capital markets. This may make negotiated avoidance of bankruptcy more difficult and increase potential bankruptcy costs.

The contention that the risks of leverage have been reduced by institutional changes also raises a theoretical question: according to the incentive-based approach, the whole point of increased leverage is to impose discipline on corporate management. If, because of changes in the financial environment, failure to make contracted interest payments becomes a minor concern, then it would seem that the disciplinary impact of debt on management will be much reduced.

CONCLUSION

The argument for higher leverage is that it imposes discipline on the managers of the corporation, leading to greater efficiency. Effectively, this greater discipline is achieved by means of a threat: if the firm does not perform up to expectations, it may well suffer insolvency and reorganization. As with the discipline of children, the advantage of a draconian threat is the good behavior it may promote; the disadvantage is that the threat may have to be carried out.

Here is an analogy often used in discussing the costs and benefits of high leverage. Suppose we want people to drive more carefully. One way to do this would be to require every car to have a dagger in the steering wheel, the point aimed directly at the chest of the driver. This would certainly promote more careful driving, since even a fender bender might have ghastly consequences. But suppose there was a sudden worsening in driving conditions—a freak snowstorm, for example—that unexpectedly put even the most careful drivers at risk of accidents. Under these circumstances, the dagger-in-the-wheel policy might well lead to more deaths and injuries than if this "discipline device" had never been used.

In this story, the dagger in the wheel is supposed to represent high corporate leverage—which under normal circumstances promotes profit maximization ("safe driving") by managers. The snowstorm is an economywide recession (or perhaps some other disturbance, like a sharp increase in interest rates). The concern is that high leverage, while possibly a boon in good times, might become a destructive force in bad times.

This trade-off poses a quandary for policymakers. Despite the criticisms and existing uncertainties, few economists would completely dismiss the claim that higher leverage can be used to improve incentives and promote efficiency. Given the importance of improving the performance of U.S. corporations in a competitive international marketplace, it would probably be a severe mistake for the government simply to ban buyouts or limit leverage. On the other hand, pro-debt biases in the tax code, the possibility that higher leverage can help shareholders "squeeze" employees and others, and the possibility of "spillovers" from financial distress all suggest that firms will take on more debt than is good for the economy as a whole.

Three types of policy responses might help the situation. First, the government should take actions to increase the accountability of managers to shareholders (for example, by eliminating legal barriers to paying managers profit-based compensation); this would reduce the need to improve incentives indirectly through high leverage. Second, banking, financial market, and antitrust regulators should carefully scrutinize highly leveraged deals that fall within their purview; it is particularly important that government-insured deposits not be the funding source for risky buyouts, unless the bank's capital is demonstrated to be adequate. Finally, biases in the tax code that favor buyouts and high leverage should be removed.

Bernanke, Ben, and John Campbell. "Is There a Corporate Debt Crisis?" Brookings Papers on Economic Activity (1988:1) pp. 83-125.

Jensen, Michael C. "Takeovers: Their Causes and Consequences," *Journal of Economic Perspectives*, vol. 2 (Winter 1988) pp. 21-48.

Jensen, Michael C., and William H. Meckling. "Theory of the Firm: Managerial Behavior, Agency Costs and Ownership Structure," *Journal of Financial Economics*, vol. 3 (1976) pp. 305-60.

Kaplan, Stephen. "Management Buyouts: Efficiency Gains or Value Transfers?" University of Chicago, unpublished (1988).

Loeys, Jan. "Low-Grade Bonds: A Growing Source of Corporate Funding," Federal Reserve Bank of Philadelphia *Business Review* (November/December 1986) pp. 3-12.

McAndrews, James J., and Leonard I. Nakamura. "Entry-Deterring Debt," Federal Reserve Bank of Philadelphia, Working Paper No. 89-15 (1989).

Roach, Stephen. "Living With Corporate Debt," *Economic Perspectives*, Morgan Stanley, November 11, 1988.

Shleifer, Andrei, and Lawrence Summers. "Breach of Trust in Hostile Takeovers," in Alan Auerbach, *Corporate Takeovers: Causes and Consequences*, Chicago: University of Chicago Press (forthcoming).

Vishny, Robert, and Andrei Shleifer. "Value Maximization and the Acquisition Process," *Journal of Economic Perspectives*, vol. 2 (Winter 1988) pp. 7-20.

Article 11

The Case for Junk Bonds

Eric S. Rosengren

Assistant Vice President and Economist, Federal Reserve Bank of Boston. This paper provides a defense of a controversial type of financing, junk bonds. It does not provide a comprehensive discussion of the opposing view. The author is grateful to Jessica Laxman, Adam Rosen, and Simeon Hyman for research assistance.

An important financial innovation of the 1980s was the emergence of original-issue junk bonds, securities of below investment grade with high initial yields to maturity. Such securities are not totally new. Fallen angels, securities that have lost their investment-grade rating, have been familiar since the inception of the corporate bond market because not all firms live up to the initial expectations of investors. Before the establishment of the original-issue junk bond market, firms that did not qualify initially as investment-grade borrowers could not issue long-term bonds. In the past these firms relied almost exclusively on short-term bank loans for debt financing, but now many such enterprises can obtain long-term financing in national credit markets.

Junk bonds are an extension of a trend to substitute publicly traded securities for bank loans, a process called disintermediation. Investment-grade firms, for example, substituted commercial paper for bank loans. As well-established firms found their credit ratings equaling or exceeding those of commercial banks, they were able to raise funds more economically by issuing instruments directly in the open market. Over time, such borrowers have become less dependent on depository institutions as a source of funds. While below-investment-grade firms have lower credit ratings than banks, by placing tradable securities directly with investors they can obtain debt with longer maturities than commonly available from banks.

Junk bonds nevertheless are under attack, with opponents arguing they facilitate excessive leverage. While junk bonds have substituted for some bank lending, both sources of debt financing have grown rapidly during the 1980s as firms have become more leveraged. Greater leverage reduces a firm's tax burden because of the tax deductibility of interest payments, but it also increases the probability of default. The recent increase in large corporate bankruptcies stems in part from firms' choice of riskier capital structure.

In response to the problems created by defaults or near defaults of highly leveraged firms, savings and loans are now prohibited from holding junk bonds. Bills before Congress would also limit other financial intermediaries' investments in junk bonds and eliminate corporate tax deductibility of interest payments on junk bonds. This article contends that such asset restrictions may be counterproductive, limiting access to public credit markets for below-investment-grade firms without reducing their demand for debt. As a result, they will turn to substitutes for junk bonds, such as bank loans, to meet their financing needs. This may limit the firms' ability to raise long-term funds, since bank loans generally have short maturities.

The first section of this article shows that junk bonds are a natural extension of the disintermediation occurring in other financial markets. The second section describes the evolution of the junk bond market. The third section argues that bank loans are close substitutes for junk bonds; therefore, regulating junk bonds alone will not prevent highly leveraged transactions. The final section concludes that further regulation of junk bonds could limit the ability of below-investment-grade firms to raise long-term funds.

I. Changing Corporate Borrowing Patterns

The major sources of debt financing for businesses are corporate bonds, commercial paper and bank loans. These instruments differ in maturity, number of borrowers, and quality of borrowers. While the corporate bond market and the commercial paper market have been major sources of debt financing, until the establishment of the junk bond market they were primarily available to large, credit-worthy companies. In 1988, about 1,000 investment-grade bonds were issued by nonfinancial corporations, with an average size of $44 million.[1] Similarly, the commercial paper market generally provides large denomination funds for firms with investment-grade ratings.

Most small and mid-sized firms are not large enough or financially strong enough to issue investment-grade debt and, therefore, depend on commercial banks for their debt financing. Table 1 shows the terms of commercial and industrial loans extended by commercial banks during the second week of November 1989, as surveyed by the Federal Reserve System.[2] As estimated from the survey, commercial

banks held approximately 142,000 loans with less than one year to maturity with an average size of $311,000, and approximately 20,000 loans with more than one year to maturity and an average size of $260,000. Thus, bank loans are generally smaller and of shorter maturity than corporate bond issues.

Only 12 percent of the commercial and industrial loans surveyed by the Federal Reserve had more than one year to maturity. Bank loans are predominantly short-term floating-rate instruments or fixed-rate loans with short maturities (the average fixed-rate short-term loan was only 30 days) because most bank

Table 1
Terms of Lending at Commercial Banks
Survey Conducted November 6–10, 1989

	Amount (Billions of Dollars)	Average Size (Thousands of Dollars)	Weighted Average Maturity
Short-Term	44.0	311	53 Days
Fixed	24.8	554	30 Days
Floating	19.3	199	117 Days
Long-Term	5.2	260	43 Months
Fixed	.9	114	49 Months
Floating	4.3	359	41 Months

Source: *Federal Reserve Bulletin*, March 1990.

liabilities are also both floating-rate and short-term. Banks can minimize their interest rate risk by issuing loans with characteristics that match those of their liabilities. While this strategy minimizes interest rate risk for banks, it increases the risks to borrowers who must fund long-term projects with short-term loans.[3]

Disintermediation

Before the development of the commercial paper market, most short-term funding for firms was provided by commercial banks. For firms that qualify for investment-grade ratings, issuing commercial paper has become a competitive alternative to bank financing. Firms have increasingly bypassed banks, with the commercial paper market expanding from $25 billion in 1979 to $85 billion by 1988. Banks have lost much of this business because they do not have a competitive advantage in providing funds, as commercial paper rates paid by investment-grade firms are virtually the same as certificate of deposit rates paid by banks. Banks specialize in evaluating and monitoring credit risk, a service not highly valued for firms where the risk of default is very low. For firms with the highest credit rating, investors are willing to supply funds at rates at or below those of banks.

Disintermediation has not been confined to corporate bonds and commercial paper issued by the most creditworthy firms. Mortgages, student loans, and consumer loans are frequently repackaged and issued directly to financial market participants. Banks have even promoted repackaging of financial assets by developing an active loan sale market, wherein commercial and industrial loans are sold without recourse to other banks in a manner similar to the underwriting services provided by investment banks. Although most of these loans have been short-term loans to investment-grade firms, they have included loans issued to firms with below-investment-grade ratings.

With so many borrowers seeking to extend their sources of credit beyond banks, the trend toward disintermediation naturally expanded to firms that sought long-term financing but did not qualify for investment-grade ratings. The breaking down of traditional banking relationships also encouraged the substitution of junk bonds for bank loans. Banks typically have provided funds to below investment-grade firms, because banks specialized in gathering and analyzing credit risks of firms. Banks frequently supplemented their lending services with cash management, payroll, and other financial services that solidified the banking relationships. Greater competition among financial intermediaries and a trend towards separate pricing of banking services have enabled firms to unbundle these activities. Thus, firms could seek long-term financing from other sources without sacrificing the banking services that firms required.

Changes in the Composition of Corporate Debt

The changing composition of corporate financing is shown in table 2. Two major trends appear in the table. First, all forms of debt financing have grown rapidly. Second, disintermediation has been important: commercial paper and high-yield debt have grown more rapidly than bank loans to businesses.

As investment-grade firms successfully bypassed banks for both their short-term and their long-term financing needs, it was inevitable that firms with lower ratings should try to do the same. While some below-investment-grade firms have issued commercial paper, most still obtain their financing from banks. However, the long-term financing needs of below-investment-grade firms have not been met by banks. Since 1979, these firms have increasingly turned to long-term financing through the high-yield bond market.

Evolution of the Junk Bond Market

The junk bond market has followed the trends occurring in bank financing. During the past decade banks have increasingly financed highly leveraged transactions such as takeovers and recapitalizations. By the end of the 1980s, these transactions represented a significant portion of commercial and industrial loans for some banks.

Table 2
Corporate Debt Outstanding

	1979		1988	
	Billions of Dollars	Percent	Billions of Dollars	Percent
Investment-Grade Corporate Bonds and Private Placements	310	55	702	48
Commercial Paper	25	4	85	6
High-Yield Bonds	28	5	183	12
Bank Loans	204	36	502	34

Source: Board of Governors of the Federal Reserve System, *Flow of Funds.*

Most junk bonds issued in 1979 financed working capital, in place of bank loans. Table 3 describes the junk bonds issued in 1979, the first year with a significant number of new issues. Of the ninety-three issues, we were able to examine prospectuses for fifty-three. An analysis of the prospectuses in conjunction with news releases and other financial reports showed that only 11 percent of the issues (10 percent of dollar value) was used exclusively for acquisitions. Proceeds of most issues were used for working capital, consistent with the trend toward greater securitization in financial markets.

In 1988, junk bond financing of acquisitions was much greater. Of the $23 billion in junk bonds categorized in this study, only 20 percent of the new issues (9 percent of dollar value) was not planned for use in acquisition financing, while 64 percent was to be used exclusively for new acquisitions or to retire

debt from previous acquisitions. The number of issues to be used for investments not related to acquisitions actually dropped. The amount of proceeds increased, however, reflecting the larger average size of junk bond issues. Most of the largest issuers in 1988 used the proceeds to finance takeovers.

Junk bonds are attractive as a financing vehicle for takeovers. Bank loans frequently have stringent underwriting standards and collateralization requirements that junk bond investors may not require if they receive a higher return. National banks and many state-chartered banks are not permitted to hold equity positions in firms, while junk bond investors may receive equity positions that enable them to share the benefits of successful ventures. To eliminate this advantage, many bank holding companies acquire equity and mezzanine financing similar to junk bonds in their nonbank subsidiaries, enabling the holding company to maintain a stake in all tiers of the transaction. Banks traditionally have been unwilling to acquire a takeover loan that represents a significant portion of their capital. However, as will be discussed later, banks are becoming more willing and able to finance takeovers.

Credit Rating Deterioration

Both the credit rating of junk bond issues and their importance to takeovers have changed substantially from 1979. Table 4 shows Standard & Poor's initial credit ratings for junk bonds issued in 1979 and in 1988: BB, B, or CCC, with BB the rating for a junk bond with the lowest probability of default and CCC the rating for a junk bond with the highest probability of default.

The proportion of rated junk bonds issued in 1979 in the higher rating categories is greater than for junk bonds issued in 1988. In 1979 only 5 percent of the total value of junk bonds issued had the lowest rating, CCC, and those issues were smaller than the average issue. None of the categorized issues whose proceeds were used to finance takeovers in 1979 had a CCC rating. In contrast, 17 percent of the total value of junk bonds issued in 1988 had the lowest credit rating and they were the largest issues. All five of the largest issues in 1988 were used to finance takeovers or restructuring to forestall a takeover attempt. Where the proceeds could be categorized, 25 percent of the issues devoted exclusively to finance takeovers had a CCC rating, while only 9 percent of the issues not used in takeovers had a CCC rating. Furthermore, securities in the largest category, B, are now of

Table 3
Amount and Purpose of Junk Bond Issues, 1979 and 1988

	Number of Issues	Amount (Millions of Dollars)
1979 Junk Bond Issues		
All Junk Bonds	93	2,653
All Junk Bonds Categorized	53	1,733
Percent of Category:		
Proceeds used exclusively to finance takeovers	11%	10%
Portion of proceeds to finance takeover or possible future takeovers	11%	25%
Proceeds not used to finance takeovers	78%	65%
1988 Junk Bond Issues		
All Junk Bonds	223	39,182
All Junk Bonds Categorized	137	22,858
Percent of Category:		
Proceeds used exclusively to finance takeovers	64%	76%
Portion of proceeds to finance takeover or possible future takeovers	16%	15%
Proceeds not used to finance takeovers	20%	9%

Source: IDD Information Services and company prospectuses.

Table 4
Standard & Poor's Initial Ratings for Junk Bonds, 1979 and 1988

Category	Amount (Millions of Dollars)	S & P Rating (Percent)			Not Rated
		BB	B	CCC	
1979 Junk Bond Issues					
All Junk Bonds	2,652.5	14.1	43.3	4.9	37.7
All Junk Bonds Categorized	1,732.8	16.1	32.5	7.6	43.8
Proceeds used exclusively to finance takeovers	165	24.2	54.5		21.2
Portion of proceeds used to finance takeovers or possible future takeovers	425	14.1	37.6		48.2
Proceeds not used to finance takeovers	1,142.8	15.7	27.4	11.5	45.5
1988 Junk Bond Issues					
All Junk Bonds	39,181.5	8.4	66.7	17.4	7.5
All Junk Bonds Categorized	22,858.2	8.3	64.9	21.7	5.0
Proceeds used exclusively to finance takeovers	17,390.7	6.8	64.3	24.6	4.4
Portion of proceeds used to finance takeovers or possible future takeovers	3,393.7	5.9	77.0	14.7	2.4
Proceeds not used to finance takeovers	2,073.8	25.3	50.6	9.4	14.7

Source: IDD Information Services and company prospectuses.

lower quality. Since 1982, Standard & Poor's has augmented the general rating with + or − to differentiate issues further. Since 1982 an increasing share of the B category has been designated B−. The higher proportion of securities with a CCC or B− rating shows that the rating agencies believe that the quality of original junk bond issues has been declining.

Given the lower credit ratings for recently issued junk bonds, one can probably expect a default rate higher than in the 1979 sample, particularly if the economy does not continue to perform as well as it has over the past ten years. A significant proportion of junk bonds issued in 1979 defaulted, despite their better initial credit ratings (table 5). Of the issues whose status could be verified, 23 percent have defaulted or have been converted under distressed conditions. This is consistent with findings by Asquith, Mullins and Wolff (1989), who analyzed a smaller sample of junk bonds from 1979. None of the bonds initially used to finance takeovers defaulted, however. Table 6 shows the defaults, classified by initial rating. No clear relationship emerges between

initial ratings and defaults, with bonds with the lowest rating having the lowest default rates. In a larger sample, however, lower initial ratings might indicate a higher probability of default.

The trend toward more acquisition-related financing and lower credit standards is not unique to junk bonds. Banks have also become increasingly aggressive lenders for takeovers and restructuring. The number of highly leveraged transactions financed by banks, and the number of highly leveraged loans past due, have been increasing. Despite the loss potential of highly leveraged debt, both for holders of junk bonds and for banks, these loans can be profitable. Defaults do not mean that all the principal is lost, only that the timely payment of interest is not made. Most troubled firms restructure, resulting in some losses to debt holders but still paying a significant proportion of the principal value. When creditors cannot reach agreement, the firm is forced into bankruptcy. Altman (1989) estimates that even in bankruptcy junk bonds sell for 45 percent of their face value one month after default. Banks that

Table 5
Status of Junk Bond Issues of 1979, Classified by Use

	Still Outstanding	Called	Converted or Defaulted	Status Not Verified
Total Number of Junk Bond Issues	27	29	17	20
Issues Categorized	17	17	6	13
Proceeds used exclusively to finance takeovers	4	0	0	2
Portion of proceeds used to finance takeovers	1	1	1	3
Proceeds not used to finance takeovers	12	16	5	8

Source: IDD Information Services and company prospectuses.

hold more senior debt positions would expect substantially higher payments from firms in default. Despite defaults, with the very high interest rates that these loans and junk bonds pay, lenders that carefully monitor the risks of their portfolios can earn high profits.

III. Regulating Junk Bonds

Recent legislation prohibits financial intermediaries such as national banks and savings and loans from holding junk bonds after an adjustment period to liquidate existing positions. Proposals to eliminate the tax deductibility of interest paid on junk bonds would further discourage the issuance of these securities. These asset restrictions have been focused on junk bonds because of their use in highly leveraged transactions and their association with takeovers,

particularly hostile takeovers. Alternative debt financing is available, however, and few highly leveraged transactions will be prevented by legislation narrowly focused to discourage investors from holding junk bonds. This section argues that such asset restrictions are not effective because bank loans are close substitutes for junk bonds and these restrictions do not alter the incentives firms have to assume more leverage.

The importance of junk bonds for financing takeovers is often overstated. Table 7 provides the number and value of junk bond issues, corporate acquisitions and hostile takeovers from 1985 to 1988. The total value of junk bonds issued includes those issued for other purposes as well as those issued for takeovers and restructuring. The value of acquisitions includes publicly announced takeover values as ascertained by *Mergerstat Review*. The table overstates the role of junk bonds in acquisitions, since other

Table 6
Status of Junk Bond Issues of 1979, Classified by Initial S & P Credit Rating

Initial Credit Rating	Still Outstanding	Called	Converted or Defaulted	Status Not Verified
BB	4	3	2	0
B	15	10	8	8
CCC	1	4	1	2
NR	7	12	6	10
TOTAL	27	29	17	20

Source: IDD Information Services.

Table 7

Number and Value of Junk Bond Issues, Net Merger Announcements, and Hostile Takeovers

| Year | Junk Bonds | | | Net Merger Announcements | | Successful Hostile Takeovers | |
	Number of Junk Issuers	Number of Junk Issues	Value (Millions of Dollars)	Number	Value (Millions of Dollars)	Number	Value (Millions of Dollars)
1988	169	223	39,181.5	2,258	246,875.1	27	38,474.4
1987	263	321	37,801.2	2,032	163,686.3	18	18,630.3
1986	369	442	45,604.2	3,336	173,136.9	15	7,613.7
1985	257	328	20,694.5	3,001	179,767.5	14	8,232.3

Source: *Mergerstat Review*, IDD Information Services.

junk bonds are included and those acquisitions whose value could not be ascertained are not included. In 1988, net merger announcements totaled $247 billion, while junk bonds issued for all purposes totaled $39 billion: the value of junk bonds relative to the total value of acquisitions had dropped to 16 percent in 1988 from a high of 26 percent in 1986.[4] The data suggest that most takeovers are financed by sources other than junk bonds.

Acquisitions are financed mostly by bank loans, internal funds and investment-grade debt. Of the ten most active acquirers from 1978 through 1985 (*Mergerstat Review* 1986), one firm had no debt outstanding and the other nine all qualified for investment-grade rating. These acquirers included Merrill Lynch & Co., General Electric, and W.R. Grace & Co. Junk bond restrictions will not diminish other important sources of acquisition financing, such as bank lending or investment-grade debt issues.

Hostile Takeovers and Junk Bonds

Successful hostile takeovers comprise less than 1 percent of the total number of takeovers, yet they have been the source of much policy debate. They are also frequently associated with junk bonds, even though hostile takeovers are usually financed by other sources of funds.[5] Table 8 shows the initial financing for nineteen successful hostile takeovers from 1985 through 1987 (40 percent of the successful hostile takeovers during this period) for which financial information was available. Sixteen of the nineteen hostile acquisitions used no junk bonds initially. Investment-grade bonds and internal funds were used in seven. The primary source of initial financing

was bank loans, used in thirteen of the cases and accounting for over 50 percent of the total amount raised for initial financing. Recently the importance of bank loans has increased further as a number of large takeovers have been structured to avoid using junk financing. As was shown in table 7, the total value of newly issued junk bonds in 1988 was $6 billion less than in 1986, while the value of acquisitions in 1988 was $73 billion more than in 1986.

In the case of the hostile takeovers shown in table 8, many of the bank loans were liquidated quickly, either through asset sales or issuance of new debt or equity. At the end of one year, however, junk bonds and non-rated debt accounted for only 20 percent of the initial price of the successful takeovers. Junk bonds are a significant source of funds, but a majority of successful hostile takeovers are financed by other means.

In hostile takeovers, bank loans and junk bonds are very close substitutes as a source of financing. Almost 50 percent of initial issues of junk bonds in table 8 were retired by the following year, in a manner very similar to bridge loans. While many bank loans are converted to junk bonds in the year following the acquisition, investment-grade debt, asset sales, and internal funds are also major ways of retiring bank loans.

Effects of Discouraging Junk Bond Financing

Restrictions on junk bonds will change the composition of debt financing without necessarily reducing acquisitions significantly. Bank loans and investment-grade debt will still be available to finance takeovers, and the incentives for firms to acquire

Table 8
Financing of Nineteen Successful Hostile Takeovers between 1985 and 1987[a]

	At Time of Transaction	One Year After Transaction			Percent of Total Cost of Transaction[b]
		Newly Issued	Retired	Net Total	
Junk Bonds					
Total Dollars	595.5	1,355	281.8	1,668.7	11.86
Number of Takeovers	3	4	2		
Investment-Grade Bonds					
Total Dollars	1,875	604	1.1	2,477.9	17.19
Number of Takeovers	3	3	1		
Bank Loans					
Total Dollars	7,747.9	160	5,531.5	2,376.4	16.49
Number of Takeovers	13	2	13		
Privately Placed and Nonrated Debt					
Total Dollars	1,252.83	675.5	550.4	1,377.9	9.56
Number of Takeovers	6	2	4		
Commercial Paper					
Total Dollars	500		500		
Number of Takeovers	1	0	1	0	
Stock Sales					
Total Dollars	1,760		200	1,560	10.83
Number of Takeovers	5	0	1		
Internal Funds					
Total Dollars	330	560	60	830	5.76
Number of Takeovers	4	5	1		
Asset Sales					
Total Dollars		3,417		3,417	23.71

[a]Complete information was available for only 19 of the 47 successful hostile takeovers from 1985 to 1987.
[b]Total cost of transactions was $14.4 billion.
Source: IDD Information Services and bond prospectuses.

other firms will remain. Enterprising lawyers, accountants, and investment bankers will find substitutes for junk bond financing.

If the purpose of restricting junk bonds is to reduce corporate leverage, it is unlikely to achieve its goal. From the mid 1970s to the present, corporate leverage rose with banks, commercial paper, and investment-grade bonds providing most of the debt. Leverage today is comparable to that of the late 1960s and early 1970s, a period when all debt consisted of bank loans and investment-grade bonds, and original-issue junk bonds were unknown. The availability of junk bond financing is not a major reason for higher leverage.

If the purpose of restricting financial intermediaries from holding junk bonds is to limit their exposure to risk, it is not likely to be effective. "Safe" assets such as government bonds and real estate loans can cause an intermediary to fail if the institution is not appropriately diversified. First Pennsylvania failed because of capital losses on government securities. Banks in Texas and New England have learned that large losses can occur on real estate loans. Despite these losses, one would not advocate prohibiting banks from holding government bonds and real estate loans. Instead, banks should carefully monitor the risk inherent in their portfolios of assets relative to their capital positions, and if they are overexposed, seek further diversification.

In commercial and industrial lending, banks essentially provide debt financing for businesses lacking investment-grade ratings. Historically, banks have profited from such lending despite the high risk of default, by monitoring their credit risk and diversifying their portfolios. Similarly, junk bonds, if appropriately monitored, can compensate investors for their higher default risk. They provide access to public capital markets for firms that previously relied solely on banks and other financial intermediaries for their external financing. In addition, junk bond financing is longer-term than that commonly available from bank loans.

Junk bonds can improve the diversity of a bank's portfolio. Most bank lending is tied to the region where the bank is located. Diversification outside the region requires setting up expensive loan offices or purchasing loans that other banks do not want to keep in their portfolios. Just as the development of the secondary mortgage market made mortgage loans more liquid, junk bonds make commercial and industrial loans more liquid. The secondary mortgage market was actively promoted by public policy, however, while public policy if anything has deterred the growth of the junk bond market. Regulators frequently restrict the investments of institutions. Not allowing poorly capitalized institutions to purchase junk bonds may be advisable, but not allowing well capitalized institutions to purchase junk bonds may limit their ability to diversify.

IV. Conclusion

Disintermediation, whereby firms obtain funds directly in financial markets rather than from banks, can encourage a more efficient transfer of funds from lenders to borrowers. For example, the secondary market for mortgage loans insulated the housing market from many of the recent problems in the savings and loan industry. The purchasing of liquid

mortgage instruments permitted mutual funds, pension funds, and insurance firms to increase their participation in home financing.

Until recently, only firms with investment-grade credit ratings could raise funds directly from credit markets. These firms have such low default risk that they can obtain funds at or below the rates on certificates of deposit. As a result, they rely much more heavily on commercial paper and corporate bonds than on bank loans. Less established companies have not had such access, relying instead on short-term, floating-rate bank loans. The original-issue junk bond market has provided below-investment-grade firms an opportunity to raise long-term funds in national credit markets. By issuing "junk" debt instruments, these firms are able to attract investors who previously had not actively financed commercial activities by relatively small firms.

Despite the advantages to below-investment-grade firms of disintermediating loans, opponents have sought to discourage investors by limiting which intermediaries can hold junk bonds and by eliminating the tax deductions for interest paid on junk bonds. Such asset restrictions do not discourage leverage or takeovers. However, they will encourage firms to substitute bank loans for junk bonds, because bank loans and junk bonds are close substitutes. These restrictions will not alter the motives for holding debt but will limit access by below-investment-grade firms to long-term financing through national credit markets.

[1] These figures are approximations from the U.S. Securities and Exchange Commission, *SEC Monthly Statistical Review*, vol. 48, no. 2, February 1989, as follows:

Public Non-Convertible Bond Offerings

	Amount $ billions	Number
Total Business	$ 224.5	3927
Less: Financial and Real Estate	−139.1	−2625
Foreign	−4.5	−36
Junk Bonds	−37.1	−214
Total Nonfinancial Investment-Grade Bonds	$ 43.8	1052

[2] The survey does not include mortgage loans or foreign loans. Construction and land development loans are included in

the survey but not reported in the table because they are not available by maturity.

[3] Borrowers can reduce this interest rate risk by hedging with interest rate futures or interest rate swaps (Felgran 1987). If borrowers can get long-term commitments from banks, with the aid of swaps they can create, at some transactions cost, an instrument that mimics long-term bonds. The Federal Reserve lending survey (table 1) shows, however, that long-term fixed or floating-rate agreements by banks are still relatively uncommon.

[4] "Net merger announcements" is calculated as total announcements in the year minus cancelled transactions in the year. As long as cancellations are stable over time, acquisition announcements should be a reasonable approximation for completions. Cancellations as a percent of gross announcements were 7 percent in 1985, 1987 and 1988 and 6 percent in 1986.

[5] The term "successful hostile takeovers" refers to tender offers by acquirers who successfully purchased the firm despite opposition of incumbent management. The list of successful hostile takeovers is taken from *Mergerstat Review*.

References

Altman, Edward. 1989. "Measuring Corporate Bond Mortality and Performance." *Journal of Finance*, vol. 44, September, pp. 909–921.

Asquith, Paul, David Mullins, Jr. and Eric Wolff. 1989. "Original Issue High Yield Bonds: Aging Analyses of Defaults, Exchanges and Calls." *Journal of Finance*, vol. 44, September, pp. 923–954.

Blume, Marshall. 1987. "Risk and Return Characteristics of Lower Grade Bonds," *Financial Analysts Journal*, vol. 43, July/August, pp. 26–33.

Drexel Burnham Lambert. 1989. *High Yield Market Report.*

Felgran, Steven D. 1987. "Interest Rate Swaps: Use, Risk, and Prices." *New England Economic Review*, November/December, pp. 22–32.

Kopcke, Richard W. and Eric S. Rosengren. 1989. "Regulation of Debt and Equity." In *Are the Distinctions Between Debt and Equity Disappearing?* Kopcke and Rosengren, eds., Federal Reserve Bank of Boston Conference Series No. 33.

Mergerstat Review. Various Years. Merrill Lynch Business Brokerage & Valuation, Inc.

Article 12

Why Are So Many
New Stock Issues Underpriced?

Anthony Saunders*

Each year hundreds of small firms approach the capital market to issue equity for the first time. These firms are usually growing so fast, or have so many profitable investment projects available to them, that traditional sources of funds (bank loans, retained earnings, and the owners' own equity) are often insufficient to finance their expansion.

Because of this need for finance at a crucial stage in their growth, it is important for these firms that the prices of their shares reflect the

*Anthony Saunders is a Professor of Finance at New York University's Stern School of Business. He wrote this article while he was a Research Adviser to the Federal Reserve Bank of Philadelphia.

true value of company assets or growth opportunities. In particular, if their shares are sold too cheaply, these firms will have raised less capital than was warranted by the intrinsic values of their assets. In other words, their shares will have been "underpriced."

Considerable evidence shows that new or initial public equity offerings (IPOs) are underpriced on *average*. That is, the prices of firms' shares offered to the public for the first time are, on average, set below the prices investors appear willing to pay when the stocks start trading in the secondary market. That is, in the parlance of investment bankers, small firms appear to leave behind considerable "money on the table" at the time of a new issue.

Why small firms raise fewer funds in the new-issue process than the market indicates they should is a crucial public policy issue. Clearly, some degree of market imperfection or lack of competition could cause such an outcome. For example, if, by restricting commercial banks' participation in the market, the Glass-Steagall Act of 1933 has allowed investment bankers to enjoy a type of monopoly (market) power over new equity-issuing firms, then this would suffice to explain underpricing. Alternatively, underpricing may be the premium the issuing firm must pay for having little information about itself to offer potential investors. In that case, underpricing would have little to do with the regulatory structure of the investment banking industry.

Let's examine the reasons for IPO underpricing and evaluate the degree to which underpricing is due to Glass-Steagall restrictions. What is the evidence on the degree of underpricing of U.S. IPOs? What are the various explanations for underpricing? And what are the implications of these explanations, and of the associated empirical evidence, for commercial and investment bank regulation?

EVIDENCE ON UNDERPRICING

In "firm commitment" underwriting ("firm" in that the investment banker guarantees the price), an investment banker (and his syndicate) will undertake to buy the whole new issue of a firm at one price (the *bid* price, or BP) and seek to resell the issue to outside investors at another price (the *offer* price, or OP). In doing so, the investment banker offers a valuable risk-management service to the issuing firm by guaranteeing to purchase 100 percent of the new issue at the bid price (BP). The return for the investment banker in bearing underwriting risk—that is, the risk that investors will demand less than 100 percent of the issue when it is reoffered for sale to the market—is the spread between the public offer price and the bid price (OP - BP) plus fees and commissions. (Here,

and throughout this article, the term "investor" refers to those who buy shares through the investment banker at the offer price.) Thus, the investment banker's spread plus fees and commissions may be viewed as the *direct* cost of going public.

However, there is also potentially an *indirect* cost of going public, measured by the degree to which the issue is underpriced. For example, if the BP is $5 per share and the OP is $5.25 per share, then the underwriter's spread is 25 cents per share. However, suppose that on the first day of trading in the secondary market the share price (P) closes at $7 per share. This indicates that the share has been underpriced in the new-issue process and that, potentially, the firm might have raised as much as $7 per share had it been priced "correctly." This implies that the issuing firm has borne an additional *indirect* new-issue cost of $1.75 per share ($7.00 - $5.25), because the investment banker has set the offer price below the price the market was willing to pay on the first day of trading.

Thus, more formally, the "raw" percentage degree of underpricing (UP) of an IPO can be defined as:

$$(1) \qquad UP = [(P - OP) / OP] \times 100$$

where:

OP = offer price of the IPO
P = price observed at the end of either the first trading day, week, or month

If UP is positive, the issue has been underpriced; if UP is zero, the issue is accurately priced; and if UP is negative, it has been overpriced. The expression for UP is also the expression for a percentage rate of return. Thus, equation (1) can be viewed as the one-day (or one-week or one-month) *initial* return on buying an IPO (that is, UP = R, the initial return on the stock).

Returns calculated by equation (1) are deemed raw returns. However, researchers also compute excess (market-adjusted) returns, as well. The reasons for this are easy to see. Given a lag between the setting of the offer price and the beginning of trading on an exchange (anywhere from one day to two weeks or more), the price observed in the market on the first day of trading may be high (low) relative to the offer price simply because the stock market as a whole has risen (fallen) over this period. Thus, in analyzing underpricing, reseachers need to control for the performance of the stock market in general. More specifically:

$$(2) \qquad R_m = [(I_1 - I_0) / I_0] \times 100$$

where:

R_m = return on the market portfolio

I_1 = level of the general market share index at the time of listing (first day, first week, or first month)

I_0 = level of the market share index at the time offer is announced

If R_m is positive, the market has been going up in the time between the setting of the offer price and the listing of the stock on the stock exchange. If R_m is negative, the market has been falling. Excess market or risk-adjusted initial returns (EX) can therefore be defined as:[1]

$$(3) \qquad EX = R - R_m$$

According to equation (3), underpricing occurs only when R is greater than R_m.

The findings of 22 studies that examine the degree of underpricing are summarized in the table on p. 10. Although the time periods, sample sizes, and ways of calculating initial returns (especially raw versus market-adjusted) differ widely across these studies, each finds underpricing on average. For example, studies that use a one-week period to calculate the difference between the offer price and the market price of an IPO find underpricing ranging from 5.9 percent to as much as 48.4 percent.[2]

Thus, an important empirical fact is that U.S. IPOs are underpriced on average, resulting in small firms raising less capital than is justified by the markets' ex post valuation of their shares.

WHY ARE NEW ISSUES UNDERPRICED?

Several reasons have been proposed in the institutional, finance, and economics literature as to why underpricing occurs. Although this article will not discuss all the proposed reasons, it concentrates on four views that have received much publicity. The first view attributes underpricing to "monopoly power" enjoyed by investment bankers. The second regards Securities and Exchange Commission regulations as the primary cause. And the third and fourth see underpricing as a problem of imperfect information among contracting parties—especially between investors and issuers.

---

[1] For a detailed discussion of excess returns, see Robert Schweitzer, "How Do Stock Returns React to Special Events?" this *Business Review* (July/August 1989) pp. 17-29. For IPOs, researchers adjust the initial return on the stock by deducting the return on the market. This is equivalent to assuming that a new IPO's returns move exactly with the market's. That is, they have a unit degree of systematic risk (or their β is 1). The reason for this assumption is that since IPOs have no past history of returns, one cannot estimate directly the IPO's β at the time of issue. The only researcher

who has tried to address this problem was Ibbotson (1975), who developed an ingenious method of constructing synthetic β's for IPOs.

[2] It should be noted that these are one week's returns and are thus very large. These underpricing "costs" swamp the direct costs of a new issue, which are, on average, in the range of 2 to 5 percent of the issue's dollar size.

The Monopoly Power of Underwriters. One possible explanation for pervasive underpricing is the monopoly power the investment banker enjoys over the issuer.[3] Given that commercial banks are barred from entering into corporate equity underwriting (a result of the Glass-Steagall Act, which effectively separated commercial banking from investment banking), investment bankers may have a degree of monopoly power that they use to earn "rents" by underpricing new issues. Of course, competition among investment banks would limit the extent of this monopoly power.

But how real is this monopoly power? Compared to U.S. commercial banks, U.S. noncommercial banking firms and foreign banks have always faced fewer restrictions on entry into investment banking. Moreover, thrifts also can enter investment banking. In recent years, for example, nonbank firms such as General Electric and Prudential have entered the investment banking industry via acquisitions, as has Franklin Savings Bank, a thrift. This potential competition presumably places a limit on the degree of monopoly power enjoyed by investment bankers.

In addition, foreign banks were not subject to Glass-Steagall regulations until passage of the International Banking Act of 1978. Even then, those already possessing investment banking powers had them grandfathered. The emphasis on investment banks is due to their traditional dominance of the underwriting market and to their potential economies of scope (cost savings from offering a combination of services) in extending to their underwriting customers a broader range of financial services.

If investment bankers have monopoly power

over the new issuer, they might use it to increase both the spread between the offer price and bid price (the underwriters' spread) as well as the degree to which the offer price is set below the markets' true valuation (P). A monopolist investment banker might have the incentive to underprice, since by doing so he can increase the probability of being able to sell the whole issue to outside investors (thereby minimizing his underwriting risk) while earning a high investment banking spread (OP - BP) on the issue.[4]

Clearly, if this was the prime reason for underpricing, it would tend to make a case for allowing commercial banks into the underwriting business. This argument would be based on the expectation that pro-competitive effects would reduce the average degree of underpricing.[5] But this argument would, of

---

[3]For a discussion of the reasons for and effects of investment bankers' potential monopoly power, see Ibbotson (1975) and Pugel and White (1984).

---

[4]Implicitly, this argument presumes that investment bankers are risk-averse. This is reasonable, given the private nature of many companies, their limited capital bases, and the potential for a large loss if they take a "big hit" (loss) on an underwriting. For example, many U.S. investment bankers suffered significant losses in underwriting an issue of British Petroleum shares at the time of the October 1987 stock market crash.

[5]A different monopoly-based argument, advanced in Baron (1982), is that investment bankers possess monopoly power through their private access to *information* about the likely size of the demand for a new issue. Since issuers are viewed as being relatively uninformed about the nature of this demand, they can easily be exploited by the investment banker. Indeed, since the issuer has no way of knowing ex ante the size of investor demand, the underwriter has an incentive to save resources on distribution and search ("shirking") by simply underpricing enough to ensure that the whole issue is sold. In this context, the presence of potential competitors, such as commercial banks, and the importance of maintaining a reputation might be viewed as potential controls on the investment bankers' temptation to shirk. This presumes, however, that commercial banks, if they entered into underwriting, have the same abilities to "place" (sell to investors) a new issue as investment bankers do. In reality, it might take commercial bankers a number of years to build up the same placement powers.

course, be tempered by the need to maintain safety and soundness of the banking system, which could be lessened if the spread (P - OP) is small enough to risk inability to sell the entire issue.[6]

Due-Diligence Insurance. A second reason given for why underwriters underprice IPOs is the fear of potential legal problems stemming from overpriced issues. Underwriters, along with company directors, are required to exercise "due diligence" in ensuring the accuracy of the information contained in the prospectus they offer to investors.[7] Since passage of the Securities Acts of 1933 and 1934, both underwriters and directors may be held legally responsible under SEC regulations for the accuracy of this information.

Investors who end up holding heavily overpriced issues may well have an incentive to sue the underwriter and/or the company directors for publishing misleading or incomplete information in the prospectus. The investors could contend they were misled into believing this was a "good" issue rather than a "bad" one. To avoid any negative legal effects, as well as adverse publicity and damage to reputation, a risk-averse underwriter may try to keep investors happy by persistently underpricing IPOs. Hence, some researchers believe that the legal penalties for due-diligence failures are what have created incentives for investment bankers to underprice.

The Problem of the "Winner's Curse." The academic literature has paid a great deal of attention to a theory first advanced by Rock (1986) and extended by Beatty and Ritter (1986) and McStay (1987), among others. This theory considers underpricing as a competitive out-

---

[6] Since P is not known with certainty, a small spread (P - OP) risks occasional negative spreads, in which case the underwriting firm suffers a loss.

[7] See, for example, Tinic (1988).

come in an IPO market in which some investors are viewed as informed while a larger group is viewed as uninformed. As a result, underpricing is directly related to the degree of information imperfection—or, more specifically, information asymmetry—in the capital market and to the costs of collecting information. Both this theory and the one that follows view underpricing as a way of resolving the problem of costly information collection.

In Rock's model, there are two types of IPOs: good issues and bad issues. Informed investors, defined as those who expend resources collecting information on IPOs, will bid only for those issues that are good. (This search effort is assumed to allow the informed investor to assess exactly the true value of the IPO.) Those investors who are uninformed, however, will not engage in expensive search, but rather will bid randomly across all issues, good and bad. It is further assumed that informed investors are never sufficiently large as a group to be able to purchase a whole issue.

First, consider a good issue. In this case, both informed and uninformed investors will bid for the issue (the uninformed in a random manner). Because both groups bid for the issue, it is likely to be oversubscribed, so that any single *individual* bidder (informed or uninformed) will get fewer shares than he bid for. Thus, for good issues, uninformed investors get only partial allotments.

Next, consider bad issues. In this case, informed investors will not bid at all. The only bidders will be the uninformed. Moreover, owing to the absence of competing informed bidders, any individual bidder will more likely achieve his full allotment (or a higher probability of an allotment). That is, the uninformed bidder suffers from the problem of the "winner's curse": he achieves a large allotment for bad IPOs and a small allotment for good IPOs.

Rock's argument is that, because of the winner's curse, IPOs have to be underpriced on average so as to produce an expected return for the uninformed investor that is high enough to attract investment in IPOs regardless of whether the issue is good or bad.[8] That is, underpricing is a phenomenon perfectly consistent with competitive market conditions in a world of imperfect information flows. Thus, monopoly power is rejected as an argument explaining underpricing.

Underpricing as a Dynamic Strategy. In the most recent literature, underpricing is seen as a dynamic strategy employed by issuing firms to overcome the asymmetry of information between issuing firms and outside investors.[9] Implicitly, underpricing is viewed as a cost to be borne by the issuing firm's insiders to persuade investors to collect (or aggregate) information about the firm and in that way establish its true value in the secondary market. Moreover, the better the firm (a "good" issue), the more it will be underpriced relative to the bad issue.

Specifically, a good firm will underprice its issue to attract outside investors.[10] Investors (such as analysts) collect information about the firm and, in the secondary market, establish its true value above its offer price. The owners of the firm benefit from this strategy because once the true (higher) market value is established, the owners have an incentive to "cash in" by coming out with new (further) secondary offerings at the higher market price. Thus, the cost or losses of underpricing the IPO are offset by the benefits from cashing in on the secondary offering.[11]

By comparison, a bad firm—one that knows it is a bad firm—will have the opposite incentives. In particular, the firm may seek to price the IPO as high as possible, since it knows that once investors collect information and discover that it is a "bad" firm, its stock's price will fall on the secondary market.[12]

As in the Rock model, these types of dynamic-strategy models view underpricing as a phenomenon that is consistent with competition in a world of imperfect information among issuing firms and investors. The difference is that, here, IPO underpricing is viewed as a cost to be borne by good firms, which is offset by the revenue benefits from making a secondary ("seasoned") offering later on at a higher price.

IMPLICATIONS FOR BANK REGULATION

What do these models imply for bank regulation and, in particular, the Glass-Steagall Act? If underpricing is indeed due to information imperfections in the capital market—especially between firms and investors—it is difficult to see how commercial banks' entry into underwriting will have much effect, unless these banks somehow collect more information and alleviate the degree of information imperfection in the market. Since the modern theory of banking views banks as major collectors and users of information, increased production of information about small firms may indeed be a benefit from repealing Glass-Steagall.

However, a better test of whether Glass-

---

[8] Technically, the *conditional* expected return for the uninformed investor, across both good and bad issues, must be at least as great as the risk-free rate.

[9] See, for example, Chemmanur (1989) and Welch (1988).

[10] In these models, the investment banker plays a largely passive function, operating as an agent on behalf of the principal (the firm). The failure of the investment banker to take a more active role may be seen as a weakness of these information-based models.

---

[11] Welch (1988) offers preliminary evidence that these issues that are more underpriced tend to follow up more quickly with a secondary (seasoned) offering.

[12] This is not to imply that the bad firms necessarily overprice. However, the theory has the *aggregate* implication that the greater the porportion of good to bad issues in the market, the greater the degree of underpricing on *average*.

Steagall has undesirable costs is whether it confers monopoly power on existing investment banks that is reflected in the degree of underpricing. That is, what, if any, is the empirical evidence linking underpricing to the monopoly power of investment banks?

One implication of the monopoly-power hypothesis[13] is that an underwriter, because of his expertise and more precise knowledge of the issuing firm's true value, can save effort (shirk) by ensuring maximum sales through underpricing while still earning a high underwriting spread (OP - BP). However, even in a world of asymmetric information, presumably firms would learn that they are being exploited and, if competition exists, would switch to other underwriters. In contrast, monopoly power would imply that issuing firms would fare as well with one investment bank as with another and that underwriters could ignore all problems or considerations related to maintaining a reputation.

Beatty and Ritter (1986) have sought to test this reputation–monopoly power effect. That is, do investment bankers who heavily underprice in one period lose business from issuing firms in the next? Beatty and Ritter's results tended to confirm that the more an investment banker underpriced in one period, the greater his loss of business in the next—a result suggesting that monopoly power is temporary at best.

A second implication of the monopoly-power hypothesis is that the investment banker—to avoid risk—will have a greater incentive to underprice relatively risky issues so as to ensure maximum sales. For example, it can be argued that the more uncertain are firms' uses of the proceeds of the issue (for example, to pay off existing debt, to develop new projects, and so on), the riskier the issue. Or, alternatively, the more variable the after-market returns on an issue—measured by the standard deviation of returns over a period subsequent to listing on the stock exchange—the riskier the issue. Thus, we would expect underpricing to increase as the number of potential uses of proceeds, and the volatility of its (expected) price in the after-market, grows.

Beatty and Ritter (1986) found a positive relationship between number of uses of proceeds and underpricing; Ritter (1984) and Miller and Reilly (1987) found a positive relationship between the standard deviation of after-market returns and the degree of underpricing. Both these results are consistent with the monopoly-power hypothesis; however, it *must* be noted that both findings are also consistent with the competitive-market, information-imperfection "winner's curse" theory of Rock (1986).[14]

A third potential implication of the monopoly-power model is that the degree of underpricing should have been less prior to passage of Glass-Steagall—that is, the pre-1933 *average* degree of underpricing should have been less than the post-1933 average degree. In a recent study, Tinic (1988) tested the degree of underpricing in the period 1923-30 and compared it with the period 1966-71. He found that underpricing was higher in the 1966-71 period. While Tinic interpreted these results as consistent with the due-diligence-insurance hypothesis—that is, the passage of the Securities Act of 1934, which forced investment banks to underprice to avoid potential lawsuits—they are also consistent with the monopoly-power hypothesis. That is, in a period preceding Glass-Steagall (when commercial banks had greater power to

---

[13] See Baron (1982), who developed a theory of investment banker monopoly power based on the inability of issuers to accurately monitor the investment bankers' effort in placing new shares with investors.

[14] That is, the greater the risk or uncertainty about the issue, the greater the cost of becoming informed and thus the greater the degree of underpricing required in equilibrium.

underwrite corporate securities),[15] the degree of underpricing was less than in a period following the Glass-Steagall separation of powers.

A fourth implication of the monopoly-power hypothesis is that IPOs of investment banks (for example, Morgan Stanley going public) should *not* be underpriced, since the investment bank brings its "own firm" public. Looking at 37 IPOs of investment banks that went public in the 1970-84 period and participated in the distribution of their own issues, Muscarella and Vetsuypens (1987) find an average degree of underpricing of *8 percent* on the first day of trading. At first sight this tends to contradict the monopoly-power hypothesis as the sole reason for underpricing; however, it could be argued that 8 percent underpricing is less

than the median or mean underpricing found in the majority of studies listed in the table below and that monopoly power may offer a partial explanation for underpricing.

Nevertheless, the results favoring monopoly power as the major determinant of new-issues underpricing appear somewhat weak. Indeed, the evidence is largely consistent with the existence of competitive markets in which investors have incomplete or imperfect infor-

[15]This was particularly true in 1927-33, when commercial banks had the same powers as investment banks. Since technology and the structure of the financial services industry are continuously changing, a more valid test might have been to compare underpricing in the period *immediately following* passage of the Glass-Steagall Act.

Initial Returns, According to Various Studies

Study	Sample Period	Sample Size	Initial Returns 1 Week	Initial Returns 1 Mo.
Reilly/Hatfield (1969)	1963-65	53	9.9%	8.7%
McDonald/Fisher (1972)	1969-70	142	28.5%	34.6%
Logue (1973)	1965-69	250	—	41.7%
Reilly (1973)	1966	62	9.9%	—
Neuberger/Hammond (1974)	1965-69	816	17.1%	19.1%
Ibbotson (1975)	1960-71	128	—	11.4%
Ibbotson/Jaffe (1975)	1960-70	2650	16.8%	—
Reilly (1978)	1972-75	486	10.9%	11.6%
Block/Stanley (1980)	1974-78	102	5.9%	3.3%
Neuberger/LaChapelle (1983)	1975-80	118	27.7%	33.6%
Ibbotson (1982)	1971-81	N/A	—	2.9%
Ritter (1984)	1960-82	5162	18.8%	—
	1977-82	1028	26.5%	—
	1980-81	325	48.4%	—
Giddy (1985)	1976-83	604	10.2%	—
John/Saunders (1986)	1976-82	78	—	8.5%
Beatty/Ritter (1986)	1981-82	545	14.1%	—
Chalk/Peavy (1986)	1974-82	440	13.8%	—
Ritter (1987)	1977-82			
Firm commitment		664	14.8%	—
Best efforts		364	47.8%	—
Miller/Reilly (1987)	1982-83	510	9.9%	—
Muscarella/Vetsuypens (1987)	1983-87	1184	—	7.6%

mation about new firms. While new issues did appear to be *less* underpriced before Glass-Steagall (consistent with the monopoly-power hypothesis), evidence suggests that those investment banks that excessively underprice today lose future business from prospective issuing firms and that investment banks' own IPOs are also underpriced on average (although less so than those of other firms). The gains from allowing commercial banks to compete directly with investment banks for corporate equity underwritings may come less from creating more potential competition than from collecting, producing, and disseminating more information about small firms in the new-issue process. This conclusion suggests that allowing banks into investment banking activities may indeed bring about price changes that benefit the public; however, those changes may be smaller and occur for different reasons than once thought.

REFERENCES

Baron, D.P. "A Model of the Demand for Investment Banking and Advising and Distribution Services for New Issues," *Journal of Finance* (1982) pp. 955-77.

Beatty, R., and J. Ritter. "Investment Banking, Reputation, and the Underpricing of Initial Public Offerings," *Journal of Financial Economics* (1986) pp. 213-32.

Block, S., and M. Stanley. "The Financial Characteristics and Price Movement Patterns of Companies Approaching the Unseasoned Securities Market in the Late 1970s," *Financial Management* (1980) pp. 30-36.

Chalk, A.J., and J.W. Peavy. "Understanding the Pricing of Initial Public Offerings," Southern Methodist University Working Paper 86-72 (1986).

Chemmanur, T.J. "The Pricing of Initial Public Offerings: A Dynamic Model With Information Production," mimeo, New York University (1989).

Giddy, I. "Is Equity Underwriting Risky for Commercial Bank Affiliates?" in I. Walter, ed., *Deregulating Wall Street* (New York: John Wiley, 1985).

Ibbotson, R.G. "Price Performance of Common Stock New Issues," *Journal of Financial Economics* 3 (1975) pp. 235-72.

Ibbotson, R.G. "Common Stock New Issues Revisited," Graduate School of Business, University of Chicago, Working Paper 84 (1982), unpublished.

Ibbotson, R.G., and J.J. Jaffe. "'Hot Issue' Markets," *Journal of Finance* 30 (1975) pp. 1027-42.

John, K., and A. Saunders. "The Efficiency of the Market for Initial Public Offerings: U.S. Experience 1976-1983," unpublished (1986).

Logue, D.E. "On the Pricing of Unseasoned New Issues, 1965-1969," *Journal of Financial and Quantitative Analysis* (1973) pp. 91-103.

McDonald, J.G., and A.K. Fisher. "New-Issue Stock Price Behavior," *Journal of Finance* (1972) pp. 97-102.

McStay, K.P. *The Efficiency of New Issue Markets*, Ph.D. thesis, Department of Economics, U.C.L.A. (1987).

Miller, R.E., and F.K. Reilly. "An Examination of Mispricing, Returns, and Uncertainty for Initial Public Offerings," *Financial Management* (1987) pp. 33-38.

Muscarella, C.J., and M.R. Vetsuypens. "A Simple Test of Baron's Model of IPO Underpricing," Southern Methodist University Working Paper 87-14 (1987a).

Muscarella, C.J., and M.R. Vetsuypens. "Initial Public Offerings and Information Asymmetry," Edwin L. Cox School of Business, Southern Methodist University, unpublished (1987b).

Neuberger, B.M., and C.T. Hammond. "A Study of Underwriters' Experience With Unseasoned New Issues," *Journal of Financial and Quantitative Analysis* (1974) pp. 165-77.

Neuberger, B.M., and C.A. LaChapelle. "Unseasoned New Issue Price Performance on Three Tiers: 1975-1980," *Financial Management* (1983) pp. 23-28.

Pugel, T.A., and L.J. White. "An Empirical Analysis of Underwriting Spreads on IPO's," Working Paper 331, Salomon Brothers Center for the Study of Financial Institutions, Graduate School of Business Administration, New York University (September 1984).

Reilly, R.K., and K. Hatfield. "Investor Experience With New Stock Issues," *Financial Analysts Journal* (September/October 1969) pp. 73-80.

Reilly, R.K. "Further Evidence on Short-Run Results for New Issue Investors," *Journal of Financial and Quantitative Analysis* (1973) pp. 83-90.

Reilly, R.K. "New Issues Revisited," *Financial Management* (1978) pp. 28-42.

Ritter, J. "The 'Hot Issue' Market of 1980," *Journal of Business* 57 (1984) pp. 215-40.

Ritter, J. "The Costs of Going Public," University of Michigan Working Paper 487 (1987a).

Ritter, J. "A Theory of Investment Banking Contract Choice," University of Michigan Working Paper 488 (1987b).

Rock, K. "Why New Issues Are Underpriced," *Journal of Financial Economics* 15 (1986) pp. 187-212.

Tinic, S. M. "Anatomy of Initial Public Offers of Common Stock," *Journal of Finance* 43 (1988) pp. 789-822.

Welch, I. "Seasoned Offering, Imitation Costs and the Underpricing of Initial Public Offerings," University of Chicago Working Paper (1988).

Article 13

AN INTRODUCTION TO MEZZANINE FINANCE AND PRIVATE EQUITY

by John R. Willis and David A. Clark, Continental Bank

The rapid growth of the mezzanine finance market in recent years is part of the restructuring movement that has swept across Corporate America in the 1980s. Although much corporate restructuring is taking place inside companies, the most visible signs of change are the leveraged transactions—the management buyouts, recapitalizations, and leveraged takeovers—that seem to receive daily attention from the press. Leveraged transactions, as their name suggests, involve the financing of a business operation with a relatively small amount of equity capital and a relatively large amount of debt. Mezzanine finance has become one of the two major financing tools for executing such highly leveraged transactions; the other, of course, is its better-known close cousin, high-yield ("junk") bonds.

Like junk bonds, mezzanine finance occupies a position in the middle level (hence the name "mezzanine") of the capital structure—that is, somewhere between the senior debt at the top and the common equity layer at the bottom. Also like many junk bond investments, a mezzanine investment often involves holdings in more than one position; it can take the form of subordinated debt, junior subordinated debt, or preferred stock (or some combination of the three), together with an equity-like claim such as a warrant.

Further like the junk bond market, the mezzanine market is flourishing because more operators and principals are seeking operating companies in which to invest, more institutions are willing to make large capital commitments for untraditional but highly promising investments, and more intermediaries have emerged to match operators with investors.

One clear result of this process is that operating companies seem to be commanding higher prices than ever before. Such acquisition premiums, combined with the desire to concentrate equity ownership in as few hands as possible, have led to a widening of the financing "gap" between the senior debt and the available conventional equity. In the larger deals, this gap has been closed by the evolution of the large, efficient public market for junk bonds. The private mezzanine market has arisen to meet the requirements of transactions in the small to middle market—those up to, say, $200 million.

In this article, we begin by providing a brief look at the history of leveraged transactions (also known as "structured financings"), compare the conventions and practices in the mezzanine finance market with those of the junk bond market, and then illustrate the mezzanine financing technique with two examples.

SOME BACKGROUND

The most direct line of descent from modern structured financings traces back to the old practice of new owner-managers' buying out the founder's interest in a business. Although certainly prevalent in the 1960s and before, such transactions were then primarily restricted to small firms seeking to ensure their continuity after the founder's departure, or at least to provide liquidity for the founder or his estate.

Up until the late 1960s, the financing for such old-fashioned management buyouts typically took the form of the "asset-based" bank loan. In such cases, the lending bank was typically fully secured by all of the firm's assets—most notably, receivables, inventory, and plant and equipment. But, as the size of these buyouts became progressively larger, asset-based loans became insufficient to fund the entire purchase price. And the market responded by creating, in effect, a new financing vehicle to overcome this obstacle. Some very aggressive insurance companies, in search of a higher risk-reward profile than the one provided by their customary secured investments, agreed to provide a portion of acquisition financing in the form of an unsecured subordinated loan in return for equity participation. Thus were the beginnings of mezzanine finance.

In the early 1970s, we also saw the beginnings of a practice that has reached full development in the 1980s: the sales by conglomerates of divisions or smaller operations to their line managers together with financial principals. As these deals got progressively larger, and as a parallel movement arose to take public companies private through leveraged buyouts, the demand for "intermediate" financing greatly expanded. A milestone was reached in 1979, when Kohlberg, Kravis & Roberts ("KKR") acquired Houdaille Industries for $343 million. This was the first such deal to exceed $100 million in financing. After the Houdaille transaction, market activity accelerated. Other major players such as Forstmann Little entered the field and buyouts in the range of $200-400 million became more and more common.

The development of the so-called "jumbo" deals did not occur until the 1983-1984 period, when corporate raiders began to emerge. The $1.5 billion recapitalization of Metromedia, although a slight variation on the theme of the LBO, was the largest transaction at the time. Since then, structured financings have become ever larger and more commonplace, culminating in KKR's recent acquisition of RJR-Nabisco for $24.8 billion.

What has brought about the growth of such leveraged transactions? There have been a number of factors at work, but some are clearly more fundamental to the process than others.

First, there was the emergence of firms like KKR and Forstmann Little that specialize in arranging such buyouts. In addition to these two premier firms, there are now scores more. The better-known names include Wesray and Clayton & Dubilier. Also, most of the major Wall Street firms such as First Boston, Morgan Stanley, Lazard Frères, Merrill Lynch, and Shearson Lehman Hutton have put together their own equity deal funds. To provide an indication of the current size of this market, KKR's fund exceeds $5.5 billion, Forstmann Little's has reached $2.5 billion and Lazard Frères' has surpassed $1.5 billion. The total amount of capital available for LBOs is now estimated at $30 billion.

A second major market force that has fueled the growth in structured financings has been the development of the "junk bond" market. This market has grown from around $8 billion in 1976 to well over $180 billion today. It seems clear that many of the large hostile transactions we have witnessed in recent years have been made possible only by the development of this market for publicly traded, subordinated, below-investment grade debt. Mezzanine finance, as we shall discuss later, has provided a means to finance relatively smaller transactions, and is typically used only in "friendly" transactions.

A third major element in the rise of structured financings was the tremendous amount of liquidity available within the international banking system. LBOs and other structured financings became a more attractive investment for banks than conventional alternatives such as loans to major U.S. corporations, to sovereign borrowers in developing countries, and to the real estate and oil and gas sector. Such untraditional bank investments in leveraged transactions have taken the forms of mezzanine finance and private equity, as well as the more familiar senior loans.

A fourth major element in the growth of leveraged transactions has been foreign investment in the U.S. The long decline in the dollar's value since its peak in early 1985 has led to a tremendous surge in the purchase of American companies by foreign corporations.

The factors we have described thus far all relate to the capital or "supply" side of the equation. What is really driving this large-scale mobilization of capital for leveraged transactions, however, are the perceived opportunities to earn large profits by recapitalizing and restructuring corporations. The presence of these opportunities, combined with the financial innovations that have allowed such transactions to take place, has put increasing pressure on corporate management to increase returns to shareholders. In some cases, this has meant corporate acquisitions of competitors with the aim of achieving consolidation within a shrinking industry, such as we have witnessed in the oil, tobacco, automotive, and food industries. It has also led, however, to the breaking up of large conglomerates into smaller pieces, most of which have been sold to single-industry firms if not to their own operating management.

An important result of this pressure from shareholder activists is an increasing trend for companies to recapitalize themselves to forestall the threat of takeover. For companies in mature businesses with lots of operating cash flow and more capital than they can profitably invest, recapitalizations that retire large amounts of stock with debt are an efficient means of returning capital to investors while increasing management's ownership of the equity. LBOs similarly provide incumbent management with a means of deflecting shareholder unrest while concentrating equity ownership.

Having offered this brief survey of leveraged transactions, let's now take a look at the role of the mezzanine market in financing corporate recapitalizations.

WHAT IS MEZZANINE FINANCE?...

A mezzanine issue, as stated earlier, occupies one or more intermediate positions in the corporate capital structure between the senior debt and the common equity. A mezzanine investment typically takes the form of subordinated debt, junior subordinated debt, or preferred stock (or some combination of each). It also virtually always includes equity participation in some form, whether as warrants, stock appreciation rights, or common stock.

It is almost always placed privately, and carries an intermediate term that ranges from 5 to 12 years. If it is entirely debt, a mezzanine issue generally carries a coupon of 400 to 700 basis points over treasuries, depending on the risk of the transaction, the degree of subordination, and market conditions. Mezzanine issues also have taken the form of securities that don't pay current cash interest—such as zero coupons and PIKs (payment in kind). And

because mezzanine finance also typically includes an equity component, the decision to invest in a mezzanine issue generally combines aspects of both a conventional credit decision and an investment decision.

In practice, a mezzanine issue is designed to fill the financing "gap" between the amount the senior lender will provide and the amount of equity capital the principal (and his backers) are able and willing to commit. From the issuer's standpoint, mezzanine finance may appear to be very expensive borrowing. But, because the decision to use mezzanine financing typically follows an understanding that the senior debt capacity has been exhausted, the issuer may choose to view it as inexpensive equity—since his only alternative may be to raise additional equity from outside sources and thus further dilute his ownership.

Neither of these perspectives on the "cost" of mezzanine finance tells the real, or at least the complete, story. In truth mezzanine finance is neither "expensive debt" nor "cheap equity." But, like the convertible bond issues they resemble, mezzanine issues occupy a middle ground between debt and common equity on the risk-reward spectrum; and, as such, their real "cost of capital" is considerably higher than that of senior debt, but considerably lower than that of straight equity.

In practice, mezzanine investors say they expect returns in the range of 20-30 percent. And, given that private investors in the equity alone typically look for annual returns around 35-50 percent, this 20-30 percent range can be taken as a reasonable estimate of the "cost" of mezzanine capital. Where investors' expectations fall within this range will likely depend on the risk of the transaction. The higher the proportion of equity promised, of course, the higher the expected return; and thus the higher the cost of the mezzanine capital.

...AND HOW DOES IT DIFFER FROM JUNK BONDS?

To provide a more detailed picture of the mezzanine finance market, let's set it against its "public" counterpart, the high-yield or junk bond market.

Junk bonds are typically public securities. The size of junk bond issues often exceeds $100 million and they trade in relatively liquid secondary markets. Investors in junk bonds include mutual funds, savings and loans, insurance companies, and pension funds.

Mezzanine issues, by contrast, are much smaller, and typically fall in the range of $3 to $40 million. They are privately placed or directly negotiated by the issuer with a private purchaser. And although the equity component will sometimes have registration rights, mezzanine investments are generally highly illiquid and bought with the expectation of being held until maturity. Because of this lack of liquidity, mezzanine issues are likely to have much tighter covenants limiting the issuer's flexibility to sell assets, take on additional debt, or distribute cash to investors. There are also typically stricter requirements for reporting and corporate maintenance than in the case of junk bond issues.

The junk bond market is, of course, far larger than the mezzanine market. Estimates by Drexel Burnham put the volume of outstanding junk bonds at the end of 1988 at roughly $180 billion. Although there are no reliable estimates of the size of the mezzanine market (because it is private), our best guess would fall in the range of $10-30 billion.

But if the sizes of the two markets are quite different, changes in the availability and cost of funding in the mezzanine market closely parallel those in the junk bond market. The correlation between conditions in these markets has been so strong that we can reasonably use the high-yield market as a surrogate for the mezzanine market.

As shown in Exhibit 1, the volume and cost (measured as a spread over treasuries) of junk bonds has proven to be sensitive to major "events," such as the stock market scandals and the stock market crash of 1987. It is also sensitive to sharp rises in interest rates as can been seen, for example, in April 1987. At such times, junk bond yields have risen dramatically and new issues have all but disappeared. But the market has also proved to be highly resilient, with yields and volume returning to normal levels in fairly short order. These developments, as suggested, have been mirrored by those in the mezzanine market.

Equity Participation

Unlike most junk bonds, mezzanine issues, as mentioned earlier, almost always include an equity component. Warrants are typically the preferred form of equity participation, by investors and issuers alike.

Let's take a moment to look at some of the major features of these warrants. Perhaps most important, the exercise price of these warrants is generally nominal. And thus the value of the warrant is at least equal in value to that of the common equity.

Although such warrants typically have a 10-year life, the targeted "exit horizon" is much shorter, generally in the range of 3 to 6 years. There are also generally put provisions that allow the investor to sell the warrants back to the issuer—as well as call provisions that allow the issuer to redeem them—well before maturity. A common arrangement gives the mezzanine investor a put option allowing it to "put" the warrants back to the issuer at an agreed-upon exit value beginning at the end of year 4. The exit value is usually based on the appraised value using a discounted cash flow formula or an agreed-upon multiple of operating income. In return for granting this put option, the issuer typically seeks to negotiate a call option —one that generally begins a year after the put option can first be exercised—to redeem the warrants for a price in the range of 100-110 percent of assessed fair market value. The mezzanine investor may also negotiate registration rights on its shares, as well as so-called "piggy back" registration rights allowing it to sell its shares along with an equity offering by the issuer.

THE CRITERIA

What kinds of companies are good candidates for mezzanine financing? Below is a list of criteria that we at the Continental Bank use in evaluating investment opportunities.

■ Companies with strong, proven operating management at key levels (either already in place or, if the key manager is selling, identified elsewhere).
■ Companies manufacturing and selling products which are not subject to rapid technological change.
■ Companies which manufacture a proprietary product and enjoy a strong market position either locally or nationally.
■ Companies whose manufacturing efficiencies establish them—or have the potential to establish them—among the "low-cost" producers within an industry.
■ Distribution concerns or companies that manufacture and sell products used in industrial markets. Some consumer products companies with widely accepted consumer use could also be considered, provided that an inordinate amount of advertising dollars are not required to keep the product visible.
■ Companies with cash flow predictability that are normally not subject to wide or prolonged cyclical swings in profitability.
■ Companies whose current balance sheet provides room for additional leverage in the new capital structure.

EXHIBIT 1

HIGH YIELD DEBT NON-
CONVERTIBLE BOND
OFFERINGS BY MONTH

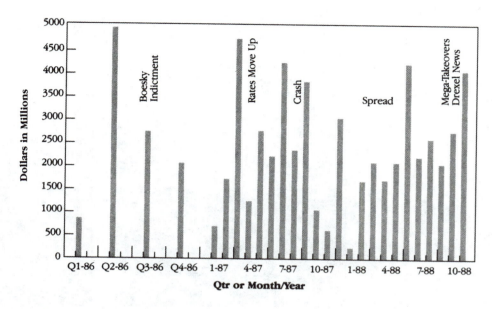

HIGH YIELD MARKET
(AVERAGE YIELD COMPARED TO
TEN YEAR TREASURY)

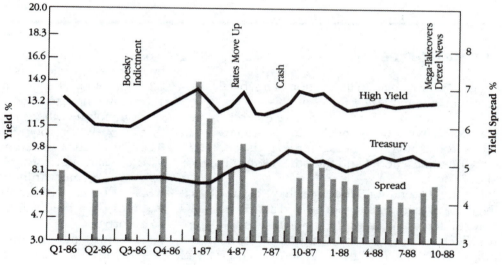

■ A purchase price, including existing debt, of not more than 8 times operating cash flow. Exceptions to this rule are made for turnaround opportunities or if a strong break-up program is an integral part of the logic of the acquisition.

■ Operations not subject to significant import threats or other unmanageable economic risks.

■ Companies which have demonstrated the ability to maintain acceptable margins even in economic downturns.

■ Companies with good asset quality and, preferably, a weighted balance in favor of current assets rather than large investment in fixed assets.

■ Companies that possess quantifiable liabilities.

EXHIBIT 2

EBIT (Operating) Model

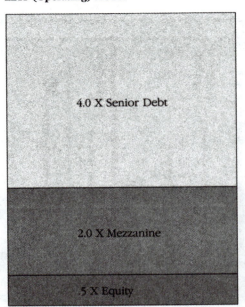

4.0 X Senior Debt

2.0 X Mezzanine

.5 X Equity

Capital Structure (Balance Sheet) Model

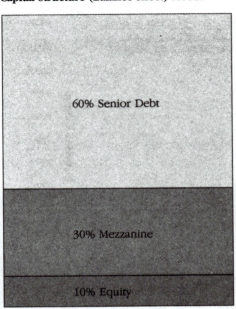

60% Senior Debt

30% Mezzanine

10% Equity

THE PROTOTYPE

Let's now turn to an illustration of a typical transaction involving mezzanine debt.

As shown in Exhibit 2, there are essentially two ways of viewing the standard capital structure that arises from a buyout. One is referred to as the "EBIT" or "Operating" Model and the other as the "Balance Sheet" Model.

In the "Operating" Model, we have assumed that the price paid for the buyout is fixed at 6.5X earnings before interest and taxes. (This pricing formula simply reflects the use of a "rule of thumb" —one that is modified, in practice, by considering a number of factors such as the stability of operating cash flows, the prospects for growth, and the current level of interest rates.) The amount of the senior debt is equal to 4X EBIT, the amount of mezzanine finance is half the amount of senior debt, or 2X EBIT, and the equity corresponds to the remaining fraction of the purchase price.

Expressed in terms of percentages, the senior capital thus represents slightly more than 60 percent of total capital, mezzanine finance accounts for just over 30 percent, and the remaining 8 percent or so is the equity layer. In this sense, the "Operating

Model" shown in Exhibit 2 has roughly the same financing proportions as the "Balance Sheet" model (also known in the industry as the standard "60-30-10") shown next to it.

Some of the other rules of thumb that fall out of the "60-30-10" prototype include the following:

■ Senior interest coverage of 1.75X EBIT
■ Total cash interest at 1.25 EBIT (which would apply to the mezzanine debt at the margin)
■ Senior bank debt amortization in 7-8 years
■ Senior debt paid out before junior debt begins to amortize
■ Mezzanine debt amortized in 10-12 years.

To show how these conventions might be applied, consider the simple case of XYZ company with revenues of $200 million and an EBIT of $20.5 million. Assuming the company is valued at about 6.5X EBIT, let's say the purchase price turns out to be $133 million. In this case, the "60-30-10" standard would produce a capital structure consisting of about $80 million in senior debt, $40 million in mezzanine finance, and $13 million in equity.

To make the example slightly more realistic, let's also assume that $20 million of the mezzanine debt is senior subordinated coupon debt, and that the other $20 million is junior subordinated PIK'd debt—

that is, it doesn't pay interest in cash, but instead increases the principal amount of the debt on which interest will eventually be paid.

Who would be the providers of capital in such a deal and what would be their expectations and requirements?

The most likely source of the senior debt are commercial banks. The interest rate would typically float (say, at LIBOR plus 2½ %) and closing fees would run about 2 percent. The debt would be amortized over a period no longer than 8 years, and the lenders would seek to reduce their exposure by taking security in the assets, requiring covenants subordinating other capital, and distributing part of the loan to other investors.

Sources of the mezzanine finance, whether the senior or the junior subordinated debt, would include the sellers themselves, both public and private "high yield" or "mezzanine" funds, LBO or other private equity funds, as well as most of the institutions providing senior debt. The senior subordinated debt would pay a fixed coupon 400-500 basis points over comparable treasuries as well as an equity participation (usually in the form of warrants). The debt would be unsecured, have limited covenant protection, and have a 10-12 year term (with some provision for exit after 3-7 years). Underwriting fees would run 2-4 percent.

The junior debt, in this case, pays no coupon (but instead makes payments in kind). The implied yield on the debt ranges from 600-800 basis points over treasuries; and the debt is likely to have warrants or be convertible into common stock. There is even less covenant protection, and fees run on the order of 2-5 percent.

Providers of the equity include, besides management, other private investors, public and private equity funds, insurance companies, pension funds, investment banks, and commercial banks. Such investors often seek board representation, have return expectations of 40-50 percent per annum, and look for a 3- to 7-year exit horizon.

In the above example, let's assume the negotiation process ends up producing the following capital structure (in millions):

Senior debt	$80	LIBOR + 2.5%
Mezzanine	$40	22-25% return expectations
Sub. Coupon Debt	$20	14.50% interest plus warrants
Sub. PIK Debt	$20	16.00% implied interest plus warrants
Outside equity	$12	40% return, 70% of company
Management	$1	50% return, 10% of company

Now, having outlined this hypothetical deal, the expectations of different investors, and the capital structure that has resulted from the negotiation process, let's see how such a deal might turn out. Assume that, after five years, the company is sold for the same 6.5X EBIT multiple for which it was originally purchased. If we also assume that EBIT has grown at a compounded rate of 10 percent per year, and thus increased from $20 to $33 million at the end of year 5, then the sale price turns out to be roughly $215 million.

Under this scenario, which could be characterized as a successful transaction, the returns to the various investors would be as follows. The senior debt of course earns its 2.5% over LIBOR (11.5% in this example) for five years. The subordinated coupon debtholders end up owning 6.6 percent of the company, and earn an annual IRR of 21 percent. The subordinated PIK debtholders end up owning 15% of the company, and earn an IRR of 27 percent. The outside equity, which ends up owning 67% of the company, earns an annual IRR of 49 percent. And management, on an original investment of $1 million, ends up owning 11% of the company, and earns an annual IRR of 69 percent.

A CASE STUDY IN MEZZANINE FINANCING

Having set forth some rules of thumb in the above illustration, let's now look at an actual example of a mezzanine financing—one that the Continental Bank recently had a hand in.

By way of background, our client is the manager of a West Coast radio broadcasting company owning four pairs (AM/FM) of stations. Two years earlier, the manager bought the stations together with an investor group. And, as a result of a limited initial investment and earn-out provisions, he had increased his ownership to 12 percent of the company.

Having achieved this level, the manager then became interested in buying out the investor group and acquiring a much larger stake in the company. We were asked to play a role both as adviser and as placement agent for both the senior and the junior debt in the transaction that eventually took place.

The equity investors were willing to be cashed out for a "fair" return. The manager and the investor group agreed on a purchase price of $45 million ($18 million for the equity, $26 million for debt repayment, and about $1million in fees), thus providing the equity investors a 45 percent rate of return over a period less than two years. Investors in the mezzanine debt would earn a return of 27 percent with the value of the coupon (PIK'd) plus warrants for 10 percent of the company.

An interesting aspect of this case was the fact that the subordinated PIK'd debt had a "window" in its no-call provision that allowed refinancing at the two-year point—and only then. Because this expensive debt could not later be refinanced, the principal had a strong incentive to "turn" the deal at the two-year mark; and this consideration in fact determined the timing of the buyout.

Working with financial institutions that arranged the senior financing, we devised a structure for the $45 million buyout that was as follows (in millions):

SOURCES		USES	
Cash	$ .75	Stock Purchase	$ 18.00
Bank Revolver	1.50	Debt Refinancing	25.80
Bank Term	28.50	Closing Costs	1.20
Mezz, PIK	14.25		
TOTAL	$ 45.00		$ 45.00

Note that this transaction was designed to be accomplished without the infusion of any additional outside equity (although the equity component associated with the mezzanine debt would amount to 30% of the company). The manager intended simply to roll his entire 12 percent stake into the deal. Based on the buyout price of $18 million for the 88 percent of the company owned by the investor group, the implied value of the manager's 12 percent was $2.2 million. But the manager felt that his equity was worth considerably more, and his reasoning was as follows: The trailing EBIT of the company was $4.5 million, and thus the purchase price of $47.2 million represented a multiple of 10.5X operating cash. Because the comparable multiple in sales of similar companies was in the 11-12X range, he wanted to capitalize the $4.5 million EBIT at 11.5 times to yield a value of $51.75 million for the entire firm. This $51.75 million value compares to a $47.2 million value for the entire firm. Therefore the implied value is an additional $4.5 million above the $2.2 million rolled into the deal, producing an implied equity value of almost $7 million.

Our job was to help the manager convince an equity-oriented mezzanine investor that this $7 million of implied equity was indeed real—and that the company's operations could support a capital structure with $45 million in debt. If we were unsuccessful, the principal would have had to attract additional equity capital—perhaps as much as $3 million, in which case the principal would have ended up owning about 33 percent of the company instead of the 100 percent (again, minus the implied 30 percent equity portion of the mezzanine) he wanted.

The deal modelled out as follows:

CAPITAL STRUCTURE (AS MULTIPLE OF OPERATING PROFIT)

	Actual		Implied	
	Amount	Multiple	Amount	Multiple
Senior Debt	$ 30.0	6.7X	$ 30.0	6.7X
Mezzanine	14.2	3.2X	14.2	3.2X
Equity	2.2	.5X	6.7	1.5X
		10.4X		11.4X

Using either the "implied" or the "actual" case, the debt-to-EBIT multiples are more aggressive than the 4/2/.5 prototype presented earlier (as they would have to be, given a purchase price of over 10X). And the coverage ratios, with senior interest coverage at 1.36 and total interest coverage, at .90, are also considerably lower than the standard 1.75 and 1.25.

Having structured the deal in this manner, we decided that while we would need to find both aggressive senior lenders and mezzanine investors, the real key to the deal would be in finding the right mezzanine player. We agreed to approach three insurance companies and three private mezzanine funds, all of which we identified as equity-oriented investors interested in the communications business. For the senior financing, we approached three regional banks and two industrial commercial finance companies.

After much negotiation and due diligence, we closed the deal largely on the terms outlined above. The senior financing was provided by a regional bank at 2½ percent over LIBOR, with some principal amortization and a balloon at 8 years. There was substantial covenant protection, security in all assets, and subordination (through both inter-creditor agreements and sub-debt documents) of all other claims. The mezzanine layer was provided by an insurance company, and involved an unsecured, subordinated PIK'd issue carrying a coupon of 15 percent and having a 10-year maturity. It also included warrants for 30 percent of the company.

As a result of the use of mezzanine financing, the manager acquired his company without giving up direct outside equity (although he will end up having the mezzanine investor as a 30 percent partner). His expectation is that he will earn over 100 percent per annum on his investment of 2.2 million, and that he will either sell or restructure the company in the next five years.

A CASE INVOLVING PRIVATE EQUITY

Our client in this case was a mid-western manufacturing company in a mature, slow-growth industry. The opportunity was brought to us by an operating professional with many years of experience in the industry. He had worked with the Continental Bank in his prior role as CEO of a much larger concern, and he now approached our equity group as a potential financial partner.

After reviewing the history and prospects of the company and its industry, we both structured and participated in the financing of the transaction. Also, because of the fragmented nature of the industry, we agreed to use the company as a vehicle to pursue strategic add-on acquisitions within the industry.

In valuing the company, we relied on their historical performance, industry and competitive analysis, extensive due diligence, and the input of our partner. Given the mature nature of the business, we believed that the target company's revenues would grow at a rate slightly in excess of inflation, with a reasonable increase in gross margins brought about by improvements in production and changes in the product mix. Operating margins were also expected to benefit from moderate reductions in G&A and better use of distribution channels.

In arriving at a purchase price we typically try to pay less than 7X trailing EBITA (earnings before interest, taxes, and amortization) for companies that are underperforming in their industry. In this case, we paid $63.6 million or 5.9X trailing EBIT (which also amounted to 7.5X the average EBIT of the preceding two years). We believed this to be a fair price for the business because of its predictable growth prospects, product reputation, and identifiable production enhancements and product mix changes.

Working with the senior and subordinated lenders, we devised a structure for the $63.6 million as follows:

SOURCES

	Amount	%
Senior Debt	$39.6	62.3%
Sen. Sub. Debt 14.25%	16.0	25.2%
Pref. Stock (10% PIK)	7.2	11.3%
Common Equity	0.8	1.2%
	63.6	100%

USES

	Amount	%
Purchase Price	30.8	48.4%
Existing Debt	26.2	41.1%
Fees	1.4	2.3%
Noncompete	5.2	8.2%
	63.6	100%

The senior debt carried a current interest rate of LIBOR plus 2.5%, with approximately 50 percent in the form of a revolving line of credit and the remainder in the form of a six-year term loan at LIBOR plus 3%. The EBITA senior interest coverage was 1.97X in year one, increasing to 5.53X by year five.

The subordinated debt had an eight-year life with a current interest rate of 14.25%. Total interest coverage was 1.36X in year one, rising to 3.02X by year five. The subordinated debt was scheduled to be repaid in three equal annual payments beginning in year six.

The subordinated debt also carried warrants for 15% of the company. To allow mezzanine investors to realize the value of those warrants, the investors were given the right to put them back to the issuer at the end of year 4 at their appraised market value. In return for this put option, the issuer was given a call option giving it the right to redeem the warrants at the end of year 5, again at appraised market value.

Based on an EBIT exit multiple of 6.5X, the mezzanine investors expected an internal rate of return on their investment of 22.4%. The table on the next page outlines the equity investment in the transaction together with the different investors' expectations.

The equity invested in the transaction was contributed in the following proportions: 10% by management, 30% by the investor, and 60% by an affiliate of Continental. In addition, management was given options to purchase an additional 5% of the company as a further incentive. Both the direct investment and the options granted management will vest according to a tenure- and performance-based formula over 5 years.

Contributed	Prfrd	Common	Fully Diluted Equity Ownership (1)	IRR (1)
Mezzanine	0.0	0.0	15.0% (2)	22.4%
Investor Group	2.1	0.3	30.0% (3)	54.0%
Continental	4.4	0.4	42.8% (3)	43.1%
Management	0.7	0.1	11.4% (4)	57.1%
	7.2	0.8	100.0%	

(1) Based on an exit multiple of 6.5X 5th-year EBIT.
(2) In the form of warrants
(3) As diluted by the mezzanine ownership and management options.
(4) Includes 5% management options exercised in year 5.

The deal was structured with preferred as well as common equity to provide our operating partners with a "capital appreciation carried interest," both for originating the deal and as partial compensation for their active management of the company on an ongoing basis. This is accomplished through the 9-to-1 preferred/common structure, which has the added virtue of ensuring that all parties are returned their invested capital before any carried interest is received.

The use of mezzine finance and private equity gave the operator the ability to leverage his own equity capital and to acquire control of this attractive company.

IN CLOSING

The mezzanine finance market is an important financing innovation that has arisen to fill the financing "gap" between the senior debt financing and the available equity financing in relatively small leveraged transactions—generally with purchase prices in the range of $25-250 million. By combining more conventional subordinated debt with PIK securities that pay no interest and with equity-like features such as warrants, mezzanine financing appears to have significantly enlarged the debt capacity of companies in mature businesses with stable cash flows. In so doing, it has also furthered an economy-wide movement toward greater concentration of ownership among operating managers and investor groups, which in turn is increasing corporate profits and efficiency.

■ JOHN WILLIS

is Senior Vice President of the Continental Bank and runs its Mezzanine Finance and Private Equity groups.

■ DAVID CLARK

is Vice President and works in the Bank's Private Equity Group.

Has Financial Market Volatility Increased?

By Sean Becketti and Gordon H. Sellon, Jr.

There is a widespread perception that financial market volatility has increased during the 1980s. While the collapse in stock prices in October 1987 has drawn the most attention, many investors and financial market analysts believe that the volatility of interest rates and exchange rates has risen as well.

If financial market volatility has increased, there may be important consequences for investors and policymakers. Investors may equate higher volatility with greater risk and may alter their investment decisions in light of increased volatility. Policymakers may be concerned that financial market volatility will spill over into the real economy and harm economic performance. Alternatively, policymakers may feel that increased financial volatility threatens the viability of financial institutions and the smooth functioning of financial markets.

Sean Becketti is a senior economist at the Federal Reserve Bank of Kansas City and Gordon H. Sellon, Jr. is an assistant vice president at the bank. Deana VanNahmen, a research associate at the bank, provided research assistance.

The purpose of this article is to examine the claim that financial volatility has increased in the 1980s. That is, are the volatilities of returns on stocks, bonds, and exchange rates historically high in the 1980s? The article finds that financial market volatility has indeed increased; yet the nature of the volatility, its magnitude, and its persistence are very different across markets.

The first section of the article examines why financial market volatility is important to investors and policymakers. The second section provides statistical evidence on the volatility of returns in the stock, bond, and foreign exchange markets. The third section discusses the response of investors and policymakers to increased financial volatility.

Why volatility matters

Financial markets and institutions play a key role in the economy by channeling funds from savers to investors. Some volatility in the prices of financial assets is a normal part of the process of allocating investable funds among competing uses. Excessive or extreme volatility of stock prices, interest rates, and exchange rates may be detrimental, however, because such volatility may impair the smooth functioning of the financial system and adversely affect economic performance.

Stock market volatility

Much of the recent concern over financial market volatility has centered on the stock market and the collapse in stock prices that occurred on October 19, 1987. The 508 point drop in the Dow-Jones average on October 19 was the largest one-day percentage drop in history. Stock market volatility of this magnitude could harm the economy through a number of channels.[1]

One way that stock price volatility hinders economic performance is through consumer spending. For example, immediately after the October 19 drop in stock prices, economic forecasters predicted sharply weaker economic growth. These analysts believed that the fall in stock prices would reduce consumer spending. The sizable fall in consumer wealth was expected to directly lower consumer spending. In addition, a weakening in consumer confidence could contribute to a further spending reduction.[2]

Stock price volatility may also affect business investment spending. Investors may perceive a rise in stock market volatility as an increase in the risk of equity investments. If so, investors may shift their funds to less risky assets. This reaction would tend to raise the cost of funds to firms issuing stock. Moreover, small firms and new firms might bear the brunt of this effect as investors gravitated toward the purchase of stock in larger, well-known firms.[3]

Extreme stock price volatility could also disrupt the smooth functioning of the financial system and lead to structural or regulatory changes. For example, the commissions studying the October 19 stock price collapse focused their attention on the stock-order execution and market-making systems. Systems that work well with normal price volatility may be unable to cope with extreme price changes. Indeed, the system itself may contribute to volatility if investors are unable to complete stock transactions. Changes in market rules or regulations may be necessary to increase the resiliency of the market in the face of greater volatility.[4]

Interest rate volatility

The 1980s have also seen increased concern over interest rate volatility. In the early 1980s, rising inflationary expectations, restrictive monetary policy, and removal of interest rate ceilings contributed to high and volatile interest rates. Like stock market volatility, extreme interest rate volatility may hurt economic performance and disrupt the smooth functioning of the financial system.

One way in which interest rate volatility may harm the economy is through business investment spending. Investors may see an increase in the volatility of interest rates as an increase in the risk of holding bonds and other debt instruments. If investors shift their portfolios toward lower risk assets, firms may find it more costly to fund investment projects. The resulting fall in investment spending would reduce economic growth.

Interest rate volatility could also have a direct impact on monetary policy. If higher rate volatility causes investors to change their investment portfolios, the demand for money may also change. To the extent that monetary policy is based on an assumed stable relationship between money and economic activity, changes in money demand due to rate volatility could complicate monetary policy.[5]

Greater interest rate volatility could also weaken the financial system if this volatility threatens the viability of financial intermediaries.[6] Increased interest rate volatility is a serious problem for depository intermediaries, such as savings and loans, that have long-term assets and short-term liabilities.[7] An increase in rate volatility can lead to periodic liquidity crises for some of these institutions and may threaten the solvency of others. Regulatory actions, such as an increase in capital requirements, may be necessary to protect these institutions from increased volatility of interest rates.

Exchange rate volatility

In 1973 the major industrialized countries abandoned the Bretton Woods system of fixed exchange rates in favor of a floating rate system. Since 1973 there has been continuing concern that exchange rate volatility under the new system might adversely affect international trade and capital flows.[8]

Like volatility in the stock market and interest rates, exchange rate volatility may create uncertainty about future profits, which impairs long-term investment decisions. Companies involved in international trade may be reluctant to commit to long-term investment projects if they fear that exchange rate changes might significantly reduce profits.

A second way that exchange rate volatility might impede international trade is through higher prices for exports and imports. If companies add a risk premium to the prices of internationally traded goods because of exchange rate uncertainty, consumers may reduce the amount of the higher priced goods they demand and slow the growth of world trade.

Finally, exchange rate variability may alter international capital flows. Long-term capital flows may be reduced by greater exchange rate uncertainty, impeding the efficient flow of resources in the world economy. At the same time, increased exchange rate volatility may promote short-term, speculative capital flows. These speculative capital flows may complicate monetary policy. Central banks may be forced to intervene frequently in exchange markets or to adjust monetary policy to prevent these capital flows from having adverse effects on the domestic economy.

Measuring financial market volatility

Because financial volatility matters to investors and policymakers, it is important to examine the claim that volatility has increased during the 1980s. This section presents evidence supporting the view that volatility has increased across financial markets in the 1980s. However, the nature, the magnitude, and the persistence of the increase in volatility differ across markets.

Stock market volatility

Most discussions of stock market volatility center on the large price movements on and around October 19, 1987. To put these events in proper perspective, however, it is useful to examine stock market volatility over a longer time span.

Viewing the stock market over a longer time horizon, some observers have concluded that the volatility of stock returns in the 1980s is not

CHART 1
Volatility of stock returns, 1918-88

Standard deviation

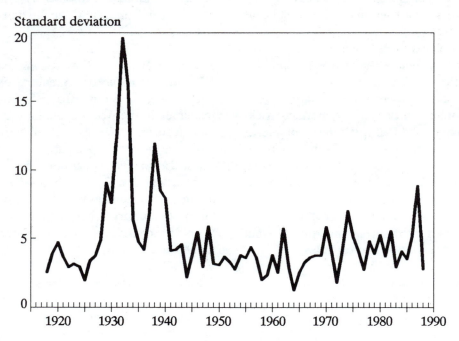

Note: In this chart, volatility is measured by the annual standard deviation of monthly stock returns. See endnote 9 for details.

Source: Center for Research in Security Prices.

unusual. For example, Chart 1 shows the volatility of stock returns from 1918 to 1988. The measure of volatility used in this chart is the annual standard deviation of the monthly returns in the Standard and Poor 500 Composite Stock Price Index.[9] According to this chart, record stock market volatility occurred in the 1930s. Compared with the 1930s, stock market volatility in the 1980s does not appear abnormal.[10]

The relevance of this extended historical comparison is open to question, however. Most observers regard the economic turbulence of the 1930s as an extraordinary historical episode, one unlikely to be repeated. Thus, a more recent

perspective on volatility may be in order. Examining Chart 1 from 1950 to 1988 shows that stock market volatility in 1987 was the highest in the postwar period.

Focusing on October 19, 1987, suggests a way of resolving these differing opinions on stock market volatility. The key feature of the October 19 period is the sharp one-day movements in stock prices. Stock prices fell 108 points on Friday, October 16, and an additional 508 points on October 19 before rising 102 points on October 20. In each case, stock price changes were considerably above normal daily price movements.

CHART 2

Normal volatility of stock returns, 1918-88

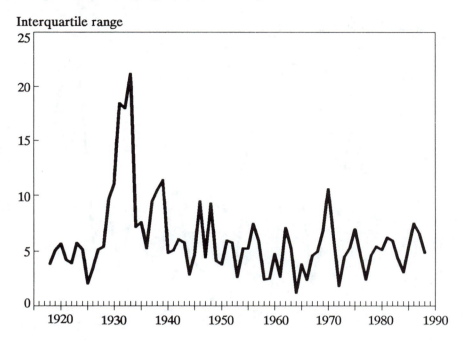

Interquartile range

Note: In this chart, volatility is measured by the annual interquartile range of monthly stock returns. See endnote 11 for details.

Source: Center for Research in Security Prices.

It is possible to think of stock market volatility as including two parts, normal volatility and jump volatility. Normal volatility refers to the ordinary variability of stock returns, that is, the ordinary ups and downs in returns. Jump volatility, on the other hand, refers to occasional and sudden extreme changes in returns.

An analogy may be useful in showing the distinction between normal volatility and jump volatility. The tidal rise and fall of the ocean resembles the normal volatility of stock returns. Tidal swings may be more or less pronounced at different times of the year, but tidal changes have a regularity and smoothness that capture the idea of normal volatility. Occasionally, however, violent weather or offshore earthquakes suddenly produce extreme changes in the level of the water and in the severity of wave actions. These disruptions are like jump volatility. In this analogy, the collapse of stock prices on October 19, 1987, was like a tidal wave.

Using a measure of normal volatility, there is no evidence that normal stock market volatility has increased in the 1980s. Chart 2 shows a measure of normal volatility that excludes extreme price changes.[11] By use of this measure, the volatility of stock prices is not historically high. Indeed, with this measure, peak stock

CHART 3
Frequency of jumps in stock returns, 1962-88

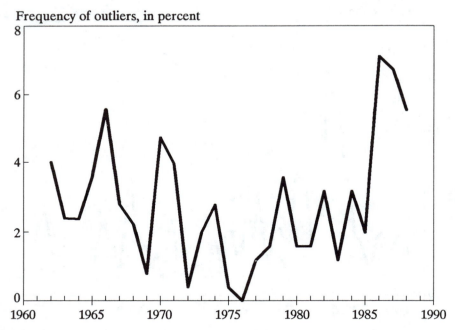

Frequency of outliers, in percent

Note: In this chart, volatility is measured by the percentage of days in each year that experienced unusually large daily stock returns, either negative or positive. See endnote 12 for details.

Source: Center for Research in Security Prices.

market volatility in the postwar period occurs in 1970, not 1987.

Jump volatility in the stock market, as measured by the frequency of extreme price changes, does seem to be higher in the 1980s, however. Chart 3 shows the percentage of daily stock returns that are extremely high or low in a given year.[12] According to this measure of volatility, the frequency of large stock price movements in 1987, as well as in 1986 and 1988, is considerably greater than in any other year since 1966. Thus, this measure of volatility suggests that jump volatility in stock returns may

have risen in the 1980s.[13] However, it should be noted that with only three years of increased volatility, additional evidence would be needed to support the view that there has been a permanent change in the jump volatility of stock returns.

Interest rate volatility

Unlike the mixed evidence regarding volatility in the stock market, all measures of interest rate volatility show sharply higher volatility in the 1980s. In the early 1980s, financial markets

CHART 4
Volatility of Treasury bill yields, 1926-87

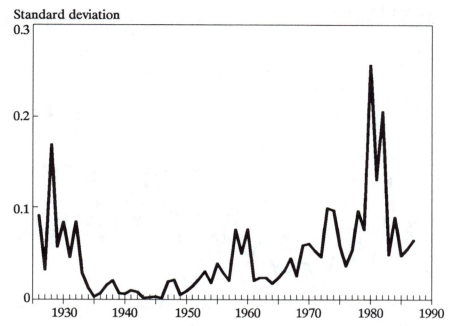

Standard deviation

Note: In this chart, volatility is measured by the annual standard deviation of monthly returns of a one-year Treasury bill index.

Source: Center for Research in Security Prices.

experienced large shifts in inflationary expectations, a change in monetary policy procedures that permitted greater short-term interest rate volatility, and widespread deregulation. These factors contributed to greater volatility of interest rates at all maturities.

The dramatic increase in the volatility of short-term interest rates during the 1980s is illustrated in Chart 4. This chart shows the annual standard deviation of the monthly returns on a one-year Treasury bill index from 1926 to 1987. As seen in this chart, short-term interest rate volatility reached record levels in the early

1980s. However, since 1982 volatility appears to have subsided to more normal levels. Thus, the increase in the volatility of short-term interest rates in the early 1980s appears to have been a temporary phenomenon.

In contrast, the increased volatility of long-term interest rates in the 1980s has been sustained. Chart 5 shows the volatility of returns on 20-year Treasury securities from 1926 to 1987.[14] According to this chart, the volatility of long-term interest rates shifted upward once in the late 1960s and early 1970s, and volatility increased again in the early 1980s. Moreover,

CHART 5
Volatility of Treasury bond yields, 1926–87

Standard deviation

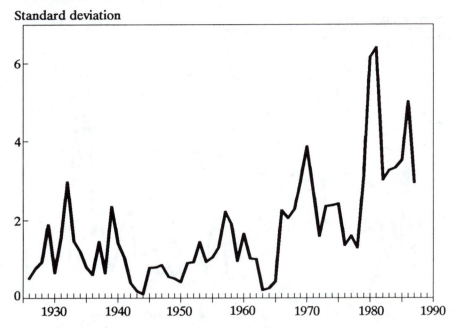

Note: In this chart, volatility is measured by the annual standard deviation of monthly returns of a 20-year Treasury bond index.

Source: Center for Research in Security Prices.

although volatility has fallen from the 1981-82 peak, it remains historically high. Unlike volatility of short-term interest rates, the volatility of long-term rates in the 1980s seems to be permanently higher.

Exchange rate volatility

The measurement and interpretation of exchange rate volatility are more complicated than for stock and bond markets. Historically, exchange rates have been subject to considerable governmental controls. In the postwar period,

for example, there have been two major exchange rate regimes, the Bretton Woods system of fixed exchange rates from 1946 to 1972, and a system of floating exchange rates since 1973. Moreover, during the floating-rate period, governments have intervened at times to stabilize foreign exchange markets or to realign currency relationships.

In moving from a fixed to a flexible system of exchange rates, exchange rate volatility should rise. Indeed, as shown in Chart 6, volatility after 1973 is significantly greater than in the earlier postwar period.[15] However, many analysts

CHART 6

Volatility of the dollar/pound exchange rate, 1950-88

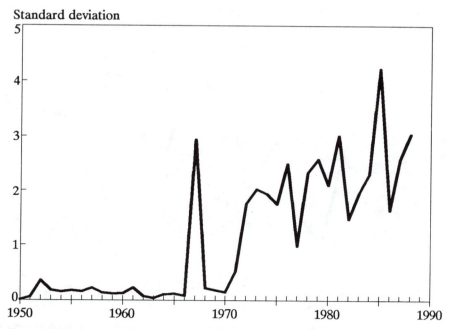

Standard deviation

Note: In this chart, volatility is measured by the annual standard deviation of monthly percentage changes in the nominal U.S. dollar/pound sterling exchange rate.

Source: Board of Governors, Financial Markets section.

expected increased volatility to be temporary until foreign exchange traders adapted to the new system. Chart 6 shows that, contrary to expectations, exchange rate volatility has shown no tendency to diminish after 1973.

A closer look at the 1973-88 floating-rate period suggests that exchange rate volatility actually increased further during the 1980s. Chart 7 shows the volatility of the trade-weighted value of the dollar.[16] Dividing the period at 1980 demonstrates that the average volatility of the dollar, shown by the horizontal line, is higher in the 1980s than in the 1970s.[17]

Thus, in the foreign exchange market as in the stock and bond markets, there is evidence of greater financial volatility in the 1980s.

Responses to increased financial volatility

In the presence of increased financial market volatility, investors may alter their investment strategies, and policymakers may pursue regulatory reforms. Investors have two options to cope with greater volatility. They can shift their investment portfolios toward less risky assets,

CHART 7
Volatility of the trade-weighted dollar, 1974-88

Standard deviation

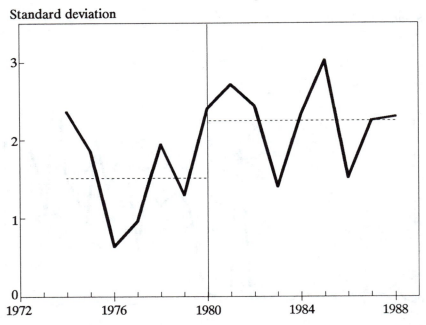

Note: In this chart, volatility is measured by the annual standard deviation of monthly percentage changes in the index of the nominal trade-weighted value of the dollar published by the staff of the Board of Governors. The horizontal dashed lines show the average volatility of the dollar before and after 1980.

Source: Board of Governors, Financial Markets section.

or they can attempt to immunize the value of their portfolios. Policymakers can also pursue either of two options. They can try to reduce volatility directly, or they can assist financial markets and institutions in adapting to increased volatility. Some investors have attempted to adjust to volatility by restructuring their portfolios. An example is the sharp drop in stock purchases by individual investors after October 19, 1987. Individual investors reduced their direct purchases of stocks and also shifted away from stock mutual funds. As a consequence, retail stock brokerages and mutual funds have

experienced reduced profitability and have scaled back operations and employment.

In the face of a general increase in financial volatility, however, investors may find it difficult to protect themselves through portfolio restructuring. For example, investors have generally considered bonds to be less risky than stocks. With increased stock market volatility, investors might prefer to shift into bonds. However, as shown in the previous section, bond market volatility has increased dramatically in the 1980s. Indeed, as shown in Chart 8, the unprecedented upsurge in volatility in the 1980s

CHART 8
Volatility of stock returns and Treasury bond yields

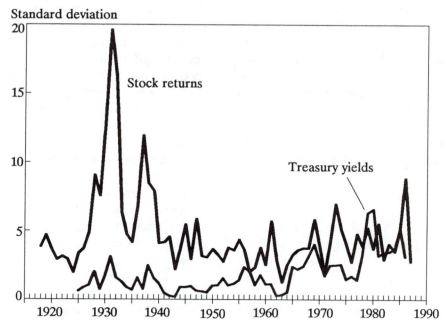

Standard deviation

Note: In this chart, volatility is measured by the annual standard deviations of monthly stock returns and 20-year Treasury bond returns.

Source: Center for Research in Security Prices.

has made fixed income investments as risky as stocks. In this environment, risk averse investors may be inclined to move away from any type of long-term investment.

The 1980s have also seen explosive growth in hedging and immunization strategies by individual and institutional investors. Individual investors, corporations, and financial institutions are increasingly using interest rate futures, swaps, and options for protection against greater interest rate volatility.[18] Similarly, stock index futures and options are now widely employed to manage stock market volatility.[19] And, cor-

porations and other institutions involved in international trade now use similar instruments to reduce their exposure to exchange rate volatility.

For the most part, policymakers have shown little inclination to attempt to reduce financial volatility directly. For example, proposals to reduce interest rate volatility and stock market volatility through regulation have received little support. Moreover, although governments have intervened in foreign exchange markets to prevent disorderly markets, they have generally rejected proposals to return to a system of fixed exchange rates.

In contrast, policymakers have attempted to increase the ability of financial markets and institutions to adapt to greater volatility.[20] For financial institutions directly exposed to increased volatility, such as depository institutions and market makers, policymakers have encouraged greater capitalization. Increased capital allows these institutions to weather greater financial volatility without incurring the liquidity and solvency problems that might disrupt the functioning of financial markets.

Summary and conclusions

The 1980s have seen increased volatility in many financial markets. The nature of the volatility, its magnitude, and its persistence differ across markets. In the stock market, there is no evidence that normal stock return volatility is different in the 1980s than in previous periods. The frequency of large one-day price movements, however, is considerably higher in each of the past three years.

The volatility of interest rates at all maturities increased sharply at the beginning of the 1980s. The volatility of short-term rates has since declined to historical levels. However, the volatility of long-term rates has continued to be unusually high. Indeed, during the 1980s the volatility of returns on long-term Treasury securities has been as great as stock volatility.

Exchange rate volatility has been considerably higher during the flexible-rate system than under the pre-1973 regime of fixed exchange rates. Even so, exchange rate volatility during the 1980s is generally higher than in the early years of floating exchange rates.

Investors and policymakers have had to adapt to increased financial volatility. Investors have shown some evidence of shifting toward less risky, short-term assets. Investors have also made increasing use of hedging and other portfolio immunization strategies. For the most part, policymakers have resisted pressures to reduce financial volatility directly through increased regulation. Instead, policymakers have attempted to improve the ability of financial markets and institutions to weather increased volatility.

Endnotes

[1] For an overview of some of the channels by which the stock market might affect the economy, see Bryon Higgins, "Is a Recession Inevitable This Year?" *Economic Review,* Federal Reserve Bank of Kansas City (January 1988), pp. 3-16.

[2] For evidence on the impact of the fall in stock prices on consumer spending, see C. Alan Garner, "Has the Stock Market Crash Reduced Consumer Spending?" *Economic Review,* Federal Reserve Bank of Kansas City (April 1988), pp. 3-16.

[3] A discussion of how financial fluctuations affect the economy is found in Mark Gertler and R. Glenn Hubbard, "Financial Factors in Business Fluctuations," *Financial Market Volatility* (Federal Reserve Bank of Kansas City, 1989), pp. 33-72.

[4] Two widely cited reports on the October 1987 stock market decline are: U.S. Presidential Task Force on Market Mechanisms, *Report of the Presidential Task Force on Market Mechanisms,* Washington, D.C., January 1988; and Working Group on Financial Markets, *Interim Report of the Working Group on Financial Markets,* Washington, D.C., May 1988.

[5] For evidence on the linkage between interest rate volatility and money demand, see C. Alan Garner, "Does Interest Rate Volatility Affect Money Demand?" *Economic Review,* Federal Reserve Bank of Kansas City (January 1986), pp. 25-37.

[6] The implications of greater interest rate volatility for financial institutions are discussed in Charles S. Morris, "Managing Interest Rate Risk with Interest Rate Futures," *Economic Review,* Federal Reserve Bank of Kansas City (March 1989), pp. 3-20. Potential costs of interest rate volatility are also discussed in Raymond Lombra and Frederick Struble, "Monetary Aggregate Targets and the Volatility of Interest Rates: A Taxonomic Discussion," *Journal of Money, Credit and Banking* (August 1979), pp. 284-300.

[7] A more detailed discussion of interest rate risk and savings and loans is contained in Charles S. Morris and Thomas J. Merfeld, "New Methods for Savings and Loans to Hedge Interest Rate Risk," *Economic Review,* Federal Reserve Bank of Kansas City (March 1988), pp. 3-15.

[8] See, for example, Keith E. Maskus, "Exchange Rate Risk and U.S. Trade: A Sectoral Analysis," *Economic Review,* Federal Reserve Bank of Kansas City (March 1986), pp. 3-15.

[9] The data in Chart 1 are obtained from the Center for Research in Security Prices (CRSP). These returns are the nominal monthly percentage capital gain in the Standard & Poor's index of 500 stocks. These returns exclude dividend yields. Statistics for the returns including dividend yields are virtually identical to those displayed in Chart 1.

The measure of volatility pictured in Chart 1 and in most of the succeeding charts is the annual standard deviation of monthly returns. This is a measure of the dispersion of monthly returns about the average return for each year. More precisely, if $r_{i,t}$ is the return for month i in year t and $\bar{r}_t$ is the average monthly return in year t, then the annual standard deviation of monthly returns for that year is

$$\sigma_t = \left(\frac{\sum_{i=1}^{12} (r_{i,t} - \bar{r}_t)^2}{11} \right)^{1/2}$$

For a more detailed look at the distribution of stock returns after 1949, see *"Stock Market Volatility,"* Carolyn D. Davis and Alice P. White, Staff Study No. 153, Board of Governors of the Federal Reserve System, August 1987.

[10] This finding that the stock market volatility of the 1980s is not unusually high when compared with the volatility of the 1930s is also reported in Robert J. Shiller, "Causes of Changing Financial Market Volatility," with *Financial Market Volatility* (Federal Reserve Bank of Kansas City, 1989), pp. 1-22.

[11] To measure normal volatility, what statisticians call a robust measure of scale is required. The statistic displayed in Chart 2 is the fourth spread, a statistic that is essentially the same as the interquartile range, the distance between the 25th and 75th percentile of the monthly returns within the year. For an explanation of the fourth spread and of its superiority to the standard deviation in measuring normal volatility, see Boris Iglewicz, "Robust Scale Estimators and Confidence Intervals for Location," *Understanding Robust and Exploratory Data Analysis,* edited by David C. Hoaglin, Frederick Mosteller, and John W. Tukey (New York: John Wiley & Sons, Inc., 1983). Note that in the special case where returns are normally distributed,

fourth spread $\approx 1.35\sigma_t$.

12 The measure of jump volatility depicted in Chart 3 is related to the measure of normal volatility shown in the previous chart. First, the fourth spread of the daily returns for each year is calculated. Then, two critical values, the upper and lower adjacent values, are calculated as follows:

upper adjacent value = 75th percentile + 1.5 (fourth spread)
lower adjacent value = 25th percentile − 1.5 (fourth spread)

Any daily returns that are either higher than the upper adjacent value or lower than the lower adjacent value are classified as outliers, that is, as extremely high or low returns relative to the rest of the daily returns in that year. Chart 3 displays for each year the number of outliers divided by the number of trading days in the year, that is, the percentage of daily stock returns that are unusually high or low. The statistical justification for this measure of outliers is discussed in David C. Hoaglin and Boris Iglewicz, ''Fine-Tuning Some Resistant Rules for Outlier Labeling,'' *Journal of the American Statistical Association*, vol. 82 (December 1987), pp. 1147-49.

13 This finding is consistent with the statistics reported in Steven P. Feinstein, ''Stock Market Volatility,'' *Economic Review*, Federal Reserve Bank of Atlanta (November/December 1987), pp. 42-47. Feinstein finds no evidence for a recent increase in the volatility of stock returns when the measure of volatility is the absolute monthly return. On the other hand, when the measure of volatility is the monthly standard deviation of daily returns, the 13 months from October 1986 through October 1987 do exhibit abnormal volatility. It is well known that the standard deviation is extremely sensitive to outliers, in this case, to jumps in daily returns.

14 The volatility of Treasury bonds is measured as the annual standard deviation of the monthly returns on a 20-year con-stant maturity Treasury bond index.

15 The volatility of exchange rates in this chart is measured as the annual standard deviation of the monthly return on the U.S. dollar/pound sterling exchange rate.

16 The volatility of the exchange rate in this chart is calculated using the index of the trade-weighted value of the dollar published by the staff of the Board of Governors. Because this measure begins in 1967, it was not used to make the longer historical comparison in Chart 6.

17 The difference in average volatilities of the trade-weighted dollar pictured in Chart 7 is statistically significant at the 5 percent level. Greater exchange rate volatility in the 1980s is also reported in Jacob A. Frenkel and Morris Goldstein, ''Exchange Rate Volatility and Misalignment: Evaluating Some Proposals for Reform,'' *Financial Market Volatility* (Federal Reserve Bank of Kansas City, 1989), pp. 185-219.

18 See, for example, Morris, ''Managing Interest Rate Risk . . . ''; Morris and Merfeld, ''New Methods for Savings and Loans . . . ''; and Gregg Whittaker, ''Interest Rate Swaps: Risk and Regulation,'' *Economic Review*, Federal Reserve Bank of Kansas City (March 1987), pp. 3-13.

19 For an introduction to stock index futures and their use as hedging instruments, see Charles S. Morris, ''Managing Stock Market Risk with Stock Index Futures,'' *Economic Review*, Federal Reserve Bank of Kansas City (June 1989), pp. 3-16.

20 There has also been increased recognition by policymakers that stable macroeconomic policies contribute to financial market stability. See, for example, Craig Hakkio, ''Exchange Rate Volatility and Federal Reserve Policy,'' *Economic Review*, Federal Reserve Bank of Kansas City (August 1984), pp. 18-31.

Article 15

Capital Market Efficiency: An Update[*]

Stephen F. LeRoy

Professor, University of California, Santa Barbara, and Visiting Scholar, Federal Reserve Bank of San Francisco. Members of the editorial committee were Adrian Throop, Michael Keeley, and Jonathan Neuberger.

Statistical evidence accumulated in the 20 years following Eugene Fama's (1970) survey raises questions about his conclusion that capital markets are efficient. Stock price volatility has been shown to exceed the volatility consistent with capital market efficiency. Other evidence —for example, the small-firm effect, the January effect, and other calendar-based anomalies of stock prices— points in the same direction. Finally, analysts find it difficult to explain stock prices even after the fact using realized values of variables which, according to efficient capital markets theory, should account for stock price changes.

Economist 1:   *"That looks like a $100 bill over there on the sidewalk."*

Economist 2:   *"Don't bother going over to check it out. If it were genuine, someone would have picked it up already."*

The theory of efficient capital markets says, most simply, that the prices of financial assets equal the discounted value of the expected cash flows these assets generate. In the context of the stock market, efficiency implies that stock prices equal the discounted value of expected future dividends. Investors are not assumed to form perfectly accurate forecasts of future dividends, but they are assumed to make effective use of whatever information they have. If capital markets are efficient in this sense, changes in stock prices should be associated exclusively with new information leading to revisions in expected future dividends: when dividend prospects improve, stock prices rise, and conversely.

Moreover, since all relevant, publicly available information is discounted in asset prices as soon as it becomes available, investors cannot construct systematically profitable trading rules based only on this information. Thus, in an efficient market there is no motive to buy stock based on favorable information; if the information is in fact favorable, the market already has discounted it. In other words, the $100 bill above could not be genuine; otherwise, it would have been picked up already.

These observations suggest that factors not identifiable with future profitability—fads, nonrational speculative bubbles, investor psychology—should not affect stock prices. In this regard, the stock market selloff on October 19, 1987, offers dramatic evidence that capital markets may not be efficient. On that single day, stock values declined by approximately a half trillion dollars, a magnitude unprecedented in absolute terms. In relative terms the selloff was comparable only to the stock market panic of October 1929 which heralded the Great Depression.

According to the efficient markets theory, the selloff could have been caused only by information made available that day (or over the preceding weekend since October 19, 1987, was a Monday) that justified a downward revision on the order of 22 percent in the present discounted value of expected future dividends. However, no economic information of an even mildly unusual nature was made public that day, let alone information that would drastically increase investors' estimates of the probability of an impending economic cataclysm. It is true that investors were worried about recession, but no more than they usually are. In any event, whatever fears of recession investors had subsequently proved unfounded, as the economy showed virtually no ill effects following the stock market collapse.

Moreover, the partial recovery of stock prices in the days following the selloff can only be reconciled with the efficient markets model if the recovery could be associated with economic news inducing investors to believe that the impending recession would, after all, not be as severe as the news that led to the selloff had indicated. Again, however, no economic news of the requisite importance was reported during the week of October 19.

This is not to say that stock price changes on the order of ten or twenty percent, even over a period as short as several days, are never associated with changes of commensurate magnitude in fundamentals. Following the June 1989 suppression of student protests in China, stock prices in Hong Kong dropped by a magnitude comparable in relative terms to the U.S. selloff in October 1987. The connection between political conditions in China and the role of Hong Kong firms in the Chinese economy is so strong that a stock price change on the order of twenty percent is not an obviously disproportionate response to the news that the Chinese government opted to suppress rather than accommodate the liberalization that the students were advocating. Therefore, there is no clear conflict between market efficiency and the selloff that occurred on the Hong Kong exchange in June 1989.

A single dramatic event like the October 19, 1987, selloff, however, does not invalidate the most important prediction of the efficient markets theory, which is that there should not exist trading rules that allow investors systematically to outperform the market. Research conducted in the 1960s and reported in Fama (1970) generally supported this implication, leading financial economists to conclude that capital market efficiency was corroborated empirically.

The more recent evidence, however, does not substantiate Fama's verdict. Detailed analysis using financial data bases developed in the 1970s, and drawing on a more extensive understanding of the empirical implications of market efficiency than was available in 1970, suggests that the October 19, 1987, selloff was not an isolated episode (although, of course, it was virtually unprecedented in magnitude). Instead, the evidence now suggests that most fluctuations in stock prices cannot be traced to changes in rational forecasts of future dividends, contrary to the prediction of the efficient markets model.

The new evidence arises from two areas of research which developed largely independently. First, analysts realized about fifteen years ago that market efficiency implied an upper bound on the volatility of stock prices. Empirical tests suggest that this bound is violated, indicating that stock prices are more variable than is consistent with market efficiency. Second, beginning about the same time analysts came to realize that stock returns display a variety of systematic patterns that are difficult to explain within a framework of rational optimization. The "variance-bounds" and "anomalies" literatures are surveyed in this paper.

Some economists view the updated evidence on market efficiency as demonstrating that the theory of efficient capital markets is wrong, and that investors are simply not as rational as efficient markets theory assumes. If so, it follows that capital markets are probably not doing a good job of resource allocation. Most economists, however, start out with a strong commitment to the assumption that people act rationally, and these economists will not reject the efficient markets model—and with it, the presumption that capital markets are doing a reasonably good job of allocating capital—unless confronted with absolutely airtight evidence against efficiency. None of the evidence reported in this paper meets such an exacting standard. Therefore those who start out with a strong predisposition in favor of capital market efficiency interpret the recent evidence as perhaps raising questions about the theory and suggesting topics for future research, but not as justifying definitive rejection.

I. The Efficient Markets Model

Contrary to the impression given above, the efficient markets model does not start out assuming that asset values equal the present value of expected future cash flows. Rather, the present-value representation is derived from the more primitive assumption that the rate of return r_{jt} on the j-th stock (more generally, the j-th asset) satisfies:

$$E\left(r_{jt} \mid I_t\right) = \rho \tag{1}$$

Here I_t comprises investors' information at t; $E(.|I_t)$ denotes the mathematical expectation of $(.)$ conditional on I_t; ρ, the expected rate of return on stock, is a positive constant, on the assumption that capital markets are perfect and investors are risk-neutral. Equation (1) says that an investor with information I_t will predict an expected rate of return equal to ρ for any asset. Since this is the same prediction that an uninformed investor would make, the efficient markets model implies that the information set I_t is useless in predicting expected rates of return. In this sense information I_t is "fully reflected" in securities prices.

For example, suppose that I_t contains the history of dividends, earnings, sales, advertising outlay, and costs for firm j up to date t, and possibly also macroeconomic variables like GNP, interest rates, commodity prices, and the money stock. Equation (1) says that no matter what values the variables in I_t take on, asset prices will depend on these values in such a way that the expected rate of return on the j-th asset is always ρ. If so, an investor who knows dividends, earnings, and so on is no better off than an investor who does not know the past history of these variables since the uninformed investor can always predict an expected rate of return of ρ without knowing I_t and is assured that his prediction will coincide with that of the informed investor, who predicts an expected rate of return of ρ for all values of I_t.

If at each date the expected rate of return on each asset is ρ, it follows that the expected rate of return on any portfolio is also ρ, since the expected rate of return on a portfolio is just a weighted average of the expected rates of return on its component securities. Accordingly, no trading rules based on information I_t can generate an expected rate of return greater than ρ. Of course, an investor in possession of information better than "the market's" information I_t could use this information to detect differentials in expected rates of return among the various assets, and consequently could construct profitable trading rules. However, efficient markets theory postulates that there do not exist investors with information better than the market's information, or more realistically, that if such investors exist, they do not affect prices.

Fama (1970) distinguished three versions of market efficiency depending on the specification of the information set I_t. Markets are "weak-form efficient" if I_t comprises past returns alone, "semi-strong-form efficient" if I_t comprises all publicly available information, and "strong-form efficient" if I_t includes insider information as well as publicly-available information.[1] It is clear that strong-form efficiency implies semi-strong form efficiency, which in turn implies weak-form efficiency, since expected returns that cannot be predicted based on a large information set surely cannot be predicted based on a small information set that is contained in the large information set. However, the reverse implications do not follow; a capital market easily could be weak-form efficient but not semi-strong-form efficient, or semi-strong-form efficient but not strong-form efficient.

The efficient markets model (1) says that rates of return on stock are unpredictable. It might appear to follow that the efficient markets model implies that stock prices are completely without structure, but that is not the case. In fact, the efficient markets model turns out to be exactly the same model as the present-value relation with which the efficient capital markets model was identified in the introduction. The derivation of this equivalence follows. Because (one plus) the rate of return is by definition equal to the sum of the dividend yield (d_t/p_t) and the rate of capital gain (p_{t+1}/p_t), (1) can be rewritten as:

$$p_t = \frac{E\left(d_{t+1} + p_{t+1} \mid I_t\right)}{1 + \rho} \tag{2}$$

Substituting $t+1$ for t, (2) becomes:

$$p_{t+1} = \frac{E\left(d_{t+2} + p_{t+2} \mid I_{t+1}\right)}{1 + \rho} \tag{3}$$

Using (3) to eliminate p_{t+1} in (2), the price of stock can be written:[2]

$$p_t = \frac{E_t\left(d_{t+1}\right)}{1 + \rho} + \frac{E_t\left(d_{t+2} + p_{t+2}\right)}{(1 + \rho)^2} \tag{4}$$

Here $E_t(.)$ is used as an abbreviated notation for $E(.|I_t)$. Proceeding similarly $n-1$ times, there results:

$$p_t = \frac{E_t\left(d_{t+1}\right)}{1 + \rho} + \frac{E_t\left(d_{t+2}\right)}{(1+\rho)^2} + \cdots + \frac{E_t\left(d_{t+n-1}\right)}{(1 + \rho)^{n-1}}$$
$$+ \frac{E_t\left(p_{t+n} + d_{t+n}\right)}{(1 + \rho)^n} \tag{5}$$

Assuming that $(1 + \rho)^{-n} E_t(p_{t+n})$ converges to zero as n approaches infinity, (5) becomes the familiar present-value equation:

$$p_t = \frac{E_t(d_{t+1})}{1 + \rho} + \frac{E_t(d_{t+2})}{(1 + \rho)^2} + \frac{E_t(d_{t+3})}{(1 + \rho)^3} + \ldots . \tag{6}$$

Further, the proof is completely reversible, implying that if the present-value relation (6) is satisfied, so is the efficient markets model (1). Samuelson (1965, 1973) and Mandelbrot (1966) were the first to state this result and to point out its relevance to efficient-markets theory.

What is striking here is that even though dividend changes in (6) can be partly forecast, the generating equation (1) implies that rates of return cannot be forecast. For example, if "the market" expects dividends to rise, the price of stock will be high relative to dividends now, so that when dividends do rise, no extra-normal return will be generated. Stockholders will earn extra-normal (sub-normal) returns only if dividends increase more (less) than had been expected. Thus if capital markets are efficient, a general expectation of a dividend increase does not imply that stocks should be bought (or, for that matter, sold), since the expected increase is already reflected in market prices.

This similarity between the efficient markets model and the "fundamentalist" model means that the much-publicized feud between Wall Streeters, who analyze stocks by computing discounted cash flows, and efficient marketers, who believe that rates of return cannot be forecast, is largely based on misunderstanding. The fundamentalist model focuses on the predictable part of prices, whereas the efficient markets model focuses on unpredictable returns, but the mathematical equivalence between the two models guarantees that there is no inconsistency.

However, the dispute is not entirely without substance: fundamentalists do not assert that prices are exactly equal to the discounted value of future dividends, but rather that prices fluctuate around the discounted value of future dividends. This apparently trivial difference is essential, since only in the latter case can profits be made by buying stocks that are priced lower than fundamentals justify, and selling stocks that appear to be overpriced. If underpriced and overpriced securities do not exist, as advocates of the efficient markets model maintain, then such trading strategies cannot succeed.

In deriving the expected present-value equation (6) from the efficient capital markets model (1), it was necessary to assume that $(1 + \rho)^{-n} E_t(p_{t+n})$ converges to zero as n

approaches infinity. This convergence assumption means that price is expected to grow more slowly than the rate at which future returns are discounted. Violation of the convergence assumption would mean that there exist speculative bubbles: even though price exceeds the discounted value of expected dividends, investors are willing to hold stocks because they anticipate that price will exceed expected dividends by an even wider margin in the future.

It is known that, in theory, speculative bubbles can exist even in simple models in which agents are assumed to be rational and to have identical preferences and endowments, and in which there is no uncertainty (Gilles-LeRoy 1989). In such countries as Japan, where stocks routinely trade at prices 50 times earnings (although such figures are difficult to interpret because accounting practices are different in Japan from those in the U.S.), it is plausible that speculative bubbles are an important determinant of stock prices. However, the same is probably not true of the U.S., where stocks trade at price-earnings multiples on the order of 10 or 15. It is not easy to devise empirical tests which can reliably detect the presence of bubbles. However, one particularly simple kind of bubble would, if it occurred, result in a sustained downward trend in the dividend-price ratio as stock prices rose without limit. Data for the dividend-price ratio in the U.S. do not display any downward trend. The absence of trend in the dividend-price ratio led West (1988a), for example, to conclude that speculative bubbles are probably not an important component of U.S. stock values.

The expected present-value model often strikes people as highly implausible. Many investors do not even consider dividend levels in their investment decisions. Instead they buy stocks that are believed likely to appreciate. Further, the stocks of many firms which do not pay, and have never paid, dividends command high prices. The proposition that rates of return cannot be forecast, on the other hand, is very appealing: the negation of (1) has the unattractive implication that there exists some information variable known to investors which they can use to construct systematically profitable trading rules. Yet the mathematical equivalence of (1) and (6) (granted the convergence condition just discussed) means that it is logically inconsistent to reject the expected present-value model while at the same time accepting the unpredictability of rates of return.

If the reasonableness of (1) is accepted, it follows that the objections to the logically equivalent (6) cannot be as compelling as they appear at first. It is perfectly natural that investors might exhibit greater awareness of capital gains than dividends, given the greater variability and unpredictability of capital gains. Although most investors do not think much about dividend yields, the hypothesis that capital gains reflect changes in dividend prospects nonetheless still holds. Also, whether a given firm has paid dividends in the past is irrelevant. What is relevant is the firm's capacity to pay dividends in the future, which is governed by the firm's earnings prospects. The expected present-value equation (6) says only that the value of a firm that investors were absolutely certain would never pay dividends in the future (even a liquidating dividend if the firm were to disband or merge into another firm) would be zero.

II. Market Efficiency and Its Implications for Volatility

The October 19, 1987, episode was not the first time stock prices had dropped sharply in the apparent absence of news of commensurate importance bearing on dividend prospects. October 19 was typical of major stock price changes in this respect, not exceptional: most stock price changes, major or minor, cannot convincingly be associated with contemporaneous changes in investors' expectations of future corporate profits (Cutler, Poterba, and Summers, 1987). To the extent that stock prices frequently fluctuate in response to variables unrelated to dividend prospects, stock prices in some sense should be more volatile than is consistent with market efficiency. This consideration led analysts to ask whether market efficiency could be shown formally to have the implication that stock price volatility should be lower than the volatility of dividends, and if so how this prediction could be tested.

Proponents of market efficiency were skeptical of this approach. They argued that since efficiency implies that prices respond instantaneously to new information, stock price volatility cannot be deemed in any sense "excessive." However, because market efficiency has been shown to imply that stock prices equal the discounted sum of expected future dividends, stock prices will behave like a weighted average of dividends over time, and an average is always less volatile than its components.[3] There is no contradiction, then, between the requirement that stock prices respond quickly to new information and the implication that the volatility of prices is related to that of the underlying dividends stream.

Results of tests of the implications of market efficiency for stock price volatility were circulated in 1975 in my paper with Richard Porter (published in 1981). The timing, incidentally, was not coincidental—our thinking on this topic was prompted by the 1974-1975 stock market drop, the most pronounced in the postwar U.S. economy up to that time. Robert Shiller reported similar volatility results in his 1979 and 1981 papers. These papers used different analytical methods, but the results were the same: stock price volatility is too great to be consistent with market efficiency.

These papers alleging excess volatility of asset prices were well-received by economists sympathetic to the idea that asset price changes are not closely linked to changes in the expected discounted value of the cash flows to which these assets give title. However, defenders of the efficient markets model were motivated to search for statistical problems with the specific econometric procedures used in the initial papers. They found several serious biases, all of which predisposed the tests to reject market efficiency. The most important papers here are Flavin (1983) and Kleidon (1986). At the same time, new volatility tests were being devised which were free of the biases that attended the initial tests (West, 1988; Mankiw, Romer, and Shapiro, 1985; Campbell and Shiller, 1988a, 1988b; and LeRoy and Parke, 1990). These new tests continued to indicate that asset prices are excessively volatile, although perhaps not by as great a margin as the initial tests suggested.

Lawrence Summers has likened the findings of the volatility tests to that of the statistical tests for a link between smoking and lung disease. Early tests indicating the presence of such a link were found to be contaminated by statistical problems which biased the outcome toward that finding. Nevertheless, subsequent tests, which were free of statistical bias, continued to support the original conclusion of a statistically significant link, although the link was shown not to be as strong as had first been thought.

The volatility test reported below, which is very simple and yet appears econometrically sound, is drawn from LeRoy and Parke (1990). Recall that the efficient markets model says that stock price equals the discounted value of expected dividends:

$$p_t = \frac{E_t(d_{t+1})}{1+\rho} + \frac{E_t(d_{t+2})}{(1+\rho)^2} + \frac{E_t(d_{t+3})}{(1+\rho)^3} + \ldots \quad (6)$$

Because there is no direct way to measure investors' information, direct observation of $E_t(d_{t+1})$, $E_t(d_{t+2})$, . . . , is not possible. This greatly complicates the derivation of the implications of market efficiency for price volatility. However, it is possible to show that the less information investors have, the higher will be the variance of the rate of return (LeRoy, 1989). Consequently, assuming markets are at least weak-form efficient, so that investors' information includes at least past returns, puts a lower bound on the amount of information investors have, therefore implying an upper bound on the variance of the rate of return.[4]

To derive the upper bound on the variance of the rate of return, it is necessary to evaluate this variance when investors predict future dividends using no information other than past returns. It is assumed that dividends follow a geometric random walk:

$$d_{t+1} = d_t \, \epsilon_{t+1} \tag{7}$$

where the ϵs are constant-mean random variables distributed independently over time. Analysts disagree about the accuracy of the geometric random walk specification. Some evidence shows it to be surprisingly accurate for such a simple specification, while other evidence suggests that in some contexts the geometric random walk specification can be misleading. For the present purpose the most attractive feature of the geometric random walk is its simplicity, which allows a very intuitive development of the variance-bounds relations. More complex characterization of dividend behavior, while allowing greater accuracy, would necessarily complicate the discussion by requiring use of more general analytical methods (Campbell-Shiller, 1988, 1988a).

When markets are at least weak-form efficient the upper bound on the variance of the rate of return on stock is the variance that would occur if investors based their dividend forecasts on past dividend behavior and nothing else. In this case the geometric random walk model implies that the best guess about future dividends is that they equal current dividends, multiplied by a trend term which depends on the mean value of ϵ. Therefore price will be given by a constant markup applied to current dividends:

$$p_t = k \, d_t \tag{8}$$

If price is proportional to dividends, the rate of return will equal the dividend growth rate multiplied by a constant which is very near one. To see this, recall the definition of the rate of return r_t as the dividend yield plus the rate of capital gain:

$$r_t = \frac{d_{t+1} + p_{t+1}}{p_t} . \tag{9}$$

Substituting $p = k \, d_t$ and $p_{t+1} = kd_{t+1}$ into (9) and using (7), we have

$$r_t = \left(\frac{k+1}{k} \right) (1 + \epsilon_{t+1}) - 1. \tag{10}$$

Because k, the price-dividend ratio, is on the order of 25, the multiplicative constant $(k+1)/k$ is not far from one, and therefore can be ignored. Thus the rate of return approximately equals the dividend growth rate, and the variances of these variables are approximately equal also.

In sum, this decreasing relation between investors' information and return volatility implies that if capital markets are at least weak-form efficient (and if dividends follow a random walk) the variance of the rate of return on stock cannot be greater than the variance of the dividend growth rate.

III. Empirical Results

Chart 1 shows the Standard & Poor's stock price index from 1926 to 1985, adjusted for inflation in commodity prices using the producers' price index. As expected, real stock prices display a pronounced upward trend over time, reflecting corporate retained earnings and, to a lesser extent, new equity issues. A very striking observation from Chart 1 is that stock price volatility has decreased between the 1930s and the 1980s. The decline from 1929 to 1932, the rise in the mid-1930s, and the decline in the years just before World War II were much more pronounced than any change occurring between World War II and the mid-1970s. This decreasing volatility of stock prices goes contrary to a common impression that stock market volatility has increased in recent decades. Another observation is that the October 19, 1987, selloff appears in Chart 1 as only a minor drop at the end of the period, rather than as the cataclysm it in fact was. The reason is that it came after nine months of rapid gains in stock prices, so that annual data show only a small drop from 1986 to 1987.

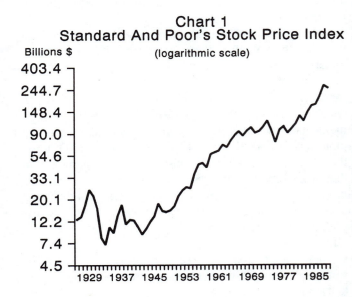

Chart 1
Standard And Poor's Stock Price Index
(logarithmic scale)

Chart 2 displays a simulated rate of return series that is representative of the pattern that would be expected under weak-form market efficiency. To generate the artificial stock prices on which the returns in Chart 2 were based, investors were arbitrarily assumed to be able to forecast dividends with perfect accuracy five years into the future. Beyond that horizon, however, they were assumed to have no information at all. Therefore they were assumed to extrapolate dividends using a constant growth rate, as implied by the geometric random walk. As would be expected in an efficient market, rates of return were higher than normal in years preceding dividend growth that was higher than normal, and lower than normal in years preceding low dividend growth. However, the relevant observation is that the rate of return has lower volatility than the dividend growth rate, conforming to the implication of market efficiency outlined above.

Chart 3 is similar to Chart 2 except that the actual rate of return on stock, rather than the simulated return based on market efficiency, is shown. Several aspects of this diagram are surprising. Most striking is the decrease in the volatility of both the rate of return on stock and the dividend growth rate from the 1930s to the 1980s. This decline in stock price volatility was noted in the discussion of Chart 1. Chart 3 makes clear that the decline in the volatility of dividend growth is even more pronounced than that in return volatility. However, for the purpose of testing the volatility implications of market efficiency, the relevant observation is that over the postwar period the rate of return on stock was much more variable than the dividend growth rate (in the prewar period the difference is not nearly as

great). This result is inconsistent with the stock market being weak-form efficient.

The volatility test just presented was chosen because it is easy to motivate intuitively. Because the test depends on strong simplifying assumptions, it may be that the finding of excess volatility arises from a violation of these assumptions rather than of market inefficiency. For example, without the simplifying random walk assumption, it is not necessarily true that the variance of the growth rate of dividends is an upper bound for the variance of the rate of return. Equally important, the version of the expected present-value model used to derive the volatility test incorporated the assumption that the discount rate is constant at ρ. Changing real interest rates over time are therefore a conceivable alternative to market inefficiency as a cause of the apparent excess volatility. However, both of these possibilities have been explored extensively in the variance-bounds literature, and so far, it appears that allowing for these more general specifications does not help explain the excess volatility. Thus, the conclusion that volatility is excessive can be justified in much more general settings than assumed here. The volatility test just reported then should be regarded as a sample from the volatility literature in which simplicity of exposition is purchased at the expense of restrictive specifications.

There are two possible sources of excess volatility in stock prices. First, investors could be overreacting to relevant information; second, they could be reacting to information which is irrelevant according to the efficient markets model. Although there do not appear to exist studies which attempt formally to apportion the excess

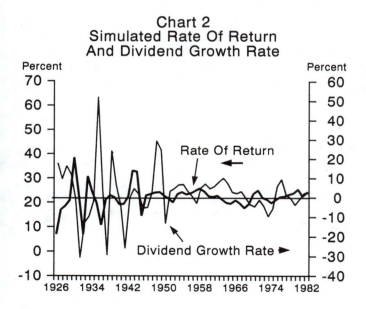

Chart 2
Simulated Rate Of Return
And Dividend Growth Rate

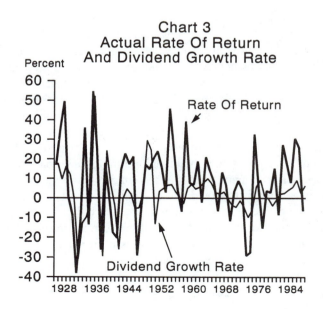

Chart 3
Actual Rate Of Return
And Dividend Growth Rate

volatility between these two sources, it seems likely that both are important.

That investors react to irrelevant information, at least, has been well established. For example, Roll (1984) documented the importance of irrelevant information in determining orange juice futures prices. Efficient markets theory implies that changes in the futures price of orange juice concentrate will reflect changes in the spot price which market participants expect will prevail at the date of the expiration of the futures contract. Roll argued persuasively that the only variable that can plausibly be viewed as giving relevant information about spot prices is weather—specifically, weather forecasts leading market participants to change their estimates of the probability of a freeze in Florida, since a freeze would adversely affect the orange crop.

Other variables which could in principle be relevant, Roll argued, would be expected to have only minor effect in the context of orange juice futures prices since current changes in supply induced by factors other than weather are of secondary importance, inasmuch as these factors do not change abruptly. For example, the number of trees bearing oranges at any time reflects planting decisions made several years earlier. Similarly, it appears unlikely that consumers' income and the prices of such substitutes as apple juice or tomato juice figure in an important way. Thus the efficient markets model predicts that weather should exert a dominant influence on futures prices. Roll verified that low temperatures in Florida were in fact associated with increases in orange juice futures prices, as expected. However, only a few percent of the total variation in futures prices can be explained in this way. In fact, Roll was unable to find any variable at all which correlated significantly with futures prices.

In his Presidential address to the American Finance Association, Roll (1988) reported the results of tests of whether the efficient markets model provides accurate *ex post* explanations for stock prices. He found that, again, irrelevant information appears to be of dominant importance. Even using such data as industry average prices and aggregate stock market indexes, Roll was able to explain *ex post* only a small fraction of the variation in prices of individual stocks.

IV. Asset Pricing Anomalies

There has always existed evidence at odds with the simplest models incorporating market efficiency. Prior to the 1970s, this conflict between theory and evidence usually was dismissed on the grounds that with relatively minor modifications, the efficient markets model could accommodate the contrary observations. For example, analysts identified trading rules that apparently could generate systematic profits, contrary to the efficient markets model. However, when these analysts allowed for brokerage charges, the profits usually evaporated.

More recently, however, analysts have recognized that there exists evidence that is not easy to square with the efficient markets model, even after making reasonable allowance for brokerage charges and other transactions costs. The "P-E anomaly" (Basu 1977, 1983) is the most prominent. It refers to the finding that stocks with low price-earnings ratios generate systematically higher rates of return than do stocks with high P-E ratios. This pattern is difficult to square with any recognizable version of the efficient markets model. In an efficient market, the stock price of successful firms should rise, but only by as much as is consistent with the firms earning normal returns in the future, and similarly with unsuccessful firms.

In contrast, it is easy to relate the P-E anomaly to the excess volatility of stock prices, at least informally. If investors overreact to news, then the stocks of successful firms will be bid to a higher multiple over earnings than is justified by the objective probability of this success continuing in the future. Subsequently the euphoria will wear off, generating low or even negative returns on average. Similarly, investors may be overeager to unburden their portfolios of losers, to the point where these stocks are discounted more than the facts justify. Subsequently such stocks on average generate higher returns than normal as their prospects improve. Correspondingly, this pattern of systematic overreaction to news would be expected to lead to price volatility in excess of that predicted by the efficient markets model. Therefore it is possible that the excess volatility of stock prices is the same thing as the P-E anomaly.

DeBondt and Thaler (1985, 1987) recently have documented a pattern similar to the P-E anomaly. They compared fictional portfolios of "winners"— stocks that had appreciated significantly in the recent past—with similar portfolios of "losers." They found that the losers strongly outperformed the market generally in subsequent years, while winners earned lower returns than the market averages. This result also suggests a pattern of overreaction, although the relation between DeBondt-Thaler's result and the P-E anomaly remains unclear.

Development of large data bases suitable for computerized study of stock prices have led to new anomalies.

Of these, the most striking is the "January effect" (Rozeff and Kinney, 1976; see Thaler, 1987, for a survey). Rozeff and Kinney found that rates of return on stock averaged 3.5 percent in January, whereas in other months returns averaged only 0.5 per cent. Several explanations involving tax-related purchases and sales of stocks have been investigated, but these explanations are not entirely convincing.

Another anomaly is the "small-firm" effect (Banz, 1981) in which small firms appear to earn higher returns than large firms, even when allowance is made for differences in riskiness. A subsequent study (Keim, 1983) showed that the January effect and the small-firm effect may be the same thing: the January effect appears only in samples that give equal weight to large and small firms. Value-weighted samples, in which small firms have much less importance relative to their role in equal-weighted samples, show little evidence of a January effect. This is exactly the pattern that would be expected if small firms account for the January effect.

Still other calendar-based anomalies have surfaced in recent years. Cross (1973), French (1980), and Keim and Stambaugh (1984), among others, have analyzed the "weekend effect," which refers to the observation that stock returns are on average negative from the close of trading on Fridays to the opening of trading on Mondays. Gibbons and Hess (1981) showed that a similar effect exists for bonds. Further, we have the "Wednesday effect": in 1968 the New York Stock Exchange was closed on Wednesdays in order to allow the back offices of brokerage houses to catch up with paperwork. Roll (1986) found that the volatility of stock prices was lower from Tuesday to Thursday when the market was closed on Wednesdays than over two-day periods over which the Exchange was not closed. This puzzle is difficult (although not impossible; see Slezak, 1988) to reconcile with market efficiency, given that as much news about corporate dividends presumably was arriving when the market was closed on Wednesdays as on other weekdays. The implication is that to some extent the trading process itself generates price volatility, a phenomenon clearly inconsistent with market efficiency. Finally, there exists a day-of-the-month effect: stock returns are positive in the days surrounding the turn of the month, but are zero on average for the rest of the month (Ariel, 1985).

Finally, Tinic and West (1984) investigated the seasonal pattern in the risk-return tradeoff. Fama and MacBeth's (1973) paper earlier had verified the prediction from finance theory that high-risk firms earn higher average rates of return than low-risk firms. Motivated by the results on the January effect, Tinic and West investigated the seasonal pattern in the correlation between risk and return which Fama-MacBeth had estimated. They found that this correlation is due entirely to the data for January. Given Keim's result that small firms earn high returns in January, and given the obvious fact that small firms are riskier than large firms, it is not surprising that the correlation between risk and expected return is strongest in January. What is surprising, however, is that the correlation between risk and return is essentially zero for the other eleven months of the year. Inasmuch as investors are risk-averse, this lack of compensation for risk in eleven of the twelve months of the year is not easy to reconcile with market efficiency.

V. Conclusions

Several essentially unrelated types of evidence that capital markets are inefficient have been discussed in this paper. Since it is not easy to think of non-trivial predictions of the efficient markets model that are borne out empirically, the burden of the evidence is negative. (Of course, trivial predictions are borne out. For example, it is true that the sustained upward trend in dividends that has occurred in the U.S. economy is associated with sustained price appreciation, as the efficient markets model predicts.)

How important this conclusion is depends on what lies behind the contrary evidence. The version of capital market efficiency adopted in the variance-bounds test reported above is grossly over-simplified (for example, equation (1) does not allow that investors are risk-averse, and therefore will demand a higher rate of return on high-risk securities than on low-risk securities). If it were to turn out that minor modification of the efficient markets model were sufficient to dispose of the contrary evidence, then the violations of market efficiency would not be important. However, most of the obvious extensions of the efficient markets model have been tried already, largely without success so far. Although it is possible that these extensions of the efficient markets model will succeed in the future, it may at some point be necessary for economists to face the uncongenial task of thinking about a world in which asset prices do not behave according to the precepts of finance and economic theory.

Economists are accustomed to thinking of prices not simply as measuring the amount of wealth that is transferred from one person to another when goods change hands, but also as guiding resource allocation. This is true as much for asset prices as for the prices of consumption goods. To see how this works in the context of asset prices, think of the petroleum market. There exists a large but far from infinite supply of oil reserves in the Middle East and other parts of the world. Other sources of energy exist, but they are at present more expensive than petroleum, at least for such purposes as automobile transportation and heating. However, when the petroleum runs out at some point in the future, the price of petroleum must be high enough to induce energy-users to shift to other energy sources. In the simplest idealized case, the price of petroleum will rise to equality with the alternate energy source just as the last gallon of oil is extracted, so that energy users are induced to shift sources at exactly the right time. Before that day of reckoning, petroleum prices must be rising to guarantee to holders of petroleum reserves a competitive return.[5] In this stylized account, the price of petroleum gives exactly the right signals to users of petroleum: they have adequate incentive to conserve, but are not induced irrationally to squander other resources so as to save petroleum. It follows that a massive program to encourage conservation or reliance on alternative sources is likely to do more harm than good, inasmuch as such a program amounts to fixing a social mechanism that is not broken.

Evidence of capital market inefficiency means that it cannot be taken for granted that asset prices are doing as good a job of rationing resources among alternative users as the foregoing account implies. The existing price of petroleum may not, after all, fully reflect the best information about petroleum reserves, alternative energy technologies, and so forth. Accordingly, the price of petroleum may not be providing the right incentives for conservation and development of alternative technologies.

It is apparent that an extreme interpretation of the evidence against capital market efficiency has the effect of opening the door to a variety of schemes to alter economic institutions. Inasmuch as such schemes generally have met with various degrees of failure in the past, we should not be too quick to jettison capital market efficiency, and with it the idea that prices determined in competitive markets do a reasonably good job of allocating resources. The evidence reviewed here suggests, rather, that economists ought to be aware that the evidence in favor of their way of thinking about the economy is far from clear-cut.

NOTES

* A more detailed version of this paper is found in LeRoy (1989).

1. Although these verbal characterizations of market efficiency are drawn directly from Fama (1970), it is not unambiguously clear that Fama identified market efficiency with the fair-game model (1); see LeRoy (1976, 1989) for discussion.

2. Used here is the rule of iterated expectations, which says that $E(E(d_{t+2} \mid I_{t+1}) \mid I_t) = E(d_{t+2} \mid I_t)$, and similarly for p_{t+2}.

3. Even though future dividends are weighted differently from current dividends because of discounting, and future dividends are not known with certainty, price behaves like an average of dividends over time.

4. The test to be described is known as the "West test" (West, 1988), although the original version of the West test is formally equivalent to one of the volatility tests derived by LeRoy-Porter (1981). (See Gilles-LeRoy, 1988.) West's derivation was independent, and he was the first actually to conduct the test. Also, West was the first to realize that the return volatility test has certain econometric advantages over price volatility tests, particularly for diagrammatic presentation. These advantages justify adoption of the West test here.

In one respect the test reported here differs from that derived by LeRoy-Porter and West. The formal derivation of the West test assumes constant-variance linear processes, which is an unsatisfactory specification in light of the upward trend in stock prices over the past fifty years. In order to correct for scale, Chart 3 instead compares the rate of return with the dividends growth rate. Formal derivation of the validity of this comparison, which is based on the linearization procedure of Campbell-Shiller (1988), is found in LeRoy-Parke (1990).

5. The implication that the prices of exhaustible resources should rise at a rate approximately equal to the real interest rate has been studied by Schmidt (1988). Schmidt found no evidence of rising prices over time, implying that holders of wealth in the form of exhaustible resources earned a zero real rate of return.

REFERENCES

Ariel, Robert A. "A Monthly Effect in Stock Returns," *Journal of Financial Economics* 17: 1985. 161-174.

Banz, Rolf. "The Relationship between Return and Market Value of Common Stock," *Journal of Financial Economics* 9: 1981. 3-18.

Basu, Sanjoy. "Investment Performance of Common Stocks in Relation to their Price-Earnings Ratios: A Test of the Efficient Market Hypothesis," *Journal of Finance* 32: 1977. 663-682.

_____. "The Relation between Earnings' Yield, Market Value and Returns for NYSE Common Stocks: Further Evidence," *Journal of Financial Economics* 12: 1983. 129-156.

Campbell, John Y. and Robert J. Shiller. "The Dividend-Price Ratio and Expectations of Future Dividends and Discount Factors," *Review of Financial Studies* 1: 1988. 195-228.

_____. "Stock Prices, Earnings, and Expected Dividends," *Journal of Finance* 43: 1988a. 661-676.

Cross, Frank. "The Behavior of Stock Prices on Fridays and Mondays," *Financial Analysts Journal:* 1973. 67-79.

Cutler, David M., James M. Poterba and Lawrence H. Summers. "What Moves Stock Prices?" reproduced, Harvard University, 1987.

DeBondt, Werner and Richard Thaler. "Does the Stock Market Overreact?" *Journal of Finance* 40: 1985. 793-805.

_____. "Further Evidence on Investor Overreaction and Stock Market Seasonality," *Journal of Finance* 42: 1987. 557-581.

Fama, Eugene F. "Efficient Capital Markets: A Review of Theory and Empirical Work," *Journal of Finance* 25: 1970. 383-416.

_____ and James D. MacBeth. "Risk, Return and Equilibrium: Empirical Tests," *Journal of Political Economy* 81: 1973. 607-636.

Flavin, Marjorie A. "Excess Volatility in the Financial Markets: A Reassessment of the Empirical Evidence," *Journal of Political Economy* 91: 1983. 929-956.

Gibbons, Michael and Patrick Hess. "Day of the Week Effects and Asset Returns," *Journal of Business* 5: 1981. 579-596.

Gilles, Christian and Stephen F. LeRoy. "Bubbles and Charges," reproduced, University of California, Santa Barbara, 1988.

Grossman, Sanford and Robert J. Shiller. "The Determinants of the Variability of Stock Market Prices," *American Economic Review* 71: 1981. 222-227.

Keim, Donald B. "Size-Related Anomalies and Stock Market Seasonality," *Journal of Financial Economics* 12: 1983. 13-22.

_____ and Robert F. Stambaugh. "A Further Investigation of the Weekend Effect in Stock Returns," *Journal of Finance* 39: 1984. 819-840.

Kleidon, Allan. "Variance Bounds Tests and Stock Price Valuation Models," *Journal of Political Economy:* 1986. 953-1001.

LeRoy, Stephen F. "Efficient Capital Markets: Comment," *Journal of Finance* 3: 1976. 139-141.

_____ . "Efficiency and the Variability of Asset Prices," *American Economic Review* 74: 1984. 183-187.

_____ . "Efficient Capital Markets and Martingales," *Journal of Economic Literature,* 1989.

_____ and William R. Parke. "Stock Price Volatility: Tests Based on the Geometric Random Walk," reproduced, University of California, Santa Barbara, 1990.

LeRoy, Stephen F. and Richard D. Porter. "The Present-Value Relation: Tests Based on Implied Variance Bounds," *Econometrica* 49: 1981. 555-574.

Mandelbrot, Benoit. "Forecasts of Future Prices, Unbiased Markets, and Martingale Models," *Journal of Business* 39: 1966. 242-255.

Mankiw, N. Gregory, David Romer, and Matthew D. Shapiro. "An Unbiased Reexamination of Stock Market Volatility," *Journal of Finance* 40: 1985. 677-687.

Roll, Richard. "Orange Juice and Weather," *American Economic Review* 74: 1984. 861-880.

_____ . "The Hubris Hypothesis of Corporate Takeovers," *Journal of Business* 59: 1986. 197-216.

_____ . "R^2," *Journal of Finance* 43: 1988. 541-566.

Rozeff, Michael S. and William R. Kinney. "Capital Market Seasonality: The Case of Stock Returns," *Journal of Financial Economics* 3: 1976. 379-402.

Samuelson, Paul A. "Proof that Properly Anticipated Prices Fluctuate Randomly," *Industrial Management Review* 6: 1965. 41-49.

_____ . "Proof that Properly Discounted Present Values Vibrate Randomly," *Bell Journal of Economics and Management Science* 4: 1973. 369-374.

Schmidt, Ronald. "Hotelling's Rule Repealed? An Examination of Exhaustible Resource Pricing," Federal Reserve Bank of San Francisco *Economic Review,* Fall, 1988. 41-53.

Shiller, Robert. "The Volatility of Long Term Interest Rates and Expectations Models of the Term Structure," *Journal of Political Economy* 87: 1979. 1190-1209.

_____ . "Do Stock Prices Move Too Much to be Justified by Subsequent Changes in Dividends?" *American Economic Review* 17: 1981. 421-436.

Slezak, Steve L. "The Effect of Market Interruptions on Equilibrium Asset Return Distributions in Dynamic Economies with Asymmetrically Informed Traders," reproduced, University of California, San Diego, 1988.

Thaler, Richard. "Anomalies: The January Effect," *Journal of Economic Perspectives* 1: 1987. 197-201.

Tinic, Seha M. and Richard R. West. "Risk and Return: January vs. the Rest of the Year," *Journal of Financial Economics* 13: 1984. 561-574.

West, Kenneth. "Dividend Innovations and Stock Price Volatility," *Econometrica* 56: 1988. 37-61.

_____ . "Bubbles, Fads and Stock Price Volatility Tests: A Partial Evaluation," *Journal of Finance* 43: 1988a. 639-656.

Article 16

Managing Interest Rate Risk with Interest Rate Futures

By Charles S. Morris

Increased interest rate volatility in the 1970s and 1980s has led to greater volatility in the returns on bonds and other fixed income assets. Consequently, investors in bonds and financial institutions with fixed income assets and liabilities on their balance sheets are now exposed to much greater risks from capital gains and losses. The problem is compounded because managing risks caused by interest rate volatility has traditionally been difficult and costly.

During the last 15 years, however, many new financial instruments have been developed to help investors manage risks caused by increased interest rate volatility. One of the most popular types of instruments is interest rate futures contracts. Interest rate futures allow investors to protect the value of their fixed income invest-

ments by providing a hedge against interest rate changes. Interest rate futures are now an important tool for investors who want to protect themselves from interest rate volatility.

This article explains how interest rate futures, when properly used in a hedging strategy, allow investors to manage interest rate risk. The first section of the article defines interest rate risk, examines its impact on investors and institutions, and discusses how interest rate risk can be managed. The second section provides an introduction to interest rate futures and discusses why they are good assets for hedging interest rate risk. The third section shows how investors and institutions can use interest rate futures to manage interest rate risk and discusses some of the other risks involved in using interest rate futures.

Interest rate risk and interest rate risk management

Bonds and other fixed income assets have become riskier investments in recent years.

Charles S. Morris is a senior economist at the Federal Reserve Bank of Kansas City. Julia Reigel, a research associate at the bank, assisted in the preparation of this article.

These assets are riskier, not because issuers are more likely to default on their obligations, but because interest rates have become more volatile. This section explains why increased interest rate volatility has increased the risk of fixed income assets, provides some examples of investors and institutions affected by greater interest rate volatility, and discusses methods of managing interest rate risk.

What is interest rate risk?

Investments in fixed income assets, such as bonds, are risky because the volatility of their prices can lead to unexpected capital gains and losses. The risk of an asset can be measured by the volatility of its returns, which is the sum of the income flows from the asset plus any changes in its price. Since the income flows from a fixed income asset, such as the coupon payments and maturity value of a coupon bond, are fixed, the riskiness of the asset depends only on its price volatility. For example, as the volatility of a bond's price rises, the bond's riskiness rises because unexpected capital gains or losses are more likely.

The primary cause of volatility in the price of a fixed income asset is interest rate volatility.[1] Indeed, the volatility in prices due to interest rate changes is commonly termed "interest rate risk." For example, when interest rates fall, the price of a bond rises; when interest rates rise, the price of a bond falls. The sensitivity of a fixed income asset's price to interest rates, that is, the degree of interest rate risk, depends largely on the asset's maturity. The longer to maturity, the larger the change in price due to a change in interest rates.[2]

Interest rate volatility has risen sharply in recent years. Chart 1 shows the volatility of interest rates on 1-year and 10-year Treasury securities from 1955 to 1988. Interest rate volatility in each year is measured by the standard deviation of the monthly interest rates during that year. The average standard deviation of 1-year interest rates over the 1979-88 period was more than twice that of the 1955-78 period, rising from 0.5 percent per month over the 1955-78 period to 1.2 percent over the 1979-88 period. The relative increase in the volatility of 10-year rates was even sharper. The average standard deviation of 10-year interest rates over the 1979-88 period was more than three times higher than that over the 1955-78 period, rising from 0.25 percent to 0.8 percent. The rise in interest rate volatility over those periods is not limited to 1-year and 10-year rates, but is typical of the volatility of interest rates at all maturities.

Who is affected by rising interest rate volatility?

Many investors and business firms are exposed to greater risks because of the increase in interest rate volatility in recent years. Examples include individual and institutional

---

[1] The riskiness of a fixed income asset also depends on the volatility of other factors that affect its price, such as the creditworthiness of the issuer and the liquidity of the asset.

[2] This assumes a uniform change in rates on all maturities. The interest rate sensitivity of a fixed income asset also depends on other factors, such as the size of the coupon payments and the dates the coupon payments are received.

CHART 1
Interest rate volatility

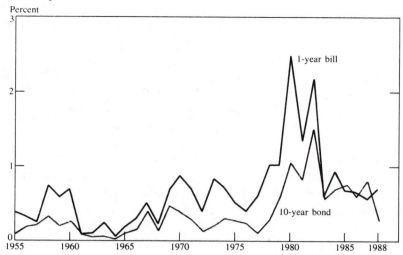

Note: Annual standard deviations of monthly constant maturity rates for 1-year U.S. Treasury bills and 10-year U.S. Treasury bonds.

Source: Board of Governors of the Federal Reserve System.

CHART 2
Bond market volatility

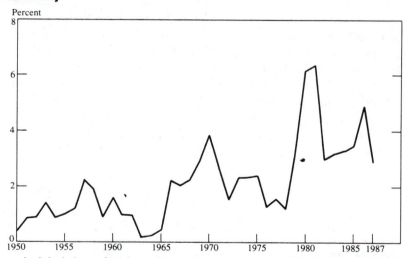

Note: Annual standard deviations of total monthly returns on a long-term U.S. Treasury bond index.

Source: Center for Research in Stock Prices.

investors in government and corporate bonds, depository institutions such as banks and savings and loans, securities dealers, mortgage banks, and life insurance companies to name a few.

One group of investors exposed to greater risks is investors in bonds. The rising risk of holding bonds is clear from Chart 2, which shows the volatility of returns on U.S. Treasury bonds from 1950 to 1987. Bond market volatility in each year is measured by the standard deviation of the monthly percentage returns on a long-term U.S. Treasury bond index during that year.[3] Bond market volatility rose from an average annual standard deviation of 1 percent per month over the period from 1950 to 1965 to 2.25 percent over the period from 1966 to 1978. Bond market volatility rose further from 1979 to 1987, averaging 4.1 percent per month.

Rising interest rate volatility has also increased the risk exposure of depository institutions, such as banks and S&Ls. When interest rates rise, the market value of their net worth generally falls; when interest rates fall, the market value of their net worth generally rises. The market value of an institution's net worth is the difference between the market values of its assets and liabilities. The effect of a change in interest rates on the market value of a firm's net worth depends on the relative interest rate sensitivities of its assets and liabilities, which primarily depend on their relative maturities.

Because the assets of banks and S&Ls generally take longer to mature than do their liabilities, the value of their assets is more sensitive to changes in interest rates than the value of their liabilities. As a result, when interest rates rise, for example, the net worth of a depository institution falls because the value of its assets falls more than the value of its liabilities.

Securities dealers are also exposed to greater risks due to rising interest rate volatility. When interest rates rise, securities dealers suffer losses like other bondholders because the value of the bonds they are holding in inventory falls.[4] Securities dealers can also suffer losses when interest rates fall, however, because they often commit themselves to delivering bonds at a future date for a fixed price when they do not have the bonds in inventory or the funds to purchase them immediately. If interest rates fall before a dealer purchases the bonds, he will suffer a loss because the price he has to pay for the bonds he has to deliver will be higher than he had expected when he made the initial commitment.

Mortgage banks are also exposed to greater interest rate volatility. A mortgage bank originates mortgages and then sells them to other investors. In general, mortgage banks hold very few mortgages on their balance sheet. They can suffer losses if interest rates rise, however, because they typically commit to a mortgage

---

[3] Although the volatility of total returns is the same as price volatility for a given bond, the volatilities are not the same when the composition of a bond portfolio changes over time because the coupon payments change. Since the composition of the portfolio that underlies the index in Chart 2 changes, the volatility of total returns is shown.

---

[4] Securities dealers make a profit on their bonds when interest rates fall. Indeed, all investors in fixed income assets make a profit when interest rates move in one direction and suffer a loss when interest rates move in the other direction. In the remaining examples, the discussion will focus on how a change in interest rates in only one direction affects an investor. The direction of the change in interest rates that is used is the one that produces a loss for the investor.

rate before the mortgage is actually closed and sold. If interest rates rise between the time they commit to a rate and the time the mortgage is sold, the value of the mortgage will fall; and mortgage banks will get a lower price than they had expected when they made the initial commitment.

A final example of a group of firms exposed to greater risks due to rising interest rate volatility is life insurance companies. For example, changes in interest rates affect life insurance companies because when interest rates fall the spread earned on Guaranteed Interest Contract (GIC) commitments falls. In recent years, life insurance companies have become heavy issuers of GICs, which are securities that guarantee a fixed interest rate on invested funds over a several-year period. GICs are generally purchased by long-term investors, such as pension funds and company thrift plans. Often, a life insurance company will commit to a rate on a GIC for a short time period before it receives the funds. Life insurance companies can suffer losses if interest rates fall during the commitment period because when they receive the funds from the GIC, they will have to invest the funds at a lower rate than they had expected when they committed to the GIC rate. As a result, the spread earned on the GIC falls.[5]

What is risk management and hedging?

Investors and business firms manage risk by

choosing the amount of risk to which they want to be exposed. The choice of how much risk to bear varies with every investor. For example, some investors will choose to accept the increased price volatility of fixed income investments of recent years, while others will take actions to reduce the riskiness of their fixed income investments. In general, though, investors will not choose to minimize risk because there are costs to reducing risk. The most important cost is that the expected return on their investment also falls when risk is reduced.

Traditionally, investors have found it difficult and costly to reduce risks caused by interest rate volatility. Investors in bonds, for example, typically could reduce interest rate risk only by selling some of their bonds and buying short-term money market instruments. Financial institutions exposed to interest rate risk had to rely on balance sheet restructuring to reduce the mismatch between the maturities of their assets and liabilities.

In recent years new financial instruments—such as interest rate futures, options on interest rate futures, and interest rate swaps—have been developed that allow investors in fixed income assets to manage interest rate risk at a relatively low cost by hedging. In general, hedging is a risk management strategy in which investors choose assets such that changes in the prices of the assets systematically offset each other. Fixed income investors can hedge the interest rate risk of an asset, such as a Treasury bond, by buying or selling hedging assets whose values change in the opposite direction to the value of the Treasury bond when interest rates change. The interest rate riskiness of a hedged Treasury bond is lower than the interest rate riskiness of the unhedged bond because the change in the value of the hedging asset due

---

[5] Viewed another way, a GIC commitment is a fixed rate liability that is not matched by an asset. When interest rates fall, the value of the GIC commitment rises, but there is no asset whose value also rises. Therefore, the insurance company's net worth falls when interest rates fall.

to a change in interest rates offsets at least some of the change in the value of the bond. It is important to realize, however, that hedging reduces price volatility because it offsets increases as well as decreases in the price of the Treasury bond.

For any given fixed income asset, the best hedging instrument for reducing interest rate risk is the one whose price is most closely related to the price of the asset when interest rates change. The more closely the prices are related, the larger the reduction in risk that is possible because changes in the price of the hedging asset are more likely to offset changes in the price of the asset being hedged.

While hedging can reduce risk, it generally cannot completely eliminate risk. Hedging will completely eliminate risk only if the values of the portfolio and hedging asset are perfectly related. However, the prices of the assets being hedged and the hedging asset are rarely perfectly related because of differences in factors such as credit quality, liquidity, maturity, and call or prepayment options. Thus, as a practical matter, hedging is an activity that permits investors to manage, but not eliminate, risk.[6]

---

[6] The risk that remains after a portfolio has been hedged is called *basis risk*. If the riskiness of a portfolio is measured by the standard deviation of the change in its value, the minimum level of basis risk that can be achieved through hedging is

$$\sigma_h = \sigma_p \sqrt{(1 - \varrho^2)},$$

where σ_p is the standard deviation of the change in the value of the unhedged portfolio, and ϱ is the correlation coefficient between the changes in the values of the portfolio and the hedging asset. The maximum percentage reduction in risk is

$$100(\sigma_p - \sigma_h)/\sigma_p = 100(1 - \sqrt{(1 - \varrho^2)},$$

which depends only on ϱ, and risk will be completely eliminated only if ϱ equals 1 or -1.

An introduction to interest rate futures

Of the variety of financial instruments used to hedge interest rate risk, one of the most popular is interest rate futures. This section describes interest rate futures, discusses the types of interest rate futures available, and explains why they are good hedging instruments.

What are interest rate futures?

An interest rate futures contract is an agreement between two parties to buy or sell a fixed income asset, such as a Treasury bond or Treasury bill, at a given time in the future for a predetermined price. For example, if in January a person buys March Treasury bond futures, he is simply agreeing to buy Treasury bonds in March. On the other hand, if in January he sells March Treasury bond futures, he is simply agreeing to sell Treasury bonds in March. Nothing is exchanged when the futures contract is written because it is only an agreement to make an exchange at a future date. The price of a futures contract is the price the buyer agrees to pay the seller for the asset when it is delivered.[7]

---

[7] The delivery dates for most interest rate futures are in March, June, September, and December. The actual delivery date varies with the contract. For example, the seller of a Treasury bond contract at the Chicago Board of Trade can deliver Treasury bonds on any day in the contract month, although the last trading day is seven business days prior to the last business day of the month. Although some interest rate futures have contract months that extend out to three years, most of the contracts traded are contracts with the nearest delivery month.

Delivery of the asset in a futures contract rarely occurs, however. The reason is futures traders can always close out the contracts they have bought or sold by taking an offsetting position in the same futures contract before delivery occurs. For example, rather than taking delivery, a buyer of ten March Treasury bond futures can settle his position by selling ten March Treasury bond futures. Similarly, a seller of ten March Treasury bond futures can settle his position by buying ten March Treasury bond futures. In 1988, Treasury bonds were delivered in less than 0.1 percent of all Treasury bond futures traded at the Chicago Board of Trade, which are one of the most widely traded interest rate futures.[8]

Since a futures trader who has settled an initial position has both bought and sold futures, his profit depends on the prices of the futures he has bought and sold. Just like any other trader, futures traders make a profit when they buy futures at a price lower than they sell futures, and they suffer a loss when they buy futures at a price higher than they sell futures. Whether a person makes a profit or suffers a loss, therefore, depends on two conditions: first, whether he initially bought or sold futures, and second, whether the price of the futures rises or falls between the time he enters the initial contract and the time he takes an offsetting position.

A buyer of futures makes a profit when the futures price rises and suffers a loss when the futures price falls. Suppose, for example, on January 10 a person buys a March Treasury bond futures contract for $95 per $100 face value of Treasury bonds, and on February 15 he settles his position by selling a March Treasury bond futures contract for $97. Under these circumstances, the person would make a profit of $2 per $100 face value of Treasury bonds because he has one agreement to buy Treasury bonds in March for $95 and another agreement to sell Treasury bonds in March for $97. On the other hand, if the price falls to $92 on February 15, he would lose $3 per $100 because he has one agreement to buy Treasury bonds for $95 and another agreement to sell Treasury bonds for $92.

In contrast, a seller of futures suffers a loss when the futures price rises and makes a profit when the futures price falls. This time, suppose on January 10 a person sells a March Treasury bond futures contract for $95, and on February 15 he settles his position by buying a March Treasury bond futures for $97. The person would suffer a loss of $2 because he has one agreement to sell Treasury bonds in March for $95 and another agreement to buy Treasury bonds in March for $97. On the other hand, if the price falls to $92 on February 15, he would make a profit of $3 because he has one agreement to sell Treasury bonds for $95 and another agreement to buy Treasury bonds for $92.

Interest rate futures are relatively new financial instruments. While futures on commodities have been trading on organized exchanges in the United States since the latter half of the 1860s, the first interest rate futures contract did not start trading until October 1975, when the Chicago Board of Trade (CBT) introduced futures on Government National Mortgage

---

[8] For some interest rate futures, such as the Eurodollar time deposit futures on the International Monetary Market exchange, all contracts must be settled by taking an offsetting position. That is, delivery of the underlying instrument is not allowed.

Association (GNMA) certificates.[9] Since then, futures on many different fixed income assets have been developed. However, there are still many fixed income assets, such as corporate bonds, on which no futures are traded.

The assets on which interest rate futures are traded span the maturity spectrum—interest rate futures on short-term, medium-term, and long-term assets are traded on several futures exchanges in the United States and abroad. The first futures contract on a short-term asset was the Treasury bill futures contract, which was introduced on the International Monetary Market (IMM) exchange in 1976. Since then, interest rate futures on other short-term assets, such as Eurodollar time deposits and 30-day interest rates, have begun trading on several exchanges, with the IMM Eurodollar futures being the most popular.[10] Interest rate futures on medium-term assets, such as Treasury notes, are also traded on several exchanges.[11] Finally, there are interest rate futures on long-term assets, such as Treasury bonds and a municipal bond index, with the CBT Treasury bond futures being the most popular.[12]

_____

[9] Although the GNMA futures contract was initially successful, it stopped trading in December 1984.

[10] Treasury bill futures are also traded on the MidAmerica Commodity Exchange in Chicago. Eurodollar futures are also traded on the London International Financial Futures Exchange. The 30-day interest rate futures contract is traded at the Chicago Board of Trade.

[11] Treasury note futures are traded on the Chicago Board of Trade exchange, the MidAmerica Commodity Exchange in Chicago, and the Financial Instrument Exchange, a division of the New York Cotton Exchange.

[12] Treasury bond futures are also traded on the MidAmerica Commodity Exchange in Chicago and the London International Financial Futures Exchange. Futures on the municipal bond index are traded at the Chicago Board of Trade.

The success of interest rate futures is shown in Chart 3. One measure of activity in a futures market is a contract's open interest—the number of contracts not yet offset by opposite transactions or delivery. Chart 3 shows the open interest in the CBT Treasury bond futures contract from 1978 to 1988. Although open interest in Treasury bond futures is fairly volatile, the trend is clearly upward. Chart 3 also shows open interest rose sharply in 1980 and 1981—the two peak years in bond market volatility (Chart 2)—suggesting that investors took advantage of the futures market for managing risk.

Why are interest rate futures good hedging assets?

Interest rate futures are good hedging assets for two reasons. First, the transaction costs of buying and selling them are relatively low. Second, interest rate futures prices are closely related to the prices of many fixed income assets when interest rates change.

The transaction costs of establishing a futures position are low because nothing is really being bought or sold—the contract is just an agreement to make a trade at a future date. When a position is established, the only outlays are broker fees and commissions and an initial margin deposit with the broker.[13] The fees paid to brokers and traders are quite small. For example, the cost of establishing and settling a position in a CBT Treasury bond futures con-

_____

[13] The margin on a futures contract is "good faith" money deposited with a broker to assure him that losses can be covered in the event of adverse price movements.

CHART 3
Treasury bond futures open interest

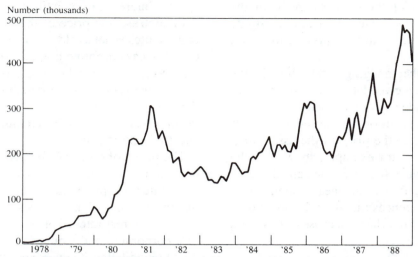

Note: Values are monthly averages of daily open interest in the nearest Chicago Board of Trade Treasury bond futures contract with at least one month until expiration.

Source: Data Resources Inc.

tract, which is based on $100,000 face value of bonds, is about $41.[14] The initial margin is also very small—the margin on a CBT Treasury bond futures used for hedging purposes is $2,000—and the margin generally earns a market.rate of interest.[15]

Interest rate futures hedge the interest rate risk of many fixed income assets successfully because interest rate futures prices are closely related to the prices of many fixed income assets. The prices are closely related because interest rate futures prices are sensitive to changes in interest rates just like fixed income asset prices. The price of any futures contract—whether it is an interest rate, exchange rate, commodity, or any other type of futures contract—is always very closely related to the

[14] See Arnold Kling, "Futures Markets and Transaction Costs," in Myron L. Kwast, ed., *Financial Futures and Options in the U.S. Economy: A Study by the Staff of the Federal Reserve System* (Washington, D.C.: Board of Governors of the Federal Reserve System, 1986), pp. 41-54.

[15] The minimum initial margin a person must deposit when establishing an open position in a futures contract and the minimum level that must be maintained is set by the exchanges and is changed from time to time. The margin level depends on factors such as the volatility of the price of the underlying instrument and the maximum daily change in the futures price the exchange allows. Margins also may

depend on whether a person is just buying or selling futures alone or is buying or selling futures to establish a hedge. The margin on an outright purchase or sale of CBT Treasury bond futures is $2,500. Although interest is generally paid on the initial margin, interest is not paid on additions to the margin account because additions represent losses that have been transferred to the accounts of parties that have gained from price movements.

price of the underlying asset.[16] Since interest rate futures are based on fixed income assets and the prices of these assets move in the opposite direction of interest rates, interest rate futures prices move in the opposite direction of interest rates.

Like any other hedging asset, though, the extent to which a given interest rate futures contract will provide an effective hedge for a fixed income asset depends on how closely the futures price is related to the price of the asset being hedged. Chart 4, for example, shows that the prices of a 30-year Treasury bond and the CBT Treasury bond futures are nearly identical.[17] The small differences that do exist are shown at the bottom of the chart. Because of this close relationship, Treasury bond futures should be very effective at hedging Treasury bonds against interest rate volatility.

In contrast, the price of the CBT Treasury bond futures is not as closely related to the price of a 30-year corporate bond as to the price of the 30-year Treasury bond (Chart 5). The difference between the corporate bond price and the futures price is clearly more variable than the difference between the Treasury bond price and the futures price.

The prices of corporate bonds and Treasury bond futures are less closely related because corporate bond prices can change for a variety of reasons other than changes in the general level of interest rates. For example, the price of a corporate bond would fall if the issuer's credit rating fell or if adverse general economic conditions led investors to believe the chances of default were more likely. The price of a corporate bond could also fall if a large investor decided to sell his share of an issue. Since these factors would not affect the price of a Treasury bond, a Treasury bond futures contract would not hedge an investor against these price changes. As a result, Treasury bond futures should be a less effective hedge for a corporate bond than for a Treasury bond.[18]

---

[16] The relationship between the price of a futures contract and the price of its underlying asset is most easily seen on the last day of trading for a particular contract, at which time the two prices must be exactly equal. In general, if there are no transaction costs and capital markets are perfect, the difference between a futures price and the price of the underlying asset can be no larger than the net cost of holding the underlying asset in inventory—inventory costs less income flows from the asset—until the futures contract expires. This relationship between the price of a futures contract and the price of its underlying asset is known as the cost of carry theory of futures prices. Prices do deviate slightly from cost of carry, though, because of transaction costs and capital market imperfections. For a detailed discussion of the relationship between interest rate futures prices and bond prices, see James M. Little, "What are Financial Futures?" in Nancy H. Rothstein and James M. Little, eds. *The Handbook of Financial Futures* (New York: McGraw-Hill Book Company, 1984), pp. 35-66.

[17] The closeness of these two prices should not be surprising. The CBT Treasury bond futures price should be very closely related to the price of its underlying asset, which is an 8 percent 20-year Treasury bond. Since 30-year Treasury bond prices and 20-year Treasury bond prices are closely related, the futures price, and the bond price in Chart 4 are closely related.

---

[18] Viewed another way, Treasury bond futures are less effective in hedging the *total* risk of a corporate bond than a Treasury bond because (1) Treasury bond futures only hedge interest rate risk, and (2) interest rate risk accounts for a smaller share of the total risk of a corporate bond than of a Treasury bond. In terms of hedging only the interest rate risk of a corporate bond—that is, changes in the price of the corporate bond due to changes in interest rates—Treasury bond futures should be fairly effective.

CHART 4
Treasury bond futures price and treasury bond price

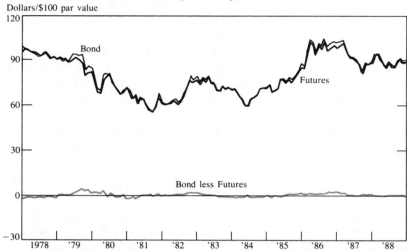

Note: The bond price is the price of the 9¼ percent 30-year Treasury bond that matures in November 2007. The futures price is the price of the nearest Chicago Board of Trade Treasury bond future with at least one month until expiration.

Source: Data Resources Inc.

CHART 5
Treasury bond futures price and corporate bond price

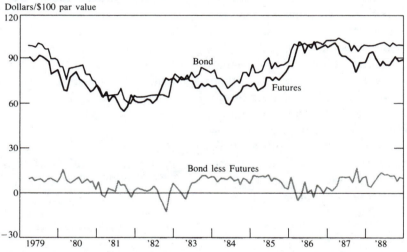

Note: Corporate bond is an A-rated 9½ percent 30-year bond of a U.S. industrial firm. The futures price is the price of the nearest Chicago Board of Trade Treasury bond future with at least one month until expiration.

Source: Data Resources Inc.

Managing interest rate risk with interest rate futures

Businesses and investors use interest rate futures in a variety of ways to manage interest rate risk. Hedging strategies can be complex, however, and this can expose investors to new risks. This section provides some specific examples of how interest rate futures are used to hedge interest rate risk and then discusses some of the other risks involved in hedging with interest rate futures.

Hedging interest rate risk with interest rate futures

Investors can hedge interest rate risk by selling or buying interest rate futures. Whether an investor sells or buys futures depends on how changes in interest rates affect the value of his portfolio.

In general, an investor who suffers losses on his investment portfolio when interest rates *rise* hedges interest rate risk by *selling* interest rate futures.[19] When interest rates rise, interest rate futures prices fall. If an investor loses money on his portfolio when interest rates rise, then, he needs to make a profit from falling futures prices. That is, he needs the gain on his futures contract to offset the loss on his original investment portfolio. Since sellers of futures make a profit when futures prices fall, the investor would hedge by selling futures. Similarly, when interest rates fall, the losses on the futures off-set the profits on the original investment portfolio.

Conversely, an investor who suffers losses on his portfolio when interest rates *fall* hedges by *buying* interest rate futures. When interest rates fall, interest rate futures prices rise. If an investor loses money on his portfolio when interest rates fall, he needs to make a profit from rising futures prices. Since buyers of futures make a profit when futures prices rise, the investor would hedge by buying futures. Similarly, when interest rates rise, the losses on the futures offset the profits on the portfolio.

Hedging a Treasury bond portfolio. Treasury bond prices fall when interest rates rise, so an investor in Treasury bonds would hedge his portfolio against changes in interest rates by selling interest rate futures. In this way, a gain or loss on the Treasury bonds would be offset by a loss or gain on the futures contracts.

An example of the reduction in price volatility that can be achieved by hedging is shown in Chart 6. This chart shows the price of a portfolio of unhedged Treasury bonds and the price of a hedged portfolio. The unhedged portfolio contains 30-year and 10-year U.S. Treasury bonds. The bonds are hedged using the CBT Treasury bond futures.[20] The value of the

---

[19] Of course, an equivalent statement of this rule is that an investor who makes profits on his investment portfolio when interest rates fall hedges interest rate risk by selling interest rate futures.

[20] This example assumes the investor wants to minimize risk. For simplicity, the value of the hedged portfolio ignores the effects of margin requirements, transaction costs, taxation, accounting practices, and regulatory requirements, all of which could affect the value of the hedge and the hedging strategy. The prices are end-of-month data, and the futures price is on the nearest contract with at least one month until expiration.

The example does not account for the possibility that risk could be reduced further by (1) using futures with contract months that are farther out, and (2) estimating the number of contracts to sell over shorter time periods and then

CHART 6
Hedging treasury bonds

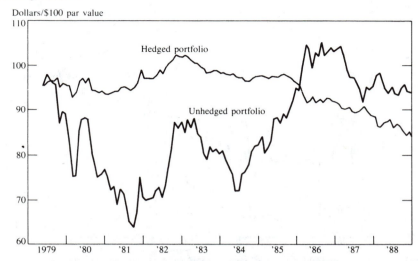

Dollars/$100 par value

Note: The bond portfolio is an equally weighted portfolio of the 30-year U.S. Treasury bond that matures in November 2007 and the 10-year U.S. Treasury bond that matures in May 1989. The hedged price is the price of the minimum risk hedged portfolio of bonds using the nearest futures contract with at least one month until expiration.

Source: Data Resources Inc.

hedged portfolio of bonds is clearly less variable than the value of the unhedged portfolio. The volatility of the price of the hedged portfolio, measured by the standard deviation of the change in price, is 60 percent lower than the volatility of the price of the unhedged portfolio.

Hedging a corporate bond. An investor in corporate bonds would hedge his portfolio against changes in interest rates by selling interest rate futures because corporate bond prices fall when interest rates rise. Corporate

bond futures do not exist, so the investor would use Treasury bond futures as a hedge. Treasury bond futures should be a less effective hedge for corporate bonds than for Treasury bonds, however, because Treasury bond futures prices are not as closely related to corporate bond prices as to Treasury bond prices.

An example of the reduction in the price volatility of a corporate bond that can be achieved by hedging is shown in Chart 7. This chart shows the prices of an A-rated 9-1/2 percent 30-year bond of a U.S. industrial company and the value of the hedged bond.[21]

---

adjusting the number of contracts to account for the changes. On the other hand, the example could be overstating the degree of risk reduction because the number of contracts sold is estimated from actual price data over the hedging period, whereas investors must estimate the number of contracts using data from periods prior to the hedging period.

---

[21] The qualifications and assumptions that applied to the hedge of the Treasury bond portfolio also apply to this example (see footnote 20).

CHART 7
Hedging corporate bonds

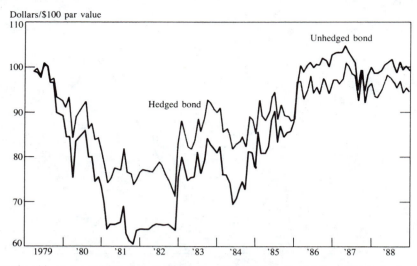

Dollars/$100 par value

Note: Corporate bond is an A-rated 9½ percent 30-year bond of a U.S. industrial firm. The hedged price is the price of the minimum risk hedged bond using the nearest futures contract with at least one month until expiration.

Source: Data Resources Inc.

The value of the hedged bond is still quite variable, but less variable than the unhedged portfolio. The standard deviation of the change in the value of the hedged bond is 8 percent lower than that of the unhedged portfolio. As expected, Treasury bond futures are a less effective hedge for corporate bonds than for Treasury bonds.[22]

Depository institutions. Depository institutions, such as banks and S&Ls, would hedge net worth against changes in interest rates by selling interest rate futures because their net worth generally falls when interest rates rise.[23]

[22] Although Treasury bond futures did not provide a good hedge for a single corporate bond, they should provide a better hedge for a portfolio of corporate bonds. The corporate bond in this example had an A rating, which suggests that credit risk is at least partly responsible for the relatively poor relationship between the bond price and the futures price. A diversified portfolio of corporate bonds, however, would be exposed to less credit risk, and therefore its price would be more closely related to the futures price.

[23] The best futures contract for hedging a depository institution's net worth is one whose price sensitivity to interest rate changes is as close as possible to the sensitivity of the institution's net worth to interest rate changes. The sensitivity of the institution's net worth to interest rate changes rises with the extent to which its asset and liability maturities are mismatched. Thus, institutions whose maturity structure is only slightly mismatched would choose futures contracts based on short-term assets, such as Treasury bills or Eurodollar time deposits. On the other hand, institutions whose maturity structure is highly mismatched would choose futures contracts based on longer term assets, such as Treasury bond and note futures.

When interest rates rise, the net worth of a typical depository institution falls because the value of its assets falls by more than the value of its liabilities. For example, suppose an S&L has assets with a market value of $100 million and liabilities with a market value of $90 million, resulting in a net worth of $10 million. If interest rates rise, the value of the assets might fall by, say, $5 million to $95 million. Since the liabilities have shorter maturities, their value would fall by only, say, $4 million to $86 million, resulting in a net worth of $9 million. But interest rate futures prices also fall when interest rates rise. So if the S&L sells interest rate futures, the gain on the futures when interest rates rise would offset some of the $1 million decline in net worth due to the rise in interest rates.[24]

Securities dealers. Securities dealers hedge interest rate risk by selling interest rate futures sometimes and buying them at other times. Securities dealers would hedge the bonds they have in inventory against changes in interest rates like any other bondholder by selling interest rate futures. On the other hand, securities dealers would hedge bonds they are committed to deliver at a future date for a predetermined price against changes in interest rates by buying interest rate futures.

To understand when securities dealers would buy futures, consider the following example. Suppose a securities dealer has agreed to deliver $10 million face value of Treasury bonds for $90.00 per $100 face value of bonds in two months, and the current price of the bonds is $89.50 per $100. If the dealer had the bonds in inventory or the funds to buy them, he would make a profit of $0.50 per $100, or $50,000. If not, though, he faces the risk that interest rates will fall and bond prices will rise. For example, if interest rates fall and bond prices rise $0.25, he would have to pay $89.75 per $100 for the bonds, and the profit on the commitment would fall 50 percent to $25,000. However, if interest rates fall, the futures price should rise. Since a person who buys a futures contract makes a profit when its price rises, the profit on the futures should offset much of the decrease in the profit on the commitment when interest rates fall.

Mortgage banks. Because the value of mortgage commitments falls when interest rates rise, mortgage bankers would hedge mortgage commitments against changes in interest rates by selling interest rate futures. For example, suppose a mortgage banker commits to a 10 percent interest rate on a $100,000 mortgage. If the mortgage closes in two months and interest rates do not change, the mortgage banker could sell the mortgage for $100,000. However, if interest rates rise, the value of the mortgage will fall. If, for example, the mortgage value falls to $98,000, the value of the mortgage commitment would fall $2,000. But since interest rates rose, interest rate futures prices would have fallen. Therefore, if the mortgage banker sells interest rate futures, the profit on the futures he sold would offset the loss on the mortgage commitment when interest rates rise.

---

[24] Of course, when interest rates fall, the value of the S&L's assets will rise more than the value of its liabilities, but the gain in net worth will be offset by a loss on the futures. In other words, like any other hedging asset, futures offset capital gains as well as capital losses. In the remaining examples, the discussion will focus on how hedging with futures offsets capital losses, but it is important to remember that futures hedges also offset capital gains.

Life insurance companies. Life insurance companies would hedge GIC commitments against changes in interest rates by buying interest rate futures. For example, suppose a life insurance company commits to a 10 percent interest rate on a GIC but will not receive the funds for two months. In addition, suppose the life insurance company expects to invest the funds in an 11 percent corporate bond. If interest rates do not change in the two-month period, the life insurance company would earn a spread of one percentage point. But if interest rates fall and the corporate bond rate falls to, say, 10.5 percent, the spread earned on the GIC would fall 50 percent to 0.5 percentage points. When interest rates fall, though, interest rate futures prices rise. Therefore, by buying futures, life insurance companies can offset declines in the spread on GIC commitments when interest rates fall.[25]

The risks of hedging with interest rate futures

Although hedging with interest rate futures allows investors to reduce interest rate risk, it generally cannot completely eliminate risk. All hedges generally contain some residual, or basis, risk. Moreover, hedging also introduces some new risks. Some of those risks are credit risk, marking to market risk, and managerial risk.

Basis risk. The risk that remains after an investor hedges his portfolio is called basis risk. An investor who hedges his portfolio with interest rate futures bears basis risk because, when interest rates change, the change in the price of the futures contract does not perfectly offset the change in the price of the asset being hedged. Fixed income asset prices can change for reasons other than changes in interest rates. As a result, the basis risk in a hedge will be relatively high when factors other than interest rates are an important source of the changes in the price of the asset being hedged.

For example, an asset's price will fall if the issuer's credit rating falls or if the asset is relatively illiquid and a large amount is sold. Since these factors would not affect the prices of interest rate futures, such as Treasury bond futures, interest rate futures cannot offset price changes caused by such factors. In fact, that is why Treasury bond futures proved to be a less effective hedging instrument for the corporate bond than for the Treasury bond portfolio in the examples used in the preceding section.

Credit risk. The credit risk in an interest rate futures hedge is not that the opposite party in the futures contract will default, but that the opposite party in the asset being hedged will default. Individuals do not have to be concerned about the opposite party defaulting on a futures contract because every futures exchange has a clearing organization that is a party to every futures contract in order to guarantee the integrity of the contract.[26] That is, the clearing house is the seller in every contract bought

---

[25] Recall that a GIC commitment is a fixed rate liability that is not matched by an asset. Therefore, net worth falls when interest rates fall because the increase in the value of the GIC commitment is not offset by an increase in the value of an asset. Since net worth falls when interest rates fall, the GIC commitment can be hedged against changes in interest rates by buying interest rate futures.

[26] The exchanges are also protected because many exchanges have limits on the amount a futures price can change within a day. The limits are equal to the minimum margin deposit that individuals must have on deposit with their broker.

and the buyer in every contract sold. But the risk remains that an investor will end up with an unhedged open futures position if there is a default on the asset being hedged.

For example, suppose an investor in corporate bonds hedges his portfolio against changes in interest rates by selling interest rate futures. If interest rates fall, the prices of the bond and futures will rise. Since futures were sold, the investor would suffer losses on the futures, but those losses would be offset by the gains on the bonds. If the bond issuer defaults, though, the investor would have the losses on his futures position but no gains to offset the losses.

Marking to market risk. Marking to market risk is the risk investors will have to cover futures losses when the contract is marked to market at the end of each day. All futures exchanges require every unsettled futures position to be marked to market every night and settled daily. That is, at the end of each day, funds are transferred from individuals who lose on their contracts to individuals who gain on their contracts so that buyers and sellers actually realize the gains and losses from daily price changes as they occur. A problem could occur for those who suffer losses on their futures position, though, because they must make immediate cash outlays. Although losses on futures contracts are generally offset by gains on the asset being hedged, investors usually do not receive those gains as they occur. Therefore, investors would either have to liquidate other investments and lose the associated income flows or pay interest on borrowed funds to cover their futures losses as they occur.

Managerial risk. Managerial risk, broadly defined, is the risk futures will be used inappropriately and result in greater, rather than less, risk. This is really a "catch all" category

that accounts for anything else that can go wrong with a hedging program. One major reason managerial risk arises is interest rate futures can be used for speculative purposes. In addition to being good assets for hedging, futures are also good assets for speculating on price movements for two reasons. First, it costs very little to open a futures position, and second, an open unhedged futures position is as risky as the underlying asset. While speculators play an important and useful role in futures markets, an institution that wants to hedge with futures must have internal controls to make sure those responsible for hedging are not speculating.

Managerial risk also arises because futures hedging strategies are complicated. Because they are complicated, it is possible for managers to make incorrect decisions that significantly lower a firm's value. For example, suppose a manager wants to minimize the interest rate risk of his bond portfolio, but he overhedges by selling too many futures contracts. If interest rates were to fall, the losses on the futures position could be much greater than the gains on the bonds. Thus, when overhedged, the riskiness of a portfolio is greater than the minimum level of risk and the return is less than that associated with the minimum level of risk. In fact, the riskiness of an overhedged portfolio can be even greater than the riskiness of the unhedged portfolio. To control this risk, it is important that managers understand the complexities of hedging with interest rate futures, the capabilities and limitations of a hedging program, and the need to continually monitor hedging programs.

Conclusion

The riskiness of investments in bonds and

other fixed income assets has increased in recent years because of increased interest rate volatility. The lack of traditional low-cost methods for managing this increase in interest rate risk led to the development of many new financial instruments that can be used to hedge interest rate risk. One of the most popular types of instruments is interest rate futures contracts. Interest rate futures are now trading on exchanges around the world, and they have become an important part of virtually every portfolio manager's tool kit for managing interest rate risk.

This article showed how interest rate futures can be used to manage interest rate risk. In many cases, interest rate risk can be substantially reduced. It must be remembered, though, that hedging with interest rate futures can be complex, and investors must thoroughly examine all aspects of interest rate futures and hedging techniques before implementing a hedging strategy.

Article 17

Managing Stock Market Risk With Stock Index Futures

By Charles S. Morris

Stock market investments always have been risky because stock returns are volatile. Stock returns are volatile because investors continually assess the effects of economic events on firm values. Some events are specific to an individual firm and therefore affect only that firm's stock price. Other kinds of events affect virtually all firms, causing the value of the entire market to change. For example, when the stock market collapsed on October 19, 1987, the price of nearly every publicly traded stock fell.

Stock investors traditionally have managed the volatility of returns due to firm-specific events by diversifying their portfolios. But diversification cannot reduce the volatility of returns caused by marketwide events like the October 1987 collapse. To protect themselves from mar-

ketwide events, stock investors traditionally have had to sell some of their portfolio and to buy other, less risky securities or to buy stocks that are influenced less by marketwide events. Such methods, however, are often costly and inconsistent with desired investment strategies.

The development over the past decade of stock index futures has given investors in stocks a new and better way to manage stock market risk. This article explains how stock index futures allow investors to manage risk by hedging the exposure of stock portfolios to marketwide events. The first section of the article discusses how stock market risks have traditionally been managed. The second section describes stock index futures and discusses the growth of stock index futures trading. The third section shows how stock index futures are used to manage market risk and explains their advantages over traditional methods of managing market risk. The fourth section discusses some of the limitations of managing risk with stock index futures.

Charles S. Morris is a senior economist at the Federal Reserve Bank of Kansas City. Julia Reigel, a research associate at the bank, assisted in the preparation of this article.

Traditional forms of risk management

Investments in stocks are risky because their returns are uncertain. Stock returns are uncertain because stock prices and dividends vary over time. Volatility in prices and dividends comes from two sources. One source is economic events specific to individual firms. The second source is economic events that affect every firm in the economy. Investors have generally found it more difficult to manage the second type of stock market risk.

Events unique to a specific firm are the primary source of volatility in an individual firm's stock returns. Indeed, the volatility in returns caused by firm-specific events is called *firm-specific* risk. For example, if a pharmaceutical company discovers a new drug, its stock price may rise. This company's discovery, however, would not directly affect any other company's stock price. If the company does not get approval to market the drug from the Food and Drug Administration, only that company's stock price would fall.

The stock returns of individual firms are also affected by marketwide events that affect the stock returns of all firms in the economy. The volatility in returns caused by marketwide events is called *market risk*. For example, an increase in interest rates might lower the earnings outlook for virtually every firm in the economy, causing all stock prices to fall.

Investors manage risk by choosing the amount of risk they are willing to incur. Some investors are willing to bear relatively high levels of risk, while others are not. In general, investors will not choose to minimize risk because there are costs to reducing risk. Because the risk and the expected return of an investment are inversely related, the main cost of reducing risk is a lower expected return.

To successfully manage risk, investors must independently manage both firm-specific risk and market risk. Firm-specific risk is traditionally managed by holding a diversified portfolio of stocks. Diversification can reduce risk because events specific to an individual firm have no direct effect on other firms. For example, suppose an investor invests in the stocks of a pharmaceutical company and an oil company. If the oil company happens to discover a new oil field and the pharmaceutical company has a new drug petition denied, the increase in the oil company's stock price could offset some or all of the decrease in the pharmaceutical company's stock price. As a result, the volatility of a diversified portfolio's returns is likely to be lower than that of any of its component stocks.

Diversification across stocks, however, cannot reduce market risk. For example, if an increase in interest rates causes all stock prices to fall, the change in one firm's stock price could not offset the change in another firm's stock price. Even the value of a completely diversified portfolio that contains every traded stock—that is, the stock market as a whole—would fall. Thus, investors must use other methods to manage market risk.

Market risk can be managed in two ways using traditional risk management techniques. One way is to adjust the share of stocks in an investment portfolio.[1] For example, an investor can decrease a portfolio's exposure to market risk by decreasing the share of stocks in the portfolio and increasing the share of other assets, such as bonds. A second way to reduce market risk is to sell stocks that have a large amount of market risk and buy stocks with a small amount of market risk. For example, the value of an S&L is very sensitive to changes in interest rates, while the value of a retail grocery store is not. Thus, an investor who has a portfolio that includes S&L stocks could reduce the portfolio's exposure to market risk by selling the S&L stocks and buying retail grocery stocks.

In contrast to diversification, these traditional methods for managing market risk are often costly and inconsistent with desired investment strategies. Adjusting portfolio shares is often inconsistent with a strategy of investing heavily in stocks. For example, the manager of a stock mutual fund must invest in stocks, but the manager cannot do so and simultaneously reduce market risk by selling stocks.

Substituting low market-risk stocks for high market-risk stocks also has several problems. First, very few stocks have a small amount of market risk because all firms are affected by marketwide events, such as changes in interest rates. Second, stocks that have a small amount of market risk might not fit into an investor's overall investment strategy. For example, an investor who has detailed knowledge about S&Ls but very little knowledge about retail grocery stores would not want to sell S&L stocks and buy retail grocery stocks. Finally, a stock with a small amount of market risk might have a large amount of firm-specific risk.

An introduction to stock index futures

The limitations of the traditional methods of managing market risk have led investors to search for new risk management techniques. Since they began trading in 1982, stock index futures have become an extremely popular tool for managing market risk. This section provides an overview of stock index futures, highlighting some of their similarities and differences with other types of financial futures.

What are stock index futures?

A financial futures contract is an agreement between two parties to buy or sell a financial asset, such as a Treasury bond or foreign currency, at a given time in the future for a predetermined price. Stock index futures are financial futures contracts in which the underlying asset is a group of stocks included in one of the major stock price indexes such as the Standard & Poor's 500 Composite Stock Price Index.

In a financial futures contract, nothing is exchanged when the contract is written because it is only an agreement to make an exchange at a future date. In a typical futures contract, the buyer of the contract agrees to take delivery of the underlying asset at the agreed price when the contract expires. The seller of the contract agrees to deliver the asset at the agreed price on the expiration date.

In most financial futures contracts, physical delivery of the asset rarely occurs. Indeed, in some futures contracts, delivery is not even permitted. In most financial futures contracts, a buyer or seller settles the contract by taking an offsetting position in the same futures contract before delivery. For example, a buyer of a March Treasury bond futures contract can offset the position by selling a March Treasury bond futures contract before the expiration date of the contract.

Stock index futures are one type of futures contract that requires traders to settle contracts by taking an offsetting position. The reason that delivery is not permitted in stock index futures is that it would be impractical for a person who, say, sells an S&P 500 index futures contract to deliver all 500 stocks in exactly the proportion in which they make up the index. Although delivery is not allowed, there is a "delivery" or expiration date for stock index futures contracts. On this date, any unsettled contracts are settled by taking an offsetting position at the price of the underlying index.

Although delivery of the underlying stocks is not allowed in stock index futures contracts, thinking about the contract as if delivery were allowed may make the concept of a stock index future more intuitive. For example, if in March an investor were to buy a June S&P 500 index futures contract, the investor would simply be agreeing to buy in June the 500 stocks in the proportion in which they make up the index. Similarly, if an investor were to sell a June S&P 500 index futures, the investor would simply be agreeing to sell the stocks in June.

Profits and losses in stock index futures

As in other futures markets, traders in stock index futures will generally earn profits or suffer losses when they settle a contract. To make a profit, futures traders must sell futures for a higher price than they pay. Whether a stock index futures trader gains or loses, therefore, depends on two conditions: whether futures were initially bought or sold, and whether the price of the futures contract rises or falls between the time the initial contract is established and the time an offsetting position is taken.

A buyer of stock index futures makes a profit when the futures price rises and suffers a loss when the futures price falls. Suppose, for example, on March 10 an investor buys a June S&P 500 index futures contract for $300 per unit of the contract, and on April 20 settles the position by selling a June S&P 500 index futures contract for $305.[2] Under these circumstances, the investor would make a profit of $5 per unit

because he offset his position by selling a futures contract for $5 more than he paid.[3] On the other hand, if the price falls to $297 on April 20, the investor would lose $3 per unit because he offset the position by selling a futures contract for $3 less than the original purchase price.

In contrast, a seller of stock index futures suffers a loss when the futures price rises and makes a profit when the futures price falls. Suppose on March 10 an investor sells a June S&P 500 index futures contract for $300 per unit of the contract, and on April 20 settles the position by buying a June S&P 500 index futures contract for $305. The investor would suffer a loss of $5 because he offset his position by buying a contract for $5 more than he initially received from selling the contract. On the other hand, if the price falls to $297 on April 20, the investor would make a profit of $3 because he offset his position by buying a contract for $3 less than he initially received from selling the contract.

Growth in stock index futures trading

Stock index futures are one of the more recent financial futures. Stock index futures are used primarily by institutional investors, such as stock mutual funds, pension funds, and life insurance companies. The first stock index futures contract began trading in February 1982, when the Kansas City Board of Trade introduced a contract based on the Value Line Index. This contract was soon followed by a futures contract based on the S&P 500 index, which began trading on the Chicago Mercantile Exchange in April 1982. A futures contract based on the New York Stock Exchange Composite Index began trading on the New York Futures Exchange in May 1982. Although other contracts have begun

CHART 1

Open interest in S&P 500 index futures

Thousands of contracts

Note: Values are monthly averages of daily open interest in the nearest S&P 500 index futures contract with at least one month until expiration.

Source: Data Resources Inc.

trading since 1982, the S&P 500 index futures is the most popular stock index futures contract.[4]

Despite their relatively short history, stock index futures have gained widespread acceptance by stock market investors. One measure of activity in a stock index futures contract is open interest in the contract—the number of contracts not yet offset by opposite transactions. Chart 1 shows the open interest in the S&P 500 index futures contract from June 1982 to December 1988. Although open interest in S&P 500 index futures is fairly volatile, the trend is clearly upward. From June 1982 to December

1987, open interest rose at an average rate of 250 percent per year. While open interest has not grown much since the end of 1987, it has remained very high, suggesting that stock index futures remain popular among investors.[5]

Managing market risk with stock index futures

Stock index futures have been successful because they have opened up new dimensions for managing market risk through hedging. In contrast to traditional methods of managing market risk, hedging with stock index futures is relatively inexpensive and is consistent with most investment strategies.

Why stock index futures can hedge market risk

Investors face market risk when marketwide events cause the value of their stock portfolios to change. The market risk of a portfolio is usually measured as the volatility of that part of the portfolio's returns that is correlated with the returns of the overall stock market.

To hedge market risk, an investor must be able to take a position in a hedging asset such that profits or losses on the hedging asset offset changes in the value of the stock portfolio when marketwide events occur. For example, when marketwide events cause the value of an investor's portfolio to fall, the investor needs to make a profit on the hedging asset. The risk reduction from hedging is not free, however. Because risk and expected return are inversely related, the primary cost is that the investor's expected return will also fall.

Stock index futures can hedge market risk effectively because changes in stock index futures prices will generally be highly correlated with changes in stock portfolio values caused by marketwide events.[6] That is, when marketwide events cause the value of the stock portfolio to change, these same events will cause stock index futures prices to change. As a result, the investor can use changes in the value of a stock index futures contract to offset—that is, to hedge—changes in the value of his portfolio caused by marketwide events.

The more diversified the portfolio, the greater the correlation between the value of the portfolio and the price of stock index futures. The reason is that the primary source of risk in a well-diversified portfolio is market risk. That is, diversification eliminates most of a portfolio's firm-specific risk. For example, Chart 2 shows the value of a well-diversified stock portfolio and the price of the S&P 500 index futures.[7] The portfolio is considered to be well diversified because market risk accounts for 99 percent of its total risk.[8] As expected, the futures price and portfolio value follow each other quite closely. Because of this close relationship, stock index futures should be very effective at hedging the risk of this portfolio.

How stock index futures hedge market risk

In general, investors who hold stock portfolios hedge market risk by selling stock index futures.[9] An investor in a stock portfolio that contains market risk suffers a loss when the market falls because the value of his portfolio will also fall. But if the market falls, stock index futures prices will fall as well. When the market falls, therefore, an investor needs to make a profit from falling futures prices to offset the loss on his portfolio. Since sellers of futures make a profit when futures prices fall, the investor would hedge by selling futures. Similarly, when the market rises, the losses on the futures contract at least partly offset the profits on the original stock portfolio. Thus, by selling stock index futures, investors can reduce the price volatility of their portfolios caused by marketwide events.[10]

The reduction in price volatility that can be achieved by hedging is shown in Chart 3. This chart compares the values of the well-diversified portfolio and the same portfolio hedged by sales of S&P 500 index futures.[11] The value of the hedged portfolio is clearly less variable than the

CHART 2
Diversified portfolio value and futures price

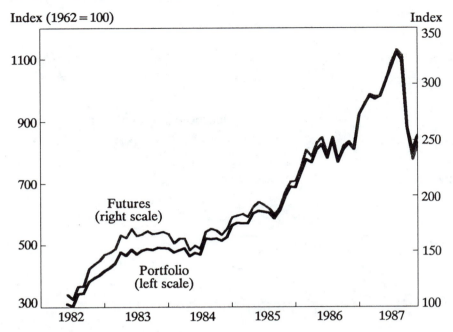

Note: The futures price is the price of the nearest S&P 500 index futures contract with at least one month until expiration. The portfolio consists of stocks of the largest firms on the New York Stock Exchange (NYSE). These firms have a market capitalization (stock prices time shares outstanding) equal to 10 percent of the NYSE capitalization.

Sources: The futures prices are from Data Resources, Inc. The portfolio values are from the Center for Research in Securities Prices.

value of the unhedged portfolio. In fact, the volatility of returns on the hedged portfolio, measured by its variance, is 91 percent lower than the volatility of the returns on the unhedged portfolio. The effectiveness of the hedge in reducing market risk is easily seen in October 1987, the month of the stock market collapse. From the end of September 1987 to the end of October 1987, the value of the unhedged portfolio fell 19 percent, while the value of the hedged portfolio fell only 6 percent.

Advantages of stock index futures over traditional techniques

Managing market risk by hedging with stock index futures does not suffer from the same problems associated with traditional methods of managing market risk. Stock index futures are relatively inexpensive and are consistent with desired investment strategies.

Relative to traditional methods of managing market risk, stock index futures are inexpen-

CHART 3
Hedging market risk

Index (1962 = 100)

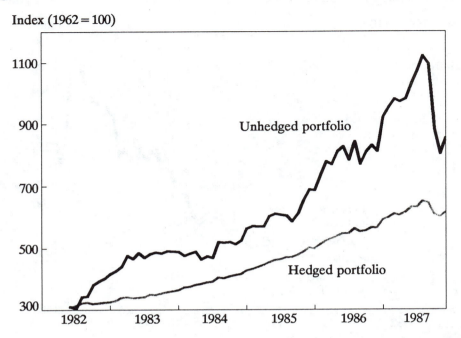

Note: The portfolio consists of stocks of the largest firms on the New York Stock Exchange (NYSE). These firms have a market capitalization (stock prices times shares outstanding) equal to 10 percent of the NYSE capitalization. The hedged value is the value of the minimum-risk hedged portfolio of stocks using the nearest S&P 500 index futures contract with at least one month until expiration.

Sources: The futures prices are from Data Resources, Inc. The portfolio values are from the Center for Research in Securities Prices.

sive because the transaction costs of establishing a futures position are low. When a position is established, the only outlays are broker fees and an initial margin deposit with the broker.[12] The fees paid to brokers and traders are quite small. For example, the cost of establishing and settling a position in an S&P 500 index futures contract is only $25.[13] Because a single S&P 500 index futures contract is worth 500 times the futures price, the total value of a contract that costs, say, $300 would be $150,000, and the $25

fee would be less than .02 of a percent of the underlying value of the contract. The initial margin is also relatively small—the margin on an S&P 500 index futures contract used for hedging purposes is $4,000. The cost of meeting the initial margin requirement is very small because investors generally can earn interest on the initial margin by using U.S. government securities to meet the margin requirement.[14]

Hedging market risk with stock index futures is also consistent with most investment strategies. In contrast to traditional methods of managing market risk, an investor who hedges market risk with stock index futures does not have to alter the composition of his portfolio. For example, stock fund managers do not have to sell part of their portfolios to reduce market risk. Nor would an investor in S&L stocks have to sell his stocks and buy low market-risk stocks with which he might not be familiar. To manage market risk by hedging with stock index futures, the investor simply has to sell the correct amount of stock index futures contracts.

Limitations of stock index futures

Despite the advantages of hedging market risk with stock index futures, there are some limitations. One important limitation is that stock index futures provide no protection against firm-specific events. In addition, the investor can be exposed to other forms of risk.[15]

Basis risk

Hedging with futures allows investors to reduce, but generally not to completely eliminate, risk. Basis risk is the risk that remains after a portfolio has been hedged. Because stock index futures only hedge market risk, firm-specific risk is the primary source of basis risk in a portfolio hedged with stock index futures.[16]

The basis risk of a hedged stock portfolio will be high when the portfolio contains a large proportion of firm-specific risk. That is, stock index futures will not be very effective in reducing the overall risk of a relatively undiversified portfolio. The reason is that firm-specific events generally have no impact on the value of the market and therefore will not affect futures prices. Because fluctuations in portfolio values

due to firm-specific events are not related to futures prices, stock index futures will not provide a good hedge for these changes in portfolio values.[17]

The significance of basis risk is shown in Charts 4 and 5. Chart 4 compares the value of a relatively undiversified stock portfolio and the price of the S&P 500 index futures contract. In contrast to the well-diversified portfolio (Chart 2) in which firm-specific risk accounted for just 1 percent of total risk, firm-specific risk accounts for 34 percent of the total risk of the portfolio in Chart 4.[18] The futures price and portfolio value are related, but not nearly as closely as are the futures price and well-diversified portfolio value.

Because the value of the relatively undiversified portfolio and the futures price are not closely related, stock index futures should be less effective at hedging the total risk of this portfolio. Chart 5 compares the values of the unhedged portfolio and the same portfolio hedged by sales of S&P 500 index futures.[19] The variance of returns on the hedged portfolio is just 27 percent lower than that of the unhedged portfolio. The relative ineffectiveness of the hedge is easily seen in October 1987. From the end of September 1987 to the end of October 1987, the value of the hedged portfolio fell 24 percent, only slightly less than the 29 percent decline in the value of the unhedged portfolio.

New risks

One new type of risk involved in futures trading is marking-to-market risk. This is the risk that arises because futures traders have to cover their futures losses at the end of each day. All futures exchanges require every unsettled futures position to be marked to market every

CHART 4

Undiversified portfolio value and futures price

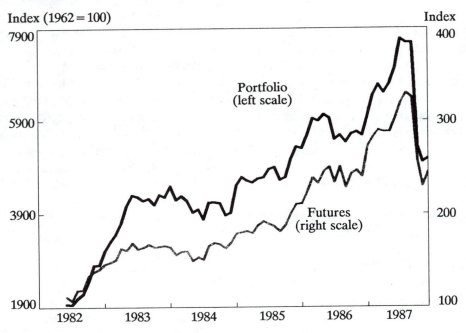

Note: The futures price is the price of the nearest S&P 500 index futures contract with at least one month until expiration. The portfolio consists of stocks of the smallest firms on the New York Stock Exchange (NYSE). These firms have a market capitalization (stock prices times shares outstanding) equal to 10 percent of the NYSE capitalization.

Sources: The futures prices are from Data Resources, Inc. The portfolio values are from the Center for Research in Securities Prices.

night and settled daily. That is, at the end of each day, funds are transferred from individuals who lose on their contracts to individuals who gain on their contracts so that buyers and sellers actually realize the gains and losses from daily price changes as they occur. A problem could occur for those who suffer losses on their futures position, though, because they must make immediate cash outlays. Although losses on stock index futures contracts are generally offset by gains on the stock portfolio being hedged, investors usually do not receive those

gains as they occur. Therefore, investors would either have to liquidate some of their investments and lose the associated income flows or pay interest on borrowed funds to cover their futures losses as they occur.

A second type of risk involved in futures trading is managerial risk. Managerial risk, broadly defined, is the risk stock index futures will be used inappropriately and result in greater, rather than less, risk. This is really a "catch all" category that accounts for anything else that can go wrong with a hedging program.

CHART 5
Hedging an undiversified portfolio

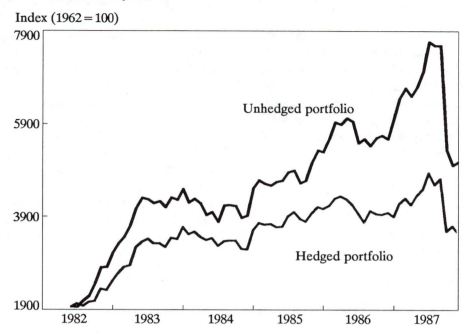

Index (1962 = 100)

Note: The portfolio consists of stocks of the smallest firms on the New York Stock Exchange (NYSE). These firms have a market capitalization (stock prices times shares outstanding) equal to 10 percent of the NYSE capitalization. The hedged value is the value of the minimum-risk hedged portfolio of stocks using the nearest S&P 500 index futures contract with at least one month until expiration.

Sources: The futures prices are from Data Resources, Inc. The portfolio values are from the Center for Research in Securities Prices.

One major reason that managerial risk arises is that stock index futures can be used for speculative purposes. In addition to being good assets for hedging market risk, stock index futures are also good assets for speculating on stock market movements for two reasons. First, it costs very little to establish a futures position, and second, stock index futures are just as risky as the market. An institution that wants to hedge with futures must have internal controls to make sure those responsible for hedg-

ing are not speculating.

Managerial risk also arises because hedging strategies involving stock index futures can become complicated. Because they can be complicated, it is possible for managers to make incorrect decisions that significantly lower a portfolio's value. For example, suppose a manager wants to minimize the market risk of a stock portfolio, but he overhedges by selling too many futures contracts. If the market were to rise, the losses on the futures position could be much greater than the gains on the portfolio. Thus, when overhedged, the riskiness of a portfolio is greater than the minimum level of risk and the expected return is less than that associated with the minimum level of risk. In fact, the riskiness of an overhedged portfolio can even be greater than the riskiness of the unhedged portfolio. To control this risk, it is important that managers understand the complexities of hedging with stock index futures, the capabilities and limitations of a hedging program, and the need to continually monitor hedging programs.

Conclusion

Stocks have always been relatively risky investments. While investors in stocks have always been able to manage the firm-specific risk component of total risk through diversification, managing the market risk component has traditionally been costly and inconsistent with desired investment strategies. The development of stock index futures, however, has provided investors in stocks with a new, low-cost tool for managing market risk. As a result, stock index futures are one of the most successful financial innovations of recent years. They have become an essential part of virtually every stock portfolio manager's tool kit for managing market risk.

This article showed how stock index futures can be used successfully to manage market risk. It must be remembered, though, that hedging with stock index futures can be complex, and investors must thoroughly examine all aspects of stock index futures and hedging techniques before implementing a hedging strategy.

Endnotes

[1] In a sense, adjusting the share of stocks in an investment portfolio is diversification, but it is diversification across different types of assets as opposed to diversification across different stocks. Throughout this article, diversification means diversification across different stocks.

[2] Actually, the quoted price of a futures contract itself is an index. The value of an S&P 500 index futures contract is $500 times the level of the index. The value of one unit of the contract, therefore, is 1/500 of the total value of the contract, or $1 times the level of the index. The total value of one contract at $300 per unit is $150,000 (500 units times $300 per unit).

[3] Because the contract is for 500 units, the actual profit is $2,500 (500 units times $5 per unit).

[4] The Value Line Index, Standard and Poor's 500 Composite Stock Price Index, and New York Stock Exchange Composite Index contracts are each worth $500 times the index level. A contract equal to $250 times the Major Market Index is traded on the Chicago Board of Trade exchange, and a contract equal to $100 times the Value Line Index (Mini Value Line) is traded on the Kansas City Board of Trade exchange.

[5] One reason open interest has leveled off is that many traders have shied away from trading stock index futures since the stock market collapsed in October 1987.

[6] These changes are highly correlated because both are highly correlated with changes in the value of the overall market. As discussed in the text, market risk is measured by the correlation between portfolio returns and market returns. Stock index futures prices are highly correlated with the value of the market because (1) broad stock indexes, such as the S&P 500 index, are used to measure the value of the market, and (2) stock index futures prices are highly correlated with the underlying index.

The price of any futures contract is always highly correlated with the price of the underlying asset. The theoretical relationship between the price of a futures contract and the price of its underlying asset is known as the cost-of-carry theory of futures prices. Prices do deviate slightly from cost of carry, though, because of transaction costs and capital market imperfections. For a detailed discussion of the relationship between stock index futures prices and stock prices, see Bradford Cornell and Kenneth R. French, "The Pricing of Stock Index Futures," *The Journal of Futures Markets* (Spring 1983), pp. 1-14.

[7] The best stock index futures contract for hedging a particular stock portfolio is the futures contract whose price is most correlated with the value of the portfolio. Stock prices move together, though, so most of the stock indexes—and therefore most of the stock index futures prices—move together. Thus, for the purposes of these examples, it makes little difference which futures contract is used. The S&P 500 index futures contract is used in all examples because it is by far the most popular of the stock index futures contracts.

[8] Total risk is measured by the variance of the portfolio's total monthly returns over the period from July 1982 to December 1987. Market risk is measured by the variance of the predicted returns from a regression of the portfolio's monthly returns on market returns over the same period. For a discussion of how market risk is measured, see Thomas E. Copeland and J. Fred Weston, *Financial Theory and Corporate Policy,* 2d ed., (Reading, Mass: Addison-Wesley Publishing Co., 1983).

The S&P 500 index is used to measure market returns. Theoretically, the market portfolio contains every asset in the economy. Since it is not possible to observe the true market returns, however, an imperfect measure must be used. While there are many broad stock indexes that can be used to measure market returns, the various indexes generally move together. As a result, the qualitative conclusions reached in the text remain the same as long as one of the broad indexes is used to measure market returns.

[9] Although this section describes how stock index futures hedge market risk, stock index futures are also often used for reasons other than purely hedging market risk. Some strategies, such as stock selection and market timing, are used in an attempt to outperform the market. Portfolio managers also use stock index futures to give them more flexibility in liquidating a portfolio. For more information on these strategies, see Stephen Figlewski, *Hedging with Financial Futures for Institutional Investors: From Theory to Practice* (Cambridge, Mass.: Ballinger Publishing Co., 1986) pp. 115-54. Stock index futures are also used in portfolio insurance strategies. For a discussion of portfolio insurance, see Peter A. Abken, "An Introduction to Portfolio Insurance," *Economic Review,* Federal Reserve Bank of

Atlanta (November/December 1987), pp. 2-25. Finally, stock index futures are used by arbitragers who try to make a profit from discrepancies between actual stock index futures prices and the prices that would be predicted from the cost-of-carry theory of futures prices. For a discussion of index arbitrage, see John J. Merrick, Jr., "Fact and Fantasy About Stock Index Futures Program Trading," *Business Review,* Federal Reserve Bank of Philadelphia (September/October 1987), pp. 13-23.

[10] Although investors in stock portfolios generally sell stock index futures to hedge their portfolios, there are times when they buy stock index futures. For example, a portfolio manager who wants to purchase some stocks but does not expect to have the necessary funds for several days faces the risk that the market will rise in the interim. The manager could hedge the risk that arises from changes in the market by buying futures. If the market rises, the loss from having to pay a higher price for the stocks will at least be partly offset by the profit on the futures. On the other hand, if the market falls, the profit from buying the stocks at a lower price will at least be partly offset by the loss on the futures.

[11] For simplicity, this example assumes that the investor wants to minimize risk. In general, investors would not *minimize* the risk of a stock portfolio with stock index futures. The reason is that the expected return on such a portfolio is the risk-free rate, which the investor could get at a much lower cost by simply investing in Treasury bills. The example also ignores the effects of margin requirements, transaction costs, taxation, accounting practices, and regulatory requirements on the value of the hedged portfolio, all of which could affect the value of the hedge and the hedging strategy. The prices are end-of-month data, and the futures price is on the nearest contract with at least one month until expiration.

The example does not account for the possibility that risk could be reduced further by (1) using futures with contract months that are further out, or (2) estimating the number of contracts to sell over shorter time periods and then adjusting the number of contracts to account for the changes. On the other hand, the example could be overstating the degree of risk reduction because the number of contracts sold is estimated from actual price data over the hedging period, whereas investors must estimate the number of contracts using data from periods prior to the hedging period.

[12] The margin on a futures contract is "good faith" money deposited with a broker to assure him that losses can be covered in the event of adverse price movements.

[13] See Arnold Kling, "Futures Markets and Transaction

Costs,'' in Myron L. Kwast, ed., *Financial Futures and Options in the U.S. Economy: A Study by the Staff of the Federal Reserve System* (Washington, D.C.: Board of Governors of the Federal Reserve System, 1986), pp. 41-54.

14 The minimum initial margin and the minimum level that must be maintained are set by the exchanges and are changed from time to time. The margin level depends on factors such as the volatility of the price of the underlying instrument. Margins also may depend on whether a person is just buying or selling futures alone or is buying or selling futures to establish a hedge. The margin on an outright purchase or sale of an S&P 500 index futures for speculative purposes is $6,500. Although investors can earn interest on the initial margin by depositing U.S. government securities, they can not earn interest on additions to the margin account because additions must be made with cash. Cash is required because additions are for losses on a contract that are transferred to the accounts of parties that have gained from price movements.

15 One risk that individuals do not have to be concerned about is the risk of the opposite party defaulting on a futures contract. The reason is that every futures exchange has a clearing organization that is a party to every futures contract in order to guarantee the integrity of the contract. In effect, then, the clearing house is the seller in every contract bought and the buyer in every contract sold.

16 Hedging a stock portfolio with stock index futures will completely eliminate risk only if the values of the portfolio and the futures are perfectly correlated. In general, the correlation is not perfect for two reasons. The primary reason is that most portfolios contain firm-specific risk. In addition, though, stock index futures do not even provide full protection from marketwide events because the value of the market is not perfectly correlated with the value of the futures contract. In other words, even if an investor were to diversify away all firm-specific risk and hold the market portfolio, the hedged portfolio would still contain some residual, or basis, risk.

17 Although stock index futures are less effective at hedging the total risk of a portfolio with a relatively large share of firm-specific risk, they are equally effective at hedging the market risk of portfolios with large or small shares of firm-specific risk.

18 Firm-specific risk is measured by the variance of the residual returns from a regression of the monthly portfolio returns on the S&P 500 index returns over the period from July 1982 to December 1987.

19 The qualifications and assumptions that applied to the hedge of the well-diversified portfolio in Chart 3 also apply to this example (see note 11).

Article 18

Interest-Rate Caps, Collars, and Floors

Peter A. Abken

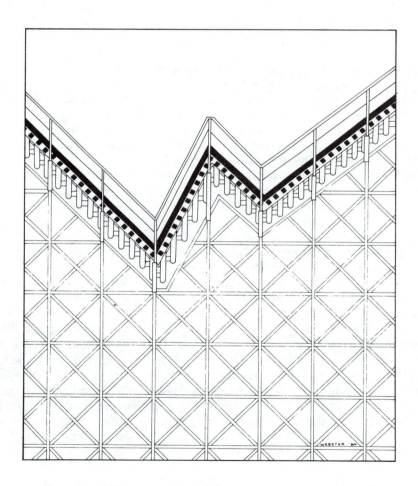

As some of the newest interest-rate risk management instruments, caps, collars, and floors are the subject of increasing attention among both investors and analysts. This article explains how such instruments are constructed, discusses their credit risks, and presents a new approach for valuing caps, collars, and floors subject to default risk.

Since the late 1970s interest rates on all types of fixed-income securities have become more volatile, spawning a variety of methods to mitigate the costs associated with interest-rate fluctuations. Managing interest-rate risk has become big business and an exceedingly complicated activity. One facet of this type of risk management involves buying and selling "derivative" assets, which can be used to offset or hedge changes in asset or liability values caused by interest-rate movements. As its name implies, the value of a derivative asset depends on the value of another asset or assets.

Two types of derivative assets widely discussed in the financial press and in previous *Economic Review* articles are options and futures contracts.[1] Another derivative asset that has become extremely popular is the interest-rate swap.[2] This article examines a group of instruments known as interest-rate caps, collars, and floors, which are medium- to long-term agreements that have proven to be highly useful for hedging against interest-rate uncertainties. In this regard, caps, collars, and floors can be thought of as insurance policies against adverse movements in interest rates.

Like interest-rate swaps, to which these instruments are closely related, caps, collars, and floors are designed to hedge cash flows over time rather than on a single date. The discussion below will show how caps, collars, and floors are related to each other, as well as how they may be constructed from the most basic derivative asset, the option. The article also shows the ways in which caps, collars, and floors are created in practice, along with the different kinds of intermediaries involved in the cap market.[3] The rationale for hedging is reviewed, as are examples of how caps, collars, and floors are used by different financial institutions. The last section of the article considers the credit risk associated with buying caps, collars, or floors and presents a new approach for determining the expected cost of default on these instruments.

The author is an economist in the financial section of the Atlanta Fed's Research Department. He thanks Igor A. Lamser of Noonan, Astley, and Pearce, Inc., for helpful discussions about the cap market and for providing data on cap rates.

What Is an Interest-Rate Cap?

An interest-rate cap, sometimes called a ceiling, is a financial instrument that effectively places a maximum amount on the interest payment made on floating-rate debt. Many businesses borrow funds through loans or bonds on which the periodic interest payment varies according to a prespecified short-term interest rate. The most widely used rate in both the caps and swaps markets is the London Interbank Offered Rate (LIBOR), which is the rate offered on Eurodollar deposits of one international bank held at another.[4] A typical example of floating-rate borrowing might be a firm taking out a $20 million bank loan on which the interest would be paid every three months at 50 basis points (hundredths of a percent) over LIBOR prevailing at each payment date. Other short-term rates that are used in conjunction with caps include commercial bank certificate of deposit (CD) rates, the prime interest rate, Treasury bill rates, commercial paper rates, and certain tax-exempt interest rates.

Data on the size of the cap market are sketchy. The International Swap Dealers Association (ISDA) conducted a survey of its members in March 1989, and 44 of the association's 97 members responded. Almost 90 percent of the respondents reported participating in the markets for caps, collars, floors, and options on swaps. As of year-end 1988, these members alone held 7,521 caps, collars, and floors, with a total notional principal of $290 billion. The volume conducted through 1988 was reported as having notional principal of $172 billion. These figures inflate the size of the market considerably because they are not adjusted for transactions among the dealers themselves, such as the purchase or sale of caps or floors to hedge existing positions in these instruments. On the other hand, the survey did not cover the entire market. Nonetheless, the figures probably still greatly overstate the size of the market, net of interdealer transactions or positions.[5] The interest-rate swaps market is vastly larger at over $1 trillion.

Most studies of caps concern agreements offered by commercial or investment banks to borrowers seeking interest-rate protection. These instruments are often tailored to a client's needs, and, particularly in the case of caps, may be marketable or negotiable. Caps, collars, and floors can also be manufactured out of basic derivative assets: options or futures contracts, or a combination of the two. The following discussion will define caps, collars, and floors in terms of option contracts, which are the simplest type of derivative asset.

Call and Put Options. An option is a financial contract with a fixed expiration date that offers either a positive return (payoff) or nothing at maturity, depending on the value of the asset underlying the option. At expiration, a call option gives the purchaser the right, but not the obligation, to buy a fixed number of units of the underlying asset if that asset's price exceeds a level specified in the option contract. The seller or "writer" of a call has the obligation to sell the underlying asset at the specified exercise or strike price if the call expires "in the money." The payoff on a call need not actually involve delivery of the underlying asset to the call buyer but rather can be settled by a cash payment. The caps market, for example, uses cash settlement. If the asset price finishes below the exercise price, the call is said to expire "out of the money."

Put options are analogous to calls. In this case, though, the purchaser has the right to sell, rather than buy, a fixed number of units of the underlying asset if the asset price is below the exercise price. The options discussed in this article will all be "European" options, which can only be exercised on the expiration date, as opposed to "American" options, which can be exercised any time before or at expiration. As will be seen, caps, floors, and collars are European-style option-based instruments, and the European interest-rate call option is the basic building block for the interest-rate cap.

Options on debt instruments can be confusing if it is unclear just what the option "price" represents. For debt instruments, the strike price is referred to as the strike level, reflecting an interest rate. Recall that the price of a debt instrument, such as a Treasury bill or CD, moves inversely with its corresponding interest rate; as the interest rate of a Treasury bill rises, its price falls. Thus, a call on a Treasury bill rate is effectively a put on its price. (To keep the exposition clear, all discussion will be in terms of options on interest rates. The strike price will be re-

ferred to as the strike level.) A call with a strike level of 8 percent (on an annual basis) on some notional amount of principal is effectively a cap on a floating-rate loan payment coinciding with the expiration of this option. (The notional amount of principal is a sum used as the basis for the option payoff computation. Cap, collar, and floor agreements do not involve any exchange of principal.)

Assume the call's payment date, known as the reset date, falls semiannually. If the interest rate is less than 8 percent on the reset date, the call expires worthless. If the interest rate exceeds 8 percent, the call pays off the difference between the actual interest rate and the strike level times the notional principal, in turn multiplied by the fraction of a year that has elapsed since purchase of the option. For example, if

---

"[C]aps, floors, and collars are European-style option-based instruments, and the European interest-rate call option is the basic building block for the interest-rate cap."

---

the actual rate of interest six months later were 10 percent and if the notional principal were $1 million, the payment received from the call writer would be 2 percent (the 10 percent actual rate minus the 8 percent strike level) x $1,000,000 x 180/360 = $10,000.

A put option on an interest payment works in a similar way and is the foundation for the interest-rate floor. The holder of a floating-rate loan could protect against a loss in interest income from the loan by buying an interest-rate put. A fall in the interest rate below the strike level of the put would result in a payoff from the option, offsetting the interest income lost because of a lower interest payment on the loan.

An option writer is basically an insurer who receives a premium payment from the option buyer when an option is created (sold). In fact, the option price is alternatively called the option premium. The same party can simultaneously write and buy options, thus creating an interest-rate collar. Before exploring this strategy further, option pricing must be reviewed briefly.

Option Pricing. An option's price before expiration depends on several variables, including the value of the underlying asset on which the option is written, the risk-free rate of interest (usually a Treasury bill that matures at the same time as the option), the time remaining before expiration, the strike price or level, and the volatility of the underlying asset price.[6] For later reference, readers should know how an option price changes in response to a change in an underlying variable, all other variables remaining constant. A call price rises (falls) when the underlying asset price, volatility, or time to expiration increases (decreases). It falls (rises)

"A cap can . . . be perceived as a series of interest-rate call options for successively more distant reset dates; a floor is a similarly constructed series of put options."

---

with an increase (decrease) in the exercise price. A put price rises (falls) with an increase (decrease) in the strike price or volatility. It falls (rises) with an increase (decrease) in the underlying asset price or interest rate. Unlike a call price, a put price is not unambiguously affected by an increase in the time to expiration, but the put price depends at any time on how far in or out of the money the put is.[7]

For an interest-rate call option, the higher the strike level compared to the current interest rate, the lower the option value. Choosing a high strike level (out-of-the-money) call is less expensive than buying an at-the-money or in-the-money call. Similarly, a low strike level (out-of-the-money) put is cheaper than one with a higher strike level.

This relationship between an option's strike level and its price (the amount the option is out of the money) is analogous to a large deductible

on an insurance policy. Such a policy is less likely to pay off and is therefore less expensive. Likewise, the cost of interest-rate "insurance" can be reduced by taking a large deductible—that is, buying an out-of-the-money option—and thereby protecting only against large, adverse interest-rate movements.

Creating an interest-rate collar is another method for reducing the cost of interest-rate insurance. The call-option premium for an interest-rate cap may be partially or completely offset by selling a put option that sets an interest-rate floor. For a floating-rate debt holder, the effect of this dual purchase is to protect against rate movements above the cap level while simultaneously giving up potential interest savings if the rate drops below the floor level.

If the cap and floor levels of a collar are narrowed to the extent that they coincide at the current floating interest rate—that is, both put and call options are at the money—the resulting collar is so tight that it is similar to a forward contract on an interest rate, which is a derivative asset that locks in the current forward rate. When the contract expires, the change in the contract's value that has occurred since the inception of the contract exactly offsets the change in the interest payment due. A rise in the floating-rate payment is matched by an equal gain in the interest paid to the contract holder; a fall in the floating-rate payment is balanced by an equal loss on the forward contract. In effect, a forward contract converts a floating-rate payment to a fixed-rate payment.

The discussion thus far has been about a single payment, yet, as mentioned earlier, actual cap, collar, or floor agreements are designed to hedge a series of cash flows, not just one. A cap can thus be perceived as a series of interest-rate call options for successively more distant reset dates; a floor is a similarly constructed series of put options. Assume that an interest payment on floating-rate debt falls due in three months, at the next reset date. If the interest rate on the reset date exceeds the strike level, the cap writer would make a payment to the cap buyer on a date to coincide with the cap buyer's own payment date on the underlying floating-rate debt.

A collar that consists of a series of at-the-money call and put options is equivalent to an interest-rate swap. Buying the cap and selling the floor transforms floating-rate debt to fixed-rate debt, whereas selling the cap and buying the floor switches fixed-rate debt into floating-rate debt. A swap that is constructed out of cap and floor agreements is called a *synthetic swap*. Caps brokers and dealers will sometimes determine rates on floors by deriving the rate from swap and cap rates, which come from instruments that are more actively traded than floors and therefore more accurately reflect current market values.

In practice, swaps are not usually put together from cap and floor agreements. Caps and floors are more readily tradable than swaps because credit risk is one-sided; swaps carry a credit risk that is two-sided in nature. Matching buyers and sellers for swaps is therefore more involved than for caps or floors.[8]

Examples of some caps, collars, and floors should help the reader understand their operation. As the foregoing single-payment-date discussion illustrates, creating these instruments amounts to an exercise in option pricing. One widely used option-pricing model, known as the Black futures option model, is used in the following examples.[9] Robert Tompkins (1989) explains caps pricing in terms of Black's model, and the examples that follow are loosely patterned on Tompkins' approach.

The chief virtue of the Black model is its simplicity and ease of use, even though it has a serious internal inconsistency when used to value debt options: the assumption that the short-term interest rate (that is, the Treasury bill rate) is constant. Options on short-term interest rates have value, though, only if those rates are less than perfectly predictable. In the last section of this paper, a more complex model that does not suffer from this shortcoming is used to price options.[10]

Eurodollar Futures and Forward LIBOR. In order to give realistic yet simple examples of caps, collars, and floors, this article assumes that the reset dates coincide with the expiration dates of Eurodollar futures contracts, which are traded at the Chicago Mercantile Exchange (CME) and the London International Financial Futures Exchange (LIFFE). Purchase of a Eurodollar futures contract locks in the interest payment on a $1 million three-month time deposit to be made upon expiration of the futures con-

tract. The interest rate on the deposit is three-month LIBOR. On the other hand, the seller of a Eurodollar futures contract is obligated to pay the specified LIBOR-based interest payment at expiration.[11]

Eurodollar futures expire in a quarterly cycle two London business days prior to the third Wednesday of March, June, September, and December. The Chicago Mercantile Exchange currently offers contract expiration months extending four years, with only March and September contracts for the fourth year.[12] The interest rate implied by a Eurodollar futures price may be regarded as a forward interest rate, that is, the three-month LIBOR expected by the market to prevail at the expiration date for each contract.[13]

The Black model uses the futures price for a particular contract expiration month as an input to determine the value of a European call and put option on that contract. In the case of Eurodollar futures contracts, the add-on yield (100 minus the futures price) is plugged into Black's formula. Another crucial variable is the volatility, which is either estimated from the historical volatility of the Eurodollar futures yield or obtained as an implied volatility from traded Eurodollar futures options.[14] Chart I shows the recent behavior of both of these volatility measures. Again, higher volatility results in higher-cost call and put options and hence more expensive caps and floors.

Table I gives two-year cap, floor, and collar prices on three-month LIBOR for two arbitrarily chosen dates, June 19, 1989, and December 14, 1987, that give reset dates which coincide with Eurodollar futures expiration dates. The first date illustrates pricing during a relatively low volatility period when the term structure of LIBOR rates, as given by the "strip" of prices on successively more distant contracts, was just about flat. The market was predicting virtually no change in short-term interest rates over this two-year horizon. In panel A of Table I, the contract expiration months are given along with the forward rates or add-on yields for each futures contract. The row labeled *time to expiration* shows the number of days from the creation of the cap, floor, or collar to the expiration date for each contract. Another input into Black's formula, the risk-free rate, is taken to be the Treasury bill or zero-coupon bond yield for which the

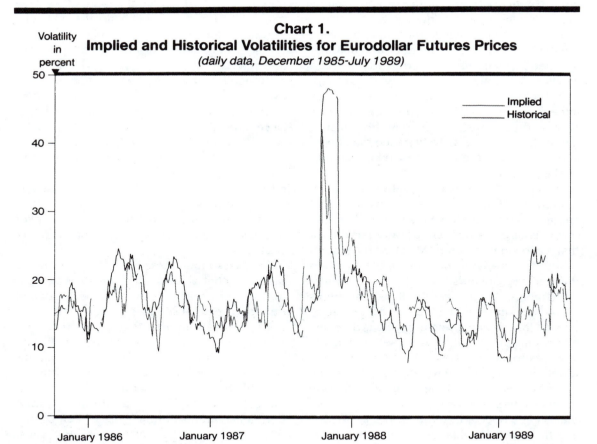

Chart 1.
Implied and Historical Volatilities for Eurodollar Futures Prices
(daily data, December 1985-July 1989)

Volatility
in
percent

Implied
Historical

January 1986　　　January 1987　　　January 1988　　　January 1989

Higher volatility, such as that exhibited around the time of the October 1987 stock-market break, results in more expensive caps, shown in Charts 2, 3, and 4.

Note: Gaps in Chart 1 result from missing observations.

Source: Chicago Mercantile Exchange.

expiration falls nearest to the futures expiration date.

The first example prices a two-year 10 percent cap, which consists of the sum of seven call options. At 10 percent, this cap is clearly out of the money. The computed call option price is expressed in basis points. The calls become progressively more expensive as the time to expiration increases, reflecting the rising time value of the calls. The shorter-maturity calls have little value because they are out of the money and, given the volatility, only a slight chance exists that they might finish in the money. Although the more distant calls are also out of the money, there is more time (and more uncertainty) about what LIBOR will do. Thus, their value is greater because of the higher probability that they might expire in the money. The

sum of these calls is the cap rate, which is 147 basis points (rounded from 147.1).[15] For a three-month contract with a nominal face value of $1 million, a one-basis-point move is worth $25 ($1 million x .01% x 90/360). Translated into dollars, 147.1 basis points is $3,677.60 (147.1 x $25), which represents the dollar cost of placing a cap for two years on a $1 million loan. This example was computed ignoring the risk of default on the cap. It also assumes that payments at reset dates, if owed, are made at the time of the reset date.

Next, a slightly out-of-the-money 7.5 percent floor is shown. The total cost is 96 basis points, or $2,396.61. As mentioned above, the cost of interest-rate protection can be reduced by creating a collar, which is sometimes referred to as a ceiling-floor agreement. In this example,

Table 1.
Examples of Two-Year Cap, Floor, and Collar Prices on Three-Month LIBOR

Panel A: June 19, 1989; Volatility, 18 percent						
	September 1988	December 1988	March 1989	June 1989	September 1989	December 1989	March 1990
Time to expiration (days)	91	182	273	364	455	546	637
Forward rate	9.02	8.84	8.64	8.71	8.77	8.87	8.86
Risk-free rate	8.46	8.47	8.54	8.56	8.59	8.59	8.56
Call prices (10.0 percent strike)	5.3	10.3	12.9	19.9	26.5	34.1	38.1
Put prices (7.5 percent strike)	.6	4.7	11.8	15.4	18.6	20.6	24.2

10 percent cap	7.5 percent floor	Zero-cost collar
Cost in basis points: 147	Cost in basis points: 96	10 percent cap implies
Cost in dollars: $3,677.60	Cost in dollars: $2,396.61	7.85 percent floor

Panel B: June 19, 1989; Volatility, 18 percent						
	September 1988	December 1988	March 1989	June 1989	September 1989	December 1989	March 1990
Call prices (11 percent strike)	.4	2.2	3.8	7.6	11.8	16.9	20.3
Put prices (7 percent strike)	.1	1.3	4.7	7.2	9.5	11.2	13.9

11 percent cap	7 percent floor	Zero-cost collar
Cost in basis points: 63	Cost in basis points: 48	11 percent cap implies
Cost in dollars: $1,575.84	Cost in dollars: $1,198.08	7.19 percent floor

Panel C: December 14, 1987; Volatility, 25 percent						
	March 1988	June 1988	September 1988	December 1988	March 1989	June 1989	September 1989
Time to expiration (days)	91	182	280	371	455	553	644
Forward rate	8.09	8.34	8.62	8.88	9.11	9.31	9.48
Risk-free rate	6.09	6.79	7.11	7.51	7.66	7.79	7.92
Call prices (10 percent strike)	2.1	12.5	28.9	45.9	62.0	78.0	91.6
Put prices (7.5 percent strike)	16.2	23.0	26.8	29.0	30.5	32.9	34.8

10 percent cap	7.5 percent floor	Zero-cost collar
Cost in basis points: 321	Cost in basis points: 193	10 percent cap implies
Cost in dollars: $8,025.53	Cost in dollars: $4,829.68	8.05 percent floor

Note: Dollar amount is for $1,000,000 in notional principal.

selling a 7.5 percent floor would substantially reduce the cost of a 10 percent cap. The combination would cost about 51 basis points, or $1,281. However, by judiciously selecting the floor level—in this case, 7.85 percent—the price of the cap can be driven to zero.[16] Marketing people delight in explaining that downside interest-rate protection (the cap) can be obtained at no cost: just sell a floor.[17] Of course, though, this strategy carries a cost. The holder of an interest-rate collar has traded away potential savings on interest-rate declines below the floor. This caveat notwithstanding, a collar for which the floor exactly matches the cap will be referred to as a *zero-cost* collar.

Panel B illustrates how the cost of caps and floors falls by selecting more out-of-the-money levels. Increasing the cap by one percentage point to 11 percent reduces the cap rate substantially to 63 basis points, or $1,575.84. Decreasing the floor by half a percentage point to 7 percent more than halves the cost to 48 basis points, or $1,198.08. A zero-cost collar with an 11 percent cap effectively lowers the floor to 7.19 percent.

The final example, reflected in panel C of Table 1, shows prices for caps, collars, and floors during the relatively high volatility period after the October 1987 stock market break. As depicted in Chart 1, Eurodollar futures' volatility surged during and after the October 21 crash; the degree of fluctuation had abated greatly by late January, although it had not returned completely to precrash levels. The implied volatility was 25 percent on December 14, 1987, as compared to 18 percent on June 19, 1989, in the earlier examples. The 10 percent cap priced in panel C is substantially more costly than the one in panel A. The cost is 321 basis points, or $8,025.53. Another important factor contributing to the higher cost is the rising structure of LIBOR forward rates. Although the futures nearest to expiration indicate a forward rate of 8.09 percent as compared to 9.02 percent in the June 19, 1989, example, the distant futures for December 14, 1987, have forward rates that are well above those for June 19. The upward sloping term structure of interest rates for December 14 reinforces the effect of higher volatility on raising cap and floor rates. The floor is more expensive as well at 193 basis points, or $4,829.68. Interestingly, the zero-cost collar with a 10 per-

cent cap is only slightly more constraining with a floor of 8.05 percent as compared to 7.85 percent in the previous example, which exhibited low volatility and flat term structure.[18]

Caps, Collars, and Floors in Practice

At first sight, creating caps, collars, and floors would appear to be a simple matter because options are traded on the Eurodollar futures contract. Selecting the appropriate strike levels and expiration dates would appear to be all one needs to manufacture a cap, collar, or floor. However, as mentioned above, Eurodollar contracts extend into the future for at most four years (which nevertheless is an unusually large number of months for a futures contract). Eurodollar futures options traded at the Chicago Mercantile Exchange currently have expiration dates ranging out only two years, in a quarterly cycle that matches that of the Eurodollar futures contracts.[19]

Another limitation of Eurodollar futures options is that only contracts expiring within the three months or so from the current date are liquid, that is, they are the only ones that are actively traded so that their prices at any time reliably reflect equilibrium values. The options also are limited to strike levels in increments of 25 basis points, whereas the futures have increments of one basis point. Unlike Eurodollar futures and options, caps, collars, and floors have been created with maturities extending as much as 10 years. Furthermore, actual caps, collars, and floors can be created on any day, not just on futures and options expiration dates. The actual use of futures and options to fashion caps, collars, and floors is neither a straightforward nor a riskless matter.

The solution to this problem is the use of existing futures and options contracts to create the desired positions synthetically. Synthesizing an options position using options or futures contracts—or a combination of the two—requires not only taking appropriate positions in the existing liquid contracts but also altering that position over time so that the value of the actual position tracks or "replicates" the desired position. This process is known as *dynamic hedging*. Theoretically, the replicating portfolio of actual futures and options contracts can exactly match the value of, say, a cap sold to a counterparty.[20] In reality, managing a replicating portfolio is a risky and costly activity.[21] Tracking errors cumulate since costly trading cannot be conducted continuously as is theoretically required and because mismatches can occur with the expiration dates and possibly also with the interest rates involved. Using Eurodollar futures to hedge a cap based on the commercial paper rate exemplifies the latter.[22]

The Over-the-Counter Market

In view of the complexities and risks of dynamic-hedging strategies, most cap, collar, and floor users prefer over-the-counter instruments. Commercial and investment banks create these instruments themselves, possibly by manufacturing them through dynamic hedging. Nonfinancial users tend to rely on the expertise of these financial institutions and are willing to pay for the convenience of interest-rate risk management products issued through an intermediary. The intermediaries may also be more willing to bear the risks associated with hedging because of the scale of their operations. In fact, Keith C. Brown and Donald J. Smith (1988) describe the increasing involvement of banks in offering interest-rate risk management instruments as the reintermediation of commercial banking. Since the 1970s, commercial banks have played less of a role in channeling funds from lenders to borrowers. With the growth of interest-rate risk management, though, their intermediary role is being restored, albeit in a different form.

Commercial banks, particularly the largest money-center banks, are better able to absorb and control the hedging risks associated with managing a caps, collars, and floors portfolio, and these institutions are better able to evaluate the credit risks inherent in instruments bought from other parties. Credit risk arises because any counterparty selling a cap, for example, is obligated to make payments if the cap moves in the money on a reset date. That counterparty could go bankrupt at some point during the course of the cap agreement and would default on its obligation. (This issue is examined in detail in the last section of this article.) By taking positions in caps, collars, and floors, commercial banks—and to a lesser extent, investment banks—act as dealers by buying and selling to any counterparties. Within their portfolio or "book" of caps and floors, individual instruments partially net out, leaving a residual exposed position that the banks then hedge in the options and futures markets. Much trading of caps, collars, and floors consists of purchases and sales of these instruments to adjust positions and risk exposures, so much of the caps market's volume is generated by inter-dealer transactions. In addition to the dozen or so commercial and investment banks in New York and London that dominate the caps market, there are about half a dozen caps brokers, who do not take positions themselves but instead match buyer and seller.[23]

Caps, collars, and floors are usually sold in multiples of $5 million, but because of the customized nature of the over-the-counter market other amounts can be arranged. Most caps have terms that range from one to five years and have reset dates or frequencies that are usually monthly, quarterly, or semiannual. Caps based on three-month LIBOR are the most common and the most liquid or tradable. From the purchaser's point of view, buying a cap that matches the characteristics of the liability being hedged might seem best. Even strike levels and notional principal amounts can be chosen to vary over the term of an agreement in a predetermined way, but good fit comes at a price. Transactions costs are higher for such tailored products, as reflected by the larger difference between bid and offer rates on uncommon caps. This wider spread also increases the cost of removing caps by selling them before their term expires. Many users opt for a liquid cap and are willing to absorb the basis risk—the risk from a mismatch of interest basis or other characteristics—in order to avoid the higher cost of a less liquid instrument.

Caps and floors are usually available at strike levels within several percentage points of the current interest-rate basis and are most commonly written out of the money. Settlement dates typically occur after reset dates, upon maturity of the underlying instrument. For example, interest on a three-month Eurodollar deposit is credited upon maturity of the deposit. A cap on three-month LIBOR would have a three-month lag between a reset date and actual settlement. Most payments for caps are made up front, although they can also be amortized. When a cap and a floating-rate loan come from the same institution, the two are usually treated as a single instrument; thus, when the floating rate exceeds the strike level, payment is limited to the strike level and the cap does not pay off directly.[24]

Long-Term Caps. During the mid-1980s, early in the development of the caps market, longerterm caps were created directly from floatingrate securities rather than synthetically. Two kinds of floating-rate instruments were used: floating-rate CDs and floating-rate notes.[25] Floating-rate notes are debt obligations usually indexed to LIBOR, and floating-rate CDs are medium-term deposit instruments that are also typically indexed to LIBOR. The innovation that sparked much activity in the caps market was the issuance of capped floating-rate notes and CDs that in turn had their caps stripped off and sold as separate instruments sometimes known as "free-standing" caps.

As an illustration, consider the floating-rate CD. Banks use ordinary CDs as well as variablerate CDs to acquire funds for the purpose of making loans and funding other balance-sheet assets. The capped floating-rate CD was promoted as a method of raising funds below LIBOR, the rate on an uncapped CD with a variable rate of interest. The reason is that, after issuing a capped floating-rate CD to a depositor, a bank could then sell the corresponding cap into the caps market and collect premium income. Because CDs of this type typically fund floating-rate loans, the bank would be fully hedged after selling the cap. Funding costs would be lowered if the premium for the cap on the floating-rate CD were less than the premium that the bank collected upon selling the cap into the market.[26] This method of creating or "sourcing" caps, floors, and collars—through capped floating-rate CDs and floating-rate notes— became extremely popular but was short-lived. Reportedly, the longer-term caps were gradually perceived to be undervalued, such that cap writers were not being compensated for the risks of having to make payments to cap holders if interest rates rose above strike levels.[27] Also contributing to the demise of this method of sourcing was a flattening of the yield curve that made floating-rate borrowing less attractive and reduced cap prices. Today, few caps, collars, or floors are created beyond the five-year maturity.

Charts 2-4 give actual cap bid and offer rates, in basis points, quoted by one major caps broker in New York. The bid rate is the rate at which the broker is willing to buy a cap; the offer rate is the rate at which the broker sells a cap. The spread between the two represents the transactions costs of matching buyer with seller. Charts 2, 3, and 4, respectively, give the rates on two-year 8 percent, three-year 10 percent, and five-year 10 percent caps. These rates are just a sample; many other strike levels are available. The strike levels quoted change over time as interest rates change. Cap strike levels that move too far in the money or out of the money are discontinued and replaced by caps with strike levels that are in greater demand. All of these series are highly correlated. They are also correlated with the volatilities shown in Chart 1, which are a major determinant of cap values.[28]

The Motivation for Hedging and Some Hypothetical Examples

With some background on the caps, collars, and floors market, the use of interest-rate risk management instruments can now be put into perspective by briefly considering the nature of hedging. Caps, collars, and floors are often talked about in terms of an insurance analogy. They are instruments that can be used to hedge assets or liabilities and thus protect against loss resulting from interest-rate risk. In practice, though, distinguishing between hedging and speculating in interest-rate risk management is sometimes difficult, especially with optionbased instruments. Discretion is required in selecting the timing of the hedge, the strike level, and the maturity of the instrument, all of which are usually predicated on some opinion of what interest rates and other variables are expected to do. Selling a cap or floor, for example, is a way to generate income on a fixedincome portfolio by collecting the premiums. The decision to sell often reflects a difference of opinion regarding the volatility implied by the

Chart 2.
Two-Year 8 Percent Cap Bid and Offer Rates
(daily data, March 1987-October 1988)

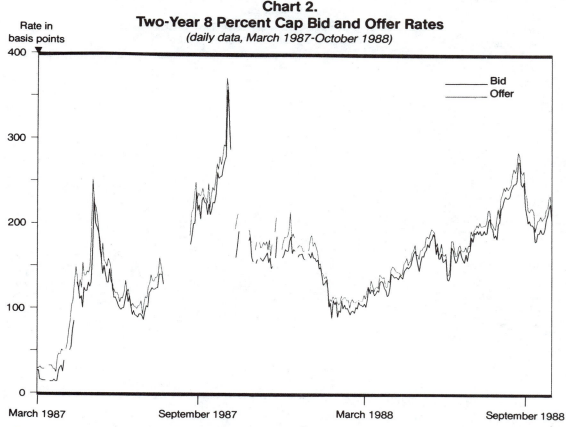

The spread between the bid and offer rates represents the transactions costs of matching buyer and seller.

Note: Gaps in Charts 2, 3, and 4 reflect days for which rates were not available.

Source: Noonan, Astley, and Pearce, Inc.

cap or floor. If a money manager thinks a cap is overvalued because the market's expectation of volatility is higher than his or her own, then selling an out-of-the-money cap might be a good move. If the money manager's judgment about volatility is correct, even small upward moves in the interest rate may not wipe out all of the premium income. At the same time, the sale provides a limited hedge against small downward moves in rates, again because of the premium receipt.

Even determining the effect of hedging can be problematic, since a firm's purchase of a cap, for example, to hedge the interest-rate risk of a particular liability could increase the variability of the firm's net worth. The financial claim being hedged may itself help offset the variability of another financial claim on the balance sheet.

The net result of a specific hedge could be to increase the interest-rate risk exposure of the firm.

A more fundamental issue is why firms hedge in the first place. A basic insight derived from the economics of uncertainty is that risk aversion leads individuals to prefer stable income and consumption streams to highly variable ones. Given an assumption of risk aversion on the part of decision makers, one can show that their welfare or utility (that is, their economic well-being) is greater over time if they enjoy smooth income or consumption opportunities rather than erratic ones.[29] Hedging is a way of improving economic well-being by trading off income or consumption in good times for greater income or consumption in bad times. Thus, a hedging strategy serves a well-defined purpose

Chart 3.
Three-Year 10 Percent Cap Bid and Offer Rates
(daily data, March 1987-June 1989)

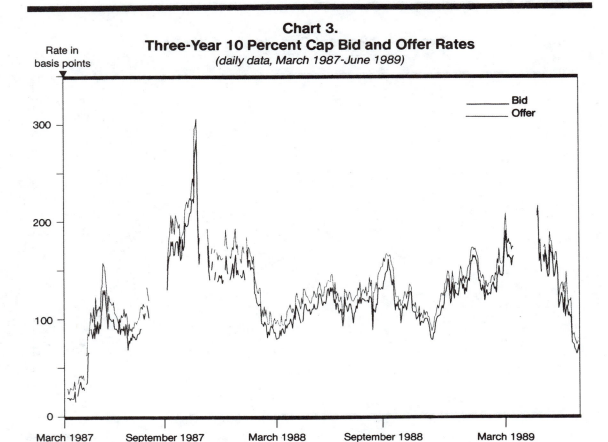

The rates depicted in Chart 3 are highly correlated with those in Charts 2 and 4, as well as with the volatilities in Chart 1.

Source: Noonan, Astley, and Pearce, Inc.

for risk-averse economic agents, such as farmers or a firm's owner-manager. The issue is less clear-cut for widely held corporations, which actually are the typical users of interest-rate risk-management tools. A corporation owned by a large number of stockholders need not operate like a risk-averse decision maker because each stockholder can insulate his or her wealth and consumption opportunities from risk, specific to the corporation's activities, by holding a diversified portfolio of assets.

Clifford W. Smith and René M. Stulz (1985) surveyed managers of widely held, value-maximizing corporations to determine the motivations behind hedging behavior. According to the researchers, managers engage in hedging of a firm's value for three basic reasons. The first explanation is tax-related; Smith and Stulz ar-

gue that, on average, a less variable pretax firm value implies a higher after-tax firm value than does a more variable pretax value. The reasoning turns on their assumption that the level of corporate tax liabilities grows at an increasing rate with rising pretax firm value because of the progressive structure of the tax code. Hedging helps reduce the variability of pretax firm value and therefore raises after-tax value. Second, Smith and Stulz maintain that hedging lowers the probability that the firm will go bankrupt and thus incur bankruptcy costs. Hedging firm value would benefit stockholders by reducing the expected future costs of bankruptcy that lower current firm value. A related point is that a firm's debt may often contain covenants that force the company to alter investment policies that the shareholders would like to see under-

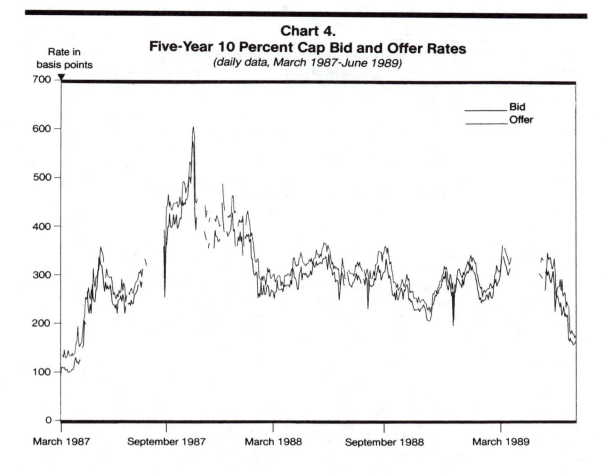

Chart 4.
Five-Year 10 Percent Cap Bid and Offer Rates
(daily data, March 1987-June 1989)

Rate in basis points

700

600

500

400

300

200

100

0

——— Bid
——— Offer

March 1987   September 1987   March 1988   September 1988   March 1989

taken. Hedging reduces the likelihood of financial distress and the limitations on managers' discretion that bond covenants may impose. A third reason for hedging is that when managerial compensation is tied to the firm's value, managers may become more risk-averse in order to maintain that value.

Participants in the Caps, Collars, and Floors Market. While the precise social value of interest-rate risk management products is not fully understood in the case of widely held corporations, such products are clearly becoming increasingly popular among corporate treasurers and other financial managers. End users of caps, collars, and floors typically include firms seeking to limit exposure to adverse movements in short-term interest rates, such as a firm that sells commercial paper to fund its purchases of inventory.

Specific market participants are depository institutions, particularly savings and loan associations (S&Ls); corporations going through leveraged buyouts (LBOs) or taking on debt to fend off hostile takeovers; and real estate developers, who are often highly leveraged with floating-rate debt. Unfortunately, the only information about these applications is anecdotal. Also, compared to the potential market, the actual market is probably very small. Many potential users are unaware of or cautious about interest-rate risk management instruments.

Any user of interest-rate swaps is potentially also a user of caps, collars, and floors. Larry D. Wall and John J. Pringle (1988) conducted a systematic search of annual reports for 4,000 firms that used interest-rate swaps in 1986. The stocks of these firms were traded on the New York

Stock Exchange, the American Stock Exchange, or the over-the-counter market. Of this sample, 250 firms were identified as swaps market participants. Over 50 percent of this group were banks, savings and loans, and other financial services firms; commercial banks alone accounted for half of these. In addition, Wall and Pringle report that "the overwhelming majority of thrifts (59 percent), manufacturing firms (69 percent), and nonfinancial, nonmanufacturing firms (77 percent) are exclusively fixed-rate payers."[30] As a conjecture, the profile of caps, collars, and floor users may be quite similar to that for swaps users. The fact that credit risks for caps and floors are one-sided, however, suggests that firms with weaker credit ratings probably use caps and floors because they cannot gain access to the swaps market on favorable terms.

Anecdotal accounts from various sources illustrate how different end users employ caps, collars, or floors in their management of interest-rate risk. Many savings and loans, for instance, have been active users of these option-based instruments. The interest-rate risk confronting S&Ls, and depository institutions generally, may be considered in terms of their net interest margins, that is, the difference between the rates at which an institution lends and borrows. S&Ls are particularly vulnerable to changes in interest rates because maturities (or alternatively, the durations) of these institutions' assets, predominantly long-term mortgages, greatly exceed the maturities of their liabilities, most often short-term time and savings deposits. Thus, a rise in rates raises the interest expense on an S&L's short-term liabilities with possibly little increase in interest earnings on its mortgages. The net interest margin narrows and could very well become negative. One solution is to convert the floating-rate interest expense on the liabilities into fixed-rate payments via an interest-rate swap. The net interest margin would then become much more stable. However, a weak credit standing could make such a swap too expensive or unobtainable. A cap on the floating-rate liabilities could be an effective alternative. An S&L's credit rating would be irrelevant to a cap writer, who bears no credit exposure.[31]

As another example, consider a commercial bank's portfolio manager who is responsible for overseeing a portfolio of floating-rate notes.

Suppose this manager believes that a large drop in short-term interest rates, currently at about 8 percent, is about to occur. He wants to protect the portfolio's earnings and therefore buys an out-of-the-money 7 percent interest-rate floor. Concerned about the cost of this protection and reasonably convinced that rates will not rise substantially, he also decides to sell a 9 percent interest-rate cap to create a collar on the portfolio. This example highlights the discretion involved in selecting a hedge. A floor could have been in place all along, but maintaining a floor reduces a portfolio's return by the amount of the premium expense. Only when the manager has strong concerns about a drop in rates is the floor purchased.

As a final example, the corporate treasurer of a consumer products firm is worried about the prospects of a rise in interest rates because her company has recently undergone a leveraged buyout. The financing strategy for the LBO included heavy reliance on floating-rate debt secured from a syndicate of commercial banks. The firm's debt-to-equity ratio has soared, and even a modest rise in rates could bankrupt the company. After the LBO the firm's credit standing was downgraded by the rating services; consequently, access to the swap market is effectively foreclosed. Buying a two-year interest-rate cap to cover the firm's floating-rate exposure seems to be a prudent action.[32] The treasurer expects earnings will be more robust after a two-year interval. Also, the protection gained for a relatively short-term horizon makes sense because during this period the firm would be downsizing and reorganizing its operations.

Credit Risk

The earlier discussion of the over-the-counter market for caps, collars, and floors alluded to the risk of default inherent in these instruments. That risk is present because the seller of a cap or floor is agreeing to fulfill a contract in the event the cap or floor moves in the money on a payment date. Since the seller is a firm, whether a commercial bank, investment bank, or nonfinancial institution, its assets are limited, and thus the company is exposed to the possibility of bankruptcy. The probability of default is rather small for the typical caps, collar, or floor writer who also typically issues investment-grade bonds into the market. Moody's Investors Service, one of the major bond rating firms, recently released a study indicating that from 1970 to 1988 the average annual rate of default by issuers of investment-grade bonds was 0.06 percent, as compared to an average annual default rate of 3.3 percent for junk bond issuers.[33] Because the consequences of default can be financially damaging, default risk receives careful analysis, particularly by counterparties entering into caps and swaps agreements. This section of the article takes a detailed look at how default risk is evaluated and how it affects the pricing of caps, collars, and floors.

The first aspect of the problem is to consider the precise nature of the default risk or, alternatively, the credit exposure. If a cap is in the money on a floating-rate reset date, the owner of the cap expects to receive a payment from the cap writer, as reviewed above. If the writer is insolvent and thus fails to make the payment, the owner is again in an unhedged position and must make the full floating-rate payment, but this is not the only consequence of default. Provided the default does not occur on the final reset date, the cap was also hedging future reset dates, which upon default are also fully exposed. Thus, credit exposure depends on the time that default occurs in the life of a cap agreement. (Note that a parallel argument can be made for floors and collars.) The cost of default to the cap buyer is the cost of replacing the original cap with a new cap from another seller. If interest rates at the default date were identical to the initial interest rates and the volatility had not changed since the original cap was purchased, the replacement cost of the cap would be zero, ignoring transactions costs and differences in credit risks. That is, the cost of a new cap for the remaining reset dates would exactly equal the current market value of the existing cap (if default had not occurred).

The next and rather complex aspect of the credit risk question to consider concerns the method of assessing credit risk when a cap is sold. Bankruptcy of a cap writer has no impact on cap buyers as long as the cap stays out of the money and the cap buyer has no intention of selling the cap before its term ends. Default occurs only when a cap is in the money and the cap writer is bankrupt. The likelihood of bankruptcy may also be related to the level of interest rates and thus dependent on the future path of these rate movements. In addition, as just discussed, a cap's replacement cost is a function of where in the life of the cap agreement default occurs. All of these factors should be weighed in evaluating what the potential cost of default could be and how that should affect the price of a cap.

Marcelle Arak, Laurie S. Goodman, and Arthur Rones (1986) propose a method of computing credit exposure for caps, collars, and floors. Their approach amounts to considering different worst-case scenarios that are defined by the degree to which a cap can move in the money. For a cap the computed exposure de-

"The cost of default to the cap buyer is the cost of replacing the original cap with a new cap from another seller."

pends on the size of the upward movement in the interest rate that could occur during each reset interval. A cap's replacement value will tend at first to increase early in the life of the instrument and then to decrease toward the end of the contract. The credit exposure is taken to be the maximum replacement value computed at the reset dates. For example, if the interest-rate volatility based on three-month LIBOR is 10 percent (as measured by the annual standard deviation), over a three-month period the volatility is $0.10 \times \sqrt{(1/4)} = 5$ percent.[34] Assuming an initial 7 percent LIBOR, three months later the upward move would· be to 7.35 [7.0 + (0.05 x 7.0)]. Given this rate and a further assumption that rates at all other maturities shifted in parallel, the cap replacement value is calculated. Another 5 percent upward move is then computed, giving a new LIBOR of 7.72 [7.35 + (7.35 x 0.05)] and again the replacement value is computed, and so forth. The credit exposure is the maximum value of the replacement cost during the cap agreement.

A more conservative evaluation of credit exposure might assume that rates rose by two standard deviations per year instead of one as in the previous example. At two-standard-deviation moves, the actual exposure would, on average, exceed the maximum computed amount only 2.5 percent of the time (as compared to exceeding it 16.5 percent of the time using a one-standard-deviation measure).[35] Arak, Goodman, and Rones give an example of the credit exposure on various collar agreements with a floor equal to 6 percent and a cap equal to 9 percent. For three-month reset intervals, the exposure is 0.44 percent of the notional principal (two-year collar), 0.82 percent (five-year collar),

---

"Computations based on worst-case scenarios implicitly overstate the actual incidence of default because of the arbitrary assumption about sequential interest-rate moves only in one direction."

---

and 2.68 percent (10-year collar).[36] By these researchers' calculations, the credit exposure on collars is rather small, especially compared to similar calculations for other instruments they consider, such as interest-rate swaps and forward contracts. These calculations are intended for commercial banks, which set credit limits for particular customers in order to manage the size of potential losses in the event of default. However, the method put forth by Arak, Goodman, and Rones is not useful for pricing caps—that is, for adjusting the price or rate for the anticipated cost of default. Computations based on worst-case scenarios implicitly overstate the actual incidence of default because of the arbitrary assumption about sequential interest-rate moves only in one direction. A more desirable approach would compute the "expected value" of default—the difference between caps not subject to default and those that are.

Caps as Default-Risky Options. Almost all of the option pricing models used to value caps ignore default risk. An exception is the model proposed by Herb Johnson and Stulz (1987), in which they derive formulas for default-risky or "vulnerable" puts and calls. Unfortunately, their formulas cannot be straightforwardly applied to caps, collars, or floors because of the time dimension involved in these options-based instruments. As has been emphasized, caps are a sequence of options—default-risky options. Fulfilling a given option contained in a cap depends on the absence of bankruptcy at earlier reset dates. If bankruptcy occurred earlier, the current option would not be honored by the cap writer. The sequential time dimension involved in valuing caps makes the mathematics formidably complex.[37]

This author has tackled the complexity of cap valuation by using computer-intensive methods to handle the intricate contingencies implied in cap, collar, floor, and swap agreements (Peter A. Abken [forthcoming]). His computer model avoids the contradictory assumption inherent in the Black model used for short-term debt options—that short-term interest rates are constant—but at the cost of trading off a simple analytical formula for a complicated computer algorithm. Nevertheless, the intuition behind the new model is simple and easily explained.

The value of a European option can be thought of as the average or expected value of its payoffs at expiration, discounted back to the present. Options are difficult to value because the payoff upon expiration is a "kinked," or discontinuous, function of the underlying asset price. A call option is worth zero if the underlying asset price at expiration is less than the strike price, and positive in value if the underlying asset price exceeds the strike price, increasing dollar for dollar with the amount above the strike. The Black-Scholes and Black formulas compute the value of a call as the expected value of the future payoffs.[38] Some payoffs are more likely to occur than others, and the formulas account for the probabilities associated with the payoffs.

Monte Carlo Simulation. One method for valuing options relies on extensive computations to determine the expected payoffs. Known as Monte Carlo simulation, this process was first applied to option pricing problems by Phelim P. Boyle (1977). The standard application involves stock option pricing. A stock price, on which an option is valued, is assumed to rise and fall randomly over time, although its value at any point can be described in terms of its statistical distribution, which is known or assumed. In standard problems the distribution for stock price changes is assumed to be fully characterized by its mean and variance. Using this information, artificial future stock-price paths, also known as *realizations,* can be created numerically by computer. By randomly generating a large enough number of price paths (tens of thousands, at a minimum) and evaluating the payoff on an option with a given strike price at a particular point in time—the option's expiration date—an average over these randomly generated payoffs can be made. The option price is given by appropriately discounting the expected future payoff into current dollars. Of course, the Black-Scholes formula accomplishes the same thing mathematically and is conceptually equivalent. To the penny, both methods will give the same price using identical assumptions regarding the statistical characteristics of stock price movements. The Monte Carlo method, though cumbersome, pays off in cases where the asset price moves in unusual ways, such as in random jumps—for example, due to a stock market crash. The Black-Scholes model rules out such movements by assumption. Cap valuation is another area where Monte Carlo methods offer a simplification over approaches that may not otherwise be mathematically tractable.

Three factors taken together contribute to the complexity of default-risky cap valuation. The first is that debt prices on instruments like Treasury bills or Eurodollar deposits vary with interest rates. Second, each constituent option in a cap is subject to default and must be valued as a default-risky option. Third, the payoff on a given option depends on the nonoccurrence of default on options from earlier periods.

The payoff of a vulnerable call option is the lesser of the firm's value or the default-free option payoff. The value of the firm is the market value of its equity (before including the value of its cap). If the value of the firm that sold the option is greater than the payoff, no default occurs. If the payoff exceeds the firm's value, the company defaults and the option holder receives the value of the firm—or some share of it, as determined by the bankruptcy courts—when

the company is liquidated. In view of the fact that a vulnerable call may pay off less, but never more, than a default-free call, the value of a vulnerable call must be less than the value of an otherwise comparable default-free call.

An additional consideration for cap valuation, as discussed above, is that default on a cap leaves the cap buyer unhedged. The exposure is the replacement value of the cap. Thus, default involves at a minimum replacement of the missed option payoff, and possibly the entire remaining value of the cap, if the firm wants to maintain the hedge. Thus, besides valuing default-risky call options, cap valuation must also evaluate such replacement costs.

The Elements of the Caps Model. To convey the basic ideas behind construction of the caps model, this section of the article sketches out

---

"An additional consideration for cap valuation . . . is that default on a cap leaves the cap buyer unhedged. The exposure is the replacement value of the cap."

---

the model, the technical details of which can be found in Abken (forthcoming). Three so-called state variables are computer-generated to implement the simulation. The options making up a cap are valued based on the underlying interest rate, as discussed earlier. The entire path of the term structure of interest rates is generated using the model developed by Stephen M. Schaefer and Eduardo S. Schwartz (1984). Two state variables are the difference or spread between the instantaneous rate and a consol rate (that is, the rate on a bond having infinite maturity), and the consol rate itself. All other intermediate-maturity discount bonds are derived by formula from these two inputs, which describe absolute and relative movements in interest rates at all maturities. The third state variable represents the value of the firm, which also fluctuates randomly over time, reflecting unpredictable changes in interest rates, earnings, and other variables that determine firm value.

The example to be considered is parallel to the one discussed earlier in Table 1, but the focus is now on credit risk. The cap model will value two-year caps on a three-month interest rate. The cap consists of seven reset dates, at each of which the firm's value is compared to the call option payoff. Default-free and default-risky caps are valued. The difference in the price or rate for these otherwise identical caps is the credit spread for default risk. The example developed below illustrates how default risk is particularly sensitive to the correlation over time between firm value and interest-rate movements.

The parameter values for the Schaefer-Schwartz model were estimated from actual

---

"[D]efault risk is particularly sensitive to the correlation over time between firm value and interest-rate movements."

---

interest-rate data on one-month Treasury bill and 30-year bond yields, which served as proxies for the instantaneous interest rate and consol interest rate, respectively. The rates were sampled weekly on Fridays from January 1983 to August 1989. The reader is referred to Abken (forthcoming) for details concerning parameter estimation and other technical details concerning the model.

A simplification used in the simulations presented in this article is that whenever a default occurs—that is, when the firm value is less than the option payoff—the replacement value of the cap is not computed. Instead, the option payoff for that reset date is set equal to the negative of the payoff. In other words, the cap owner has to cover the full floating-rate interest payment for that date. Payoffs at future reset dates are assumed to be zero. Valuing a new cap at current rates would increase the cost of default com-

pared to the procedure used here; such valuation, however, would also require separate simulations at each occurrence of default.

More Examples. Table 2 gives the results of the simulations. Three panels of this table differ only in the degree that firm value is correlated with interest-rate movements. In the Schaefer-Schwartz model, there are two elements to this correlation. Firm value can be correlated with consol rate movements or spread movements, or both. (The Schaefer-Schwartz model assumes that the spread and consol rate are uncorrelated, which is supported by empirical research.) Correlation coefficients range from -1, perfect negative correlation, to 1, perfect positive correlation. Intuitively, a cap writer whose firm value is negatively correlated with interest-rate movements poses a greater credit risk than one that is positively correlated. For a given strike level, when interest rates are high, caps are more likely to be in the money and require a payment from the writer. A negative correlation therefore means that high interest rates are associated with low firm value; hence, default is more probable than it would be for zero or positive correlations. Also, empirically short- and long-term interest rates are positively correlated. Thus, a negative correlation of firm value and long-term interest rate would also be associated with a negative correlation between the firm value and interest-rate spread (defined as the short rate less the long rate).

Panel A gives the base case of zero correlation of firm value with the interest-rate spread and with the long-term interest rate. The annual default rate for this case is set to 0.13 percent by adjusting the initial value of the firm to give this rate as the outcome of the simulations.[39] The same initial firm value is then used in panels B and C, thereby yielding new default rates due to different correlations with the term structure variables. The initial term structure has a spread of 2.7 percentage points, which was the average spread over the sample period. The short-term interest rate is initially 8 percent and the cap is written at 9 percent. As in Table 1, the option rates are given for each reset date. This table includes default-free and default-risky options; the sum over reset dates for each type is the cap rate. Because the default rate is so low, the discrepancies between default-free and default-risky option prices do not become significant

Table 2.
Default-Free and Default-Risky Cap Rates
Estimated by Monte Carlo Simulation, 9.0 Percent Two-Year Cap

Initial term structure: Short-term rate, 8.0 percent; Long-term rate, 10.7 percent

Panel A: Correlation of firm value with interest-rate spread: 0
Correlation of firm value with long-term rate: 0

Reset date number:	1	2	3	4	5	6	7
Time to expiration (weeks):	13	26	39	52	65	78	91
Default-free option rate:	7.94	17.99	26.95	35.57	43.98	51.87	59.86
Default-risky option rate:	7.94	17.99	26.95	35.53	43.81	51.34	58.71

Default-free cap rate:	244.16	Default-risky cap rate:	242.28
Standard deviation:	(1.45)	Standard deviation:	(1.43)
95 percent confidence interval:	(241.32, 247.00)	95 percent confidence interval:	(239.48, 245.08)

Credit spread in basis points:	1.89
Standard deviation:	(0.14)
95 percent confidence interval:	(1.62, 2.16)
Annual default rate:	0.13 percent

Panel B: Correlation of firm value with interest-rate spread: −0.5
Correlation of firm value with long-term rate: −0.5

Reset date number:	1	2	3	4	5	6	7
Default-free option rate:	7.94	17.99	26.95	35.57	43.98	51.87	59.86
Default-risky option rate:	7.94	17.98	26.79	34.98	42.19	48.15	53.51

Default-free cap rate:	244.16	Default-risky cap rate:	231.54
Standard deviation:	(1.45)	Standard deviation:	(1.35)
95 percent confidence interval:	(241.32, 247.00)	95 percent confidence interval:	(228.89, 234.19)

Credit spread in basis points:	12.63
Standard deviation:	(0.35)
95 percent confidence interval:	(11.94, 13.32)
Annual default rate:	0.71 percent

Panel C: Correlation of firm value with interest-rate spread: 0.5
Correlation of firm value with long-term rate: 0.5

Reset date number:	1	2	3	4	5	6	7
Default-free option rate:	7.94	17.99	26.95	35.57	43.98	51.87	59.86
Default-risky option rate:	7.94	17.99	26.95	35.57	43.98	51.87	59.86

Default-free cap rate:	244.16	Default-risky cap rate:	244.16
Standard deviation:	(1.45)	Standard deviation:	(1.45)
95 percent confidence interval:	(241.32, 247.00)	95 percent confidence interval:	(241.32, 247.00)

Credit spread in basis points:	0.0
Standard deviation:	(0.0)
95 percent confidence interval:	(0.0, 0.0)
Annual default rate:	0.0 percent

Note: Sample size for each panel: 50,000 independent draws. Cap rates expressed in basis points.

until the later reset dates. The default-free cap rate is 244.16 basis points, whereas the default-risky cap rate is 242.28. The difference of 1.89 basis points is the credit spread.

These figures are estimates and have an error associated with them. One can arbitrarily reduce that error by increasing the number of realizations used to compute the options. Quadrupling the number of realizations reduces the standard deviation by half. The simulations for each panel were generated by taking 50,000 independent sets of realizations of the state variables.[40] The standard deviation and 95 percent confidence intervals for each cap rate and the spread are reported in Table 2.

The simulation used to generate panel B was the same as that for panel A in all respects except that the correlation between firm value and interest-rate spread is −0.5 instead of zero, and the correlation between firm value and long-term rate is −0.5 instead of zero. The results show a substantial increase in the incidence of default. The base rate in panel A for zero correlations is 0.13 percent, whereas the negative correlations in panel B raise the default rate to 0.71 percent. The credit spread rises from 1.89 basis points to 12.63 basis points. As discussed previously, the reason is that firm value is likely to be low when interest rates are high. The cap writer has a greater chance of being insolvent when a payment is required. As a final example, the correlations in panel C take the opposite signs from those in panel B. The credit spread and annual default rate drop to zero. The greater chance of high firm value coinciding with cap payments reduces the likelihood of default by the cap writer; in this case, the incidence of default drops to zero.

The substantial increase in the credit spread exhibited in panel B may exaggerate default risk for two reasons. First, the cap is assumed to be unhedged by the firm. In other words, the company is taking a speculative position. Actual cap writers usually take offsetting positions in other caps or hedge by other methods, at least to some degree. Second, the model assumes that failure to cover cap payments is the only factor causing bankruptcy. For actual cap writers, the contingent liability posed by a cap is probably small compared to other items on the balance sheet. On the other hand, the computed credit spread may still be a good approximation if the cap serves as a proxy for the firm's overall balance sheet exposure to movements in interest rates.

No data on actual credit spreads are published. In conversations with the author, cap market participants place the credit spreads that have occurred in the range of 5 to 10 basis points for two- to three-year caps. The estimated spreads using the cap model are roughly in that range. Further research into actual credit spreads and refinements of the cap model should sharpen the estimation results and make the model more useful.

Conclusion

Interest-rate caps, collars, and floors are among the newest interest-rate risk management instruments. This article has given an exposition of these closely related instruments, which are options-based and designed to limit exposure to fluctuations in short-term interest rates on floating-rate assets or debt. Their applications are not limited to hedging. Like options, they are also convenient for speculating on interest-rate movements. In practice, however, the distinction between these two applications is rarely clear-cut. Several examples served to illustrate how financial managers use caps, collars, and floors.

The article also discussed the credit risks associated with caps, collars, and floors, which for the most part are over-the-counter contracts offered by one firm to another. Default risk is inherent in this kind of arrangement and can be priced. A new cap valuation model produced credit spreads that are not much different from those observed in the cap market between stronger and weaker credit risks among cap writers. Interest-rate risk management has been growing in importance for financial managers. This article may improve their understanding of the credit risk of caps, collars, and floors and help determine the cost of interest-rate protection.

Notes

[1] Recent *Economic Review* articles include Abken (1987), Feinstein and Goetzmann (1988), Kawaller, Koch, and Koch (1988), and Feinstein (1989).

[2] See Wall and Pringle (1988) for an introduction to interest-rate swaps.

[3] For brevity, the market for caps, collars, and floors will be referred to as the *cap market*.

[4] See Kuprianov (1986): 16-20, for a discussion of Eurodollar deposits and Eurodollar futures.

[5] The information on the ISDA survey was reported in *Risk* 2 (April 1989): 11.

[6] A detailed discussion of option pricing is beyond the scope of this article. A basic overview can be found in Abken (1987). See Cox and Rubinstein (1985) or Jarrow and Rudd (1983) for more thorough introductions to option pricing.

[7] See Abken (1987): 6, for more detail.

[8] See Henderson (1986) for further discussion.

[9] See Black (1976).

[10] To the author's knowledge, no published studies have compared the accuracy of different option-pricing models for pricing caps and related instruments. One reason may be that there are no publicly available data on these rates, and another is that these instruments are relatively new. Little empirical research exists on the adequacy of different interest-rate option-pricing models. Boyle and Turnbull (1989) use the Courtadon option-pricing model in evaluating collar rates, but they do not compare their rates with those from other models nor with actual market rates.

[11] Because the CME and most LIFFE Eurodollar futures are "cash-settled," a $1 million deposit is rarely made, but instead only the difference between the current, or spot, LIBOR and the contracted LIBOR times the notional principal actually changes hands.

[12] Prior to June 1989 contract months extended three years.

[13] A Eurodollar futures price is actually an index value that equals 100 minus the "add-on" yield (three-month LIBOR). Thus, the futures price and add-on yield move inversely with each other. See Kuprianov (1986): 16, for more detail on Eurodollar futures and short-term interest-rate futures generally. Both the add-on yield and the futures price are usually quoted in the financial press.

[14] See Feinstein (1989) for details on the estimation, interpretation, and uses of implied volatilities. The Eurodollar futures options are actually American options, but the early exercise feature has negligible value for the slightly out-of-the-money options usually used in estimating the implied volatilities with a European futures option formula.

[15] Sums in Table 1 may not add up due to rounding error. Cap rates are usually rounded to whole basis points. The dollar amounts are the exact amounts computed in constructing Table 1.

[16] Another way to create a zero-cost collar is to set the floor first and then determine the appropriate cap. The method discussed in the text is more common.

[17] Collars have also been offered that give the buyer a payment for taking the collar, that is, the value of the floor sold exceeds the cost of the cap purchased. See "NatWest Uses Incentives to Push Rate Collars," *American Banker*, August 2, 1989.

[18] These examples are consistent with the recent findings of Boyle and Turnbull (1989) in their examination of collars. Using a different option-pricing model than the Black model, they found that a 100 percent increase in the volatility causes the floor level to change by less than one basis point. If their findings are also valid for the Black model, most of the difference observed in the examples in the text is attributable to the difference in yield curves.

[19] Before March 1989, contract expiration dates had a maximum maturity of one year. See Chicago Mercantile Exchange (February/March 1989): 7.

[20] The term *counterparty* is standard terminology for the other party in a swap, cap, floor, or collar agreement.

[21] Another complication in using futures in a replicating portfolio is that futures contracts are marked to market daily. This situation may create cash flow problems since futures positions that lose value may be subject to frequent margin calls. Even though the replicating portfolio is used to hedge a cap, which matches it in value, the cash flows from the cap come only when it is sold and on interest payment dates.

[22] See Abken (1987) for more on the synthetic creation of options. Mattu (1986) gives examples of replicating portfolios for caps and floors.

[23] Shirreff (1986) gives an interesting though somewhat dated overview of the caps market and the various players in it.

[24] LeGrand and Fertakis (1986): 134.

[25] Floating-rate CDs are also called variable-rate CDs.

[26] See *Intermarket* (October 1986): 14, for an account of the first such sale of a cap from a capped floating-rate note (FRN). By selling a cap off an issue of $100 million in 12-year capped FRNs, Banque Indosuez of Paris lowered its interest rate by one-eighth of a point below LIBOR. Uncapped, the notes would have sold at LIBOR. The capped FRNs were issued at LIBOR plus three-eighths. On an annual basis, Indosuez therefore collected the equivalent of 50 basis points on the sale of its cap.

[27] Shirreff (1986): 29.

[28] The volatilities shown in Chart 1 are probably not the same as those used to generate the cap rates. The volatilities were obtained from a different source than the cap rates, but they should be highly correlated with the actual volatilities used to price the caps.

[29] Newbery and Stiglitz (1981) give a comprehensive discussion of risk aversion and the rationale for hedging.

[30] Wall and Pringle (1988): 22.

[31] The example given was described in terms of a "flow concept" of interest-rate risk, that is, the impact of a change in interest rates on the net interest margin. Another way to view interest-rate risk is in terms of a "stock concept," the change in the net worth of the firm. A parallel shift in the term structure of interest rates would reduce the value of an S&L's long-term mortgages more than it would reduce the value of its short-term liabilities. Net worth would be reduced or possibly turn negative. Purchasing a cap—an asset on the balance sheet—would offset loss of net worth

to some extent because it would gain value as interest rates rise. See Spahr, Luytjes, and Edwards (1988) for a good exposition of this application of caps and how they hedge interest-rate risk.

[32]Commercial banks underwriting debt for highly leveraged financings often require their floating-rate borrowers to buy caps for a portion of the debt. This hedging requirement may be stipulated in the loan covenant. See Richardson (1989): 12.

[33]See *Moody's Special Report* (1989).

[34]This method assumes that the interest rate follows a random walk with no "drift" (that is, deterministic trend movements). Changes in the interest rate from period to period are assumed to be normally distributed with constant variance (or standard deviation), implying that the statistical distribution of interest-rate movements may be completely characterized by only its mean and variance.

[35]These percentages are based on the properties of the normal distribution, which is assumed to describe interest-rate movements.

[36]Arak, Goodman, and Rones (1986): 452.

[37]Cap valuation can be formulated as a kind of compound option problem. See Geske (1977) to appreciate the complexities involved in valuing securities that are composed of sequences of options.

[38]In a discrete time model the expected value is a weighted average of all possible payoffs, each payoff multiplied by the probability of its occurring.

[39]According to Moody's study, the lowest investment-grade bonds, rated Baa (or BBB by Standard and Poor's), had average annual default rates over two-year horizons of 0.25 percent. A Standard and Poor's BBB-rated investment bank was reportedly at a disadvantage in writing caps compared to stronger writers. See Shirreff (1986): 34.

The 0.13 default rate used in the example was chosen to reflect the lower risk of default on a cap relative to a bond.

[40]The Monte Carlo simulations used a variance reduction technique called the method of antithetic variates (see Boyle [1977]). The total number of realizations was in fact 200,000 for each simulation, though only a fourth of that number came from independent draws from the random number generator. See Abken (forthcoming) for more details.

References

Abken, Peter A. "An Introduction to Portfolio Insurance." Federal Reserve Bank of Atlanta *Economic Review* 72 (November/December 1987): 2-25.

_____ . "Valuing Default-Risky Interest Rate Caps: A Monte Carlo Approach." Federal Reserve Bank of Atlanta Working Paper (forthcoming).

Arak, Marcelle, Laurie S. Goodman, and Arthur Rones. "Credit Lines for New Instruments: Swaps, Over-the-Counter Options, Forwards and Floor-Ceiling Agreements." In *Proceedings of a Conference on Bank Structure and Competition.* Federal Reserve Bank of Chicago (May 1986): 437-56.

Black, Fischer. "The Pricing of Commodity Contracts." *Journal of Financial Economics* 3 (January/March 1976): 167-79.

Boyle, Phelim P. "Options: A Monte Carlo Approach." *Journal of Financial Economics* 4 (May 1977): 323-38.

Boyle, Phelim P., and Stuart M. Turnbull. "Pricing and Hedging Capped Options." *Journal of Futures Markets* 9 (February 1989): 41-54.

Brown, Keith C., and Donald J. Smith. "Recent Innovations in Interest Rate Risk Management and the Reintermediation of Commercial Banking." *Financial Management* 17 (Winter 1988): 45-58.

"Caps and Floors." *The Banker* (February 1989): 9.

Chicago Mercantile Exchange. *Market Perspectives.* Various issues.

Commins, Kevin. "Managing Interest Rate Risk." *Intermarket* (May 1987): 28-34.

Cox, John C., and Mark Rubinstein. *Options Markets.* Englewood Cliffs, N.J.: Prentice-Hall, 1985.

Feinstein, Steven P. "Forecasting Stock-Market Volatility Using Options on Index Futures." Federal Reserve Bank of Atlanta *Economic Review* 74 (May/June 1989): 12-30.

Feinstein, Steven P., and William N. Goetzmann. "The Effect of the 'Triple Witching Hour' on Stock Market Volatility." Federal Reserve Bank of Atlanta *Economic Review* 73 (September/October 1988): 2-18.

Geske, Robert. "The Valuation of Corporate Liabilities as Compound Options." *Journal of Financial and Quantitative Analysis* 12 (1977): 541-52.

Henderson, Schuyler K. "Securitizing Swaps." *International Financial Law Review* (September 1986): 31-34.

Jarrow, Robert A., and Andrew Rudd. *Option Pricing.* Homewood, Ill.: Richard D. Irwin, Inc., 1983.

Johnson, Herb, and René Stulz. "The Pricing of Options with Default Risk." *Journal of Finance* 42 (June 1987): 267-80.

Kawaller, Ira G., Paul D. Koch, and Timothy W. Koch. "The Relationship between the S&P 500 Index and S&P 500 Index Futures Prices." Federal Reserve Bank of Atlanta *Economic Review* 73 (May/June 1988): 2-10.

Kuprianov, Anatoli. "Short-Term Interest Rate Futures." Federal Reserve Bank of Richmond *Economic Review* (September/October 1986): 12-26.

LeGrand, Jean E., and John P. Fertakis. "Interest Rate Caps: Keeping the Lid on Future Rate Hikes." *Journal of Accountancy* (May 1986): 130-36.

Mattu, Ravi. "Hedging Floating Rate Liabilities: Locks, Caps and Floors." Chicago Mercantile Exchange Strategy Paper, 1986.

Moody's Special Report. "Historical Default Rates of Corporate Bond Issuers, 1970-1988." July 1989.

Newbery, David M.G., and Joseph E. Stiglitz. *The Theory of Commodity Price Stabilization: A Study in the Economics of Risk.* New York: Oxford University Press, 1981.

Richardson, Portia. "Put on Your Thinking Cap." *Intermarket* (March 1989): 10-13.

Schaefer, Stephen M., and Eduardo S. Schwartz. "A Two-Factor Model of the Term Structure: An Approximate Solution." *Journal of Financial and Quantitative Analysis* 19 (December 1984): 413-24.

Shirreff, David. "Caps and Options: The Dangerous New Protection Racket." *Euromoney* (March 1986): 26-40.

Smith, Clifford W., and René M. Stulz. "The Determinants of Firms' Hedging Policies." *Journal of Financial and Quantitative Analysis* 20 (December 1985): 391-405.

Spahr, Ronald W., Jan E. Luytjes, and Donald G. Edwards. "The Impact of the Uses of Caps as Deposit Hedges for Financial Institutions." *Issues in Bank Regulation* (Summer 1988): 17-23.

Sutherland, L. Frederick. "Squeezing Cash: How to Make an LBO Work." *Corporate Cashflow* (June 1988): 47-50.

Tompkins, Robert. "The A-Z of Caps." *Risk* 2 (March 1989): 21-23, 41.

Wall, Larry D. "Alternative Explanations of Interest Rate Swaps: A Theoretical and Empirical Analysis." *Financial Management* (forthcoming, 1989).

Wall, Larry D., and John J. Pringle. "Interest Rate Swaps: A Review of the Issues." Federal Reserve Bank of Atlanta *Economic Review* 73 (November/December 1988): 22-37.

Section III

The Thrift Crisis and Deposit Insurance Reform

In the 1990s we are witnessing the closing of many thrift institutions. Traditionally, these savings and loan associations have been charged with providing mortgage financing for residential real estate. In addition, as depositiory institutions, they have offered insured savings accounts. With greater financial freedom for depository institutions in the 1980s, many thrift institutions began to offer commercial loans as well as home mortgages. In addition, fraud and malfeasance became more of a problem in a less restricted industry. After many of the new loans that thrifts made in the 1980s have turned sour, the taxpayer is left to honor the insurance on thrift deposits. This is the current situation of the thrift industry in the simplest terms. In this section, we examine the current turmoil in the industry and some of the plans to re-establish the industry on a sound basis.

The thrift debacle has already involved the closing of many institutions, as Leonard I. Nakamura explains in "Closing Troubled Financial Institutions: What Are the Issues?" Nakamura traces the origin of the thrift crisis and shows how insuring savings can lead to inefficient practices at depository institutions. Along the way he explains how the number of insolvent savings and loan associations rose from 14 in 1977 to 338 in 1988. Against this background, Nakamura argues that closing weak institutions is necessary for the economic health of the nation. As a critical part of this procedure, Nakamura urges new measures to place the industry on a sound footing.

The Financial Institutions, Reform, Recovery, and Enforcement Act of 1989 (FIRREA) provided funds to begin closing insolvent thrifts and to reorganize the thrift industry. Elizabeth Laderman explains the provisions of the Act in her article, "FIRREA and the Future of Thrifts." This law is important because it provides the framework for insuring funds deposited at savings and loans and at commercial banks. As part of the Act, depository institutions now face new capital requirements designed to prevent another thrift industry debacle.

In his article, "Using Market Incentives to Reform Bank Regulation and Federal Deposit Insurance," James B. Thomson analyzes the recent problems in the thrift industry. He also discusses the changes that are necessary in the industry in the light of FIRREA. Thomson argues that the solution to the thrift industry problem does not lie solely in increasing regulation. Instead, he maintains that market-oriented solutions offer better hope. Deposit insurance gives bank or thrift managers incentives to behave inefficiently because the institution does not face the discipline of market scrutiny in raising funds. In Thomson's view, the industry needs a framework that provides bank managers with incentives that encourage them to behave in a manner consistent with society's interests.

Any attempt to resolve the crisis facing depository institutions must face two issues. First, there is a need for insured deposits. Second, insuring deposits must be achieved without giving bank managers incentives to manage badly. One method of achieving this goal might be to tie deposit insurance to the risk of the institution. Risky thrifts or banks would be required to pay a higher insurance premium for their deposits than a low risk institution. This policy would give bank managers an incentive to control risk. William R. Keeton explores this approach in his article, "The New Risk–Based Plan for Commercial Banks." Keeton finds considerable merit in this framework, but he reasons that its implementation is subject to our imperfect measurement of risk and bank capital.

Article 19

Closing Troubled Financial Institutions: What Are the Issues?

*Leonard I. Nakamura**

In the final days of 1988, negotiators at the Federal Savings and Loan Insurance Corporation found themselves working nights and weekends to complete deals that would turn ailing thrifts over to new owners. By the end of the year they had placed, by General Accounting Office estimates, roughly $90 billion in thrift assets in new hands, at a loss to the FSLIC of $38.6 billion. And they were being criticized

*Leonard I. Nakamura is a Senior Economist in the Banking and Financial Markets Section of the Philadelphia Fed's Research Department.

widely for their slowness in closing insolvent thrifts, many of which had been allowed to pile up massive losses through fraud and mismanagement.

The FSLIC could ill afford more losses. Despite a rise in premium collections and a special recapitalization loan arranged by a 1987 Act of Congress, the insurance program was already $75 billion in the red at the end of 1988, according to the GAO. In the end, the FSLIC disappeared into a new entity, the Savings Association Insurance Fund, with the special act of Congress that was required to mend the safety net for thrift depositors. The cost of that legislation, the Financial Institutions Reform, Recovery, and Enforcement Act of 1989 (FIRREA),[1] has been estimated by the Administration at no less than $166 billion. The cost represents some 20 percent of the insured savings deposits the FSLIC was established to protect.

Has enough been done to prevent further costs on this scale? To find out, the Treasury Department is coordinating a FIRREA-mandated study of the deposit-insurance system. The need for such a study underscores continuing concern about the system's fundamental design. Past studies suggest that one area deserving more scrutiny is bank closure by regulators.[2] Currently, deposit insurance subsidizes risky and insolvent banks and thrifts, sharply reducing their private incentive to close or reorganize themselves. The system can be protected only by reducing the subsidy and improving regulatory closure.

The Search for the Best Closure Policy. Regulatory bank closure has two intertwined objectives. One is to protect the deposit-insurance fund and keep down the cost of deposit insurance. The other is to promote the efficiency of banking. Taken to its extreme, the first objective—protecting the deposit-insurance fund—can be met completely, and require relatively little information, if regulators always close any bank that nears insolvency. However, a brush with insolvency may be due merely to bad luck, and an unlucky efficient bank may find itself closed along with the inefficient bank. Ideally, regulators should be able to sort through the banks that come close to insolvency and keep open those banks that are well-managed and efficient. But to differentiate between efficient and inefficient banks, regulators need a great deal of information, some of it difficult to obtain.

Two key steps are necessary to improve closure policies: 1) reduce the subsidy to inefficient banks and thrifts so they are likelier to merge or close themselves without regulatory interference; and 2) improve the information available to bank regulators so that they can act in a timely, discerning manner.

This article is intended as a primer on the issues surrounding efficient closure of insured banks and thrift institutions.[3] The closure policies fall into three categories: efficient closure, general forbearance, and quick closure. Efficient closure aims to close inefficient banks that jeopardize the deposit-insurance fund. General forbearance gives banks as much time as possible to return to health. And quick closure seeks solely to protect the insurance fund.

DEPOSIT INSURANCE CAN ENCOURAGE INEFFICIENT BANKING

Before the institution of deposit insurance, depositors frequently enforced a policy of quick

---

[1]For a discussion of the FIRREA, see Richard W. Lang and Timothy G. Schiller, "The New Thrift Act: Mending the Safety Net," this *Business Review* (November/December 1989).

[2]See George J. Benston and others, *Perspectives on Safe and Sound Banking*, M.I.T. Press, Cambridge, MA (1986).

[3]Bank closure includes all of the tools regulators now use to change a bank's management: mergers and acquisitions of whole banks and of bank holding companies, as well as situations in which banks are split up and their assets sold off. Involuntary closure of a bank or thrift is officially performed by the charter issuer, which may be a state banking official, the Comptroller of the Currency, or the Office of Thrift Supervision; however, the regional Federal Reserve Bank and the deposit insurer typically coordinate closely with such officials. For example, if the regulators decide to close a bank that has borrowed funds from a Federal Reserve Bank, the Federal Reserve Bank can call the loan, placing the bank into technical insolvency. The state banking official then closes the bank, and the FDIC arranges to sell the bank's deposits and healthy assets to a sound bank, with a subsidy to make up any deficit left by unsound assets.

closure by withdrawing their deposits en masse in a bank run. However, depositors often were not able to distinguish sound banks from unsound banks, and runs could force both solvent and insolvent institutions to close their doors. By guaranteeing deposits, deposit insurance prevents bank runs.

The troubling aspect of deposit insurance is that it can encourage failing institutions to continue operating unless they are closed by regulators. An insolvent bank or thrift can continue to attract funds because the deposits are guaranteed by the insurance fund and the depositors feel protected. Thus, losses do not necessarily lead depositors to force an insured bank out of business, as would happen in the absence of deposit insurance.

On the other hand, the bank or thrift will not close itself, since to do so would leave its shareholders empty-handed. The shareholders will opt to keep the bank in business, hoping that a lucky investment or a change in the environment allows a return to profitability. Worse yet, dishonest bank managers may make loans to themselves or associates, gaining favorably priced loans at the expense of the dying institution and the deposit-insurance fund.

Inefficient Banks Have an Incentive to Stay Open. The current flat-rate premiums for deposit insurance give an inefficient, risky bank—whether insolvent or nearly so—a strong incentive to stay in business. All insured banks pay the same premiums, as do all insured thrifts: banks pay $1.20 per $1,000 of deposits, and thrifts pay $2.08 per $1,000 of deposits.[4] In exchange, the insured financial institution is able to guarantee that deposits (up to the statutory limit of $100,000 per account) will be repaid, even if the financial institution proves insolvent.

If the true riskiness of deposits is greater than its payments for insurance and any premiums necessary to attract deposits, then the financial institution is effectively being subsidized by the deposit insurer. And a subsidized institution has an incentive to stay in business even if it is inefficient.

ORIGINS OF THE THRIFT PROBLEM

The mortgage rate was around 9 percent from 1974 to 1977. It increased to 9.6 percent in 1978, then leapt each year thereafter, finally reaching 16.4 percent in November 1981. All rates went up, including the interest rates savings banks paid to depositors. As a consequence, the thrift industry as a whole lost money: the mortgages that had been made in the 1970s were not earning enough to cover the cost of funds in the early 1980s (see *Historical Data on the FSLIC*, p. 18).

There is now widespread agreement that thrift regulators, during the 1980s, permitted too many thrifts to stay open for too long. This policy of forbearance was, in fact, sanctioned by the Federal Home Loan Bank Board and by legislation such as the Garn–St. Germain Depository Institutions Act of 1982. During the early 1980s, thrifts were permitted to abandon generally accepted accounting principles in favor of a far less stringent set of accounting rules, dubbed regulatory accounting practices. As a consequence, hundreds of insolvent thrifts were able to keep their doors open.

Closing thrifts during the deep recession of the early 1980s would have been extremely difficult and expensive. At that time, almost all thrifts were losing money, and there would have been few potential merger partners. With the end of the recession in 1982, and the rapid decline in interest rates that followed, many thrifts were able to return to health. By 1986, however, interest rates were down to about 10 percent, and housing activity had rebounded. But instead of accelerating closure, the FSLIC

---

[4]Beginning in 1991, banks will pay $1.50 and thrifts will pay $2.30 per $1,000 of deposits. Thrift premiums will decline to $1.80 in 1993 and to $1.50 in 1998, at which point thrifts will again be paying the same amount as banks.

Historical Data on the FSLIC

Year	Mortgage Rate[a] (percent)	FSLIC Reserves[b] (billion $)	S&L Income[c] (billion $)	S&Ls In Operation[d] (thousands)	Insolvent S&Ls[e] (number)
1977	9.0	4.7	3.2	4.1	14
1978	9.6	5.3	3.9	4.1	10
1979	10.8	5.8	3.6	4.0	15
1980	12.7	6.5	0.8	4.0	16
1981	14.7	6.2	-4.6	3.8	53
1982	15.1	6.3	-4.1	3.3	222
1983	12.6	6.4	1.9	3.2	281
1984	12.4	5.6	1.0	3.1	434
1985	11.6	4.6	3.7	3.2	449
1986	10.2	-6.3	0.1	3.2	460
1987	9.3	-13.7	-7.8	3.1	505
1988	9.2	-75.0	-12.1	2.8	338

[a]Conventional loans on new homes, effective interest rate in percent, annual average, Federal Home Loan Bank Board (FHLBB).

[b]Total FSLIC reserves, year-end, FHLBB.

[c]Net income after taxes, FSLIC-insured savings institutions (includes FSLIC-insured savings banks), FHLBB.

[d]Number of FSLIC-insured savings institutions (includes FSLIC-insured savings banks), year-end, FHLBB.

Data for the above series through 1988 are available in convenient form in the *Savings Institutions Sourcebook 1989*, United States League of Savings Institutions.

[e]Insolvent S&Ls at year-end according to GAAP, U.S. General Accounting Office. Data through 1987 are in *Trends in Thrift Industry Performance: December 1977 Through June 1987*, May 1988; 1988 data are in *Solutions to the Thrift Industry Problem*, February 1989.

found itself with insufficient funds to close thrifts rapidly, and it permitted more and more insolvent thrifts to remain open.

A New Attitude Apparently Prevails. Now the pendulum appears to be swinging in the opposite direction, in favor of quick closure: it is now being proposed that thrifts and banks, even though solvent, be closed if their net worth—which provides a cushion against deposit-insurance losses—falls too low. For example, five academic experts on banking have called for closing depository institutions "when the market value of net worth goes below some low but positive percentage, such as 1 or 2 percent of assets."[5] But is the pendulum swinging too far? If that principle had been in place in 1981, virtually the entire savings and loan industry would have been closed. And

[5]This proposal is in Benston and others (1986), p. 309.

with few available buyers, the losses would have been enormous.

Clearly, today's first order of business is to return thrift regulators toward a standard of efficient closure, which is an important element of the FIRREA. But this closure of insolvent thrifts needs to be buttressed by more efficient decisions on closure, providing regulators with more information to help them separate the sound and unsound institutions. Though forbearance created severe problems, speeding closure alone is not a sufficient response. Improving the efficiency of closure decisions also requires increasing both the quality and quantity of the information brought to bear by regulators and other parties.[6]

HOW BANKS ARE CLOSED

How are banks actually closed? At present, bank regulators first make a preliminary identification of problem banks using the quarterly Reports of Condition and the quarterly Reports of Income required of all insured banks. Banks earmarked by these "early warning systems" are then investigated further. Bank regulators identify problem banks using a system nicknamed CAMEL, which rates banks on *c*apital, *a*sset quality, *m*anagement, *e*arnings, and *l*iquidity. Banks classified as problem banks are then told to correct deficiencies, first voluntarily and then, if necessary, through cease-and-desist orders.

Under current law, banks and thrifts can be closed only if they are deemed insolvent by the bank- or thrift-chartering regulator—the state regulator, the Comptroller of the Currency, or the Office of Thrift Supervision. Thus, the accounting rules that define solvency are an additional, and crucial, issue.

What Makes an Institution Insolvent. Any institution is insolvent when an accounting of its assets and liabilities reveals that liabilities exceed assets. Unfortunately, the proper method for accounting for assets and liabilities is not straightforward.

Suppose a thrift makes a mortgage for $100,000 at a fixed interest rate of 8 percent. The mortgage is entered into the thrift's books as an asset of $100,000 and initially earns $8,000 a year in interest. But suppose that after the loan is made, interest rates skyrocket and the fixed rate for mortgages rises to 16 percent. If the thrift were to make the mortgage again, it could earn $16,000 per year. The economic value of the old mortgage loan—discounted by the higher interest rate—falls roughly in half, to $57,000 (assuming the mortgage is held until maturity).[7] However, under "generally accepted accounting principles," referred to as GAAP, the mortgage remains on the thrift's books at its "book value" of $100,000, unless the mortgage is actually sold at the lower value, in which case the loss in value must be written off.[8]

---

[6]Passage of the FIRREA does not mean that the problems created by general forbearance are gone for good. There are strong reasons to believe that over the decade many banks and thrifts, perhaps numbering in the thousands, will close because of increasing competition among financial institutions. For a discussion of the problems facing smaller banks, see Sherrill Shaffer, "Challenges to Small Banks' Survival," this *Business Review* (September/October 1989). For an overview of the problems faced by the banking system and some suggested solutions, many of them already widely accepted, see George J. Benston and others (1986).

[7] The effect of a change in interest rates on the value of a mortgage can be calculated using discounted present value. The monthly payment on a 30-year mortgage debt of $100,000 at 8 percent interest is $714.40. The discounted value of a payment i months from now is $714.40/(1.08)^{i/12}$, and the present discounted value of the mortgage is the sum of these values as i goes from 1 to 360. When the interest rate rises to 16 percent, the denominator increases to $(1.16)^{i/12}$ and the sum falls, to $56,735.

[8]Under the looser regulatory accounting principles used by thrifts in the 1980s, the value lost when mortgages were sold did not have to be written off all at once.

The key point is that the economic value of the mortgage is what the market is willing to pay if the thrift is closed. Suppose the thrift has on its books $2 million in deposits, $2 million in mortgages at 8 percent, and $200,000 in cash on hand. Its GAAP net worth is thus $200,000. But with mortgage rates at 16 percent, the economic value of the mortgages is just $1.14 million and the thrift is then economically insolvent. If the thrift were closed and its assets sold to repay depositors, the deposit insurer would have to provide $660,000 to fully pay off the depositors.

On the other hand, mortgage rates may well return to their previous rate of 8 percent. If the thrift is well managed, it might be desirable to wait to see if interest rates will drop and the thrift can return to solvency. The corresponding danger is that the mortgages earn only $160,000 per year. If the thrift must pay more than that in interest on its deposits—as would be likely in a period of high interest rates—the thrift will lose money while the regulators delay closure.

Should Loans Be "Marked to Market"? Some argue that mortgages and other loans should be "marked to market"—that is, their accounting value should equal their economic value. The existence of secondary markets, on which existing mortgages and other loans can be bought and sold, provides a basis for pricing a wide variety of assets. For example, if bank loans to Mexico are priced on the secondary market at 65 cents on the dollar, a bank with $100 million of Mexican loans would have to report this as an asset worth $65 million.

An important caveat is that the market may not always be a good guide to asset valuation. Some secondary markets are very thin—with low-volume, infrequent trading—and may not be representative of the assets we want to value. And at times even very large markets may experience disruptions that distort value.

Under GAAP, loans are entered as assets at their book value, so an institution that is insolvent when marked-to-market may well not be technically insolvent. When this occurs, it may not be legally possible to close the bank or thrift. Moreover, if such a bank or thrift is closed by regulators, the owners often can sue the regulators, arguing that the bureaucrats have unreasonably deprived the owners of property. One step the deposit insurer can take to protect itself is to remove deposit-insurance protection from new deposits to the institution. Then the bank or thrift will typically be unable to attract new deposits and will become insolvent as its deposit base declines.

On the other hand, determining legal insolvency by marking-to-market might force regulators to close an efficiently managed bank or thrift simply because it became insolvent temporarily. And it is possible that marking-to-market itself may induce imperfect measurement of assets if the market does not accurately represent the value of the bank's assets, a situation that would exacerbate the potential mistakes of forced closure. Indeed, in the late 1970s and early 1980s, Congress and thrift regulators felt that even the GAAP rules were too harsh in the rising-interest-rate environment of that period. Unfortunately, their decision to move toward general forbearance proved extremely costly.

WHY GENERAL FORBEARANCE HAS BEEN SO COSTLY

Severe problems accompanied general forbearance. These problems are considerably more evident with hindsight than they were when the policy was being implemented in the early 1980s.

First, and probably most important, general forbearance raises the monetary losses of the insurer and thus the direct costs of deposit premiums. After all, deposit insurance subsidizes insolvent banks and thrifts, and the longer regulators allow them to stay in business, the larger the costs ultimately charged to the deposit-insurance fund.

Permits Excessive Risk-Taking by Banks. A bank that is failing may seek to avoid bankruptcy by taking greater risks. In this case, the motives to generate profit and continue in business may conflict with the traditional principles of carefully assessing the risks and returns to lending.

For example, consider the profit motives of an insolvent thrift in the Southwest that must decide whether to lend additional funds to a large real-estate developer in the area. If the whole real-estate market in the area has gone sour, the developer is likely to go bankrupt, even with the infusion of cash. But as long as the market remains bad, the thrift itself has no hope of a return to solvency. If the market does turn around, the developer will be able to repay the loan and the thrift will no longer be insolvent. The decision to make the loan pushes the thrift deeper into danger. But if the developer's venture is successful, the thrift's shareholders will be the beneficiaries. If it is not, the cost of failure will be borne entirely by the deposit insurer.

An additional risk of general forbearance is that insolvent banks are temptations for fraud. An insolvent bank is a tempting target for a crook, because it may be for sale at a low price. The crook can then make loans to his own enterprises or to cohorts at concessionary rates, siphoning dollars out of the bank.[9]

"Zombie" Thrifts Can Exacerbate the Problem. Allowing inefficient banks to remain in business under a policy of general forbearance imposes social costs on other banks and the community. When inefficient insolvent banks compete aggressively for deposits and loan business, they can harm better-managed banks, which are forced to compete in a deteriorating environment. Professor Edward Kane has dubbed such insolvent thrifts "zombie thrifts," to underscore how the "living dead" can bring about more of their own kind, multiplying the problems of the insurance system.[10]

WHY EFFICIENT CLOSURE IS SUPERIOR TO QUICK CLOSURE

Undeniably, many of the problems of forbearance can be solved by quick closure. Quick closure reduces the monetary losses of the insurer, and this has the fundamental benefit of protecting taxpayers from losses. Not incidentally, it also will tend to result in lower deposit premiums. In addition, by making it likelier that a bank encountering difficulties will be closed, quick closure guards against excessive risk-taking by banks. Fearing bad outcomes that may lead to quick closure, banks will tend to take steps to raise their capital and make less risky loans. Finally, quick closure closes banks that, because of their weak balance sheets, would be most likely to engage in risky or fraudulent behavior.

Unfortunately, quick closure increases the number of efficient banks that are closed or merged when they experience what otherwise would be a temporary setback. When efficient banks close, valuable resources to the community are lost. Goodwill and expertise, the building blocks for business centers, are sacrificed.

If a region's major industry suffers a severe blow—as when an agricultural community suffers a prolonged drought or when an oil-producing state is hit by low energy prices—both well-managed and poorly managed banks may show losses and become insolvent. Under quick closure, both types of banks would be closed, and the region would suffer an additional blow that could harm its ability to recover.

---

[9]The FIRREA widens the authority of regulators to disapprove bank and thrift directors and senior executives, and it strengthens criminal penalties for misconduct.

[10]Edward J. Kane, "Dangers of Capital Forbearance: The Case of the FSLIC and 'Zombie' S&L's," *Contemporary Policy Issues* (January 1987).

Typically, the well-managed bank will have fully reported its losses, and with sound banking practices it will be able to return to profitability in short order. But the poorly managed bank often will not have a good system for reporting its losses, and its return to profitability will be prevented because of old and new mistakes. To the extent that regulators can efficiently sort out good and bad banks, costs will be minimized and benefits to the community will be greatest.

Banks Must Not Avoid Risk. Quick closure also increases regulatory interference in bank conduct. In particular, it may have the chilling effect of making banks too averse to risk. The business of banking is to manage risk in lending through diversification and through knowledge of the business scene. It is important for banks to know that if they are fundamentally sound, they will be given the opportunity to return to profitability. That way, they will be more willing to pursue profitable but risky lending, which helps keep the U.S. economy flexible and growing.

IMPROVING PRIVATE INCENTIVES

Closing banks whenever losses are possible is obviously not the best way to regulate bank risk. The focus should be on enhancing the efficiency of closure decisions—first by increasing shareholders' incentives to close and merge inefficient banks, and then by improving the information regulators can use to identify and close inefficient banks.

A bank's shareholders are the most likely party to know when a solvent bank is losing money. Giving shareholders the right incentives to close or merge an inefficient bank increases the presumption that banks that remain open are efficient. This places less of a burden on regulators to close solvent institutions and permits them to focus more keenly on insolvent institutions.

Risk-based Deposit Premiums and Capital Requirements. One way to provide the right incentives to shareholders is to base deposit premiums on a bank's level of risk. When a nearly insolvent bank has to pay fully for its riskiness, its incentive to stay independent diminishes. Unfortunately, setting premiums to the right amount is an extremely difficult task. Current proposals, which set premiums based on the composition of the bank's assets, go only part way toward capturing the bank's riskiness, but are a step in the right direction.

Another step toward improving private incentives is risk-based capital requirements. In 1988, the United States and 11 other nations signed an agreement establishing minimum risk-based capital requirements for banks, to be phased in by 1992. Under this system, banks investing in riskier assets will have to raise additional capital, which will provide additional protection for the FDIC against losses. This will tend to discourage weak banks from taking risky positions. However, the provisions are quite broad and do not cover all forms of risk-taking; the risk of interest rate movements, for example, is not included.

Since setting risk-based deposit premiums and capital requirements properly is likely to be imperfect, it is also crucial to provide bank regulators with better information.

IMPROVING INFORMATION FOR CLOSURE

Proposals to provide regulators with better information begin with timely and accurate financial reporting. In principle, accounting practices and appraisals would use current market values of assets and liabilities to accurately reflect economic solvency. At a minimum, banks and thrifts would report the market value of assets whenever accurate pricing is possible.

If such information on economic solvency were available, then more careful consideration could be given to proposals that permit regulators to close or merge institutions that are near economic insolvency. But to avoid the undesirable effects of quick closure under such proposals, regulators would have to retain substantial discretion to keep open banks and thrifts that can show they are well managed.

The FIRREA encourages better accounting information by increasing the penalties for false reporting of assets. For the first time, the accounting firms hired by banks and thrifts can face severe penalties for countenancing false reporting.

But accurate accounting data are not enough to assure efficient closure, and the information of all parties should be brought to bear. Several current proposals make it more likely that depositors, capital markets, and even other banks will signal to regulators a lack of faith in particular banks, buttressing the early warning signals currently in use. But some of these proposals also have pitfalls.

Information from Depositors. Some depositors may know a lot about their bank and its fortunes. Large depositors at a small bank, for example, may know how its portfolio is doing because they are deeply involved in the local business environment.

Moreover, if deposit-insurance protection is reduced below 100 percent—an idea known as "co-insurance"—depositors are more likely to signal failures by removing funds from risky or failing institutions. One form of this proposal is to reduce the maximum-size deposit protected by insurance. The idea here is that the most savvy depositors are likely to be large depositors, and a run of their deposits can signal insurers of impending trouble.[11]

The drawback to co-insurance is that depositors' runs were the problem in the first place. Deposit insurance exists largely because depositors' information and incentives all too often led to failures of good banks. Co-insurance may provide a useful signal, but if depositors act on poor information, they may make aiding good banks harder rather than easier.

Information from Other Banks. Before the system of deposit insurance was created, clearing houses, which were consortia of banks, successfully propped up banks threatened by panics. They were successful largely because competitors are often in the best position to judge whether a rival bank is well managed.[12] Professor Charles Calomiris has pointed out that these consortia sometimes have acted very successfully as mutual deposit-insurance groups, precisely because banks had good information about one another.[13] Calomiris proposes to make groups of banks responsible for one another in just this way.

The mutual-insurance concept may no longer be credible, however, given the FIRREA. A key to mutual insurance is the fundamental notion that the group suffers when any bank goes under. This mutual dependence ensures that banks have a strong incentive to report bad banks. If banks interpret FIRREA to mean that taxpayers will bail out the insurance fund in the future, then the banking industry has little incentive to help construct sound rules for bank closure. If banks pay the full cost of deposit insurance, they will have a strong interest in seeing that closure is quick and efficient.

Information from Capital Markets. At present, regulators are keen observers of banks' stock prices and costs of funds, and the capital markets are thus useful in signaling bank problems. But most banks and thrifts have stocks

---

[11]For a spirited advocacy of co-insurance, see John H. Boyd and Arthur J. Rolnick's "A Case for Reforming Federal Deposit Insurance" in the *1988 Annual Report* of the Federal Reserve Bank of Minneapolis.

[12]There is a risk, however, that even a well-managed bank may be forced out of business by rivals seeking to reduce competition.

[13]Charles Calomiris, "Deposit Insurance: Lessons from the Historical Record," Federal Reserve Bank of Chicago *Economic Perspectives* (May/June 1989).

that either are not publicly traded or are traded on thin markets.

One way to obtain additional information from capital markets is to raise capital standards. This forces banks and thrifts to raise cash outside the umbrella of deposit insurance. Under FIRREA, thrifts are required to meet the higher capital standards that banks face. This requirement is forcing thrifts to raise additional equity, borrow money from capital markets, or shrink their assets. But before a thrift can convince lenders to put up new cash, its management must provide credible information that the thrift will remain profitable. While a powerful sign of creditworthiness, raising additional equity or debt is not a panacea. For example, given widespread press reports of problems in the S&L industry, good thrifts may be unable to convince outside investors that they are sound.

Limits on Assets of Banks and Thrifts. A final way to reduce the problem of insufficient information is to limit the types of assets banks and thrifts can hold. Such a move would make it easier to evaluate the performance of the institution and its management, simply by reducing the number of asset categories regulators would need information about. At the extreme end are proposals to create "safe banks," which would be restricted to holding extremely safe assets such as U.S. Treasury bills. However, an important rationale for deposit insurance is to ensure that banks and thrifts are able to lend to businesses and consumers. Preventing these loans would harm the economy's ability to allocate savings to those who would use them best.

Among the less radical reform proposals are those that suggest reining in the ability of banks and thrifts to diversify into risky assets and to limit the expansion of their powers into new areas, such as direct real-estate investment or securities underwriting. In particular, the FIRREA requires thrifts to keep nearly 70 percent of their assets in mortgage-related investments. A drawback of this requirement, however, is that it prevents possible diversification of portfolios, which, if properly managed, can reduce the risk of bank failure.

CONCLUSION

Under the current system of deposit insurance, troubled banks and thrifts do not have the right incentives to close themselves, and failing banks have incentives to jeopardize the funds with which they are entrusted. Consequently, the job of closing failing banks falls to the deposit insurer. If the deposit insurer fails to do so—or is somehow prevented from doing so—then losses from deposit insurance will inevitably multiply.

Vigorous closure of inefficient banks and thrifts is crucial to the health of our deposit-insurance system. But vigorous closure is an aim that needs to be buttressed by 1) reducing the subsidy to risky and inefficient banks and thrifts, via risk-based deposit-insurance premiums and capital requirements; 2) improving the accuracy of information provided to insurers and other regulators; and 3) giving all parties concerned more incentives to signal to insurers their lack of faith in inefficient banks and thrifts—and their faith in efficient ones.

Article 20

FIRREA and the Future of Thrifts

The Financial Institutions Reform, Recovery, and Enforcement Act of 1989 (FIRREA) provides the funds to begin closing and/or reorganizing the hundreds of insolvent savings and loan associations that contributed to the so–called thrift crisis. In addition, it alters the legal and regulatory environment for the remaining institutions by changing the laws governing the deposit insurance funds, thrift powers, bank holding company acquisition of thrifts, and capital requirements. This Letter discusses the implications of each of these new rules for the future operating environment and size of the thrift industry.

New insurance funds

FIRREA establishes two new deposit insurance funds, replacing the fund administered by the Federal Savings and Loan Insurance Corporation with the Savings Association Insurance Fund (SAIF) and the fund administered by the Federal Deposit Insurance Corporation (FDIC) with the Bank Insurance Fund (BIF). The Act places both funds under the administration of the FDIC.

These funds offer the same protection to depositors, but differ in the level of their reserve ratios (the ratio of insurance fund reserves to insured deposits) and therefore, in the size of the premia charged to their member institutions. FIRREA requires BIF and SAIF to build and maintain a "designated reserve ratio," which is now set at 1.25 percent of insured deposits. Because SAIF's reserve ratio currently is considerably lower than this target, FIRREA requires SAIF members to pay substantially higher premia than BIF members. BIF members now pay 12 cents per $100 of deposits, while SAIF members must pay 20.8 cents.

Over time, this differential will narrow, with BIF and SAIF members paying 15 and 18 cents, respectively, for each $100 of deposits between August 1994 and January 1, 1998. After January 1, 1998, this differential is expected to disappear altogether, and members of both funds will be paying 15 cents for each $100 of deposits.

However, beginning on January 1, 1995, the FDIC is permitted to raise premia for either insurance fund above the statutory levels set in FIRREA, if it determines that reserve ratios are likely to fall below the designated reserve ratio of 1.25 percent. Thus, the premium differential between SAIF and BIF may persist even after 1998.

BIF or SAIF?

The sizeable differential between SAIF and BIF premia may encourage institutions to convert their memberships from SAIF to BIF. However, depository institutions cannot convert from one deposit insurance fund to the other until five years after enactment of FIRREA, which will be August 1994. Exceptions may be made for insolvent thrifts or those in danger of default and for relatively small thrift branches.

When the moratorium is lifted, any thrift or bank can convert from one insurance fund to the other. To convert, a depository will have to change its charter, merge with an institution belonging to the other fund, or acquire a branch or branches from an institution in the other fund. The converting institution also will be required to pay both an exit fee to the fund it is leaving and an entrance fee to the fund it is joining.

FIRREA mandates that the FDIC set entrance fees sufficiently high to prevent "dilution of the fund" being entered. This means that an institution seeking to convert from SAIF to BIF likely will have to pay entrance fees approximately equal to BIF's reserve ratio. Thus if BIF succeeds in building its reserve ratio to 1.25 percent or higher by August 1994, institutions entering BIF will probably pay an entrance fee of at least $1.25 per $100 of insured deposits.

Given such a high entrance fee and assuming that the premium differential in August 1994 (when the moratorium is lifted) is only three cents per $100 per year, as FIRREA mandates, conversions from SAIF to BIF are not likely. Moreover, any exit fees charged for leaving SAIF would further discourage conversions.

Persistent differentials?

However, if thrifts expect premium differentials to persist indefinitely, a substantial number of conversions could take place, despite the hefty entrance and exit fees. Given the large number of thrift insolvencies, many may believe that SAIF premia will remain permanently higher than BIF premia in order to maintain reserves in the face of future losses.

Faced with the expectation of permanently higher premia, savings and loans with sufficient cash flow to cover the exit and entrance fees likely will convert. In fact, any thrift with a strong net worth position could be a candidate for conversion since at the very least, it should be able to borrow against its net worth to raise the money to cover exit and entrance fees.

Thus, it is possible that only the weaker institutions would be left behind in SAIF. Since weak institutions pose the greatest risks and therefore impose the greatest costs on the insurance funds, SAIF premia may have to increase to cover the higher expenses associated with a growing concentration of weak institutions. Higher premia, in turn, may encourage even more defections from SAIF and an even greater concentration of weak thrifts in SAIF.

Switching charters

Although a thrift may not convert from SAIF membership to BIF membership until August 1994, it is permitted at any time to convert to a bank for all other purposes. It needs approval for charter conversion from the appropriate regulatory agencies, but once it gains such approval, a thrift can call itself a bank and exercise bank powers. A thrift that converts to a bank charter will have the choice of staying with SAIF or moving to BIF after the moratorium on insurance fund conversion expires.

Even if a thrift chooses not to convert from SAIF to BIF, it may want to change to a bank charter because provisions in FIRREA reduce the attractiveness of a thrift charter relative to a bank charter. First, FIRREA diverts some of the earnings of the Federal Home Loan Banks in which thrifts hold stock. This will reduce the dividends thrifts receive from the Home Loan Banks. Second, FIRREA alters the activities and investments that are permissible for thrifts.

Under FIRREA's Qualified Thrift Lender (QTL) test, a thrift must have 70 percent of its tangible assets in "qualified thrift investments," which are generally housing–related assets. Formerly, thrifts were required to hold only 60 percent of their portfolio in such investments, and the list of assets deemed housing–related was broader than under FIRREA.

Historically thrifts have had tax advantages over banks that compensated them for these portfolio restrictions. These tax advantages remain, but they have not been enhanced in response to the new investment rules.

Banks, in contrast, have much broader lending powers and are not required to hold housing–related investments. A bank thus has more flexibility to take advantage of profitable investment opportunities and to diversity its portfolio.

A wall comes down

Prior to FIRREA's enactment, bank holding companies were prohibited from acquiring all but insolvent thrifts. FIRREA amends the Bank Holding Company Act to authorize the Federal Reserve to permit bank holding companies to acquire healthy thrifts.

The new rule may increase the number of thrifts purchased by bank holding companies. Many of these acquired thrifts are likely to be converted to bank charters because of the investment restrictions on thrifts and because a bank holding company may find it more efficient to run a depository institution subsidiary as a bank than as a thrift.

Thrifts that are acquired by bank holding companies also may, with certain restrictions, be merged into affiliate banks. This option will be attractive whenever the holding company can take advantage of economies associated with a larger scale of banking operations. The merged entity will have to pay SAIF premiums on the portion of deposits attributable to the thrift until August 1994, though.

New capital requirements

FIRREA introduces three new capital requirements for thrifts. First, FIRREA imposes a new minimum "leverage ratio." The leverage ratio, defined as the ratio of "core capital" to total assets, is to be no less than three percent. Core capital is the sum of common equity, noncumulative perpetual preferred stock, and minority interests in consolidated subsidiaries, minus most intangibles except purchased mortgage servicing rights and qualifying supervisory goodwill. (Supervisory goodwill is the premium above tangible net worth that may be paid for a troubled savings institution. Acquirers may be willing to pay such premium to obtain the deposit insurance guarantee.)

Second, FIRREA requires compliance with a new minimum 1.5 percent tangible–capital–to–assets ratio. Tangible capital is core capital minus supervisory goodwill and all other intangibles except qualifying purchased mortgage servicing rights.

Finally, FIRREA establishes a minimum risk–based capital requirement for thrifts. Risk weights are applied to a thrift institution's assets according to the assets' inherent riskiness. This yields the risk–adjusted asset base against which a minimum amount of capital must be held.

Goodwill

In addition to the new capital–asset ratios, new definitions of capital are in effect since FIRREA's enactment. Thrifts are no longer permitted to include most types of "goodwill" in regulatory measures of capital. Moreover, even supervisory goodwill is to be phased out of core capital by 1995. Goodwill is the difference between the market value of a firm's net worth and the value based on tangible assets only. Goodwill represents the value of a franchise, including name recognition, an established reputation, and loyal customers. For many thrifts, goodwill was booked as capital when they acquired other enterprises at greater–than–tangible asset value.

For weak thrifts, the new rules pertaining to goodwill are especially appropriate. The only source of goodwill for these thrifts was the unpriced value of the deposit insurance guarantee and the forbearance practiced by the regulators. The exclusion of goodwill from capital will thus be reflected in lower stock prices for these thrifts.

For healthy thrifts, however, excluding goodwill from regulatory capital may have undesirable effects. A healthy thrift that was operating efficiently prior to FIRREA would have chosen an optimal capital level, including goodwill. If its capital, excluding goodwill, is less than the regulatory minimum, FIRREA will force the thrift to raise additional capital. This presumably will lead to a decrease in the wealth of the thrift's shareholders, since the institution will be required to operate with greater–than–optimal capital. (It is worth pointing out that any increase in capital due to the new capital requirements would for the same reason diminish thrift shareholder wealth. From a social standpoint, however, there is an offsetting reduction in the value of potential claims on the insurance funds.)

Perhaps the only way for these shareholders to recover this lost wealth would be to sell the thrift. A purchaser should be willing to pay for the full value of the goodwill, as long as the purchaser does not also face the same regulatory capital deficiency problem as the acquiree. Thus, the new requirement concerning goodwill could lead to increased thrift takeovers, particularly by bank holding companies, which are not likely to be as capital–constrained as are thrift holding companies.

The exclusion of goodwill and the new capital–asset ratios are in sum more stringent than pre–FIRREA requirements. They will cause some thrifts that are unable to raise enough capital to close down. Many other thrifts will be able to raise the necessary capital only be selling off assets and/or slowing growth. The requirements, therefore, will cause the industry to shrink considerably, at least over the next several years.

An uncertain future

It is too early to tell whether bank holding companies will acquire healthy thrifts on a large scale, and we will have to wait five years to observe the extent of conversions from SAIF to BIF. However, it is clear that the operation of a savings and loan is a very different business from what it was less than six months ago. Higher deposit insurance premia for thrifts, restricted thrift activities, the prospect of bank holding company acquisitions of thrifts, and stiffer capital requirements all contribute to the likelihood that the thrift industry will experience considerable consolidation in the wake of the deposit insurance crisis.

Elizabeth Laderman
Economist

Article 21

Using Market Incentives to Reform Bank Regulation and Federal Deposit Insurance

by James B. Thomson

James B. Thomson is an assistant vice president and economist at the Federal Reserve Bank of Cleveland. The author thanks Edward Kane, George Kaufman, and Walker Todd for helpful comments and suggestions.

Introduction

Reform of the financial services industry became a hotly debated issue in the 1980s, and this debate continues to rage in the 1990s. Much of the debate has been generated by a growing recognition that fundamental reforms are needed in our bank and thrift regulatory systems to respond to market-driven changes in the financial services industry. Deposit-insurance reform has taken center stage in the political arena, as the Financial Institutions Reform, Recovery and Enforcement Act (FIRREA) of 1989 formally commits $159 billion of taxpayer money to resolve the thrift crisis and mandates that a study of federal deposit insurance be undertaken.

The overall objective of reform in the financial services industry should be to maximize the efficiency and stability of the banking and thrift systems while minimizing the exposure of the federal safety net, and hence the taxpayer, to losses generated by insured banks and thrifts. A plethora of reform proposals have been advanced by the banking industry, bank regulators, and the academic community. These reform proposals typically can be divided into proposals that rely on increased regulation and less discretion for bank management,[1] and proposals that rely on market-oriented solutions and increased management discretion within supervisory guidelines.[2]

The purpose of this paper is twofold. First, it presents the case for adopting market-oriented reforms to the regulatory system and to the financial safety net.[3] Second, it summarizes the literature from one perspective and presents a cohesive view on the topic. Section I reexamines the issue of whether banks are special and the

■ **1** Reform proposals that rely on increased government regulation include Corrigan (1987) and Keehn (1989). These authors propose the use of regulation as a substitute for market discipline, and hence reforms to the federal safety net. In their separate proposals, Corrigan and Keehn would allow bank holding companies to engage in virtually any financial activity so long as there is legal separation between the nonbanking activities and the insured banks in the holding company. In principle, this would capture some of the efficiencies of an integrated financial services industry without increasing the size and scope of the safety net. However, Kane's (1989b) application of principal-agent theory to regulatory agencies calls into question the substitutability of regulation and market discipline.

■ **2** Proposals that rely on increased market discipline include Cates (1989), Ely (1985, 1989), Kane (1983, 1985, 1986), Benston et al. (1986, ch. 9), Benston et al. (1989), Benston and Kaufman (1988), the Federal Reserve Bank of Minneapolis (1988), Hoskins (1989), Thomson and Todd (1990), and Wall (1989).

■ **3** For an opposing view, see Campbell and Minsky (1987), Guttentag and Herring (1986, 1988) and Randall (1989).

issue of stability in banking markets, both regulated and unregulated. In addition, section I looks at principal-agent problems associated with bank regulation (Kane [1988b]). Section II proposes reforms to our system of regulatory taxes and subsidies. Conclusions are presented in section III.

I. Stability in
Banking Markets

Those who propose reforms that rely on an increased role for regulation in determining limits on bank powers and activities—and hence a reduced role for management discretion, shareholders' control, and market discipline—assume that financial markets are inherently unstable or that banks are "special" in the sense that the social costs of bank failures significantly exceed the private costs (Corrigan [1987] and Tallman [1988]). Therefore, proponents of increased regulation are willing to trade efficiency for stability. Moreover, in principle, increased regulation protects the public purse from losses by restricting the participation of insured depository institutions in activities that are deemed to be excessively risky.

The reforms outlined in this paper assume that the opposite is true; that, left to their own devices, financial markets are stable in the sense that in the long run they exhibit an orderly process of change, and that, if there is a trade-off between efficiency and stability, it exists only in the short run.[4] Moreover, it is the system of regulatory taxes and subsidies, in our view, that makes banks "special," and not any intrinsic characteristic of banking.[5]

Are Banks Special?

The banks-are-special argument typically is based on one of two notions: either that bank failures have a high social cost or that all runs on individual banks are contagious and, therefore, the banking system is unstable. Since the issue of banking-system stability is dealt with in the fol-

lowing section, we will concentrate on the social cost of bank failures here. To argue that banks are special because there are high social costs associated with their failures, one must demonstrate two things: first, the social costs of bank failures are significantly greater than the private costs of bank failures (that is, there is an economically significant externality associated with the failure of a bank); and second, the social costs of bank failures are significantly higher than the social costs of failures of other firms.

What has been the cost of bank failures? Benston et al. (1986, ch. 2) show that for the entire period from 1865 to 1933 (the time period between the National Banking Act and the creation of the FDIC), total losses were $12.3 billion, or about 1 percent of total commercial bank assets. Losses to depositors were only about $2.4 billion, or about 0.21 percent of commercial bank deposits. Even in the Great Depression (1930-1933), the losses to depositors were only about 0.81 percent of total commercial bank deposits. So, in an environment of no federal deposit insurance and lighter regulation, the private costs of bank failures appear to have been small.

The issue of the "specialness" of banks rests on social costs, however, and not on private ones. Unfortunately, the social costs of bank failures are difficult to quantify, because measures of the size of the externalities associated with bank failures are highly subjective or do not exist.

The first of these externalities is the loss of banking services in the community or the disruption of special banking relationships. Banking relationships are considered valuable because one service performed by banks is information intermediation. In the first case, rarely does a community lose all of its banking services when an individual bank fails. Kaufman (1988) argues that in those few cases where the only bank in the area fails, it is often replaced by another bank or financial institution, often in the same location. Furthermore, liberal chartering of new banks and the relaxation of intrastate and interstate branching restrictions should take care of this problem when it does arise.

Second, most firms have relationships with more than one financial institution, and many of the lending officers of the failed institution find jobs with other banks in the area, often with the bank that replaces the failed institution (Benston and Kaufman [1986]). Moreover, as Schwartz (1987) argues, it is difficult to believe that financial institutions interested in acquiring the liabilities of failed banks would not also be interested in capturing their creditworthy customers, especially if banking relationships have value.

■ 4 The trade-off between efficiency and stability in the short run can occur only when there are no principal-agent problems associated with bank regulation or, in other words, when bank regulators are "faithful agents" as defined by Kane (1989b). Otherwise, the trade-off between efficiency and stability would not hold even in the short run. The author thanks Edward Kane for this analysis.

■ 5 For a comprehensive look at the arguments and evidence as to why banks are not special, and a list of articles on the subject, see Saunders and Walter (1987).

The second externality may be the disruption of the payments system.[6] Because banks are the conduit for payments in this country, the failure of a major depository institution could cause the failures of other banks on the payments system, topple the payments system itself, or at least shut it down for an unacceptable period of time. However, there is no reason that the failure of any institution, let alone a large one, should result in the collapse of the payments system.

Even today, the loss on assets associated with large bank failures is typically small, certainly not approaching 100 percent.[7] Therefore, banks with payments-related exposure to the failed institution should realize only a small loss, and the threat of loss from payments-system defaults should cause banks to limit their exposure to other banks that are considered to be excessively risky. After all, banks routinely do this today in the federal funds market. In addition, the lender of last resort can immunize the rest of the payments system from the failure of a single bank by lending (with a "haircut") to banks against their claims on the failed institution until those claims are realized.[8] The Federal Reserve's role in providing liquidity to financial markets during the October 1987 stock market crash illustrates how a properly functioning lender of last resort can prevent spillover effects from bank failures or from crises in individual financial markets.

The third component of social costs is the causal relationship between declines in the banking industry and in the level of general economic activity. Do declines in the banking sector cause declines in economic activity, or is the opposite true? A review of the historical evidence by Benston et al. (1986, ch. 2) and Schwartz (1987) suggests that bank failures are caused by the declines in general economic activity, whether the declines are national or regional.

Therefore, although there are economic and social costs associated with individual bank failures, these costs do not appear to be significantly larger than those for other firms. As Saunders and Walter (1987) point out, the costs of individual bank failures are much different from the costs to the economy from a collapse of the banking system, and those who argue that bank failures have high social costs often fail to recognize that difference. Thus, the argument that banks are special because of social externalities associated with their failures does not appear to be valid.

Bank Runs and Stability

Opponents of market-based banking reforms argue that the very nature of bank and thrift deposit liabilities (that is, they are redeemable at par on demand) makes free-market banking systems inherently unstable.[9] They argue that, without federal deposit guarantees, the banking system is subject to contagious bank runs. As the argument goes, deposit insurance removes or reduces the incentives for bank runs and thus stabilizes the banking system. Regulation, in turn, is needed to protect the federal deposit insurance agency, and ultimately the taxpayer, from the moral hazard embedded in federal deposit guarantees.[10]

To analyze this claim of instability, one needs to distinguish between rational and irrational bank runs. Kaufman (1988) argues that a rational bank run is one that occurs because depositors have good information that their depository institution has (or may) become insolvent. This type of run should not be contagious and, in fact, is the method the market uses to weed out weak institutions. Because rational bank runs are essentially a market-driven closure rule, they act as a form of market discipline on bank management and shareholders (Benston and Kaufman [1986]).

Kaufman (1988) describes an *irrational* bank run as one that occurs because poorly informed depositors mistakenly believe that their depository institution has (or may) become insolvent. Institutions that are truly solvent can stop an irrational run by demonstrating their solvency. Although these runs theoretically could be contagious, it is unlikely that they would be (except,

---

■ **6** Payments-system concerns are the motivation for the safe-bank proposals of Litan (1987) and others.

■ **7** Although loss rates have ranged as much as 50 percent of assets in small-bank failures, the failure of these banks is not a threat to the payments system.

■ **8** Lending with a haircut refers to the practice of making short-term collateralized loans for less than the estimated market value of the collateral. That is, the lender estimates the value of the collateral and then "takes a little off the top." This is usually done when the market value of the collateral is measured with uncertainty.

■ **9** The theoretical foundation for this viewpoint is found in Diamond and Dybvig (1983). In their model of a simple economy, Diamond and Dybvig find that government deposit insurance improves social welfare by removing the possibility of systemic bank runs. However, McCulloch and Yu (1989) show that private contracts could perform the same function as deposit insurance in the Diamond and Dybvig world. Furthermore, McCulloch and Yu find that neither the private contracts nor government deposit insurance can improve social welfare in the Diamond and Dybvig world if private capital markets exist outside the official banking sector.

■ **10** For a detailed discussion of bank runs and their positive implications for economic stability, see Kaufman (1988).

possibly, to other insolvent institutions) because other banks and thrifts have incentives to provide liquidity to solvent institutions experiencing runs. In fact, private bank clearinghouses performed this function prior to the creation of the Federal Reserve System (Gorton and Mullineaux [1987]).

Moreover, a properly functioning lender of last resort can prevent irrational bank runs from becoming systemic bank runs by providing liquidity to solvent institutions experiencing runs. In so doing, the central bank further relieves pressures on solvent institutions, while removing any potentially destabilizing effects of irrational bank runs, yet without precluding rational bank runs on insolvent institutions (Meltzer [1986] and Schwartz [1987, 1988]). One should note that bank runs were historically a statewide or systemic problem primarily in unit banking systems, where regional and therefore industry diversification of assets was artificially restricted by regulations. Thus, irrational bank runs may simply be an unintended side effect of branching restrictions, rather than a natural source of instability in free-market banking systems.

By suppressing or overriding market closure mechanisms, federal deposit insurance has reduced or removed one of the self-correcting forces that ensures the efficiency and long-run stability of banking markets. Kane (1985, ch. 3) and Thomson (1986, 1989) argue that the way federal deposit insurance is priced and administered results in government subsidization of the risks undertaken by insured banks and thrifts. This, in turn, leads to perverse incentives for risk-taking by insured institutions and decreases the stability of the financial system.

Moral Hazard and Regulation

To mitigate the moral hazard (that is, the incentives for the insured to increase their risk in order to maximize the combined value of their equity and deposit guarantees) intrinsic in deposit-insurance guarantees, strict regulations were adopted that limited the scope of activities in which banks could participate and the types of products (both asset and liability) they could offer. In other words, regulations were used as a tax to offset the perverse effects of the subsidy inherent in federal deposit insurance (Buser et al. [1981]). These regulations sought to alleviate the moral hazard problem by removing a large degree of management and shareholder discretion in the operation of depository institutions.

An unintended side effect has been that these regulations have made managers and shareholders less responsive to market incentives and have reduced the flow of capital from poorly managed institutions to well-managed ones (because all institutions are equally insured). This system most assuredly resulted in fewer bank failures from the mid-1930s through the late 1970s, but did so at the expense of the long-run stability of the financial system, as evidenced by the escalation of problems in the banking and thrift industries in the 1980s.[11] The movement of capital from marginal firms in an industry to the strongest and best-managed firms is another of the self-corrective forces that would ensure the long-run stability of our banking system.

While regulation may reduce the moral hazard associated with deposit guarantees, Kane (1988b, 1989b) shows that principal-agent problems cause other forms of moral hazard to arise.[12] In the principal-agent framework, bank and thrift regulatory agencies are viewed as self-maximizing bureaucracies whose primary task is to act as the agent for taxpayers to ensure a safe and sound banking system and to minimize the taxpayer's exposure to loss. In addition, regulators must cater to a political clientele who are intermediate or competing principals. Furthermore, regulators are sometimes motivated by their own self-interest.[13]

In Kane's (1989e) principal-agent framework, political pressures and self-interest considerations create perverse incentives for regulators that may cause them to "paper over" emerging problems in an industry instead of dealing with them early and forcefully with the hope that, by buying time to deal with each crisis, the ultimate cost of resolving it will be smaller. Policies such as "too big to let fail," capital forbearance programs, and the adoption of regulatory accounting principles (RAP) for thrifts are some of the more visible manifestations of the problem (Kane [1989b]).

■ **11** Schwartz (1987, 1988) argues that the 60 years of relative stability in our financial system were due to price stability and not to either deposit insurance or bank regulation. She argues that one cost of price-level instability is troubled depository institutions, regardless of whether they are regulated.

■ **12** For a general discussion of agency costs and pricipal-agent problems and their applications in corporate finance, see Jensen and Meckling (1976) and Jensen and Smith (1985).

■ **13** Of course, throughout this paper, it is assumed that all politicians and bureaucrats firmly believe that their actions are motivated exclusively by the public interest. The analysis provided here emphatically does *not* accuse public servants of intentionally acting in bad faith but, rather, assumes that they do not always articulate or understand their real motives.

Regulation and Stability

Government-regulated systems, such as those operative in our banking and thrift industries, attempt to achieve stability by setting up a delicate and complex web of regulatory taxes and subsidies. In the case of banks, regulation has attempted to achieve stability by limiting competition between banks and nonbank financial institutions, both through prohibitions on activities banks can engage in (Glass-Steagall restrictions) and by subsidizing bank funding (through federal deposit insurance). Regulators are charged with the task of stabilizing the banking system by delivering an optimal mix of regulatory subsidies and taxes.

As Kane (1985, ch. 5) points out, the ability of regulators to deliver an optimal mix of regulatory taxes and subsidies becomes increasingly difficult over time as competitive forces in financial markets gradually erode existing regulations and alter the size and mix of regulatory taxes and subsidies.[14] Existing regulations often are weakened, or are made completely inappropriate, or become counterproductive. In addition, subsidies inherent in fixed-rate deposit insurance, access to discount-window credit, and free finality of payments over the Federal Reserve's wire transfer system increase in size. This effect is accentuated by exogenous shocks to the financial system, such as surges of inflation or technological changes.

These market-driven changes in our system of regulatory taxes and subsidies are the beginning of the ongoing process of regulation, market avoidance, and reregulation: a process that Kane (1977, 1988a) calls the "regulatory dialectic." The response of government-regulated systems to market-driven changes in the size and mix of regulatory taxes and subsidies is to accommodate the shocks. Changes to the regulatory structure tend to lag developments in the marketplace and are typically piecemeal, usually with the purpose of either validating market innovations or reregulating areas where market forces have made existing regulations obsolete.[15] This

may include regulations designed to limit or prohibit new activities that are deemed too risky (for example, thrifts' investments in high-yield bonds), the removal of regulations that are unenforceable or politically costly to continue (for example, deposit-rate ceilings), or the modification of existing regulations (for example, risk-based capital standards for banks and RAP accounting standards for thrifts).

Essentially, the regulatory response is to deal with the symptoms of a shock without making the basic structural adjustments necessary to allow the banking system to adjust fully. This often results in policies aimed at protecting the regulator's weakest client firms at the expense of the efficient firms in the industry and, hence, the stability of the banking system. An example is the capital forbearance policies adopted by both the bank and thrift regulators during the 1980s (Barth and Bradley [1989, table 3], Caliguire and Thomson [1987], and Thomson [1987a]). Moreover, regulatory interventions in the banking system tend to thwart market-oriented forces often enough that normal market outcomes are difficult to achieve within the limited scope of activities that the regulators are willing to permit. Consequently, increased subsidies from the public purse become necessary to permit regulated entities to achieve the returns on equity that enable them to remain competitive. This system minimizes the number of failures of individual, regulated firms in the short term, but increases the efficiency loss and the aggregate public exposure to loss in the long term. Kane (1989b) points to the current thrift debacle as a vivid example of this type of regulatory behavior.

The result is a set of financial institutions that are special or unique only in terms of the regulatory taxes and subsidies to which they are subject. In other words, it is the restrictions on organizational form, where they can do business, and what businesses they can be in, coupled with access to federal deposit guarantees, to the Federal Reserve's discount window, and to the Federal Reserve-operated payments system that make depository institutions special. Additionally, banks and thrifts are less efficient and less able to adapt to changes in the economy than they would be if they were more subject to market incentives, and the resulting banking system is less stable in the long run than one governed by market principles.

■ **14** Regulatory subsidies arise because banks and thrifts are not charged the fair value of the risk-bearing services provided to them by the federal safety net. Regulatory taxes represent the reduction in the value of a bank or thrift due to constraints placed on its profit-maximization function through regulation.

■ **15** The difference between the market and regulatory adjustment process is equivalent to the difference in exchange-rate adjustments under floating and fixed exchange rates. Under a floating-exchange-rate regime, supply and demand factors in markets cause nearly continual adjustment of the exchange rate. Under a fixed-exchange-rate regime, the official exchange rate is maintained for long periods of time, with large adjustments made periodically.

II. Market-Oriented Reforms

The alternative to increased regulation is a system of reforms that relies more heavily on market forces to shape the structure of the financial services industry.[16] Market-oriented reforms, such as a reduction in the scale and scope of the federal safety net, improved information systems (including the adoption of market-value accounting and early dissemination of information), and the adoption of a timely, solvency-based closure rule for banks and thrifts, would increase the efficiency and long-run stability of the banking system. Rather than blocking or attempting to circumvent market forces, these reforms would rely on market forces to reestablish the trade-off between risk and return in financial services, so that those who benefit from the gains of risky strategies would also bear the losses when these strategies did not pan out. Therefore, there would be less of a need for regulations, as distinct from reliance on market forces, to protect the public purse from losses.

In its most extreme form, market-oriented reforms would establish a free-market banking system with no remaining vestiges of the federal safety net (discount-window access, deposit insurance, and direct access to the Federal Reserve payments system). The market would determine the structure and scope of financial intermediaries' activities, and market-determined closure rules would prevail. The role of the government would be limited to collecting and disseminating information and to enforcing property rights by resolving contractual disputes. However, reforms to the federal safety net necessary for a free-market banking system are unlikely to be implemented. Kane (1987), echoing Downs (1957), argues that subsidies, like those embodied in the financial safety net, tend to become viewed as entitlements by the subsidized industry. Industry trade associations and other special interest groups lobby Congress vigorously to protect their narrow interests, while society's interests are sufficiently diffuse that they cannot defeat special interest lobbies.

One caveat to note is that the following proposed reforms have transitional or "switching" costs that must be dealt with. This is especially true of deposit-insurance reforms. These transitional costs would be less of a problem if the reforms were applied to an industry that is already healthy. Obviously, this is not the case for either our banking industry or the thrift industry.

It must be recognized that the transitional costs, which include the cost of recapitalizing, reorganizing, or closing insolvent and unsound institutions, cannot be avoided forever regardless of whether reforms are adopted. Moreover, as demonstrated so vividly by the thrift crisis, the sooner these costs are dealt with, the smaller they are likely to be (Kane [1989b, ch. 3] and Barth and Bradley [1989]). Therefore, the realization of the switching costs should not be seen as an impediment to reform, but rather as an important first step in implementing any set of reforms. FIRREA represents a partial realization of these switching costs; however, considerably more needs to be done before a comprehensive package of deposit insurance and regulatory reforms can be implemented.

Deposit-Insurance Reform

Restoring market discipline as an effective constraint on bank and thrift activities is the main purpose of deposit-insurance reform. The coverage and pricing of federal deposit guarantees must be changed so that federal bank and thrift insurance funds do not subsidize risk in the financial system.

To restore market discipline to banking, federal deposit insurance coverages must be limited, and remaining coverage must be correctly priced.[17] At the very least, deposit insurance should be cut back to strict observance of the current statutory limit of $100,000. Furthermore, this limit should be applied per depositor, rather than to each insured deposit account. Coverage should not be extended in any circumstance to explicitly uninsured depositors, unsecured creditors, or stockholders of banks and their parent holding companies. In other words, the failures of all insured institutions should be handled in a manner that reduces the regulators' and insurers' incentives to minimize insured deposit payouts while maximizing long-term exposures to uninsured claims.

Kane (1985, ch. 6) proposes that strict enforcement of the current limit would require some changes to the failure-resolution policies of the FDIC and might require statutory constraints on

---

■ **16** This section draws heavily on Benston et al. (1986), Benston and Kaufman (1988), and Kane (1985, 1986, 1987, 1989a, 1989b, 1989c, 1989d).

■ **17** Merton (1977, 1978) shows how option pricing can be used to model and value deposit guarantees. Using Merton's results, Thomson (1987b) shows how information regarding the market prices of uninsured and partially insured deposits can be used to construct risk-based deposit-insurance premiums for insured deposit balances. Ronn and Verma (1986) show how option pricing can be used to derive estimates of the value of deposit insurance using stock-market data and different closure assumptions.

the authority of the FDIC to rescue large insolvent financial institutions.[18] These constraints would preclude the use of failure-resolution techniques such as open-bank assistance and purchase-and-assumption transactions, which provide de facto coverage to de jure uninsured claimants.[19] Such changes would give the "too big to let fail" doctrine the decent burial it deserves and would restore some measure of market discipline to banking.

However, to truly reap the benefits of deposit-insurance reform, the statutory limits on coverage should be reduced to levels significantly below the current $100,000 ceiling. Kane (1986) and Thomson and Todd (1990) suggest that a reduction in the limit from $100,000 to $10,000 (indexed to the Consumer Price Index) would be consistent with a social desire to provide a safe haven for the savings and transactions balances of small savers while reestablishing large depositors as a source of discipline on banks' risk-taking. Thomson and Todd (1990) point out that a $10,000 ceiling exceeds the average (arithmetic mean) insured deposit account in both banks and thrifts (about $8,000) and that depositors with balances in excess of $10,000 already have access to U.S. Treasury bills, which are close substitutes for federally guaranteed bank deposits.

In addition to lowering the insured deposit ceiling, several authors have suggested that a coinsurance feature could be added for additional deposit balances above the full-insurance level.[20] For example, if the deposit insurance ceiling were set at $10,000, the FDIC could provide 90 percent coverage for balances between $10,000 and $50,000 and 70 percent coverage for balances in excess of $50,000. Other, apparently more drastic, variations on this theme are possible; the original (1933) interim deposit insurance scheme provided for only 50 percent coverage for balances in excess of $50,000, for example. Presumably, if mandatory closure rules were adopted,

private insurance markets would develop to provide coverage for the coinsurance deductible portion of the deposit for those depositors who desired full protection.

An important feature of coinsurance is that it would establish minimum recoveries on deposit balances in excess of the fully insured limit. This would remove an important constraint on the FDIC's ability to resolve bank failures quickly without extending forbearances to uninsured depositors. With coinsurance, the federal deposit guarantor would not need to estimate in advance the losses to the uninsured depositors. It would simply apply the coinsurance haircut to depositors' balances. If the institution's total losses did not exceed the haircut amount, the receiver would rebate to the uninsured depositors their share of the difference. Thus, coinsurance would alleviate financial hardship for uninsured depositors by paying them a predetermined portion of their deposits up front.

The Role of the Discount Window

For deposit-insurance reform to be truly effective, the Federal Reserve should avoid using its discount window to support the solvency (capital replacement) of, or to delay the closing of, an insolvent bank or thrift (Kane [1987]). Benston et al. (1986, ch. 5) maintain that solvency support or capital replacement lending by Federal Reserve Banks is simply another way for regulators to extend de facto guarantees to uninsured depositors and other creditors of depository institutions: it provides an opportunity for these claimants to liquidate their claims at par, thereby increasing the ultimate cost (loss upon liquidation) to either the lender of last resort, the deposit insurance fund, or the receiver.

This loss arises because, if good assets are pledged to the lender of last resort to fund early redemption at par of some (usually the largest) uninsured claims, then the pool of good assets remaining to cover eventual payments to insured depositors and other uninsured claimants is reduced. The effect of this practice is analogous to the effect of a leveraged buyout (LBO) announcement on outstanding corporate bonds of the LBO target: the pool of assets available to cover outstanding bonded debt service is reduced to cover LBO debt service. Rating agencies have no choice but to downgrade outstanding bond issues, and those bonds decline in secondary market value.

■ **18** For expressions of skepticism that regulators would allow big banks to fail, even if explicit deposit-insurance coverage were reduced or, in advance, said to be strictly enforced, see Trigaux (1989) and Passell (1989).

■ **19** The failure-resolution policies of the FDIC are the process through which implicit guarantees are issued to uninsured depositors, general creditors, subordinated creditors, and even stockholders. For a discussion of FDIC failure-resolution policies, see Benston et al. (1986, ch. 4), Caliguire and Thomson (1987), Kane (1985, ch. 2), and Todd (1988b).

■ **20** Coinsurance was a feature in the original FDIC Act (see Todd [1988a]). Kane (1983) suggested coinsurance as part of a six-point deposit-insurance reform proposal. Baer (1985) suggested it as part of a proposal for mixed private and public coverage of deposits. More recently, Cates (1989), the Federal Reserve Bank of Minneapolis (1988), and the Federal Reserve Bank of Cleveland (Hoskins [1989]) have embraced the concept of coinsurance.

To prevent the use of the discount window for purposes other than *liquidity* support for solvent institutions (the originally intended and the only theoretically sound purpose, according to Todd [1988a]), the following guidelines should be followed. First, the discount window should be available only to demonstrably solvent institutions, with the loans fully secured by sound and fairly evaluated collateral. Heavy and frequent borrowers at the window should be required to demonstrate their solvency, and loans should not be extended or renewed once an institution is determined to be insolvent.

Second, discount-window advances should be made at unsubsidized rates with a penalty for loans made to heavy or frequent borrowers. Finally, the discount window should not be seen as a substitute for the maintenance of a reasonable amount of liquidity by even solvent financial institutions, except in extraordinary circumstances.

Information and Market-Value Accounting

Kane (1989b, ch. 6) asserts that better information systems are needed to increase the effectiveness of both government regulation and market-oriented regulation of depository institutions. Currently, our regulatory system suppresses information about depository institutions, which results in information flows to market participants that are both noisy and "lumpy."[21] Noisy and lumpy information flows do not allow markets to make several small corrective adjustments as new information comes in; instead, they cause the market to make larger and more dramatic adjustments as market participants attempt to process new information. This, in turn, leads to the appearance that markets overreact to new information as it arrives.

To improve the informational efficiency of markets, several authors have advocated the use of market-value accounting (Kane [1985, chs. 5 and 6; 1987, 1988a], Benston et al. [1986, ch. 8], Benston et al. [1989], and Benston and Kaufman [1988]). Traditional accounting systems like GAAP (generally accepted accounting principles) and RAP result in unnecessary noise in the information system because they allow firms to carry assets and liabilities at their par value (usually, historical cost) and do not reflect the subsequent changes in their market value. Therefore, Thomson (1987a) argues that GAAP and

RAP may not be good measures of the true solvency of a bank or thrift, that both GAAP and RAP tend to be high-biased measures of solvency for banks and thrifts experiencing solvency problems, and that the degree of error in GAAP and RAP measures increases as solvency deteriorates.

Berger et al. (1989) correctly point out that market-value accounting systems themselves are not perfect, as there are many assets and liabilities on the balance sheets of banks and thrifts for which estimates of market value are not readily available. However, Benston and Kaufman (1988) and Mengle (1989) argue that it is possible to adjust asset and liability values for changes in interest rates and that, as markets develop for securitized bank assets, the ability to make reasonable, market-based adjustments to the value of similar assets in bank portfolios increases. Market-value accounting is not a panacea and still results in noisy information streams. Nonetheless, it is a less-noisy information stream than the one that flows from both GAAP and RAP. Over time, market-value accounting should become less noisy as financial markets evolve.

In addition to the use of market-value accounting, Benston et al. (1986, ch. 7) suggest that the regulatory community move from suppression to timely dissemination of information. FIRREA takes an important step in this direction as it mandates that cease-and-desist orders, supervisory agreements, and other regulatory actions are to be published by the appropriate supervisory agency. Hoskins (1989) goes even further in advocating that banks and thrifts should have the right to release their examination ratings and reports to the public.[22] Finally, annual audits by independent accounting firms should be required for all financial institutions. For small, well-capitalized institutions for whom this rule could prove to be a financial hardship (for example, consolidated entities with less than $100 million in assets), outside audits could be required only every second or third year.

Both of these changes in the current information system would increase the effectiveness and efficiency of market-based oversight of depository institutions and would increase the stability of the financial system. Markets would be better able to discriminate among financial institutions and to force corrective action much sooner than

■ 21 The information flows are lumpy in the sense that large amounts of information are arriving at discrete intervals, as opposed to smaller amounts of information arriving nearly continuously.

■ 22 Mandatory release of examination ratings and reports by the regulators is a sufficient, but not necessary, condition for the timely dissemination of information about the condition of insured institutions. If banks and thrifts are allowed to release their examination ratings and reports to the public, then institutions with high ratings would have incentives to signal their condition to the market.

is currently possible, thereby reducing the probability of bank runs (Pennacchi [1987]). Consequently, systemic stability would be improved, as the size and the volatility of the market correction would be smaller. Better information systems also would reduce the ability of regulators to conceal problems in the financial services industry as they emerged.

Deregulation and Timely Closure of Insolvent Institutions

Under a market-based incentive system, the role for supervision and regulation would be radically different. Regulators would be assigned the task of enforcing a few basic rules (for example, minimum capital requirements, periodic reporting and public disclosure requirements, outside audits, and market-value accounting), and monitoring efforts would be directed at ensuring that those rules were observed. Any individual or financial institution able to meet these minimum guidelines would be granted a bank charter. Institutions that failed to meet these guidelines would be required either to close or to adjust their operations to comply.[23]

This approach, proposed by Benston and Kaufman (1988) and Benston et al. (1989), recognizes that a bank's management has the skills, information, and incentives to make optimal use of its resources, while bank regulators do not. As long as supervisors tolerated failure (either through market closure or a solvency-based closure rule), any financial service or activity could be performed by any financial institution, as long as it could do so within the minimum operating guidelines.

Unlike the current approach toward bank regulation, which often seeks to suppress market forces, this approach attempts to complement and enhance market discipline. Allowing managers and stockholders to make the decisions governing the operation of their institution, including scope of activity and institutional structure, would make them more responsive to market incentives. The perverse incentives currently facing managers and owners of weak and barely solvent institutions would be neutralized by supervisory interference as the condition of the institution deteriorated.[24] The most extreme case of supervisory interference would be the closure or forced sale of institutions that deteriorated to the point where they violated the minimum operating standards.

This approach would lead to a more efficient and stable financial system than pure regulation. Fewer resources would be expended in the enforcement and evasion of outdated rules by regulators and regulatees, respectively, and those who took the risks would bear the consequences of those decisions. Organizational form and activities would be dictated by markets.

Since market forces would be allowed to operate unfettered, efficiency and stability would be enhanced: private capital would be reallocated by market forces to the best-managed institutions and away from the weak and poorly managed ones, which would be allowed to fail. Timely release of information to markets under the supervisory approach would allow financial distress in an institution to be detected more quickly, constraining the growth of marginally solvent and insolvent institutions. Market recognition of financial distress would lead to an orderly outflow of funds and an increase in the cost of funds for troubled institutions, which, in turn, would lead to more orderly and timely closure of insolvent institutions and a reduction in their ultimate failure-resolution costs.

III. Conclusion

At the August 9, 1989 signing ceremony for FIRREA, President Bush proclaimed, "We will keep the federal deposit insurance system solvent and help serve those millions of small savers who make America great ..." while "...ensuring the taxpayers' interests will always come first ...."[25] Accomplishing both of these objectives will require great effort in any case, but might be impossible without market-oriented reforms of the financial structure such as those described here.

Moreover, as Kane (1989c, 1989e) argues, the Bush plan from which FIRREA evolved was not based on a comprehensive theory of how the

■ **23** Prior to 1933, the solvency test applied in bank closing cases was *either* incapacity to pay obligations as they matured or balance-sheet insolvency. Since then, the Office of the Comptroller of the Currency has tended to use *only* the former "maturing obligations" test, although the statutory basis for the latter "balance-sheet" test remains intact. Compare 12 U.S.C. Section 191 (balance-sheet or maturing obligations) with Section 91 (usually interpreted as "maturing obligations" only).

■ **24** The Benston and Kaufman (1988) and Benston et al. (1989) proposals set up several different trigger points for increasing supervisory interference as the institution slides toward insolvency and allows regulators to close the institution before it becomes insolvent.

■ **25** See "Bush Remarks: 'First Critical Test' Has Been Passed," *American Banker*, August 10, 1989, p. 4.

losses in the thrift industry occurred and were allowed to grow so large. Consequently, because the Bush plan (and, by inference, FIRREA) fails to correct the incentive-incompatibility problems in the current deposit-insurance contract that caused the current thrift crisis, there is a high probability that taxpayers will be faced with another deposit-insurance crisis in the near future.

It is hoped that the study of federal deposit insurance mandated by FIRREA, and currently under way at the U.S. Treasury Department, will address the fundamental structural flaws in the federal safety net and, in particular, in federal deposit insurance. The purpose of any reforms to the federal safety net and to our system of bank regulation should be to increase the efficiency and long-run stability of the banking system while protecting the public from financial loss. The market-oriented reforms put forth in this paper would go a long way toward achieving these goals.[26]

■ **26** The reforms set forth in this paper are aimed at increasing market discipline primarily through increased depositor and stockholder discipline on insured banks and thrifts. Another way to increase market discipline on banks is through the use of subordinated debt (see Baer [1985], Benston et al. [1986, ch. 7], and Wall [1989]) and surety bonds (see Kane [1987]). For conflicting evidence of the ability of subordinated-debt holders to discipline bank risk-taking, see Avery et al. (1988) and Gorton and Santomero (1990). Ely (1985, 1989) would use banks to discipline each other through a system of cross-guarantees for their liabilities.

References

Avery, Robert B., Terrence Belton, and Michael Goldberg. "Market Discipline in Regulating Bank Risk: New Evidence from the Capital Markets," *Journal of Money, Credit, and Banking,* vol. 20 (November 1988), pp. 597-610.

Baer, Herbert. "Private Prices, Public Insurance: The Pricing of Federal Deposit Insurance," Federal Reserve Bank of Chicago, *Economic Perspectives,* September/October 1985, pp. 41-57.

Barth, James R., and Michael Bradley. "Thrift Deregulation and Federal Deposit Insurance," *Journal of Financial Services Research,* vol. 2 (September 1989), pp. 231-59.

Benston, George J., R. Dan Brumbaugh, Jr., Jack M. Guttentag, Richard J. Herring, George G. Kaufman, Robert E. Litan, and Kenneth Scott. *Blueprint for Restructuring America's Financial Institutions.* Washington, D.C.: The Brookings Institution, 1989.

Benston, George J., Robert A. Eisenbeis, Paul M. Horvitz, Edward J. Kane, and George G. Kaufman. *Perspectives on Safe and Sound Banking: Past, Present, and Future.* Cambridge, Mass.: MIT Press, 1986.

Benston, George J., and George G. Kaufman. "Risks and Failures in Banking: Overview, History, and Evaluation," in George G. Kaufman and Roger C. Kormendi, eds., *Deregulating Financial Services: Public Policy in Flux.* Cambridge, Mass.: Ballinger Publishing Co., 1986, pp. 49-77.

———. "Risk and Solvency Regulation of Depository Institutions: Past Policies and Current Options," *Monograph Series in Finance and Economics,* New York University, 1988.

Berger, Allen N., Kathleen A. Kuester, and James O'Brien. "Some Red Flags Concerning Market Value Accounting," in *Proceedings from a Conference on Bank Structure and Competition,* Federal Reserve Bank of Chicago, May 1989, pp. 515-46.

Buser, Steven A., Andrew H. Chen, and Edward J. Kane. "Federal Deposit Insurance, Regulatory Policy, and Optimal Bank Capital," *Journal of Finance,* vol. 36 (March 1981), pp. 51-60.

Caliguire, Daria B., and James B. Thomson. "FDIC Policies for Dealing with Failed and Troubled Institutions," Federal Reserve Bank of Cleveland, *Economic Commentary,* October 1, 1987.

Campbell, Claudia, and Hyman P. Minsky. "How to Get Off The Back of a Tiger, or, Do Initial Conditions Constrain Deposit Insurance Reform?" in *Proceedings from a Conference on Bank Structure and Competition,* Federal Reserve Bank of Chicago, May 1987, pp. 252-71.

Cates, David C. "Market Discipline: The Key to Deposit Insurance Reform." Paper presented before the American Bankers Association's Deposit Insurance Task Force, Washington, D.C., July 27, 1989.

Corrigan, E. Gerald. "Financial Market Structure: A Longer View," Federal Reserve Bank of New York, *Annual Report,* January 1987.

Diamond, Douglas W., and Philip H. Dybvig. "Banking Runs, Deposit Insurance, and Liquidity," *Journal of Political Economy,* vol. 91 (1983), pp. 401-19.

Downs, Anthony. *Economic Theory of Democracy.* New York: Harper and Row, 1957.

Ely, Bert. "Yes—Private Sector Depositor Protection is a Viable Alternative to Federal Deposit Insurance," in *Proceedings from a Conference on Bank Structure and Competition,* Federal Reserve Bank of Chicago, May 1985, pp. 335-53.

———. "Privatizing Depositor Protection: More Feasible than Ever." Washington, D.C.: Ely and Company, Inc., May 2, 1989.

Federal Reserve Bank of Cleveland. "Banking Deregulation: Examining the Myths," *Annual Report,* 1988.

Federal Reserve Bank of Minneapolis. "A Case for Reforming Federal Deposit Insurance," *Annual Report,* 1988.

Gorton, Gary, and Donald J. Mullineaux. "Joint Production of Confidence: Endogenous Regulation and the Nineteenth Century Commercial-Bank Clearinghouses," *Journal of Money, Credit, and Banking,* vol. 19 (November 1987), pp. 457-68.

Gorton, Gary, and Anthony M. Santomero. "Market Discipline and Bank Subordinated Debt," *Journal of Money, Credit and Banking,* vol. 22 (February 1990), pp. 117-28.

Guttentag, Jack M., and Richard J. Herring. "Disaster Myopia in International Banking," *Essays in International Finance,* 164 (September 1986), Princeton University.

———. "Prudential Supervision to Manage Systemic Vulnerability," *Proceedings from a Conference on Bank Structure and Competition,* Federal Reserve Bank of Chicago, May 1988, pp. 602–33.

Hoskins, W. Lee. "Reforming the Banking and Thrift Industries: Assessing Regulation and Risk." 1989 Frank M. Engle Lecture in Economic Security, presented to the American College, Bryn Mawr, Pennsylvania, May 22, 1989.

Jensen, Michael C., and William H. Meckling. "Theory of the Firm: Managerial Behavior, Agency Costs and Ownership Structure," *Journal of Financial Economics,* vol. 3 (1976), pp. 305–60.

Jensen, Michael C., and Clifford W. Smith. "Stockholder, Manager, and Creditor Interests: Applications of Agency Theory," in Edward I. Altman and Marti Subrahmanyam, eds., *Recent Advances in Corporate Finance.* Homewood, Ill.: Richard D. Irwin, 1985, pp. 93–131.

Kane, Edward J. "Good Intentions and Unintended Evil: The Case Against Selective Credit Allocation," *Journal of Money, Credit, and Banking,* vol. 9 (February 1977), pp. 55–69.

———. "A Six-Point Program for Deposit-Insurance Reform," *Housing Finance Review* (July 1983), pp. 269–78.

———. *The Gathering Crisis in Federal Deposit Insurance.* Cambridge, Mass.: MIT Press, 1985.

———. "Confronting Incentive Problems in U.S. Deposit Insurance: The Range of Alternative Solutions," in George G. Kaufman and Roger C. Kormendi, eds., *Deregulating Financial Services: Public Policy in Flux.* Cambridge, Mass.: Ballinger Publishing Co., 1986, pp. 97–120.

———. "No Room for Weak Links in the Chain of Deposit Insurance Reform," *Journal of Financial Services Research,* vol. 1 (September 1987), pp. 77–111.

———. "Adapting Financial Services Regulation to a Changing Economic Environment," in *Advances in the Study of Entrepreneurship, Innovation and Economic Growth,* vol. 2 (1988a), JAI Press Inc., pp. 61–94.

———. "How Market Forces Influence the Structure of Financial Regulation," in William S. Haraf and Rose Marie Kushmeider, eds., *Restructuring Banking and Financial Services in America.* Washington, D.C.: American Enterprise Institute for Public Policy Research, 1988b, pp. 343–82.

———. "How Incentive-Incompatible Deposit-Insurance Funds Fail." National Bureau of Economic Research Working Paper No. 2836, February 1989a.

———. *The S&L Insurance Mess: How Did It Happen?* Washington, D.C.: The Urban Institute Press, 1989b.

———. "Defective Regulatory Incentives and the Bush Initiative," *Independent Banker* (November 1989c), pp. 30–35.

———. "Changing Incentives Facing Financial-Services Regulators," *Journal of Financial Services Research,* vol. 2 (September 1989d), pp. 265–74.

———. "The High Cost of Incompletely Funding the FSLIC Shortage of Explicit Capital," *Journal of Economic Perspectives,* vol. 3 (Fall 1989e), pp. 31–47.

Kaufman, George G. "The Truth About Bank Runs," in Catherine England and Thomas Huertas, eds., *The Financial Services Revolution: Policy Directions for the Future.* Boston, Mass.: Kluwer Academic Publishers, 1988, pp. 9–40.

Keehn, Silas. "Banking on the Balance, Powers and the Safety Net: A Proposal," Federal Reserve Bank of Chicago, 1989.

Litan, Robert E. *What Should Banks Do?* Washington, D.C.: The Brookings Institution, 1987.

McCulloch, J. Huston, and Min-Teh Yu. "Bank Runs, Deposit Contracts, and Government Deposit Insurance." Unpublished manuscript, August 1989.

Meltzer, Allan H. "Financial Failures and Financial Policies," in George G. Kaufman and Roger C. Kormendi, eds., *Deregulating Financial Services: Public Policy in Flux.* Cambridge, Mass.: Ballinger Publishing Co., 1986, pp. 79–96.

Mengle, David L. "The Feasibility of Market Value Accounting for Commercial Banks." Working Paper 89-4, Federal Reserve Bank of Richmond, 1989.

Merton, Robert C. "An Analytic Derivation of the Cost of Deposit Insurance and Loan Guarantees: An Application of Modern Option Pricing Theory," *Journal of Banking and Finance,* vol. 1 (June 1977), pp. 3–11.

_____ . "On the Cost of Deposit Insurance When There are Surveillance Costs," *Journal of Business,* vol. 51 (July 1978), pp. 439–52.

Passell, Peter. "Economic Scene: Are Banks Broke, Too?" *New York Times,* August 23, 1989.

Pennacchi, George G. "Market Discipline, Information Disclosure, and Uninsured Deposits," in *Proceedings from a Conference on Bank Structure and Competition,* Federal Reserve Bank of Chicago, May 1987, pp. 456–72.

Randall, Richard E. "Can the Market Evaluate Asset Quality Exposure in Banks?" Federal Reserve Bank of Boston, *New England Economic Review,* July/August 1989, pp. 3–24.

Ronn, Ehud I., and Avinash K. Verma. "Pricing Risk-Adjusted Deposit Insurance: An Options-Based Model," *Journal of Finance,* vol. 41 (September 1986), pp. 871–95.

Saunders, Anthony, and Ingo Walter. "Are Banks Special?" *Journal of International Security Markets* (Winter 1987), pp. 171–76.

Schwartz, Anna J. "The Lender of Last Resort and the Federal Safety Net," *Journal of Financial Services Research,* vol. 1 (September 1987), pp. 1–17.

_____ . "The Effects of Regulation on Systemic Risks," in *Proceedings from a Conference on Bank Structure and Competition,* Federal Reserve Bank of Chicago, May 1988, pp. 28–34.

Tallman, Ellis. "Some Unanswered Questions About Bank Panics," Federal Reserve Bank of Atlanta, *Economic Review,* November/ December 1988, pp. 2–21.

Thomson, James B. "Equity, Efficiency, and Mispriced Deposit Guarantees," Federal Reserve Bank of Cleveland, *Economic Commentary,* July 15, 1986.

_____ . "FSLIC Forbearances to Stockholders and the Value of Savings and Loan Shares," Federal Reserve Bank of Cleveland, *Economic Review,* 3rd Quarter 1987a, pp. 26–35.

_____ . "The Use of Market Information in Pricing Deposit Insurance," *Journal of Money, Credit, and Banking,* vol. 19 (November 1987b), pp. 528–32.

_____ . "Economic Principles and Deposit Insurance Reform," Federal Reserve Bank of Cleveland, *Economic Commentary,* May 15, 1989.

_____ , and Walker F. Todd. "Rethinking and Living with the Limits of Bank Regulation," *The Cato Journal,* vol. 9 (Winter 1990—forthcoming).

Todd, Walker F. "Lessons of the Past and Prospects for the Future in Lender of Last Resort Theory," in *Proceedings from a Conference on Bank Structure and Competition,* Federal Reserve Bank of Chicago, May 1988a, pp. 533–77.

_____ . "No Conspiracy, but a Convenient Forgetting: Dr. Pangloss Visits the World of Deposit Insurance," Cato Conference Paper, November 2, 1988b.

Trigaux, Robert. "Isaac Reassesses Continental Bailout," *American Banker,* July 31, 1989.

Wall, Larry D. "A Plan for Reducing Future Deposit Insurance Losses: Puttable Subordinated Debt," Federal Reserve Bank of Atlanta, *Economic Review,* July/August 1989, pp. 2–17.

Article 22

The New Risk-Based Capital Plan For Commercial Banks

By William R. Keeton

Since the beginning of the decade, banks have been required to satisfy minimum capital-asset ratios independent of risk. While these capital requirements have boosted capital-asset ratios, they have failed to prevent an increase in the overall risk of the banking industry—an increase that some observers blame on the stimulus to risk-taking from fixed-rate deposit insurance. Hoping to gain better control over bank risk-taking, regulators have decided to tie banks' capital requirements to their estimated risk while retaining an absolute floor on capital. The new capital standards will be phased in gradually, taking full effect at the end of 1992.

Will the new plan control risk in the banking industry? Some critics argue the plan will not raise capital requirements enough for risky banks. Others claim the floor on capital will prevent the plan from reducing capital requirements enough for safe banks. Still others argue that banks may not respond as intended to the change in their capital requirements—specifically, banks facing higher requirements may take actions that increase their risk instead of reducing it, while banks facing lower requirements may fail to respond at all.

This article explains the new plan and evaluates its likely effectiveness in controlling risk. The article concludes that the plan will affect a relatively small number of banks, but that these banks are likely to respond in the desired way, improving the regulation of bank risk-taking. The first section gives the historical background of the plan. The second section reviews the key elements of the plan and shows how capital requirements will be determined. The third section estimates the impact of the plan on banks' capital positions and considers banks' likely response to those changes. The

William R. Keeton is a senior economist at the Federal Reserve Bank of Kansas City. He is indebted to John O'Keefe of the FDIC Office of Research and Statistics for providing the data for this article.

last section draws on these results to assess the plan's likely effectiveness.

I. HISTORICAL BACKGROUND OF THE NEW PLAN

The current system of capital requirements dates back to the beginning of the decade. Before the 1980s, banks were not required to meet an explicit capital-asset ratio. Instead, regulators used "moral suasion" to induce banks they considered undercapitalized to increase their capital-asset ratios. Although this informal approach to capital regulation worked well for many years, it failed to prevent a gradual decline in bank capital after the 1960s, especially at large banks. Formal capital requirements were imposed in 1981 to reverse that decline.

The current requirements take the form of minimum capital-asset ratios that are independent of risk. At first, requirements varied by size of bank and differed among the three bank regulators—the Federal Reserve, the Federal Deposit Insurance Corporation (FDIC), and the Office of the Comptroller of the Currency (OCC).[1] By 1985, however, the three regulators had agreed to subject all banks to the same requirements, using two measures of capital. The first measure was called "primary" capital and consisted of equity, loan loss reserves, perpetual preferred stock, and mandatory convertible debt. This measure was intended to

reflect a bank's cushion against unforeseen losses, and thus, its protection against failure. The second measure was called "total" capital and included other items that help limit the FDIC's losses in the event of failure—items such as subordinated debt and limited-life preferred stock.[2] Since 1985, the minimum capital-asset ratios have been 5.5 percent for primary capital and 6.0 percent for total capital. However, a bank can be pressured to exceed these minimums if examiners determine it is unusually risky.

Although the current capital requirements helped reverse the decline in bank capital, they failed to prevent an increase in overall risk in the banking industry. During the 1980s, banks shifted away from assets with little or no default risk, such as Treasury securities, to assets with significant default risk, such as commercial loans. Also, the rate of chargeoffs and delinquencies increased sharply, suggesting that bank loans had become riskier. Finally, over the course of the decade, banks greatly increased their off-balance sheet commitments and guarantees, such as letters of credit, loan commitments, and interest rate and currency swaps. These off-balance sheet instruments were not subject to capital requirements but in

---

[1] The OCC supervises nationally chartered banks, the Federal Reserve supervises state-chartered banks belonging to the Federal Reserve System, and the FDIC supervises state-chartered banks not belonging to the Federal Reserve System.

[2] Preferred stock is stock on which dividends must be paid before any dividends on common stock can be paid. Perpetual preferred stock has no maturity date, while limited-life preferred stock does. Mandatory convertible debt is debt that must be converted to common or preferred stock at some future date. Subordinated debt is debt which can be repaid only after the FDIC and uninsured depositors have been paid in full. For further details on the components of primary and secondary capital and the computation of required capital, see Gilbert, Stone, and Trebing 1985.

some cases exposed banks to significant default risk.[3]

Confronted with these developments, the three regulators began to consider ways of improving the regulation of bank capital. Regulators did not question the need for some form of minimum capital requirement. However, they became convinced that risk would be better controlled by basing each bank's requirement on the riskiness of its activities.

In principle, risk-based capital requirements should improve control over risk-taking in three ways—by reducing risky banks' chances of failing without driving up safe banks' cost of funds, by rewarding banks for shifting to safer activities, and by discouraging risky banks from outgrowing safe banks. Forcing a bank to hold more capital and fewer deposits increases its cushion against losses and reduces its chance of failure. But because deposits have unique transactions features that make them cheaper than equity, forcing a bank to hold more capital also increases its cost of funds. With risk-based requirements, regulators can force risky banks to maintain a greater cushion against losses without forcing safe banks to incur an unnecessarily high cost of funds.[4] Risk-based requirements can also

reduce banks' incentive to engage in risky activities by forcing them to hold more capital than they prefer but allowing them to reduce their capital as they shift to safer activities. Finally, even if banks do not shift to safer activities, risk-based requirements can reduce total risk-taking by decreasing risky banks' share of the market. Basing capital requirements on risk raises the cost to risky banks of obtaining new funds and reduces the cost to safe banks, inducing risky banks to grow slower and safe banks to grow faster.

Besides seeking greater control over risk, regulators both here and abroad saw risk-based capital requirements as a way to harmonize capital standards for multinational banks. In international markets, banks subject to loose capital standards had a competitive advantage over banks subject to strict capital standards. Eliminating these differences in capital standards required not only a common definition of capital but also a way of accounting for differences in the riskiness of banks' portfolios.

The new risk-based capital plan took several years to develop.[5] Regulators in the

---

[3] The increase in asset risk is documented for large banks in Furlong 1988. Furlong also finds that the increase in asset risk more than made up for the increase in capital, raising the risk of failure. Evidence on the growth of off-balance sheet activity can be found in General Accounting Office 1988.

[4] The transactions advantage of deposits is emphasized in Orgler and Taggart 1983. Some economists dispute this view, arguing that transactions services can be "unbundled" from deposits (Black 1975 and Fischer 1983). However, there are other reasons why deposits may be a cheaper source of funds than equity, making it undesirable to set a high capital

requirement for safe banks. For example, equity may have to be raised from outside investors who demand a low share price because they fear that the original owners will manage the bank inefficiently or understate the bank's profits (Jensen and Meckling 1976 and Townsend 1979). Deposits could also be cheaper than equity due to the tax-deductibility of interest. In this case, though, there would be no net gain to society from allowing a safe bank to lower its capital— the reduction in the bank's cost of funds would be offset by a decrease in tax revenues.

[5] It should be noted that risk-based capital requirements were not an entirely new idea. Before the imposition of formal capital requirements, regulators often used risk-adjusted formulas to evaluate the adequacy of banks' capital. The most complicated of these was the Federal Reserve's ABC (Analyzing Bank Capital) formula, which was developed in the mid-1950s and used for 20 years. For further details, see Crosse and Hempel 1973.

United States and other countries began working on a common set of risk-based requirements in 1986. After lengthy negotiations, a final agreement was reached in June 1988 by the Basle Committee, a group of banking officials from 12 industrial nations meeting under the auspices of the Bank for International Settlements. In early 1989, the Federal Reserve, FDIC, and OCC issued virtually identical plans implementing the agreement, setting deadlines of December 1990 for partial compliance and December 1992 for full compliance. The Basle plan focuses exclusively on credit risk and ignores other forms of risk, such as interest rate risk and liquidity risk. Recognizing these shortcomings in risk measurement, the three U.S. regulators decided to maintain a minimum capital-asset ratio, to ensure that banks with low measured risk but high true risk held enough capital.

II. DESCRIPTION OF THE NEW PLAN

This section describes the new risk-based capital plan in detail. The section first summarizes the key elements of the plan and then shows how a bank's minimum capital requirement is determined.

Key elements of the plan

The new risk-based capital plan contains three key elements—a new definition of eligible capital, a risk-based capital requirement, and a leverage requirement.[6]

Definition of capital. An important feature of the plan is that capital is redefined to put greater emphasis on equity and less on loan loss reserves. Two new measures of capital are introduced: a narrow measure that replaces primary capital and a broad measure that replaces the current definition of total capital.

The narrow measure is called Tier 1, or "core," capital and consists primarily of tangible equity—equity net of intangible assets such as goodwill. The main difference between core capital and primary capital is that core capital excludes all loan loss reserves. This change was made because loan loss reserves are often established to cover losses the bank is already expecting, making them unavailable to absorb unexpected losses. Core capital is also more restrictive than primary capital in that it excludes mandatory convertible debt and cumulative perpetual preferred stock.[7]

The broad measure is again called total capital and equals the sum of core capital and "supplementary" capital. The latter measure, also known as Tier 2 capital, includes subordinated debt, loan loss reserves up to 1.25 percent of risk-adjusted assets, and other items counted as primary capital but not core capital. The main difference between the new and current definitions of total capital is that the new definition includes only a limited amount of loan loss reserves, while the current definition includes all loan loss reserves.

---

6 The Federal Reserve and OCC versions of the plan were published in *Federal Register* 1989a and the FDIC version

in *Federal Register* 1989b. The Federal Reserve also issued a separate version for bank holding companies that differs slightly in the definition of eligible capital.

7 Cumulative preferred stock is preferred stock on which unpaid dividends are not "forgiven." In other words, the dividends accumulate over time and must be paid in full before any dividends can be paid on common stock.

Risk-based requirement. The most important innovation in the plan is to tie banks' capital requirements to their estimated credit risk. The first step in the procedure is to allocate assets among four risk categories, each with a different weight designed to reflect the degree of credit risk. The lowest category carries a zero weight and consists of items that have no default risk whatsoever, such as cash, U.S. government securities, and mortgage-backed securities directly guaranteed by the Government National Mortgage Association (Ginnie Mae). The next category has a weight of 20 percent and includes assets believed to have positive but very low default risk—assets such as interbank deposits, general obligation municipal bonds, and mortgage-backed securities guaranteed by the Federal National Mortgage Association (Fannie Mae) or the Federal Home Loan Mortgage Corporation (Freddie Mac). The third category has a weight of 50 percent and includes municipal revenue bonds and first mortgages on homes. The last category carries the maximum weight of 100 percent and lumps together all remaining securities and loans.

A bank's credit risk from off-balance sheet activities is treated in a similar manner. The face value of each off-balance sheet instrument is first converted to an on-balance sheet "credit equivalent" reflecting the bank's credit exposure. For example, a standby letter of credit backing a customer's commercial paper is counted in its entirety, on the grounds that it exposes the bank to the same default risk as a direct loan to the customer. By contrast, only half of the unused portion of a home equity credit line is counted as a credit exposure because the bank does not face any credit risk unless the credit line is drawn down. Once off-balance sheet items have been converted to

credit exposures, they are assigned to one of the four risk categories based on the type of guarantee and the identity of the other party.

The next step in computing a bank's risk-based requirement is to compute "risk-adjusted" assets—the sum of assets and off-balance sheet credit exposures, with each item weighted by the risk weight for its category (0, 20, 50, or 100 percent). A bank that had no off-balance sheet commitments and invested entirely in U.S. government securities would have no risk-adjusted assets because U.S. government securities carry a weight of zero. On the other hand, a bank that had no off-balance sheet credit commitments and invested only in business and consumer loans would have the same risk-adjusted assets as total assets because business and consumer loans carry the maximum weight of 100 percent. Finally, a bank that invested heavily in business and consumer loans and also made substantial off-balance sheet commitments would have more risk-adjusted assets than total assets because off-balance sheet exposures are included in risk-adjusted assets but not in total assets.

In the last step, the bank's risk-based requirement is computed as a percentage of its risk-adjusted assets. Two requirements must be met, corresponding to the two measures of capital—core capital must equal at least 4 percent of risk-adjusted assets, and total capital must equal at least 8 percent of risk-adjusted assets. These minimums do not go into effect until the end of 1992. However, by the end of 1990, banks must satisfy interim ratios of 3.25 percent for core capital and 7.25 percent for total capital.

Leverage requirement. The plan will continue to place a floor on bank capital in the form of a minimum ratio of capital to total assets.

This ratio has come to be known as the "leverage ratio" but is no different in concept from the minimum capital-asset ratios currently in force. Regulators have indicated that the new leverage requirement will be expressed in terms of the new capital definitions and will go into effect in December 1990, the deadline for partial compliance with the risk-based requirements.

As of this writing, regulators have not decided how high the leverage ratio should be or whether there should be separate ratios for core capital and total capital. From the beginning, the OCC has argued for a low leverage requirement and the FDIC for a high requirement. In September, the OCC formally proposed a leverage ratio of 3 percent for core capital, with no separate ratio for total capital.[8] Because total capital cannot be less than core capital, the OCC proposal would imply an effective floor of 3 percent for total capital. The FDIC did not object to the 3 percent leverage ratio for core capital but argued that there should be a separate and higher leverage ratio for total capital to prevent banks from reducing their capital excessively. The Federal Reserve did not take a position on the issue until late November, when it came out in favor of a 3 percent leverage ratio for core capital alone.[9]

---

[8] Passage of the S&L bailout bill in August increased pressure on the OCC to decide on a leverage ratio, due to a provision in the bill that S&Ls meet the same capital standards as national banks, which are supervised by the OCC. A draft of the OCC proposal was issued in early September, and the final proposal was published two months later in *Federal Register* 1989c.

[9] See Board of Governors 1989. In its statement, the Federal Reserve emphasized that some banks would be expected to operate above the minimum requirements. For further details, see footnote 11.

How a bank's capital requirement will be determined

How much capital must a bank hold, given that it faces both a risk-based requirement and a leverage requirement? The leverage requirement will be the relevant constraint for some banks and the risk-based requirement for others. Which requirement is relevant for a particular bank depends on how high its risk-adjusted assets are relative to its total assets.

The interaction of the risk-based requirement and leverage requirement is illustrated in Figure 1 for core capital, the narrower of the two capital measures. The horizontal axis measures the ratio of risk-adjusted assets to total assets. For convenience, this ratio will be called the "risk ratio." The vertical axis measures the ratio of core capital to total assets.

To satisfy the risk-based requirement, banks with higher risk ratios must maintain higher ratios of core capital to total assets. In Figure 1, the risk-based requirement is shown by the upward-sloping line. All banks must maintain a minimum ratio of core capital to risk-adjusted assets of 4 percent. However, the higher a bank's risk ratio, the greater its risk-adjusted assets will be relative to total assets, and thus, the more core capital it will have to hold relative to total assets. As shown in the figure, a bank with a risk ratio of 1.0 must hold core capital equal to 4 percent of total assets. However, a bank that has a risk ratio of zero because it invests entirely in cash and Treasury securities will not have to hold any core capital to satisfy the risk-based requirement. And at the other extreme, a bank that has a risk ratio greater than 1.0 because it has substantial off-balance sheet exposures will have to hold core capital in excess of 4 percent of total assets.

FIGURE 1
Minimum requirement for core capital

Ratio of core capital to total assets (percent)

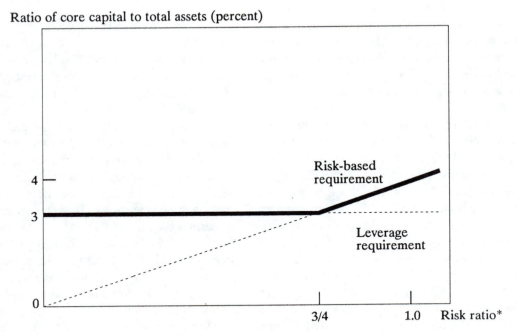

*Ratio of risk-adjusted assets to total assets.

In contrast to the risk-based requirement, the leverage requirement is a constant percentage of total assets. Because the leverage requirement is independent of the risk ratio, it is given by a horizontal line in Figure 1. For purposes of illustration, the leverage ratio is assumed to be 3 percent, as proposed by the OCC and the Federal Reserve.

Because a bank must satisfy both the risk-based requirement and the leverage requirement, its minimum capital requirement will always be the greater of the two. In Figure 1, this means the minimum requirement is given by the heavy kinked line. If the bank has a high

risk ratio (a ratio greater than 3/4), the risk-based requirement will exceed the leverage requirement; therefore, the bank's minimum capital requirement will equal the risk-based requirement. However, if the bank has a low risk ratio (a ratio less than 3/4), the leverage requirement will exceed the risk-based requirement; therefore, the leverage requirement will be the relevant constraint.

Figure 2 shows how a bank's minimum requirement for total capital is determined. The vertical axis of this diagram measures the ratio of total capital to total assets. To satisfy the risk-based requirement, banks must hold total capital

FIGURE 2
Minimum requirement for total capital

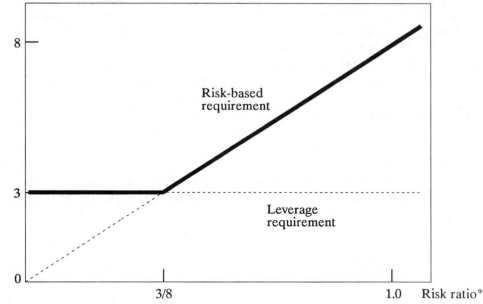

Ratio of total capital to total assets (percent)

Risk-based
requirement

Leverage
requirement

3/8   1.0   Risk ratio*

*Ratio of risk-adjusted assets to total assets.

equal to at least 8 percent of their risk-adjusted assets. Thus, the minimum ratio of total capital to total assets satisfying the risk-based requirement varies with the risk ratio, equaling 8 percent only for banks with risk ratios of 1.0. For purposes of illustration, Figure 2 assumes the leverage ratio for total capital is 3 percent, as implied by the OCC and Federal Reserve proposals. As in the case of core capital, the bank's minimum requirement for total capital equals the greater of the risk-based requirement and the leverage requirement. Thus, the risk-based requirement is the relevant constraint for banks with high risk ratios (in this case, ratios above

3/8) and the leverage requirement the relevant constraint for banks with low risk ratios (ratios below 3/8).[10]

Finally, regulators will continue to pressure a bank to exceed its minimum capital require-

---

[10] The reason the critical ratio is only half as great for total capital as for core capital is that the leverage requirement is the same while the risk-based requirement is twice as steep. As a percent of total assets, the risk-based requirement equals the risk ratio times the required percentage of risk-adjusted assets—4 percent for core capital and 8 percent for total capital. Thus, the critical risk ratio at which the risk-based requirement just equals the 3 percent leverage requirement is 3/4 for core capital but only 3/8 for total capital.

ment if the bank is judged to be unusually risky. After conducting an on-site examination, for example, regulators could conclude that a bank's management or overall financial condition was sufficiently poor to warrant a level of capital greater than the minimum. Such a bank would be pressured to move above the heavy kinked lines in Figures 1 and 2, so as to reduce its risk of failure.[11]

III. IMPACT ON BANKS

Since the purpose of risk-based requirements is to raise requirements for some banks and reduce them for others, the plan will naturally affect banks in different ways. This section shows which banks will face higher requirements, which banks will face lower requirements, and how banks will likely respond to the changes in their capital positions.

Overview

The principal factors that will determine how particular banks are affected by the plan are their risk ratio, their reliance on loan loss reserves, and their ability to meet current requirements. The accompanying box illustrates the different ways in which the plan will affect banks' capital positions. Banks that have high risk ratios or rely heavily on loan loss reserves

to meet current capital requirements will suffer a worsening in their capital positions. Such banks will end up with smaller surpluses, bigger shortfalls, or shortfalls instead of surpluses. On the other hand, banks that have low risk ratios and do not rely heavily on loss reserves will gain from the plan, ending up with bigger surpluses, smaller shortfalls, or surpluses instead of shortfalls. Compliance with current requirements also matters because banks that have shown themselves unable to meet current requirements are unlikely to be allowed to take advantage of a reduction in requirements.

Table 1 classifies all banks operating in June 1989 according to whether they meet the current requirements, whether they meet the new requirements, and whether their capital position improves or worsens as a result of the plan.[12] The estimates assume a 3 percent core-capital leverage ratio, with no separate leverage ratio for total capital. The groups are also illustrated in Figure 3. Each point in the diagram corresponds to a different group and indicates the group's average risk ratio and average ratio of total capital to total assets, using the new definition of total capital. In each

---

[11] In November, the Federal Reserve said that the only banks it planned to allow to operate at the minimum were those that were assigned the top CAMEL rating of 1 by examiners and were not experiencing or anticipating significant growth. Under the CAMEL system, banks are rated by examiners from 1 to 5 based on their capital adequacy, asset quality, management, earnings, and liquidity. See Board of Governors 1989.

[12] The estimates are based on data from the June 1989 Reports of Income and Condition, and were provided by John O'Keefe of the FDIC. Because the risk categories and capital components do not exactly match the variables in the Reports of Income and Condition, a number of assumptions had to be made in computing risk-adjusted assets and Tier 1 and Tier 2 capital. These assumptions are available from John O'Keefe on request. All averages reported below are weighted averages, with each bank weighted by its total assets. Also, the definition of total assets used throughout is ''adjusted total assets.'' This is the measure used in the current requirements and equals average book assets over the previous quarter, plus end-of-quarter loan loss reserves, minus disallowed intangibles.

TABLE 1
**Classification of banks by capital position
June 1989**

	Number of banks	Average total assets[1]	Percent of assets
Group 1: Fail both current and new requirements			
a. Bigger capital shortfall[2]	289	274	2.5
b. Smaller capital shortfall[2]	112	165	.6
Group 2: Satisfy current requirements but fail new requirements	290	3,042	27.6
Group 3: Fail current requirements but satisfy new requirements	95	82	.2
Group 4: Satisfy both current and new requirements			
a. Bigger capital surplus[2]	9,630	90	27.1
b. Smaller capital surplus[2]	2,528	531	42.0
All banks	12,944	247	100.0

case, the number in parentheses is the number of banks in the group.

Group 1 consists of banks that fail both the current and new requirements. Two subgroups can be identified. The first includes 289 banks that will face a bigger shortfall of total capital under the plan. As shown in Table 1, these banks are slightly above average in size and account for 2.5 percent of all bank assets. The second subgroup includes 112 banks that will face a smaller shortfall of total capital. These banks are below average in size and hold 0.6 percent of all bank assets.

Group 2 includes 290 banks that satisfy the current requirements but fail the new requirements—banks that will face a shortfall of capital instead of a surplus. Because these banks average over $3 billion in assets, they account for a relatively large share of all bank assets, 27.6 percent.

FIGURE 3
Group averages

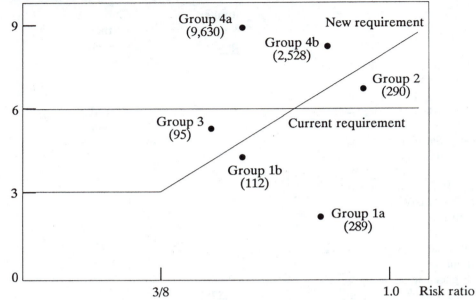

Ratio of total capital to total assets (percent)*

*Using new definition of total capital.

Group 3 consists of 95 banks that fail the current requirements but satisfy the new requirements—banks that will face a surplus of capital instead of a shortfall. Besides being few in number, these banks are small in size. Thus, they account for only 0.2 percent of total bank assets.

Finally, Group 4 consists of banks that satisfy both the current and new requirements. This group, which includes the vast majority of banks, can also be divided into two subgroups. First are 9,630 banks that will face a bigger surplus of total capital. Due to their small average size, these banks account for only 27.1

percent of bank assets. The second subgroup includes 2,528 banks that will face a smaller surplus of total capital. These banks are much larger than banks in the first subgroup and thus account for a bigger share of assets, 42.0 percent.

The rest of this section shows how the plan will affect each of the four groups and considers how banks in each group are likely to respond.[13]

13 Although the main question of interest is how the impact of the plan will vary across banks, it is worth noting that capital standards will be tightened in the aggregate, even with

Group 1

The subgroup of 289 banks facing a bigger capital shortfall rely heavily on loan loss reserves to meet current requirements. As shown in Table 2 and Figure 3, the average risk ratio of this subgroup is 0.79, putting their risk-based requirement for total capital only slightly above the current 6 percent requirement.[14] But their reliance on loan loss reserves causes their total capital to fall from 3.6 percent of assets under the current definition to 2.4 percent under the new definition. Thus, the shortfall of total capital rises sharply, from 2.4 percent of assets under the current requirements to 3.9 percent under the new requirements. Reflecting their lack of equity, they also face a shortfall of core capital equal to 1.8 percent of assets.

The subgroup of 112 banks facing a smaller capital shortfall have lower risk ratios and rely less heavily on loan loss reserves. Their average risk ratio is 0.61, yielding a risk-based requirement for total capital well below 6 percent of assets. Also, their total capital falls only slightly under the new definition. Thus, even though they lack sufficient capital to meet the new requirements, their shortfall of total capital falls from 1.4 percent of assets to 0.6 percent of assets. And in contrast to the first subgroup, they face a surplus of core capital of 0.9 percent.

TABLE 2
Group 1: Fail both current and new requirements

	(a) Subgroup with bigger shortfall	(b) Subgroup with smaller shortfall
Risk ratio[1]		
On-balance sheet	.69	.57
Off-balance sheet	.10	.04
Total	.79	.61
Ratio of total capital to total assets (percent)		
Current definition	3.6	4.6
New definition	2.4	4.5
Ratio of total-capital surplus to total assets (percent)		
Current requirement	−2.4	−1.4
New requirement	−3.9	−0.6
Ratio of core capital to total assets (percent)	1.5	3.9
Ratio of core-capital surplus to total assets (percent)	−1.8	0.9

[1] Ratio of risk-adjusted assets to total assets
Source: FDIC

a leverage ratio of only 3 percent. In particular, the surplus of total capital falls from 2.3 percent of total assets under the current requirements to 1.3 percent of total assets under the new requirements.

[14] As a percent of total assets, the average risk-based requirement for the group is $0.79 \times 8.0 = 6.3$ (the average risk ratio times the required percentage of risk-adjusted assets).

Although the plan tightens standards for the first subgroup and weakens them for the second, neither subgroup is likely to be much affected by the plan. Most of these banks are financially troubled—either they have recently suffered heavy losses depleting their capital, or their future prospects are so bleak they cannot raise capital. The banks with a bigger capital shortfall will not find it any easier to meet the new requirements than the current ones. And because they are already under close supervision, the banks with a smaller shortfall may find that the amount they have to boost their capital depends less on the formal requirement than on regulators' judgment as to how much capital they need.

Group 2

As shown in Table 3 and Figure 3, the 290 mostly large banks in Group 2 are distinguished by their high risk ratios.[15] The average risk ratio of 0.94 is higher than for any other group, due partly to the concentration of assets in high-risk categories but mostly to heavy off-balance sheet activity—the off-balance sheet component of 0.22 compares with an average of 0.13 for all banks. The high risk ratio results in a high risk-based requirement. And because banks in Group 2 rely heavily on loan loss reserves, their total capital falls from 7.6 percent of assets to 6.6 percent. Thus, instead of a surplus of total capital of 1.6 percent, they face a shortfall of 0.8 percent. The shortfall does not extend to core capital because core capital accounts for three-fourths of total capital and only half as much core capital is needed to satisfy the requirement.

Banks in Group 2 are likely to respond to the shortfall of total capital partly by reducing

---

[15] The group includes 248 banks that fail the risk-based requirement but satisfy the leverage ratio, 37 banks that fail both the risk-based requirement and leverage ratio, and 5 banks that satisfy the risk-based requirement but fail the leverage ratio.

TABLE 3

Group 2: Satisfy current requirements but fail new requirements

Risk ratio[1]	
On-balance sheet	.72
Off-balance sheet	.22
Total	.94
Ratio of total capital to total assets (percent)	
Current definition	7.6
New definition	6.6
Ratio of total-capital surplus to total assets (percent)	
Current requirement	1.6
New requirement	−0.8
Ratio of core capital to total assets (percent)	4.9
Ratio of core-capital surplus to total assets (percent)	1.2

[1] Ratio of risk-adjusted assets to total assets
Source: FDIC

---

their risk ratios. In other words, they will cut back on off-balance activities and shift toward assets in lower risk categories, such as home mortgages and U.S. government securities. If a bank left its portfolio unchanged, it would have to increase its capital-asset ratio to comply with the risk-based requirement. In Figure 3, the bank would have to move up until it reached the kinked line representing the new requirement. At that point, however, the bank's capital-asset ratio would be higher than it preferred. As a result, the bank would have an incentive to reduce its risk ratio and move down the kinked line to a point closer to its desired capital-asset ratio.

Besides reducing their risk ratios, banks in Group 2 are likely to increase their capital-asset ratios. If a bank did not increase its capital-asset ratio—if the bank simply moved to the left in Figure 3—it would have to reduce its risk ratio well below the level it preferred. Thus, banks are more likely to adjust to the plan by simultaneously reducing their risk ratios and raising their capital-asset ratios than by doing either alone.

The increase in capital-asset ratios will be achieved at least partly through a reduction in assets. Because the higher capital requirement will raise their cost of funds, banks will have an incentive to shed less profitable assets until they can earn enough on remaining assets to cover the increased cost. Thus, instead of raising their capital-asset ratios by substituting capital for deposits, banks are likely to liquidate assets and use the proceeds to reduce deposits and borrowings. Furthermore, since banks will also want to reduce their risk ratios, the assets most likely to be liquidated are those in high-risk categories. For example, banks may sell some of their consumer and business loans, reducing their risk ratios and increasing their capital-asset ratios at the same time.

A final response of banks in Group 2 may be to shift to riskier assets within categories. The increase in capital requirements will raise the effective cost of making loans, forcing banks to increase their loan rates. Large, well-known borrowers may respond to these higher loan rates by seeking credit in the open market.[16] As a result, banks may have to make

---

16 Some banks might continue originating loans to their large customers but sell the loans on the open market.

a higher proportion of their loans to smaller, lesser-known borrowers. Since these borrowers are likely to be riskier than the borrowers who turn to the open market, the average risk of banks' loan portfolios may increase.

Although such a shift in loan composition cannot be ruled out, the shift is likely to be at least partly offset by the favorable effect of increased capital on banks' incentive to make risky loans. To the extent banks in the second group increase their capital-asset ratios, their shareholders will have more to lose from risky loans that fail to pay off. Thus, even though they may be forced to make more of their loans to lesser-known borrowers, they will have more incentive to screen their loan applicants carefully and reject the ones that are willing to pay high rates but have a high chance of defaulting.

Group 3

The 95 banks in the third group have too little capital to satisfy current requirements but have a low enough risk ratio to exceed the new requirements. As shown in Table 4 and Figure 3, the average risk ratio of 0.52 yields a low risk-based requirement for the group. In addition, the group is little affected by the redefinition of total capital. Thus, instead of facing a shortfall of total capital equal to 0.4 percent of assets, the group will enjoy a surplus equal to 1.2 percent of assets. It does not follow, however, that banks in Group 3 will be allowed to reduce their capital. Since most of the group are financially troubled banks that are already under close regulatory scrutiny, they will probably be pressured by regulators to exceed their formal capital requirements.

TABLE 4
Group 3: Fail current requirements but satisfy new requirements

Risk ratio[1]	
On-balance sheet	.50
Off-balance sheet	.02
Total	.52
Ratio of total capital to total assets (percent)	
Current definition	5.6
New definition	5.4
Ratio of total-capital surplus to total assets (percent)	
Current requirement	−.4
New requirement	1.2
Ratio of core capital to total assets (percent)	4.7
Ratio of core-capital surplus to total assets (percent)	1.8

[1] Ratio of risk-adjusted assets to total assets
Source: FDIC

Group 4

Banks in the last group will be affected very differently by the plan according to whether they face a bigger or smaller surplus of total capital.

Bigger capital surplus. The 9,630 banks in the first subgroup have low risk ratios and rely relatively little on loan loss reserves. As shown in Table 5 and Figure 3, the average risk ratio is only 0.61, reflecting both a high share of assets in low-risk categories and a low level

TABLE 5
Group 4: Satisfy both current and new requirements

	(a) Subgroup with bigger surplus	(b) Subgroup with smaller surplus
Risk ratio[1]		
On-balance sheet	.58	.71
Off-balance sheet	.03	.13
Total	.61	.84
Ratio of total capital to total assets (percent)		
Current definition	9.1	8.6
New definition	9.0	8.1
Ratio of total-capital surplus to total assets (percent)		
Current requirement	3.1	2.6
New requirement	4.0	1.4
Ratio of core capital to total assets (percent)	8.2	6.3
Ratio of core-capital surplus to total assets (percent)	5.2	2.9

[1] Ratio of risk-adjusted assets to total assets
Source: FDIC

of off-balance sheet activity. Also, total capital is virtually unchanged by the new definition. The surplus of total capital thus rises from 3.1 percent of assets to 4.0 percent. And thanks to a high equity level, the subgroup enjoys a large surplus of core capital equal to 5.2 percent of assets.

The only banks that will respond to the lower capital requirement will be those that are currently constrained, in the sense of holding more capital than they would in the absence of any requirement. The banks most likely to be in this position are those that exceed current requirements only slightly—in Figure 3, the ones just above the horizontal line at 6 percent. But as the diagram shows, the subgroup as a whole exceeds current requirements by a wide margin—more than three percentage points. Some banks may maintain surpluses this large because they are worried about falling below the minimum unexpectedly and having to raise capital in a hurry to satisfy regulators. Such banks would react to the plan just like other constrained banks.[17] Given how large the average surplus is, however, it seems likely that many banks are unconstrained, choosing the high capital levels they do, not because they fear falling below the minimum, but because they desire capital for its own sake.[18]

The main way constrained banks will respond to the plan is by reducing their capital-asset ratios. In Figure 3, banks will move downward until they either reach their desired capital-asset ratio or bump up against the kinked line. This adjustment is likely to be achieved at least partly through an increase in assets. Because the reduction in capital requirements will lower their cost of funds, banks will have an increased incentive to expand. Thus, rather than raising more deposits and using all the proceeds to retire equity, they are likely to use some of the proceeds to acquire additional assets.

Some constrained banks may also reduce off-balance sheet exposures and shift to lower risk categories. As Figure 3 shows, any bank that had a risk ratio greater than 3/8 and reduced its capital-asset ratio the maximum amount would end up constrained by the risk-based requirement. That is, it would bump up against the positively sloped segment of the kinked line. Such a bank would have an incentive to lower its risk ratio so as to reduce its risk-based requirement and move even closer to its desired capital position. Once the risk ratio reached 3/8, however, the leverage requirement would take over and the bank would have no reason to lower its risk ratio any further.

Smaller surplus of total capital. Compared with the first subgroup, the 2,528 banks in the second subgroup have higher risk ratios and rely more heavily on loan loss reserves. The average risk ratio of 0.84 yields a high risk-based requirement, and the limit on loan loss reserves reduces total capital by half a percentage point. However, the initial level of total capital is high. Thus, the surplus of total capital is reduced but not eliminated, falling from 2.6 percent of assets to 1.4 percent.

Although banks in the second subgroup will not have to respond to the change in

---

[17] The possibility that capital may serve as a buffer against falling below the minimum is discussed in Keeley 1988 and Wall and Peterson 1987.

[18] Some banks may fear losing intangible assets, such as the bank charter, if they are forced to close (Marcus 1984 and Keeley 1989). If banks in this position also thought they would be unable to raise enough new capital to cover losses and avert failure, they might hold high capital even without any capital requirement. It should also be noted that some banks may hold surplus capital because they are pressured to do so by regulators—for example, because they are considered risky despite their low risk ratios. Such banks would presumably not be allowed to reduce their capital-asset ratios.

requirements, some may do so anyway. Under the plan, the subgroup will enjoy only a moderate surplus of total capital. Some banks may regard their reduced surplus as too small to protect them from falling below the minimum. Such banks will either increase their capital-asset ratios to restore their surpluses or reduce their risk ratios to keep their requirement from going up so much. In Figure 3, they will move up or to the left, farther above the kinked line. However, other banks may not care if their margin of safety is reduced and thus may not respond at all.

IV. EFFECTIVENESS IN CONTROLLING RISK

How successful will the plan be in its ultimate objective of controlling risk? This section concludes that the plan will have significant favorable effects but that these beneficial effects will be limited by the imperfect measurement of capital and risk.

Favorable effects

The most favorable effect of the plan will be to induce a substantial number of risky banks to increase their capital-asset ratios, shift to safer activities, and shrink their assets. Several hundred large banks with high risk ratios will face a capital shortfall as a result of the plan. And at least some other banks with high risk ratios will satisfy the new requirements but find their capital surplus reduced too much for comfort. The majority of these banks probably have high true risk due to the nature of their activities. By inducing them to increase their capital-asset ratios, the plan will limit their chance of failure. And by inducing them to shift toward

safer activities and shrink, the plan will reduce total participation in risky activities by the banking industry.

A second, less certain benefit of the plan will be to allow some safe banks to reduce their capital-asset ratios and grow faster. With a 3 percent leverage ratio for core capital and no separate leverage ratio for total capital, three-fourths of all banks will face a lower capital requirement and increased capital surplus due to their low risk ratios. Many of these banks probably have low true risk. To the extent they are now forced to hold more capital than they prefer, letting them decrease their capital-asset ratio will reduce their cost of funds without appreciably increasing their risk of failure. And by encouraging them to grow faster, the plan will decrease the average risk of the banking industry. It is uncertain, however, how many safe banks will actually reduce their capital-asset ratios and grow more rapidly. Most of the banks already exceed requirements by a wide margin, suggesting they may not respond to the change at all.

Limitations

The idea behind risk-based capital requirements is to make banks with a greater chance of unexpected losses hold a greater cushion against those losses, so as to limit their risk of failure and cost to the FDIC. An ideal risk-based capital plan would therefore include two components—a measure of capital reflecting the bank's true cushion against unexpected losses and a measure of risk reflecting the bank's true chance of experiencing unexpected losses. The new plan is lacking on both counts.

The reason the plan fails to measure capital adequately is that it relies on book-value accounting. Under book-value accounting, assets and liabilities are recorded at historical cost, and capital is not adjusted for subsequent changes in their true market values. As a result, book capital can understate or overstate a bank's cushion against unexpected losses. If, for example, a bank finances long-term securities with shorter term deposits and interest rates subsequently rise, the market value of the securities will decline more than the market value of the deposits. Book capital will be unchanged, but the bank will be less protected against future losses because its portfolio will be worth less. Similarly, if a bank's loans become delinquent and the bank fails to increase its loan loss reserves enough to cover its higher expected losses, the true value of its loan portfolio will decline but book capital will remain the same. Thus, as before, the bank's book capital will overstate its true protection against failure.[19]

One reason the plan fails to measure the risk of unexpected losses accurately is that it focuses exclusively on credit risk. The plan completely ignores interest rate risk—the risk that future changes in interest rates will affect the market value of the bank's assets differently than the market value of its liabilities. Even if the book values of assets and liabilities were adjusted for the effect of past interest rate changes, it would be desirable to make banks that were highly exposed to future interest rate changes hold more capital.

The plan also measures credit risk imperfectly. No distinction is made between loans to highly creditworthy borrowers and loans to borrowers with little credit history or collateral. Also, a highly diversified loan portfolio is treated the same as a portfolio of loans concentrated in one industry or region, even though the concentrated portfolio has greater risk of unexpected default losses.

The fact that banks' capital and risk of unexpected losses are both measured imperfectly means that the risk-based requirement will be too high for some banks and too low for others. Among the banks that will face a capital shortfall are some that should not have to increase their capital or alter their mix of activities—banks whose true likelihood of failure is low. And among the banks that will face an increased capital surplus are some that should not be allowed to decrease their capital—banks whose true likelihood of failure is high.

The leverage requirement will help limit the damage from imperfect measurement of capital and risk, but only by blunting the favorable effects of the plan on risk-taking. On the positive side, a leverage requirement will prevent banks with low risk ratios but high probabilities of failure from reducing their capital-asset ratios excessively. On the negative side, however, even a 3 percent leverage ratio will force some truly safe banks to hold too much capital and will limit banks' incentive to shift to safer activities. With a lower leverage ratio, more banks might specialize in low-risk mortgage lending. And if there were no leverage ratio at all, some banks might give up lending and become deposit-taking specialists, providing transactions services only and investing in government securities with the

---

[19] Not surprisingly, empirical studies find that a risk-adjusted capital requirement would perform significantly better if capital were adjusted downward to reflect delinquent or classified loans. See, for example, Belton 1985 and Chessen 1987.

same maturity as their deposits.

The only way of resolving the dilemma over the leverage requirement is to move closer to market-value accounting and estimate the risk of unexpected losses more accurately. In announcing the risk-based capital plan, regulators acknowledged the plan's deficiencies in measuring risk and expressed their resolve to remedy those deficiencies over time. As such refinements are made, it may be possible to lower or eliminate the leverage ratio, so as to realize the full benefits of risk-based capital requirements.

V. SUMMARY

The new risk-based capital plan was adopted to stem an increase in the overall risk of the banking industry. In principle, risk-based capital requirements should improve control over risk-taking in three ways—by reducing risky banks' chances of failing without driving up safe banks' cost of funds, by rewarding banks for shifting to safer activities, and by discouraging risky banks from outgrowing safe banks.

As to be expected, the impact of the plan will vary greatly across banks. Several hundred large banks engaged in risky activities will face a higher capital requirement as a result of the plan. A much larger number of small banks engaged in safe activities will face a lower capital requirement; but because most of these banks already exceed requirements by a substantial margin, it is uncertain how many will respond. On balance, the plan should affect enough banks in the desired way to improve the regulation of bank risk-taking. However, the full benefits of the plan will not be realized until the measurement of capital and risk is improved.

The impact on banks' capital surplus or shortfall

The diagram below shows how the plan will affect the surplus or shortfall of total capital at two hypothetical banks, one with a high risk ratio and the other with a low risk ratio. The diagram is the same as Figure 2, except that it includes a horizontal line at 6 percent representing the current requirement for total capital. For each bank, the x represents the bank's total capital under the current definition and the dot its total capital under the new definition. In both cases, the dot lies below the x, reflecting the tendency for the limit on loan loss reserves to reduce a bank's total capital.

The bank on the right enjoys a surplus of total capital under current requirements (the x lies above the horizontal line corresponding to the current requirement). However, the bank's high risk ratio results in a high risk-based requirement. Also, its total capital is reduced by the limit on loan loss reserves. As a result, the bank faces a shortfall of total capital under the new requirements (the dot lies below the kinked line corresponding to the new requirement).

The bank on the left enjoys a surplus of capital under both the current and new requirements. Although its total capital is reduced by the limit on loan loss reserves, it has a low risk-based requirement due to its low risk ratio. As a result, the bank enjoys a bigger surplus under the new requirements than the current requirements (the dot lies farther above the kinked line than the x lies above the horizontal line).

FIGURE A1

Impact on capital positions

Ratio of total capital to total assets (percent)

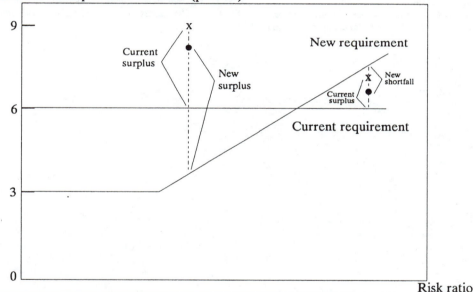

References

Belton, Terrence M. 1985. "Risk-Based Capital Standards for Commercial Banks." Paper presented at the Federal Reserve System Conference on Banking and Financial Structure, Atlanta, September 19-20, 1985.

Board of Governors of the Federal Reserve System. 1989. Press Release, November 22.

Black, Fisher. 1975. "Bank Funds Management in an Efficient Market," *Journal of Financial Economics*, September.

Chessen, James. 1987. "Risk-Based Capital Comes to the Fore," *Issues in Bank Regulation*, Spring.

Crosse, Howard D. and George H. Hempel. 1973. *Management Policies for Commercial Banks*, 2d ed. Englewood Cliffs: Prentice-Hall. Chap. 5.

Federal Register. 1989a. Vol. 54, no. 17, January 27.
_____ . 1989b. Vol. 54, no. 53, March 21.
_____ . 1989c. Vol. 54, no. 212, November 3.

Fischer, Stanley. 1983. "A Framework for Monetary and Banking Analysis," *Economic Journal*, March.

Furlong, Frederick T. 1988. "Changes in Bank Risk-Taking," Federal Reserve Bank of San Francisco, *Economic Review,* Spring.

General Accounting Office. 1988. "Off-Balance Sheet Activities," March.

Gilbert, R. Alton, Courtenay C. Stone, and Michael E. Trebing. 1985. "The New Bank Capital Adequacy Standards," Federal Reserve Bank of St. Louis, *Review,* May.

Jensen, Michael and William Meckling. 1976. "Theory of the Firm: Managerial Behavior, Agency Costs, and Ownership Structure," *Journal of Financial Economics,* October.

Keeley, Michael C. 1988. "Bank Capital Regulation in the 1980's: Effective or Ineffective?" Federal Reserve Bank of San Francisco, *Economic Review,* Winter.
_____ . 1989. "Deposit Insurance, Risk, and Market Power in Banking." *Proceedings of Conference on Bank Structure and Competition,* Federal Reserve Bank of Chicago, May.

Marcus, Alan J. 1984. "Deregulation and Bank Financial Policy," *Journal of Banking and Finance,* December.

Orgler, Yair E. and Robert A. Taggart, Jr. 1983. "Implications of Corporate Capital Structure Theory for Banking Institutions," *Journal of Money, Credit, and Banking,* May.

Townsend, Robert M. 1979. "Optimal Contracts and Competitive Markets with Costly State Verification," *Journal of Economic Theory,* October.

Wall, Larry D. and David R. Peterson. 1987. "The Effect of Capital Adequacy Guidelines on Large Bank Holding Companies," *Journal of Banking and Finance,* December.

Section IV

Management and Policy Issues for Financial Institutions

Financial institutions today face a vastly different world than they did a decade ago. The liberalization of financial institution regulation and the innovation that has swept the financial markets imply an entirely different realm of managerial options and concerns. This section analyzes some of the most important issues that confront financial institutions as we approach the next century. The decisions that financial institution managers make today will determine the strength of their institutions in the decade ahead.

Linda Aguilar surveys the persistent difference among various types of financial institutions in her article, "Still Toe–to–Toe: Banks and Nonbanks at the End of the 80s." With an industry that is considerably free from regulation, banks must compete with diverse nonbank financial institutions, including the financial subsidiaries of auto companies and retailers, in addition to commercial finance companies and insurance companies. Aguilar concludes that commercial banks have been at least holding their own in the competition.

Alone among industrialized nations, the U.S. has no nationwide bank, due to substantial restrictions that keep banks from operating in more than one state. Robert T. Clair and Paula K. Tucker trace the history of the interstate banking idea in their article, "Interstate Banking and the Federal Reserve: A Historical Perspective." As Clair and Tucker point out, the Federal Reserve initially opposed interstate banking, but now favors the idea. The authors also believe that allowing banks to operate interstate will help to control risk.

With less regulation and the prospect of banks operating nationwide, there is considerable concern about the fate of small banks. Sherril Shaffer examines the status of small banks in "Challenges to Small Banks' Survival." Shaffer concludes that several thousand small banks face a significant challenge to their survival. According to Shaffer, these small banks face cost disadvantages compared to larger banks. To survive, these small banks must be aggressive in finding a market niche and in controlling costs.

Most ATMs (automated teller machines) are owned jointly as part of a network. Elizabeth Laderman examines this practice in her paper, "Shared ATM Networks: An Uneasy Alliance?" Laderman examines some of the costs and benefits inherent in such a system. The program offers obvious cost advantages, but Laderman discusses some conflicts inherent in sharing these systems that process over 400 million transactions per month.

Economists often analyze the relationship between a principal and an agent. For example, shareholders (principals) hire managers (agents) to operate a corporation to benefit the shareholders. However, there can be conflicts between the interests of the shareholders and managers. A manager might buy an unnecessary corporate jet, for instance, because the shareholders pay for the jet, but the manager enjoys its use. Loretta J. Mester examines these potential principal-agent conflicts in a banking setting in her article, "Owners Versus Managers: Who Controls the Bank?"

Venture capital is capital provided to small high–risk firms, usually in the start–up phase of the firm's operation. The venture capitalist usually holds a substantial equity interest in the firm. Although banking regulation is much relaxed, banks still cannot hold controlling amounts of equity in firms. In "Banking and Venture Capital," Randall Johnston Pozdena discusses this restriction on bank operations. He shows that these restrictions may impede the flow of capital to new firms.

While prohibitions on equity control of corporations by banks may be a problem for venture capital, banks have been very active in lending for leverage buyouts (LBOs). These loans can be of enormous size and high risk as James B. Thomson discusses in "Bank Lending to LBOs: Risks and Supervisory Response." Because of potential hazards associated with such lending, bank regulators have a legitimate concern about the risks and magnitudes of this lending.

While recent years have seen great change in the financial industry, new changes are on the horizon. Herbert L. Baer considers one kind of change that is likely to intensify in his paper, "Foreign Competition in U.S. Banking Markets." As Baer points out, foreign banks already have a large position in some key U.S. banking markets. He predicts that this trend will continue.

One of the problems that plagued banks in the 1980s was default by foreign nations. In 1982 Mexico declared that it could not service its nearly $80 billion of foreign debt. Other nations quickly followed suit. Chien Nan Wang considers the implications of this debt for the banking industry in "The Costs of Default and International Lending." Wang reviews the continuing attempts of banks and borrowers to resolve the debt crisis and notes that the struggle will likely continue for many years.

Article 23

Still toe-to-toe: Banks and nonbanks at the end of the '80s

Market shares, loan volumes, and ROIs suggest that banks are competing skillfully and successfully with the competition— and not just in traditional banking services

Linda Aguilar

The 1980s have been a decade of change for the financial services industry. The industry has been deregulated geographically and on a product-line basis following the passage of the Depository Institutions Deregulation and Monetary Control Act of 1980, the Garn-St Germain Act of 1982, and the Competitive Equality Banking Act of 1987. Several important decisions by the Federal Reserve Board expanded the nonbank powers of bank holding companies to include underwriting municipal revenue bonds, asset-backed securities, and corporate bonds. Following the lowering of geographic barriers by most states, the banking industry has undergone considerable consolidation.

One segment of the financial services industry—savings and loan associations—has been "bailed out," following the passage of the Financial Institutions Reform, Recovery, and Enforcement Act in 1989. Indeed, several crises, including that in the thrift industry and several large bank failures, were resolved.

Also, during the 1980s, the distinction between investment banks and commercial banks became blurred as commercial banks responded to competition from the capital markets by increasing loans sales, providing financial guarantees, and directly placing securities for customers.[1] The distinction between commercial banking and other lines of commerce also became very fuzzy as nonbank providers of financial services, including nondepository-based providers, increasingly offered products and services that compete with those of com-

mercial banks. Many predicted disaster for banks as the barriers between banking and "nonbanking" fell.

By 1985, the Federal Reserve Bank of Chicago had published three studies on nonbank competition. The last (1985) examined the period 1981–83.[2] This study found that "the banking industry has shown an amazing degree of resiliency in the face of [nonbank competition]."[3] Results showed the auto- and industrial-based firms making inroads into financial services and the industrial-based firms being "formidable competitors;" the traditional financial services industry was in a state of flux; but the insurance sector was not seen as a threat. Retailers appeared to be meeting with success in their "experiments" in offering financial services.

Given the changes in the financial services industry that have occurred throughout the 1980s, the changing macroeconomic environment, and the fact that many nonbanks were still novices in providing financial services when the last study was completed, a re-examination of the activities of the major nonbank providers of financial services is useful. This latest analysis of nonbanks does not differ dramatically from the 1985 study. Banks continue to show great adaptability and resourcefulness in the face of their new and less trammeled competition. The predicted horrors from nonbank competition have not developed. How-

Linda Aguilar is an analyst at the Federal Reserve Bank of Chicago. The author thanks Christine Pavel and Herbert Baer for comments, and Carl Quinn for invaluable assistance in collecting data.

ever, the study does differ from its predecessors in three respects.

First, there has been a change in the firms used as the basis for the study. Some former nonbank competitors (Dana and Montgomery Ward) were excluded because they did not meet this study's size criterion of finance receivables greater than $3 billion. Armco, formerly included as an industrial-based firm, is no longer in the financial services business. Over the 1984–85 period, Armco was forced to divest most of its insurance operations in order to avoid financial ruin. Also, some firms, such as Weyerhaeuser, Metropolitan Life, and four other insurance companies, were added.

Second, the "diversified financial services firms" are no longer as diversified. They have, therefore, been reclassified as either consumer finance or commercial finance companies. For example, Borg Warner Acceptance Corporation was purchased by Transamerica and renamed Transamerica Commercial Finance, moving Transamerica from a diversified financial services firm to a commercial finance company.

Third, two banking "peer groups" were developed for comparison purposes (see Table 1). In previous studies, comparisons were made among the nonbanks, the top 15 bank holding companies (BHCs), and all domestic, insured commercial banks. In this study, the large BHCs are broken out by the ratio of their commercial or consumer loans to total loans and lease finance receivables. By doing this, a primarily commercial-oriented BHC such as Bankers Trust, with 57 percent of its total loan portfolio devoted to commercial loans, is not grouped together with a primarily consumer-oriented BHC such as Barnett Banks, with 84 percent of its total loans and lease finance receivables devoted to consumer lending. The top ten BHCs whose commercial loans are greater than 40 percent of total loans compose one BHC peer group. The other peer group includes the top ten BHCs with consumer loans greater than 50 percent of total loans. The commercial-oriented BHC peer group holds 21 percent of the total loans and lease finance receivables of all commercial, insured banks

---

TABLE 1

List of 28 nonbank firms and 20 large bank holding companies

Nonbanks

Auto companies:	Commercial finance companies:	Insurance companies:
General Motors Acceptance Corp.	General Electric Financial Services	The Prudential
Ford Motor Credit Co.	ITT Financial Corp.	Aetna
Chrysler Financial Corp.	IBM Credit	The Travelers
	Westinghouse Credit	Metropolitan Life
Consumer finance companies:	Weyerhauser Financial Services	Teachers Insurance and
	Heller International	Annuity Association
American Express Co.	Transamerica Corp.	The Equitable
Sears, Roebuck & Co.		Cigna
J.C. Penney Co.		John Hancock
Associates		CNA Financial Corp.
Household International		American General
Beneficial Corp.		
Avco Financial Services		
Commercial Credit		

Bank holding companies

Consumer:	Commercial:
Citicorp	Chase Manhattan Corp.
Security Pacific Corp.	Manufacturers Hanover Corp.
Wells Fargo & Co.	Chemical New York Corp.
First Interstate Bancorp.	J.P. Morgan & Co.
Bank of New England Corp.	First Chicago Corp.
NCNB Corp.	Bankers Trust New York Corp.
Barnett Banks, Inc.	Bank of Boston Corp.
Banc One Corp.	Marine Midland Banks, Inc
First Union Corp.	Mellon Bank Corp.
Citizens and Southern Corp.	Bank of New York Co..

(domestic and foreign offices). The consumer-oriented BHC peer group holds 10 percent.

Methodology and data

The nonbank groups include a total of 28 firms (see Table 1): auto makers (GM, Ford, and Chrysler), consumer finance companies, commercial finance companies, and insurance companies. As mentioned earlier, the nonbank criterion for inclusion in this study was finance receivables outstanding greater than $3 billion.

The data used throughout the study are from the Federal Reserve Board's databases, annual reports, income statements, and other publicly available data. Data for 1987 are used as the most current period and performance and growth comparisons are over the 1982–1987 period.

As in previous studies, each nonbank group's loan composition and growth, profitability, and market presence are analyzed and compared. As shown in Table 2, the largest consumer- and commercial-oriented BHCs have increased their combined share of total private sector finance receivables from 48 percent to 54 percent due mainly to the growth of consumer loans among the 10 largest consumer-oriented BHCs. These BHCs increased their total loans outstanding by over 20 percent per year, largely through mergers and acquisitions. At the same time, slow growth in consumer as well as in commercial loans among the ten insurance companies contributed greatly to the 6 percentage point loss for the 28 nonbanks in this study.

Most nonbanks groups offer financial services to both consumers and businesses, and in this study, the split between *total* nonbank commercial and consumer lending is fairly even. However, each nonbank group does have its primary niche. Consumer loans are a larger part of the portfolio for the auto and consumer finance companies, and commercial loans dominate the holdings of the insurance and commercial finance companies.

Consumer lending

In providing financial services to individuals, commercial banks compete among themselves and with thrift institutions. They also compete with manufacturers, retailers, consumer finance companies, and insurance companies. Commercial banks compete with these firms in offering transactions and savings accounts, investments, and loans. Nonbanks have

proven to be formidable competitors in lending areas, but in a deregulated environment, commercial banks as well as other depository institutions have successfully competed with nonbank providers of deposit substitutes.

Deposit accounts are offered through depository institutions—commercial banks, S&Ls, and credit unions. Nondepository-based firms offer money market mutual funds (MMMFs) and non-term life insurance premiums, which are close substitutes for deposit accounts. MMMFs were introduced in 1972 and grew rapidly in the high-interest rate environment of the late 1970s. By 1982, MMMFs stood at $242 billion.

In late 1982, Money Market Deposit Accounts (MMDA) were authorized. The MMDA is a federally insured savings account offered by banks and thrifts. It is directly equivalent to and competitive with money market mutual funds.

Seven weeks after their introduction, balances in MMDAs surpassed $242 billion, largely due to high introductory rates offered by many institutions. By mid-1983, balances in MMMFs declined to $180 billion. During 1984 and 1985, MMMFs grew, albeit at a slower rate than MMDAs (see Figure 1), and in the spring of 1986, the MMMF growth rate began to surpass that of MMDAs. As of October 1989, balances in MMDAs were $473 billion, and balances in money market funds were $400 billion.[4]

Although MMMFs are primarily offered through brokerage firms, some insurance companies offer them as well. In addition, insurance companies offer another deposit-like product, the non-term life insurance policy, which contains an insurance component as well as an investment component. The advantage of insurance premiums over most bank deposits is that they are long-term and ongoing in nature. People use insurance as financial protection, rather than as a savings instrument *per se* and, thus, are more reluctant to withdraw or cash in policies. Therefore, they provide insurance companies a steady stream of income.[5]

Many nonbank firms also offer deposit accounts through their nonbank banks, i.e., banks that either accept all types of deposits and make only consumer loans or accept only nontransactions deposits and make all types of loans. As of year-end 1987, 10 of the 28 nondepository-based firms in this study owned a

TABLE 2

Financial services at a glance: 1987
(Billions of dollars)

	No.	Total finance receivables	Market share	Change from 1982	Commercial loans	Market share	Change from 1982	Consumer loans	Market share	Change from 1982	Financial services earnings	
											NI	ROI
Auto	3	$162.8	14.8	2.1	$53.4	10.1	2.6	$109.4	19.0	--	2.4	7.6
Consumer finance	9	115.2	10.5	(1.2)	20.7	3.9	(2.0)	94.5	16.5	(2.0)	2.9	5.6
Comm. finance	6	63.3	5.7	1.0	58.2	11.1	4.5	5.2	.9	(1.5)	1.7	6.1
Insurance	10	163.9	14.9	(8.3)	119.3	22.6	(7.9)	44.6	7.8	(6.8)	7.4	2.0
Total nonbanks	28	$505.2	45.9	(6.4)	$251.5	47.7	(2.8)	$253.7	44.2	(10.3)	14.4	3.9
Consumer BHCs	10	$329.2	29.9	5.3	$114.4	21.7	1.4	$214.8	37.4	7.6	(.5)	5.7
Commercial BHCs	10	266.5	24.2	1.1	161.2	30.6	1.4	105.4	18.4	2.7	(4.5)	4.7
Total BHCs	20	$595.8	54.1	6.4	$275.6	52.3	2.8	$320.2	55.8	10.3	(5.0)	5.1
TOTAL		$1,101.0			$527.1			$573.9				

nonbank bank and another four owned savings and loans.

While nondepository-based firms do offer deposit-like products, commercial banks and thrift institutions remain the primary suppliers of these products. In lending, however, depository institutions no longer dominate. Table 3 shows the breakdown of various consumer loans by holder. At year-end 1987, over 40 percent of all residential mortgage loans were held by federal mortgage agencies or by various investors in the form of mortgage-backed securities. Also, over one-third of all auto loans were held by finance companies, and nearly one-quarter of all revolving credit was held by retailers.

Table 4 illustrates that only four of the ten largest non-real estate consumer lenders are commercial banking firms. GMAC heads the list with over $55 billion of consumer loans, followed by Citicorp, Ford Credit, and American Express. In fact, three of the four top providers of consumer finance are nonbank firms. Furthermore, the four largest nonbank providers hold almost twice the consumer receivables of the four commercial banks. Two of the commercial banking firms are not consumer-oriented BHCs and one of the largest nonbank providers of consumer loans is not primarily consumer focused.

The following two sections examine, in more detail, the role of selected nonbank providers of financial services to consumers relative to that of consumer-oriented BHCs.

Auto companies

The three leading U.S. auto makers, through their captive finance companies, are among the largest nonbank providers of consumer credit. In 1987, they held over $100 billion in consumer installment loans, which is equal to 18 percent of total consumer installment loans outstanding in the United States and greater than the $82 billion held by the consumer-oriented BHC group. Over 90 percent of consumer loans held by the auto financing arms are made to support the parents' primary line of business.

Each of the three auto financing arms were initially formed to facilitate the sale of the parent's products. In addition to auto loans, which account for 75 percent of their loan portfolios, they provide lease financing to dealers, wholesale financing of inventories, and term loans to dealers for capital improvements and other big ticket items. However, in recent years, each of the three has diversified into non-auto-related financial services as well.

General Motors began its consumer finance operations in 1919 when it formed General Motors Acceptance Corporation (GMAC). In 1925, it diversified into auto-related insurance, and in 1981 it entered the leasing business. GMAC Mortgage Corporation, formed in 1985, purchased the $11 billion loan-servicing portfo-

FIGURE 1

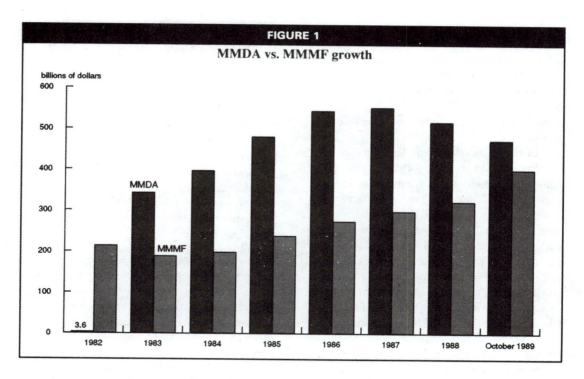

MMDA vs. MMMF growth

lio of Minneapolis-based Norwest Corporation and the $7.4 billion mortgage business of CoreStates to become one of the nation's largest mortgage servicers. By year-end 1988, GMAC Mortgage serviced a nearly $26 billion mortgage portfolio and ranked as the second largest mortgage servicer in the nation.[6]

Ford Credit was originally formed in 1959 to provide wholesale financing and to purchase retail installment sales contracts from Ford dealers. In 1960, the Ford Leasing Development Company was formed to provide lease financing to car and truck leasing companies. It

entered direct consumer lending in 1966. Through its insurance subsidiaries, Ford provides group credit life and credit disability insurance as well as its extended service plan. Its Diversified Finance division negotiates large, private investments in preferred stocks, leases of and loans secured by transportation equipment, and real estate loans secured by first and junior mortgages.

In 1985, Ford Motor Co. acquired First Nationwide Financial Corporation, whose subsidiary, First Nationwide Savings, was the 8th largest savings and loan association with 177

TABLE 3

Market share of various consumer loans by sector: 1982–1987

	1–4 family mortgage loans		Auto loans		Revolving credit		Other consumer loans	
	1982	1987	1982	1987	1982	1987	1982	1987
Commercial banks	15.9	27.0	45.2	40.6	54.6	62.0	38.4	39.9
Finance companies	n.a.	1.8	37.5	36.7	n.a.	n.a.	30.9	22.5
Savings institutions	41.7	27.3	n.a.	6.4	n.a.	8.3	9.4	17.9
Credit unions	n.a.	n.a.	17.3	16.3	n.a.	4.2	18.8	16.6
Retailers	n.a.	n.a.	n.a.	n.a.	39.3	23.2	2.5	3.1
Life insurance cos.	1.5	0.6	n.a.	n.a.	n.a.	n.a.	n.a.	n.a.
Other	40.9	43.3	n.a.	n.a.	6.1	2.3	n.a.	n.a.

Source: Board of Governors of the Federal Reserve System.
n.a.—not available.

offices in 4 states.[7] In 1989, Ford acquired Associates Corp.[8] Through Associates' bank subsidiary, Ford will gain a major presence in the credit card industry. If First Nationwide and Associates were consolidated with Ford Motor Credit, only 42 percent of Ford Motor Credit's finance receivables would be auto-related.

In 1964, Chrysler Credit Corp. and an insurance subsidiary were formed to provide auto financing and physical damage and comprehensive insurance. In 1985, Chrysler began acquiring more diversified financial businesses with the purchase of Finance America (renamed Chrysler First) and E.F. Hutton Credit Corporation (renamed Chrysler Capital Corporation).

Chrysler First provides consumer loans, small business loans, and inventory financing for national manufacturers' dealers. In 1987, Chrysler Capital acquired NFC Leasing which sells, leases, and refurbishes computers and computer peripherals, adding not only another financial service to its credit but a nonautomotive one as well. In 1987, 32 percent of Chrysler's total assets were nonautomotive.

Despite the fact that auto-related financing still accounts for most of the auto captives' business, commercial banks as a group have a larger share of the auto loan market.[9] However, since as early as 1978, the captives have been stealing market share from the commercial banks. In 1978, commercial banks held 60 percent of all auto loans outstanding; by 1982 their share dropped to 45 percent; and by 1987, the commercial banks held only 41 percent. The auto makers had picked up most of this decrease with a 6 percentage point increase in their auto loan portfolios over the 1982–87 period. Chrysler's performance over the 1982–1987 period was the best of the big three with total finance receivables increasing from a mere 5 percent of the combined auto makers auto loans outstanding to 16 percent in 1987.

During the 1982–87 period, the auto financing arms periodically offered special-rate financing to boost sales and credit financing.[10] At one point during the early 1980s, commercial banks were in effect forced out of the market because of a shift in interest-rate relationships. High funding costs and state-mandated ceilings on consumer loans reduced banks' auto loan portfolios by 12.5 percent and their market share fell from 58 to 45 percent during the 1980–82 period.

TABLE 4
Consumer lenders study group: 1987*
(Millions of dollars)

GMAC	$55,050
Citicorp	44,399
Ford Credit	38,147
American Express	28,884
Sears	26,068
Chase Manhattan	16,752
Prudential	14,795
Chrysler	12,236
Manufacturers Hanover	11,652
Security Pacific	10,798

*Includes credit card and all consumer installment loans except mortgages.

The auto makers initially responded to commercial banks' retrenchment by standing ready to provide credit as needed. In 1981, they began to offer low-rate financing on certain slow-selling models. By November of 1982, about 50 percent of their normal sales mix was eligible and by first quarter of 1983, almost all cars were eligible. However, this tactic was not without a downside. The increase in liabilities that allowed them to offer the incentives began to put pressure on their balance sheets.

In 1983 when the economy began to improve, commercial banks rejoined the market, and the auto makers stopped the special-rate programs and began to concentrate on getting their balance sheets in order. Throughout 1985, special-rate financing was offered sporadically, mostly when sales needed a boost.

By 1986, consumers began to realize that special-rate financing and dealer rebates no longer had to be grabbed up at first offer and that if no incentive was currently being offered, they just had to wait a bit and one would be. Also, many consumers had made car purchases and would not be buying another car for a while. In essence, the timing of sales rather than an increase in sales was being affected. The effectiveness of the program as a means of increasing sales began to slack off.

Despite the strain that incentive-rate financing may have had on their financial statements, the auto finance companies were more profitable in 1987 than their commercial banking rivals. Average return on investment (ROI) for the three auto financing arms was 7.6 percent in 1987.[11] ROI for the consumer-oriented BHC group was 5.7 percent and included negative net income of $450 million.[12]

Overall, it appears that the auto finance companies still do well at what they were originally formed to do—finance the products of their parents. Commercial banks and credit unions combined still finance a greater proportion of auto loans than the auto makers, but the growth of the auto financing arms has far exceeded the growth of auto finance receivables of commercial banks and credit unions. In addition, through diversification into mortgage loans, insurance, equipment leasing, and credit card lending, they are making inroads into other industries' financial services as well.

Consumer finance companies

Along with the auto companies, some consumer finance companies rank among the largest providers of financial services to individuals. The consumer financial services sector in this study comprises nine firms, and includes five traditional consumer finance companies, such as Household International and Commercial Credit; two retailers, Sears and J.C. Penney; a travel-related services firm, American Express; and a commercial-turned-consumer finance company, ITT Financial Corp. Firms in this category provide financial services to businesses as well as consumers, but over 80 percent of their loans held are consumer loans, totaling $94 billion in 1987, approximately 45 percent of the total consumer loans of the consumer-oriented BHC group.

Many of the traditional financial services firms have been in operation for most of this century. What started as primarily personal and real-estate-based lending now includes sales finance contracts (such as private label retail revolving charges) and asset-based financing. For example, Household International has a consumer segment that offers banking services and credit insurance products; a commercial segment that consists of investments in leveraged leases, term preferred stocks, and equipment loans and leases; and an insurance segment that provides ordinary life, annuity, and specialty insurance products.

Commercial Credit offers personal unsecured loans, real estate or home equity loans, commercial insurance, and specialty insurance products such as director's and officer's liability, special events coverage, and fidelity insur-

ance for financial institutions. In 1983, Commercial Credit bought 99.5 percent of the First National Bank of Wilmington, Delaware (recently renamed Primerica) which offers credit card services as well as loans by mail.

Sears is the largest issuer of retail credit cards and J.C. Penney is the second largest.[13] Sears is engaged in retail credit, insurance, real estate brokerage, and investment services through its four primary business units. Sears has in most cases been the first nonbank to enter a particular financial services market. Sears began its consumer sales financing in 1911, eight years before General Motors began financing car sales. It was also first in expanding into insurance by establishing Allstate Insurance Co. in 1931. In 1985, Sears purchased both Coldwell Banker and Dean Witter, solidifying its place as a giant in the financial services industry.

Each of Sears' four primary businesses offers some form of financial services. In its merchandising operations, the standard Sears credit card provides both revolving and installment-type credit to consumers. In addition to providing consumer credit through the Discover Card, its Dean Witter subsidiary offers auto, home equity, and other consumer loans. Coldwell Banker has an advantage in the mortgage loan arena by being able to offer mortgage loans along with real estate sales.

Yet all recent accounts indicate that Sears is having its share of growth and expansion problems. ''Financial supermarkets'' are beginning to trim operations.[14] In particular, Sears is eliminating its entire in-store Coldwell Banker operations and cutting in half the number of Dean Witter in-store units. In 1989, Sears announced the sale of Coldwell Banker's Commercial Group.

On the other hand, the Discover card is doing quite well. In a recent study of over 4,000 consumers, the number of households with Discover cards increased by 2.1 million, or 14 percent, in 1989. According to a MasterCard International spokesperson, the big advantage of the Discover card is that there is no annual fee.[15] The 1 percent cash rebate is also attractive.

The bulk of J.C. Penney's finance receivables comes from its retail credit card and major purchase plans. J.C. Penney Financial Corp, a wholly owned, consolidated subsidiary, provides the financing of operations for its parent.

In addition, J.C. Penney National Bank offers Visa and MasterCard credit programs.

American Express, with $655 million in net income in 1987 from its travel-related services and total net income of $533 million, ranks second only to Sears in the financial services industry. American Express is the largest issuer of travel and entertainment cards. American Express Travelers Cheques have been in existence since 1890. The American Express Green Card was created in 1958.

American Express also engages in investment banking and brokerage, private banking, life and health insurance, and financial planning and asset management through Shearson Loeb Rhoades, acquired in 1981, and Investors Diversified Services, acquired in 1984. In both the January 1988 and 1989 issues of *Fortune*, American Express was voted the most admired firm in the diversified financial services industry, with all four business segments offering financial services.

ITT Financial Corp. is just one of ITT's nine business segments. ITT Financial Corp. was incorporated in 1974 as the result of a merger of two previously acquired finance companies, Aetna Finance and Thorp Finance. ITT Financial Corp. offers both consumer and commercial financing, but until 1985 the commercial finance segment was always the larger of the two. In both 1987 and 1988, consumer finance receivables were approximately 56 percent of total receivables. Financial services offered include personal loans and home equity loans; commercial financing for manufacturers, retail dealers, and distributors of consumer and commercial durable goods; capital equipment financing and residential real estate financing; and credit-related insurance.

The majority of the consumer finance companies' loans are real estate loans, which include first and second mortgages and home equity loans, and consumer installment credit, which includes bank card receivables. The nine consumer finance companies in this study also provide some commercial financial services although commercial loans account for only 18 percent of their combined portfolio. Furthermore, consumer loans for these firms have increased 134 percent over the 1982–87 period, almost four times as fast as their commercial loans. Total finance receivables more than doubled.

Despite this growth, the consumer finance group lost one percentage point market share when compared to the entire study group. The consumer-oriented BHC group increased consumer finance receivables 230 percent and total finance receivables 179 percent. Consequently, market share for the consumer-oriented BHC peer group increased 5 percentage points from 25 to 30 percent.

The nine consumer finance companies combined had ROI of 5.6 percent in 1987, which is comparable to the consumer-oriented BHC peer group's 5.7 percent. However, even though their profitability ratios are comparable, the consumer finance companies are not posing much of a threat to the banking industry. This is confirmed by their loss of market share. This loss is due, at least in part, to the fact that most consumers maintain a transactions account at a commercial bank, savings and loan, or credit union and, therefore, have an existing relationship with a depository institution. Therefore, even though consumer finance companies are equally profitable, the particular niche they once enjoyed in terms of consumer loans appears to be eroding.

Commercial lending

As in providing financial services to individuals, U.S. commercial banking firms also compete with many other firms than just domestic commercial banks in the commercial finance arena. They compete with foreign banking firms, the capital markets, and nonbank firms. U.S. branches of foreign banks now hold over 15 percent of all U.S. commercial loans outstanding, almost double their share in 1984. Between 1975 and 1986, banks' share of short-term debt of large corporations fell from nearly 50 percent to 27 percent due to competition from the capital markets.[16]

In addition, the importance of nonbank suppliers of financial services to businesses has increased. The third and fifth largest commercial lenders are nonbank firms, and the largest commercial real estate lenders are insurance companies, not banks. Also, five of the largest leasing firms, among those firms in this study, are nonbanks. General Electric Financial Services, GMAC, and IBM rank first, second, and third, respectively.

The following sections examine in more detail the role of selected large nonbank firms in providing financial services to business.

Several of the firms, including General Electric Financial Services and Westinghouse Credit, gained experience in financial services as captive finance companies, but have ceased providing support for the sale of their parents' products and have become independent financiers.

Commercial finance companies

The commercial finance companies included in this study are subsidiaries of some of the largest corporations in America—General Electric, Westinghouse, IBM, and Weyerhaeuser. Heller and Transamerica are also included because they are primarily commercial lenders.[17]

The six firms in the commercial finance segment had $58 billion in commercial lending in 1987, equalling nearly one-fourth of the total commercial lending of the 28 nonbanks and 36 percent of the commercial lending of the commercial-oriented BHC peer group.

GE is by far the largest provider of financial services to business among the commercial finance companies. General Electric Financial Services (GEFS) is GE's financial services unit, and consists of GE Capital Corporation (GECC), Employers Reinsurance Corporation, and an 80-percent interest in Kidder, Peabody Group, Inc. Despite its origin as a captive finance company, almost all of the products GECC provides financing for are non-GE.

More than half of GEFS's finance receivables are time sales and loans for retail merchants, commercial and industrial loans, commercial and residential real estate financing, and manufactured housing time sales and inventory financing. In its commercial and industrial financing, GEFS is one of the leading financiers of leveraged buyouts. Also, GEFS provides commercial real estate financing in the form of first and second mortgages, construction loans and equity investments. The remainder of GEFS's finance receivables are primarily from its leasing activities for vehicles, containers and aircraft. In vehicle fleet leasing, GEFS owns and manages more than 400,000 vehicles.

Westinghouse Credit was founded in 1954 as a financing source for Westinghouse appliance dealers. It now focuses exclusively on the commercial finance market. Over one-third of Westinghouse's finance receivables are from commercial real estate. Its second largest line of business is lease financing for major capital equipment such as commercial and corporate aircraft.

IBM Credit was founded in 1981 to finance the sales and leasing of IBM equipment. By year-end 1982, finance receivables exceeded $1 billion, primarily from installment payment receivables. By 1987, finance receivables were nearly $6 billion, with lease financing comprising nearly two-thirds of the total.

Weyerhaeuser, primarily a lumber company, is engaged in financial services through its two unconsolidated subsidiaries, Weyerhaeuser Real Estate (WRECO) and Weyerhaeuser Financial Services. The financial services subsidiary was formed in December of 1987 as a holding company for Weyerhaeuser Mortgage Company, Republic Federal Savings and Loan, and GNA Corporation, an annuity, insurance, and securities firm.

Commercial leasing accounts for a large part of the financial services offered by the six commercial finance companies studied. Weyerhaeuser, through its S&L and mortgage company subsidiaries, is the only lender in this segment that engages in consumer lending. Over the 1982–87 period, commercial lending for the six firms increased 237 percent, nearly twice as fast as that of the commercial-oriented BHC group.

GEFS's growth accounts for much of the sector's gain in market share. Since 1982, GEFS has increased commercial lending over fourfold. Total commercial finance receivables outstanding for GEFS in 1987 were $33.3 billion, making it the largest commercial lender of the 28 nonbanks. Its commercial loan portfolio is larger than any individual BHC's portfolio with the exception of Citicorp.

While profitability ratios are not strictly comparable across groups, the commercial finance companies, on average, appear to be have been more profitable than their banking counterparts. The commercial finance companies had ROI of 6.1 percent in 1987, compared to the commercial-oriented BHC peer group's ROI of 4.7 percent. The profitability of the largest BHCs has been adversely affected by the poor performance of their loans to less developed countries (LDCs).

As mentioned earlier, the commercial finance companies include some of America's largest corporations and represent a unique grouping of highly competitive, highly concentrated firms. While their market shares are relatively small, the six commercial finance companies in this study are quite profitable and have been growing very rapidly for years. Therefore, in and of themselves, they represent a threat to the banking industry.

Insurance companies

The ten insurance companies in this study are among the largest providers of commercial financial services. In total, these ten firms held $119 billion in commercial loans in 1987, approximately 75 percent of the commercial loans held by the commercial-oriented BHC group. The commercial loans on the books of the insurance companies are primarily real estate-based. Indeed, six of the largest providers of funding for real estate are insurance companies.

Many of the insurance companies surveyed have diversified into noninsurance activities. For example, Prudential's 1987 annual report lists residential mortgages, credit card services, retail securities and commodities brokerage, and investment and merchant banking as services offered. Metropolitan's menu reads similarly—Century 21 Real Estate Corp., MetFirst Financial Company, MetLife Capital Credit Corp., and MetLife Securities, Inc. John Hancock discusses four lines of business in its 1987 annual report—consumer insurance products, consumer financial services, employee benefits services, and investment and pension services. Aetna's breaks down similarly.

Insurance is still the core business of Equitable, Travelers, Cigna, and CNA Financial. Each of these firms, with the exception of CNA, offers mutual funds. Equitable also offers discount brokerage services and in a joint venture with Merrill Lynch, distributes life and annuity products through Merrill Lynch's marketing organization. Travelers, primarily through subsidiaries, offers investment banking, mortgage origination, and other services.

American General delineates six business units—four insurance, one consumer credit, and one mortgage and real estate. Consumer credit is offered through three consumer credit subsidiaries and mortgage and real estate services are offered through another three subsidiaries.

Teacher's Insurance and Annuity Association (TIAA) offers insurance and investment services to the educational community through a variety of investment funds, annuities, and other income options.

Insurance companies compete with financial institutions in three major ways. First, through non-term premiums, they take in quasi-deposits; second, most offer investment options such as mutual funds, and, through subsidiaries, credit cards; third, they invest premiums and other deposits in the capital markets.

On the investment side, insurance companies compete in the financial services arena primarily in commercial lending through their investment portfolios, with commercial mortgage loans being the overwhelming component. Of the nonbank segments, insurance companies are the largest commercial lenders with nearly half of the total 1987 commercial loans of the 28 nonbanks.

While the insurance companies are some of the largest providers of financial services, they are also some of the slowest growing. For example, Equitable's finance receivables grew by 1 percent, and Metropolitan's fell 4 percent over the 1982–87 period. In both cases the companies were slowed by little or no growth in commercial mortgage or real estate loans. Also, of the study group, the insurance sector realized the only significant *decrease* in market share.

On a company-by-company basis, performance was stable with most companies' net income in the $250 million to $400 million range. Two notable exceptions were Equitable with losses of $57 million and John Hancock with net income of only $6 million. ROI for the insurance sector, at 2.0 percent in 1987, is the lowest of the nonbank sectors.[18]

As far as making inroads into the banking industry, the insurance companies for the most part are not a threat. Their insurance operations continue to provide them with plentiful resources, but their diversification into more profitable financial services has been slow. As stated in the Chicago Fed's 1985 study, the insurance companies have more to fear from financial institutions entering the insurance market than vice versa.

Summary

Commercial banking firms continue to show resiliency in competing with nonbanks. The commercial-oriented BHC group as well as the consumer-oriented BHC group increased their market shares of total finance receivables at the expense of the 28 nonbanks surveyed.

The banking firms' increase in market share, however, may have come at the expense of profitability. The commercial-oriented BHCs averaged 4.7 percent ROI in 1987 and the consumer-oriented BHCs averaged 5.7 percent. Of the 28 nonbanks surveyed, the consumer finance companies ROI was 5.6 percent; the auto financing arms 7.6 percent; the commercial finance companies 6.1 percent; and the insurance firms 2.0 percent.

The money center banks have been hit hard by their involvement in LDC debt. A major reason financial institutions have reported negative income is due to their efforts to reduce LDC debt exposure. Were it not for provisions for LDC debt taken in 1987, ROI would have been 1.7 percentage points greater. Apparently, the money centers are not through making provisions for their LDC debt. In late 1989, the money center banks began another round of reserving for this burdensome debt.

Banks still have an edge over nonbanks in several areas. First, they have the advantage of experience, which carries considerable weight with many consumers. Also, banks have deposit insurance, another attractive difference in the eyes of consumers. As banks and other financial services industries become more deregulated and more intertwined, banks will be able to use these strengths to their advantage.

On the other hand, nonbanks have an edge as well. Several industries, such as insurance and financial services, have extensive distribution networks which make their products more readily available to the masses. A new product or service from either of these industries can often reach a much larger group than can a similar product or service of a regional banking entity.

Nonbanks also are beginning to realize the benefits of time. Financial services offerings by nonbanks are much more commonplace than they were 30 years ago. Generations are growing up with financial services readily available from a variety of sources. Mass media marketing, consumer education, and other marketing techniques have helped both banks and nonbanks grow.

The bottom line is still that banks are, at the very least, holding their own against the competition. Since 1983, banks have operated in a much less regulated environment and proven that, when allowed to compete on equal footing, they can be quite successful. Past mistakes—namely, LDC lending and some real estate lending—may hamper them somewhat in the future. However, as banks gain broader powers, especially in insurance brokerage and underwriting, we may see the banking industry running well ahead of the nonbanks.

FOOTNOTES

[1] See Herbert L. Baer and Christine A. Pavel, ''Does regulation drive innovation?,'' *Economic Perspectives*, Federal Reserve Bank of Chicago, March/April 1988; and Betsy Dale, ''The grass may not be greener: Commercial banks and investment banking,'' *Economic Perspectives*, Federal Reserve Bank of Chicago, November/December 1988.

[2] Christine Pavel and Harvey Rosenblum, ''Banks and nonbanks: The horse race continues,'' *Economic Perspectives*, Federal Reserve Bank of Chicago, May/June 1985.

[3] Pavel and Rosenblum, p. 15.

[4] Board of Governors of the Federal Reserve System.

[5] *Life Insurance Companies as Financial Institutions*, Life Insurance Association of America, Prentice-Hall, p. 2.

[6] *American Bank Top Numbers, 1989 Update*, American Bank-Bond Buyer.

[7] First Nationwide is not consolidated with Ford Credit in this study. If it were, Ford's 1987 finance receivables would increase to $63.5 billion.

[8] Associates is a consumer finance company and is examined separately in the consumer finance section of this article because Associates was not owned by Ford when this study was initiated.

[9] This may seem an unreasonable comparison since there are only three auto finance companies and over 14,000 banks, but the three auto finance companies are able to offer their services through their network of 37,000 dealerships (see *Automotive News*, February 16, 1987, p. 56.).

[10] Most of the following section dealing with special rate financing is from Charles A. Luckett, ''Recent trends in automobile finance,'' *Federal Reserve Bulletin*, June 1986.

[11] Return on investment is defined as after-tax net income plus interest expense divided by total assets.

[12] Because commercial banking firms and the captive finance companies do not engage in all of the same activities, their profitability is not strictly comparable.

[13] Based on receivables outstanding. See *The Nilson Report*, September 1989.

[14]Lisabeth Werner, "Financial Supermarkets Suffer Setback," *American Banker*, April 4, 1989, p. 1+.

[15]Rebecca Cox, "Discover Seen Making Inroads in Banking Cards," *American Banker*, September 29, 1989, p. 1.

[16]Baer and Pavel, p. 4.

[17]Heller is owned by Fuji Bank, Ltd., a Japanese banking organization.

[18]For the insurance group, dividends paid by mutual companies to policyholders are also added to net income as an expense.

REFERENCES

Baer, Herbert L. and Christine A. Pavel, "Does regulation drive innovation?" *Economic Perspectives*, Vol. XII, No. 2, Federal Reserve Bank of Chicago, March/April, 1988, pp. 3-15.

Board of Governors of the Federal Reserve System, *Federal Reserve statistical release*, No H.6(508) Washington, DC, November 9, 1989.

Cox, Rebecca, "Discover Seen Making Inroads on Bank Cards," *American Banker*, September 29, 1989, p.1.

Dale, Betsy, "The grass may not be greener: Commercial banks and investment banking," *Economic Perspectives*, Vol. XII, No. 6, Federal Reserve Bank of Chicago, November/December 1988, pp. 3-13.

H.S.N. Consultants, Inc., *The Nilson Report*, No. 460, Los Angeles, CA, September 1989.

Life Insurance Association of America, *Life Insurance Companies as Financial Institutions*, New Jersey: Prentice-Hall, 1962.

Luckett, Charles A., "Recent trends in automobile finance," *Federal Reserve Bulletin*, June 1986, pp. 355-365.

Pavel, Christine and Harvey Rosenblum, "Banks and nonbanks: The horse race continues," *Economic Perspectives*, Vol. IX, No. 3, Federal Reserve Bank of Chicago, May/June 1985, pp. 3-17.

Rose, Peter S., *The Changing Structure of American Banking*, New York: Columbia University Press, 1987.

Werner, Lisabeth, "Financial Supermarkets Suffer Setback," *American Banker*, April 4, 1989, pp. 1+.

Article 24

Robert T. Clair
Senior Economist
Federal Reserve Bank of Dallas

Paula K. Tucker
Economic Analyst/Writer
Federal Reserve Bank of Dallas

Interstate Banking and the Federal Reserve: A Historical Perspective

I do not believe that we will ever reach a point in this country where we will have perfection in our banking legislation. We are, of course, in a changing economy and, looking over the past hundred years, we have found that no one has been able to develop a perfect system of money and banking.

—Marriner S. Eccles, Chairman
Federal Reserve Board
in congressional hearings
on the Banking Act of 1935

For much of its history, the United States has had a banking system like no other in the industrialized world. Since the early 1800s, the U.S. banking system has been highly fragmented, consisting of numerous small banks without extensive branch systems. Banking organizations that expanded across state lines were extremely rare, and none had established nationwide networks. It is this lack of nationwide banks that distinguishes the banking system in the United States from the banking systems of other countries. Interstate geographic restrictions on banking have been lifted only recently, fostering the development of regional and, ultimately, nationwide banking.

Interstate banking raises several issues that directly affect the Federal Reserve's mandate to maintain a safe and sound banking industry. Supporters have promoted interstate banking as a method for banks to diversify their risks. Opponents have argued that interstate banking permits banks to become "too big to fail"; that is, the Federal Deposit Insurance Corporation (FDIC) will not close a large bank for fear of repercussions to other banks. Thus, permitting banks to grow through interstate banking may diminish incentives for soundness. Debates have also addressed whether interstate banking would increase bank efficiency or promote a concentration of banking power resulting in a higher cost and a misallocation of credit. The Federal Reserve has been an important player in the interstate banking debate because it has been the traditional regulator of bank holding companies, the corporate organizational form that would likely be used to establish an interstate banking network.

Over its 75-year history, the Federal Reserve's position has evolved from opposition to support of interstate banking. This article discusses interstate banking in a historical context and suggests the sources of the initial opposition to interstate banking. The authors document the softening of the Federal Reserve's opposition over the years and present evidence of the Fed's currently supportive position. This evolution results largely from disentangling the issue of interstate banking from other issues, such as monopolistic power and political influence resulting from the concentration of financial power.

The origins of interstate financial organizations in the United States date back to the late eighteenth century. Two main forms of interstate organizations developed at different times: interstate branching and interstate banking. Interstate branching developed first with the chartering of the First Bank of the United States in 1791. Interstate branching permits a bank to operate branch offices in states other than the state in which the head office is located. Interstate banking, which began to develop in the late 1800s, allows banking organizations to operate fully chartered banks in more than one state.

In this article, interstate branching and interstate banking will be considered as a single issue; however, the differences between the two are not inconsequential. Interstate branching has the potential to be a more efficient organizational form that could provide better banking services to certain customers. Advantages would include more efficient deposit-taking services for national organizations and the reduction or complete elimination of the need for cash concentration and check collection services. Because branches are typically less costly to establish than separately chartered banks, interstate branching would offer more banking offices than interstate banking.

Interstate banking: guilt by association

The fact that the United States did not have interstate banking for much of its history and that today it does not have full interstate banking is directly related to opposition to the first two national banks. Early in U.S. history banks were chartered by special acts of either state or federal legislatures. In the eighteenth and early nineteenth centuries, a national bank charter implied that the bank was chartered by federal authority and was empowered to operate nationwide. Following the passage of the National Banking Act of 1864, national banks were chartered by federal authority, which Congress had delegated to the Office of the Comptroller of the Currency. Bank operations, however, were restricted to a single location, the polar extreme of a nationwide operation.

Congress chartered two national banks. The First Bank of the United States — chartered from 1791 to 1811 — encountered opposition, and Congress failed to renew its charter. Congress later chartered the Second Bank of the United States in 1816, which operated for 20 years until President Andrew Jackson vetoed the congressional bill to renew its charter.

These two national banks faced opposition because of the characteristics of their charters. The banks were granted exclusive national charters; therefore, they enjoyed a monopoly in the provision of nationwide banking services. Be-

cause their charters permitted them to establish branches across state lines, they operated with a distinct advantage over state-chartered banks. Both the First and Second Banks were very large organizations, and their size was at least partially attributable to the government's role in subscribing a large part of their capital stock. The Second Bank controlled more than one-third of all banking assets at the time (Chandler 1959, 137). In both instances, some bank directors, several of whom were appointed by the federal government, neglected to dismiss political factors when making bank decisions.

The problems inherent in the structures of the First and Second Banks of the United States could have been addressed largely by eliminating their monopolistic positions. Had more national charters been granted, competition might have reduced some of the criticisms directed at these banks. For example, arguments of undue concentration of financial power would have been more difficult to substantiate if several large national banks were operating. Proponents of easier monetary conditions would have found it more difficult to focus their attacks if the supply of bank notes had been controlled by not one but by several banks.

Another problem in the chartering of the monopolistic national banks was that the banks were politically active. The chartering of the First and Second Banks was a contested political issue between the Federalists, led by Alexander Hamilton, and the anti-federalists. The Federalists supported the ratification of the Constitution and wished to see strong centralized power in the federal government. They supported the federal chartering of banks and preferred to see the United States develop a commercial and industrial economy. The anti-federalist forces, including Thomas Jefferson's Democratic-Republican party, supported greater political power vested in the states. Jefferson and his supporters wanted the states to issue bank charters and they preferred to see the United States develop an agricultural economy.

Given the political differences between the two groups, it is not surprising that charges of favoritism were lodged regarding the banking operations of the nationally chartered banks. Lester V. Chandler reported accusations that the First Bank "was dominated by Federalists and that it discriminated against anti-Federalists in making loans" (Chandler 1959, 135). The charges against the Second Bank were more direct; it granted loans to influence votes. Furthermore, the president of the Second Bank, Nicholas Biddle, openly opposed President Andrew Jackson (Chandler 1959, 137).

The exercise of political power by these organizations was often erroneously attributed to their size. Certainly their size increased their political power, but the fact that they exercised the power at all is more likely the result of their monopolistic charters. If these banks had been in competition with other national banks, then their failure to grant loans to anti-federalists only would have created profitable opportunities for their competitors to exploit.

The primary factor affecting the exercise of political power by the First and Second Banks was the federal government's role as a stockholder. The government owned one-fifth of the capital stock of both of these banks. Five of the directors of the First Bank were appointed by the government and included members of Congress and well-known Federalists (Johnson 1988, 8, and Holdsworth and Dewey 1910, 34). With regard to the Second Bank, the President of the United States, with Senate approval, appointed five of the twenty-five directors (Hammond 1957, 244). One of the presidential appointees to the board of directors, Nicholas Biddle, was president of the Second Bank from 1823 to 1839 (Hammond 1957, 291).

Additional opposition came from state-chartered banks that saw the First and Second Banks as interlopers on their own government-granted monopolies. State-chartered banks of this era were also established by special acts of state legislatures. The requirement of legislation posed a significant barrier to entry that lessened competition. The national charters of the First and Second Banks created the right to establish interstate branches, and thus, created new competition for state banks. The state banks had every incentive to support political forces opposed to the national banks.

It might be argued that state banks both won and lost their fight against the Second Bank of the United States. Shortly after the demise of the Second Bank, many states enacted banking incorporation laws that granted bank charters to anyone meeting general requirements, thereby ending the practice of special charters through acts of legislation. These new laws eliminated an important barrier to entry in the banking industry and helped eliminate the monopolistic power of the specially chartered banks. By vigorously pointing out the evils of monopoly, state banks set the stage for their own loss of protection from competition.

The history of the First and Second Banks unfortunately left interstate branching (and interstate banking) guilty by association. The First and Second Banks were criticized because of their monopolistic power and their exertion of undue political influence. Their opponents also condemned interstate organization and size, neither of which were at the root of the problem. Interstate banking creates opportunities for large banks to develop; however, size alone is not a sufficient condition to establish monopolistic power, especially if there are no barriers to entry.

State banks argued against interstate organization, focusing primarily on the distribution of credit within the country. Opponents of interstate banking argued that interstate banks would redirect credit away from rural areas into cities. There is little empirical or theoretical evidence to support this argument. Money should flow to where it earns the highest return regardless of the banking structure (Scheld and Baer 1986, 75–76).[1]

Events surrounding the First and Second Banks dramatically influenced banking legislation and regulation. Most states passed beneficial legislation to establish bank incorporation laws that reduced barriers to entry and increased competition in banking. The fear of concentration of financial power and undue influence, however, fostered detrimental restrictions designed to limit bank growth. Government-imposed geographic restrictions against branch banking limited the size of banks. It was thought, perhaps erroneously, that these laws would also force banks to lend in their local communities. Country banks placed some of their deposits in interest-earning accounts

---

[1] It should be noted, however, that to the extent the First and Second Banks used their monopolistic position to play politics with their loan decisions, there may have been cases where loans were granted to urban Federalists and denied to rural anti-federalists.

at city banks if these deposits offered higher returns than local loans.

The restrictions against branch banking resurfaced following the passage of the National Banking Act of 1864. Although the text of the legislation contained no references to branch banks, the Comptroller of the Currency's interpretation of the act prohibited national banks from establishing branches. This prohibition resulted from fear that national banks would establish interstate banking operations and represent a concentration of financial power. In 1922, the Office of the Comptroller of the Currency reversed its position and began to approve branches. With the McFadden Act in 1927, Congress removed any ambiguity concerning the power of national banks to establish branches. The act permitted national banks to establish branches within the city of their head office operations if state banks could do the same. In 1933 amendments to the act permitted national banks to branch wherever state banks in the same state were allowed to branch. The McFadden Act, however, by its definition of permissible branching, effectively prohibited the establishment of interstate branches.

The combination of bank incorporation laws and branching restrictions in many states produced a highly fragmented banking system of small banks. Branching was relatively rare with only 87 banks operating a total of 119 branches in 1900 (Cagle 1941, 118). In 1913 there were 26,664 national and state banks holding $22,056 million in assets. There were 19,197 state banks accounting for more than 70 percent of all commercial banks. The average size of a state bank was $574,000 in assets, less than half the size of an average national bank (Board of Governors of the Federal Reserve System 1959, 35–44).

Interstate banking at the time of the Federal Reserve's creation

When Congress established the Federal Reserve System in 1913, some banks were attempting to build interstate networks. The industry was fragmented, but consolidation began with the development of two new types of multibank organizations: chain banks and group banks. These new banking structures were primarily methods to circumvent intrastate branching restrictions and

thereby reduce the fragmentation of the banking industry. To a lesser extent, these new structures were also used to create interstate organizations. Both of these structures were networks of separately chartered banks and, hence, these interstate networks represented the first form of interstate banking in U.S. history.

Chain banking is an informal form of multiple-office banking in which three or more banks are owned or controlled by the same individual or individuals. Organizationally, the banks are formally unrelated to one another and each has a completely independent charter. Stockholders who are common to all the banks in the chain effectively control these banks. These stockholders need not hold 100 percent of the stock of each bank, only a controlling share.

Chain banks date back to at least 1890. Their unique structure and the relative lack of regulation concerning chain banks makes it difficult to trace their development. Chain banks were primarily an alternative to branch offices in states where branching was restricted. The first chain banks began in the Northwest and South. Chain banking grew rapidly from 1900 to 1920. Growth peaked in 1925. By the end of 1931, when the first accurate data on chain banks became available, 176 chains were operating 908 banks with aggregate assets of $927 million. Over time the number of chains and the number of their associated banks declined, but their financial size grew. By the end of 1945, when the number of chains had dropped to 115 operating 522 banks, their total deposits had risen to $4,628 million.

Some early chain banks crossed state lines, establishing interstate banking organizations. For example, in 1926 the Witham-Manley chain included 175 banks operating in Georgia and Florida (Lamb 1962, 56). By the end of 1939 there were 18 interstate chains (Cagle 1941, 127). C.E. Cagle states that "… under existing legislation neither group nor chain systems are prohibited from taking in banks from the Atlantic to the Pacific. Although no chain or group system operates banks from coast to coast, many have banking offices in several States" (Cagle 1941, 140).

While it did not become totally extinct, chain banking eventually evolved into group banking, a more formal structure of multiple-office banking. In this structure a controlling organization, usually a holding company, holds controlling stock, often 100 percent, in the affiliated banks. Each bank is a separately chartered bank with its own board of directors and its own corporate identity. The holding company provides supervision and assistance in developing loan and investment policies. The main advantage of the group bank over that of a chain bank is that the holding company can raise capital in the financial markets so that the group bank's growth is less constrained. In contrast, chain banks were limited by the financial resources of the individual or individuals who formed the chain. Furthermore, because it involves a corporation, a group bank's control over its affiliated banks is presumably perpetual, while chain banks often dissolve following the estate settlement of one of the key stockholders.

The exact date of origin of group banking is somewhat uncertain, primarily because no distinction was made between group and chain banks in banking data collected prior to the late 1920s. Cagle reports that one bank holding company was formed prior to 1900, even before the creation of the Federal Reserve System.[2] The major expansion of group banking occurred in the late 1920s, coincident with the stock market boom. The major bank holding companies found a ready market for their securities. By 1931 there were 97 group banking systems operating 978 banks with an additional 1,219 branch offices.

Early in their development, group banks were used to establish interstate banking organizations. W. Ralph Lamb reports that at least six large bank holding companies crossed state lines. When Transamerica Corporation was formed in 1928, the founders intended to establish six regional holding companies that would serve the entire nation. An article titled "Branch, Chain, and Group Banking: December 1929" (Board of Governors of the Federal Reserve System 1930, 148) reports that 10 of the 34 largest group banking organizations operated in more than one state. One of these was a Minneapolis-based group-banking system controlling banks in eight states.

Early Federal Reserve policy toward interstate banking

Early in its history, the Federal Reserve System viewed the development of interstate banking negatively. The issue of interstate banking was often intertwined with the issue of branch banking and the fear of concentration of financial power, whether justified or not. Simultaneously, the Federal Reserve also had to handle the issue of Federal Reserve System membership. Every piece of banking legislation was considered not only for its intrinsic merits, but also for whether it would encourage or discourage Fed membership; an example is the Fed's position concerning branching for national banks.

In 1924 Congress held hearings on the branching privileges of national banks. National banks operated at a disadvantage in many states because state banks were permitted to operate branch offices while national banks were restricted to operating a single office. Eventually the law was changed by the McFadden Act in 1927, which restricted national banks to operating branch offices in the city of their head office in states that permitted branching.[3]

Nationwide branching was discussed during the 1924 hearings preceding the McFadden Act. The testimony of two members of the Federal Reserve Board, Governor D. R. Crissinger and Vice Governor Edmund Platt, indicated that extensive interstate branching or banking would not be considered a positive development. Their objections seem to be based on arguments of undue concentration of financial power. While they did not object to branching across state lines, they opposed extensive national branching networks. Despite these objections, the Fed not

---

[2] W. Ralph Lamb, however, reports that, "[T]he Marine Bancorporation, formed in Seattle during the summer of 1927, was the first independently capitalized bank holding corporation organized primarily for that purpose." Sydney Hyman reported that the 1928 formation of the First Security Corporation "was the first time the [holding company device] was used in banking."

[3] The McFadden Act was later amended in 1933 to permit national banks the same branching privileges as existed for state banks located in the same state.

only supported the limited easing of branching restrictions on national banks included in the McFadden Act but also supported statewide branching for national banks. Because national banks were required to be members of the Federal Reserve System, the Fed did not want any restrictions that might discourage a bank from operating under a national charter and thereby discourage membership.

When Vice Governor Platt testified to the House Committee on Banking and Currency, he was asked by Congressman W. F. Stevenson of South Carolina about the advisability of permitting national banks in New York City to establish branches in New Jersey. Platt responded, "If the State law allowed banks in the city of New York to establish branches in contiguous territory, I would see no reason why they should not go to Newark provided the people of New Jersey would agree to it" (U.S. Congress 1924, 211). While this statement indicates that Platt would support interstate branching, he limited his support only to branches that would operate in a relatively close proximity to the head office of the bank. Congressman William Williamson of South Dakota summarized Platt's position as, "You are not going so far as to advocate nation-wide branches for Federal Banks, the only suggestion being that it might be wise to permit a branch in a locality contiguous to the city, even if it were necessary to cross the State line?" Platt agreed (U.S. Congress 1924, 219).

Governor Crissinger was hostile toward interstate branching and was not particularly supportive of intrastate branching. Crissinger told the committee:

> I do not believe that this country is ready for national branch banking systems. Personally I would be opposed to them.... I further am of the opinion that the country is not ready for State-wide branch-banking systems in all the States. (U.S. Congress 1924, 231)

Crissinger's opposition to chain banking, especially involving interstate banking, was made clear by the following exchange with Chairman Louis T. McFadden:

> *The Chairman....* So it is my understanding that at least one of those five banks out there is not confining its activities to branches, but they are attempting to control through the chain-banking method not only California but other States. They are proposing to expand that way. I do not know what you think about it, but it strikes me that is breeding a dangerous situation in banking.
>
> *Mr. Crissinger.* I agree with you.
>
> *The Chairman.* It has been clear to me for some time that this committee ought to consider some kind of a restriction on chain banking. It is a menace in this country.
>
> *Mr. Crissinger.* The board has no restrictions on it, because we have no authority to put restrictions on it. But it is notorious that we have banks in the system that not only own the stock of the member banks but they have allied institutions which own stock in various banking concerns in this country and some out of this country. (U.S. Congress 1924, 236)

Crissinger, however, believed that federal law should not abrogate state law on branching. He recommended that national banks in a given state receive the branching privileges permitted to state banks in that state, a position that would encourage, or at least not discourage, Fed membership. The Fed was opposed to extensive interstate organizations regardless of whether the vehicle was branch banking or group banking.

Regulation of the bank holding companies

After their rapid growth in the late 1920s, group banks came under greater scrutiny. Both federal regulators and legislators sought to obtain greater control over these new organizations outside the current structure of bank regulation. The Federal Reserve System used its control over granting membership to restrict member banks from obtaining control of other banks. The Fed's limitations on member banks, however, only further discouraged membership.

The range of suggested legislation was extreme. Some proposals called for "death sentence" legislation for group banks that would break up existing holding companies. Others suggested "freeze" legislation that would have prevented any further acquisitions by holding companies. Such extreme suggestions usually came from unit banks, the competitors of group banking systems. The legislation that was eventually passed in 1933 was intended to provide the Federal Reserve with the ability to control but not to prohibit the further expansion of the group banking systems.

The first important piece of legislation dealing with group banking systems was the Banking Act of 1933. This act is primarily remembered for requiring the separation of investment banking and commercial banking and for establishing the Federal Deposit Insurance Corporation. With regard to group banking, this act defined a "holding company affiliate" as any company "(1) which owns or controls, directly or indirectly, either a majority of the shares of capital stock of a member bank or more than 50 per centum of the number of shares voted for the election of directors of any one bank at the preceding election, or controls in any manner the election of a majority of the directors of any one bank; or (2) for the benefit of whose shareholders or members all or substantially all the capital stock of a member bank is held by trustees" (Lamb 1962, 174). Group banking systems were now referred to as holding company affiliates.

Regulatory control over the holding company affiliates was established through the granting of a "voting permit." The Banking Act of 1933 required that a holding company affiliate obtain a voting permit from the Federal Reserve Board to vote its shares of member bank stocks. To obtain a voting permit the holding company affiliate must agree to regular reporting and examination, to separation of investment from commercial banking, to maintain liquid reserves, to limit dividends to actual earnings, and to be subject to the same criminal penalties as pertained to member banks with regard to false entries.

The primary regulatory concern about the existence of holding company affiliates, or bank holding companies as they later came to be known, was that these holding companies should not financially weaken their affiliated member banks. For example, the amount of credit that could be extended by the affiliated member banks to the holding company was limited to 10 percent of capital stock. Another view was that bank holding companies should not be able to undertake any activities that would have been prohib-

ited for banks. This restriction was a very narrow prohibition against the ownership of a majority interest in both a member bank and an entity principally engaged in investment banking (Huertas 1988, 744). There was nothing in the Banking Act of 1933, however, that would prevent further interstate banking. As Lamb reiterated the idea stated by Cagle, "nothing prohibited group systems from taking in banks from the Atlantic to the Pacific prior to the 1956 legislation" (Lamb 1962, 177).

While the Banking Act of 1933 was important as the first piece of legislation to regulate bank holding companies, it was hopelessly inadequate to achieve regulation as some members of Congress had intended. The act had several major loopholes that permitted many of the bank holding companies to avoid regulation entirely. First, the act applied to a holding company only if at least one of its affiliates was a member bank. Consequently, group banks comprised of only state-chartered nonmember banks were not affected by the legislation. In some instances members of group banking systems withdrew from the Federal Reserve System to avoid the need to obtain a voting permit. Furthermore, the definition of holding company was too restrictive because it was possible to control an affiliated bank by owning much less than 50 percent of the stock. In addition, the act applied only if the bank holding company desired to vote its shares. In some cases, the control of the affiliated banks was possible without the voting of shares. In 1952 more than 40 percent of bank holding companies were not subject to federal regulation (Lamb 1962, 177).

A softening of Federal Reserve opposition: discord on the Board

Federal Reserve policy regarding interstate banking softened by the early 1930s. In 1926, Governor Crissinger stated quite clearly that he had little use for chain or group banks extending across state lines. By 1933, however, many of the interstate group banks had provided valuable services during the period of financial crisis. In many instances the strength of the bank holding company was used to stabilize its affiliated banks, demonstrating the potential for the bank holding company structure to reduce bank failures.[4] In more than one instance, bank holding companies acquired failed banks and re-established banking services, which helped the effected communities recover (Lamb 1962, 94–97). The positive contributions made by the bank holding companies during this period helped temper the 1933 legislation from the previous suggestions of "death penalties" or "freezes."

Opinions of the members of the Federal Reserve Board were not uniform with regard to interstate banking. Furthermore, in the discussion of legislation in the 1930s, the issue of interstate banking overlapped considerably with the issue of branching. When testifying in 1930, Roy A. Young, Governor of the Federal Reserve Board, made it clear that he was representing only his opinion and not a unanimous opinion of the Board with his statement to the committee.

Young supported the position of John Pole, Comptroller of the Currency, which proposed that the national banks be permitted to branch within a trade area that might exceed state boundaries. Young stated his view of how this might work to the committee.

> So I have come to the same conclusions that the Comptroller of the Currency has, that a trade area is the proper thing at the moment. To describe a definite trade area is extremely difficult. If the Federal reserve act intended to have the Federal reserve system do it, I might say that they did it as well as they could with 12 regional banks, and we have since extended that by the establishment of 25 branches, and even that is not 100 per cent perfect. (U.S. Congress 1930, 501)

Young's statement implies a willingness to permit national banks to branch across state lines just as the Federal Reserve Districts cross state lines. He also stated a preference for interstate branching as opposed to interstate banking through chain and group banks.

Diversity of opinion on the Federal Reserve Board continued after Eugene Meyer became

Governor following Young. Meyer was willing to support branching on a limited scale, although it is unclear whether he would have supported either interstate branching or banking. During his testimony in a Congressional hearing in 1923, Meyer stated, "Branch banking may be good or it may be bad. It may be good if carried on in a limited way and bad if permitted on an extensive scale" (Krooss 1969, 2679). Meyer reread this quotation into the *Congressional Record* in the early 1930s, suggesting that his position had not changed. But the Board could not reach an agreement on the issue, and this lack of unanimity was stated clearly by Meyer when testifying to the Senate Committee on Banking and Currency.

While Young's supportive opinion and the diversity of opinion on the Board indicated a softening of the resistance to interstate banking, the Fed's position reversed sharply in the early 1940s. In the 1943 Annual Report of the Board of Governors of the Federal Reserve System, the Board recommended "that immediate legislation be enacted preventing further expansion of existing bank holding companies or the creation of new bank holding companies. Such legislation should be so designed as to prevent any such company from using the corporate device to circumvent and evade sound banking principles, regulatory statutes, and declared legislative policy." Surprisingly, this recommendation occurred when Marriner S. Eccles was the Chairman of the Board of Governors. Before he joined the Board of Governors, Eccles was credited as possibly the first banker to establish an interstate multibank holding company.

The Transamerica case

The Federal Reserve's recommendation for "freeze" legislation was driven by the desire to halt the expansion of one particular bank holding company. The Board's statement was clear that most bank holding companies are cooperative in the regulatory process. The statement then focused on the "exceptional case" where the corporate device was used to challenge the Board's ability to regulate, to expand into extraneous businesses including industrial and manufacturing concerns, to circumvent state branching laws, and to concentrate financial power and permit

---

[4] Nonetheless, there were failures among the affiliated banks of bank holding companies. From 1930 to 1933, 200 affiliated banks with deposits of more than $1 million suspended operations.

financial manipulation. While the Board did not name the "exceptional case," this proposal for legislation was aimed at Transamerica Corporation.

Transamerica Corporation was founded in 1928 and operated by Amedeo P. Giannini. Beginning with the Bank of Italy, and later the Bank of America, Giannini redefined the provision of banking services, especially in expanding access to the banking system to the average individual. He was a pioneer in the establishment of extensive branch networks and retail banking, and he supported nationwide branch banking.

Many of the charges made by the Board hardly seem like accusations. Certainly, Giannini was establishing extensive branch networks, but the Board had supported statewide branch banking in the past. Transamerica was hardly "the exceptional case" in maintaining a structure that permitted it to operate without a Federal Reserve voting permit, nor was it the only holding company that owned nonbanking businesses.

The Board's arguments regarding Transamerica appear to be based on fear of undue concentration of financial power that might be used to exploit monopolistic power in banking and in other industries. Again, as in the case of the First and Second Banks of the United States, the issues of monopoly and undue influence became intertwined with interstate operations and size. Important differences existed between these two situations. The First and Second Banks held statutory monopolies and faced limited competition. Transamerica Corporation, in contrast, built its sizable organization while in competition with other existing banks and while facing potential competition from new entrants. The Transamerica situation is complicated further by the twist of separating banking and nonbanking enterprises.

Beginning in 1945 the Board of Governors proposed specific bills to regulate bank holding companies. Hearings were held on many of these bills, but it was not until 1956 that the Bank Holding Company Act was finally passed. The delay in passing legislation may be attributed to the change in the political agenda during the transition from the Roosevelt to the Truman administrations. Roosevelt's administration had to deal with the Great Depression and World War II, while Truman's was more focused on the transition to a peace-time economy. A clash of the personalities

of regulators, politicians, and bankers also may have been involved.

Henry Morgenthau, Jr., was the Secretary of the Treasury from 1934 to 1945. In the late 1930s, Morgenthau asked the federal regulators of banks, including the Federal Reserve Board, to review their position on the concentration of financial power arising in bank holding companies. Morgenthau was particularly concerned about the rapid growth of Transamerica Corporation, a bank holding company in California that owned Bank of America, other banks in several states, and a variety of nonbanking companies. While the federal regulators agreed that bank holding companies needed greater regulation, no compromise could be established as to which agency should regulate them. Meanwhile, Transamerica Corporation continued to expand its operations.

In 1943 the Federal Reserve Board, together with the Comptroller and the FDIC, notified Transamerica that they would decline permission for Transamerica to directly or indirectly acquire any more banking offices. Eccles met with Transamerica officers and obtained a "stand-still" pledge from Giannini. Despite the pledge, Transamerica resumed acquiring banks, which was legal under federal law at the time. The agencies refused to permit Transamerica to convert these banks into branches of Bank of America.

By late 1945, Transamerica's expansion spurred the Board to investigate the possibility of initiating an antitrust suit against Transamerica, and the Board contacted the Justice Department for its opinion. Attorney General Thomas C. Clark responded that the evidence would probably not support a case against Transamerica under the current legal standards. Because the judicial approach seemed blocked, the Federal Reserve Board pursued a legislative solution, proposing bills to regulate bank holding companies.

By the time the proposed legislation for bank holding company regulation was prepared, Morgenthau was no longer Secretary of the Treasury. The Secretary in 1946 was John W. Snyder. The change in the Secretary was important because Snyder was more favorably disposed toward Transamerica Corporation. Snyder personally had brought the work done by Giannini in directing credit to post-war Europe to the attention of President Truman (James and James 1954,

478–79). It is likely that Snyder's unwillingness to support the bank holding company legislation prevented its passage for several years; Snyder was a master at hindering legislation he opposed.

Snyder left the Treasury Department in 1953 following Eisenhower's presidential victory. Hearings on a banking holding company bill were held in 1955 and a bill limiting bank holding company activities was passed in 1956.

During this period of blocked legislation from 1945 to 1955, the Federal Reserve did not stand idle with regard to Transamerica. Following a new judicial interpretation of antitrust law, the Board in 1947 again requested the attorney general to evaluate the potential of an antitrust suit against Transamerica. Two significant events followed. First, Snyder had requested that the attorney general advise him of all matters concerning Transamerica. The attorney general sent the Board's request to Snyder where it was held without action. Second, the joint agreement between the Federal Reserve, the FDIC and the Comptroller refusing to grant any permits to Transamerica to convert banks into branches was breaking down. The Comptroller, under what appears to be pressure from Snyder, began to grant Transamerica's requests. The Board assessed the situation and in November 1947 investigated Transamerica Corporation for violation of the Clayton antitrust laws. This case was not fully resolved until 1953 when the United States Court of Appeals set aside the Board's ruling against Transamerica.

---

[5] It is unfair to condemn Transamerica Corporation for controlling 79 percent of the banking deposits in Nevada. In 1933, the governor of Nevada approached Transamerica and requested that they take over a chain of failed banks. While the chain was beyond redemption, Giannini entered the state through the purchase of an existing bank and established a branching network (Fischer 1962, 52). Giannini's efforts are credited with greatly aiding the state's economic recovery.

[6] It is unclear why Eccles expanded this "axiom" to require the divestment of the nonbanking corporations. Certainly a prohibition on the lending by a banking affiliate to any other affiliate in the bank holding company would have been effective.

Federal Reserve softens policy

Despite the Federal Reserve's reaction to Transamerica Corporation, its position on bank holding companies and particularly on interstate banking through holding companies was neutral in the late 1940s and early 1950s. The issue of the regulation of bank holding companies was clouded by the Transamerica case, which was focused on the degree of bank concentration and, to a lesser extent, the mixing of banking and commerce. In his 1947 testimony to the Senate Committee on Banking and Currency, Eccles reported that Transamerica controlled 43 percent of total deposits in California, nearly 45 percent of the deposits in Oregon, and 79 percent of the deposits in Nevada.[5] Eccles believed that such concentration "destroys the whole principle of competitive banking" (U.S. Congress 1947, 26). Eccles also listed a number of the nonbanking enterprises owned by Transamerica and stated that it is "axiomatic that the lender and the borrower or potential borrower should not be dominated or controlled by the same management" (U.S. Congress 1947, 15).[6]

The Board's harsh position against bank holding companies in 1943 moderated substantially by 1947 when hearings were held on proposed bank holding company legislation. The proposed legislation did not restrict interstate banking through bank holding companies at all. Possibly the clearest statement of Federal Reserve policy with regard to bank holding companies came from Eccles during his testimony before the Senate Committee on Banking and Currency in May 1947. In describing the proposed bill, Eccles stated:

What this bill does is to exercise control over holding companies. ...There were certain evils and abuses which had developed in this field and there was an attempt on the part of Congress to regulate the situation, to give the Board power to regulate bank-holding companies. ...But we are not proposing here, and we think if we did propose it that we would not succeed, and see no use for proposing the death sentence or what may be known as the freeze. ...[W]e are not asking Congress to hold in this bill that the holding company is necessarily an evil. It can be abused, but in a great many, indeed in most of the instances, they have not abused their power. (U.S. Congress 1947, 21)

The proposed 1947 bill did not call for any restriction on interstate banking. The Fed appears to have accepted interstate banking as being permissible for a bank holding company. This is not totally surprising since Eccles had been an interstate banker prior to his joining the Federal Reserve, and the advantages of geographical diversification were presented as far back as the 1924 testimony of Vice Governor Platt.

By not requesting either a "death penalty" or a "freeze," it is clear that the Fed's position changed substantially since the call for legislation in the Annual Report of 1943. The proposed legislation in 1950 showed that Federal Reserve policy was essentially unchanged from the 1947 statement made by Eccles. In testimony for the 1950 proposed bill, Thomas B. McCabe, the new Chairman of the Board of Governors, stated that the new bill was very similar to the 1947 bill.

Another banking bill was introduced in 1952 that would have restricted interstate banking via the bank holding company. Specifically, Section 5(d) of H.R. 6504 prohibited any bank holding company from acquiring a bank located outside the state in which the bank holding company maintained its principal offices; furthermore, bank holding companies would be prohibited from acquiring any more banks in states that did not permit the operations of branches. This change was a substantial departure from the bank holding company bills proposed in 1947 and 1950.

The Federal Reserve was openly against such provisions in the 1952 bill. Twice the Fed's position was stated in the committee hearings. The first statement was in a letter submitted to the committee by William McChesney Martin, Jr., Chairman of the Board of Governors. The second was given in testimony to the Senate committee by Governor J. L. Robertson. Robertson stated:

> [T]he prohibition against expansion across State lines would mean that a State would be deprived of any right to express its policy as to the operation within its borders of a bank holding company having its principal office in another State....In our opinion, the States should be left entirely free to deal with bank holding company operations on a basis different from that on which they deal with

branch banking operations and to express their policy as to the operation of out-of-State holding companies within their borders. (U.S. Congress 1952, 25)

The Federal Reserve Board's position regarding interstate banking via the holding company device shifted from uncertain to supportive following the Banking Act of 1933 until the early 1950s. The reason for supporting interstate banking appears to have shifted over the years. Platt and Young recognized the positive aspects of diversification, but by 1955 Robertson supported the position by citing states' rights.

The Bank Holding Company Act of 1956

After more than a decade of proposed bills and hearings, the Bank Holding Company Act of 1956 was passed. The two main purposes of the act were to regulate further expansion of bank holding companies and to require the divestment of their nonbanking activities. Interstate banking was not the primary focus of the act, but an important legislative change in the act dictated the development of interstate banking in the United States until today.

The Banking Holding Company Act of 1956 evolved from a series of House and Senate bills. In 1955 the House of Representatives passed a bill, H.R. 6227, which would have prohibited any further interstate acquisitions by bank holding companies (Lamb 1962, 195). As stated above, the Federal Reserve Board opposed the restriction. Most of the debate concerning the restriction focused on the issue of states' rights and whether it was appropriate for Congress to dictate to the states whether a holding company can acquire a bank in their state. In the end, however, the restriction remained in the bill reported out by the House committee and passed by the House.

The Senate committee held hearings on several proposed bills concerning bank holding companies, including the House bill in the summer of 1955. The Senate bills included S. 880 and S. 2350. The first bill, S. 880, prohibited further interstate acquisition, similar to the House bill. The second bill, S. 2350, however, did not mention a restriction. In February 1956 the Senate committee produced a compromise bill, S. 2577, in which further interstate acquisitions were not prohibited. This bill was reported out of committee and sent to the Senate.

The issue of interstate banking was reintroduced during Senate debate on the bill. Senator Paul A. Douglas of Illinois introduced what is now known as the Douglas amendment, which prohibits further interstate acquisition unless the state involved specifically authorizes it by law. Douglas was opposed to big banks, which he believed failed to serve the needs of small businesses and borrowers. This argument is a variation of the argument that large banks would drain deposits away from rural areas to fund financial activity in the money centers. He stated that he was "unhappy" that the current bill permitted the already existing interstate bank holding companies to continue to operate their current networks of banks. The amendment was first proposed by the American Bankers Association and was heavily supported by the Independent Bankers Association. Despite the Federal Reserve's opposition, which was cited by Senator Robertson during the Senate debate, the Douglas amendment was passed and became part of the Bank Holding Company Act of 1956.

The passage of the Douglas amendment set the tone for interstate banking for the next two decades. The bank holding companies with existing interstate networks continued to operate their networks, a distinct competitive advantage over other banks. Because no state had passed a law that specifically authorized interstate acquisition, the Douglas amendment was effectively a prohibition against further interstate banking until 1978.[7] The passage of the Bank Holding Company Act of 1956 shifted the issue of interstate banking out of Congress and into state legislatures.

Development of state laws authorizing interstate banking

Maine was the first state to pass laws permitting interstate banking, thus ending the effective prohibition against expanded interstate banking

brought about by the Bank Holding Company Act of 1956 via the Douglas amendment. Effective January 1, 1978, Maine permitted interstate banking on a national reciprocal basis; that is, out-of-state bank holding companies were permitted to acquire Maine banks if Maine bank holding companies were granted similar privileges in the acquiring bank holding company's state (Amel 1988, 24).

Maine was alone, however, in its effort to establish interstate banking until 1982 when both New York and Alaska passed interstate banking laws. The New York law, which became effective June 28, 1982, was similar to Maine's in providing for interstate banking on a national reciprocal basis. Alaska's law differed in that effective July 1, 1982, it permitted open entry for all states; that is, there was no reciprocity requirement.

Open-entry interstate banking law as was passed in Alaska was more likely in states where banks were facing financial difficulties. First, bank holding companies in these states were not in a position to make acquisitions; hence, reciprocity was less important. Second, the absence of a reciprocity requirement created a larger market for the acquisition of troubled institutions and higher acquisition prices. In addition, there were often restrictions that entry be made through the acquisition of existing banks. Third, some states with troubled financial institutions established interstate banking permitting only failed institutions to be acquired. This approach increased the ease with which regulators could deal with a troubled institution but protected the existing bank holding companies from undesired takeover attempts. Alaska, a large energy-producing state, was feeling the pain of the decline in oil prices in 1982 and its effect on the Alaskan banking industry, which influenced the decision to pass open-entry legislation.

Interstate banking activity accelerated from 1983 to 1985 with the creation of regional interstate pacts. Large banks within the region supported the law because it afforded them the potential advantages of interstate banking without competition from the money-center banks. The first pact was the New England pact encompassing Connecticut (1983), Maine (1978), Massachusetts (1983), New Hampshire (1987), Rhode Island (1984), and Vermont (1987). (The year in paren-

---

[7] There were some minor exceptions permitting additional acquisitions by specified bank holding companies in certain states.

thesis indicates when interstate banking took effect.) Because Maine was in this pact and Maine permitted interstate banking on a national reciprocal basis, Connecticut and Massachusetts put in place anti-leapfrogging clauses. Banks in these two states were worried about competing with the large money-center banks of New York. They envisioned the money-center bank holding companies acquiring a Maine bank holding company and then using the Maine bank holding company to make acquisitions throughout New England. The anti-leapfrogging clauses prevented the entry of New York banks into these two states.[8]

Other regional pacts began to develop shortly thereafter. In 1984 Kentucky passed an interstate banking law to establish a regional pact of Mid-Central states. Ohio, Tennessee, and Virginia joined this pact in 1985, and Illinois, Indiana, and Missouri joined in 1986. West Virginia finally joined the pact in 1988.

A third regional pact for Southeast states began in 1985 with interstate banking laws passed in the District of Columbia, Florida, Georgia, Maryland, North Carolina, Tennessee, and Virginia. South Carolina passed an interstate banking law the next year, and in 1987 Alabama and Louisiana joined the pact, followed by West Virginia in 1988.

Interstate banking continued to develop on a state-by-state basis. Additional regional pacts were formed and other states passed open-entry or national reciprocal legislation. The current status of interstate banking laws and their outlook for the early 1990s is presented later in this article. During this development of state laws permitting interstate banking, one federal law was passed that provided a limited liberalization of interstate banking. In October 1982 Congress passed the Garn-St Germain Depository Institutions Act of 1982. The act is primarily associated with the additional deregulation of interest rates on deposits, but one provision of the act authorized out-of-state acquisition of failed or failing banks and thrifts. The Garn-St Germain Act did not encourage interstate acquisitions but authorized them only to minimize the cost of dealing with failing institutions to the FDIC and the FSLIC.

Federal Reserve supports the development of interstate banking

The Federal Reserve saw as favorable that states were removing barriers to interstate banking. There was concern that regional pacts would create uneven development and consequently an unequal quality of banking services across the country. In testimony to the Senate Committee on Banking, Housing, and Urban Affairs on September 13, 1983, Chairman of the Board of Governors Paul Volcker stated:

These state actions are constructive in breaking down outmoded barriers but they also dramatically illustrate the haphazard and unequal development of interstate activity. A closely integrated economy requires and deserves more uniform rules in this important area....Similar doubts arise about the logic of proposals that a Providence, Rhode Island bank be able to purchase a bank two states and 150 miles away in southern Vermont, but that an Albany, New York bank 30 miles away be prohibited....For want of any better rule to assure gradualism and to take state preferences into account in the evolution of interstate banking, regional compacts have had an appeal to some as a transitional device. We are concerned, however, about the implications for a kind of balkanization of the process that could discriminate against banking organizations in some states and, without serving a legitimate local purpose, limit the ability of banks wishing to sell or merge to find an appropriate partner. (Volcker 1983, 30–31)

---

[8] The regional nature of interstate banking and the concern over the money-center banks dates back to the very beginning of group banking and interstate acquisitions. Lamb states that the conservative banks of Minnesota had close relationships with their city correspondent banks, especially in times of emergencies. Rumors surfaced that banks from New York and Chicago were attempting to gain control of the city correspondents in Minneapolis in order to gain access to the Twin City trade area. The Minnesota bankers chose to organize their key correspondents into group banks. The first was the Northwest Bancorporation in January 1929, and First Bank Stock Corporation was formed three months later.

Because many of the regional compacts were structured as temporary arrangements with eventual shifting to national reciprocal interstate banking, some of these concerns about regional compacts were probably overstated. The regional compacts were justified on the grounds of permitting the large regional banks to consolidate their positions prior to permitting the entrance of the much larger money-center banks.

Current Chairman of the Board of Governors Alan Greenspan also supports interstate banking. Prior to becoming Fed Chairman, Greenspan published a paper on the advantages of deregulation of product and geographic barriers. In that work he stated:

> Geographic diversification can similarly work to reduce risk. Assuming that capital remains adequate, there is no reason to expect lending in another state will be inherently more risky than lending in an institution's home state. Indeed, by diversifying to another regional and economic base, a bank has the opportunity to reduce its overall risk. (Greenspan 1987a, 16)

Chairman Greenspan has not changed his position on interstate banking since joining the Federal Reserve. In a statement before the House subcommittee on telecommunications and finance, Greenspan stated:

> Already 10 states have adopted full interstate banking, 13 states have provided for it after a transition period, and 8 additional states permit interstate acquisition of troubled banks. This constructive trend, especially when fully developed, will result in better service to customers and a strengthened banking system. (Greenspan 1987b, 4)

Current status of interstate banking in the United States

By 1989 the vast majority of states had passed some type of legislation enabling interstate banking. The status of interstate banking laws in the United States in April 1989 is shown on Map 1. The various types of legislation have been grouped into four categories, with the darkest shading of green indicating the most liberal laws concerning interstate banking. Nine states have passed legislation permitting acquisitions by bank holding companies from any other state, which is often referred to as open-entry and is the most liberal type of legislation. Nine states permit reciprocal interstate banking on a nationwide basis. Reciprocity implies that out-of-state bank holding companies are permitted to make acquisitions in a given state only if they are located in a state that grants similar privileges to bank holding companies located in the other state. For example, for an out-of-state bank holding company to make an acquisition in New York, it must be headquartered in a state that would permit New York bank holding companies to make acquisitions.

The most common form of interstate banking legislation is the regional compact, which is labeled regional reciprocal on the map. In a regional compact interstate banking is limited only to states specified in the enabling state legislation and reciprocity is required. These compacts are usually limited to adjacent states or to states that are contiguous to adjacent states. The regional compacts overlap in some states. Twenty-five states utilize regional compacts and some are quite large, including as many as twelve states. Interstate acquisitions are not permitted in seven states as of the date of this publication.

Substantial changes in interstate banking laws will occur in the next few years. Seven states that passed legislation for regional compacts also specified the shifting to more liberal interstate banking laws at a specified "trigger" date in the future. Many of these "trigger" dates are approaching. Furthermore, two states have recently passed legislation that will become effective in the next year. By 1993 nine more states, including some of the most populous, will permit either open-entry interstate banking or reciprocal interstate banking on a nationwide basis. The status of interstate banking in 1993 based on legislation that has already been passed is presented in Map 2.

A comparison of the two maps shows some striking regional shifts in interstate banking law. By 1993 the vast majority of the West and Southwest will permit national interstate banking on either an open-entry or national reciprocal basis. Similarly, most of the Great Lakes region will permit reciprocal interstate banking on a national basis by 1993. The areas showing the least change are the Southeast regional interstate compact and the New England regional compact. Prohibitions against interstate banking appear to be concentrated in the Great Plains states.

Summary

For most of its 75-year history, the Federal Reserve has supported interstate banking. Beginning with Crissinger in 1924, interstate banking was described as "a menace." By the early 1930s, however, various members of the Board were willing to accept group banks and interstate banking. Young even described the growth of group banks as "a natural development." This shift in attitude, together with the positive contributions of group banks during the Great Depression, led

to only a minor degree of regulation of these banks in the Banking Act of 1933.

Federal Reserve policy shifted sharply in the late 1930s and early 1940s in response to the rapid expansion of the Transamerica Corporation. Eccles described bank holding companies as a device "to escape the supervisory powers." Eccles' position moderated as legislation was proposed to close the loopholes that permitted some bank holding companies to escape supervision. By 1947 Eccles made it clear that he believed that bank holding companies were "not necessarily evil." The prevailing opinion of the Federal Reserve seemed to shift to one of regulated expansion with support for interstate expansion. In fact,

Map 1
Interstate Banking Regulation, April 1989

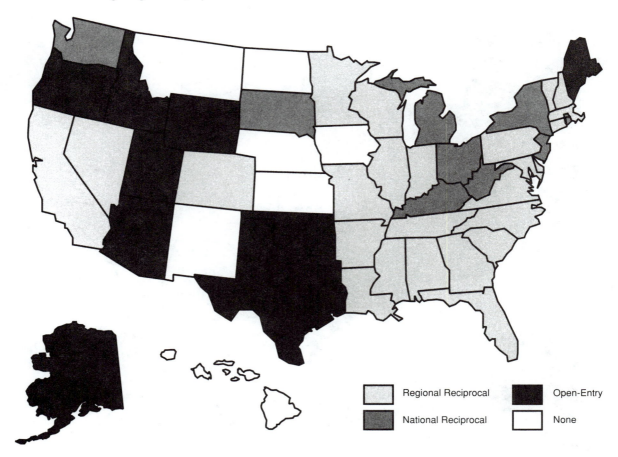

Regional Reciprocal   Open-Entry

National Reciprocal   None

SOURCE OF PRIMARY DATA: *American Banker*, 4 April 1989, 10.

when Congress suggested the prohibition of any further interstate expansion, Governors McCabe, Martin, and Robertson all voiced their opposition. Their opposition, however, was not sufficient to defeat the Douglas amendment to the Bank Holding Company Act of 1956, which prohibited further interstate acquisition unless specifically authorized by state law.

The Douglas amendment effectively stopped further interstate banking for two decades. In the late 1970s and early 1980s, however, state laws were enacted to permit interstate acquisitions. The Federal Reserve's position fully supported interstate banking. Volcker described these laws as breaking down "outmoded barriers." Volcker was concerned, however, that many states were passing laws that permitted interstate acquisition in limited geographical areas, and he preferred instead a system of full national interstate banking. Volcker recognized the concern that interstate banking would alter the nature of the U.S. banking system, and he responded to that concern.

I recognize the traditional and historic concern about local control of banking, the importance of healthy community banks, and the dangers from excessive concentration of resources. Fortunately, we have a good deal of experience within large states about the ability of small banks to survive and prosper alongside relative giants—and for the good

Map 2
Interstate Banking Regulation in 1993

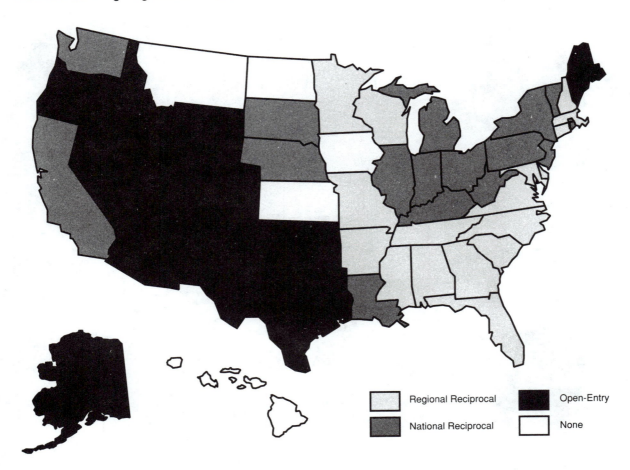

Regional Reciprocal

National Reciprocal

Open-Entry

None

SOURCE OF PRIMARY DATA: Amel (1988).

reason that they can operate efficiently and establish solid relations with local consumers and businesses....[P]roperly implemented and controlled I see no danger that the United States would be bereft of large numbers of smaller banks, or that, with appropriate safeguards, excessive concentration would become a problem. (Volcker 1983, 32)

Alan Greenspan, the current Chairman of the Federal Reserve, has described interstate banking as a "constructive trend" that will provide the country with "a strengthened banking system."

The change in the Federal Reserve's position over the years is likely the result of disentangling the issue of interstate banking from fears of concentration and undue influence of large banks. This disentangling occurred both inside and outside the Fed and spanned the chairmanships of several Fed leaders. Interstate banking has proven to be helpful in achieving the goals of the Federal Reserve. The safety and soundness of the banking industry will likely be enhanced since interstate banking provides additional opportunities for diversifying risks. It has also proven to be an effective mechanism for injecting needed capital into weak banks in economically depressed regions (*see the box: Interstate Banking in the Eleventh District*). The establishment of interstate networks will help banks be more efficient in providing services to their customers who also operate nationally. It is also likely to improve the efficiency of the nation's payment system by reducing the number of checks that must be cleared through the Federal Reserve (*see the box: The Effect of Interstate Banking on Federal Reserve Check Clearing*).

Interstate Banking in the Eleventh District States

Interstate banking is well advanced in the Eleventh Federal Reserve District. After entering into the Southeast regional compact in 1987, Louisiana has since moved to nationwide interstate banking on a reciprocal basis. An out-of-state bank holding company must acquire an existing bank, as *de novo* entry is prohibited. New Mexico currently permits interstate banking only for the acquisition of failing banks, but on January 1, 1990, it will permit open entry to banks from all states. New Mexico also prohibits *de novo* entry and further requires that the acquired bank be at least five years old at the time of acquisition. Texas currently permits open entry to banks from all states and also prohibits *de novo* entry. Texas law requires that the acquired bank have been in existence as of July 15, 1986, or in operation for at least five years prior to acquisition.

The push toward national interstate banking and the prohibitions against *de novo* entry result from the problems facing banks in the Southwest in the later half of the 1980s.

After the decline in energy prices and the collapse of the real estate market, many banks in this region faced loan losses sufficient to cause many of them to fail. The enactment of interstate banking laws improved the ability of regulators to deal with these failures and offered opportunities for banks that had not failed to diversify their operations and capital resources through interstate mergers.

Interstate mergers in Texas represent both the disposition of failed banks and the acquisition of healthy banking organizations. NCNB Corporation acquired First Republic-Bank, the state's largest bank, through an FDIC-assisted merger. BancOne Corporation of Columbus and Equimark Corporation of Pittsburgh also entered the Texas market by acquiring failed banks. In contrast, other banking organizations entered the Texas market through the acquisition of healthy banks including Chemical Banking Corporation of New York City; First Interstate Bancorp, Inc., of Los Angeles: Northern Trust Company of Chicago and Comerica Incorpoated of Detroit.

The Effect of Interstate Banking on Federal Reserve Check Clearing

The expansion of interstate banking in the U.S. will not only change the nation's banking system but also will cause significant changes in the Federal Reserve's payments system. The Federal Reserve currently clears about 15 billion of the estimated 40 billion checks written in the United States annually and is the only check clearing system serving the entire nation. In a study titled "Interstate Banking: Impacts on the Payments System" (September 1986), authors Allen Berger, David Humphrey, and Joanna Frodin, estimate the effects of interstate banking on the U.S. payments system.

Of the 40 billion checks written annually in the United States, about 28 billion end up in a bank other than where they originated and must be cleared. To be cleared, the average check is processed through an average of 2.4 financial institutions, one of which is usually part of the Federal Reserve. Depending upon whether the check originated inside or outside of a bank's Federal Reserve check processing zone, the check will be sent down one of seven check-clearing paths. Each path consists of a mix of private sector and Federal Reserve processing and/or transportation. Thirty-one billion checks remain inside the zone of the bank on which they are drawn; and, of these, Federal Reserve facilities perform processing, transporting, or both, on about 8 billion checks. When a check is first deposited outside its originating zone, however, its chances of being processed, transported, or both by the Fed increase substantially. In this instance, 7 billion of the 9 billion out-of-zone checks pass through a Federal Reserve facility.

Berger, Humphrey, and Frodin hypothesize that three factors are important in determining what portion of checks written are cleared or transported for clearing by the Federal Reserve: bank concentration, the average bank's size measured by its deposits, and the geographic dispersion of bank deposits.

Bank concentration is the number of banks serving a particular market; the more concentrated a market, meaning the fewer banks are serving it, the less demand for Federal Reserve check-clearing services. As bank size measured by total deposits increases, there is also less demand for Federal Reserve check-clearing services. Bank geographic dispersion is measured as the extent that the deposits of banks headquartered in a particular zone are held at bank offices outside this zone. The authors hypothesized that greater dispersion reduces demand for Federal Reserve check clearing. The development of interstate banking is expected to increase bank concentration, average bank size and bank geographic dispersion. Therefore, interstate banking is expected to reduce the volume of checks cleared through the Federal Reserve.

The estimation of the effects of nationwide interstate banking indicates the Federal Reserve's market share of check processing volume would decline from 37.5 percent to between 15 percent and 21 percent. This estimate is based on the assumption that 25 percent of total deposits in the nation will be held at banks with nationwide operations. The movement to nationwide interstate banking would also shift the demands for Federal Reserve services away from check processing toward accepting checks that have been fine sorted (already processed before delivery to the Fed) and toward increased use of the Federal Reserve's transportation network.

The total impact on the Federal Reserve payments system, however, would not be as large or as rapid as the numbers might suggest. Greater acceptability of checks is estimated to result in check volume growth of 4.8 percent after complete interstate banking, in addition to the normal growth of check usage of about 4.28 percent annually. The effect on the Federal Reserve, the authors note, would be a decline in volume of about 1 percent to 3 percent annually for about ten years.

References

Amel, Dean F. (1988), "State Laws Affecting Commercial Bank Branching, Multibank Holding Company Expansion, and Interstate Banking," (Washington, D.C.: Board of Governors of the Federal Reserve System, October).

Berger, Allen N., David B. Humphrey, and Joanna H. Frodin (1986), "Interstate Banking: Impacts on the Payments System," Research Papers in Banking and Financial Economics (Washington, D.C.: Board of Governors of the Federal Reserve System, September).

Board of Governors of the Federal Reserve System (1930), "Branch, Chain, and Group Banking: December 1929," *Federal Reserve Bulletin* 16 (April): 144–57.

———— (1943), *Thirtieth Annual Report* (Washington, D.C.: Board of Governors of the Federal Reserve System).

———— (1959), *All-Bank Statistics, United States 1896–1955* (Washington, D.C.: Board of Governors of the Federal Reserve System).

Bolger, Thomas F. (1981), "The McFadden Study: An Unsound Proposal for Community Banks," *Journal of Retail Banking* 3 (March): 41–44.

Cagle, C.E. (1941), "Branch, Chain and Group Banking," In *Banking Studies*, edited by E.A. Goldenweiser, Elliot Thurston, and Bray Hammond, 113–40 (Washington, D.C.: Board of Governors of the Federal Reserve System).

Carstensen, Peter C. (1989), "Public Policy Toward Interstate Bank Mergers: The Case for Concern," *Ohio State Law Journal* 49: 1397–1437.

Chandler, Lester V. (1959), *The Economics of Money and Banking,* 4th ed. (New York: Harper & Row).

Congressional Record (1956), 84th Cong., 2d sess., 102, pt. 5: 6856–63.

Eccles, Marriner S. (1951), *Beckoning Frontiers: Public and Personal Recollections.* Edited by Sidney Hyman (New York: Alfred A. Knopf).

Federal Reserve Committee on Branch, Group, and Chain Banking (1932), *Branch Banking in the United States.*

Fischer, Gerald C. (1961), *Bank Holding Companies* (New York: Columbia University Press).

Frieder, Larry A., and others (1985), *Commercial Banking and Interstate Expansion: Issues, Prospects, and Strategies* (Ann Arbor, Mich.: UMI Research Press).

Greenspan, Alan (1987a), "The Case for Deregulation of the Banking Industry," *American Banker,* 4 June, 15–16.

———— (1987b), "Greenspan Urges Congress to Tackle Regulatory Issues," Testimony before a House Subcommittee on Telecommunications and Finance on Oct. 5, 1987, *American Banker,* 13 October, 4, 12, 20.

Hammond, Bray (1957), *Banks and Politics in America from the Revolution to the Civil War* (Princeton: Princeton University Press).

Holdsworth, John Thom, and Davis R. Dewey (1910), *The First and Second Banks of the United States,* prepared for the National Monetary Commission (Washington, D.C.: Government Printing Office).

Huertas, Thomas F. (1988), "Can Banking and Commerce Mix?" *The Cato Journal* 7 (Winter): 743–62.

Hyman, Sidney (1976), *Marriner S. Eccles: Private Entrepreneur and Public Servant* (Stanford: Stanford University Graduate School of Business).

James, Marquis, and Bessie Rowland James (1954), *Biography of a Bank: The Story of Bank of America* (Westport, Conn.: Greenwood Press).

Johnson, Roger T. (1988), *Historical Beginnings ...The Federal Reserve* (Boston: Federal Reserve Bank of Boston).

Klebaner, Benjamin J. (1958), "The Bank Holding Company Act of 1956," *The Southern Economic Journal* 24 (January): 313–26.

Krooss, Herman E., ed. (1969), *Documentary History of Banking and Currency in the United*

States, vol. 4 (New York: Chelsea House Publishers).

Lamb, W. Ralph (1962), *Group Banking: A Form of Banking Concentration and Control in the United States* (New Brunswick, N.J.: Rutgers University Press).

Lown, Cara S., and John H. Wood (1989), "Are Reserve Requirement Changes Really Exogenous? An Example of Regulatory Accommodation of Industry Goals," Federal Reserve Bank of Dallas Research Paper no. 8911 (Dallas, July).

McCall, Alan S., and Donald T. Savage (1981), "The Interstate Banking Debate: Another Viewpoint," *Journal of Retail Banking* 3 (September): 31–38.

O'Driscoll, Gerald P., Jr. (1988), "Bank Failures: The Deposit Insurance Connection," *Contemporary Policy Issues* 6 (April): 1–12.

Scheld, Karl A., and Herbert Baer (1986), "Interstate Banking and Intrastate Branching: Summing Up," In *Toward Nationwide Banking: A Guide to the Issues,* edited by Herbert Baer and Sue F. Gregorash, 75–83 (Chicago: Federal Reserve Bank of Chicago).

Spong, Kenneth (1985), *Banking Regulation: Its Purposes, Implementation, and Effects,* 2d ed. (Kansas City, Mo.: Federal Reserve Bank of Kansas City).

Tippetts, Charles S. (1929), *State Banks and the Federal Reserve System* (New York: D. Van Norstrand Company).

U.S. Congress. House Committee on Banking and Currency (1924), *Consolidation of National Banking Associations, Etc.: Hearings on H.R. 6855,* 68th Cong., 1st sess. (Washington, D.C.: Government Printing Office).

——— (1930), *Branch, Chain, and Group Banking: Hearings on H. Res. 141,* 71st Cong., 2d sess. (Washington, D.C.: Government Printing Office).

—— (1935), *Banking Act of 1935: Hearings on H.R. 5357,* 74th Cong., 1st sess. (Washington, D.C.: Government Printing Office).

——— (1952), *Control and Regulation of Bank Holding Companies: Hearings on H.R. 6504,* 82d Cong., 2d sess. (Washington, D.C.: Government Printing Office).

——— (1955), *Control and Regulation of Bank Holding Companies: Hearings on H.R. 2674,* 84th Cong., 1st sess. (Washington, D.C.: Government Printing Office).

U.S. Congress. Senate Committee on Banking and Currency (1932), *Operation of the National and Federal Reserve Banking Systems: Hearings on S. 4115,* 72d Cong., 1st sess. (Washington, D.C.: Government Printing Office).

——— (1935), *Banking Act of 1935: Hearings Before a Subcommittee on S. 1715 and H.R. 7617,* 74th Cong., 1st sess. (Washington, D.C.: Government Printing Office).

——— (1947), *Providing for Control and Regulation of Bank Holding Companies: Hearings on S. 829,* 80th Cong., 1st sess. (Washington, D.C.: Government Printing Office).

——— (1950), *Bank Holding Bill: Hearings Before a Subcommittee on S. 2318,* 81st Cong., 2d sess. (Washington, D.C.: Government Printing Office).

——— (1955), *Control of Bank Holding Companies: Hearings Before a Subcommittee on S. 880, S. 2350, and H.R. 6227,* 84th Cong., 1st sess. (Washington, D.C.: Government Printing Office).

——— (1956), *Control of Bank Holding Companies: Hearings on Amendments to S. 2577,* 84th Cong., 2d sess. (Washington, D.C.: Government Printing Office).

——— (1958), *Bank Holding Company Act: Report of the Board of Governors Federal Reserve System,* 85th Cong., 2d sess. (Washington, D.C.: Government Printing Office).

Volcker, Paul A. (1983), "Statement before the Committee on Banking, Housing and Urban Affairs of the U.S. Senate" (Washington, D.C.: Board of Governors of the Federal Reserve System, 13 September).

Article 25

Challenges to Small Banks' Survival

*Sherrill Shaffer**

The annual number of bank failures in the U.S. has climbed dramatically in recent years. In the 32 years from 1943 through 1974, the number of bank failures nationwide requiring disbursements by the Federal Deposit Insurance Corporation never rose as high as 10 per year.[1] Since 1979, by contrast, the annual number

of failures has never been lower than 10 and has exhibited an almost exponential increase. A disproportionate number of such failures have occurred among the nation's smallest banks. It makes sense, therefore, to take a closer look at the health of the smallest banks and at their prospects for the 1990s.

Some indicators appear to suggest an optimistic picture. When interest rates were deregulated in 1980, and later when interstate banking began to proliferate, many people were concerned that the dozen or so largest banks (the multinationals) would swallow up most of the smaller banks. Fewer banks in each market, it was feared, might decrease competition. This

*Sherrill Shaffer, a Research Officer and Economist, heads the Banking and Financial Markets Section of the Philadelphia Fed's Research Department.

[1]Here, and throughout the article, a bank "failure" is defined to include not only liquidations but also forced mergers and open bank assistance—in short, any response to a distressed bank that involved a cost to the FDIC.

sort of massive consolidation has not occurred, however. The multinationals have been less acquisitive than some feared. Even though the mid-sized regional banks have been steadily buying up smaller competitors, there are still over 13,000 commercial banks nationwide, and a bit less than 10,000 separate banking organizations even allowing for multibank holding companies.

Several factors make it unlikely that the giant multinational banks will expand significantly at the expense of the smaller regional or community banks in the near future. In fact, compared with the multinationals, regional banks have exhibited superior growth and profitability over the past few years. Among other things, new regulations adopted in 1988 require off-balance-sheet items, such as loan commitments and standby letters of credit, to be accompanied by proportional amounts of equity capital.[2] Because multinationals have a large amount of such items, these regulations have further limited their ability to expand rapidly within the next few years; for a bank that barely meets the regulation, any expansion must be accompanied by a corresponding new issue of capital, and the cost of raising capital makes expansion less profitable for such banks.

The aggregate failure statistics and the recent behavior of the multinational banks might seem to suggest contradictory conclusions about the viability of the smallest banks. Resolving the issue requires a deeper look.

HOW HEALTHY
ARE THE SMALLEST BANKS?

Two sets of evidence can help us determine how viable the smallest banks are in today's market: statistical estimates of banking cost functions, and actual performance data.

Statistical Cost Studies. Dozens of studies

[2]See Moulton (1987).

on economies of scale in the banking industry have been carried out over the past 35 years. Many have been summarized in a handful of excellent survey articles.[3] Focusing on the question of whether expenses tend to rise less than proportionately with bank size, each of these studies measures the statistical relationship between historical data on size and total expenses. Various measures of bank size have been employed, such as assets, deposits, or the number of accounts; however, an essential element in all is to make allowance for the prices each bank must pay for its inputs, such as wages and rents. In general, all of the studies find that there is some minimum efficient size of bank. A bank falling below that level typically faces higher average costs than a larger bank and is therefore less able to compete effectively in the marketplace.

Much controversy exists over the exact threshold of efficient size. Most recent studies, which generally exclude banks with total assets larger than $1 billion, conclude that the minimum efficient scale lies somewhere in the range between $50 million and $200 million in total assets. Some estimates are outside this range, however. At least one puts the figure as low as $25 million in assets, while several studies of the largest banks have found a minimum efficient scale as large as 1,000 times this size.[4]

All studies agree that banks smaller than $25 million in assets are, on average, less efficient than larger banks, and nearly all agree that the true minimum efficient scale is at least $50 million.[5] On the basis of historical experience it

[3]See Gilbert (1984), Mester (1987), and Clark (1988).

[4]See Shaffer (1984, 1988), Hunter and Timme (1986), and Shaffer and David (1986).

[5]Sometimes these comparisons are complicated by the use of nominal rather than real (inflation-adjusted) measures of size, so that a figure of $25 million in 1975 dollars would correspond to perhaps twice that figure in 1988 dollars. Some studies measured bank size in terms of

seems fairly certain that, on average, banks with total assets below the range of $25 million to $50 million are handicapped by higher costs relative to larger banks. Since roughly one-third of all U.S. banks are smaller than $25 million and nearly 60 percent are smaller than $50 million, this finding could have potentially serious implications. At the same time, it is important to keep in mind that these patterns describe *average* banks and do not rule out the possibility that some individual small banks can be as cost efficient as larger ones.

Small-Bank Performance. Massive evidence from statistical cost studies thus suggests that as many as half of the nation's banks may be under financial pressure due to inefficiencies associated with small size. This finding is consistent with the recent pattern of bank failures alluded to earlier. Is there more specific evidence that would either corroborate or refute the implications of the cost studies?

It is sometimes claimed that there are at least two different types of banking customers.[6] Some want a full array of services while some want personalized service. A large bank may have an advantage over a smaller one in the range of services it can provide, but a small bank may have an advantage in offering personalized service. In that case a small bank, by catering to the second type of customer, may be able to match the profitability of a larger bank despite the overall cost structure.

Let's consider actual performance data for banks of various size categories. The ideal measure of performance would reflect both

profitability and risk, since a riskier bank must earn a higher return to compensate its owners for bearing the risk. In practice, no single statistic perfectly reflects these two factors, but a general picture can be obtained by looking at several measures. The rate of return on assets reflects raw profitability unadjusted for risk. The rate of return on equity would adjust the rate of return on assets for one component of risk, the leverage ratio, if equity is measured by market value rather than book value; however, the true market value of equity is not available for all banks, and there are other components of risk besides leverage. Therefore, return on equity, while useful to examine alongside the return on assets and other statistics, is not by itself a completely satisfactory measure of performance.

The rate of default on loans made by a bank indicates the average credit quality of its assets, the soundness of the bank's management and lending decisions, and the long-run prospects for the bank's survival. Two common measures of default are net charge-offs, reflecting actual defaults, and noncurrent loans, which have stopped repaying according to schedule but have not yet been officially written off by the banks. The number of failed banks within each size category, of course, provides an after-the-fact measure of health.

Some surveys from the financial press and other sources suggest the more comforting message that the community banks have been outperforming the multinational banks.[7] But

deposits, further complicating a cross-study comparison since assets typically exceed deposits by over 25 percent (1987 aggregate U.S. figure); thus, a minimum efficient scale of $25 million in deposits would imply a larger minimum efficient scale in terms of assets.

[6]Of course, it is an oversimplification to speak of only two types of consumers, but the point remains valid for a richer variety of tastes.

[7]For example, Rose (1988), in an article titled "Small Banks Recover; Big Banks Languish," reports survey data indicating a 1987 average return on assets of .81 percent for banks smaller than $100 million, .66 percent for banks with assets of $100 million to $1 billion, and .81 percent for banks larger than $1 billion. Danker and McLaughlin (1987) report that banks smaller than $100 million earned higher returns on assets than banks with assets between $100 million and $1 billion in every year from 1981 to 1984, and that both groups outperformed the giant money-center banks in every year from 1981 to 1986.

such conclusions are misleading, at least in part because they are based on too coarse a gradation of size categories; the "smallest banks" are defined as all those with assets smaller than $100 million or even $300 million.

What the Numbers Show. A finer gradation of size categories portrays a different picture. Figures 1 through 5 show various measures of profitability, loan quality, and failure rates for all insured U.S. commercial banks smaller than $500 million that were continuously in operation throughout each respective year. These banks are broken down into five size categories, with the smallest two being $0-25 million and $25-50 million.

Relative to banks with assets between $25 million and $500 million, banks smaller than $25 million show a discouraging and worsening picture.[8] From 1986 through 1988, these smallest banks, compared with larger banks, on average earned only two-thirds to three-fourths the rate of return on assets and as low as half the rate of return on equity. At the same time, they suffered up to 50 percent more noncurrent (problem) loans as a

percentage of total loans and over twice the net charge-off (loan loss) ratio, indicating more serious problems of credit quality than those faced by the larger banks. Thus, the smallest banks are less profitable than larger banks, even before adjusting for risk; any form of adjusting for risk reveals an even bleaker picture. As a percentage of banks in their peer group, small banks experienced a failure rate that was three to four times as high as that among larger banks.[9,10]

This picture was also present, if to a slightly

---

[8]Figures 2 through 5 depict the median values of each item. The median was chosen in preference to the mean because it is less sensitive to outliers. A Wilcoxon rank sum test, used to test equality of the medians across size categories for 1988 data, shows that all figures for each of the smallest two size categories were significantly different from those for larger banks, at the 2 percent level or better. While no tests for statistical significance were performed for earlier years, the magnitude and consistency of the gaps suggest that those differences are also meaningful in most cases.

[9]While it is possible that some banks change size categories immediately prior to failure, this possibility is unlikely to bias the figures, for two reasons. First, any size change associated with distress can go in either direction: a failing bank may shrink as it tries to liquidate assets (for instance, to accommodate an outflow of deposits), or else management may choose to expand assets in an attempt to "grow out of trouble." Both patterns are observed and tend to offset each other in the aggregate. Second, the size categories are broad enough that, on average, a bank would need

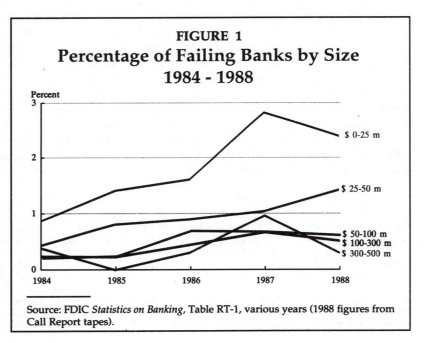

FIGURE 1
Percentage of Failing Banks by Size
1984 - 1988

Source: FDIC *Statistics on Banking*, Table RT-1, various years (1988 figures from Call Report tapes).

more moderate degree, at least as far back as 1984. Figures available for the years prior to 1984 suggest that some of these problems have persisted even longer while others have emerged only recently. In every year from 1979 through 1983, banks with assets smaller than $25 million experienced a lower rate of return on equity and higher average loan losses than banks with assets of between $25 million and $500 million.[11] Since 1981, the smallest banks have even suffered heavier relative loan losses

than the very largest banks.[12] However, it was only in 1982 and 1983 that the average rate of return on assets for the smallest banks began to fall below the level for larger banks.[13]

Structural patterns over time tell a similar story (see Table 1). The annual decline in the number of banks smaller than $25 million has exceeded 300 in every year but one since at least 1980. Until 1984, however, this decline was matched by an increase in the number of larger banks, indicating that much of the decline represented a mere redistribution as some of the smaller banks grew. But with more failures concentrated among the smallest banks in recent years, this is no longer the case. In the four years from 1984 to 1988 the number of FDIC-insured commercial banks with assets of less than $25 million fell by 30 percent.

These patterns are consistent with an ongoing and accelerating shake-out of inefficient banks from the industry, resulting from intensified competition of the 1980s.[14] Actual performance data, therefore, bear out the concern prompted by the combination of economies of scale and increasing market competition.

to double or halve its size in order to change categories. Regulators almost always close down a failing bank before changes of this magnitude can occur.

[10]There may be other reasons besides economies of scale why small banks fail more often than large banks. For example, large banks have the potential to diversify more completely, thereby lowering their financial risk. However, any such factors would only compound the challenges facing a small bank.

[11]See Wall (1984), pp. 20 and 22.

[12]See Wall (1984), p. 20.

[13]See Wall (1984), p. 21.

[14]It is unlikely that these comparisons are noticeably distorted by spotty performance from new banks included in the smallest size category; the figures in Table 1 exclude banks that were in operation less than a full year. Similarly, some of the statistical cost studies excluded banks less than five years old and reached similar conclusions. Moreover, the pattern persists to a lesser degree into larger size ranges, such as $25 million to $50 million.

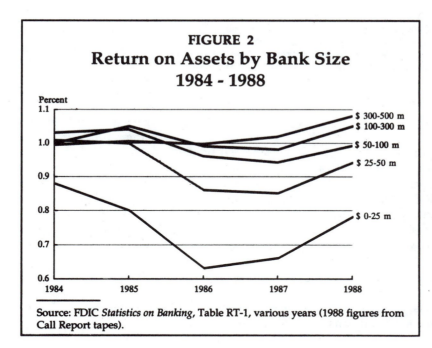

FIGURE 2
Return on Assets by Bank Size
1984 - 1988

Source: FDIC *Statistics on Banking*, Table RT-1, various years (1988 figures from Call Report tapes).

Number of Banks by Size Category
$0-500 Million in Assets[*]
(Percentage change from previous year in parentheses)

Year	Size Categories				
	$0-25M	$25-50M	$50-100M	$100-300M	$300-500M
1988	3948 (-13.6%)	3380 (-6.0)	2730 (-3.1)	1845 (0.0)	331 (5.4)
1987	4571 (-7.0)	3596 (-3.5)	2817 (-2.2)	1845 (1.1)	314 (-2.8)
1986	4914 (-7.8)	3725 (-0.1)	2880 (3.3)	1825 (3.6)	`323 (9.5)
1985	5327 (-5.6)	3729 (-0.4)	2788 (2.2)	1762 (7.1)	295 (15.2)
1984	5645 (-3.0)	3742 (-0.1)	2728 (3.2)	1645 (4.2)	256 (-0.8)

[*]U.S. FDIC-insured commercial banks operating throughout the year (year-end figures). Size categories are total assets in nominal dollars. Rescaling the categories to real dollars would make some difference, since $1 in 1984 was worth $1.09 by 1987 (based on the GNP deflator, Table B-3, *Economic Report of the President*, 1989). However, the essential conclusion of the comparison would remain the same.

Source: FDIC *Statistics on Banking*, Table RT-1, various years; 1988 figures are from Call Report tapes and the FDIC.

TURNING UP THE HEAT

If indeed the smallest banks have always been intrinsically handicapped by higher costs, then why are patterns of distress and failure consistent with that view only now emerging? The answer lies in recent changes in banking markets, in regulation, in technology, and in consumer sophistication. In former decades, banking markets were relatively localized, insulated from external pressures by a comprehensive web of regulations. In such an environment, many small banks could survive, even though they were less efficient than some of their rivals. However, the degree of competition across the industry has increased sharply in recent years and will likely continue to increase.

Market forces had initiated the competitive pressures even before deregulation began. Following the 1966 lowering of the ceilings on the interest rates that banks were allowed to pay on deposit accounts, the market responded by creating money-market mutual funds as an alternative to bank accounts, allowing depositors to take advantage of higher interest rates. The impetus to switch intensified during the decade of the 1970s as inflation and interest rates rose. Predictably, consumers responded by withdrawing a significant amount of their funds from the commercial banking sector and placing it in these new institutions that were not subject to the same regulations. The entry of large non-bank financial firms or conglomerates, such as Sears and Merrill Lynch, into the market for bank-like services has intensified the competitive pressure on commercial banks. Finally, competition from foreign banks and financial firms has been on an upsurge, responding to the increased globalization of financial markets in general and the attractiveness of the U.S. market in particular.

Sometimes viewed as the cause of the increased competition, deregulation has to some extent enabled banks to meet the competitive pressures already imposed by the market. This was the main result of the interest rate deregulation that was phased in following the passage of the Depository Institutions Deregulation and Monetary Control Act of 1980—the banks were now able to compete for deposit funds on an equal basis with money-market mutual funds. This increased ability to deal with competition from outside the banking industry, however, has been at the cost of increased competition among banks. Interstate banking and liberalized intrastate branching laws in certain states have intensified the competition among banks and have eroded traditional geographic market boundaries. Moreover, limited deregulation of the products and services that banks are allowed to offer has been accompanied by a certain amount of product-line deregulation for thrift institutions that permits them to compete more fully with commercial banks.

Boundaries of local markets have also been weakened by technological advances, such as more widespread applications of electronic funds transfer, which allow many banking services to be provided from a distance. Regional networks of automated teller machines are commonplace. Numerous banking services also are available by mail, allowing a potentially nationwide market for those services; credit cards are perhaps the most widespread type of service marketed in this way.

Accompanying these changes has been the increasing sophistication of the average bank customer. Experience with recent periods of high interest rates and uncertainty over future rates have made depositors and borrowers more inclined to shop around rather than rely on a single long-term banking relationship. People have also become more comfortable with banking at a distance. Accordingly, even banks in remote areas of the country are less insulated from outside competition than before, and those that are less efficient are beginning to pay the penalty. Barriers that once protected small banks from their more efficient rivals are either gone or are disappearing fast.

Deregulation is not the villain here; it was a necessary response to changing market conditions. By the same token, increased competition should not be viewed as bad either. Competition generally carries with it the benefits of more favorable prices to consumers, along with higher quality service, relative to a situation in which local monopolists or ineffi-

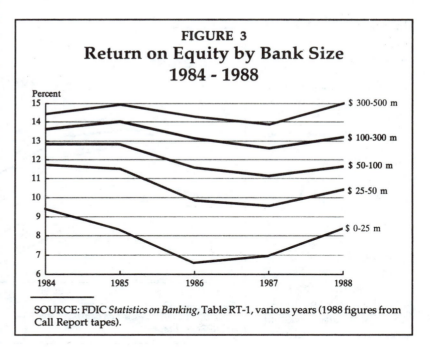

FIGURE 3
Return on Equity by Bank Size
1984 - 1988

SOURCE: FDIC *Statistics on Banking*, Table RT-1, various years (1988 figures from Call Report tapes).

cient producers control the market. Thus, even if competitive pressures have potentially painful consequences for inefficient producers, it is generally better for the economy as a whole to recognize and eliminate the inefficiencies rather than continue to subsidize them through paying higher prices commensurate with the higher costs.

WHAT IS LIKELY TO HAPPEN?

The evidence suggests that banks with assets smaller than $25 million to $50 million are, on average, less efficient than somewhat larger banks. Increasing competition is intensifying the pressure on these banks either to become efficient or to leave the market. Performance data and failure rates support this view. By 1985, the annual number of failures had risen to over 100, of which 77 were smaller banks with total assets of less than $25 million. Some 200 banks failed in 1987, of which 130 had less than $25 million in assets and 167 had less than $50 million. In 1988, out of 221 failed banks, 100 had less than $25 million in assets while 148 had less than $50 million. If all this is true, then what are the likely consequences for the structure of the U.S. banking industry?

As of year-end 1988, there were 13,114 FDIC-insured commercial banks in the United States. Of these, 3,948 (or 30 percent) had total assets of less than $25 million. A total of 7,328 (or 56 percent) had assets of less than $50 million. According to statistical cost studies, these are the banks that historically have had costs above the industry average. If all of these banks encounter direct competition from larger, more efficient banks, then in the long run, any individual bank with above-average costs will be driven out of the market if it fails to contain its costs or find a way to insulate itself from the competition.

Even if the most extreme restructuring were to occur (meaning if all banks smaller than $50 million in assets were to disappear), the nation would still be left with over 5,700 commercial banks, not to mention other depository institutions such as savings and loan associations. This number, while dramatically smaller than at present, should be more than enough to maintain a high degree of competition in the production of financial services, assuming an ongoing vigilant enforcement of antitrust laws within local markets. Thus, there appear no compelling grounds for concern over the impact on competition one way or the other.

Of course, no one is predicting that 3,948 (or 7,328) banks will necessarily disappear from the scene. The consequences may be far less

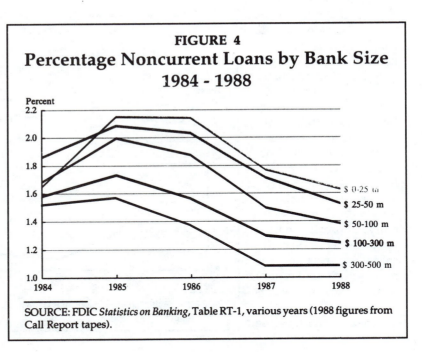

FIGURE 4
Percentage Noncurrent Loans by Bank Size 1984 - 1988

SOURCE: FDIC *Statistics on Banking*, Table RT-1, various years (1988 figures from Call Report tapes).

severe, even if the designated size thresholds are accurate and reliable predictors of bank viability. For instance, imagine that all banks with less than $25 million in assets were recombined to form larger banks, each with $25 million in assets. These banks total 3,948 and together accounted for $60.35 billion in assets as of year-end 1987. If these 3,948 banks were recombined to form banks with exactly $25 million each, there would be only 2,414 such banks ($60.35 billion divided by $25 million), a decline of 1,535.

Similarly, banks smaller than $50 million in assets together account for $182.4 billion in assets. If all these banks were recombined into banks having exactly $50 million each, the total number would be 3,648. In this scenario, the number of banks would decline by 3,680—still a large number, but only about half the total number of banks in this size category.

Thus, apart from other factors, a naive interpretation of the statistical cost studies would predict that competition could lead to some combination of mergers and failures that would reduce the number of banks in the U.S. over time by some 1,500 to over 3,600. Among the stylized assumptions in this assessment are perfect competition among all banks, perfectly efficient restructuring, and an unalterable minimum efficient scale in the range of between $25 million and $50 million in total assets. The first assumption probably errs on the side of overstating the likely structural shift, while the last two may well understate the shift. On balance, it would be difficult to assess whether the naive interpretation is overly pessimistic or overly optimistic. At least two recent studies anticipate a more drastic consolidation of industry structure than suggested here, leaving as few as perhaps 2,000 to 4,000 banks nationwide.[15]

WHAT CAN SMALL BANKS DO?

Are several thousand of the nation's banks really doomed to be bought up by larger banks or else fail? The answer is not so simple. Clearly, a typical small bank these days does face a major challenge. But, depending on various demand factors, there may be ways in which such a bank could respond to this challenge creatively and productively. Even assuming there is an *overall* cost disadvantage that the bank cannot change, smaller banks may be able to take advantage of some potentially offsetting factors. There may be a

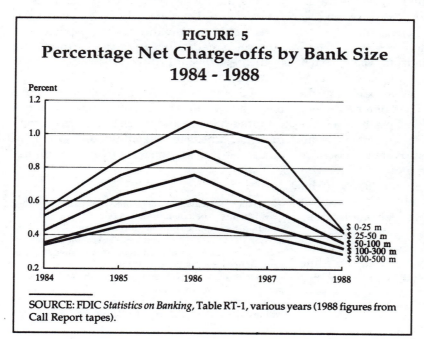

FIGURE 5
Percentage Net Charge-offs by Bank Size
1984 - 1988

$ 0-25 m
$ 25-50 m
$ 50-100 m
$ 100-300 m
$ 300-500 m

SOURCE: FDIC *Statistics on Banking*, Table RT-1, various years (1988 figures from Call Report tapes).

[15]See Kaufman et al. (1983) and Miller (1988).

subset of banking services for which the small bank is not at a cost disadvantage. Alternatively, or in addition, there may be some customers who are willing to pay for the type of services that a small bank, but not a large bank, can easily provide.

If either condition is present, then a small bank could try to identify and stake out a profitable market niche. The key is for the bank not to attempt everything that a large bank might do, but rather to focus its business in a way that capitalizes on some specialized expertise of its staff. This strategy is useful whether the bank hopes to overcome an overall cost disadvantage, to appeal to a particular group of consumers, or both.

Regarding the first possibility, at least one study finds statistical evidence that certain types of specialization by small banks (such as locating in a small geographic market and deemphasizing large commercial and industrial loans) may overcome overall cost disadvantages.[16] Unfortunately, evidence is sparse and mixed concerning which subsets of banking services may minimize or reverse the cost disadvantage of a typical small bank.

Even if specialization fails to reduce costs, a small bank may find specialization beneficial if certain customers are willing to pay extra for the special things that a small bank can do better than a large bank. The point here is not just *which* services are offered but how a service is offered; knowing its customers is an often-cited example. This advantage not only allows the bank to offer more personalized service, which to some customers is worth a bit extra, but also confers a potential edge in credit quality control over the relatively anonymous screening procedures of a larger bank.

A cautionary note must be sounded in either case: the bank should avoid focusing on a line of business that may be fashionable now but won't survive a downturn. Nor should it undertake an emphasis that would be unsustainable if a key officer or employee were to leave the bank.

Over and above any specialization, small banks must become familiar with and take advantage of new technological or financial developments that could allow them to reduce costs or risks and thereby compete on a more even footing with the larger institutions. The development of relatively inexpensive desktop computers provides capabilities formerly limited to expensive mainframes, and associated software is commercially available that in years past would have required costly in-house development. With these tools, some back-office operations could be performed more efficiently. Calculating "what if" scenarios to evaluate alternate business plans or economic shifts can also be a productive use of these machines to reduce costs or risks. "Expert systems" software can even supplement (but not replace!) the usual evaluation of loan applications, improving the control of credit risk.[17] It is not clear, however, whether such innovations would narrow the existing gap between large and small banks' costs and performance, or merely prevent further erosion of the position of small banks.

On the financial side, relatively new instruments allow banks much better control of interest rate exposure and other forms of risk than in earlier times. Intelligent use and pricing of adjustable rate mortgages is by now a familiar

---

[16]See Shaffer (1985).

[17]Expert systems software walks the user through a questionnaire to obtain information relevant to a particular situation, then applies proven procedures and standards to analyze the situation and produce a case profile and recommendation. It is more efficient than an operating manual, since the program will omit questions that prior answers imply to be irrelevant, and more flexible than a rigid set of guidelines, in that a wider range of possibilities can be considered and more sophisticated techniques applied within a short amount of time. See Bestor (1987) and Turner (1987).

response to the possibility of fluctuating interest rates combined with a short average maturity of liabilities. But community banks may also stand to benefit from appropriate use of interest rate swaps and even asset securitization.[18] These new instruments, and others like them, may well become part of every banker's standard tool kit. It is important for small banks to learn not only the potential but also the pitfalls of the techniques behind such instruments. As an initial step, some of the techniques can be effectively implemented using only one or a few standardized instruments, such as Treasury bill futures to hedge interest rate risk. Sophistication of this sort may not benefit a small bank more than a large bank, but at least it could help a small bank not to fall further behind the large banks.

Finally, it is possible to take advantage of networking economies while remaining a small bank. Using a third-party vendor for some services, such as payroll data processing, can sometimes cut costs. A "bankers' bank," a correspondent bank, or even a Federal Reserve Bank can sometimes provide certain back-room services at a savings.[19] A more ambitious step would be to affiliate with several other like-minded small banks by forming a multibank holding company, an alternative that many small banks would view as preferable to being absorbed into an existing large organization with an incompatible focus.

[18]See Findlay (1987) and Nadler (1987).

[19]Shaffer (1985) has found evidence that the use of correspondent banking services can enable a typical small bank to reduce or overcome an overall cost disadvantage.

CONCLUSION

Statistical cost studies, failure rates, and performance data agree: several thousand of the nation's smallest banks are facing a significant challenge to their long-run survival. Specialized market niches can offer some protection to these banks, and there are other defensive steps they can take. But current figures on asset quality and failure rates indicate that the challenge has not been adequately met.

The reality is that a substantial number of banks may disappear from the industry over the next decade or so. Small banks must recognize that it is no longer "business as usual" and take greater advantage of the possible opportunities. Bank regulators, when considering particular mergers and acquisitions involving small banks, have already been assessing what cost a blocked merger proposal will have on the health—or survival—of the banks involved.

At least part of the challenge to small banks appears to stem from intrinsically higher costs than large banks face. What translates this cost handicap into a challenge to survival is the increasing competition in banking markets. We cannot reverse this trend of the past two decades, nor even the trend of the past decade toward deregulation of the banking industry. Even if these trends could be reversed, it would not be advisable to do so. To the extent that true inefficiencies exist, it is to the common good to replace them with efficiently provided banking services.

In any case, the degree of consolidation anticipated should not lessen competition. There would still be on the order of 10,000 banks in the United States. Rather, what should emerge from the process is a stronger, more cost-efficient industry that meets the nation's financial needs even more effectively than before.

References

Bestor, Jennifer L. "Using Expert Systems to Improve Lenders' Performance During Mergers and Acquisitions," *The Journal of Commercial Bank Lending* (March 1987) pp. 10-16.

Clark, Jeffrey A. "Economies of Scale and Scope at Depository Financial Institutions: A Review of the Literature," Federal Reserve Bank of Kansas City *Economic Review* (1988) pp. 16-33.

Danker, Deborah J., and Mary M. McLaughlin. "The Profitability of U.S.-Chartered Insured Commercial Banks in 1986," *Federal Reserve Bulletin* 73 (1987) pp. 537-51.

Findlay, David M. "Swap Applications for Community Banks," *The Journal of Commercial Bank Lending* (December 1987) pp. 9-14.

Gilbert, R. Alton. "Bank Market Structure and Competition: A Survey," *Journal of Money, Credit and Banking* 16 (1984) pp. 617-44.

Hunter, William C., and Stephen G. Timme. "Technical Change, Organizational Form, and the Structure of Bank Production," *Journal of Money, Credit and Banking* 18 (1986) pp. 152-66.

Kaufman, George, Larry R. Mote, and Harvey Rosenblum. "Implications of Deregulation for Product Lines and Geographic Markets of Financial Institutions," *Journal of Bank Research* 14 (1983) pp. 8-21.

Mester, Loretta J. "Efficient Production of Financial Services: Scale and Scope Economies," this *Business Review* (January/February 1987) pp. 15-25.

Miller, Stephen M. "Counterfactual Experiments of Deregulation on Banking Structure," *The Quarterly Review of Economics and Business* 28 (1988) pp. 38-49.

Moulton, Janice M. "New Guidelines for Bank Capital: An Attempt to Reflect Risk," this *Business Review* (July/August 1987) pp. 19-33.

Nadler, Paul S. "Implications of Securitization for the Community Bank," *The Journal of Commercial Bank Lending* (November 1987) pp. 19-25.

Rose, Sanford. "Small Banks Recover; Big Banks Languish," *American Banker* 153 (February 9, 1988) pp. 1, 4.

Shaffer, Sherrill. "Scale Economies in Multiproduct Firms," *Bulletin of Economic Research* 36 (1984) pp. 51-58.

Shaffer, Sherrill. "Competition, Economies of Scale, and Diversity of Firm Sizes," *Applied Economics* 17 (1985) pp. 467-76.

Shaffer, Sherrill. "A Revenue-Restricted Cost Study of 100 Large Banks," Federal Reserve Bank of New York, *Research Paper No. 8806* (1988).

Shaffer, Sherrill, and Edmond David. "Economies of Superscale and Interstate Expansion," Federal Reserve Bank of New York, *Research Paper No. 8612* (1986).

Turner, George J. "How an Outside Expert Views Expert Systems," *The Journal of Commercial Bank Lending* (January 1987) pp. 8-11.

Wall, Larry D. "Commercial Bank Profitability in 1983," Federal Reserve Bank of Atlanta *Economic Review* 69 (1984) pp. 18-29.

Article 26

Shared ATM Networks:
An Uneasy Alliance?

The United States has approximately 82,000 automated teller machines (ATMs) which process over 400 million banking transactions per month. About 85 percent of these transactions occur on ATMs that are part of a "shared ATM network." Banks and other depository institutions form these networks to share ATMs with one another and with institutions that do not own ATMs.

Shared ATM networks benefit banks and ATM users alike. Sharing lowers the unit costs of operating an ATM network by increasing the number of transactions conducted at each ATM within the network. Sharing also expands the geographic area within which customers can obtain transaction services. In addition, it enables small banks to provide some "big bank" services.

To achieve these benefits, shared networks require some degree of cooperation among participating financial institutions. Such cooperative agreements can be complex and unstable. This *Letter* discusses the characteristics of these cooperative agreements and their implications for the welfare of consumers in connection with a recent complaint that has been brought against a shared ATM network.

The costs of shared networks
The fixed costs associated with owning and operating a large network of ATMs are considerable. By spreading these fixed costs over a large volume of transactions, a bank can lower the unit cost of operating a network. However, only very large banks generate sufficient transaction volume to profit from a proprietary network of geographically dispersed ATMs. In most cases, moreover, even large banks find off-premise ATMs (those that are not located at a bank branch) unprofitable, since these off-premise machines do not generate sufficient transaction volume to justify the added expenses.

Shared networks, in contrast, enable banks to spread the fixed costs of an ATM network over a larger volume of transactions, thereby lowering the unit cost of transactions. Likewise, shared networks can make off-premise ATMs profitable. As a result, even many of the nation's largest banks have joined shared systems in recent years. Under sharing arrangements, then, each bank continues to own and operate its ATMs, but agrees to allow other banks' customers to use its machines.

Just as ATMs themselves are subject to falling unit costs, so is the sharing technology. The main element in the sharing technology is the "switch," which facilitates the transfer of transactions between shared network members. Transactions carried out by one bank's customer on another bank's ATM, referred to as "foreign transactions," are routed from the ATM, through the switch, and on to the data processor of the customer's bank. The switch has a large fixed cost, so switch costs per transaction fall as the number of foreign transactions increases, up to a large number of foreign transactions.

The existence of falling unit costs in the switch means that *every* member of a shared network benefits from an increase in foreign transactions originated at *any* member's ATM, and suffers from a decrease in foreign transactions. The shared network's costs per switched transaction, which have to be met by member "switch" fees, thus should vary inversely with the number of foreign transactions.

Cooperation in shared networks
To achieve the benefits of sharing, all shared networks require cooperation among banks that are otherwise competitors. For instance, member banks must agree on certain technological specifications for their ATMs to permit the transmission and processing of foreign transactions. In addition, members may be required to meet

certain security standards or advertising practices to protect the public image of the network as a whole.

In most shared networks, cooperation is formalized through the organization of the network as a joint venture. In these networks, equity ownership and control of the decision-making processes regarding membership access, organizational structure, and specific details of network operation are shared between some or all of the members.

Cooperation in shared networks often extends to agreements on certain types of fees and prices. In addition to setting the switch fee and other network fees, shared networks set the "interchange" fee which members pay to *each other* (as opposed to the network owners) to cover the costs of foreign transactions. The interchange fee is paid by the customer's bank to the ATM-owning bank and is the same for all members. In turn, the bank that is charged the interchange fee often will pass this fee on to the customer who initiated the foreign transaction.

Shared networks set fixed interchange fees to avoid each individual member negotiating with each individual ATM-owner. The large number of bilateral negotiations necessary in such a situation likely would be prohibitively expensive to define and implement. Moreover, if some pairs of members could not reach agreement, the shared network could no longer offer universal access to all customers of all members.

A fatal flaw?
Cooperative agreements between competing firms presumably increase the profits of the firms that are a party to the agreement. However, such arrangements often generate conflicting interests which threaten the existence of the agreement since they create an opportunity for individual members of the group to increase profits even more by violating the agreement that all other members are honoring. Ultimately, of course, the agreement will disintegrate if each member separately ignores it, thinking that all other members will hold to it. If this happens, all the members will be worse off than if they all had honored the agreement.

Shared networks have not been able to completely avoid the internal conflicts that are inherent in cooperative agreements. In 1987, a member of a regional network raised objections to the joint fixing of interchange fees in shared networks. More recently, a member of a large national shared network has challenged the network's prohibition of "surcharges," fees that ATM owners charge directly to customers of other banks for foreign transactions. These fees are in addition to any interchange fees the non-ATM owning bank may pass on to its customer.

The shared network is being sued by the network member on the grounds that it fixes prices in violation of antitrust laws. The bank claims that the interchange fee is not sufficient to compensate it for the full value of the foreign transactions carried out at its own heavily-trafficked off-premise ATMs. Despite the objections of the network, this bank has started to charge customers of other network members a $1.00 surcharge every time they use one of the bank's ATMs in airports, casinos or hotels.

This type of infringement is typical of breaches of cooperative agreements. The recalcitrant member benefits only if the other members of the group continue to honor the agreement. A lone bank that imposes a surcharge will benefit when the surcharge raises revenues more than it raises costs. Although the number of transactions routed through the switch would fall, it would not fall by an amount sufficient to significantly raise per transaction member fees. However, if all members were to impose a surcharge, the decrease in foreign transactions could be substantial, and per transaction member fees then would rise significantly. This is why virtually all shared networks prohibit surcharges.

Bad news for ATM users?
Thus, the widespread imposition of surcharges could have an adverse impact on consumers. The introduction of surcharges would raise the price of foreign transactions both directly, through the surcharge, and indirectly, through the rise in the per unit network cost of foreign transactions.

If the costs of sharing rise too much, the shared network could break up, increasing the costs of *all* ATM transactions, not just foreign transactions. Moreover, surcharges could lead to the break-up of shared ATM networks because banks might be reluctant to remain in sharing arrangements in which they have no control over the price that their customers pay to use other banks' ATMs. It is possible that banks could regain control by negotiating with ATM owners and setting up contracts on a case-by-case basis, but this may be prohibitively expensive.

On the other hand, permitting ATM-owning banks to levy surcharges may have some beneficial effects, as well. It is possible, as advocates of surcharges argue, that the number of ATMs installed would increase. Under current shared network practices, the interchange fee is the only compensation that an ATM owner receives for the costs of a foreign transaction. Thus, the supply of ATMs is restricted by the fixed interchange fee. If ATM owners in shared networks were permitted to impose a surcharge and thus were able to capture the full value of ATMs installed at popular locations, it is likely that more ATMs would be installed at such locations.

Surcharges unlikely

Even if the courts rule that shared ATM networks must allow surcharges, there is reason to believe that surcharges will not become widespread or be very large. An increase in the price of foreign ATM transactions due to a surcharge would decrease the number of these transactions. If demand for foreign transactions were quite sensitive to changes in price, revenues to the ATM owner imposing the surcharge could fall. Moreover, a substantial decrease in demand at one bank's ATMs might not affect network costs very much, but would increase that bank's *own* per unit costs that are not shared with other network members. Therefore, demand that is quite sensitive to price changes would help to minimize surcharges.

Only in cases where demand is relatively insensitive to price changes would ATM owners possibly benefit from surcharges. For example, the number of transactions conducted at an ATM in a casino is not likely to be too sensitive to an increase in the price if the location cannot support an additional, competing ATM. Only banks with ATMs at such exclusive locations would be able to profit from surcharges. The number of such exclusive locations likely is small, given the ubiquity of off-premise ATMs owned by different banks. This suggests that most banks do not have an incentive to impose surcharges, which means, in turn, that ATM networks are inherently stable.

Prohibitions on surcharges probably were needed when shared networks were getting established and there were fewer off-premise ATMs, and hence more market power associated with each one. Now that off-premise ATMs are more commonplace, competition likely could take the place of outright prohibitions in holding down surcharges.

Elizabeth Laderman
Economist

Article 27

Owners Versus Managers: Who Controls the Bank?

*Loretta J. Mester**

"Let's remember when we talk about hostile takeovers, the hostility is between the managements of the two organizations, not between the shareholders of either. In fact, the problem that exists is that too often, in my judgment, the managements try to protect themselves from, in effect, their own shareholders, who are essentially their bosses."

Alan Greenspan, Chairman of the Federal Reserve Board, testifying before the Senate Banking Committee in February 1988 on Bank of New York's hostile-takeover bid for Irving Bank.

On October 5, 1988, Bank of New York's year-long struggle to take over Irving Bank Corporation ended when Irving announced it would accept BONY's tender offer. While not

*Loretta J. Mester is a Senior Economist in the Banking and Financial Markets Section of the Federal Reserve Bank of Philadelphia's Research Department.

the first hostile takeover in the banking industry, the BONY-Irving transaction is the largest the industry has experienced to date. Although Irving claimed during the battle that such hostile takeovers would "promote serious instability in the industry," the Federal Reserve has taken the position that it will treat hostile bids no differently from friendly bids in assessing whether or not to permit a takeover.

Why do some managers, as Chairman Greenspan stated, try to "protect themselves" from their own shareholders? If managers are hired to act on behalf of the stockholders, the firm's owners, then why wouldn't the goals of both always be aligned? Or if managers were inclined to act on their own behalf and not on the owners' behalf, why wouldn't the market ensure the replacement of such managers and so deter any self-serving actions?

The agency theory of the firm can be used to analyze the relationship between a firm's owners and managers. It asks whether there are sufficient mechanisms in place that will induce managers to take actions in the best interests of owners, or whether managers will be able to act in their own interests at the expense of owners. If agency problems exist, are there ways in which owners can control managers?

The conventional theory of the firm makes no distinction between the managers of a firm and its owners: the firm is treated as a single entity that acts to maximize its stock market value (and so its long-run economic profits). But this view applies only to small firms that are tightly run by entrepreneurial owners willing to take risks. Many firms today, including banks, are complex organizations. More banks are members of holding companies, holding a larger percentage of assets than ever before.[1]

At the same time, ownership of the bank is becoming more dispersed—that is, most shareholders own only a small fraction of the bank's shares. In today's larger, more complex banking corporation, decisions are made not by a single individual but by officers and directors, who do not, without inducement, have the same goals as the stockholders. Because outside directors on the bank's board have no managerial responsibilities, their goals are less likely to differ from those of the stockholders they represent. But inside directors are managers whose goals do differ from bank owners. And more control in the hands of inside directors means more chance of conflict, or so-called agency problems.

Recent empirical studies of the banking industry indicate that agency problems do exist. Agency theory suggests certain prescriptions that would help minimize the conflict between bank managers and bank stockholders. These prescriptions include the Fed's position on treating hostile takeovers no differently from friendly takeovers.

THE OWNER-MANAGER RELATIONSHIP IS A PRINCIPAL-AGENT ONE

The relationship between bank owners and bank managers is just one example of a principal-agent relationship. A principal delegates an agent to take some action on his behalf, often because the agent is an expert. A person who hires a real estate agent to sell his house, a performer who hires an agent to find her interesting acting roles, or a litigant who hires an attorney to try his case in court are all principals who are hiring agents. In fact, the word "attorney" means agent. (See the Bibliography for several excellent articles on agency theory.)

Several principal-agent relationships are found in banks. The bank acts as an agent for its depositors: when depositors place their money in a bank account rather than investing directly in firms, they are delegating to the bank the responsibility of monitoring the performance of each firm to which the bank lends depositors' money.[2] Borrowers are also agents for the

---

[1] In 1987, 68.3 percent of commercial banks were in bank holding companies (BHCs), holding 91.9 percent of the industry's assets. This is a substantial increase from 1977, when 26.5 percent of banks were in BHCs, holding 68.2 percent of the assets.

[2] Mitchell Berlin discusses the role of the bank as a delegated monitor in "Bank Loans and Marketable Securities: How Do Financial Contracts Control Borrowing Firms?" this *Business Review* (July/August 1987) pp. 9-18.

bank: typically, the firm selects the projects it will develop with the money it has borrowed. But banks can also be thought of as agents for borrowers, since the bank works on the firm's behalf in obtaining funding for the firm's project. Finally, as in other kinds of firms, the managers of the bank act as agents for the bank's owners, making decisions about the bank's everyday operations.

Because the agent can be a specialist, there are efficiency gains in the principal-agent relationship. Rather than doing some job for himself, the principal is better off hiring an agent who is an expert in the field. However, these gains must be weighed against the problems that arise in the principal-agent relationship. Problems can arise if the goals of the agent differ from the goals of the principal, and if the agent and principal have different information relevant for the decisions the agent is supposed to make on behalf of the principal. Both conditions must be present for there to be a problem. Suppose, for instance, that the agent had the same goals as the principal. In this case there would be no problem—the agent, in working on his own behalf, would also be doing what the principal wants.

But the goals of the principal and agent are not always aligned. For example, an attorney who is paid a flat fee regardless of the outcome of a case might not put forth her best effort to win on the litigant's behalf. Of course, if the litigant could see how hard the attorney was working and knew enough law to determine whether the attorney was pursuing the best strategy to win, then the litigant could fire the attorney for shirking. Knowing this, the attorney would be compelled to work hard in order to get paid. But typically the principal is ignorant of some relevant information—the litigant can't tell how hard the attorney is working and, even if he could, he doesn't know enough law to determine whether the attorney is doing the best possible job. (If the litigant knew enough law, he wouldn't have to hire the attorney.)

The benefits in the principal-agent relationship derive from the specialized knowledge of the agent. But the fact that the principal and agent have different information causes a problem if the two have different goals. One way to solve the problem is to bring the aims of the agent in line with the aims of the principal. For example, if instead of paying the attorney a flat fee, the litigant paid a fee contingent on the outcome of the case, then the attorney would have the incentive to try her best to win. (Many contracts between attorneys and their clients are written this way.)

The two conditions necessary for a principal-agent conflict—divergent goals and different information—are present in the owner-manager relationship. The owners of widely held firms want to maximize their firm's market value. Typically, these owners hold a portfolio of stock in many firms. If their portfolios are well diversified, they won't be concerned about the riskiness of any one firm.[3] Managers, however, have their own goals that may not coincide with value maximization. Managers want to maximize their own welfare, which may mean diverting some of the firm's resources for their own use. For example, managers may want to spend money on perquisites like large staffs and expensive offices—so-called expense preference behavior.

In addition, managers of large firms are often paid more than managers of small firms. While this could be related to the greater difficulty of managing a large firm, it also gives a manager the incentive to maximize the firm's size rather than its value. For example, a loan officer's compensation might be tied to the number of loans he makes, not to their quality

---

[3]In fact, if the owners of a firm that is leveraged can declare bankruptcy and have limited liability, they may want to take on more risk. The owners would benefit from a risky action if it paid off, but could declare bankruptcy and avoid the full cost of the action if it didn't.

and so not to the value produced by his portfolio. The manager of a large firm may also find that he has better employment opportunities than the manager of a small firm—another incentive to maximize size rather than value.

Unlike diversified shareholders of widely held firms, managers will be concerned about the riskiness of the firm. The manager may have developed skills and studied techniques that can't easily be used in another firm. If so, then if the firm goes bankrupt, the manager would suffer a high cost by losing his job. Since a manager can't be diversified like the firm's owners can be (that is, he can't hold a portfolio of employers), he may take on less than the value-maximizing amount of risk.[4]

Just as in the litigant-attorney relationship, it is difficult for the firm's owners to see all the actions the manager takes on their behalf. And even if owners see the actions, it is difficult for them to know if these actions are proper for the situation, since managers know more about the firm than the owners. (Recall that one reason to hire a manager is for his expertise.) Therefore, unless controlled, managers will not always act to maximize the wealth of shareholders. Managers will divert resources for their own use to provide themselves with perks and will act too conservatively in order to avoid the risk of unemployment.

Owners Versus Managers in Banks. These same issues characterize the owner-management relationship in today's large, complex

banking organization. But the conflicts between owners and managers can also explain why small banks often act in a very risk-averse manner. In these small banks, the owners are the managers. They can be thought of as owners who also manage their bank, but it's better to view them as managers who also own the bank. That is, their interests are closer to those of a typical manager than to those of shareholders in a widely held firm. Owner-managers in small banks often have a taste for managing and therefore try to act in a manner that would preserve their positions as bank managers. This would include acting very conservatively—maintaining high capital-to-asset ratios, for example—in order to avoid bankruptcy.[5]

Banking is a regulated industry, and the regulators want to ensure its safety and soundness. Thus, it might seem that regulators would prefer the objectives of managers, since managers prefer less risk. However, regulators also want to ensure an efficient banking industry. They don't want to support bad managers who divert bank resources for their personal use. To the extent that the goals of managers and owners can be aligned, bad management would be weeded out and the industry would become more efficient. Regulations already in place, such as risk-based capital requirements, can help control risk-taking in banking.[6]

The fact that banks are regulated adds another place for the conflict between owners and managers to emerge. Periodically, banks must report their balance sheet information to regulators. Shareholders of the bank have an incentive for *downward window dressing*, that is, tak-

---

[4]However, there are reasons why managers might take on more risk than the shareholders would like. For example, a manager who directs a risky project that turns out to be successful may increase his attractiveness to other firms. See Stiglitz [6]. Also, if the firm is near bankruptcy, a manager has nothing to lose by taking on a very risky project in an attempt to keep the firm solvent and retain his job. So he has the same incentives as stockholders in leveraged firms that are near bankruptcy. See Eric Rasmussen, "Mutual Banks and Stock Banks," *Journal of Law and Economics* 31 (October 1988) pp. 395-421.

[5]For example, in 1987, the capital-to-asset ratio of banks with assets of at most $100 million was 11.64 percent, while that of banks with assets of over $1 billion was 8.15 percent.

[6]But some regulations, such as flat-rate deposit insurance, exacerbate the conflict between bank managers and stockholders over the optimal level of risk-taking.

ing actions at the end of a reporting period that allow the bank to report lower values for assets and liabilities than their average values over the reporting period. Downward window dressing reduces the cost of meeting capital requirements, lowers the cost of deposit insurance (which is based on the bank's reported liabilities), and may reduce the cost of capital to the bank by raising the bank's apparent capital adequacy ratio and thereby making the bank look safer. So, downward window dressing raises the value of the bank, which is the aim of shareholders.

Managers, on the other hand, have an incentive for *upward window dressing*, since their compensation is often tied to the size of the bank. Also, since upward window dressing reduces the reported capital adequacy ratio, regulators may then require a capital infusion into the bank that would lower the chance of bankruptcy and the risk of managers losing their jobs.[7] Thus, in regulated firms like banks, the direction of window dressing, expenditures on perks, and risk-taking behavior are three areas where the conflict between owners and managers may appear.

WHAT CONTROLS THE BEHAVIOR OF MANAGERS?

While managers and owners have divergent goals, it is not clear that managers can pursue their own goals at the expense of owners. There are some controls that limit the ability of managers to follow the beat of their own drummer. These controls fall into two groups: labor market controls and capital market controls.

Labor Market Controls. Managers want to act in their own best interests; however, if their interests can be made to coincide with those of stockholders, then by acting for themselves they will be acting for stockholders. For example, if a manager's compensation is tied to

the value of the firm's stock, then she will want to act to raise the value of the stock—which is what the owners want. But even though more corporations are including stock in managerial compensation packages, bank size rather than performance still appears to be the largest determinant of pay scales in the banking industry.[8,9] Perhaps a better incentive for a manager is her reputation. Managers with good reputations will have an easier time finding other jobs, if they need to, and will have better employment opportunities than managers with poor reputations.

Capital Market Controls.[10] Other controls on the behavior of managers work through the capital markets. One potential control on managers is the stockholders' meeting. However, these meetings are rarely effective since they are usually controlled by management. Also, stockholders who are well diversified usually don't bother to attend the meetings and vote since they don't have very much of their wealth tied up in any one firm. Good management is what economists call a public good—all the stockholders benefit from good management, but no individual stockholder

---

[7]This is discussed in Allen and Saunders [8].

[8]This was reported by J. Richard Fredericks and Jackie Arata in *Montgomery Securities Annual Banking Industry Compensation Review*, May 5, 1987. In studying compensation at 33 banks in 1985 and 1986, they found no correlation between the compensation of the top five highest-paid employees and the performance of the bank.

[9]Joseph Stiglitz [5] observes that most stock-option plans were instituted not so that managers would bear more risk, but as supplements to their salaries. Thus, the incentive effects of these plans are questionable. However, a Bank Administration Institute survey of 839 banks with assets under $500 million found a positive correlation between bank performance and the presence of an annual bonus program. Of course, it is not clear which came first, the award program or better performance. See W. Frank Kelly, "Bank Performance and CEO Compensation," Bank Administration 62 (November 1986) pp. 52-56.

[10]Most of the discussion in this section and the next follows Stiglitz [5] and Jensen [2].

has an incentive to ensure that management is good because the personal gain from doing so is not great enough. Other shareholders can get a "free ride" if one shareholder decides to become an active participant in the stockholder meetings. Large shareholders, however, can exert control on the management—they find it worth their effort—but usually have to be compensated in some way for taking on the risk of not being diversified; for example, they may receive a high fee for being on the board of directors.[11]

One control on the management of nonfinancial corporations involves banks themselves. Like large shareholders, banks have an incentive to monitor the performance of firms to which they have made substantial loans, in order to avoid default. Unlike equity holders, who cannot control their funds once invested, banks have more control of their funds: they set the terms of their loans and can decide not to reinvest in the firms once the loans mature.

The interbank loan market and certificate of deposit (CD) market provide a similar control on banking firms, especially money-center banks, which rely greatly on purchased funds. Federal funds transactions (overnight interbank loans) are not collateralized, so banks that find themselves in trouble (perhaps due to the negligence of management) must pay a premium for such funds. Also, the large, negotiable CDs of large banks trade on a no-name basis. That is, even though CDs differ with respect to the quality of the issuing bank, dealers quote a single price for large-bank CDs and don't specify names when trading them. However, if a bank is in trouble, traders will refuse to trade the bank's CDs on a no-name basis. Once singled out, the bank will have to pay a premium for funds. (Continental Illinois, for example, was dropped from the no-name

[11]See Stiglitz [5], p. 144.

list when it ran into trouble in 1982.) In addition to hurting shareholders (by lowering the market value of the bank), these "punishments" have a direct negative impact on managers by hurting their reputations, by reducing the amount available for perquisites, by lowering compensation to the extent it is tied to market performance, and by increasing their chance of unemployment due to bankruptcy.

The Threat of Takeover Is a Capital Market Control on Managers. The 1980s have seen a new wave of corporate mergers, acquisitions, and takeovers. The pros and cons of these takeovers are being debated, especially the extensive use of debt financing characteristic of recent takeovers, and the wealth transfers from employees (many of whom lose their jobs) to shareholders of the acquired firm (who gain the takeover premium).

A potential benefit of a well-functioning takeover market is that the threat of a takeover, in which management is usually replaced, can discipline managers to act in the interests of the firm's shareholders. The idea here is that if the firm's market value could be enhanced with better management, then someone could purchase the firm by buying the outstanding shares from the current shareholders. He could then remove the bad management, make the proper decisions to maximize the firm's value, and gain from that increase in value.

For several reasons, however, this takeover threat won't necessarily be effective in controlling management. And even if takeovers are effective in replacing bad management, there are several ways in which managers can avoid this discipline.

For instance, takeovers may not work because of information problems. A firm may be performing poorly because the current management is bad or because the past management was bad. That is, management might be doing the best it can given what it has to work with. Only the insiders of a weak firm know which is the case, and if they hold enough stock in the firm to determine the outcome of any takeover attempt, they'll sell only if the offer is more than the firm is worth. In other words, successful takeovers will be overpriced takeovers, in which case the new stockholder will not gain.

As with the stockholders' meetings, there are free-rider problems associated with takeovers. Suppose takeovers work and eliminate inefficient management; then the shareholders who didn't sell their shares get a free ride and gain from the firm's increased stock price. Each shareholder reasons this way, believing she doesn't have enough stock to affect the success of the takeover attempt. Therefore, it is in her interest to hold onto her shares. If everyone does this, the takeover won't be successful.

Another free-rider problem occurs if it is costly to find badly managed firms, which are good takeover targets. Someone who has expended the resources to find such a firm and then makes a bid thereby announces to other potential bidders that the firm is a good target. The ensuing bidding war drives to zero any expected profits from taking over the firm, so the first bidder who expended the resources to find the target firm earns a negative expected profit, even if he's successful in taking over the firm. Therefore, there is no gain in finding good takeover targets.[12]

While extreme, these cases point out that it is not easy to complete a successful takeover. However, if bidders can find a way to keep some of the gains from a successful takeover for themselves (rather than sharing them with others) they will have an incentive to search out firms with inefficient management and attempt a takeover.[13] But even if the takeover market would otherwise work smoothly, there are ways in which managers of targeted firms can deter takeovers. By thwarting potential acquirers, these actions help entrench managers who may not be acting in the shareholders' interests.[14]

For example, managers of a targeted firm can swallow a *poison pill,* that is, they can take some action that will make the firm an unattractive candidate for takeover. The action is something that the firm wouldn't do if it were not threatened with a takeover. One poison pill is for the targeted firm itself to take over another firm in order to increase the possibility of antitrust litigation if its potential acquirer succeeds. Other poison pills include financial restructuring of the firm, issuing "poison pill preferred stock" that raises the cost of a takeover, or selling off some assets that attracted the bidder.

In the Bank of New York-Irving fight, Irving's board voted a poison pill that gave shareholders certain rights to buy stock at half price in the event of a hostile merger. They added a "flip in" amendment that allowed the measure even if the hostile investor did not attempt an immediate merger. BONY filed suit against this defense and a state court invalidated it. The decision was appealed and the Appellate Division of the New York Supreme Court upheld it, which led to the takeover's final resolution.

---

[12]Event studies find that in recent takeovers the excess returns to acquired firms are usually positive, while those to acquiring firms are often negative or zero. See Robert Schweitzer, "How Do Stock Returns React to Special Events?" in a forthcoming issue of this *Business Review.*

[13]See Andrei Shleifer and Robert W. Vishny [4].

[14]These defensive tactics may, however, actually improve the takeover market. Eliminating a bidder can help solve the bidding-war free-rider problem discussed above and encourage other firms to study the possibility of taking over the firm. The increased likelihood of more bids may be enough to compensate shareholders for the elimination of a potential acquirer and the costs of discouraging him. See Andrei Shleifer and Robert W. Vishny, "Greenmail, White Knights, and Shareholders' Interest," *Rand Journal of Economics* 17 (Autumn 1986) pp. 293-309.

Another way a firm can prevent a takeover involves *greenmail*. The payment of greenmail refers to a targeted stock-repurchase plan in which managers repurchase the stock of a subgroup of shareholders at a premium over the market price. Greenmail can be used to avert a takeover—if offered enough, the potential acquirer will sell the shares it has accumulated back to management. Usually, the potential acquirer also signs an agreement prohibiting the purchase of any of the firm's stock for a period of time, sometimes as long as five years.

Like greenmail, *golden parachutes* can be used to deter takeovers by raising their cost. A golden parachute is a large severance payment made to top managers who are replaced after a takeover. By lowering the costs to managers of losing their jobs, the parachutes also hinder the threat of takeover in controlling managers. They may also induce the manager to cave in and sell the firm at too low a price, or even to seek out buyers for the firm. On the other hand, the parachutes may benefit shareholders by facilitating a takeover. If the managers who have to decide whether or not to fight the takeover have golden parachutes, they will be less inclined to fight—and this can benefit shareholders. Also, by lowering the costs to managers of investing in education and training worth little outside the firm, the parachutes may increase the efficiency of managers.

On balance, then, whether golden parachutes are harmful or beneficial to stockholders depends on who receives them and how they are structured. If the parachutes are paid to the managers involved in negotiating the terms of the takeover with a potential acquirer, and if their value is tied to the increase in the firm's market value that may occur after a takeover, then parachutes benefit shareholders. Otherwise, they are probably detrimental to shareholders.

In general, restrictions on the type or number of potential acquirers of a firm make takeovers less likely and limit the ability of the takeover threat to discipline management. For example, there are two principal ways for a corporation to acquire a commercial bank. It can either acquire a controlling interest in the bank's stock or it can merge with the bank. But mergers are prohibited between nonbank corporations and commercial banks, and some states restrict corporate acquisitions of bank stock. Also, banks in states that prohibit branching are less attractive merger partners than are banks in branching states, all else equal, and prohibition of interstate banking eliminates out-of-state banks as potential bidders, making takeovers less likely. Thus, in banking, the threat of takeovers may not ensure that managers work on behalf of their shareholders.[15] However, the recent breakdown of these restrictions—for example, regional interstate banking pacts—suggests that the takeover threat should become more effective in the future.

HOW EFFECTIVE ARE THE CONTROL MECHANISMS IN THE FINANCIAL SERVICES INDUSTRY?

Although there are many potential mechanisms for ensuring that managers act on behalf of stockholders, these controls are imperfect and costly. Just how well do these controls work in the financial services industry? Are managers able to pursue their own goals at the stockholders' expense, or are they disciplined to act in a way that maximizes the value of the firm? Empirical studies suggest that there are agency problems in financial firms: managers are able to pursue their own interests and do not always act in an efficient, value-maximizing manner. (The Bibliography includes references to the studies discussed below.)

Several studies of the commercial banking industry find evidence that managers spend excessively on perquisites, such as large staffs. That is, they spend more than the profit-maxi-

[15]This is the focus of Christopher James [11].

mizing amount. Michael Smirlock and William Marshall present evidence that larger banks, whose management is presumably harder to control, exhibit such expense preference behavior. In a study of states that limit the acquisition market for banks by limiting the amount of bank stock a corporation can own, Christopher James finds that bank managers in these states spend more on perquisites than do managers of banks in states that permit corporate holdings of bank stock. This is evidence that takeovers can discipline managers.[16]

In a study last year, the author investigated the savings and loan industry for evidence of expense preference behavior. Savings and loans are organized either as stock-issuing institutions or as mutual institutions. Although the owners of a mutual S&L are, in theory, its depositors, these owners have virtually no control over management. Thus, managers of mutual S&Ls should be more able to follow their own pursuits than managers of stock S&Ls. The author's study finds that the mutual S&Ls are operating with an inefficient mix of inputs and outputs. While this could be due to the impact of regulations and to the fact that mutual S&Ls are not able to issue stock in order to expand, it is more likely evidence that managers are consuming some of the firm's resources as perquisites.

In addition to spending excessively on perquisites, managers have the incentive to act more conservatively than shareholders would like and to engage in upward window dressing. Anthony Saunders, Elizabeth Strock, and Nickolaos G. Travlos find evidence that banks with diffuse ownership—that is, no one shareholder holds a large number of shares—are more conservative than other banks whose shareholders can be expected to exert more influence on the decisions of managers. Linda Allen and Anthony Saunders find evidence of upward window dressing in banks located in states with takeover barriers and in banks whose managers have no large equity holdings.

To sum up these studies, in cases where the agency theory predicts that managers of financial firms will work on their own behalf rather than on the shareholders' behalf, there is evidence that they do so.

PRESCRIPTIONS TO REMEDY AGENCY PROBLEMS

There is evidence that managers of financial firms are able to pursue their own interests rather than the interests of shareholders. The agency theory of the firm suggests several ways in which the goals of managers and shareholders could be better aligned, which would lead to higher efficiency and help resolve agency problems.

Bank managers and directors could be encouraged to own stock in the companies they manage. In this way, they would directly benefit from the decisions they make that increase the market value of the bank. Since outside directors' goals are more coincident with shareholders', increasing the power of outside directors to remove managers could induce better behavior by managers. But this may not have much effect if it is difficult to find directors with enough knowledge to determine whether the management should be replaced. Finally, decreasing the barriers to takeovers—including state prohibitions on corporate acquisition of commercial bank stock, laws prohibiting interstate banking and branching, and laws restricting hostile takeovers—will increase the effectiveness of the takeover threat as a device to control managers; so will the Federal Reserve's position to treat hostile takeovers in banking no differently from friendly takeover bids.

[16]However, the methodology of the studies by Smirlock and Marshall and by James, as well as that of earlier banking studies, is critiqued in Loretta J. Mester, "A Testing Strategy for Expense Preference Behavior," Working Paper 88-13/R, Federal Reserve Bank of Philadelphia, December 1988.

Some argue that today's takeovers are too often funded by high-risk junk bonds or other sources of debt that can lead to macroeconomic instability by increasing the number of bankruptcies when a recession hits.[17] And there is evidence that while shareholders of the target firm gain in a takeover, their gain is at the expense of employees who lose their jobs or are forced to take wage cuts.[18] Clearly, not all takeovers are in the best interests of society. However, it should be remembered that an actual takeover is not necessary to induce managers to act efficiently—the *threat* of a takeover is what is needed. If restrictions on takeovers are reduced, making the possibility of a takeover a real threat to inefficient managers, these managers will be induced to maximize the value of their firms. Easing restrictions on takeovers could actually lead to a reduction in the number of acquisitions by reducing the number of inefficiently managed firms, which are among the prime takeover targets.

---

[17]See F.M. Scherer, "Corporate Takeovers: The Efficiency Arguments," *Journal of Economic Perspectives* 2 (Winter 1988) pp. 69-82.

[18]See Shleifer and Vishny [4].

Bibliography

There are many excellent articles on the agency theory of the firm. Several of the articles cited in the text are included in this bibliography.

[1] Kenneth J. Arrow, "The Economics of Agency," in *Principals and Agents: The Structure of Business*, John W. Pratt and Richard J. Zeckhauser, eds. (Boston: Harvard Business School Press, 1985) pp. 1-35. This is an excellent overview of the principal-agent relationship. In fact, all of the articles in this book are recommended.

[2] Michael C. Jensen, "Takeovers: Their Causes and Consequences," *The Journal of Economic Perspectives* 2 (Winter 1988) pp. 21-48. An excellent overview of the takeover as a capital market control on managers, this article discusses such potential takeover deterrents as greenmail and golden parachutes.

[3] Michael C. Jensen and William H. Meckling, "Theory of the Firm: Managerial Behavior, Agency Costs and Ownership Structure," *Journal of Financial Economics* 3 (1976) pp. 305-360. This article discusses agency theory and the financial structure of firms.

[4] Andrei Shleifer and Robert W. Vishny, "Value Maximization and the Acquisition Process," *The Journal of Economic Perspectives* 2 (Winter 1988) pp. 7-20. The authors review the agency theory of the firm and the role of hostile takeovers in disciplining managers.

[5] Joseph E. Stiglitz, "Credit Markets and the Control of Capital," *Journal of Money, Credit, and Banking* 17 (May 1985) pp. 133-152. This is an excellent introduction to the conflicts between owners and managers, and the effectiveness of certain controlling devices.

[6] Joseph E. Stiglitz, "Ownership, Control, and Efficient Markets: Some Paradoxes in the Theory of Capital Markets," in *Economic Regulation: Essays in Honor of James R. Nelson,* Kenneth D. Boyer and William G. Shepherd, eds. (East Lansing, MI: Michigan State University Press, 1981) pp. 311-340. The author discusses managerial incentives for risk-taking.

[7] The Symposium on Takeovers, in *The Journal of Economic Perspectives* 2 (Winter 1988), includes several papers, in addition to those by Jensen and by Shleifer and Vishny, on the role of takeovers as an external control mechanism.

Empirical studies of agency problems in financial firms include:

[8] Linda Allen and Anthony Saunders, "Incentives to Engage in Bank Window Dressing: Manager vs. Stockholder Conflicts," Working Paper No. 471, Salomon Brothers Center for the Study of Financial Institutions, Graduate School of Business Administration, New York University, June 1988.

[9] Franklin R. Edwards, "Managerial Objectives in Regulated Industries: Expense-Preference Behavior in Banking," *Journal of Political Economy* 85 (1977) pp. 147-162.

[10] Timothy H. Hannan and Ferdinand Mavinga, "Expense Preference and Managerial Control: The Case of the Banking Firm," *Bell Journal of Economics* 11 (Autumn 1980) pp. 671-682.

[11] Christopher James, "An Analysis of the Effect of State Acquisition Laws on Managerial Efficiency: The Case of the Bank Holding Company Acquisition," *Journal of Law and Economics* 27 (April 1984) pp. 211-226.

[12] Loretta J. Mester, "Agency Costs in Savings and Loans," Working Paper No. 88-14/R, Federal Reserve Bank of Philadelphia, November 1988.

[13] Anthony Saunders, Elizabeth Strock, and Nickolaos G. Travlos, "Ownership Structure, Deregulation and Bank Risk Taking," Working Paper No. 443, Salomon Brothers Center for the Study of Financial Institutions, Graduate School of Business Administration, New York University, October 1987.

[14] Michael Smirlock and William Marshall, "Monopoly Power and Expense-Preference Behavior: Theory and Evidence to the Contrary," *Bell Journal of Economics* 14 (Spring 1983) pp. 166-178.

Article 28

Banking and Venture Capital

At present, the ability of banks in the United States to invest in commercial enterprises is limited. Although they are allowed to extend loans to industrial firms, they may not hold controlling amounts of equity in such firms nor simultaneously lend to a commercial firm and hold its equity. An earlier *Letter* argued that these restrictions on bank powers may handicap the ability of banks to finance productive business ventures in our economy.

This *Letter* discusses the importance of risk control mechanisms in lending to business ventures. Venture capital financing techniques illustrate the kinds of control mechanisms needed to finance risky projects safely. A comparison of the financial instruments used by venture capitalists with those available to U.S. banks suggests that banks' limited powers may contribute to low rates of business investment in our economy.

The hazard of lending
Both venture capital firms and commercial banks are in the business of funding commercial ventures. They both assess and manage the risks associated with their investments, but they differ significantly in the types of instruments they are permitted to use to manage risk.

Banks in the U.S. generally are restricted by regulation to providing pure external debt financing to a firm. ("External" here refers to funding that is provided by those who do not have access to the information about a firm's prospects that is available to the firm's "insiders," or managers.) In addition to the normal uncertainty concerning the payoffs associated with risky projects, external finance is risky because of information asymmetries and the "moral hazard" problem inherent in this type of lending. Specifically, since borrowing firms have a better understanding of their prospects than do outsiders, they may exploit this information asymmetry to obtain financing terms that do not adequately compensate the lender for the risks being undertaken.

In addition, external creditors also face risks associated with a "moral hazard" problem. Specifically, borrowers have an incentive to use funds obtained from external sources to finance a riskier project than originally envisioned since any upside benefits are captured entirely by the equity holders of the firm, while downside risks are shared with the lender. The thinner is the equity position of the firm's insiders, the greater is this moral hazard problem.

To control these risks associated with pure debt financing, U.S. banks generally limit their loan clients to well-capitalized, established firms selling established products or to firms with ample collateral. Unfortunately, these are precisely the firms best positioned to bypass the bank loan market altogether by issuing their debt directly to investors in the form of commercial paper or bonds. The high net worth of these firms reduces the moral hazard problem for outside debt holders, and in recent years, improvements in information and instrumentation technology have helped to reduce problems with information asymmetries and have made direct placement of debt more feasible.

At the other end of the spectrum of potential loan clients are entrepreneurial firms selling new products. They are, by definition, firms with little or no current cash flow to support debt obligations. High quality information may be impossible or very costly to obtain externally, and the thin veneer of equity typically provided by the entrepreneur creates a serious moral hazard problem that must be controlled by the outside investor. On account of the significant informational and moral hazard challenges these firms pose, loans to such firms are not attractive investments for banks, despite the high expected returns.

Venture capitalists
The venture capital industry has evolved as a specialist in intermediation to these thinly-capitalized, entrepreneurial firms. Unlike banks,

venture capitalists are largely unrestricted in terms of the financial relationship they may establish with their customers. Venture capitalists thus are able to devise instruments to control the informational and moral hazard problems inherent in such lending.

Not surprisingly, simple coupon debt is an uncommon mode of venture finance, except for the financing of mature venture firms. Where debt is issued, it takes the form of a hybrid of debt and equity that combines equity conversion or detachable stock warrant features with the underlying debt. Like the mixed debt/equity ("strip") financing employed in industrial takeovers in recent years, such instruments let the lender participate in the "upside" of any risk-taking. In the process, the entrepreneur's incentive to exploit the moral hazard problem is partially dampened.

For the riskiest ventures (that is, the ones that are very thinly-capitalized and have no earnings track record), simple combinations of outside debt and equity do not provide sufficient control. Such firms are very difficult to monitor externally, and the risk that inside equity holders will exploit outside financiers simply is too great to be held in check by the rather blunt powers afforded lenders or simple equity holders.

As a result, venture capitalists typically seek financing mechanisms that provide additional control and insider-like information. This financing generally takes the form of convertible preferred stock. The preferred stock position gives the venture capitalist some debt-like priority over common stock holders, while the requirement that the preferred stock be convertible to common equity provides opportunities to enjoy the greater upside potential of common stock.

The preferred stock position often includes special rights, such as liquidation priority, which offers priority over other equity holders in liquidation, and thereby provides the venture capitalist with worst-case, downside protection. In addition, the preferred stock often includes redemption rights, which are intended to encourage on-going performance. These rights require that the firm cash out the venture capitalist at a premium over the value of the initial investment if, by a certain time, performance has been less

than anticipated. This feature gives the entrepreneur an incentive to pursue the project aggressively.

In addition to embedding these control features in their outside positions, venture capitalists usually obtain inside (management) rights in return for their significant equity positions. These may be the right to appoint one or more directors or to serve as an officer of the company. These management rights are an important hallmark of venture capitalism, and provide channels for both information and control.

The role of banks

That the venture capital industry employs instruments other than simple debt raises the logical question whether the economy would benefit if banks enjoyed similar flexibility in their financial relationships with firms. At present, commercial banks are confined to a shrinking middle ground between the direct placement debt market and the market served by financiers like venture capitalists, who enjoy equity powers. On the one hand, direct placement activity has diminished banks' role in funding low-risk credits, while restricted equity powers limit their ability to safely monitor (and therefore, provide funding to) higher-risk credits. As a result, net new bank lending to business has trended down (in inflation-adjusted terms); in contrast, the flow of venture capital financing commitments and bond financing has exhibited a general upward trend. (See the chart.)

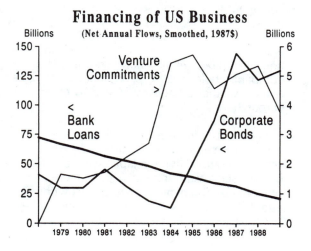

Financing of US Business
(Net Annual Flows, Smoothed, 1987$)

If banks were given expanded equity powers, the broadest opportunities for banks likely would not be in venture capital *per se*, but in more extensive involvement with their current credit customers. In Germany and Japan, for example, where banks' powers are less restricted, banks provide roughly twice the proportion of total industrial credit that banks in the U.S. provide.

Nonetheless, it is also likely that banks would become more involved in providing true venture funding. Indeed, since banks perform the same essential monitoring function as the venture capitalist, and have superior access to debt and equity markets, they may even come to dominate traditional venture financing channels.

Foreign evidence

Evidence from other countries appears to confirm the potential for a significantly increased role for banks in venture finance if current restrictions on equity-holding and exercise of control were relaxed. In France, Germany, and Italy, for example, where banks do enjoy such powers, they provided 35, 45, and 65 percent of total venture funding in 1985, respectively. By comparison, banks provide less than five percent of venture funding in the United States, and this primarily arises from the activity of Small Business Investment Company (SBIC) subsidiaries. (SBICs are special entities licensed by the Small Business Administration to pass through debt funding.)

In Japan, banks nominally have narrower powers than do the European banks, but institutional arrangements provide a channel for risk control analogous to that provided by venture capital institutions in the U.S. Specifically, large portions of industry are interconnected through group affiliations (*kieretsu*) and cross-shareholding relationships (*mochiai*), and banks and insurance companies hold over 40 percent of all corporate equity. Another 30 percent is held by other corporations.

On account of these relationships, it is not surprising that attempts to initiate U.S.-style venture capital activity in Japan generally have been unsuccessful. It appears that much new product development in Japan occurs within established firms, where the risk of funding new ventures is controlled by existing relationships.

Implications for the economy

The key concern, of course, is not who supplies funding to industry, but whether the overall cost of capital is reduced by one funding structure or another. Here, both theory and casual empirical evidence suggest that the U.S. economy may be handicapped in this regard by restrictions on bank powers.

It is clear from finance theory that unresolved information asymmetries are costly to the economy. As Myers and Majluf have demonstrated, the existence of information asymmetries leads to underinvestment since firms are unable to obtain financing sufficient to pursue all worthwhile projects; "outside" investors' lack of information causes them to withhold funding, effectively raising the cost of capital. To the extent that improved equity and control powers at banks would resolve information asymmetries, the cost of capital would be reduced, and investment in the economy enhanced.

International comparisons appear to lend some support to this view. Estimates by Ando and Auerbach, for example, suggest that the Japanese cost of capital may have been as little as half that in the U.S. in the 1967-83 period. Since they carefully control for other factors and still the cost difference persists, Ando and Auerbach conclude that the difference may have been due to the "lower risk" of comparable investments in Japan. This is consistent with the notion that the *kieretsu* and *mochiai* relationships are effective mechanisms of risk control.

It is also interesting to note that both Germany and Japan have higher rates of expenditure on research and development than the U.S. does, and that spending on plant and equipment is roughly twice as great in Germany and Japan as in the U.S., adjusting for the sizes of the respective economies. Whether this laggard performance is a manifestation of an "underinvestment" phenomenon related to inadequate risk-control powers of banks, of course, is difficult to ascertain. It may suggest, however, that as energetic as it is, our unique venture capital industry may not be an adequate substitute for banks with broader financing powers.

Randall Johnston Pozdena
Vice President

Bank Lending to LBOs: Risks and Supervisory Response

by James B. Thomson

An increased use of debt financing has been a hallmark of the financial restructuring of corporate America that has taken place in the mid- and late 1980s. An organization that develops from a corporate reorganization now commonly has 80 to 90 percent of its financing in the form of debt, in contrast to the 30-percent debt-to-assets ratio that prevailed in the previous two decades. Because of the high degree of leverage employed in these deals, they are often referred to as leveraged buyouts (LBOs), a form of highly leveraged financings.

The news media, Congress, and the regulatory community have all focused considerable attention on LBOs in recent months, largely because of the use of this financing arrangement to fund corporate takeovers. Media interest has been heightened by the size and volume of recent deals, particularly the reported $25.3 billion that the firm of Kohlberg, Kravis & Roberts paid for RJR Nabisco. The total volume of LBO deals for 1988 exceeded $98 billion.

Congressional attention concerns the use of LBOs in takeover deals that involve a major restructuring of the acquired company. The result in such deals may be layoffs and plant closings in communities where the acquired firm is the major, and sometimes only, employer. Some members of Congress are also wary of the LBO market's potential effect on consumer and small-business credit and on the stability of the financial system itself. Furthermore, because the tax code makes debt financing relatively less expensive than equity financing, Congress is concerned that tax considerations alone may be a major motivation behind many of the LBO deals. The LBO situation is so important that only the $100 billion thrift-industry bailout and deposit-insurance reform take precedence over it on the 101st Congress's agenda for regulatory reform in the financial sector.

Bank regulators are becoming increasingly interested in bank participation in LBO lending because of the dramatic increase in LBO credits on bank portfolios. The Comptroller of the Currency estimates that of the $150 billion to $180 billion in LBO debt outstanding, $80 billion is held by U.S. banks.[1] Most of this exposure has been accumulated in recent years. In fact, estimates of total bank lending for LBOs in 1988 may exceed $48 billion (excluding $15 billion in bank loans to RJR Nabisco).

Leveraged buyouts (LBOs), a popular method of corporate restructuring in the past decade, have attracted significant attention among the news media, Congress, and bank regulators. The huge size of recent takeover deals and the dramatic increase in LBO credits on bank portfolios have raised concerns about the risks of LBO financing. This article examines these risks and discusses the current response of bank supervisory authorities to the increased use of funding by leveraged buyouts.

In addition, analysts estimate that LBO credits on bank portfolios equal 18 percent of the total dollar volume of commercial and industrial loans and 50 percent of bank capital.[2] Concentration of LBO exposure is uneven; one published estimate of LBO exposure for the 10 most active banks in the LBO market cites a range from 40 to 140 percent of equity capital.[3]

Bank regulators are concerned about the impact of increased LBO exposure on bank soundness and, ultimately, on the regulatory safety net. High levels of leverage are thought to be associated with both increased risk and larger expected returns than most loans to less-leveraged customers. Assuming the current system of federal deposit insurance remains intact, federal deposit guarantees may cause banks to underprice the risk of LBO credits and to book more LBO loans for their portfolios than they would in the absence of deposit guarantees.[4] Because of these incentives, it is likely that LBO-related credits will be a point of exposure in the banking system.

This *Economic Commentary* looks at the risks associated with LBO lending and the current response of federal bank regulators to banks' increasing participation in this market. First, we will provide a brief overview of LBOs. Then we will examine the risks associated with lending to these highly leveraged companies. Finally, we will outline the current response of federal bank regulators to the increased participation of banks and bank holding companies in funding LBOs.

■ A Brief Primer on LBOs

What degree of leverage must a firm have in order for its financial restructuring to be defined as an LBO? There seems to be no consensus: Bankers Trust defines a firm as highly leveraged if it has 70 percent debt financing, while the Federal Reserve System is now using 75 percent debt financing as a general examination guideline.[5]

The degree of leverage that constitutes a highly leveraged firm is a relative concept. For example, the J.P. Morgan deal that created U.S. Steel in 1901 was considered to be highly leveraged because it resulted in a debt-to-assets ratio of 35 percent.[6] Although a debt-to-assets ratio of 80 percent is not uncommon in a country like Japan, a U.S. firm with this ratio is considered to be highly leveraged.

Even though the transactions that have drawn the majority of attention lately are the multibillion-dollar deals like RJR Nabisco, the data presented in table 1 show that the bulk of the $98.3 billion of LBO deals last year were relatively small. Of the 304 deals in 1988 identified as LBOs by Venture Economics, Inc., roughly 88 percent had a transaction price under $500 million, 19 deals were between $500 million and $1 billion, and 17 deals exceeded $1 billion. The average size of LBO transactions in 1988 was $327 million. The multibillion-dollar deals dominated the market in terms of total dollar lending, however, accounting for nearly 57 percent of the $98.3 billion in total transactions.[7]

Making loans to highly leveraged firms is not a new activity for banks. Banks have lent to highly leveraged firms in the middle market (deals under $500 million) for years. Most loans guaranteed by the Small Business Administration can be defined as highly leveraged financings. However, the syndication of loans for leveraged buyouts of national and multinational companies is a more recent phenomenon.

LBOs typically have three tiers of financing. The first tier is senior debt, which makes up 50 to 60 percent of the total and mainly consists of secured bank loans. The second tier is mezzanine financing, which consists of unsecured debt and makes up roughly 30 percent of the total. These debentures are considered highly speculative investments (junk bonds). The last tier of financing is equity, which usually makes up 10 to 20 percent of total financing. Some of the equity in the reorganized firm may be held by nonbank subsidiaries of bank holding companies.

■ Risks Associated with LBO Credits

LBO financing is a natural market for banks. Loans to support LBO transactions carry many of the same risks of more traditional commercial loans, so banks should be in an excellent position to assess and assume these risks. However, the larger degree of leverage in LBO financing accentuates the risk of default, because there is less equity in the firm to absorb unexpected earnings losses. It is therefore essential that the lender conduct a sufficient analysis of the proposed transaction and of the creditor, and that it appropriately price the risks of these loans.

TABLE 1 LEVERAGED BUYOUTS IN 1988 BY TRANSACTION SIZE[a]

Transaction Size	Number of Buyouts	Percent of Total	Dollar Volume[b]	Percent of Total $
Under $50 million	105	34.5%	$2,206.6	2.2%
$50 million - $99.9 million	58	19.1%	4,086.8	4.2%
$100 million - $499.9 million	105	34.5%	22,334.0	22.7%
$500 million - $999.9 million	19	6.3%	13,961.0	14.2%
Over $1 billion	17	5.6%	55,687.0	56.7%
Totals	304	100.0%	$98,275.4	100.0%

a. Deals announced or consummated in 1988.
b. Millions of dollars.
SOURCE: *Buyouts*, vol. 2, issue 1, Venture Economics, Inc., January 11, 1989, page 2.

Lending analysis should be focused primarily on reasonable projections of cash flows and secondarily on collateral values. Recent experience with real-estate lending in Texas and with agricultural loans in the Midwest illustrates the problems that can arise when lending is based on inflated asset values and not on accurately projected cash flows.

However, the valuation of collateral and cash flows may be difficult, as the value of a firm's stock may double or triple when a takeover deal is announced. Furthermore, cash-flow projections are often based on a radically reorganized firm and on overly optimistic assumptions about cost-cutting measures and asset sales. These uncertainties make it difficult to use historical cash flows to project future cash flows.

The recent expansion of lending to highly leveraged firms has occurred during the relatively stable macroeconomic environment of the mid-1980s. Although banks' loss experience on LBO-related loans is not materially higher than for more traditional commercial loans, it is unclear how LBO credits will perform in a less stable macroeconomy. How much can interest rates rise before some highly leveraged firms can no longer meet their debt payments? What effects would an economic downturn (especial-

ly a prolonged recession) have on many highly leveraged firms' abilities to service their debt from operating income? A large part of a bank's LBO portfolio could conceivably go under if interest rates rise dramatically or if there is a severe economic downturn. The concern is that a bank may not be able to adequately hedge against macroeconomic risks in its LBO-related loan portfolio.

Although macroeconomic risk may not be mitigated by diversifying the LBO portfolio, diversification is important. Even in a robust macroeconomy, regional- or industry-specific problems can affect the ability of an LBO firm to service its debt. Through diversification, the impact of these problems on the bank's LBO portfolio is minimized.

■ **Current Supervisory Response**
Currently, federal bank authorities both supervise and regulate risks posed to the banking system from the LBO portfolios of banks. Because no additional restrictions have been imposed on the activities of banks participating in the LBO market, only the existing regulations for bank lending pertain to LBO loans.[8] Moreover, much like the approach taken to reign in daylight overdrafts in the payments system, banks are being asked to define, manage, and impose internal limits on

their own LBO risk exposure.[9] Regulators, using their supervisory authority, would take action against a bank only if its internal procedures were deemed inadequate. Federal supervisors would emphasize management skills and portfolio composition in evaluating a bank or bank holding company's LBO exposure.

In their evaluation, bank examiners look for an internal definition of an LBO credit: can the bank identify its LBO portfolio and LBO loan exposure? In addition, are there procedures in place for evaluating the risk of LBO loans? Does management have the ability to evaluate the target company's management and operating controls?

Banks are also expected to have in place specific procedures to deal with defaults, including procedures to monitor their risk exposure to both individual and aggregate LBO credits. In addition, the banks must have established policies, procedures and documentation to handle the special legal problems associated with LBO lending.[10] Finally, the adequacy of internal controls will be examined. For instance, has management established prudent and reasonable limits on the total amount of exposure and the type of exposure to LBO credits (on both a bank and a consolidated holding company basis)?

In conjunction with their evaluation of management, bank examiners will pay particular attention to the composition of the LBO portfolio. Specifically, they will look at the quality of the credits and the overall diversification, as well as the bank's total capital exposure to the LBO portfolio, on both a firm and industry basis. In the context of the overall asset portfolio, total LBO loans may be treated as a specific concentration of credit.

Another concern of bank regulators is the syndicated loans in a bank's LBO portfolio. To the extent that the lead banks in the LBO loan syndicate primarily perform an investment banking function and retain only a small percentage of the loans on their books, the banks purchasing the loans must conduct their own independent evaluation of the loan. Examiners will scrutinize this part of the portfolio to determine the adequacy of internal procedures for evaluating and managing the risks of the syndicated loans. In addition, examiners are concerned with banks' potential higher risk of obtaining liens on collateral and participating in any debt renegotiation.

■ **LBO Loans and Risk-Based Capital Standards**

Bank regulators view capital as the last line of defense between unexpected earnings losses on a bank's portfolio and both uninsured bank depositors and the regulatory safety net. The traditional approach to capital regulation has been to set a uniform capital-to-assets ratio for all banks, regardless of their risk, and to control portfolio risk through supervision and regulation. This approach has been criticized for two reasons. First, regulators do not know with much precision how much capital an individual bank (let alone *all* banks) needs to hold to protect against insolvency. Second, the amount of capital required to protect the federal deposit insurance funds and uninsured depositors from loss varies from bank to bank depending on risk. In response to the second criticism, bank regulators in the United States and in the other major developed countries have recently announced new international capital standards for banks.[11] These new standards require banks to hold a level of capital that corresponds to the credit risk in their portfolio.

The new capital standards partition a bank's asset portfolio into four risk categories according to perceived default risk. The amount of capital a bank must hold against a particular asset (or activity) is then determined by its risk category. The premise behind this approach is that banks should be allowed to choose the risk of their portfolio without regulatory interference, so long as increased risk to depositors and to the federal deposit insurance funds is offset by increased capital protection.

Critics of the new capital guidelines claim that they do not explicitly recognize the increased risk associated with LBO-related loans. Under the current risk-based capital standards, loans to highly leveraged companies are placed into the same risk category as more traditional commercial and industrial loans. This means that a bank must hold the same amount of capital to back up an LBO-related credit as it would a similar credit to a less-leveraged firm.

Admittedly, the standards are not perfect because they do not take into account all risks. However, risk distinctions beyond those contained in the regulatory framework are difficult to define with precision. Additionally, regulating risk runs the danger of introducing unwanted effects on credit allocation. More important, the risk-based ratio is only a first step in assessing capital adequacy. As is the case with other loans, the quality of LBO-related loans and investments must also be taken into account.

Moreover, the final risk-based capital guidelines are the result of negotiation and compromise between bank regulators in the nations adopting the new capital standards. Given the differences in capital structure for non-financial firms across countries (as noted earlier, Japanese firms tend to be much more leveraged than U.S. firms), it would be difficult to gain a consensus among nations to adopt capital guidelines that differentiate among loans according to the leverage of the borrower. Consequently, it is unlikely that LBO-related loans will be assigned their own risk class under the international capital guidelines.

■ **Conclusion**

LBO financing is a natural market for banks to engage in, and they are in an excellent position to assess and assume this risk. With returns on LBO loans as much as four percentage points higher than those available on more traditional commercial loans, it appears that the higher risk may currently be offset by higher expected returns.[12]

The high debt-to-equity ratio in the resulting firm leaves little or no margin for error when evaluating and pricing these loans, however. Lenders therefore need to adopt adequate controls and procedures for evaluating, pricing, and managing the risks of this type of lending activity. As long as banks adopt appropriate internal controls, bank regulators should reasonably expect that supervision—not regulation—is the appropriate approach to LBO-related lending.

■ **Footnotes**

1. See Barbara A. Rehm, "Regulators Mull Changes in Fees on LBO Loans: Bank Exposure to Firms in Debt Raises Concerns," *American Banker*, January 31, 1989, page 1.

2. See Nancy J. Needham, "Son of LDCs: Banks Are Borrowing Trouble with Loans to LBOs," *Barron's*, December 26, 1988, page 13.

3. See Sarah Bartlett, "Bankers Defend Buyout Loans But Investors Fret," *The New York Times*, October 28, 1988, page D1.

4. As I discussed in an earlier article, the current system of federal deposit guarantees subsidizes risk-taking behavior by banks. The value of the subsidy increases with the risk of the bank. Therefore, banks will tend to hold riskier portfolios than they would if there were no deposit insurance subsidy. See James B. Thomson, "Equity, Efficiency, and Mispriced Deposit Guarantees," *Economic Commentary*, Federal Reserve Bank of Cleveland, July 15, 1986.

5. However, not all loans to companies with 75 percent debt financing are classified as LBOs by the Federal Reserve. In addition to the leverage criteria, the loans must be for the purpose of acquiring or reorganizing the firm to be considered as LBO credits by the Federal Reserve System.

6. See George Anders, "Shades of U.S. Steel: J.P. Morgan Paved the Way for LBOs: Bidding for RJR Nabisco Has Precedents Dating Back to the Turn of the Century," *The Wall Street Journal*, Midwest Edition, November 15, 1989, page A1.

7. See *Buyouts*, vol. 2, issue 1, Venture Economics, Inc., January 11, 1989.

8. Additional reporting requirements for LBO loans may be required. The Y-9 report for bank holding companies may include a line item for LBOs in the near future. Furthermore, the federal bank regulators may change the accounting treatment of fees on LBO credits. See Barbara A. Rehm, op. cit.

9. For a discussion of the payments system and daylight overdrafts, see E.J. Stevens, "Reducing Risk in Wire Transfer Systems," *Economic Review*, Federal Reserve Bank of Cleveland, Quarter 2 1986, pages 17-22; and E.J. Stevens, "Pricing Daylight Overdrafts," *Working Paper* 8816, Federal Reserve Bank of Cleveland, December 1988.

10. Unique legal problems can arise during the first year of an LBO loan, mostly concerning fraudulent conveyance, equitable subordination, and state bulk transfer laws.

11. For a more detailed discussion of the new capital guidelines, see Janice M. Moulton, "New Guidelines for Capital: An Attempt to Reflect Risk," *Business Review*, Federal Reserve Bank of Philadelphia, July/August 1987, pages 19-33.

12. See Stan Hinden, "Executive Urges LBO Loan Curbs: Moody's Official Sees History as a Warning," *The Washington Post*, February 2, 1989, page F2.

James B. Thomson is an assistant vice president and economist at the Federal Reserve Bank of Cleveland. The author would like to thank Lawrence Cuy, William Osterberg, and Mark Sniderman for helpful comments.

The views stated herein are those of the author and not necessarily those of the Federal Reserve Bank of Cleveland or of the Board of Governors of the Federal Reserve System.

Article 30

Foreign competition in U.S. banking markets

Foreign penetration of U.S. wholesale banking already exceeds that of most other industry groups; unless market capitalization ratios for U.S. banks go up—or down for foreign banks—this trend is likely to continue.

Herbert L. Baer

 The global integration of the world's banking markets seems an inevitable, if not an already accomplished, fact. However, the accommodations that global integration will force upon U.S. banks may well be more disruptive and anxiety-inducing than those experienced in other sectors of the U.S. economy that have been integrated into the global marketplace. This article discusses the extent and nature of foreign competition in U.S. banking and argues that the increasing importance of foreign banking organizations is primarily a consequence of their superior capitalization.

Banking in perspective

Firms in most sectors of the U.S. economy have been free to sell their products in a nationally integrated market. And, despite tariff protection, these sectors have been subject to foreign competition for many years. In contrast, for most of its history, the American banking system has been simply a collection of local banking markets tied together by a correspondent banking network and the existence of large domestic corporate customers. For many bank customers, interstate competition, let alone international competition, has been rare. Indeed, as recently as twenty-five years ago, foreign and U.S. branches of foreign banks accounted for only 1.5 percent of total commercial lending by banks. At that same time, imports of manufactured and semi-manufactured goods were about 7 percent of the supply of U.S. manufactures.

The fragmented nature of U.S. banking is likely to place U.S. banks in a weak position as they compete for market share in an increasingly global market for banking services. Indeed, by 1988 foreign banking organizations accounted for 28 percent of wholesale banking in the United States (see Figure 1). Thus, foreign penetration of U.S. wholesale banking markets exceeds the levels achieved in primary metals, in electronic equipment, and in the transportation equipment sector. A higher level of foreign penetration been achieved in only one broad industry group—leather goods. In short, U.S. wholesale banking has gone from an extremely protected position in the 1960s to a quite exposed position in the 1990s.

Accessing the U.S. market

Foreign banks provide services to U.S. customers through branches located in the United States, through subsidiary banks chartered in the United States, and through offices outside the United States. Legally, foreign-owned banks chartered in the United States are subject to exactly the same regulations as a domestically owned bank chartered in the United States. If the owner of the bank is a bank or some other corporation, then the owner is generally treated as a bank holding company for regulatory purposes. However, in practice, some attempt is made to accommodate differences in banking practices across countries. For instance, foreign banks that

Herbert L. Baer is an assistant vice president at the Federal Reserve Bank of Chicago.

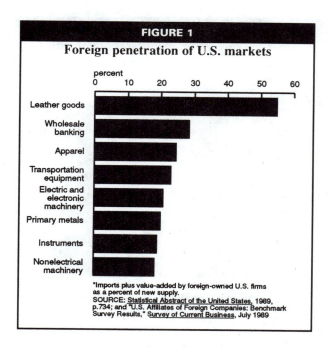

FIGURE 1

Foreign penetration of U.S. markets

percent

Leather goods

Wholesale banking

Apparel

Transportation equipment

Electric and electronic machinery

Primary metals

Instruments

Nonelectrical machinery

*Imports plus value-added by foreign-owned U.S. firms as a percent of new supply.
SOURCE: Statistical Abstract of the United States, 1989, p.734; and "U.S. Affiliates of Foreign Companies: Benchmark Survey Results," Survey of Current Business, July 1989

have controlling interests in commercial firms are permitted to own bank subsidiaries in the United States. At the other extreme, foreign banks lending to U.S. customers from overseas offices are entirely free of U.S. regulation. Foreign-owned banks can also serve U.S. customers using a third approach—setting up a branch in the U.S. In this case, the U.S. branch's assets and liabilities are commingled with the rest of the bank's assets and liabilities. Capital requirements and lending limits are set by regulators in the bank's home country. However, the branch is subject to examination by the licensing state.

Market shares

Foreign banking organizations play virtually no role in the retail segment of the U.S. banking market. However, they are playing an increasingly important role in the wholesale banking market.

Commercial lending

The share of commercial and industrial (C&I) lending accounted for by U.S. branches of foreign banks has risen from 8.6 percent in 1980 to 14.4 percent in 1988 (see Figure 2). All of this increase is accounted for by branches of Japanese banks. In 1980, the U.S. branches of Japanese banks accounted for 2.7 percent of all C&I lending. By 1988, their share had risen to 8.5 percent. Over the same

period, the market share of the U.S. branches of other foreign banks remained steady at 5.9 percent. The growth in C&I lending by foreign-owned banks chartered in the United States has been less dramatic, rising from 4.4 percent in 1980 to 6.3 percent in 1988. In contrast to the striking inroads made by branches of Japanese banks, the share of Japanese-owned U.S. banks has been relatively small, rising from 0.1 percent in 1980 to 2.4 percent in 1988.

The volume of C&I lending to U.S. firms through banking offices located outside the United States is more difficult to come by. The Bank for International Settlements (BIS) reports total foreign bank exposure to U.S. nonbank borrowers (including government and corporate bonds) while the Federal Reserve reports total loans by foreign firms (bank and nonbank) to nonfinancial firms. Neither source permits a breakdown by nation. However, using either definition, borrowing from offshore offices has grown dramatically. Using the Federal Reserve numbers, which include borrowings from banks and nonbanks, the share of C&I lending accounted for by offshore offices has risen sixfold from 1.2 per cent in 1980 to 7.6 percent in 1988.

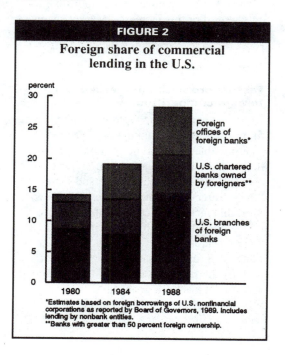

FIGURE 2

Foreign share of commercial lending in the U.S.

percent

Foreign offices of foreign banks*

U.S. chartered banks owned by foreigners**

U.S. branches of foreign banks

1980   1984   1988

*Estimates based on foreign borrowings of U.S. nonfinancial corporations as reported by Board of Governors, 1989. Includes lending by nonbank entities.
**Banks with greater than 50 percent foreign ownership.

Guarantees

Guarantees in the form of standby letters of credit (SLOC) represent another important wholesale banking product. When a bank writes a SLOC, it guarantees that the customer will meet a financial commitment. SLOCs are used to guarantee a wide array of financial agreements. Examples include loans, commercial paper, bonds, asset-backed securities, and futures margin payments. The market for SLOCs, while smaller than the market for C&I lending, is clearly sizeable. As of December 1988 there were a total of $288 billion in SLOCs outstanding to U.S. customers versus $660 billion in commercial loans. There are a number of reasons why banks may choose to intermediate indirectly through the issuance of SLOCs rather than through direct lending (Baer and Pavel, 1987). These include avoidance of reserve requirements, deposit insurance premiums, or other regulatory factors that place the bank at a disadvantage relative to its customer in raising funds and declines in the credit quality of the issuing bank (Benveniste and Berger, 1987).

The growth in SLOCs issued by foreign banking organizations has been explosive (see Figure 3). In 1980 U.S. branches of foreign banks accounted for only 10 percent of all SLOCs issued to U.S. customers. By 1988, they accounted for 53 percent. Moreover, in contrast to the market for C&I loans, branches of Japanese banks have been responsible for only a third of this increase. Market shares of banks based in Switzerland, West Germany, France, and the United Kingdom have all grown dramatically.

Factors promoting increased foreign competition

What explains the rapid growth in competition from foreign banking organizations? One possible factor is the continued integration of the nonfinancial portion of the U.S. economy through greater trade and increased foreign direct investment in the U.S. However, this increase is capable of explaining only a portion of the observed increase in the market shares of foreign banking organizations. U.S. imports have been growing at roughly 7.6 percent a year and foreign direct investment has been growing at 14 percent a year. However, total C&I loans outstanding have been growing at 8 percent a year. This

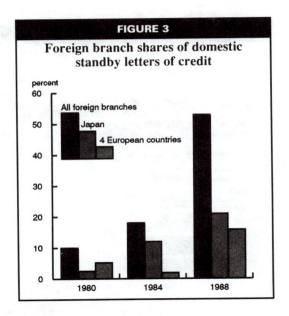

FIGURE 3

Foreign branch shares of domestic standby letters of credit

means that, at best, taking into account the increased integration of the U.S. economy into the global economy would only explain half the growth in the share of C&I for foreign banking organizations. At worst, global integration of nonfinancial activities accounts for none of the growth in market share experienced by foreign banking organizations. Other data support the contention that the growth in foreign banking organizations is not simply the result of increased foreign trade and foreign direct investment.

Sales of domestic C&I loans by U.S. commercial banks account for a significant portion of the competitive inroads being achieved by foreign banking organizations. Banks voluntarily sell loans to other institutions (including foreign banks) to avoid violating lending limits; to achieve a more diversified loan portfolio; to reduce capital requirements; or to take advantage of lower funding costs available at other institutions. Loans are purchased by other banks because they seek to diversify their portfolios; because their ability to raise deposits exceeds their ability to generate loans directly; because they are attempting to develop a banking relationship with a customer; or because they are able to raise funds at a lower rate than the seller (see Pavel and Phillis, 1987). By all accounts, loan sales were relatively unimportant prior to the early 1980s. In 1985, the first year for which formal figures are available, loans sold to U.S.

branches of foreign banks accounted for 1.9 percent of total C&I loans outstanding and 24 percent of total loans held by U.S. branches of foreign banks. By 1988, they accounted for 2.5 percent of total C&I loans. Thus, U.S. banks have been directly responsible for over two-fifths of the 5.8 percentage point increase in the market share of U.S. branches of foreign banks that occurred between 1980 and 1988 (Board of Governors of the Federal Reserve System, various years).

Some observers have been concerned that the rapid penetration of the U.S. wholesale banking market by foreign firms is the result of lax regulation by foreign governments (for instance, Walters, 1987). Excessive regulation of banks in their home markets has certainly played a role in the growth of the Eurodollar activities of U.S. banks (Baer and Pavel, 1987) and the Eurodollar and Euroyen activities of Japanese banks (Terrell, Dohner, and Lowrey, 1989). However, the links between lax regulation in a foreign bank's home markets and its competitive position in the domestic U.S. market is less well documented. Fears regarding the competitive advantages conveyed by lax regulation at home may be justified, particularly with respect to banks owned by foreign governments. And although no objective rankings exist, this concern would also appear to be valid where privately-owned foreign banks enjoy stronger guarantees from their governments than U.S. banks enjoy from the U.S. government. Whatever the particulars of the complaint, it ultimately boils down to the assertion that foreign banks are able to hold less capital per dollar of risk or pay less for the capital that they raise.

If this complaint is correct, then we would expect that those banks that have made the greatest inroads into the U.S. market—that is, the large Japanese banks (known as "city" banks)—would be the least capitalized of the major international banks. Yet, as Figure 4 shows, the large Japanese city banks, as a group, have the highest ratio of market capitalization (share price times number of shares outstanding) to assets of all the major international banks. As of January 1990, the lowest figure for a Japanese bank is about 16 percent while two have ratios over 20 percent.

The major U.S. money center banks, in contrast, have much lower market capitalization ratios. The highest market capitalization ratio for a U.S. money center bank is about 9.5 percent, while three money center banks have market capitalization ratios of under 3 percent. Banks based in Switzerland, West Germany, and the United Kingdom lie between the extremes of the U.S. and Japanese banks.

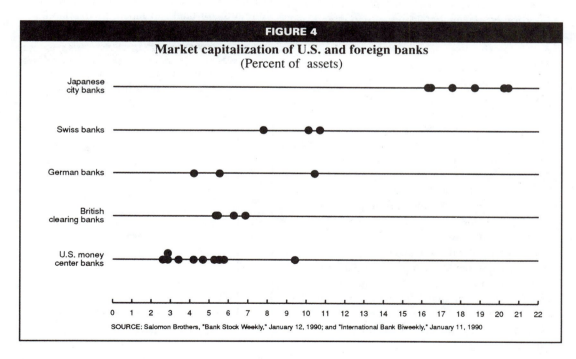

FIGURE 4

Market capitalization of U.S. and foreign banks
(Percent of assets)

SOURCE: Salomon Brothers, "Bank Stock Weekly," January 12, 1990; and "International Bank Biweekly," January 11, 1990

While the market capitalization of Japanese banks is extraordinarily high, their reported book values are relatively low, with the major Japanese banks reporting book capital ratios ranging from 2.5 to 3.0 percent in early 1990. Much of the discrepancy between the relatively low book values of Japanese banks and their relatively high market values is accounted for by unrecognized gains on their holdings of equity investments in Japanese nonbanking firms (Hanley et al., 1989). Japanese banks are permitted to hold up to a five percent interest in a nonbanking firm. The Japanese city banks are members of "keiretsus" or clubs that are the postwar successors to the powerful "zaibatsus." Banks frequently hold equity positions in other firms belonging to the keiretsu and it is not uncommon for a bank to be a firm's leading shareholder (Tokyo Keizai, 1989). A bank will also hold equity stakes in firms that are not members of its keiretsu.

The value of the equity portfolios of the large city banks has soared in the last decade along with the dramatic increase in Japanese (as well as worldwide) share prices (see Figure 5). By 1988, unrealized gains on securities accounted for 45 percent of the market capitalization of Japanese city banks. Unrealized gains on real estate, while not currently disclosed, are also likely to account for a nontrivial portion of the gap between the market and book values of Japanese banks because each has an extensive branch network and Japanese real estate values are high relative to those in other countries. The remainder of the discrepancy is accounted for by discounted future earnings on banking activities. And, while book earnings of Japanese banks are low by Western standards the discount rates applied to these earnings are also typically quite low (French and Poterba, 1990).

Even ignoring the unbooked value of Japanese real estate and the present discounted value of future earnings—i.e., counting only book equity and unrealized gains on securities net of unrealized gains on LDC debt—Japanese banks, as a group, are the most heavily capitalized banks in the world. In 1988, the least capitalized Japanese city bank had an adjusted book value of 6.4 percent while the best capitalized city bank had an adjusted book value of 12.6 percent. Clearly,

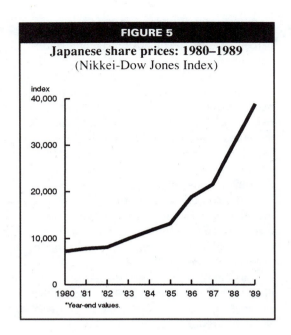

FIGURE 5

Japanese share prices: 1980–1989
(Nikkei-Dow Jones Index)

*Year-end values.

the impressive growth of Japanese banks cannot be explained by too little capital.

Too much of a good thing?

If too little capital does not explain the rapid growth of Japanese banks in the United States perhaps it is worth considering whether the high level of capital can explain their relatively high growth. Figure 6 plots the growth in international assets and market capitalization ratios for banks in Japan, Switzerland, the

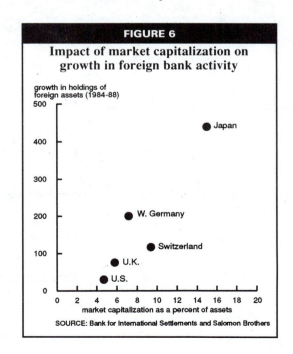

FIGURE 6

Impact of market capitalization on growth in foreign bank activity

SOURCE: Bank for International Settlements and Salomon Brothers

United Kingdom, the United States, and West Germany. Banks from France and Italy are excluded because their ownership by a national government makes it difficult to measure their true capital. Figure 6 suggests that the success of Japanese banks is only the most dramatic example of a more general principle—banks that have high market capitalization ratios have made greater inroads in foreign markets than have banks with relatively low market capitalization ratios. Swiss and German banks, which also have relatively high market capitalization ratios due to unrecognized gains on equity portfolios, have also been expanding into foreign markets at a relatively rapid rate.

At the November 1989 conference on globalization, a well-known economist remarked that he had never met a bank that had too much capital. Many in the audience chuckled at this remark with knowing agreement. In the context of American money center banking, where large windfall profits have been fairly rare while losses due to regional downturns and poor performance by third-world borrowers have been large relative to capital, the remark is correct.

How should a bank holding an equity portfolio that experiences a significant appreciation respond? One possible response would be to realize some of the unrecognized gains and pay the proceeds to the bank's shareholders through a special dividend. In the case of Japanese banks, however, both the shareholders and the bank want to avoid paying a special dividend. The bank owns much of its equity holdings as a direct result of its membership in its keiretsu. If the bank sells off its shareholdings in these firms, it risks weakening its ties to and influence over the keiretsu. The taxation of dividend income for individual investors is also an issue since dividend income is taxable while income from capital gains is not (Spicer and Oppenheimer, 1988). Furthermore, any capital gains realized when the bank sells securities are taxable at a rate of 52 percent (Hanley et al., 1989).

Clearly, there are strong incentives to avoid realizing capital gains in the absence of offsetting losses. As long as the discrepancy between the bank's current and "potential" share price is less than the tax that would be paid on the special dividend, bank shareholders prefer to realize the capital gain by selling the bank's shares rather than by having the bank pay a special dividend. Thus, for Japanese banks, strategy and shareholder tax avoidance both point toward retaining any capital gains within the bank.

The bank's decision to retain its capital gains places it in the position of having too much capital. If the bank's portfolio was previously in equilibrium, the bank now is able to issue uninsured liabilities at a lower rate than before. It is also able to take larger exposures to borrowers while maintaining the same level of diversification in its portfolio. The shift toward highly leveraged transactions by large U.S. and British firms in the latter half of the 1980s has accentuated this effect and surely explains a significant portion of the rapid growth of Japanese banks in the United States.[1]

Even if the bank is forced to raise book capital, it will still have strong incentives to grow. It can either increase book equity by realizing capital gains or by simply issuing additional securities. In contrast to banks with relatively low market capitalization, it will find securities issuance inexpensive, in large part because the issuance of additional securities does not generate an offsetting loss of government guarantees.[2] As Edward Kane points out elsewhere in this issue, this factor explains why Japanese banks have had little trouble raising additional equity.

However, the decision to retain capital gains within the bank may also give managers the leeway to pursue goals that do not maximize shareholder value. One common tactic in such situations is to pursue rapid growth both internally and through acquisition. This has proved common in nonbanking firms and there is no reason to believe that banks would behave any differently given the opportunity (Jensen, 1986). However, the conglomerate merger wave of the 1960s was reversed in the 1970s and 1980s as shareholders came to realize that these mergers were not in their interests. It is equally likely that inroads by foreign banks that have been driven by runaway management will be reversed in the next decade.

Conclusions

Many explanations have been advanced to explain the rapid growth of foreign banking organizations in the United States over the past decade. Some have argued that this growth simply reflects the increasing globalization of financial markets while others have argued that it is the result of the relatively lax regulation of foreign banks that permits them to operate with too little capital. The facts support neither explanation. Increased trade and foreign direct investment are capable of explaining only a portion of recent inroads made by foreign banking organizations while data on market capitalization suggest that the fastest growing foreign banking organizations, the Japanese city banks, are four to five times better capitalized than the typical U.S. money center bank.

The rapid growth of foreign banking organizations in the U.S. is best understood as a result of three events. First, Japanese banking organizations experienced a rapid increase in market capitalization due to rapid increases in the value of their equity portfolios. Second, the increasing importance of large-value highly leveraged transactions conveyed an advantage to well-capitalized banks able to lend large amounts of money quickly. Third, the market capitalization of the largest U.S. banks suffered repeated reverses due to a series of regional downturns and the failure of many LDC borrowers to repay loans as scheduled. According to this view, foreign inroads will ease only if asset growth or declines in the value of the equity portfolio bring the market capitalization ratios of Japanese banks back to the levels of the early 1980s, or if the market capitalization ratios of major U.S. banks rise significantly.

FOOTNOTES

[1]Kane (1990) and (1988) makes a similar point.

[2]When a bank is poorly capitalized and deposit insurance is mispriced, the deposit insurance can account for a substantial portion of the bank's market value. Issuance of new equity reduces the value of the deposit insurance and hence the overall value of the bank's equity. Existing shareholders must compensate new shareholders for this decline in value. This makes new equity expensive to issue.

REFERENCES

Baer, Herbert L., and Christine A. Pavel, ''Does Regulation Drive Innovation?,'' Federal Reserve Bank of Chicago, *Economic Perspectives*, Vol. 12, No. 2, March/April 1988, pp. 3-15.

Benveniste, Lawrence M., and Allen N. Berger, ''Securitization with Recourse: An Instrument that Offers Bank Depositors Sequential Claims,'' *Journal of Banking and Finance*, Vol. 11, No. 3, September 1987, pp. 403-424.

Board of Governors of the Federal Reserve System, *Senior Loan Officer Opinion Survey on Bank Lending Practices*, October 1989, August 1988, June 1987, February 1986, June 1985, mimeo.

French, Kenneth R., and James M. Poterba, ''Are Japanese Stock Prices Too High?,'' Center for Research in Research in Security Prices, *Working Paper*, W.P. 280, February 1990.

Hanley, Thomas H., John D. Leonard, Diane B. Glossman, Ron Napier, and Steven I. Davis, *Japanese Banks: Emerging Into Global Markets*, New York: Salomon Brothers, September 1989.

Kane, Edward J., ''How Market Forces Influence the Structure of Financial Regulation,'' in William Haraf and Rose-Marie Kushmeider (eds.), *Restructuring Banking and Financial Services in America*, Washington, D.C.: American Enterprise Institute for Public Policy Research, 1988.

Kane, Edward J., ''Incentive conflicts in the international regulatory agreement on risk-based capital,'' Federal Reserve Bank of Chicago, *Economic Perspectives*, Vol. 14, No. 3, May/June 1990, pp. 33-36.

Pavel, Christine A., and David Phillis, ''Why Commercial Banks Sell Loans: An Empirical Analysis,'' Federal Reserve Bank of

Chicago, *Economic Perspectives*, Vol. 11, No. 3, May/June 1987, pp. 3-14.

Spicer Oppenheim International, *The Spicer and Oppenheim Guide to Securities Markets Around the World,* New York: John Wiley and Sons, 1988.

Terrell, Henry S., Robert S. Dohner, and Barbara R. Lowrey, ''The U.S. and U.K. Activities of Japanese Banks, 1980-1988,''

Board of Governors of the Federal Reserve System, *International Finance Discussion Papers*, No. 361, September 1989.

Tokyo Keizai, *Japan Company Handbook,* Tokyo, Winter 1989.

Walters, Dennis, ''Stunned U.S. Banks Fear Deeper Market Inroads by Foreign Firms,'' *American Banker,* January 26, 1987, p. 29.

Article 31

The Costs of Default and International Lending

by Chien Nan Wang

In August 1982, Mexico announced that it was unable to service its nearly $80 billion foreign debt. Brazil, Argentina, Venezuela and other debtor countries soon announced their own debt-servicing difficulties.

Initially, it was feared that these borrowers might flatly refuse to repay their debts, thus repudiating their loan obligations. Because debt repudiation could severely hurt both creditors and debtors, the threat became the focus of what became known as the 1982 less-developed-country (LDC) debt crisis.

Between 1983 and 1986, creditors, debtors, and the International Monetary Fund (IMF) generally were able to work together to manage the debt problems, keeping interest payments on schedule by restructuring old loans and by making new loans in what can be described as a process of "cooperative interruptions."[1]

However, in 1986, Peru limited debt-service payments to not more than 10 percent of its export revenues. More strikingly, in February 1987, despite an ongoing effort to reschedule and refinance its debt, Brazil unilaterally delayed interest payments. In addition to Brazil, seven other Latin American countries, together with several smaller African countries, delayed interest payments in 1987. However, as will be discussed later, most of these interrupted payments were renegotiated, with inter-

est payments resuming within a year, through a set of arrangements that has been described as a "conciliatory default."[2] Earlier this year, Brazil again announced several measures designed to delay the repayment of its debts.

Conciliatory default, cooperative interruptions, and outright debt repudiation can each be regarded as a type of debt servicing failure—that is, of a borrower's failure to service and repay its debt as originally specified in the loan agreement. There are important distinctions among the types of debt-service failure. Outright repudiation is the most extreme form of noncooperative default, and occurs rarely. In contrast, both conciliatory default and cooperative interruption are characterized by important elements of mutual agreement, or at least acceptance of the need to modify the original loan agreement. Of these two, the latter procedure is the most amicable. However one describes the process, the international debt-service difficulties of recent years raise questions that are worth exploring.

First, any type of debt servicing failure can hurt creditors and debtors alike. Creditors see their capital eroded, threatening their solvency; debtors damage their own creditworthiness, perhaps impairing their ability to borrow again. Given such significant costs, how do borrowers choose the appropriate response to their debt servicing problems?

During the past few years, a number of less developed countries (LDCs) have had difficulty repaying their foreign debt. Sometimes payments have been suspended or delayed— making it necessary for debtors and creditors to renegotiate or reschedule loan payments. These problems have raised questions about the costs and benefits of different types of debt repayment negotiations and their implications for the future of international lending. This article investigates these questions.

Second, international lending to LDCs currently is declining. Declining capital inflows make it even more difficult for LDCs to service their debts and to finance their growth. Considering the huge amount of old debt and the uncertain prospects for future repayment, it is difficult to restore lenders' incentives to make new loans. Even if overall indebtedness were reduced to a more manageable level, for example, how could lenders really be confident that debtors would not default again in the future? Finally, do widespread problems with international debt service reveal a fundamental weakness in the structure of international private lending that does not exist in purely domestic lending?

The key to answering these questions centers on the benefits and costs of default in its various forms. This *Economic Commentary* investigates these aspects of default, using the current LDC debt problem to illustrate several issues that seem especially important for future international lending.

■ The Benefits and Costs of Default

International credit agreements involving the direct or indirect obligations of governments present the most difficult problems for creditors. The ultimate defenses for creditors against nonpayment —such as seizure of collateral and recourse to legal proceedings—are not fully available in international lending, so that repayment from sovereign debtors is not strictly enforceable.

A country may choose not to repay, even if it can. When unwillingness to repay motivates a sovereign debtor's debt-service decision, this decision is usually made after comparing the costs and benefits involved in a continuum of options ranging from timely debt service to extreme forms of default. One such option may be to alter the terms of repayment.

The primary benefit of altering the terms of repayment is the ability in the short run to save foreign exchange for domestic consumption and promotion of economic growth. The amount of foreign exchange saved is larger in repudiation cases than in conciliatory defaults because the former reduces the debt-servicing load for a longer period of time than the latter. While conciliatory default relieves or delays full debt-service payments for a period of time, cooperative interruption still assumes a certain amount of debt servicing for that period, thus reaping fewer benefits.

Debtors may also think that altering debt-service obligations will enhance domestic political tranquility. It is reasonable for debtors to believe that reducing debt service will permit increased domestic consumption and improve the resident population's immediate living standard. Altering the terms

of debt-service agreements may help consolidate the political regime, particularly for countries with pressing demands for a higher living standard. The longer-run effect is less certain. The costs of default may make it impossible to maintain a higher growth profile that will improve the future living standard, although this will depend on the severity and the effectiveness of the creditors' sanctions.

Altering debt-service agreements, while perhaps economically and politically attractive, is not cost-free, however. The costs and benefits for the debtor depend importantly on a wide range of factors, including the ability to negotiate new terms with lenders. In extreme cases of unilateral default, the borrower often faces trade and financial sanctions that impede the ability of the debtor country to maintain its overall consumption level when its income is low and then to repay when its income is high. Profitable investment opportunities may also be lost, and trade credit may be reduced or eliminated. Trade embargoes imposed by the lender's government may cause severe damage to countries dependent on trade, which includes most major debtors.

Default may also result in seizure of a defaulter's foreign assets or exports. Sovereign immunity from foreign interference with commercial transactions once was a basic principle in international law. However, the 1976 Foreign Sovereign Immunity Act (FSIA) in the U.S. and the 1978 State Immunity Act (SIA) in the United Kingdom established the legal liability of foreign governments for their acts of a purely commercial nature.

FSIA and SIA are crucial statutes because most international loan contracts are signed under U.S. or British law. As a result, borrowing countries typically waive sovereign immunity in commercial loan contracts.

There have been several instances in which a sovereign defaulter's foreign assets were seized by creditors. In

1979, for example, Morgan Guaranty Trust Company successfully attached the Iranian government's stake in Fr. Krupp AG through the German courts. Also, in 1981, the Cuban ship I Congresso del Partido was seized by Chilean plaintiffs for a default by Cubazucar, the state sugar monopoly. In general, however, the relatively limited resort to seizure by creditors suggests that it is a useful option only in the most extreme circumstances of debt-resolution failure.

■ The Uncertain Costs of Default

Economic issues, such as debt repayments, are only one dimension of a country's overall relationship with debtors, so that it may be difficult to define the national interest of the creditor's country narrowly enough to impose sanctions. Disagreements may exist either between various interest groups within a creditor country or between creditor nations about whether or not to sanction a defaulter. For example, exporters, nonexporters, regional banks, and multinational banks within the creditor country may take different positions on proposed sanctions. Finally, economic sanctions, if imposed, may be of limited effectiveness, because trade and financial flows are multilateral. Factors such as these and others may operate to reduce the threat of default penalties from the debtor's perspective. If debtors regard efforts to alter debt-service terms as unlikely to provoke a strong response, they are likely to press forward with some initiatives.

It may also be a misconception to believe that all foreign economic interests would unite to cut off future loans to a defaulting country. A permanent interruption of debt service on medium-term bank debts, for example, would cut a country off from new medium-term bank loans for a substantial period. However, if the debt service interruption is either temporary or occurs within a framework of ongoing negotiation and of acceptance by the borrower of the need to resume debt service, then eventual renegotiation of the loan contract is likely to restore access to credit. In such a setting, the reactions of nonbank foreign traders, multinational direct investors, and providers of short-term, direct-trade finance to a defaulting country might not be as serious. Foreign equity investors could very well retain their equity intact, and trade credits might still be serviced.

Trade retaliation against a defaulting nation is another option available to creditors, although such restrictions are most effective when applied by the creditors' governments. Moreover, the impact of trade embargoes is often diluted by trade with other countries and triangular-trade arrangements through third-country firms.[3]

The effectiveness of legal sanctions against sovereign defaulters is also limited. Although the legal position of creditors against the sovereign immunity defense has been improved substantially since 1976, the practical remedies for creditors still are limited.

For example, the Act of State principle, an established tenet of U.S. law, prevents U.S. courts from passing judgment on foreign countries' actions in cases involving our national interest. Execution of judgment under the legal process also usually does not apply to foreign diplomatic, military, and central bank properties in the U.S. Private property of individual foreign nationals located in the creditor country also is usually protected. Finally, legal actions may be avoided simply because they diminish the debtor's incentive to renegotiate the debt.

The argument that sovereign nations can avoid or reduce the cost of altering the terms of debt sevice implies that the benefits of such efforts may often be greater than the costs. While outright permanent and unilateral abrogations of lending agreements are uncommon, cooperative interruptions and conciliatory default, as part of an ongoing effort to reduce debt-service obligations, have occurred often since 1982. However, the infrequency of outright debt repudiation suggests that both debtors and creditors saw benefits in renegotiation and new repayment terms.

There are two other factors that seem to be important explanations of the willingness of debtor countries to renegotiate new repayment terms. National pride and a sense of fairness often require making the necessary payments: However, a borrowing country may simply be unable to generate enough foreign exchange through export expansion, import reduction, or acquisition of new capital to repay its debts, thus becoming unable to make the capital transfer.

Both the reputation factor and the transfer problem have been important underlying factors in the default and repayment experiences following the onset of the LDC debt crisis. During this period, most LDC debtors tightened their belts in order to generate sufficient trade surpluses to service their debts, both for preventing sanctions and for maintaining their reputations.

After the 1982 debt crisis, extensive debt restructuring was negotiated, usually requiring debtors to adopt International Monetary Fund (IMF) adjustment programs. These restructuring packages included lowering interest terms and stretching out interest or principal payment schedules, which increased the benefits of interrupting the debt servicing in a cooperative way. The restructuring packages also included refinancing arrangements that lowered the costs of cooperative interruptions. Therefore, debtors, after examining the costs and benefits, did not choose repudiation.

■ **Changing Situation**
Recently, lending to LDCs has been shrinking. In 1983, new bank lending to developing countries was $34.3 billion; in the first half of 1987, new lending fell to $3.4 billion. Reduced lending reduces the benefits to debtors of debt service because not much new financing is likely to be forthcoming whether they repaid or not. Also, the longer that debt stalemates continue, the longer would the benefits of withholding debt service accrue to debtor countries for enhanced economic growth, living standards, and political

stability. A probable result of these changes in the cost-benefit effect was the 1987 Brazilian interest moratorium. More than 10 other LDCs also delayed interest payments in the same year.

Brazil's interest moratorium did not last, however; Brazil and its creditors were able to negotiate lower fees and interest on restructured loans, and assemble new-money financing packages. The possibility that creditors would seek more extreme measures in order to maintain their reputation for debt-repayment enforcement also may have contributed to the reluctance of Brazil to remain in arrears.

For some countries in arrears, private medium-term financing virtually ceased, and short-term trade credits also declined. Peru, for example, has received few new agreements on short-term trade credits since its default. As for Brazil, it reportedly experienced difficulties in obtaining trade financing. (According to Brazil's Finance Minister, Mailson Ferreira da Nobrega, Brazil's 1987 interest moratorium was a mistake because it created new economic uncertainty and affected credit flows from abroad.)[4]

The bank trade credit loss for Brazil was estimated to be a moderate 20 percent. Once Brazil publicly expressed its intention to renew debt servicing, a record-high $82 billion restructuring package was assembled by Brazil's bank creditors. This event illustrates that, overall, the costs of debt service interruptions can be low as long as debtors show evidence of a cooperative attitude.

■ **Conclusion**
After the 1982 debt crisis, difficulties in securing debt repayment in the terms as originally agreed upon has emphasized the risks in international lending, and has contributed to a decline in lending. In 1983, involuntary bank lending to Latin America was $13.3 billion; it dropped to $2.0 billion in the first three quarters of 1987. In 1981, voluntary bank lending to Latin America was

$24.3 billion; in 1987, it fell to only $0.1 billion in the first three quarters.[5]

Various financial plans have been advanced to resolve the ongoing LDC debt repayment and economic growth problems. The proposals are divided between plans favoring an increase in lending to buy time and to finance structural reforms, and plans favoring a reduction in debt that is compatible with the debtor's ordinary servicing capacity. No matter how the current LDC debt and economic growth problems are managed, in the long run the difficulties encountered in enforcing international loan agreements seem likely to limit lenders' confidence in the likelihood of complete repayment.

The debt servicing difficulties of the past several years have increased lender's perceptions of risks to such a degree that a resumption of international lending may require basic and complicated structural changes in the framework of lending itself. Making these changes will prove to be very difficult, but if the volume of lending could be increased as a result, then both borrowers and lenders would benefit accordingly.[6]

Creditor and debtor nations will continue to struggle with their debt resolution efforts for many years. Parties on both sides will undoubtedly search for new ways to prevent overborrowing and overlending from repeating. They will also continue to calculate the costs and benefits of defaults on current obligations, and act accordingly.

■ **Footnotes**

1. See IMF Staff, *Recent Developments in External Debt Restructuring* (Washington D.C.: IMF, 1983, 1985), Occasional Paper, No. 25, 40.

2. Anatole Kaletsky is probably the first person to use the term "conciliatory default." Refer to the discussion of the costs of default in his book, *The Costs of Default* (New York: Priority Press Publications, 1985).

3. See Gary C. Hufbauer and Jeffrey J. Schott, *Economic Sanctions in Support of Foreign Policy Goals* (Washington D.C.: Institute for International Economics, 1983).

4. See "Brazil's Reversal of Debt Strategy," New York Times, February 22, 1988.

5. See IMF Staff, International Capital Markets (Washington D.C.:IMF, 1988), World Economic and Financial Surveys Series.

6. Various sanctions can deter defaults and enable lenders to extend credit to developing countries. See Jonathan Eaton and Mark Gersovitz, "Poor Country Borrowing in Private Financial Markets and the Repudiation Issue," Princeton Studies in International Finance, No. 47, June 1981.

Chien Nan Wang is an economist at the Federal Reserve Bank of Cleveland. The author would like to thank John Davis, William Gavin, Owen Humpage, Mark Sniderman, E.J. Stevens, and Walker Todd for helpful comments.

The views stated herein are those of the author and not necessarily those of the Federal Reserve Bank of Cleveland or of the Board of Governors of the Federal Reserve System.

Section V

International Financial Markets and Instruments

While the 1980s may have been the decade of debt and financial innovation, the 1990s promise to be a decade of internationalization and globalization. This is particularly true in finance. Already East and West Germany have achieved monetary union. Now Europe stands on the brink of much greater integration of the economies of countries in the European Community. Experts are virtually unanimous in foreseeing much greater interaction among the financial systems of different countries. In some sectors, such as the futures market and the stock market, globalization has already been achieved in some measure. While the preceding sections have often touched on international issues, the articles in this section deal squarely with financial issues of global concern.

In "Globalization in the Financial Services Industry," Christine Pavel and John N. McElravey survey the current status of globalization in financial services. They also examine how future movements toward globalization are likely to proceed. They find that globalization has already been achieved to a large extent for wholesale banking markets, and they foresee an increasing pace to globalization, particularly in Europe.

Increasingly, securities markets are electronic. When trading securities can be accomplished by the remote control of computer and telephone, the physical impediments to globalization are no longer critical. However, full globalization also requires a uniform clearing system. The clearing system in a securities market records the transaction, assigns the traded securities to the proper party, and credits the payment. In their article, "Standardizing World Securities Clearance Systems," Ramon P. DeGennaro and Christopher J. Pike examine the movement to standardize clearing systems. They find that the large volume of international trading already strains the existing system. However, DeGennaro and Pike note that attempts are underway to improve the system.

Faced with markets that are quickly becoming global, regulation of the financial system must become global as well. Otherwise, the regulation will be irrelevant, or it will impede the functioning of the market. One aspect of this financial regulation falls in the macroeconomic sphere. Already some governments work together in international currency and debt markets. W. Lee Hoskins evaluates the costs and benefits of this type of governmental coordination in his article, "International Policy Coordination: Can We Afford It?."

The European Community includes some of the largest and most important countries of Europe, such as Great Britain, West Germany, France, Italy, and Spain. In 1992, many restrictions on cross–border business will fall. Norman S. Fieleke assesses the likely impact of these changes in his article, "Europe in 1992." The European Community represents the U.S.'s largest export market and its integration may lead to greater economic activity throughout the world. By the same token, Fieleke notes that the European Community might allow economic freedom within its own sphere, but erect barriers to trade with outside nations.

If the Community instituted such policies, the consequences for countries such as the U.S. could be severe. However, Fieleke does not regard such a possibility as a serious threat.

One of the most critical issues in international finance is the entire question of foreign currency and the rate of exchange between currencies. Jane Marrinan evaluates the factors that affect the exchange rate in her paper, "Exchange Rate Determination: Sorting Out Theory and Evidence." Noting some conflict between theory and the actual behavior of exchange rates, Marrinan reviews the behavior of exchange rates in the last two decades. Her conclusions offer little hope that theory will quickly match the actual behavior of exchange rates.

Article 32

Globalization in the financial services industry

The pace has been most rapid at the wholesale, bank-to-bank and bank-to-multinational level; at the retail customer level, globalization will soon quicken, particularly in Europe.

Christine Pavel and John N. McElravey

Globalization can be defined as the act or state of becoming worldwide in scope or application. Apart from this geographical application, globalization can also be defined as becoming universal. For the financial services industry, this second meaning implies both a harmonization of rules and a reduction of barriers that will allow for the free flow of capital and permit all firms to compete in all markets.

This article looks at how global the financial services industry already is, and will likely become, by examining the nature and trends of globalization in the industry. It will also draw lessons from global nonfinancial industries and from recent geographic expansion of banking firms within the United States.

Financial globalization is being driven by advances in data processing and telecommunications, liberalization of restrictions on cross-border capital flows, deregulation of domestic capital markets, and greater competition among these markets for a share of the world's trading volume. It is growing rapidly, but primarily at the intermediary, rather than the customer, level. Its effects are felt at the customer level mainly because prices and interest rates are influenced by worldwide economic and financial conditions, rather than because direct customer access to suppliers has increased. However, globalization at the customer level will soon become apparent, at least in Europe after 1992, when European Community banking firms will be allowed to cross national borders.

Trends in other industries and lessons from interstate banking in the United States suggest that as financial globalization progresses, financial services will become more integrated, more competitive, and more concentrated. Also, firms that survive will become more efficient, and consumers of financial services will benefit considerably. Reciprocity is likely to be an important factor for those countries not already part of a regional compact, as it has been for interstate banking to proceed in the United States.

International commercial banking

The international banking market consists of the foreign sector of domestic banking markets and the unregulated offshore markets. It has undergone important structural changes over the last decade.

Like domestic banking, international banking involves lending and deposit taking. The primary distinction between the two types of banking lies in their customer bases. Since 1982, international lending and deposit taking have both been growing at roughly 15 percent annually. At year-end 1988, foreign loans and foreign liabilities at the world's banks each totalled more than $5 trillion. The extent, nature, and growth of international banking, however, are not the same in all countries.

When she wrote this article, Christine Pavel was an ecnomist at the Federal Reserve Bank of Chicago. She is now an assistant vice president at Citicorp North America Inc. John N. McElravey is an associate economist at the Federal Reserve Bank of Chicago.

Figures 1 and 2 show the ten countries whose banks have the largest shares of foreign banking assets and liabilities. Combined, these ten countries account for nearly three-quarters of all foreign assets and liabilities. Nearly half of all foreign banking assets and liabilities are held by banks in the United Kingdom, Japan, the United States, and Switzerland, up from 47 percent in 1982. This increase is almost entirely due to the meteoric rise in foreign lending by Japanese banks.

Perhaps the most notable event in international banking has been the rapid growth of Japanese banks. This extraordinary growth can be traced to deregulation in Japan, as well as to its banks' high market capitalization, the country's high savings rate, and its large current account surplus. Japanese foreign exchange controls and restrictions on capital outflows were removed in 1980. This allowed the banks' industrial customers to go directly to the capital markets for financing. The loss of some of their best customers, along with deposit rate deregulation and stiffer competition from other types of institutions, reduced profits.[1] To improve their profitability and to service Japanese nonfinancial firms that had expanded overseas, Japanese banks moved into new markets abroad. While a large part of the business of Japanese banks abroad is with Japanese firms, Japanese banks have been very successful lending to foreign industrial firms because of a competitive advantage conferred by a more favorable regulatory environment. Japan's capital requirements have been relatively easy, allowing banks to hold assets at 25 to 30 times book capital.[2] Japan's share of all foreign assets and liabilities rose from 4 percent in 1982 to more than 14 percent in 1988, surpassing the U.S. and second only to the U.K.

While many banks have significant international operations, only a few are truly international in scope. More than one-half of the total banking assets and liabilities in Switzerland, nearly one-half of total banking assets and liabilities in the United Kingdom, and over one-quarter of total banking assets and liabilities in France are foreign. In contrast, less than 25 percent of the balance sheets of German, Japanese, and U.S. banks consist of foreign assets and liabilities.

The United Kingdom and Switzerland have long been international financial centers. For more than 100 years Swiss bankers have been raising loans for foreigners. The largest Swiss banks, in fact, try to maintain a 50–50 split between their foreign and domestic assets for strategic and marketing reasons.[3] Deregulation, or the lack of regulation in some cases,

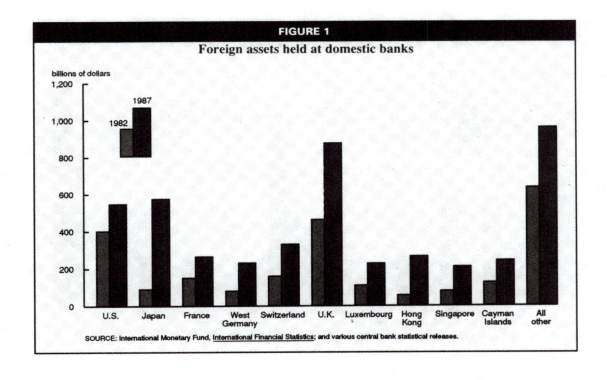

FIGURE 1

Foreign assets held at domestic banks

billions of dollars

SOURCE: International Monetary Fund, International Financial Statistics; and various central bank statistical releases.

and the restructuring of the British financial system have made London a powerful international financial center. More than half of all banking institutions in the U.K. are foreign-owned, and 59 percent of all assets of banks in the U.K. are denominated in foreign currency.[4]

At the aggregate level, the proportion of bank assets that are claims on foreigners is roughly equivalent to the proportion of liabilities that are claims of foreigners. This is not true of individual countries. Some countries' banks lend more to foreigners than they borrow from them. Foreign assets of German banks are almost twice the size of foreign liabilities, and Swiss banks hold about 34 percent more foreign assets than liabilities. For banks in these countries, the combination of international orientation and their country's high domestic saving rates makes them strong net lenders. Banks in the United States, Japan, and France, however, have more foreign liabilities than foreign assets, although in each case the difference is less than 5 percent.

U.S. banks have not always been net foreign borrowers. In 1982, foreign deposits at U.S. banks accounted for less than 13 percent of total liabilities, while foreign assets accounted for over 20 percent of total assets. Foreign deposits at U.S. banks have more than doubled over the 1982–87 period, growing far

more rapidly than domestic deposits. Foreign assets increased only 37 percent over that time and more slowly than domestic assets. This is due largely to the reduction in LDC lending and to the writing down of LDC loans by U.S. banks.

Foreign deposit growth also outpaced domestic deposit growth at Japanese banks. In 1982, foreign deposits accounted for 9 percent of total liabilities, and by 1987, they accounted for 18 percent. Similarly Japanese banks booked foreign assets about twice as fast as domestic assets over the 1982–87 period.

Offshore banking centers

A considerable portion of international banking activity occurs in unregulated offshore banking centers commonly known as the Euromarkets.[5] The Euromarkets, unlike the domestic markets, are virtually free of regulation. Euromarkets consist of Eurocurrency deposits, Eurobonds, and Euro-commercial paper. Eurocurrency deposits are bank deposits denominated in a foreign currency, and account for 86 percent of banks' foreign-owned deposits.

The development of Eurocurrency deposits marked the inauguration of the Euromarket in the mid-1950s. Eurocurrency deposits grew at a moderate rate until the mid-1960s when they began to grow more rapidly.[6] At that

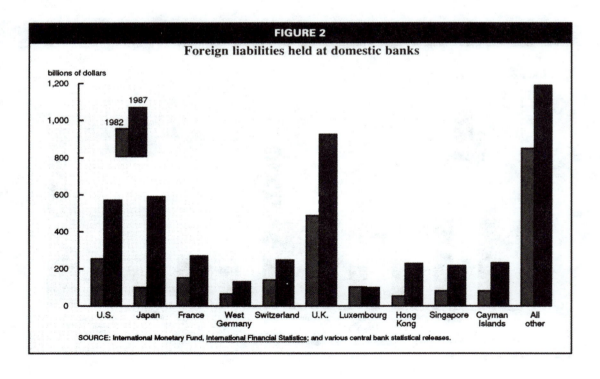

FIGURE 2

Foreign liabilities held at domestic banks

billions of dollars

SOURCE: International Monetary Fund, International Financial Statistics; and various central bank statistical releases.

time, the U.S. government imposed severe controls on the movement of capital, which "deflected a substantial amount of borrowing demand to the young Eurodollar market."[7] These U.S. capital controls were dismantled in 1974, but the oil crisis of the 1970s helped to fuel the continued growth of the Eurocurrency market. The U.S. oil embargo made oil-exporting countries fearful of placing their funds in domestic branches of U.S. banks. In the late 1970s and early 1980s, high interest rates bolstered the growth of Eurocurrency deposits, which are free of interest-rate ceilings and not subject to reserve requirements or deposit insurance premiums. From 1975 to 1980, Eurocurrency deposits grew over threefold.

Since 1980, Eurocurrency deposits have continued to grow quite rapidly, reaching a gross value of $4.5 trillion outstanding in 1987 and a net value of nearly $2.6 trillion (net of interbank claims). Eurodollar deposits, however, have not grown as rapidly. During the early 1980s, Eurodollars represented over 80 percent of all Eurocurrency deposits outstanding, but by 1987, they represented only 66 percent (see Figure 3). The declining importance of Eurodollar deposits can be explained, at least partially, by the decline in the cost of holding noninterest-bearing reserves against domestic deposits in the United States.[8]

Many Eurocenters have developed throughout the world. They have developed where local governments allow them to thrive, i.e., where regulation is favorable to offshore markets. Consequently, some countries with relatively small domestic financial markets, such as the Bahamas, have become important Eurocenters. Similarly, some countries with major domestic financial markets have no or very small offshore markets. In the United States, for example, the offshore market was prohibited until 1981 when International Banking Facilities (IBFs) were authorized.

Japan did not permit an offshore market to develop until late in 1986. Until then the "Asian dollar" market consisted primarily of the Eurocenters of Singapore, Bahrain, and Hong Kong. Now Japan's offshore market is about $400 billion in size, over twice as large as the U.S. offshore market, but still smaller than that in the United Kingdom.[9]

The interbank market

The international lending activities of most banks, aside from the money centers, are concentrated heavily in the area of providing a variety of credit facilities to banks in other countries. Consequently, a large proportion of banks' foreign assets and liabilities are claims on or claims of foreign banks. Eighty percent of all foreign assets are claims on other banks.[10] This ratio varies somewhat by country; however, since 1982, it has been increasing for all the major industrialized countries.

Similarly, nearly 80 percent of all banks' foreign liabilities are claims of other banks.[11] In Japan, 99 percent of all foreign liabilities at banks are deposits of foreign banks. Swiss banks are the exception, where only 28 percent of foreign liabilities are claims of banks.

The Swiss have a long history of providing banking services directly to foreign corporate and individual customers, which explains their relatively low proportion of interbank claims. A favorable legal and regulatory climate aided the development of a system that caters to foreigners, especially those wishing to shelter income from taxes. Confidentiality is recognized as a right of the bank customer, and stiff penalties can be imposed on bank officials who violate that right. In effect, no information about a client can be given to any third party.[12]

Since a very large portion of foreign deposits are Eurocurrency deposits, it is no surprise that about half of all Eurocurrency deposits are interbank claims. Eurocurrency

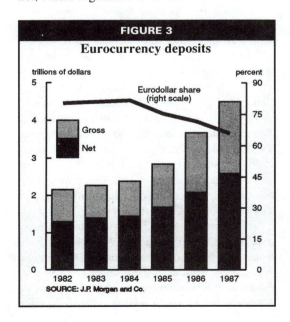

FIGURE 3

Eurocurrency deposits

trillions of dollars

percent

Eurodollar share (right scale)

Gross

Net

1982 1983 1984 1985 1986 1987

SOURCE: J.P. Morgan and Co.

deposits are frequently re-lent to other, often smaller, banks in the interbank market.[13]

The Japanese have become very large borrowers in the interbank market in response to domestic restrictions on prices and volumes of certain activities. Japanese banks operating overseas have been funding their activities by borrowing domestically (from nonresidents) in one market (e.g., the U.K.), and lending the funds through the interbank market to affiliates in other countries (e.g., the U.S.).[14]

Foreign exchange trading

Foreign exchange (forex) trading is another important international banking activity. Informal estimates place daily foreign exchange trading at $400 billion.[15] Like the loan markets, forex markets are primarily interbank markets. The primary players involved in the United States are the large money center and regional commercial banks, Edge Act corporations, and U.S. branches and agencies of foreign banks. Forex trading also involves some large nonbank financial firms, primarily large investment banks and foreign exchange brokers. However, according to the Federal Reserve Bank of New York's *U.S. Foreign Exchange Market Survey* for April 1989, 82 percent of the forex trading volume of banks was with other banks. Foreign exchange trading in New York grew at about 40 percent annually since 1986 to reach more than $130 billion by April 1989. In contrast, foreign trade (imports plus exports) has been growing at only about 6 percent annually since 1982 (3 percent on an inflation-adjusted basis).

The German mark is the most actively traded currency, followed by the Japanese yen, British pound, Swiss franc, and Canadian dollar. Since 1986, however, the German mark has lost some ground to the Japanese yen and the Swiss franc.[16]

The explosion of forex trading can, at least partly, be explained by the high rate of growth in cross-border financial transactions. Capital and foreign exchange controls were reduced or eliminated in a number of countries during the 1980s.

An international banking presence

There are several ways that commercial banks engage in international banking activities—through representative offices, agencies, foreign branches, and foreign sub- sidiary banks and affiliates. In addition, in the United States, commercial banks may operate International Banking Facilities (IBFs) and Edge Act corporations, which unlike the other means, do not involve a physical presence abroad. The primary difference among these types of foreign offices centers on how customer needs are met (often because of regulation). For example, agencies of foreign banks are essentially branches that cannot accept deposits from the general public, while branches, as well as subsidiary banks, can offer a full range of banking services.

U.S. branches and agencies of foreign banks devote well over half of their assets to loans, about the same proportion as the domestic offices of U.S. commercial banks. U.S. commercial banks, however, hold a much larger proportion of their assets in securities and a much smaller proportion in customer's liability on acceptances.[17] This latter situation reflects the international trade financings of U.S. foreign offices.

U.S. offices of foreign banks compete with domestic banks primarily in commercial lending and, to a lesser extent, in real estate lending.[18] However, a significant portion of the commercial loans held at U.S. offices of foreign banks were purchased from U.S. banks, rather than originated by the foreign offices themselves.[19]

Both U.S. offices of foreign banks and domestic offices of U.S. commercial banks primarily fund their operations with deposits of individuals, partnerships and corporations (IPC).[20] Offices of foreign banks currently gather 23 percent of these deposits from foreigners, and nearly all of these deposits are of the nontransaction type.

The presence of foreign banks in the United States has been increasing. The ratio of foreign offices to domestic offices in the United States has increased from 2.8 percent in 1981 to 4.4 percent in 1987. Similarly, the ratio of assets of foreign banking offices in the United States to assets of U.S. domestic banks has increased over 5 percentage points since 1981 to nearly 21 percent in 1987.[21]

The presence of U.S. banks abroad, however, has been falling since 1985. At that time, U.S. banks operated nearly 1,000 foreign branches.[22] Similarly, the number of U.S. banks with foreign branches peaked at 163 in 1982 and began to fall in 1986. By 1988, the number of banks with foreign branches had fallen to 147. On an inflation-adjusted basis, total assets of foreign branches of U.S. banks fell 12 percent since 1983 to $506 billion in 1988. The number of IBFs and Edge Act Corporations has also been waning. Edge Acts numbered 146 in 1984 and were down to 112 by 1988.[23] This retrenchment reflects the lessening attractiveness of foreign operations as losses on LDC loans have mounted.

Implications of Europe after 1992

The presence of foreign banking firms in European domestic markets will likely increase over the next few years as the 12 European Community states become, at least economically, a "United States of Europe." The EC plans to issue a single license that will allow banks to expand their networks throughout the Community, governed by their home country's regulations.[24]

Since banking powers will be determined by the rules of the home country, banks from countries with more liberal banking laws operating in countries with more restrictive banking laws will have an advantage over their domestic competitors. Consequently, the most efficient form of banking will prevail. Countries with more fragmented banking systems will need to liberalize for their banks to compete with banks from countries with universal banking.

While reciprocity will not be important for nations within the EC, it will be an issue for banks from countries outside the EC, especially those from Japan and the U.S. As financial services companies in Europe begin to operate with fewer restrictions, there will be competitive pressure on the U.S. and Japan to remove the barriers between commercial and investment banking. To be most efficient, firms operating in various markets want similar powers in each market. The EC, as previously noted, solved this problem with a Community banking license. Thus, the EC's efforts at regulatory harmonization may hasten the demise of Glass-Steagall in the U.S. and Article 65 in Japan.[25]

The implications for European banking will be similar to the experience in the United States following the introduction of interstate banking in the early to mid-1980s. Since that time, the U.S. commercial banking industry has been consolidating on nationwide, re-

gional, and statewide bases through mergers and acquisitions. Acquiring firms tend to be large, profitable organizations with expertise in operating geographically dispersed networks, while targets tend to be smaller, although still relatively large firms, in attractive banking markets. Large, poorly-capitalized firms will also find themselves to be potential takeover targets.

What these lessons imply for Europe in 1992 is that the largest and strongest organizations with the managerial talent to operate a geographically dispersed organization will become Europe-wide firms, while smaller firms will have a more regional focus and others will survive as niche players. In addition, just as different state laws have slowed the process of nationwide banking in the United States, language and cultural barriers will slow the process in Europe as well. The overall result of a more globally integrated financial sector in Europe, and elsewhere, will be that the organizations that survive will be more efficient, and customers will be better served. Also, it is very likely that the 1992 experience will improve European banks' ability to compete outside of Europe.

Size is not, and will not be, a sufficient ingredient for survival. In general, firms in protected industries, such as airlines, tend to be inefficient. Large banking organizations based in states with restrictive branching and multibank holding company laws tended to be less efficient than their peers in states that allow branches and, therefore, more competition. In addition, commercial banking organizations that operated in unit banking states had little expertise in operating a decentralized organization, and tended to focus primarily on large commercial customers. Consequently, these banking firms have not acquired banks far from home.

The process of consolidation has already begun within European countries and within Europe as firms prepare for a single European banking market. Unlike the Unites States' experience of outright mergers and acquisitions, however, the European experience centers on forming "partnerships." Partnerships have been formed Europe-wide, even though the most recent directive on commercial banking permits branching, because of the difficulties in managing an organization that spans several cultures and languages. Apparently, financial services firms want to get their feet wet first, rather than plunge into European banking and risk drowning before 1992 arrives. But also, until regulations among countries become more uniform, partnerships and joint ventures allow financial firms to arbitrage regulations.

The formation of partnerships and joint ventures is not only a European phenomenon. Indeed, U.S. firms have entered into such agreements with European and Japanese companies. For example, Wells Fargo and Nikko Securities have formed a joint venture to operate a global investment management firm, and Merrill Lynch and Société Générale are discussing a partnership to develop a French asset-backed securities market.

The experience of nonfinancial firms suggests that this arrangement can be a good way to establish an international presence. For example, in 1984, Toyota and General Motors entered into a joint manufacturing venture in California. Through this venture, the Japanese were able to acquaint themselves with American workers and suppliers before opening their own plants in the U.S. Since then, Toyota has opened two more manufacturing plants on its own in North America, and there is speculation in the auto industry that they will buy GM's share of the joint venture once the agreement ends in 1996.[26]

Another case of international expansion through joint ventures can be found in the petroleum industry. Oil companies from some oil-producing countries have been quite active in recent years buying stakes in refining and marketing operations in the United States and Europe. These acquisitions give producers an outlet for their crude in important retail markets, and refiners get a reliable source. Saudi Arabia purchased a 50 percent stake in Texaco's eastern and Gulf Coast refining and marketing operations in November 1988. The state-owned oil companies from Kuwait and Venezuela have joint ventures with European oil companies as well.[27] If joint ventures between financial services firms are as successful as nonfinancial ones have been, then global financial integration will benefit.

International securities markets

International securities include securities that are issued outside the issuer's home country. Some of these securities trade on foreign exchanges. Issuance and trading of international securities have grown considerably since 1986, as has the amount of such securities outstanding.

Greater demand for international financing is stimulating important changes in financial markets, especially in Europe. Regulations and procedures designed to shield domestic markets from foreign competition are gradually being dismantled. London's position as an international market was strengthened by the lack of sophistication of many other European markets. Greater demand for equity financing in Europe has been encouraged by private companies, and by governments privatizing large public-sector corporations. These measures to deregulate and, therefore, improve the efficiency, regulatory organizations, and settlement procedures are a response to competition from other markets, and the explosion of securities trading in the 1980s.[28]

It is estimated that the world bond markets at the end of 1988 consisted of about $9.8 trillion of publicly issued bonds outstanding, a nearly $2 trillion increase since 1986.[29] At year-end 1988, two-thirds of all bonds outstanding were obligations of central governments, their agencies, and state and local governments. This figure varies considerably across countries. Over two-thirds of bonds denominated in the U.S. dollar and the Japanese yen are government obligations, but less than one-third of bonds denominated in the German mark are government obligations, and only 10 percent of bonds denominated in the Swiss franc represent government debt.[30]

The international bond market includes foreign bonds, Eurobonds, and Euro-commercial paper. Foreign bonds are bonds issued in a foreign country and denominated in that country's currency. Eurobonds are long-term bonds issued and sold outside the country of the currency in which they are denominated. Similarly, Euro-commercial paper is a short-term debt instrument that is issued and sold outside the country of the currency in which it is denominated.

The Japanese are the biggest issuers of Eurobonds because it is easier and cheaper than issuing corporate bonds in Japan. Japanese companies issued 21 percent of all Eurobonds in 1988.[31] Ministry of Finance (MOF) regulations and the underwriting oligopoly of the four largest Japanese securities firms keep the issuance cost in the domestic bond market higher than in the Euromarket. The ministry would like to bring this bond market activity back to Japan, so it has been slowly liberalizing the rules for issuing yen bonds and samurai bonds (yen bonds issued by foreigners in Japan). So far, the impact of these changes has been small.[32]

International bonds accounted for almost 10 percent of bonds outstanding at the end of 1988 and over three-quarters are denominated in the U.S. dollar, Japanese yen, German mark and U.K. sterling (see Figure 4). These countries represent four of the largest economies and financial markets in the world.

The importance of international bond markets has increased considerably for many countries. As Table 1 shows, international bonds account for nearly half of all bonds denominated in the Swiss franc and over one-third of all bonds denominated in the Australian dollar. International bonds account for over 21 percent of bonds denominated in the British pound, up dramatically from less than 1 percent in 1980. The rise in importance of international bonds for these currencies can, at

least in part, be explained by the budget surpluses in the countries in which these currencies are denominated and, therefore, the slower growth in the debt obligations of these countries' governments.

The value of world equity markets, at $9.6 trillion in 1988, is about equal to the value of world bond markets. Three countries—the United States, Japan, and the United Kingdom—account for three quarters of the total capitalization on world equity markets, and they account for nearly half of the 15,000 equity issues listed on the world's stock exchanges (see Figure 5).

American, Japanese, and British equity markets are the largest and most active. American and British markets are very open to foreign investors, but significant barriers to foreign competitors still exist in Japan.

Stocks have, historically, played a relatively minor role in corporate financing in many European countries. Various regulatory and traditional barriers to entry made these bourses financial backwaters. The stock exchanges in Switzerland, West Germany, France, and Italy have only recently taken steps to modernize in order to compete against exchanges in the U.S. and the U.K. It was estimated that about 20 percent of daily trad-

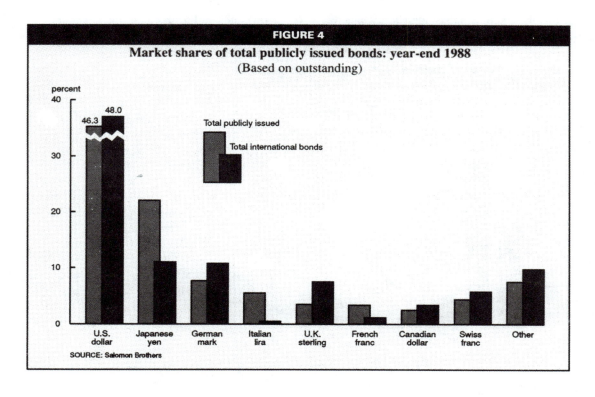

FIGURE 4

Market shares of total publicly issued bonds: year-end 1988
(Based on outstanding)

SOURCE: Salomon Brothers

TABLE 1

International shares of the world's major bond markets

(Percent based on outstanding)

	1980	1985	1988
U.S. dollar	4.4	8.8	10.5
Japanese yen	1.6	3.2	5.0
German mark	12.6	11.2	14.2
U.K. sterling	0.9	9.4	21.3
Canadian dollar	3.1	5.5	13.7
Swiss franc	27.3	42.3	49.2
Australian dollar	n.a.	9.5	36.2

SOURCE: Salomon Brothers

firms have traditionally relied more heavily on bank credit and bonds than on equity to finance growth. The integration of banking and commerce in Germany has contributed to this reliance. German banks, "through their equity holdings, exert significant ownership control over industrial firms."[34]

The fragmented structure of the West German system, which consists of eight independent exchanges each with its own interests, also helped check development. Over the last several years, though, rivalries between the exchanges have been somewhat buried, and they have been working to improve their integration and cooperation. One way is through computer links between exchanges to facilitate trading. A transaction that cannot be executed immediately at one of the smaller exchanges can be forwarded to Frankfurt to be completed. Overall, German liberalization efforts have been moderately successful, adding about 90 new companies to the stock exchange between 1984 and 1988.[35]

Active institutional investors, such as pension funds, which have a major position in the U.S. markets, have no tradition in the German equity market. Billions of marks in pension funds are on the balance sheets of German companies, treated as long-term loans from employees.[36] Freeing these funds in a deregulated and restructured market could have a profound effect on Germany's domestic equity markets.

ing in French equities was done in London in 1988.[33] French regulators hope that their improvements will lure some of that trading back to Paris.

West German equity markets, until recently, provided a good illustration of the kinds of barriers that keep stock exchanges small, inefficient, and illiquid. Access to the stock exchange was effectively controlled by the largest banks, which have a monopoly on brokerage. Under this arrangement, small firms were kept from issuing equity, thus remaining captive loan clients. Large German

Issuance of international securities

The issuance of international securities was mixed in 1988. Issuance of international bonds was relatively strong, while issuance of international equities, at $7.7 billion in 1988, was off considerably from 1987, but almost triple 1985 issuance.[37]

The contraction of international equities was driven by investors, and reflects their caution. Following the stock market crash in October 1987, portfolio managers reportedly focussed, and have continued to focus, on low-risk assets and on domestic issues.[38] Lower volatility of share prices on the world's major

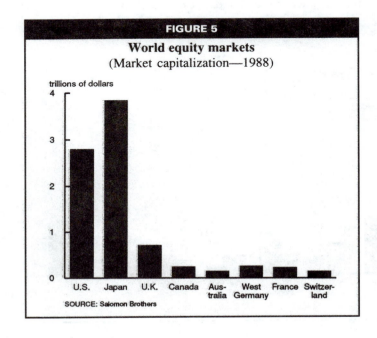

FIGURE 5

World equity markets

(Market capitalization—1988)

trillions of dollars

SOURCE: Salomon Brothers

exchanges, however, would likely aid a rebound in the appetite for and in the issuance of international equities.

Some important structural changes took place in international financial markets between 1985 and 1987. A sharp increase in issuance for the U.K. translated into substantially greater market share of international equity issuance, from 3.7 percent in 1985 to 33.0 percent in 1987. This increased share of international activity reflects the deregulation and restructuring of the London markets that occurred in the fall of 1986, improving their place as an international marketplace for securities. Even with the retrenchment in 1988, London maintained its leading role, with twice the issuance of second-place U.S.[39]

Over this same three-year period, Switzerland's international equity issuance translated into a substantially smaller market share, falling from 40.7 percent to 6.0 percent. This sharp decline in market share, from undisputed leader to fourth, reveals Switzerland's failure to keep pace with deregulation in other countries. For years, a cartel system dominated by its three big banks has set prices and practices in the stock markets. It is only recently that competition from markets abroad has forced the cartel to liberalize its system.[40]

In contrast to the international equities markets, issuance of international bonds was very strong in 1988, following a sharp contraction in 1987 entirely due to a 25.5 percent decline in Eurobond issuance.[41] Eurobonds account for about 80 percent of international bond issues, and nearly two-thirds of all international issues are denominated in three currencies—the U.S. dollar, Swiss franc, and the Deutschemark. Nearly 60 percent of international bonds are issued by borrowers in Japan, the United Kingdom, the United States, France, Canada, and Germany.

The long-time importance of the United States and the U.S. dollar in the international bond market has been dwindling. In 1985, 54 percent of all Eurobonds were denominated in U.S. dollars, but by 1988 only 42 percent were in U.S. dollars.

Similarly, U.S. borrowers issued 24 percent of all international bonds in 1985, but issued only 8 percent in 1988. The impetus behind this decline lies in part with the investors who prefer low-risk securities and are leery of U.S. bonds because of the perceived increase in "event risk" associated with restructurings and leveraged buyouts. Also, no doubt, developments such as the adoption of Rule 415 by the Securities and Exchange Commission (shelf registration) have encouraged U.S. firms to issue domestic securities by making it less costly to do so.

Trading in international securities

The United States is a major center of international securities trading. Foreign transactions in U.S. markets exceed U.S. transactions in foreign markets by a ratio of almost 7 to 1. This is a result of several factors. The United States has the largest and most developed securities markets in the world. U.S. equity markets are virtually free of controls on foreign involvement. SEC regulations on disclosure dissipate much uncertainty concerning the issuers of publicly listed securities in the United States while less, or inadequate, regulation in other countries makes investments more risky in those foreign markets. The market for U.S. Treasury securities has also been very attractive to foreign investors. In fact, large purchases of these securities by the Japanese have helped finance the U.S. government budget deficit.

Both foreign transactions in U.S. markets and U.S. transactions in foreign markets have been increasing at a very rapid pace. Foreign transactions in U.S. equity securities in U.S. markets plus such transactions in foreign equities in U.S. markets grew at almost 50 percent annually to exceed $670 billion in 1987.[42] Foreign transactions in U.S. stocks on U.S. equity markets have been increasing faster than domestic transactions; in 1988, foreign transactions accounted for 13 percent of the value of transactions on U.S. markets, up from 10 percent in 1986 (see Table 2).

Foreign transactions have increased in securities markets abroad as well; however, they have not, in general, kept pace with domestic trading. Consequently, foreign transactions as a percentage of all transactions has declined over the 1986-88 period for Japan, Canada, Germany, and the United Kingdom. Nevertheless, transactions by U.S. residents in foreign equity markets were estimated at about $188 billion in 1987, nearly 12 times as much as in 1982.[43]

TABLE 2

Foreign transactions in domestic equity markets: Share of domestic trading
(Percent of total volume)

	1985	1988
Japan	8.7	6.5
Canada	29.5	21.6
Germany	29.9	8.7
U.S.	9.7	13.1
U.K.	37.3	20.8
France	38.0	43.5
Switzerland	4.6	6.3

SOURCE: Salomon Brothers

Foreign transactions in U.S. bonds and foreign bonds in U.S. markets in 1988 increased to more than 13 times their 1982 level (see Figure 6). This trading boom was fueled mainly by growth in transactions for U.S. Treasury bonds, which accounted for about 84 percent of total foreign bond transactions in 1988, up from 63 percent in 1982. These transactions in U.S. Treasury bonds accounted for almost three-quarters of all foreign securities transactions in U.S. markets in 1988.

Bond transactions in other countries by nonresidents also increased dramatically. In Germany, for example, the value of such transactions increased by 300 percent over the 1985-88 period and now account for over half of the value of all transactions in German bond markets.[44] Foreign bond transactions by U.S. residents reached an estimated $380 billion in 1987, six times greater than the 1982 figure.

Derivative products

Globalization has affected derivative financial products in two ways. First, it has spurred the creation and rapid growth of internationally-related financial products, such as Eurodollar futures and options and foreign currency futures and options as well as futures and options on domestic securities that trade globally, such as U.S. Treasury securities. Trading hours on some U.S. futures and options exchanges have been expanded to support cross-border trading of underlying assets, such as Treasury securities. Second, globalization has lead to the establishment of futures and options exchanges worldwide. Once the exclusive domain of U.S. markets, especially in Chicago, financial derivative products are now traded in significant volumes throughout Europe and Asia.

The number of futures contracts on Eurodollar CDs and on foreign currencies as well as the number of open positions has increased rapidly (see Figure 7). The number of futures contracts on Eurodollar CDs traded worldwide increased almost 70 percent annually since 1983 to reach over 25 million in 1988. This compares with a 20 to 25 percent annual growth rate for Eurodollars.[45] Similarly, nearly 40 million futures and options contracts on various foreign currencies were traded worldwide in 1988, up from 14 million in 1983. This growth rate is roughly equivalent to that of forex trading.

The rapid increase in the volume of trading of internationally-linked futures and options contracts has largely benefited U.S. exchanges, which are the largest and sometimes the only exchanges where such products are traded. Nevertheless, the share of exchange traded futures and options volume commanded by the U.S. exchanges has dropped from 98 percent in 1983 to about 80 percent in 1988.

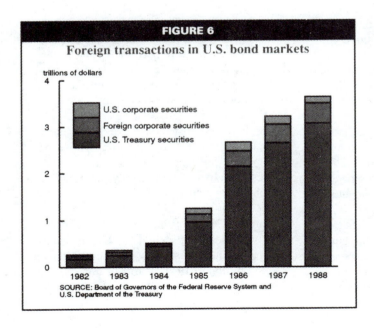

FIGURE 6

Foreign transactions in U.S. bond markets

trillions of dollars

- U.S. corporate securities
- Foreign corporate securities
- U.S. Treasury securities

SOURCE: Board of Governors of the Federal Reserve System and U.S. Department of the Treasury

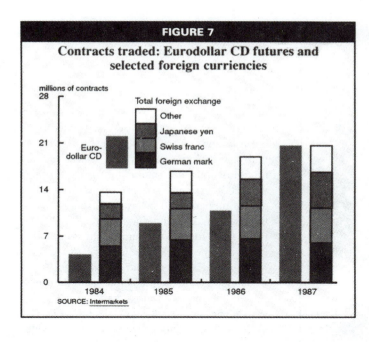

FIGURE 7

Contracts traded: Eurodollar CD futures and selected foreign curriencies

millions of contracts

Total foreign exchange
Other
Japanese yen
Swiss franc
German mark

Eurodollar CD

1984   1985   1986   1987

SOURCE: Intermarkets

petition from London for business that the Germans felt should be in Frankfurt. LIFFE began trading futures on West German government bonds in September 1988, and, as of year-end 1989, it was the second most active contract on the exchange, trading about 20,000 contracts daily. It has been estimated that anywhere from 30 to 70 percent of this London-based trading is accounted for by the German business community.[50]

When an exchange is established, its product line usually includes a domestic government bond contract, a stock index futures contract, and, sometimes, a domestic/foreign currency futures or option contract. Therefore, the number of contracts listed on foreign exchanges that compete with contracts on U.S. exchanges is small relative to the number of contracts traded throughout the world.

The U.S. exchanges' most formidable competitors are LIFFE and SIMEX (Singapore International Monetary Exchange). LIFFE competes with U.S. exchanges for trading volume in U.S. Treasury bond futures and options and in Eurodollar futures and options. SIMEX also competes for trading volume in Eurodollar futures as well as in Deutschemark and Japanese yen futures. But the SIMEX contracts are also complements to U.S. contracts in that a contract opened on the U.S. (Singapore) exchange can be closed on the Singapore (U.S.) exchange.

As shown in Figure 8, LIFFE commands less than 3 percent of trading volume in T-bond futures and options and Eurodollar options. Similarly, less than 3 percent of all Deutschemark futures trading occurs on SIMEX. LIFFE and SIMEX, however, are much more significant competitors for Eurodollar futures volume. SIMEX accounts for 7.5 percent of trading volume and LIFFE accounts for 6.5 percent.

Furthermore, in only three years, SIMEX managed to capture over 50 percent of the annual trading volume in the yen futures contract. The relatively greater success of SIMEX with the yen contract reflects the importance

These 18 percentage points were primarily lost to European and Japanese exchanges.

In the past four years, 20 new exchanges have been established, bringing the total to 72.[46] Many of these new exchanges are in Europe. In addition, foreign membership at many exchanges is considerable. For example, over two-thirds of LIFFE's (London International Financial Futures Exchange) membership is based outside of the United Kingdom.[47]

Two notable additions to futures and options trading are Switzerland and West Germany. The Swiss Options and Financial Futures Exchange (SOFFEX) was established in March 1988, and is the world's first fully-automated, computer-based exchange.[48] SOFFEX trades index options on the Swiss Market Index, which consists of 24 stocks traded on the three main stock exchanges in Geneva, Zurich, and Basle. Critics of the system contend that there is a lack of liquidity on the underlying stocks, thus limiting its effectiveness. Swiss banks control brokerage and can match trades internally with their own clients. This leaves a small amount for open trading on the exchange.[49]

The Germans will begin trading futures and options in 1990. The exchange will trade bond and stock-index futures, and options on 14 high-turnover German stocks. Trading will be executed entirely by computer, as on its Swiss counterpart. The main reason the government approved the new exchange was com-

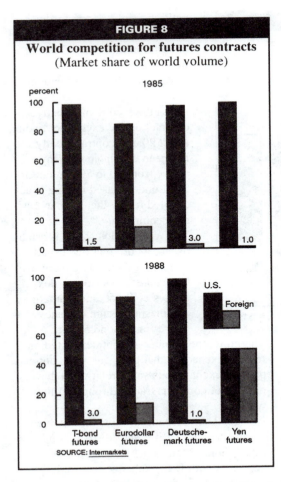

FIGURE 8

World competition for futures contracts
(Market share of world volume)

1985

percent

1.5   3.0   1.0

1988

U.S.

Foreign

3.0   1.0

T-bond   Eurodollar   Deutsche-   Yen
futures   futures   mark futures futures

SOURCE: Intermarkets

of trading in the same time zone as one side of a foreign exchange transaction. In June 1989, a yen/dollar futures contract was launched in Tokyo, along with a Eurodollar contract. The experience of SIMEX suggests that the yen contract will attract market share away from SIMEX rather than from the CME because Singapore and Tokyo are in the same time zone. The above experiences suggest that once deutschemark futures begin trading on the German exchange, some proportion now traded in London will move to Germany.

24-hour trading

True 24-hour trading exists in only a few markets, and is most valuable for assets whose investors span several time zones. Major currencies are traded around the clock in at least seven major money centers. Precious metals, especially gold bullion, and oil, which trade in New York, London and Singapore, are traded 24 hours a day. U.S. Treasury bonds are traded around the clock as well, but overseas markets are thin. Twenty percent of the busi-

ness at the French futures exchange in Paris (Matif) is conducted outside of normal trading hours, indicating how important the extended hours can be.[51]

To a lesser extent, stocks of about 200 major multinational firms are traded in foreign markets as well as in their domestic markets, but foreign trading volume does not compare with that in domestic markets. One reason is that most information about a firm is revealed while domestic markets are open.

In preparation for the increase in round-the-clock trading and due to perceived competition from foreign exchanges, the National Association of Securities Dealers, the Chicago Mercantile Exchange, and the Chicago Board of Trade have made plans to extend their normal trading hours through computerized systems. The New York Stock Exchange is considering trading stocks electronically outside of normal trading hours, and the Cincinnati Stock Exchange and the CBOE are planning 24-hour electronic trading systems. The trading hours for foreign currency options on the Philadelphia Stock Exchange begin at 7:45 a.m. (Eastern Standard Time) to encompass more of the London business day.

International investment banking

As financial markets become more globally integrated, foreign investment banks are attempting to play larger roles in domestic markets. Overall, they are meeting with mixed results.

Foreign investment banks in the United States

Foreign-based investment banks have made some inroads into U.S. domestic capital markets. For the first time, two foreign firms ranked among the top ten advisers for U.S. mergers and acquisitions in the first quarter of 1989. Kleinwort Benson and S.G. Warburg, ranked sixth and seventh, respectively, according to the value of deals.[52] They placed ahead of Merrill Lynch and Kidder Peabody. No Japanese firms ranked among the top M&A advisers, although Fuji Bank of Japan has an ownership interest in Kleinwort Benson.

The Japanese are making a concerted effort to penetrate the U.S. investment banking market, but they have met with little success. The Big Four—Nomura Securities, Daiwa Securities, Nikko Securities, and Yamaichi

Securities Company—expanded in the United States in the mid-1980s, but have scaled back personnel due to unprofitable U.S. operations. Two of the Big Four—Nomura and Yamachi—have been trying to model their U.S. operations as identifiable Wall Street companies, and not just subsidiaries of Tokyo firms, by their appointment of Americans to head their U.S. operations. Nomura's strengths have been its primary dealership in U.S. government securities and U.S. stock trading unit, primarily for Japanese purchase. Nomura's weaknesses, however, are its lack of financial product development and its trading skills.

The Japanese have been more successful in U.S. derivative markets. In April 1988, Nikko Securities became the first Japanese securities firm to acquire a clearing membership at the Chicago Board of Trade (CBOT). Since then, fifteen others have joined the CBOT. The Chicago Mercantile Exchange (CME) has seventeen Japanese companies as members. Nikko, Daiwa, and Yamaichi are members of both the CBOT and CME. Recently, Nomura announced a cooperative agreement with Refco, one of the world's largest futures merchants. Consummation of the deal will assist Nomura in learning futures trading.

U.S. investment banks' activities abroad

Merger and acquisition activity has been slowing in the United States, prompting Wall Street firms to look to foreign markets. According to a 1988 survey, U.S. firms accounted for slightly more than half of all cross-border merger and acquisition activity. The most active U.S. investment banks were Shearson Lehman Hutton (57 deals), Goldman Sachs (46), and First Boston (34).[53]

U.S. investment banks represented about 12 percent of all mergers and acquisitions for European clients in 1988. The most active U.S. firms in this category were Security Pacific Group (37 deals), Shearson Lehman Hutton (26), and Goldman Sachs (22). Security Pacific has acquired two foreign investment banks, one Canadian and one British.[54]

U.S. firms expect to find some business in Asia as well. The newly formed investment bank, Wasserstein Perella, for example, recently dispatched merger and acquisition teams to Japan to set up the Tokyo joint venture, Nomura Wasserstein Perella.

In the area of securities underwriting, U.S. firms are quite strong. Seven of the top ten underwriters of debt and equity securities worldwide are U.S. firms; however, only three U.S. firms rank among the top underwriters of non-U.S. securities. Merrill Lynch was the top underwriter of all debt and equity offerings worldwide during the first half of 1989.[55]

The strength of U.S. firms abroad lies primarily in Europe. Foreign securities firms in Tokyo have found it difficult to establish themselves. Thirty-six of the 51 Tokyo branches of foreign securities houses lost a total of $164 million for the six months ending March 1989.[56] As a result of these losses, many foreign firms have cut back their Tokyo operations, concentrating on a particular product or service. Twenty-two out of the 115 Tokyo stock exchange members are foreign firms. Another 29 foreign securities houses have opened branch offices in Tokyo. Nevertheless, the Big Four dominate the Tokyo exchange, accounting for almost 50 percent of daily business. The foreign firms account for only 4.5 percent of this daily business.[57]

Three American investment banks, Salomon Brothers, Merrill Lynch, and First Boston, have been able to develop profitable operations in the Tokyo market. All three American firms attribute their success in part to a well-trained staff, and to hiring Japanese college graduates to fill positions. Salomon posted a $53.6 million pretax profit as of March 31, 1989. It also made a $300 million capital infusion, which has helped to make Salomon a challenger to the Big Four in bond trading.[58]

The U.S. government has been pressuring for greater access for U.S. firms to Japanese capital markets since 1984. For instance, Japanese government securities are predominantly sold through closed syndicates, in which foreign firms account for only about 8 percent of the total. Change has been slower than foreign investment banks and governments would like, but some progress has been made. The Japanese sold 40 percent of its 10-year bonds at an open auction in April 1989.[59]

Conclusion

Financial markets and financial services are becoming more globally integrated. As businesses expand into new markets around the world, there is greater demand for financing to follow them. All major areas of international finance have grown far more rapidly than foreign trade in recent years. Trading of securities in U.S. markets by nonresidents, trading volume of foreign currency futures and options, and foreign exchange trading have been growing at 40 percent or more a year. This rapid growth of international financial transactions reflects the growth in cross-border capital flows.

The major markets for domestic as well as international financial services are the United States, Japan, and the United Kingdom, although it is beginning to make more sense to talk about the dominant markets as the United States, Japan, and Europe. The reduction of regulatory barriers and harmonization of rules among countries have allowed more firms to compete in more markets around the world. These markets are also competing against each other for a share of the world's trading volume.

Today, a very large part of financial globalization involves financial intermediaries dealing with other, foreign, financial interme-

diaries. Consequently, prices in one market are affected by conditions in other markets, but, with a few exceptions, of which commercial lending is the most notable, customers do not have direct access to more suppliers. Again, this could change as Europe moves toward economic and financial unification.

Lessons from industries such as automobiles and petroleum, as well as lessons from geographic expansion in the United States, indicate that the financial services industry will become more consolidated, with firms from a handful of countries garnering substantial market share. International joint ventures will be common and often precursors to outright acquisitions. For smaller firms to survive as global competitors, they will have to find and service a market niche.

As the financial services industry and financial markets become more globally integrated, the most efficient and best organized firms will prevail. Also, countries with the most efficient—but not necessarily the least—regulation will become the world's major international financial centers.

FOOTNOTES

[1]"Japanese Finance," Survey, *The Economist*, December 10, 1988, pp. 3 and 10.

[2]Ibid.

[3]Thomas H. Hanley, et. al., "The Swiss Banks: Universal Banks Poised to Prosper as Global Deregulation Unfolds," *Salomon Brothers Stock Research*, June 1986.

[4]See David T. Llewellyn, *Competition, Diversification, and Structural Change in the British Financial System*, 1989, unpublished xerox, p. 1.

[5]Christopher M. Korth, "International Financial Markets," in William H. Baughn and Donald R. Mandich, eds., *The International Banking Handbook*, Dow Jones-Irwin, 1983, pp. 9-13.

[6]During the Cold War, the U.S. dollar was the only universally accepted currency, and the Russians wanted to maintain their international reserves in dollars, but not at American banks for fear that the U.S government might freeze the funds. Therefore, the Russians found some British, French and German banks that would accept deposits in dollars. See Korth, p. 11.

[7]Christopher M. Korth, "The Eurocurrency Markets," in Baughn and Mandich, p. 26.

[8]Herbert L. Baer and Christine A. Pavel, "Does regulation drive innovation?," *Economic Perspectives*, Vol. 12, No. 2, March/April 1988, pp. 3-15, Federal Reserve Bank of Chicago.

[9]"Japanese banking booms offshore," *The Economist*, November 26, 1988, p. 87.

[10]*International Financial Statistics*, International Monetary Fund, various years.

[11]Ibid.

[12]This does not apply in criminal cases, bankruptcy, or debt collection. The disclosure of secret information to foreign authorities is not allowed, unless provided for in an international treaty. In such a case, which is an exception, the foreign authorities could obtain only the information available to Swiss authorities under similar circumstances. See Peat, Marwick, Mitchell & Co., *Banking in Switzerland*, 1979, pp. 35-6.

[13]Eurobanks have specific rates at which they are prepared either to borrow or lend Eurofunds. In London, this rate is known as LIBOR (the London Interbank Offer Rate). LIBOR dominates the Eurocurrency market.

[14]Henry S. Terrell, Robert S. Dohner, and Barbara R. Lowrey, "The Activities of Japanese Banks in the United

Kingdom and in the United States, 1980-88," *Federal Reserve Bulletin*, February 1990, p. 43.

[15]Michael R. Sesit and Craig Torres, "What if They Traded All Day and Nobody Came?," *Wall Street Journal*, June 14, 1989, p. C1.

[16]*U.S. Foreign Exchange Market Survey*, Federal Reserve Bank of New York, April 1989, pp. 5-7.

[17]"Report of Assets and Liabilities of U.S. Branches and Agencies of Foreign Banks," Table 4.30, *Federal Reserve Bulletin*, June 1989, Board of Governors of the Federal Reserve System; and *Annual Statistical Digest*, Board of Governors of the Federal Reserve System, Table 68.

[18]Ibid.

[19]*Senior Loan Officer Opinion Survey on Bank Lending Practices for August 1989*, Board of Governors of the Federal Reserve System.

[20]See footnote 17.

[21]*Annual Report*, Board of Governors of the Federal Reserve System, Banking Supervision and Regulation Section, various years; authors' calculations from Report of Condition and Income tapes, Board of Governors of the Federal Reserve System, various years.

[22]Ibid.

[23]Ibid.

[24]"European banking: Cheque list," *The Economist*, June 24, 1989, pp. 74-5.

[25]The Glass-Steagall Act is the law that separates commercial banking from investment banking in the U.S. Article 65 is its Japanese equivalent.

[26]James B. Treece, with John Hoerr, "Shaking Up Detroit," *Business Week*, August 14, 1989, pp. 74-80.

[27]*Standard and Poor's Oil Industry Survey*, August 3, 1989, p. 26.

[28]"European Stock Exchanges," *A supplement to Euromoney*, August 1987, pp. 2-5.

[29]Rosario Benvides, "How Big is the World Bond Market?—1989 Update" *International Bond Markets*, Salomon Brothers, June 24, 1989.

[30]Ibid.

[31]"Look east, young Eurobond," *The Economist*, September 16, 1989, pp. 83-4; "Japanese paper fills the void," *A supplement to Euromoney*, March 1989, p. 2.

[32]See *The Economist*, Sept. 16, 1989, pp. 83-4.

[33]"La grande boum," *The Economist*, October 1, 1988, pp. 83-4.

[34]Christine M. Cumming and Lawrence M. Sweet, "Financial Structure of the G-7 Countries: How Does the United States Compare?," Federal Reserve Bank of New York, *Quarterly Review*, Winter 1987/88, pp. 15-16.

[35]"Sweeping away Frankfurt's old-fashioned habits," *The Economist*, January 28, 1989, pp. 73-4.

[36]Ibid.

[37]*Financial Market Trends*, OECD, February 1989, pp.85-6.

[38]Ibid.

[39]Ibid.

[40]"A smooth run for Switzerland's big banks," *The Economist*, June 17, 1989, pp. 87-8.

[41]*World Financial Markets*, J.P. Morgan & Co., November 29, 1988.

[42]"Foreign Transactions in Securities," Table 3.24, *Federal Reserve Bulletin*, June 1989, Board of Governors of the Federal Reserve System.

[43]Ibid.

[44]Various central bank statistical releases.

[45]The underlying instrument is worth $1 million.

[46]"US exchanges fight for market share," *A supplement to Euromoney*, July 1989, p. 9.

[47]Elizabeth R. Thagard, "London's Jump," *Intermarkets*, May 1989, p. 22.

[48]See *A supplement to Euromoney*, August 1987, p. 28.

[49]Ginger Szala, "Financial walls tumble for German investors," *Futures*, January 1990, p. 44.

[50]Ibid., p. 42.

[51]See Thagard, p. 23.

[52]Ted Weissberg, "Wall Street Seeks Global Merger Market: IDD's First-quarter M&A Rankings," *Investment Dealers Digest*, May 8, 1989, pp. 17-21.

[53]"The World Champions of M&A," *Euromoney*, February 1989, pp. 96-102.

[54]Ibid.

[55]Philip Maher, "Merrill Lynch Holds on to Top International Spot," *Investment Dealers Digest*, July 10, 1989, pp. 23-25.

[56]"Japan proving tough for foreign brokerage," *Chicago Tribune*, September 11, 1989, section 4, pp. 1-2

[57]Ibid.

[58]Ibid.

[59]Ibid.

Article 33

Standardizing World Securities Clearance Systems

**by Ramon P. DeGennaro and
Christopher J. Pike**

The international trading of corporate securities has flourished in the past decade. In just several years, the volume of this international trade has increased tenfold (see figure 1), accompanied by heavy investment in automated systems to handle the expanded sales and purchases of the securities. This automation, however, has had only a limited impact on the timeliness and accuracy of international settlement.

Trading volumes continue to swell, and each country has continued to operate under its own settlement procedures. No two securities markets settle trades in precisely the same way; each adheres to unique standards and time frames. Without common standards or compatible clearance systems, the result has been an increasing difficulty in operating securities clearance systems, which match trades and transfer securities and funds—the nuts and bolts of securities exchange.

Lack of coordination among securities exchange markets not only slows trade, but also is costly. Securities houses bear the risk of deals not being concluded on time—and the additional cost if they are not concluded at all. London exchanges, for example, spent $25 million to $33 million each in 1987 on the interest payments for borrowings against unsettled deals.[1]

The stock market crash of October 1987 highlighted the inefficiency, economic costs, and risk inherent in the current international system. Fully 40 percent of all transactions failed to settle by contract date at the time of the crash, increasing the pressure to reform and standardize trading procedures.[2] All countries recognize the problem, but there has as yet been no coordination in the efforts to reform and standardize international securities trade.

Within the past year, one international organization, the Group of Thirty (G-30), has made specific recommendations for the clearance and settlement of international securities trades.[3] A private-sector group, the G-30 comprises bankers, investors, traders, regulators, and bank officials concerned with the basic mechanisms underlying the international financial system.

The group's recently evolved Steering Committee, composed of members from eight countries, has been mandated to propose suggestions for improving world securities markets by 1992, coinciding with the plan for establishing a single internal market in Europe by that date. Unlike the European Economic Community's goal of free access to all types of markets within its 12 member states, the G-30's recommendations focus specifically on reducing the risk and cost of trading in

The dramatic increase in the volume of international securities trading has strained the present system of settling trades. The costs and risks of such trading can no longer be ignored. An international organization, the Group of Thirty, has recommended changes in the structure of financial markets to minimize these problems.

FIGURE 1 INTERNATIONAL STOCK TRANSACTIONS
    Sales and purchases by U.S. investors

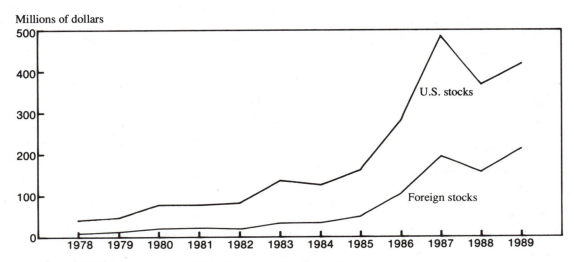

SOURCE: *Treasury Bulletin*, December 1989; and *NYSE Fact Book*, New York Stock Exchange, 1989.

financial markets worldwide. The group offers a challenging framework for improving the current situation in world securities markets.

■ The G-30 Report

In its March 1989 report, "Clearance and Settlement Systems in the World's Securities Markets," the G-30 set forth a nine-step strategy for reducing the risk and increasing the efficiency of international securities clearance and settlement (see box 1). A secondary, but necessary, intermediate goal is to foster standardization among the groups involved in securities transactions. Of the nine specific recommendations in the G-30 report, the United States is already in compliance with seven.

A U.S. Steering Committee has recently reviewed the areas in which the United States is not in compliance: moving to a t+3 (trade date plus three business days) settlement period for corporate securities, and adopting a same-day funds payment schedule for settlement of those trades.[4] Same-day funds earn interest from the day received. Currently, some investors pay for corporate securities with next-day funds, which do not earn interest and cannot be used for settlement until the following day.

The Steering Committee's proposal, issued in March 1990, urges that the United States shift to the same-day funds transfer process, instead of its current next-day funds payment standard.[5]

■ The Current Settlement Process

Presently, stock trades in the United States do not result in immediate delivery of the security in exchange for payment. Current procedures call for delivery on t+5, five business days later. During those five business days, both the buyer and seller (or their intermediaries) are at risk: either party could conceivably fail to honor its commitment. The longer the time before securities are exchanged for cash, the greater the likelihood that the value of the securities will change, increasing the incentives for one party to default. Many market participants have concluded that the increasing volume and volatility of financial markets makes the risk too great to ignore.

The most direct way to address this problem is to reduce the time between the trade date and the exchange of securities for cash. However, several important steps must occur during that time. First, the brokers must confirm the transaction by notifying their cus-

tomers of the terms of the trade. The customers, in turn, must affirm, or agree to those terms as communicated by the broker. Next, the trade is cleared, which creates statements of obligation. One party must deliver securities, while the other must deliver funds. Finally, the trade is settled, at which time both parties discharge the obligations created at clearance.

These steps must occur in proper sequence, and none of them is automatic or immune to error. Shortening the time between the trade date and settlement of that trade leaves less room for inefficiency and mistakes. This emphasizes the need for dealers and brokers to submit all trades for confirmation by day t+1, and for customers to have access to an interactive affirmation system.

The problems of international securities transactions are still more complex, because markets do not yet have standardized procedures. For example, although the United States does not yet settle by t+3, it does at least use rolling settlement. Trades are settled five business days from the trade date, regardless of the time of the trade. In contrast, France uses a monthlong account period. All trades during the account period settle on the same day. The

The nine recommendations of the Group of Thirty, designed to reduce the risk and lower the cost of trading securities internationally.

1. Comparisons should be established between direct market participants (brokers, exchange members) by day t+1.

2. Indirect market participants should be members of a positive-affirmation comparison system by 1992.

3. Each country should have a central securities depository (CSD, used to immobilize securities) by 1992.

4. Each country should implement a netting system by 1992, unless volume is low enough to permit otherwise.

5. A delivery versus payment system should be in place by 1992.

6. Payment in same-day funds should be adopted.

7. Rolling settlement should be adopted. No later than 1990, final settlement by t+5 should be the rule. The ultimate goal is t+3 by 1992.

8. Securities lending as a means of expediting settlement should be encouraged.

9. The numbering of securities and message codes should be standardized.

differing systems mean that trades between French and U.S. investors encounter yet another layer of cost, risk, and potential error. This lack of standardization adds to the problems financial markets face in limiting risk and lowering costs.

The United States must also institute changes to conform to a second recommendation by the G-30, the proposal to settle all trades in same-day funds. From the perspective of the financial markets, same-day funds are safer. The additional risk of paying with next-day funds can be large enough to disrupt trading: many banks refused to deliver securities to Drexel Burnham Lambert's broker-dealer subsidiary after the parent corporation entered Chapter 11 unless they were paid with same-day funds.[6]

■ **The Transition Phase and Potential Pitfalls**

Markets throughout the world are not likely to incorporate the G-30's recommendations smoothly, including the implementation of settlement by day t+3 or the use of same-day funds. Some markets must incur substantial up-front costs and may not view the benefits as sufficiently large. An important advantage of the G-30's recommendations is that none of the nine is new; all are in place in various markets throughout the world. For example, in the U.S. Treasury bill market, trades are settled either on the trade date or on the next business day, well before t+3, and settle in same-day funds. The problems facing other financial markets concern implementation and coordination, not invention.

Although the required procedures are already in place in some markets, the problems of implementation and coordination can be real and large. For example, the apparent 40 percent reduction in the settlement period from five days to three is in fact even more extreme. With five business days between the trade date and the settlement date, brokers and other market participants could rely on an intervening weekend to catch up with paperwork. This will not always be possible with settlement

due at t+3, making affirmation and confirmation by t+1 even more important.

The G-30 also recognizes that consistently making delivery of physical securities by t+3 is impossible. Book-entry systems, in which computer entries entirely replace paper certificates of ownership, are the best method for recording and transferring ownership. A good alternative is a central securities depository (CSD), such as the Depository Trust Company. CSDs are financial intermediaries that hold all paper certificates immobile in a central location, recording and transferring ownership by means of computer entries. Book-entry systems or CSDs offer cost savings as well as faster transfers. One problem with such systems is that some local laws, both in the U.S. and abroad, require the use of physical securities. Unless the appropriate authorities change these laws, they will impede the movement toward book-entry systems and could block their constituents' access to financial markets.

In addition, the G-30 has refrained from addressing political problems—at the corporate, national, and international levels—that are likely to arise. For example, using next-day funds permits clearing banks to earn float; they retain use of the funds for one more business day. In 1985, the American Bankers Association estimated that same-day settlement could cost the banking industry $3 billion in lost float. The industry cannot forgo that much income annually, and its members will be forced to change their clearing fees to compensate. Brokerage firms may need fewer employees and have lower profit margins under the automated systems needed to meet the G-30's recommendations. Even if total employment in the brokerage industry remains constant, the nature of jobs will change. The implementation process will eliminate certain jobs, while increasing the need for others. Employees whose jobs are in jeopardy may resist and successfully delay the necessary changes.

Some countries have many of the recommended procedures already in place, while others must invest large sums both in capital improvements and in training personnel. France has essentially completed the process of dematerializing physical securities in favor of a book-entry system, while England has not yet even immobilized securities in a CSD.

Will some countries resist implementing portions of the recommendations? If so, what will this mean for standardizing trading terms and for transactions across national boundaries? Markets that fail to conform to common standards will suffer cost and risk disadvantages relative to other markets, and investors will choose to use the markets that do adopt the G-30 recommendations.

Finally, the G-30 has identified many of the risks inherent in the proposed system, and notes that they can be surmounted using methods already in place in other markets. For example, markets can develop central clearinghouses to guarantee that transactions settle according to the terms of the trade. To protect itself from the possibility of its members failing to perform, the clearinghouse can incorporate a risk-sharing arrangement similar to those that futures exchanges already use.

What the G-30 cannot do is uncover all possible risks other entities may bear because of the proposed system. For example, under present trading systems, the buyer and seller offer a faceless commitment to perform, since they do not know each other at the time of the trade. Shortening the period between the trade date and the execution of the trade tends to limit the risk of this arrangement, but ensuring delivery by the target date of t+3 will require more borrowing (and lending) of securities, which is not riskless. In this case, the G-30's recommendations may not reduce total risk, but they do make the credit commitment more explicit. They reduce the risk of the faceless commitment between the buyer and seller, while increasing the risk between the borrower and lender.

■ **Conclusion**

Large increases in trading volume have strained the current system of settling international securities trades and have driven up the costs and risks of such transactions. In addition, advances in computers and communications technology have made international trading a common occurrence, introducing new sources of cost and risk to financial markets. The Group of Thirty's recommendations are an attempt both to coordinate and to accelerate the evolution of worldwide financial markets in response to the changing nature of international trading.

■ **Footnotes**

1. See "Back Office to the Fore," *The Economist,* March 25, 1989, pp. 84, 90.

2. See "Faster, Better and More Profitable," *The Banker,* August 1989, pp. 22, 24.

3. See "Clearance and Settlement Systems in the World's Securities Markets," Group of Thirty, London, March 1989.

4. See "Compressing the Settlement Period," Group of Thirty, U.S. Working Group Draft Report, November 8, 1989.

5. See Karen Gullo, "Faster Securities Settlement Urged," *American Banker,* March 5, 1990, p. 3.

6. Ibid.

Ramon P. DeGennaro is a visiting scholar and Christopher J. Pike is a research assistant at the Federal Reserve Bank of Cleveland.

The views stated herein are those of the authors and not necessarily those of the Federal Reserve Bank of Cleveland or of the Board of Governors of the Federal Reserve System.

Article 34

International Policy Coordination: Can We Afford It?

by W. Lee Hoskins

Policymakers and economists today embrace the argument that increased openness among the world's economies justifies--if not necessitates--a closer coordination of nations' economic policies. Their automatic, almost unthinking, acceptance of this idea reflects both the undeniable fact that growing trade and capital flows now tightly link the world's markets and an unwavering association of words like *cooperation* and *coordination* with images of harmony, peace, and prosperity. Only a fool would question the need for policy coordination, contend proponents of international cooperation. Are we not, after all, in the same boat, affected by each other's policies? We must pull together if we hope to progress.

The matter is not quite so simple. In a rush to enumerate the possible benefits of cooperation, we have neglected to recognize some of the potential costs. For those of us who believe that free markets guarantee the highest possible standard of living, the words *cooperation* and *coordination* ring like euphemisms for collusion against market outcomes and sound a threat to a proven source of lasting prosperity.

My concerns stem most recently from attempts at, and continued calls for, close global coordination of macroeconomic policies, but my fears have roots in other international developments, including policies dealing with the international debt situation. To be sure, certain types of cooperation are beneficial--indeed essential--to the smooth functioning of markets, but governments, through cooperation, often attempt to supplant markets and avoid market discipline. As such, we should keep a wary eye on proposals for global cooperation.

■ The Function of Markets and the Role of Government

Competitive markets are unique social machines that produce an efficient allocation of the world's resources and the highest possible standard of living. The price mechanism relays information to all components of the market, while the profit mechanism forces prices and costs to their minimum.

The globalization of markets offers enormous potential for international cooperation--a potential both to enhance markets and to supplant markets. We must not accept proposals for international policy coordination without a critical assessment of their potential costs as well as benefits.

Through these mechanisms, competitive markets foster a special type of economic cooperation, in which participants readily understand the objectives and in which markets maintain discipline quickly and without discrimination. This cooperation within markets rewards innovations and efficiencies and removes waste. It confers net benefits on participants in excess of what they could otherwise secure. Economists have recognized these qualities of open, competitive markets since the time of Adam Smith, and realize that the global scale of markets only serves to enhance them.

Markets require an institutional framework to reduce the inevitable frictions that will result as participants interact. In market economies, the institutional structure includes laws that guarantee property rights, including contracts, and laws that protect other rights of individuals. Moreover, a medium of exchange with reasonably predictable purchasing power can enhance the smooth functioning of the market mechanism. These institutions reduce transaction costs and allow markets to achieve economies of scale.

The market machinery does not always work perfectly, however. Sometimes markets do not fully internalize the benefits, costs, or risks associated with private activities to the responsible parties, or a "free rider" problem exists. Frequently, economic shocks, starting in one market, can disrupt a wide range of economic activity as they ripple throughout the economy. Sometimes the nature of goods or the characteristics of production confer monopoly powers on individuals. At other times, we make adjustments to the market, sacrificing efficiency, to correct for inherent inequities among individuals.

The need to create an institutional framework, and at times to adjust the market machinery, provides a role for governments in market economies. International cooperation can enhance this role in a closely integrated, global market. Government intervention, whether singular or cooperative, can guide an economy toward its ultimate objective of maintaining the highest standard of living when it enhances the functioning of private markets and when it dampens the transmission of severe, disruptive economic shocks.

Unlike the market, however, the machinery of government includes no automatic mechanisms for maximizing output and minimizing costs. Rather than promoting efficiency and improving this important social engine, governments often slow and impede the market's proper function. We have come to recognize problems with governmental intervention in markets at the national level, but we often seem unwilling to accept that government intervention at the international level can impede the functioning of global markets just as easily.

■ Government Versus Market Objectives

Students of government dismiss the view that elected officials seek to maximize the common good. Policymakers, in their own self-interest, promote the desires of their constituencies, which often conflict with market outcomes. The world economy today is tied in a web of tariffs, taxes, subsidies, and regulation that, more often than not, lacks purpose other than to secure rents for certain influential segments of society.

This tendency of elected government officials to define the common good in terms of their own self-interest and the interests of their constituencies should cause us to question all government policies. Do these policies strengthen the institutional framework that enhances the market's performance? Do they provide adjustments to the market that help secure a high, sustainable standard of living? Or, alternatively, do these policies serve to supplant well-functioning markets with administrative and regulatory mechanisms that interfere with market discipline and market performance at the expense of real economic growth?

■ Interdependence and the Benefits of Global Coordination

The current perceived need for global policy coordination stems from evidence that markets for goods, services, and capital are now more open, or globally integrated, than in the past.[1] Advances in transportation and in communications have increased the degree of international openness by making production and distribution on a global scale more feasible.[2] The liberalization of trade and capital movements has permitted producers and investors to take fuller advantage of these advances. Indeed, trade flows have increased relative to GNP in nearly all major developed countries, and capital flows can be a large proportion of national savings and investment.[3]

Greater openness has enhanced economic interdependence among nations. Changes in economic variables in one country have a more immediate, stronger influence on economic variables in another. A tendency to underestimate the growing importance of interdependent markets has caused surprises in recent years. Inflows of foreign capital, for example, lessened the expected impact of large budget deficits on real interest rates in the United States.

A concern most often cited by advocates of coordinated macroeconomic policies is that global interdependence has increased the risks of *systemic failure*. This term eludes precise definition, but it implies a complete collapse of the financial system and currency markets, emanating from the actions of only one country or events in a single market. In an integrated world economy, individual countries might not be able to insulate themselves against such contagion and its enormous costs.

Observers often point to two recent events as evidence of the increased risks of systemic failure. One is the international debt crisis, which gained wide recognition in late 1982. The debt crisis threatened not only large banks, but also many midsized regional banks and small banks through their lending arrangements with debtor countries and through their domestic and international correspondent-banking relationships. The repercussions of widespread defaults could have had serious global implications. The stock-market collapse of October 19, 1987 offers a second, more recent, example of the risks of systemic failure. This collapse spread rapidly through stock markets around the world, posing a threat to global economic growth and stability. Although unscathed from these recent experiences, the world remains vulnerable to similar types of events.

In listing the arguments for closer international policy coordination, I also should note that this global interdependence, which complicates economic interactions and increases the risks of systemic failure, often serves to discipline policymakers. Nations that have adopted inflationary policies have seen the market's disapproval quickly reflected in capital flows, in exchange-rate movements and, with some delay, in trade patterns. Similarly, the increased ease with which manufacturing and financial firms can move about the globe places a check on regulation and taxation. Simply stated, greater international interdependence increases the opportunities for investors and traders to protect their wealth from the misguided policies of individual countries.

Proponents of global policy coordination argue that because of increased economic integration, the chances of achieving substantial benefits through mutual cooperation are greater now than at any other time. In many respects, they are correct. The potential benefits from the mutual reduction of trade restraints and from the further liberalization of capital movements undoubtedly grow as markets expand. I applaud such market-enhancing international cooperation as GATT and the U.S.-Canadian Free Trade Agreement.[4] The removal of artificial restraints on markets can increase the standard of living worldwide. Moreover, one cannot deny the value of shared information, common purpose, and coordinated efforts during those rare periods of clear economic crisis. In today's economic environment, such shocks can ripple through markets quickly and forcefully.

In contrast to these efforts, many of the recent proposals for global policy cooperation call for a detailed harmonization--a fine tuning on a grand scale--of monetary, fiscal, and regulatory policies among the major developed countries. Recent meetings of the Group of Seven (G7) countries, for example, have focused on developing a set of "objective indicators"--including unemployment, inflation, current-account balances, exchange rates, and money growth--that could trigger policy changes in participant countries. Others have recommended target-zone arrangements or fixed-exchange-rate regimes, which presuppose a willingness to coordinate basic macroeconomic policies closely.[5] Some advocates of coordination have sought solutions for the international-debt situation that involve greatly expanded roles for governments and quasigovernmental international organizations.

■ Market Adjustments and the Costs of Cooperation

The evolving importance of globally integrated markets creates both the enormous potential for nations to benefit from cooperation and the great danger that such cooperation could entail substantial costs by subverting markets for political ends.

Consider, for example, recent allegations that the G7 countries are relying on a loose system of reference zones for exchange rates and on a set of economic indicators to guide their decisions about the compatibility of macroeconomic policies and about the appropriateness of adjustments. One can find little concrete evidence that these reference zones and indicators actually have influenced macroeconomic decisions in the separate G7 countries. This judgment might not be entirely fair. The G7 has never announced a complete set of "indicators" along with their relative weights in policy discussions, nor has it revealed reference zones for exchange rates. Furthermore, we do not know what policy would otherwise have been.

To date, most of the cooperative efforts have attempted to stabilize exchange rates; the industrialized countries have not focused their attack on the fundamental problems underlying their current-account imbalances. Under the guise of cooperation and exchange-rate stabilization, the United States and the other major industrialized countries have financed a growing share of the U.S. current-account deficit through official reserve flows. While some might contend that this slowed the adjustment process to a manageable pace, one could argue just as forcefully that this official financing has avoided the adjustments that the exchange market ultimately will demand--specifically, an increase in U.S. private savings and a substantial reduction in the U.S. budget deficit. I doubt that cooperation has led countries to adopt markedly better policies, or that it has reduced exchange-market uncertainty. Failing this, it has imposed substantial costs.

Similar arguments apply to the developing-country-debt situation. To be sure, quick U.S. actions in providing bridge loans helped to avoid outright defaults in some instances, and the cooperative efforts of governments and of the International Monetary Fund helped to initiate adjustment programs in many debtor countries and to secure rescheduling agreements from banks. These actions reduced the risks of systemic failure.

Many have argued, however, that this cooperation between debtor and creditor governments also has helped many banks to avoid the repricing of their assets, but has done little to ease developing countries' debt burdens or to foster a lasting adjustment in debtor countries. Substantiating this appraisal, developing-country debts trade far below their book values in secondary markets, as does the stock of highly exposed banks in equity markets. These policies have not significantly reduced uncertainties associated with the long-term prospects for uninterrupted debt service and probably have increased the overall real-resource costs of adjustment.

■ **Coordination and the Costs of Uncertainty**
In addition to the potentially large real-resource costs, which I have thus far attributed to the tendency of governments to supplant markets, international coordination could create additional costs by generating market uncertainty. Private

market participants base decisions, in part, on the expected actions of governments. When future policies are uncertain, market participants attempt to hedge by raising prices or by avoiding actions that might leave them vulnerable to policy changes. Recent proposals for detailed international policy coordination could actually increase uncertainties, if they create doubt about the willingness and ability of governments to implement them.

Nations willingly cooperate when all benefit. Mutual gains most likely result when cooperation is narrow in scope, when the number of participants is small, and when the resulting policies promote the smooth functioning of markets. Bilateral trade agreements are an example. When cooperation is more complex, however, as in the case of macroeconomic policy coordination, success often requires that countries take actions contrary to some of their individual interests. Compliance then entails burdens, which countries historically have attempted to avoid or to shift.

Consider our experiences with macroeconomic policy coordination since 1985. In light of the sparse U.S. progress toward lowering our budget deficits, our part of the bargain, one could argue that the dollar's depreciation has shifted more of the adjustment burden onto our trading partners--an outcome that was not completely the result of international coordination and cooperation. Because international policy coordination--unlike markets--often lacks a credible system for enforcement and burden-sharing, it can create uncertainties about the extent of compliances.

Even if nations are willing to coordinate broad policy objectives, many observers doubt that they

can. The sharp differences among economists about the true state of the economy, and about the inter-relationships among policy levers and economic variables, are almost legendary. If economists cannot agree on how the economy works, can we expect governments to agree on and implement coordinated, effective macroeconomic policies? One also might wonder about the outcome if the world cooperated, but adopted the wrong model of how the world works. This, of course, is a problem at the national level, but international cooperation could greatly increase the costs of an error.[6]

Many of the proposals for detailed international coordination remind me of policymakers' "fine tuning" efforts of the 1960s and 1970s, when they attempted to achieve many targets simultaneously. The thrust of policies shifted frequently, and those policies generally missed on all accounts. The markets' mistrust of policymakers was reflected in an inflationary psychology that complicated and extended the fight against inflation. If we now make domestic objectives subject to international targets and events, economic agents once again could lose confidence in the willingness and the ability of policymakers to pursue important domestic goals.

■ **Conclusion**
Governments obviously play an essential role in a market economy. That markets today extend across national boundaries does not alter this role; indeed, global markets enhance it. We should explore opportunities for international cooperation that enhance the performance of markets and reduce the risks of systemic failure, but we must consider both the benefits and costs of such policies.

Many have advocated a greatly expanded role for international policy coordination. They argue that as markets become increasingly integrated, the potential benefits from such coordination become enormous. I caution that such policies often seek to supplant markets and to avoid market discipline, risking enormous costs in terms of real economic growth and efficiency.

Much of the current thrust toward global cooperation is concerned with macroeconomic policy coordination. Given the political and economic realities of the world today, I believe that a move toward detailed coordination of macroeconomic policies would not improve, but could very well jeopardize, our standard of living.

Instead, I would urge countries to adopt, to announce, and to steadfastly maintain long-term nominal targets for policy, consistent with zero inflation and long-term real growth potential. This would not stabilize exchange rates, but it would remove much of the uncertainty about future policy that contributes to exchange-rate volatility. Flexible exchange rates would adjust, making the plans of individual nations compatible, and would provide a buffer to external policy errors and shocks. Such broad, individually instituted targets would be credible, predictable, and--most important--capable of maintaining the integrity of private markets.

■ Footnotes

1. A perceived need for policy coordination is not new. For a discussion of central-bank cooperation in the 1920s, see Stephen V. O. Clarke, *Central Bank Cooperation 1924-31*. New York: Federal Reserve Bank of New York, 1967.

2. For a discussion of factors increasing world integration, see Richard N. Cooper, "Economic Interdependence and Coordination of Economic Policies." In Ronald W. Jones and Peter B. Kenen, eds., *Handbook of International Economics*, Vol. 2. Amsterdam: North-Holland Publishing Co. (1985): 1195-1234.

3. On the growth of trade and capital flows, see Norman S. Fieleke, "Economic Interdependence between Nations: Reason for Policy Coordination?" *New England Economic Review*, Federal Reserve Bank of Boston (May/June 1988): 21-38.

4. Through successive rounds of negotiation, the General Agreement on Trade and Tariffs (GATT) has achieved multilateral reductions in trade barriers.

5. See John Williamson, "The Exchange Rate System," *Policy Analyses in International Economics*, No. 5. Washington, D.C.: Institute for International Economics, September 1983. See also Ronald McKinnon, "Monetary and Exchange Rate Policies for International Financial Stability: A Proposal." *Journal of Economic Perspectives*, vol. 2, no. 1 (Winter 1988): 83-103.

6. See Jeffrey A. Frankel and Katharine Rockett, "International Macroeconomic Policy Coordination When Policymakers Do Not Agree on the True Model." *American Economic Review*, vol. 78, no. 3 (June 1988): 318-340.

W. Lee Hoskins is president of the Federal Reserve Bank of Cleveland. The material in this Economic Commentary is based on a speech presented to the Denver Association of Business Economists in Denver, Colorado, on December 9, 1988.

Article 35

Europe in 1992

With the approach of the 1990s, the world is witnessing a remarkable conjuncture of movements toward economic integration, movements aimed at tearing down barriers to commerce both within and between nations. Within nations, deregulation or liberalization of markets has been widespread in recent years. Between nations, the recent U.S.-Canada Free Trade Agreement, the emerging European common market, and the Uruguay Round of Multilateral Trade Negotiations seem likely to further the economic integration of vast areas if not the world economy.

The focus of this article is on the European Community internal market. The 12 member nations of the EC (European Community) are now striving to realize the full promise of the 1957 Treaty of Rome (the European Economic Community's founding charter), which called for a Community-wide market free of restrictions over the movement of goods, services, persons, and capital, and for progressively "approximating," or harmonizing, the economic policies of the member states. Much progress toward these goals has been made. By July 1, 1968, a customs union had been established among the original six members of the EC, as France, Germany, Italy, Belgium, the Netherlands, and Luxembourg had abolished tariffs on trade among themselves and had imposed a common tariff schedule on imports from other countries. Subsequently, Denmark, Ireland, the United Kingdom, Greece, Spain, and Portugal have joined the union.

Not only have EC members formed a customs union, but they have taken some noteworthy steps toward approximating their economic policies. For example, a Common Agricultural Policy was adopted in 1962. And the establishment of the European Monetary System in 1979 was a significant move toward monetary integration, as most of the member countries undertook to limit fluctuations in exchange rates between their currencies to rather narrow, publicly announced ranges.

Although the EC states have approximated some of their economic

Norman S. Fieleke

Vice President and Economist, Federal Reserve Bank of Boston. Valerie Hausman provided research assistance.

policies and have achieved a customs union, they have yet to complete the next stage of economic integration—the common market. A detailed program for attaining this stage was set forth by the EC Commission (the EC's executive body) in June 1985 in a White Paper entitled, "Completing the Internal Market." The EC Council (the EC's supreme decisionmaking body) promptly committed the EC to carry out the White Paper's program by the end of 1992.

The White Paper lists 300 specific areas (subsequently reduced to 279) for action by 1992. The proposed actions are intended to eliminate the obstacles to an integrated market, which the Paper divides into three kinds of barriers—physical, technical, and fiscal. A genuine European Community, without internal economic frontiers, is the desired result, with freedom of movement for goods, services, persons, and capital.

What has sparked this renewed drive toward economic integration within the EC? What might be the consequences, not only for the EC but for the rest of the world, and particularly for U.S. business?

Why a Common Market?

Between the formation of the customs union in 1968 and the adoption of the White Paper in 1985, little progress was made toward a common market in the EC. The hostile economic climate of the 1970s—with the oil shocks of 1973–74 and 1978–79, the high inflation rates, and the recessions—led the member country governments to focus more on protecting their constituencies from external forces than on dismantling economic barriers. What, then, revitalized the process of economic integration?

One factor has been the improvement in EC economic conditions during the 1980s. Another stimulus has been mounting frustration with the obstacles to intra-EC transactions. For example (Calingaert 1988, pp. 6–7):

> As members of the European Community Youth Orchestra traveled within the Community, they had to carry documentary evidence of their instruments' country of origin and often had to deposit the value of their instruments when leaving their home country to satisfy customs authorities that they had not exported the instruments.
>
> A European television manufacturer had to make seven types of television sets to meet member country standards, which required 70 engineers to adjust new models to individual country requirements and cost an additional $20 million per year.

Another motivation for further integration is to rectify the EC's slow growth and high unemployment, a condition partly traceable to structural rigidities that has been labelled "Euro-sclerosis." This particular motivation has been heightened by anxiety that the EC is becoming less competitive in the world economy and is lagging behind Japan and the United States in economic performance. Establishment of a common market is seen as a tonic that will enhance efficiency, largely by promoting competition within the EC and by fostering the development of production facilities large enough to achieve the economies associated with large-scale production.

The prospect of substantial gains has fired the

Establishment of a common market is seen as a tonic that will enhance efficiency in economic performance.

---

imagination of EC officials and of many other Europeans. To convey their enthusiasm, it is worth quoting a few paragraphs from *A Frontier-Free Europe*, a publication of the Commission (1988b, pp. 8–9, 16–17).

> This tremendous challenge is galvanizing Europeans as no other has done over the last four decades. Everyone has more or less accepted the ugly truth that continued inertia will lead the member countries of the Community into inexorable international decline. . . .
>
> Yesterday the Twelve were manifestly apathetic, unassertive and disunited. . . . They had failed once again to take the Community's birth certificate—unity is strength—to its logical conclusion. . . . With 'Deadline 1992' the hour of resurgence has come. In an appointment with history, the European Community is gambling on the ability of Europeans to rise to a challenge, on that spirit which, down the centuries, has made them great on the international scene. . . .
>
> . . . the large frontier-free market can make a vital contribution to the recovery and competitiveness of industry and commerce and act as a motive force for European union. . . .
>
> Support for integration . . . is no longer confined to dreamers and old-fashioned romantics. It is coming from pragmatic Europeans, confronted day in day out with the absurdity of 12 national markets every bit as compartmentalized as they were in medieval times. . . .

The need to create a market comparable with that of the United States is obvious. . . . Our present structure of nation-States is costing us enormous sums of money and making it easier for our competitors to divide and rule. Europe is now trailing the U.S. and Japan in key areas of high technology. We must pool our efforts to narrow the gap.

In the same vein, another EC publication prophesies, "After the 'American challenge' of the 1960's and the subsequent emergence of Japan onto the world stage, the 1990's promise to be the decade of a revitalized Europe" (Commission of the European Communities: Spokesman's Service, p. 10).

Is this just empty rhetoric? Or are the potential gains truly large, and is the EC really mobilizing to achieve them? And what barriers must be removed in order to complete the internal market?

Completing the Market: Barriers That Must Go

The barriers targeted for removal by the White Paper can be divided into eight categories, some of which overlap.[1]

(1) *Border controls.* At the borders between EC member states are physical controls that regulate the passage of people and goods. Such controls are necessitated by certain differences in laws and regulations between member states. For example, widely differing indirect tax rates (including excise and value-added rates) require tax adjustments at the borders to ensure that goods crossing over are taxed at the rates of the countries they are entering, so as to minimize competitive distortions. Differing health regulations for plant and animal products also require controls to ensure that such products satisfy the regulations of the country the products are entering. These controls impose significant delays and other costs. Harmonization of the differing laws and regulations (including tax rates) would of course be one way to obviate the need for such controls.

(2) *Limitations on movement of people and their right of establishment.* An important illustration of this kind of barrier is that academic degrees and professional qualifications acquired in one EC member country have not, as a rule, been readily recognized in other member countries. Thus, it has been difficult for professionals to transfer the practice of their occupations from one state to another. In addition, border controls are maintained to combat terrorism, drug trafficking, and illegal immigration by non-EC residents.

(3) *Differing indirect taxation regimes.* As already noted, the existence of differing tax rates and systems is one reason for the maintenance of border controls. Thus, the EC Commission has proposed that the same excise tax rates should be adopted by all EC countries and that value-added tax rates should diverge by no more than 5 to 6 percentage points between countries, a divergence that the Commission believes would be essentially neutral in its effect (Calingaert 1988, pp. 42–43).

(4) *Lack of a common legal framework for business.* The operation of business enterprises in the EC has been governed largely by differing national laws and regulations, introducing complications into cross-border business activity involving mergers, joint ventures, patents, copyrights, and so forth.

(5) *Controls on movement of capital.* Eight of the EC states have maintained some degree of control over capital movements to or from other member states.

(6) *Heavy—and differing—regulation of services.* The service industries, such as transportation and especially finance, have been subjected to regulation that has considerably raised the cost of the services provided and that has also differed significantly from one member state to the next.

(7) *Divergent product regulations and standards.* Often a product has had to meet differing standards in different EC countries.

(8) *Protectionist public procurement policies.* In procuring goods and services, the public authorities in the various EC countries have generally granted preferential treatment to domestic suppliers in a number of ways, including the procedures through which bids are solicited and contracts are awarded.

These eight categories of barriers comprise a formidable phalanx. It is not surprising that substantial gains from their removal are forecasted by a recent study.

The Potential Gains: Some Quantitative Estimates

In order to obtain quantitative estimates of the economic benefits that could flow from the common market, the EC Commission arranged for a major study, the results of which were published only last year. A massive research effort, the study involved 200 people, took two years to complete, and cost about $5 million. It is the only comprehensive analysis available of the potential gains to the EC from completing the internal market. Carried out under the general direction of Paolo Cecchini, a former EC Commission official, the study is summarized in a slim volume widely known as the "Cecchini report" (Cecchini 1988).

In the study the potential gains to the EC from market integration are evaluated using both microeconomic analysis, which focuses on the effects on producers and consumers, and macroeconomic analysis, which focuses on the effects on major components of the gross domestic product (GDP). With both analytical approaches, the starting point is the removal of the market-fragmenting barriers targeted in the White Paper. Their removal will lower the costs of doing business—a favorable supply-side shock—and prices are expected to go down with costs under the pressure of wider competition across the newly unified market. The reduction in prices will stimulate demand and, therefore, output, and the increase in output will lead to further reductions in costs as economies of larger-scale production are realized.

In the microeconomic analysis, two approaches are employed: a price-convergence approach and a welfare-gains approach. The price-convergence approach assumes that the removal of barriers will greatly reduce the substantial price differences often observed for a given product between EC countries. Across countries in 1985, the average before-tax price variation from the EC mean price was 15.2 percent for consumer goods and 12.4 percent for capital equipment. Much greater price dispersion was observed for some individual items, such as glass and crockery (21 percent), boilermaking equipment (22 percent), tea (27 percent), ladies' linen and hosiery (31 percent), and books (49 percent). And glaring price differences (tax inclusive) are reported within the service sector: 28 percent in road and rail transport, 42 percent in electrical repairs, and 50 percent in telephone and telegraph services.

As barriers to arbitrage across countries are relaxed, prices should converge, and intensified competition across frontiers should lower the general average. Thus, the analysis assumes that in sectors where barriers are currently low, any price peaks will be brought down to the EC average, and that in sectors with high barriers, prices will settle at the average of the prices prevailing in the two EC countries with the lowest price levels. On the further assumption that output remains unchanged, this line of analysis concludes that total savings from the drop in prices would be about 4.8 percent of EC gross domestic product—a one-time, once-and-for-all gain.

This gain estimated by the price-convergence ap-

proach is conservative in that it takes no account of (1) the increases in output that would accompany the increased demand stimulated by price reductions or (2) the further cost- and price-reducing effects of larger scale production. By contrast, the welfare-gains approach does allow for these ramifications. It is more comprehensive than the price-convergence approach in another respect as well: it takes into account the profit losses that may be suffered by some currently protected producers as well as the gains to consumers and other producers. In the welfare-gains approach, a gain for consumers (or "consumer surplus") stems from lower prices and larger purchases, and this gain is partly offset by a drop in profit for producers subjected to new competition. Another gain, with no offsetting losses, results from enhanced operational efficiencies throughout the EC.[2]

Table 1 itemizes the net welfare gains estimated by this approach. "Barriers directly affecting intra-EC trade" are essentially customs formalities and related delays. "Barriers to production" are those that impede entry into a national market by a foreign firm. Among such production barriers are the preferential treatment granted by government purchasing offices to native producers, differing national regulatory practices, and differing national standards for products. The estimated maximum gain, nearly 6.5 percent of GDP, is substantially larger than the 4.8 percent of GDP estimated with the price-convergence

Table 1

Potential Gains in Economic Welfare for the European Community Resulting from Completion of the Internal Market

Source of Gain	Gain as Percentage of GDP
1. Removal of barriers directly affecting intra-EC trade	.2 to .3
2. Removal of barriers to production	2.0 to 2.4
3. Greater economies of scale, and intensified competition reducing inefficiencies and monopoly profits	2.1 to 3.7
Total	4.3 to 6.4

Source: Paolo Cecchini, *The European Challenge: 1992*, p. 84.

Table 2
Estimated Medium-Term Macroeconomic Consequences for the European Community from Market Integration Processes

	Process				Total	
Nature of Consequence	Removal of Customs Formalities	Opening of Public Procurement	Liberalization of Financial Services	Supply-side Effects	Average Value	Spread
Change in GDP (%)	.4	.5	1.5	2.1	4.5	3.2 to 5.7
Change in Consumer Prices (%)	−1.0	−1.4	−1.4	−2.3	−6.1	−4.5 to −7.7
Change in Employment (thousands)	200	350	400	850	1,800	1,300 to 2,300
Change in Budgetary Balance (percentage point of GDP)	.2	.3	1.1	.6	2.2	1.5 to 3.0
Change in External Balance (percentage point of GDP)	.2	.1	.3	.4	1.0	.7 to 1.3

Source: Paolo Cecchini, *The European Challenge: 1992*, p. 98.

approach; but even the 6.5 percent figure might be too low, since it does not allow for the impact of new business strategies and technical innovation that could be stimulated by integration of the market.

Shifting from the microeconomic to the macroeconomic perspective, the study's analysis of potential gains from market integration focuses on the major components of GDP. As can be seen in table 2, the macroeconomic analysis proceeded by quantifying the effects of easing barriers in customs procedures, in public procurement, and in financial services, and by quantifying various supply-side effects entailing greater business efficiency. The greatest gains are estimated from the liberalization of financial services and from supply-side effects.

The gains from liberalizing financial services stem from the resulting intensification of competition and associated reduction in the prices of financial services. Transmission of lower financial services costs throughout the economy is estimated to reduce prices generally, stimulating demand (both domestic and external) and output. This favorable effect will be amplified by increased investment in response to the lower cost of credit. More general supply-side effects come from the business sector's response to the more competitive environment—from more efficient techniques and greater economies of scale.

In total, the macroeconomic consequences of EC market integration are expected to be very favorable.

It is estimated that GDP will be boosted by 4.5 percent, with 1.8 million new jobs, while consumer prices will simultaneously be lowered by 6.1 percent. The aggregate government budget balance is expected to improve by an amount equivalent to 2.2 percentage points of GDP, as government revenues rise with GDP and procurement costs are eased with the opening of public procurement to wider competition. Benefiting from improved competitiveness, the EC's current-account balance with the rest of the world is estimated to improve by the equivalent of 1 percentage point of GDP. Again, these are one-time, or once-and-for-all, gains, and their realization is likely to require 5 or 6 years once the market-integration program is complete.

The nature of these gains—especially the drop in consumer prices and the improvements in public finances and the external balance—suggests that still greater gains might be achieved were EC governments to pursue more expansionary fiscal policies. Thus, policies that reduced the improvement in government budget balances to 0.7 of a percentage point of GDP might boost the medium-term increase in GDP to 7 percent, with 5 million new jobs and no inflation, according to the Cecchini report (pp. 99–102).

As the basic study makes clear, such gains are contingent on removal of all essential barriers to market integration. Retention of only a few key barriers would suffice to restrain competition. In the words of the study, "Implementation of half of the actions proposed in the White Paper will deliver much less than half of the total potential benefits" (Commission of the European Communities 1988a, p. 22).

With such sizable total gains in prospect, the question arises how the gains will be distributed among the EC member countries. The study offers no quantitative estimates of this distribution. Economic theory suggests that proportionately larger gains will accrue to the smaller countries, especially those that have recently joined the EC and have had relatively high protection from external competition. Initially, however, such countries could suffer losses, as could various regions within the EC, until the firms and workers exposed to keener competition made adjustments such as adopting new techniques or acquiring new skills. Should some EC members suffer losses from the integration process, the EC has policy instruments, such as structural funds, that could be used to help them recover (Commission of the European Communities 1988a, p. 21).

Potential Gains for Countries Outside the EC

If market integration does yield the growth spurt projected for the EC in the Cecchini report, rising EC income could lead to increased imports and thus to higher levels of economic activity in the rest of the world. The boost to GDP in the rest of the world would be considerably smaller than that inside the EC, however, and like that within the EC, would be a one-time phenomenon. Indeed, the net impact on the rest of the world could be contractionary, since the Cecchini report expects the rest of the world to expe-

---

EC market integration could lead to higher levels of economic activity in the rest of the world.

---

rience a deterioration in its trade balance with the EC unless EC governments pursue relatively expansionary macroeconomic policies.

· Another potentially favorable result for the rest of the world is a lower rate of inflation, induced by the projected deflationary impact of EC market inte-

gration. This, in turn, could lead to lower interest rates if inflationary expectations were revised downward. And the rest of the world would experience more favorable terms of trade with the EC, if the real cost of goods purchased from the EC went down. This outcome, too, is far from certain. The expected growth spurt in the EC could generate an investment boom, pushing interest rates upward rather than downward and raising rather than lowering the real cost of goods exported from the EC in the near term. In this case, though, economic growth in the rest of the world could receive a larger boost, as the EC's external trade balance would likely deteriorate.

Still another gain for the rest of the world is possible, although it is even more speculative and imponderable than the preceding gains. As we have noted, one motivation underlying EC market integration is to narrow a perceived lag in EC economic performance behind Japan and the United States. Such competition among nations, if conducted without protectionist devices, can benefit all involved. Perhaps the United States, for example, will be spurred by the European challenge, as it has been by the Japanese challenge, to reconsider and improve some of its ways of doing business.

The Specter of Fortress Europe

As the foregoing discussion suggests, the consequences of EC market integration for the rest of the world are highly problematic, even on the assumption that the EC completes its internal market without resorting to intensified protection against the rest of the world. Now suppose that as the EC allows the winds of competition to blow more freely across its members' frontiers, it simultaneously erects substantially more barriers against competition from the rest of the world, so as to mitigate the overall competitive shock and the degree of internal adjustment that will be required. This outcome, which is rather widely feared, would have damaging consequences for the rest of the world, and perhaps for the EC as well.

Were the EC to turn inward in this way, international economic cooperation in general would surely be undermined. For example, efforts to coordinate macroeconomic policies among the EC, Japan, and the United States would probably suffer. More certainly, the Uruguay Round of Multilateral Trade Negotiations, undertaken to liberalize international trade in both goods and services, would be imperiled if the EC's protectionist course became manifest before the completion of the Round, now scheduled for 1990.

A heightening of the EC's protectionist barriers would tend to negate the benefits that could otherwise accrue to the EC itself from integrating its internal market. After all, realization of those benefits is deemed to depend heavily upon a widening of competition within the market. Insofar as the strengthening of internal competition is offset by the blockage of

---

Were the EC to erect more barriers against outside competition, the consequences could be damaging for the rest of the world and perhaps for the EC as well.

---

competition from abroad, the benefits will be choked off near the source.

If completion of the internal market in this fashion would yield little benefit for the EC, the rest of the world would benefit even less, and might well be harmed. For example, intensification of EC protectionism would militate against the reduction of costs and inflation within the EC and thus would do little to lower inflation abroad. Other countries might also experience a worsening of the terms on which they traded with the EC, as EC demand for their goods and services was damped by the heightened barriers, although this outcome would depend on the circumstances, including the nature of the barriers and the foreign response to them.

If protectionism were to transform the EC into "Fortress Europe" as it completed its internal market, how might the transformation occur? What measures would work the transformation? Because internal market integration implies removal of barriers between EC member countries but not necessarily between the EC and other countries, EC members might typically agree that all should impose against other countries the harshest of the barriers currently prevailing in any EC member country, while simultaneously eliminating such barriers against movements of goods, services, people, or capital among themselves.

To illustrate, the individual states of the EC currently maintain as many as 1,000 separate quantita-

tive restrictions on imports (including the so-called "voluntary" restraints that some countries impose on their exports to EC countries), mostly on imports from Japan, the Asian newly industrialized countries, and the East European nonmarket economies (Calingaert 1988, p. 83). To prevent imports in excess of any restriction that it has promulgated, each EC country must monitor the flow of the restricted goods that comes to it via other EC members as well as from other sources. However, such border controls over intra-EC trade, with the associated delays and other costs, are inconsistent with EC market integration. To eliminate the border controls and complete the internal market, therefore, EC members must abolish the restrictions or establish a uniform set, to be applied by all the members acting as one, on imports from the rest of the world.

The most important of these restrictions relate to textiles and automobiles. For both of these commodity categories, it is likely that uniform EC restrictions will replace the prevailing individual member restrictions, resulting in no less overall protection than that now in force. Exports from the United States in these two categories are currently exempt from the restrictions, but automobiles from the United States might be covered in the future. Now it is automobiles from Japan that are targeted. If Japanese-brand automobiles manufactured in the United States were to be exported to the EC in sizable volume, the EC surely would consider encompassing them within the restrictions (Calingaert 1988, pp. 83–84).

Of even greater concern for the United States is the possibility of another variety of EC protectionism. This protectionism would take the form of denying "national treatment" for U.S. firms seeking to enter the EC through subsidiaries. The principle of national treatment—meaning government treatment of foreign-owned subsidiaries that is no less favorable than that accorded domestically owned firms—has been endorsed by all 24 member countries of the Organization for Economic Cooperation and Development, including the EC countries. But some EC officials and documents have espoused a different principle, the principle of reciprocity. Under a strict interpretation of reciprocity, subsidiaries to be established in the Community by firms located in a nonmember country would be granted the benefits of the integrated market only if EC subsidiaries in that nonmember country enjoyed similar benefits.

Some measure of reciprocity has been called for in proposed EC directives on financial services, especially with respect to investment services and life insurance, and also to some extent with respect to banking. In regard to banking, it would not be possible for the United States to offer to EC banks opportunities comparable to those that EC banks have in their home markets. U.S. laws and regulations do not permit banks, either domestically or foreign-owned, to establish branches or subsidiaries nationwide, and banks in the United States are also subjected to other restrictions—for example, on securities activities—that do not apply to banks in the EC. (What the United States can and does offer is national treatment, or equality of competitive opportunity for banks regardless of nationality of ownership.) Thus, a strict interpretation of reciprocity could put U.S. banks at a competitive disadvantage in the Community.

The principle of reciprocity could be applied by the EC within certain sectors such as banking, or could be applied on an overall basis, with the EC granting national treatment in sectors such as banking in return for new opportunities for EC firms abroad in other sectors. The overall approach would be more consistent with the traditional practice in multilateral trade liberalization, in which the negotiating parties generally settle for an overall balance of concessions rather than a balance sector by sector. For the EC to demand sector-by-sector reciprocity as it integrated its internal market would be especially inimical to the achievement of a more liberal international economic order.

Rather than explicitly denying national treatment to foreign firms, the EC might engage in roughly equivalent practices, the effect of which would be protectionist even if the motivation were not. For example, the set of regulations and product standards to be adopted by the EC as part of the integration process could render foreign firms less competitive in the EC market. The purpose of EC regulations and standards is generally to assure some minimum quality, and concerning that general goal there can be little dispute. But if EC authorities refused to recognize product tests administered abroad, foreign manufacturers would face the expense of shipping their products to the EC for testing and sale without the assurance of certification.

Aside from difficulties with the certification process, non-EC firms could be disadvantaged by the EC standards themselves. A good illustration is the controversy between the EC and the United States over U.S. meat produced with the aid of growth hormones. Growth hormones are widely used in meat production in the United States, but not in the EC. The EC recently banned imports of such meat for human consumption on the grounds that it poses a health hazard. Arguing that scientific inquiry reveals no hazard, the United States has retaliated with 100 percent duties on selected U.S. imports of EC food products whose total import value approximates the $100 million of banned U.S. meat exports.

The Likelihood of Fortress Europe

It is much easier to conjure up the specter of Fortress Europe than to determine whether the Fortress will materialize. What is the likelihood that the EC will become more protectionist as it completes its internal market?

In his classic, *The Customs Union Issue*, Jacob Viner opined that "with respect to most customs union projects the protectionist is right and the free-trader is wrong in regarding the project as something, given his premises, which he can logically support" (Viner 1950, p. 41). Viner believed that the external barriers of the typical customs union would be adjusted so as to offset—indeed, more than offset—any overall decline in protection associated with heightened competition among the members. It would be hard to prove that the EC has followed such a protectionist course from its inception, particularly with respect to tariffs on manufactured goods. With respect to other forms of protection the record is not so good, especially in recent years.

Moreover, some EC documents and official statements are worrisome. In July 1988, Willy de Clercq, then the EC Commissioner for External Relations, asserted that the new common market will "give us the negotiating leverage to obtain . . .overall reciprocity" (de Clercq 1988). Similarly, the Cecchini report warns, "If the fruits of the European home market are to be shared internationally, there must also be a fair share-out of the burdens of global economic responsibility, with market opening measures extended internationally on a firm basis of clear reciprocity" (Cecchini 1988, p. xx). And the White Paper declares that "the commercial identity of the Community must be consolidated so that our trading partners will not be given the benefit of a wider market without themselves making similar concessions" (Commission of the European Communities 1985, para. 19). Not only will the EC seek global reciprocity (an overall balance of concessions), but according to Mr. de Clercq, it will seek sectoral reciprocity in certain sectors not covered by the General Agreement on Tariffs and Trade, particularly the services sector (de Clercq 1988).

Concern is warranted not only by such official pronouncements, but also by EC trade policy, which, as in some other countries, has turned more protectionist and discriminatory over the past two decades. Much of the heightened protection and discrimination has taken the form of various nontariff interventions. In particular, the EC has made increasing use of selective, quantitative import restrictions (including "voluntary" export restraint agreements), especially to limit manufactured imports from developing countries. In addition, it has subsidized EC exports, notably exports of agricultural goods whose production is also protected by variable import levies, and it has employed countervailing and antidumping duties more vigorously (Henderson 1989, pp. 13–14). In light of this seeming predisposition toward protectionism, it would not be surprising if competitive pressures generated by the removal of barriers to trade within the EC were eased by the elevation, or at least the maintenance, of similar barriers against competition from without. Thus, completion of the EC's internal market may well entail at least the preexisting degree of EC protection against foreign competition.

Any shift toward greater protection by the EC is likely to be slight, however, so that the specter of Fortress Europe will probably remain little more than a specter. As EC authorities are well aware, even minor heightenings of protectionist barriers have provoked retaliation from the injured trading partners, and the prospect of such retaliation is a strong deterrent. To put much the same point more positively, the EC, like most other trading entities, has much more to gain from an open, integrated international economy than from one fragmented by protectionist barriers. Indeed, that conclusion flows from the same line of reasoning that is used to justify the completion of the EC internal market. And the EC has many good logicians.

U.S. Business and the Common Market

U.S. business has a sizable stake in the EC. In 1988 the United States exported $130 billion in goods and services to the EC, one-third more than to Canada, our second largest export market. Because most export sales are of merchandise and because detailed

Table 3

U.S. Exports of Domestic and Foreign Merchandise to Canada and the European Community in Total and by Leading End-Use Categories, 1982 and 1988[a]

Millions of U.S. Dollars

Category[b]	Canada		European Community	
	1982	1988	1982	1988
Grand total	37,799	68,747	51,255	74,679
Total foods, feeds, and beverages	1,966	2,225	8,839	5,689
Agricultural foods, feeds, and beverages	1,801	1,994	8,653	5,561
Total industrial supplies and materials	9,054	12,615	16,650	19,734
Nonagricultural except fuels	6,361	10,043	9,648	14,463
Chemicals, excluding medicinals	1,979	3,170	3,648	6,019
Capital goods except automotive	10,173	16,547	19,628	36,997
Nonelectrical machinery, including parts and attachments	8,194	12,581	14,643	25,581
Industrial and service machinery	3,727	5,055	5,284	7,329
Computers, peripherals, and semi-conductors	1,335	3,853	4,926	12,080
Transportation equipment, except automotive	1,107	2,168	3,588	8,935
Civilian aircraft, parts and engines, excluding special category	925	1,915	3,124	8,434
Automotive vehicles, parts and engines	9,310	19,634	954	2,162
Passenger cars, new and used	2,345	6,266	76	643
Automotive parts, engines and bodies	6,211	10,585	778	1,364
Consumer goods (nonfood), except automotive	2,141	3,452	3,872	7,228
Domestic exports, n.e.c., and reexports	5,156	14,271	1,312	2,680

[a] Special category military-type goods are not included.
[b] Categories shown are those in which total exports to Canada and the EC were $5 billion or more in 1988.
Source: National Institutes of Health, COMPRO data base.

data are available on the merchandise categories, tables 3 and 4 present statistics for the leading merchandise categories. The data are shown for Canada as well as the EC, not only because Canada is the second largest U.S. export market but because the two nations have recently concluded a free trade agreement.

As shown in the tables, for merchandise alone, total EC and Canadian purchases of U.S. exports were not vastly different in 1988. However, except for automotive vehicles, parts, and engines—in which sectoral free trade between Canada and the United States has contributed to close integration of the national industries—the EC is a much more important export market for the United States in every merchandise category listed in the tables. Especially noteworthy are the EC shares of U.S. worldwide exports in the categories of computers, peripherals, and semiconductors, and of civilian aircraft, parts, and engines (table 4).

Firms invade foreign markets not only by exporting but by acquiring facilities in those markets. Thus, U.S. multinational firms have many affiliates, including branches and subsidiaries, in Canada and the EC, and the sales of these affiliates are much larger than U.S. exports to either area, especially in the case of the EC (table 5). While not all such sales are to Canadian or EC residents, the preponderance surely are.[3] Between 1982 and 1986 (the latest year for which data are available at this writing), the biggest increases in these affiliate sales were in manufacturing industries, although the increase within wholesale trade in the EC also merits mention.

As can be seen in table 6, the EC affiliates of U.S. firms account for almost half of the sales of all foreign affiliates of U.S. companies. In nearly every industry listed the EC is significantly more important for these sales than Canada is. A comparison of tables 6 and 4 suggests that the EC absorbs a much larger share of these total affiliate sales than of total U.S. merchandise exports.[4] These phenomena may well be heightened by the completion of the EC internal market and the implementation of the free trade agreement between Canada and the United States. The EC internal market will probably serve to raise U.S. direct investment and sales within the market relative to U.S. ex-

Table 4

U.S. Merchandise Exports to Canada and the European Community in Total and by Leading End-Use Categories, as a Percentage of U.S. Exports Worldwide by Category, 1982 and 1988[a]

	Canada		European Community	
Category[b]	1982	1988	1982	1988
Grand total	17.2	21.5	23.3	23.3
Total foods, feeds, and beverages	6.2	6.8	27.7	17.9
Agricultural foods, feeds, and beverages	5.9	6.6	28.2	18.4
Total industrial supplies and materials	14.6	14.5	26.8	22.7
Nonagricultural except fuels	16.5	15.6	25.1	22.5
Chemicals, excluding medicinals	12.6	12.4	23.3	23.6
Capital goods except automotive	13.5	14.3	26.1	32.0
Nonelectrical machinery, including parts and attachments	14.7	15.2	26.2	31.0
Industrial and service machinery	16.4	17.9	23.2	26.0
Computers, peripherals, and semi-conductors	10.7	12.0	39.5	37.5
Transportation equipment, except automotive	9.2	9.6	29.7	39.7
Civilian aircraft, parts and engines, excluding special category	9.4	9.2	31.8	40.7
Automotive vehicles, parts and engines	58.3	61.2	6.0	7.1
Passenger cars, new and used	74.5	69.3	2.4	7.1
Automotive parts, engines and bodies	60.2	61.2	7.5	7.9
Consumer goods (nonfood), except automotive	13.7	13.4	24.7	28.0
Domestic exports, n.e.c., and reexports	56.6	60.4	14.4	11.3

[a] Special category military-type goods are not included.
[b] Categories shown are those in which total exports to Canada and the EC were $5 billion or more in 1988.
Source: National Institutes of Health, COMPRO data base.

Table 5

Sales of Canadian and European Community Affiliates of U.S. Multinational Companies, by Selected Industries, 1982 and 1986

Millions of U.S. Dollars

Industry[a]	Canadian Affiliates		EC Affiliates[b]	
	1982	1986	1982	1986
All industries	120,327	132,594	370,542	430,377
Petroleum	28,642	18,479	104,685	74,118
Oil and gas extraction	d	d	d	12,048
Crude petroleum (no refining) and gas	d	d	9,918	11,233
Petroleum and coal products	19,046	d	63,138	44,228
Integrated refining and extraction	17,233	10,640	35,128	18,841
Refining without extraction	d	d	27,796	25,275
Petroleum wholesale trade	3,645	2,178	23,023	11,553
Manufacturing	56,911	75,521	160,609	226,068
Food and kindred products	5,258	5,655	16,337	23,998
Grain mill and bakery products	1,214	1,465	6,454	9,990
Chemicals and allied products	8,265	10,493	30,451	40,705
Industrial chemicals and synthetics	4,240	4,638	13,791	18,289
Drugs	1,122	1,521	6,583	10,395
Primary and fabricated metals	3,202	3,880	9,284	12,232
Fabricated metal products	2,155	2,575	6,586	7,917
Machinery, except electrical	4,994	5,615	28,416	47,924
Electric and electronic equipment	4,323	4,704	11,928	24,174
Transportation equipment	19,108	34,075	36,867	36,760
Motor vehicles and equipment	18,086	32,383	d	35,036
Other manufacturing	11,761	11,099	27,325	40,274
Tobacco manufactures	d	d	d	10,648
Instruments and related products	1,079	1,024	8,602	10,482
Wholesale trade	9,788	10,984	58,645	75,460
Durable goods	7,001	8,315	36,935	43,013
Nondurable goods	2,788	2,670	21,711	32,447
Finance (except banking), insurance and real estate	6,349	7,499	8,361	11,888
Insurance	4,629	5,600	d	6,410
Services	2,403	2,611	9,413	15,520
Business services	810	966	5,387	9,850
Other industries	16,234	17,499	28,829	27,323
Transportation, communication and public utilities	d	2,349	d	18,884
Retail trade	10,530	12,399	7,189	5,978

[a] Identifiable industries in which Canadian and EC affiliate sales totaled $10 billion or more in 1986.

[b] EC includes 10 countries because data for Spain and Portugal are not available.

d: Data were suppressed for confidentiality reasons.

Source: U.S. Bureau of Economic Analysis, *U.S. Direct Investment Abroad: Preliminary 1986 Estimates*, June 1988, table 7; and *U.S. Direct Investment Abroad: 1982 Benchmark Survey Data*, December 1985, p. 112.

ports to it, because market completion plans call for a reduction in barriers to commerce within the EC but not between the EC and other countries. By contrast, the U.S.-Canada free trade agreement mandates the removal or reduction of many barriers to trade between the two nations.

What firms will benefit most from EC market integration? In general, the prime beneficiaries will be those firms that are highly competitive within the EC and that face substantial cross-border and other costs and barriers associated with EC market fragmentation. The lowering of these internal barriers and costs will enable such firms to compete more effectively across the Community. Should the EC maintain or elevate its barriers against external competition, these same firms will become even more profitable, at least in the short or medium term. Thus, it is understandable that the financial press has reported something of a scramble by firms to position themselves advantageously within the EC.

If completion of the EC internal market generates a growth spurt, as forecasted by the Cecchini report, EC demand for U.S. (and other) exports likely will also spurt, even if the EC maintains or slightly intensifies its protection against external competition. On the other hand, the Cecchini report expects EC firms to enjoy lower costs as a result of the market integration. Such enhanced competitiveness on the part of EC producers would enable them to accommodate some of the increase in EC demand that might otherwise generate U.S. exports. Similarly, U.S. firms would encounter stiffer competition from EC firms in

Table 6

Sales of Canadian and European Community Affiliates of U.S. Multinational Companies as a Percentage of U.S. Foreign Affiliate Sales Worldwide, by Selected Industries, 1982 and 1986

| | Percent of Total Sales, All U.S. Foreign Affiliates | | | |
| | Canadian Affiliates | | EC Affiliates[b] | |
Industry[a]	1982	1986	1982	1986
All industries	12.9	14.2	39.6	46.2
Petroleum	8.7	9.2	31.8	37.1
Oil and gas extraction	d	d	d	30.5
Crude petroleum (no refining) and gas	d	d	19.6	32.0
Petroleum and coal products	14.0	d	46.4	52.0
Integrated refining and extraction	30.0	32.4	61.2	57.4
Refining without extraction	d	d	35.7	49.0
Petroleum wholesale trade	3.2	3.6	20.0	18.9
Manufacturing	15.8	16.8	44.7	50.2
Food and kindred products	13.5	12.7	41.9	53.9
Grain mill and bakery products	9.7	9.9	51.8	67.3
Chemicals and allied products	11.9	13.1	43.8	50.7
Industrial chemicals and synthetics	12.8	12.6	41.6	49.8
Drugs	8.6	8.4	50.2	57.5
Primary and fabricated metals	14.0	16.3	40.5	51.4
Fabricated metal products	16.1	18.3	49.1	56.2
Machinery, except electrical	10.8	7.9	61.2	67.3
Electric and electronic equipment	13.9	10.2	38.3	52.5
Transportation equipment	22.0	30.7	42.4	33.2
Motor vehicles and equipment	21.6	30.2	d	32.7
Other manufacturing	18.6	15.1	43.2	54.9
Tobacco manufactures	d	d	d	79.7
Instruments and related products	8.5	6.4	67.4	65.7
Wholesale trade	8.0	7.3	47.8	50.5
Durable goods	9.6	9.6	50.6	49.7
Nondurable goods	5.6	4.2	43.7	51.5
Finance (except banking), insurance and real estate	22.2	20.5	29.2	32.5
Insurance	27.6	26.6	d	30.4
Services	11.8	10.2	46.4	60.9
Business services	8.0	6.5	53.1	66.6
Other industries	21.4	25.2	38.0	39.4
Transportation, communication and public utilities	d	9.4	d	75.2
Retail trade	38.6	43.1	26.4	20.8

[a] Identifiable industries in which Canadian and EC affiliate sales totaled $10 billion or more in 1986.

[b] EC includes 10 countries because data for Spain and Portugal are not available.

d: Data were suppressed for confidentiality reasons.

Source: U.S. Bureau of Economic Analysis, *U.S. Direct Investment Abroad: Preliminary 1986 Estimates*, June 1988, table 7; and *U.S. Direct Investment Abroad: 1982 Benchmark Survey Data*, December 1985, p. 112.

other markets, including the U.S. market, not only during the EC growth spurt but over the longer run.

EC officials, however, often argue that U.S. firms will excel in the competitive struggle. One EC publication puts it as follows:[5]

> U.S. businesses are well placed to exploit the benefits of a unified market. First of all, their subsidiaries incorporated in the Community will profit from the removal of barriers to the same extent as purely European companies. American companies are already used to operating in both a global and a large domestic marketplace, so may have less trouble adapting to the new environment than indigenous companies.
>
> U.S. exporters will find themselves selling into a single market with a generally uniform set of norms, standards, and testing and certification procedures. They will no longer have to face 12 different sets of requirements or intra-Community border controls. . . .
>
> In fact, many people of the Community are afraid that the main beneficiaries of the internal market could well prove to be the Japanese and American companies operating in Europe.

Progress in Completing the Market

It was in June 1985 that the EC Commission released its White Paper detailing a program for completing the internal market by the end of 1992. The undertaking is formidable even at the technical level, and at the political level has encountered opposition from many who would be affected adversely. What progress has been made?

A single quantitative measure is not feasible, but a crude idea of overall progress is conveyed by the percentage of White Paper subject areas that have been acted upon. As of January 30, 1989, the EC Commission had submitted proposals for more than four-fifths of the subjects covered in the White Paper, and the Council of Ministers—the EC's supreme decisionmaking body—had adopted more than two-fifths of the measures that will eventually be required. Areas in which little progress had been made include freeing the movement of people and reconciling the differences in indirect taxation and in plant and animal health regulation.[6]

Much skepticism exists that the EC nations will resolve all their differences—especially on sensitive matters such as taxation—so as to complete the internal market fully. Certainly it is most unlikely that all of the White Paper's program will be in effect by the end of 1992. But the endeavor should not be labeled a failure on those grounds alone. It has been said more than once that "1992 is a process, not an event." By the end of 1992, that process probably will have made substantial progress in integrating the European market.

Conclusion

Motivated largely by frustration with internal economic barriers and by a desire to gain in international economic stature, the EC is well embarked upon a massive effort to establish a Community-wide market free of restrictions over the movement of goods, services, persons, and capital. The potential gains to the EC from such market integration could amount to more than 6 percent of the Community's GDP, with much smaller gains for the rest of the world.

Despite some disturbing omens, it seems unlikely that the EC will transform itself into a protectionist "Fortress Europe" as it unifies its internal market. One deterrent is the threat of retaliation from the rest of the world. Another is the risk that the inefficiencies associated with such protectionism would offset the efficiencies to be reaped from internal market integration.

Viewed as a collectivity, the EC is the largest export market for the United States. Similarly, EC affiliates of U.S. multinational firms account for nearly half of the sales of all foreign affiliates of U.S. companies. The firms to benefit most from EC market integration will be those that are highly competitive within the EC and that have been encumbered by substantial cross-border and other costs and barriers associated with market fragmentation.

Barring a near miracle, the EC internal market will not be completed on schedule by the end of 1992. While there is no guarantee of eventual success, a delay of some years would mean little in such a grand undertaking.

[1] This is the classification used by Calingaert (1988, pp. 20–27).

[2] In a recent theoretical inquiry, Ian Wooton (1988, p. 537) concludes that the welfare of a customs union is enhanced by establishment of a common market as long as the common external tariff structure is set correctly.

[3] See U.S. Bureau of Economic Analysis, *U.S. Direct Investment Abroad: 1982 Benchmark Survey Data*, 1985, p. 225, for local as well as total sales by majority-owned nonbank affiliates of nonbank U.S. parents for 1982.

[4] The same is true if exports are defined to include services as well as merchandise.

[5] "A Europe Without Borders by 1992: Answers to Some Questions," *European Community News*, No. 23/88 (September 15, 1988), p. 4.

[6] "E.C. Commission Evaluates Progress of 1992 Program," *European Community News*, No. 31/88 (November 10, 1988).

References

Calingaert, Michael. 1988. *The 1992 Challenge from Europe: Development of the European Community's Internal Market*. Washington, D.C.: National Planning Association.

Cecchini, Paolo. 1988. *The European Challenge: 1992*. Brookfield, Vt.: Gower Publishing Company.

Commission of the European Communities. 1985. "Completing the Internal Market: White Paper from the Commission to the European Council."

———. 1988a. *European Economy*, No. 35, March.

———. 1988b. *A Frontier-Free Europe*.

Commission of the European Communities: Spokesman's Service. [no date]. *The EC's 1992 Strategy: Market Integration and Economic Growth*.

de Clercq, Willy. 1988. "1992: The Impact on the Outside World." Speech presented in London, July 12.

EC Office of Press and Public Affairs. 1988a. "A Europe Without Borders by 1992: Answers to Some Questions." *European Community News*, No. 23/88, September 15.

———. 1988b. "E.C. Commission Evaluates Progress of 1992 Program." *European Community News*, No. 31/88, November 10.

Henderson, David. 1989. *1992: The External Dimension*. New York: Group of Thirty.

U.S. Bureau of Economic Analysis. 1985. *U.S. Direct Investment Abroad: 1982 Benchmark Survey Data*. Washington, D.C.

Viner, Jacob. 1950. *The Customs Union Issue*. New York: Carnegie Endowment for International Peace.

Wooton, Ian. 1988. "Towards a Common Market: Factor Mobility in a Customs Union." *Canadian Journal of Economics*, vol. XXI, August, pp. 525–38.

Article 36

Exchange Rate Determination: Sorting Out Theory and Evidence

The behavior of the current account and the value of the dollar relative to other currencies have been focal points of much policy discussion during the eighties. Since 1973, and especially from 1982 to the present, exchange rate movements have not been consistent with the predictions of several popular economic models. This conflict between theory and observation poses a problem in determining the most appropriate role of the exchange rate in the formation of monetary policy. Any policy suggestion, even one of "do nothing," must be based on some idea of how the exchange rate is determined. Since none of the theoretical models based on economic fundamentals does well in explaining recent exchange rate movements, we could abandon them altogether in favor of "nonfundamental" explanations. Rather than do that, this paper addresses the more constructive questions:

What aspects of each class of models give rise to the apparent inconsistencies with the observed data? and

What aspects of each class show the most promise of increasing our understanding of exchange rate behavior?

To provide a foundation for addressing these questions, we next define some basic concepts and briefly consider the behavior of exchange rates since the early 1970s.

Some Definitions

A nominal bilateral exchange rate is the price of one country's currency in terms of another country's currency, such as the price of French francs in terms of dollars. When traders in foreign exchange markets (primarily commercial banks trading interest-bearing bank deposits) agree on a foreign exchange transaction, they also agree on when that transaction will take place. For transactions settled immediately (within two business days), the price at which the currencies are

Jane Marrinan

Assistant Professor, Economics Department, Boston College. The author was an Economist at the Federal Reserve Bank of Boston at the time this article was written. She would like to thank Norman S. Fieleke and Steven Sass for helpful comments and suggestions. Lawrence D. Herman provided valuable research assistance.

exchanged is called the spot exchange rate. A forward exchange rate is a prenegotiated rate for an exchange of currencies to take place at some date in the future—say, 30, 60, or 90 days.

Since currency is not the final object of consumption, economic agents making consumption and investment decisions often want to know the value of the currency in terms of its real purchasing power. Using nominal bilateral exchange rates, individuals can translate different countries' prices into comparable currency units. Once the prices of home goods and imports are expressed in a common unit, households and firms can compute relative prices of goods and services. Often it is these relative prices of real goods and services that are important in making investment and spending decisions.

One important relative price is a country's real exchange rate. This is the nominal exchange rate adjusted for price level differences across countries. It measures the number of typical foreign consumption baskets needed to purchase a typical domestic consumption basket.[1] The real exchange rate, ultimately determined by real factors such as resource endowments, consumer tastes, government spending and production technology, is of interest because it reflects the cost of living in the United States relative to the foreign country. Using the consumer price indices in each country, the real rate can be expressed as the foreign price level measured in dollars divided by the U.S. price level.

If S_t is the DM/dollar spot exchange rate at time t, P_t^* the price level in Germany at time t, P_t the price level in the United States at time t, then the real DM/dollar exchange rate can be expressed as

$$Q_t = S_t(P_t/P_t^*).$$

It is actually the behavior of the real exchange rate that lies at the heart of many discussions regarding the appropriate role of the nominal exchange rate in the conduct of monetary policy. Proponents of using deliberate monetary policy to achieve greater stability of the nominal rate hope to dampen large and persistent swings in the real exchange rate. This reflects their view that much of the fluctuation in real exchange rates represents departures from some appropriate equilibrium level.

The alternative view suggests that most of the important real exchange rate movements are the result of real disturbances to the economy. Current and expected future changes in investment opportunities, government purchases, tax rates and the like

Chart 1

Contemporaneous Three-Month-Forward Exchange Rate and Spot Exchange Rate for the Deutsche Mark

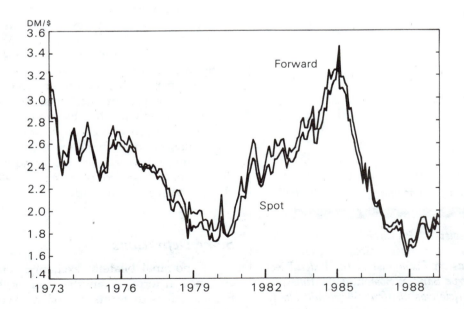

Observations are for the last business day of each month.

Source: Board of Governors of the Federal Reserve System.

alter relative prices in the economy, including the real exchange rate. If real disturbances are the predominant source of real exchange rate movements, then it is questionable whether it is advisable or even feasible to use monetary policy in an attempt to alter nominal rates as a means to alter real rates.

In order to evaluate these two positions and the underlying models on which they are based, we begin by looking at how exchange rates, both nominal and real, have behaved during the floating rate regime.

Empirical Behavior of the Exchange Rate

Prior to 1973 most nominal exchange rates were pegged to the U.S. dollar and their values were typically held for long periods within very narrow bands of central parity through official intervention by central banks. Exchange rate behavior was characterized by infrequent, relatively large changes in parity in response to fundamental disequilibrium. The 1970s witnessed the adoption of much more flexible exchange rates by the major industrial economies. Although this move had long been advocated by most economists, by the mid 1970s many agreed that exchange rates were more volatile under the floating rate regime than they had anticipated. Moreover, it became clear that existing theoretical and empirical models of the exchange rate did not provide reliable descriptions of exchange rate dynamics. Researchers thus directed much attention to the analysis of exchange rate movements.

Empirical studies of the short-term behavior of major currency exchange rates during the floating rate period have revealed the following general characteristics:[2] First, month-to-month variability in bilateral spot exchange rates is frequently large and changes are almost entirely unpredictable. Neither the forecasts of market participants as revealed by the forward discount or survey data,[3] nor simple time series models, nor theoretically sophisticated models based on market fundamentals[4] appear able to appreciably and consistently outpredict a simple random walk model of exchange rates.[5]

Second, there is a strong positive correlation between spot and contemporaneous forward exchange rates. For maturities of forward contracts extending out to one year, spot and forward rates tend to move in the same direction and by approximately the same amount in percentage terms. This can be seen in chart 1, which plots the DM/$ spot and contemporaneous three-month forward rate using monthly data. The contemporaneous correlation between these two series is .99. Although it may seem intuitive to think of the forward rate as the market's expectation of the future spot rate, by shifting the forward rate of chart 1 ahead by three months one can see that it is a very poor predictor. (See chart 2.) In fact, an important anomaly during the early 1980s is that for many currencies the forward premium or discount on the dollar has tended to systematically mispredict even the direction in which the dollar exchange rate actually moved during the subsequent month (Kaminsky and Peruga 1988; Obstfeld 1987; Lewis 1988). Chart 3 shows the one-month-forward premium or discount and actual percentage change in the spot rate for the U.S. dollar versus the deutsche mark, monthly June 1973 through April 1989.

A third widely noted empirical regularity is that short-term variability of nominal exchange rates has been significantly greater than the variability of relative national price levels. Therefore, short-term movements in real rates are highly correlated with nominal rate movements and have been highly persistent in the sense that the real rate takes a long time to begin returning to its original level.[6]

Fourth, there is strong evidence that the variability, not only of nominal rates, but also of real exchange rates, differs across alternative nominal exchange rate systems (Mussa 1986; Stockman 1983; Edison and Melvin 1988). As table 1 points out, short-term variability of real exchange rates among the five major industrial country currencies is substantially greater during the floating rate period than during the Bretton Woods era (except for the franc/mark rate, which actually was more nearly pegged than floating during the latter period). Although the floating rate period was in fact characterized by greater variability of underlying real disturbances, the differences between the regimes cannot be explained entirely by the size of these exogenous shocks (Stockman 1983). Karl Brunner and Allan Meltzer point out that "the findings raise a question about whether the additional variability [of real rates] is an excess burden, borne under floating rates, a response to policy differences in a fluctuating rate regime, or a substitution of exchange rate variability for other effects of underlying variability."[7]

These features of exchange rate data suggest a number of questions that any plausible model should be able to explain: why do expected changes in exchange rates seem to be so small relative to unexpected changes? why are real and nominal rates so

Chart 2

Spot Exchange Rate for the Deutsche
Mark and Three-Month-Forward
Rate Advanced Three Months

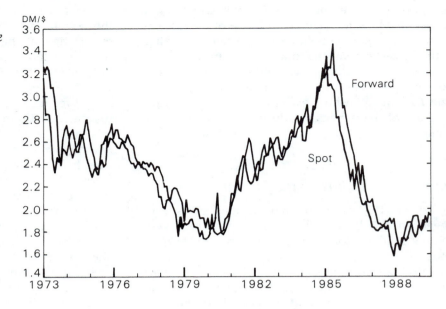

Observations are for the last business
day of each month.

Source: Board of Governors of the
Federal Reserve System.

Table 1

Standard Deviations of Monthly Real
Exchange Rate Changes

	Peg (January 1957– March 1971)	Float (March 1973– May 1988)
Dollars per yen	.0031	.0333
Dollars per French franc	.0189	.0329
Dollars per deutsche mark	.006	.0353
Dollars per pound	.0106	.0319
Yen per French franc	.0192	.029
Yen per deutsche mark	.0065	.0308
Yen per pound	.0108	.0324
French francs per deutsche mark	.023	.0166
French francs per pound	.003	.004
Deutsche marks per pound	.0121	.0297

Source: Hali Edison and Michael Melvin, "The Determinants And
Implications of the Choice of an Exchange Rate System." Forthcoming in an American Enterprise Institute volume.

highly correlated? why do most of the changes in real exchange rates persist for very long periods of time? and what accounts for the difference in behavior of the real rate across regimes? All in all this is a tall order for any class of models. A key issue in all explanations or models of exchange rate behavior is how expectations about future exchange rates are formed, so we consider this issue briefly before discussing major classes of models.

The Role of Expectations

One major insight to come from the numerous empirical studies is that exchange rates exhibit behavior very similar to the behavior of other assets traded in highly organized markets. The general principle governing the behavior of asset prices is that the current price is very closely linked to the market's expectation of the future worth of that asset. If, for example, people expect a substantial increase in the price of an asset in the future, they would have a strong incentive to purchase and hold that asset, putting upward pressure on its current price as well. Thus, current asset market models of the exchange rate are explicitly dynamic and forward-looking: they incorporate the factors that are expected to affect the foreign exchange market in the future as well as those that affect it now. Since prices move not only with current developments, but in anticipation of future developments, there is no clear correlation between exchange rate movements and contemporaneous movements in those forces thought to determine the exchange rate. This compounds the difficulty of pinpointing the sources even of historical movements in exchange rates.

Most modern exchange rate theories include as part of their structure the hypothesis that expectations are rational, or model consistent. In formal analysis, the term expectation is a conditional mathematical expectation. This is the mathematical average or expected value of a variable based on a given set of information. In day-to-day life, people form expectations subjectively based on casual observation or vague intuitive feelings about the likely outcome of some future event. Because costs are usually associated with being wrong, these subjective expectations tend to coincide with the conditional mathematical expectation based on all relevant and available information, that is, expectations tend to be rational.

Since a rational expectation of a variable is just a conditional average over a number of possible values that the variable can take, the expectation will often be incorrect. The difference between the realized value of a variable and the expected value (or average) of the variable is referred to as a shock or a disturbance. A shock or unanticipated change is unanticipated in the sense that it differs from what agents predicted based on the information available to them, not in the sense that they failed to recognize that it might occur. While it may be impossible to avoid being wrong about individual events, if expectations are rational people will not repeatedly make systematic errors.

Within the context of an economic model, rational expectations means that the way agents form expectations about the future value of a variable is the same way that the particular model says that the variable is determined. Economists do not believe that people actually go through the complicated calculations of solving a model to arrive at the appropriate conditional mathematical expectation. Rather, economic agents behave *as if* they know the model representing the activities they are dealing with, so that the model is a reasonably good summary of a less

Chart 3

One-Month-Forward Discount on the Dollar and Actual Change in the DM/$ Spot Rate

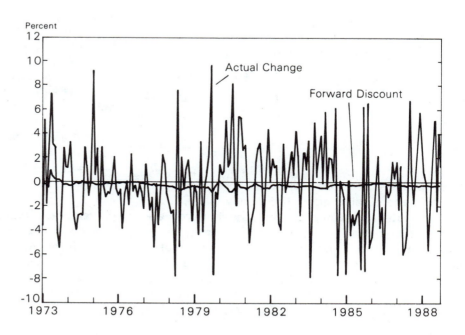

Observations are for the last business day of each month.

Source: Data Resources, Inc.

formal thought process.

The sections that follow will briefly describe how three of the leading theoretical models of exchange rate determination have attempted to account for the behavior of exchange rates and summarize their implications for the formulation of policy. Since there exist a number of variants of each of the three classes of models, rather than discuss specific predictions this study will attempt to identify which core elements of each class appear compatible with the facts and which hypotheses are clearly incorrect. The approaches differ in their views of what market disturbances predominate and how they operate to influence the actual behavior of the exchange rate. The discussion begins with a class of monetary models that were developed during the 1970s.

Monetary Models

Since the exchange rate is the relative price of two monies, the monetary approach emphasizes those factors that directly affect national money markets. Flexible price monetary models have been used primarily to analyze the influence of actual and anticipated movements in money supplies and demands on nominal exchange rates. The two essential features of the simplest version of the monetary

---

The monetary approach emphasizes those factors that directly affect national money markets.

---

model include the concept of purchasing power parity, PPP, and equilibrium in the money market.

Absolute PPP contends that the nominal exchange rate between two countries' currencies is equal to the ratio of their national price levels. This suggests that any change in the exchange rate between two currencies just equals the difference in their inflation rates. Another implication is that the real exchange rate, $Q_t = S_t(P_t/P_t^*)$, must always be constant and equal to 1.

Combining this concept of PPP together with equilibrium in the domestic and foreign money mar-

kets, the monetary approach expresses the current exchange rate directly in terms of current and expected future money market conditions. Using PPP, the nominal exchange rate is first written as the ratio of national price levels. The equilibrium national price levels can then be solved by equating real money supply to money demand in each of the two countries. This allows the spot rate to be expressed explicitly in terms of current relative money supplies and factors affecting money demands.

Most monetary models assume that money supplies are determined (exogenously) by each country's central bank and follow a random process. The demand for real money balances depends on factors such as real income and interest rates where the nominal interest rate incorporates an inflation premium. Since PPP predicts that percentage changes in exchange rates are completely explained by differences in national inflation rates, an increase in expected inflation in the United States will generate an expectation that the dollar will depreciate. If a currency is expected to depreciate, investors will be willing to hold it—or, more precisely, assets denominated in the currency—only if they are compensated by higher interest rates on those assets. This implies that the equilibrium spot exchange rate depends not only on current money supplies and money demand factors, but also on the expectation of next period's exchange rate. Since the exchange rate expected at any date in the future depends on expected future money market conditions, the spot exchange rate can be expressed in terms of the entire expected future path of money supplies and variables affecting money demands.

This view of the foreign exchange market highlights the essential role of expectations in determining exchange rates and provides a natural rationale for the high correlation between movements in the spot and forward rates. The monetary model also builds in a high degree of exchange rate volatility. A current change in the money supply, for example, can have a more than proportionate effect on the contemporaneous exchange rate if it leads the market to expect more money growth and currency depreciation in the future.

A serious deficiency of the simple monetary model is its failure to recognize that those things that affect money demand will also generally have repercussions in output markets. Unless the direct effects of real changes in output markets are considered explicitly, and not just through their effects on money demand, the model can give somewhat contorted predictions. A change in government spending or a drought, for instance, can alter relative prices in the economy as well as alter aggregate money demand. More generally, any disturbance that causes a change in relative prices may cause violations of PPP (which assumes relative prices to be constant) and its resulting implication that the real exchange rate is a constant. PPP has been studied extensively, and empirical research has documented significant violations of the doctrine. By regarding the real rate as a constant the model cannot explain either the observed high correlation between movements in nominal and real exchange rates during the floating rate era or the difference in the behavior of the real rate between the fixed and the floating rate regimes.

Disequilibrium Macroeconomic Model

A commonly accepted alternative to the simple monetary approach of analyzing exchange rate movements is a disequilibrium macroeconomic model that highlights differential speeds of adjustment in asset markets and commodity markets.[8] According to this view, nominal prices of domestic output adjust slowly over time largely because of long-term wage and price contracting. Asset markets, on the other hand, clear continuously in response to new information or changes in expectations. Continuous clearing of the foreign exchange market requires uncovered interest parity: the deposits of all currencies must offer the same expected rate of return when measured in a common currency unit.[9]

As a direct consequence of this rigidity in factor and output pricing, a purely nominal disturbance can cause short-run deviations from PPP and nominal exchange rate "overshooting." Although the nominal spot exchange rate remains in equilibrium by adjusting continuously to equalize international rates of return, the short-term change in the equilibrium spot exchange rate exceeds, or overshoots, the long-term change in the equilibrium spot exchange rate. The mechanism producing this result is as follows.

Following an unanticipated permanent expansion in the U.S. money supply, nominal prices in the economy, including the dollar price of foreign currencies, will all eventually rise in proportion to the money supply increase. However, because commodity prices do not adjust immediately, households and firms hold more money than they require. Until prices have time to adjust, attempts to get rid of excess money balances by lending them will temporarily drive down the domestic interest rate below the foreign rate. In order for this decline in the domestic interest rate to be consistent with equilibrium in the foreign exchange market, traders must expect an appreciation of the dollar that would generate capital gains to compensate for the lower interest payments. Future appreciation requires that the value of the

---

The disequilibrium and flexible price monetary models cannot deal properly with the nature of the risk that individuals bear.

---

dollar initially overshoot or be temporarily driven below its new long-run equilibrium level.

The initial downward jump in the exchange rate will be unexpected since the increase in the money supply was unanticipated. However, after the sharp fall, the exchange rate is expected to move up again smoothly as output prices adjust. Thus, in response to monetary disturbances the spot exchange rate can fluctuate far more than relative national price levels. Further, because of sluggishness in nominal price adjustments, changes in the spot exchange rate move the real exchange rate. This corresponds well with both the observation that real and nominal exchange rate changes are highly correlated and the observation that the real rate is more volatile under the floating regime than it was under the fixed.

In this context, when economists say that the exchange rate is "undervalued" or "overvalued," what they really mean is that at current prices the nominal exchange rate implies a disequilibrium level of the real exchange rate. Everyone understands that in the long run changes in real factors will change equilibrium exchange rates. Prices will eventually adjust to reflect long-run productivity trends, permanent changes in tax policies, or new investment opportunities. However, the more slowly nominal prices adjust to a change in economic conditions, the longer it will take to eliminate the difference between the current real exchange rate and its new long-run equilibrium level. This allows for the possibility that an activist monetary policy designed to influence the nominal exchange rate can effectively move the real rate closer to its equilibrium level. A more active policy would be appropriate only if the correlation between nominal and real rates is exploitable by the monetary authority (as is the case if prices adjust slowly), if we have a good notion of what the long-run equilibrium rate is, and if we could predict and analyze sources of real exchange rate shifts. Otherwise errant monetary policies themselves may induce misalignments.

The sluggish price model may have a certain claim to realism since there do appear to be frictions in the economy that give rise to slow adjustment of some prices. However, it comes up against a number of problems. If exchange rates respond quickly to new information while commodity prices adjust only with a lag, then we would expect changes in the spot exchange rate to be useful predictors of future changes in nominal price levels. This is not the case (Diba 1986). The model also suggests that changes in real exchange rates arising either from real or from nominal disturbances should have a large predictable component associated with price adjustment following the disturbance. If monetary disturbances or transitory real disturbances predominate, then the real rate will eventually return to its mean. But most of the changes in the real rates cannot be predicted and there is little evidence that they tend to reverse themselves (Huizinga 1987; Kaminsky 1988). In defense of the disequilibrium approach Paul Krugman (1988) has argued that the statistical evidence may be somewhat misleading. He suggests that ". . . a random walk will in fact be harder to reject the stickier are prices, and hence the more slowly the real exchange rate reverts to its long-run equilibrium."

A more specific challenge to the model is to explain the medium-term movements in exchange rates during the 1980s. During the first half of the 1980s the value of the dollar appreciated dramatically in real and nominal terms and then subsequently depreciated after peaking in February 1985. Many economists have argued that the appreciation was due chiefly to large increases in the U.S. government budget deficit as a percent of GDP. In the disequilibrium model (as in some other models), a fiscal deficit would raise domestic interest rates, and lead to a dollar appreciation and to deterioration of the current account. While the direction of movement is correct, this explanation cannot account for the magnitude of the actual exchange rate changes that occurred. If market participants had correctly anticipated the stance of future fiscal policies, then the forward premium or interest differential should have pre-

dicted the large dollar appreciation. But forward premiums were in fact far smaller than actual dollar exchange rate movements. This suggests that either the forward premium does not adequately capture the expected rate of change in the exchange rate or exchange rate movements were dominated by unpredictable events.

Not only have forward premium forecast errors been large, but the errors were predictable with information available at the time the forward rate was set. To explain this phenomenon several hypotheses have been advanced. One explanation is that market participants do not form expectations rationally but make systematic or avoidable mistakes. This is the conclusion reached by Jeffrey Frankel and Kenneth Froot in their analysis of market survey data (1987). They argue that market participants systematically underpredicted the strength of the dollar during the early 1980s, behavior that is inconsistent with rational expectations.

Rather than reject rational expectations, a number of other authors have suggested that during this period a "peso problem" existed. This occurs when the market believes some small probability exists that a major change in the economic environment might occur. As long as the change does not materialize, expectations may appear biased after the fact even if ex ante they were rational.[10]

Another widely recognized explanation of the systematic errors is that the forward rate differs from the market's expectations of the future spot rate due to the existence of a risk premium. If some or all of the predictable component of the forward premium forecast errors is properly attributable to a risk premium, then the model's assumption of uncovered interest parity must be relaxed. The question then becomes whether the behavior of the risk premium is consistent with a well-defined theory.

General Equilibrium Models

A number of recent models have attempted to interpret the qualitative and quantitative features of observed exchange rate fluctuations in a general equilibrium framework. The relations between changes in exchange rates, the current account, domestic investment, government budget deficits and other variables are derived in an intertemporal framework in which markets clear through price as well as quantity adjustments. This is not to say that in the real world all prices actually do adjust to clear all markets instantaneously. These are hypothetical constructs designed to determine whether sluggish nominal price adjustment is an *essential* ingredient in understanding key features of exchange rate behavior. It is difficult to assess the extent to which exchange rate fluctuations are attributable to nominal price rigidities without first understanding the sorts of fluctuations that would be observed in the absence of market failures. This research program challenges the currently popular view that much of the fluctuation in real exchange rates results, primarily as disequilibrium phenomena, from nominal exchange rate fluctuations.

The idea of the equilibrium approach is quite simple. Changes in prospective future economic comi-

---

One reason empirical models have a hard time explaining exchange rate movements in terms of economic fundamentals is because the exchange rate is not related to these variables in any simple and systematic manner.

---

ditions or current changes to the supplies or demands of goods alter real quantities like consumption, investment and the current account. These real disturbances will also alter equilibrium relative prices including the real exchange rate. Large swings in real exchange rates and the current account do not necessarily represent misalignments. They may simply reflect the natural adjustment of agents' consumption, saving and investment decisions in response to changing conditions in an uncertain economic environment.[11]

Since the real exchange rate is the nominal exchange rate adjusted for price level differences across countries, changes in the real rate can be realized either through changes in the nominal rate, changes in the relative price levels, or changes in both. How the nominal exchange rate responds depends on the monetary policies of the central banks. If the central banks attempt to stabilize their domestic price levels, volatility in the real exchange rate resulting from real disturbances will induce comovements in the nomi-

nal rate. In other words, rather than nominal exchange rate changes causing real exchange rate changes, the causation may be running in the opposite direction. Repeated real disturbances move both the real and the nominal exchange rates. This can theoretically explain both the high correlation between real and nominal exchange rates and the greater volatility of nominal exchange rates relative to nominal price levels.

The general equilibrium models are actually part of a broader class of models of the New Classical School. Rather than postulating anecdotal behavioral relationships or mechanical price adjustment rules, the new classical approach attempts to account for decisions in a way consistent with the idea of optimizing behavior. This does not suggest that there are no frictions in the economy that call for active government intervention to improve the functioning of the system. It does, however, require that the economic environment be explicitly spelled out in terms of the motivations and constraints (including budget or borrowing constraints, the availability of information, and the like) that economic agents face. Because the equilibrium models are more highly developed, it is possible to pose questions that cannot be precisely formulated in the other approaches. Explicitly stochastic models make clear the distinction between how agents respond to anticipated shifts in fundamentals as opposed to unanticipated shifts, and the distinction between permanent and transitory disturbances.

One reason empirical models have such a hard time explaining exchange rate movements in terms of economic fundamentals such as the trade balance, output, money supply or international interest rate differentials is because the exchange rate is not related to these variables in any simple and systematic manner. Not only the magnitude, but even the direction of concurrent movements in the exchange rate, the balance of trade, and other variables will depend on the nature of the underlying disturbance impinging on the economy. Alan Stockman, who has developed a number of equilibrium models, has argued that the empirical record suggests that real disturbances have been the primary source of real exchange rate movements (Stockman 1988). The evidence, however, is far from conclusive. Even with the benefit of hindsight the equilibrium models are hard pressed to identify exactly which real factors were responsible for the pattern and size of exchange rate movements during the 1980s.

One aspect of the economy that cannot be properly dealt with in the disequilibrium and flexible price monetary models is the nature of the risk that individuals bear and how they respond to perceived changes in the uncertainty of their environment. It has long been recognized that the price a risk-averse trader will pay for an asset depends, not only on the expected income stream of the asset, but also on expected future variations in that income stream. In uncertain environments there will be a risk premium implicit in the forward and the spot exchange rates that will in general vary over time. Understanding the nature and variability of the risk premium can help in analyzing the sources of variability in the spot rate.

Intertemporal optimization models, assuming risk-averse agents, have attempted to do this by exploring how changes in the uncertainty of mone-

---

Since we have not well identified the sources of exchange rate movements, determining what to do about such movements is a difficult issue.

---

tary policies, government spending and rates of technological change affect both the level and volatility of spot and forward exchange rates (Hodrick 1987; Flood 1988). These models distinguish between how investors react to new information about the risk environment and to predictable changes in the risk environment. Moreover, since the risk premium in the forward rate depends on information available at the time the forward contract is written, this approach can in principle explain the finding that the forward premium forecast errors are predictable. Whether or not the predictable component actually reflects a risk premium or expectational errors is still unresolved.

While these models have provided theoretical insight into the nature of the risk premium, they do not lend themselves to easy empirical evaluation for at least two reasons. The first is that the models themselves are highly stylized. In order to remain analytically tractable they have adopted rudimentary government sector and monetary policy rules and very simple structures of available trader information

used in forming expectations. The second difficulty is that risk premiums are not directly observable or easily quantifiable. To test the theory it is necessary to find a good measure, not only of conditional expectations (this is a problem common to all the exchange rate models), but also of the conditional variances of future money supply growth rates, productivity growth rates and government spending shares. Tests of the theory so far have not done very well. Variability in those things thought to determine the risk premium seems to be too small to explain it except at implausibly high degrees of risk aversion. (This finding of course depends on whether the risk premium has accurately been measured.)

Summary and Conclusion

By now it may seem that the only thing we actually do know about exchange rate behavior is that we know very little. In fact, we also understand that economists have good reason to legitimately disagree on how to interpret the exchange rate experience of the past 15 years. While we are still in an ongoing stage of advancing alternative hypotheses, we are better equipped to determine which if any of the alternatives are at least compatible with (and possibly responsible for) the facts and why some hypotheses might properly be discarded.

Out, for example, goes the age-old idea that the exchange rate will adjust to maintain purchasing power parity. PPP will not hold in the short run if prices are sticky and, if there are permanent changes in relative prices, is not even a good benchmark in the long run. Also, we should not be surprised at the poor econometric results of monetary models based on macroeconomic fundamentals since they do not take into account the reasons for shifts in factors affecting money demand. Because exchange rates, international interest rate differentials, and the trade balance or current account are all determined endogenously, there will not necessarily be simple and historically consistent relationships among them. In any specific instance, evaluating the "theoretically sensible" relation among these variables requires that we first identify the underlying factor causing them to move.

Two quite plausible fundamentals-based hypotheses are still in the running to explain why variability of nominal exchange rates has been greater than variability of national price levels: changes in real exchange rates (resulting from real disturbances) are accomplished through changes in the nominal exchange rate while monetary authorities act to stabilize aggregate price indices, or monetary disturbances result in nominal exchange rate overshooting because goods prices adjust slowly. These same two hypotheses can in principle also explain the high correlation between real and nominal exchange rate changes. Despite considerable research on this subject, the relative importance of these two types of shocks is an empirical question that remains unresolved.

The greater the uncertainty in the economy, the greater will be prediction errors. More troubling than frequent prediction errors would be the finding that they are systematically biased. The systematic bias found in forward rate forecast errors could mean that the market does not process information efficiently or could instead reflect shifting risk premia. Because we do not have a good method of measuring market expectations, distinguishing between these two hypotheses is difficult. If risk premia are large and variable, then expected future developments may be less important in accounting for exchange rate variability than the uncertainties surrounding the course of future developments. Fundamental interpretations of the unquestionably large real dollar appreciation and subsequent depreciation must therefore identify credible sources of uncertainty in the economy.

Standard theories of exchange rate behavior have inspired a search for causes of dollar movements in

---

The greater the uncertainty in the economy, the greater will be prediction errors.

---

terms of new information about economic fundamentals—shifts in consumer tastes, monetary or fiscal policies, or production technologies. The inability of econometricians to find shifts in these variables that can explain short-run dollar movements has resulted in an appeal by some economists to psychological factors unrelated to fundamentals. One interpretation of the recent experience is that the foreign exchange market has worked poorly so that exchange rates have become excessively volatile, at times moving far out of line with market fundamentals. This reflects, for example, the feeling that rational beliefs about the future course of economic fundamentals could not credibly explain the full rise of the dollar in the 1980-85 period. If the culprit were a speculative bubble driven by self-fulfilling anticipations but unrelated to economic fundamentals, then the case for relying on market forces to set exchange rates would be weakened. We would then have to grapple with the question of how exchange rates *should* be set.

However, the controversy over the sources of exchange rate movements goes beyond fundamental versus nonfundamental explanations. Even among economists who believe that the data reflect the decisions of rational agents who care about fundamentals, there is little consensus on whether monetary or real factors have been more important, how rapidly prices in the economy adjust, and how important risk considerations are.

Since we have not well identified the sources of exchange rate movements, determining what to do about such movements is a difficult issue. It entails recognizing what key frictions might lead exchange rate variability to impose social costs, evaluating whether these costs are greater than those that would ensue under greater fixity of exchange rates, and determining what policies and institutions might be set in place to influence exchange rates in a stabilizing way (Frenkel and Goldstein 1989).

Active exchange rate management could affect economic welfare either positively or negatively by altering information that traders and policymakers extract from exchange rates. Even if exchange rate fluctuations do impose social costs, central bank intervention to achieve greater fixity of exchange rates may not be the best way to reduce these costs, especially if stabilization of the dollar is achieved at the expense of other monetary goals. If exchange rate fluctuations reflect uncertainties surrounding fiscal policies or aggregate economic fluctuations, pursuing domestic monetary policies aimed at stabilizing exchange rates will not necessarily eliminate the uncertainty. Rather, stability of both government and monetary policies and coordination of policies across countries would go further in reducing some of the uncertainty that agents face.

Appendix

It is often stated that the (natural log of) the spot exchange rate is well approximated by a random walk in the short run. What exactly does this mean? A sequence of observations over time on the variable Z follows a random walk if each successive change in the variable is drawn independently from a probability distribution with mean 0. The variable Z_t thus evolves according to:

$$Z_t = Z_{t-1} + U_t$$

where U_t is an independent random variable. Because the expected value of U_t is zero, period to period variability in Z is due entirely to unanticipated changes. Therefore, for a forecaster who wishes to predict the future realization Z_{t+1}, the expected position of the series in the next period is just its current position. If we think of the process as starting at some origin Z_0, then the position of the series at any time t can be written as the sum of its initial position and its successive changes as:

$$Z_1 = Z_0 + U_1$$
$$Z_2 = Z_0 + U_1 + U_2$$
$$\cdot$$
$$\cdot$$
$$Z_t = Z_0 + U_1 + \ldots U_t.$$

These changes are permanent in the sense that on average there is no tendency for a change to be followed by other changes that either reinforce or reverse the original change.

If there is a long-run uptrend or downtrend in the behavior of Z_t, then the random walk model is easily modified to include drift by adding a constant, say K, each period:

$$Z_t = Z_{t-1} + K + U_t$$

meaning that on average the process will tend to move in the direction of the sign of K and the forecaster will take this into account when forming her expectation.

It should be noted that even if the univariate time series process is a random walk, this does not rule out the possibility that future changes can be predicted using a broader information set. A random walk univariate process simply indicates that lagged values of the variable itself cannot be used to predict future changes.

---

[1] The real exchange rate can be defined in a number of ways but always entails pricing some bundle of goods in terms of some other bundle of goods, for example, the price of domestically produced tradable goods in terms of foreign-produced tradable goods. Which definition is most appropriate to use in any particular analysis will in general depend on the question under consideration.

[2] In addition to the empirical regularities discussed here, Michael Mussa (1979) discusses a number of other regularities in the behavior of exchange rates during the 1970s. These include the relationships between exchange rates and interest rates, trade balance and money supplies and demands.

[3] See Frankel and Froot (1987).

[4] Meese and Rogoff (1983, 1985) explore both the in- and out-of-sample predictive performance of the log-linear monetary models of the 1970s and find that the models fail to beat a random walk representation, even when ex post right-hand-side variables are used.

[5] See the appendix for a discussion of a random walk.

[6] See Huizinga (1987) for an analysis of the persistence of changes in real exchange rates.

[7] Quotation is from the Introduction of *Real Business Cycles, Real Exchange Rates, and Actual Policies*, Carnegie-Rochester Conference Series on Public Policy, vol. 25, 1986.

[8] This approach, which is a dynamic extension of the static Mundell-Flemming model, was originated by Rudiger Dornbusch (1976).

[9] This assumes that traders' preferences are well approximated by risk neutrality so they do not require a risk premium.

[10] Lewis (1988) advances another alternative. She analyzes the effect upon forecast errors due to a change in the process of fundamentals that the market does not immediately recognize. Since the market does not immediately recognize the change, forecast errors are on average wrong during a period when the market is rationally learning.

[11] Alan Stockman (1987, 1988) provides a number of simple examples which illustrate the effects of various real disturbances on the current account, exchange rate and other variables.

References

Bilson, John F. O. 1984. "Exchange Rate Dynamics." In *Exchange Rate Theory and Practice*, John F.O. Bilson and Richard C. Marston, eds., pp. 175–198. University of Chicago Press.

Campbell, John Y. and Richard H. Clarida. 1987. "The Dollar and Real Interest Rates." In *Empirical Studies of Velocity, Real Exchange Rates, Unemployment and Productivity*, K. Brunner and A.H. Meltzer, eds., pp. 149–215. Carnegie-Rochester Conference Series 27.

Cumby, Robert E. and Maurice Obstfeld. 1984. "International Interest Rate and Price Level Linkages under Flexible Exchange Rates: A Review of Recent Evidence." In *Exchange Rate Theory and Practice*, pp. 121–152. See Bilson 1984.

Diba, Behzad T. 1986. "Monetary Disturbances, Price Rigidities, and Exchange Rate Fluctuations: An Empirical Study." Mimeo, Georgetown University, August.

Dornbusch, Rudiger. 1976. "Expectations and Exchange Rate Dynamics." *Journal of Political Economy*, vol. 84, December, pp. 1161–76.

———. 1988. "Real Exchange Rates and Macroeconomics: A Selective Survey." *NBER Working Paper No. 2775*.

Edison, Hali and Michael Melvin. 1988. "The Determinants and Implications of the Choice of an Exchange Rate System." Forthcoming in an American Enterprise Institute volume.

Flood, Robert P. 1988. "Asset Prices and Time-Varying Risk." *International Monetary Fund Working Paper*.

Frankel, Jeffrey A. "International Capital Mobility and Exchange Rate Volatility." In *International Payments Imbalances in the 1980s*, Norman S. Fieleke, ed., pp. 162–188. Federal Reserve Bank of Boston Conference Series No. 32.

Frankel, Jeffrey A. and Kenneth A. Froot. 1987. "Using Survey Data to Test Standard Propositions Regarding Exchange Rate Expectations." *The American Economic Review*, vol. 77, March, pp. 133–153.

Frankel, Jeffrey A. and Richard Meese. 1987. "Are Exchange Rates Excessively Variable?" In *NBER Macroeconomics Annual 1987*, pp. 117–162.

Frenkel, Jacob A. and Morris Goldstein. 1989. "Exchange Rate Volatility and Misalignment: Evaluating Some Proposals for Reform." NBER Working Paper No. 2894.

Froot, Kenneth A. and Jeffrey A. Frankel. 1989. "Forward Discount Bias: Is It An Exchange Risk Premium?" *Quarterly Journal of Economics*, February, pp. 139–161.

Hodrik, Robert J. 1987. "Risk, Uncertainty and Exchange Rates." NBER Working Paper No. 2429.

———. 1988. "U.S. International Capital Flows: Perspectives from Rational Maximizing Models." NBER Working Paper No. 2729.

Hodrik, Robert J. and Sanjay Srivastava. 1984. "An Investigation of Risk and Return in Forward Foreign Exchange." *Journal of International Money and Finance*, vol. 3, April, pp. 5–29.

Huizinga, John. 1987. "An Empirical Investigation of the Long-Run Behavior of Real Exchange Rates." In *Empirical Studies of Velocity, Real Exchange Rates, Unemployment and Productivity*. See Campbell and Clarida 1987.

Kaminsky, Graciela. 1988. "The Real Exchange Rate Since Floating: Market Fundamentals or Bubbles?" International Economics Research Center Discussion Paper No. 15, University of Pennsylvania.

Kaminsky, Graciela and Rodrigo Peruga. 1988. "Credibility Crises: The Dollar In The Early Eighties." International Economics Research Center Discussion Paper No. 17, University of Pennsylvania.

Krugman, Paul R. 1988. "Equilibrium Exchange Rates." Prepared for the Conference on International Policy Coordination, Kiawah Island, October 27–9.

Krugman, Paul R. and Maurice Obstfeld. 1988. *International Economics: Theory and Policy*. Scott, Foresman and Company.

Levich, Richard M. 1985. "Empirical Studies of Exchange Rates: Price Behavior, Rate Determination and Market Efficiency." In *Handbook of International Economics vol. II*, pp. 979–1041.

Lewis, Karen K. 1988. "Changing Beliefs about Fundamentals and Systematic Rational Forecast Errors: with Evidence from Foreign Exchange Markets." Mimeo, New York University, May.

Lucas, Robert E., Jr. 1982. "Interest Rates and Currency Prices in a Two Country World." *Journal of Monetary Economics*, vol. 10, pp. 335–360.

Mark, Nelson C. 1988. "Real and Nominal Exchange Rates in the Long Run: An Empirical Investigation." Ohio State University working paper.

Meese, Richard A. 1986. "Empirical Assessment of Foreign Currency Risk Premiums." In *Financial Risk: Theory, Evidence and Implications*, Courtenay C. Stone, ed., pp. 157–180. Proceedings of Eleventh Annual Economic Policy Conference of the Federal Reserve Bank of St. Louis, Kluwer Academic Publishers (1989).

Meese, Richard A. and Kenneth Rogoff. 1983. "Empirical Exchange Rate Models of The Seventies: Do They Fit Out of Sample?" *Journal of International Economics*, February, pp. 1–24.

———. 1985. "Was It Real? The Exchange Rate–Interest Differential Relation, 1973–1984." NBER Working Paper No. 1732.

Mussa, Michael. 1979. "Empirical Regularities in the Behavior of Exchange Rates and Theories of the Foreign Exchange Market." Carnegie-Rochester Public Policy Conference No. 11, pp. 9–57.

———. 1984. "The Theory of Exchange Rate Determination." In *Exchange Rate Theory and Practice*, pp. 13–78. See Cumby and Obstfeld 1984.

———. 1986. "Nominal Exchange Rate Regimes and the Behavior of Real Exchange Rates: Evidence and Implications." Carnegie-Rochester Conference Series on Public Policy 25, pp. 117–214.

Obstfeld, Maurice. 1987. "Peso Problems, Speculative Bubbles, Risk." NBER Working Paper no. 2203, April.

Obstfeld, Maurice and Alan C. Stockman. 1985. "Exchange Rate Dynamics." In *Handbook of International Economics vol. II*, pp. 917–977.

Singleton, Kenneth. 1987. "Speculation and the Volatility of Foreign Currency Exchange Rates." Carnegie-Rochester Series on Public Policy 26, pp. 9–56.

Stockman, Alan C. 1983. "Real Exchange Rates Under Alternative Nominal Exchange Rate Systems." *Journal of International Money and Finance*, vol. 2, August, pp. 147–166.

———. 1987. "The Equilibrium Approach to Exchange Rates." Federal Reserve Bank of Richmond *Economic Review*, March/April, pp. 12–30.

———. 1988. "Exchange Rates, the Current Account, and Monetary Policy." Written for the American Enterprise Institute Monetary Policy Project.

Stockman, Alan C. and Harris Dellas. "International Portfolio Nondiversification and Exchange Rate Variability." Forthcoming in *Journal of International Economics*.

Stockman, Alan C. and Lars E.O. Svensson. 1987. "Capital Flows, Investment, and Exchange Rates." *Journal of Monetary Economics*, vol. 19, March, pp. 171–201.

Stulz, Rene M. 1987. "An Equilibrium Model of Exchange Rate Determination and Asset Pricing with Nontraded Goods and Imperfect Information." *Journal of Political Economy*, vol. 95, October, pp. 1024–1040.

Svensson, Lars E.O. 1985a. "Currency Prices, Terms of Trade, and Interest Rates: A General Equilibrium Asset-Pricing, Cash-in-Advance Approach." *Journal of International Economics*, vol. 18, February, pp. 17–41.

———. 1985b. "Money and Asset Prices in a Cash-in-Advance Economy." *Journal of Political Economy*, vol. 93, no. 5, October, pp. 919–944.

Sources

"Monetary Aggregates: A User's Guide," John R. Walter, Federal Reserve Bank of Richmond *Economic Review*, January/February 1989, pp. 20–28.

"Money and Velocity in the 1980s," John B. Carlson and John N. McElravey, Federal Reserve Bank of Cleveland *Economic Commentary*, January 15, 1989, pp. 1–4.

"What Is an 'Acceptable' Rate of Inflation?—A Review of the Issues," Michelle R. Garfinkel, Federal Reserve Bank of St. Louis *Review*, July/August 1989, pp. 3–15.

"The Stock Market and Inflation: A Synthesis of the Theory and Evidence," David P. Ely and Kenneth J. Robinson, Federal Reserve Bank of Dallas *Economic Review*, March 1989, pp. 17–29.

"Payments System Risk: What Is It and What Will Happen If We Try To Reduce It?," R. Alton Gilbert, Federal Reserve Bank of St. Louis *Review*, January/February 1989, pp. 3–17.

"The U.S. as a Debtor Country: Causes, Prospects, and Policy Implications," Stephen A. Meyer, Federal Reserve Bank of Philadelphia *Business Review*, November/December 1989, pp. 19–31.

"Is America Being Sold Out?," Mack Ott, Federal Reserve Bank of St. Louis *Review*, March/April 1989, pp. 47–64.

"Setting the Discount Rate," E. J. Stevens, Federal Reserve Bank of Cleveland *Economic Commentary*, July 15, 1989, pp. 1–6.

"The High–Yield Debt Market: 1980–1990," Richard H. Jefferis, Jr., Federal Reserve Bank of Cleveland *Economic Commentary*, April 1, 1990, pp. 1–6.

"Is There Too Much Corporate Debt?," Ben Bernanke, Federal Reserve Bank of Philadelphia *Business Review*, September/October 1989, pp. 3–13.

"The Case for Junk Bonds," Eric S. Rosengren, Federal Reserve Bank of Boston *New England Economic Review*, May/June 1990, pp. 40–49.

"Why Are So Many New Stock Issues Underpriced?," Anthony Saunders, Federal Reserve Bank of Philadelphia *Business Review*, March/April 1990, pp. 3–12.

"An Introduction to Mezzanine Finance and Private Equity," John R. Willis and David A. Clark, *Journal of Applied Corporate Finance*, Summer 1989, 2:2, pp. 77–86.

"Has Financial Market Volatility Increased?," Sean Becketti and Gordon H. Sellon, Jr., Federal Reserve Bank of Kansas City *Economic Review*, June 1989, pp. 17–30.

"Capital Market Efficiency: An Update," Stephen F. Leroy, Federal Reserve Bank of San Francisco *Economic Review*, Spring 1990, pp. 29–40.

"Managing Interest Rate Risk with Interest Rate Futures," Charles S. Morris, Federal Reserve Bank of Kansas City *Economic Review*, March 1989, pp. 3–20.

"Managing Stock Market Risk with Stock Index Futures," Charles S. Morris, Federal Reserve Bank of Kansas City *Economic Review*, June 1989, pp. 3–16.

"Interest–Rate Caps, Collars, and Floors," Peter A. Abken, Federal Reserve Bank of Atlanta *Economic Review*, November/December 1989, pp. 2–24.

"Closing Troubled Financial Institutions: What Are the Issues?," Leonard I. Nakamura, Federal Reserve Bank of Philadelphia *Business Review*, May/June 1990, pp. 15–24.

"FIRREA and the Future of Thrifts," Elizabeth Laderman, Federal Reserve Bank of San Francisco *Weekly Letter*, January 19, 1990, pp. 1–3.

"Using Market Incentives to Reform Bank Regulation and Federal Deposit Insurance," James B. Thomson, Federal Reserve Bank of Cleveland *Economic Review*, 1990:1, pp. 28–40.

"The New Risk–Based Plan for Commercial Banks," William R. Keeton, Federal Reserve Bank of Kansas City *Economic Review*, December 1989, pp. 40–60.

"Still Toe–to–Toe: Banks and Nonbanks at the End of the 80s," Linda Aguilar, Federal Reserve Bank of Chicago *Economic Perspectives*, January/February 1990, pp. 12–23.

"Interstate Banking and the Federal Reserve: A Historical Perspective," Robert T. Clair and Paula K. Tucker, Federal Reserve Bank of Dallas *Economic Review*, November 1989, pp. 1–20.

"Challenges to Small Banks' Survival," Sherrill Shaffer, Federal Reserve Bank of Philadelphia *Business Review*, September/October 1989, pp. 15–27.

"Shared ATM Networks: An Uneasy Alliance?," Elizabeth Laderman, Federal Reserve Bank of San Francisco *Weekly Letter*, February 23, 1990, pp. 1–3.

"Owners Versus Managers: Who Controls the Bank?," Loretta J. Mester, Federal Reserve Bank of Philadelphia *Business Review*, May/June 1989, pp. 13–23.

"Banking and Venture Capital," Randall Johnston Pozdena, Federal Reserve Bank of San Francisco *Weekly Letter*, June 1, 1990, pp. 1–3.

"Bank Lending to LBOs: Risks and Supervisory Response," James B. Thomson, Federal Reserve Bank of Cleveland *Economic Commentary*, February 15, 1989, pp. 1–5.

"Foreign Competition in U.S. Banking Markets," Herbert L. Baer, Federal Reserve Bank of Chicago *Economic Perspectives*, May/June 1990, pp. 22–29.

"The Costs of Default and International Lending," Chien Nan Wang, Federal Reserve Bank of Cleveland *Economic Commentary*, March 1, 1989, pp 1–4.

"Globalization in the Financial Services Industry," Christine Pavel and John N. McElravey, Federal Reserve Bank of Chicago *Economic Perspectives*, May/June 1990, pp. 3–18.

"Standardizing World Securities Clearance Systems," Ramon P. DeGennaro and Christopher J. Pike, Federal Reserve Bank of Cleveland *Economic Commentary*, April 15, 1990, pp. 1–4.

"International Policy Coordination: Can We Afford It?," W. Lee Hoskins, Federal Reserve Bank of Cleveland *Economic Commentary*, January 1, 1989, pp. 1–5.

"Europe in 1992," Norman S. Fieleke, Federal Reserve Bank of Boston *New England Economic Review*, May/June 1989, pp. 13–26.

"Exchange Rate Determination: Sorting Out Theory and Evidence," Jane Marrinan, Federal Reserve Bank of Boston *New England Economic Review*, November/December 1989, pp. 39–51.